Social and Personality Development

Essays on the Growth of the Child

William Damon is the author of
Social and Personality Development: Infancy through Adolescence

Social and Personality Development

Essays on the Growth of the Child

Edited by **William Damon**
CLARK UNIVERSITY

W • W • NORTON & COMPANY • New York • London

Cover illustration: *Boys in a Pasture* by Winslow Homer. c. 1874.
Courtesy, Museum of Fine Arts, Boston. Charles Henry Hayden Fund.

Library of Congress Cataloging in Publication Data
Main entry under title:
Social and personality development.
    1. Child development—Addresses, essays, lectures.
2. Infant psychology—Addresses, essays, lectures.
3. Child psychology—Addresses, essays, lectures. 4. Adolescent psychology—Addresses, essays, lectures. 5. Socialization—Addresses, essays, lectures. I. Damon,
William, 1944   . [DNLM: 1. Child development. 2. Personality development. 3. Socialization. 4. Social adjustment. WS 105 S678]
HQ767.9.S654   1983   155.4   83-12130

ISBN 0-393-95307-6

W. W. Norton & Company, Inc., 500 Fifth Avenue,
    New York, N.Y. 10110

W. W. Norton & Company Ltd., 37 Great Russell Street,
    London WCIB 3NU

1 2 3 4 5 6 7 8 9 0

To Louis Meyers and Jesse Louis Damon

Contents

Part V   Children's Peer Relations   217

Part VI   Individuality and Self in Childhood   279

Part VII   Adolescent Social and Moral Development   365

Preface

The readings in this volume were chosen to provide a state-of-the-art account of social and personality development during the first two decades of life. Many of the readings are classic studies that remain unsurpassed in the insights they provide. Others are recent breakthroughs that have significantly expanded our understanding of psychological development. Each of the readings has been chosen to illustrate a particular aspect of social and personal growth during infancy, childhood, or adolescence.

This book of readings follows the chronological organization of its companion text, *Social and Personality Development: Infancy through Adolescence*. Like the text, this book has parts devoted to each major age period between birth and maturity. Consequently, it is possible from these readings to trace the developmental connections between social behavior in infancy and the subsequent challenges and achievements of childhood and adolescence. The companion text makes these developmental connections explicit; but this set of readings paints the same picture for readers wishing to draw the links for themselves. Therefore this book can either be used alone or supplemented by the text.

The readings are organized under part headings designed to highlight the complementary aspects of social and personality development at each age period. These complementary aspects are (1) the integration of the individual into the social world, and (2) the self-identification of the individual as a unique person with a coherent personality. Among the topics included in the first aspect are the child's relations with adults, the child's relations with peers, and the range of socialization experiences in family, school, and society that influence the child while growing up. Included in the second aspect of social and personality development are the individual's search for identity and the processes of personality formation. These two aspects of development are complementary because they influence and support each other as the individual grows and acquires new capabilities.

Parts I and II, IV and V, and VII—devoted to infancy, childhood, and adolescence, respectively—are "social-relational" in content: leaving III, VI, and VIII to treat "individuality" in these three stages. Prior to each part, I have provided some introductory comments in order to outline my own integration of the material. A more extensive treatment of this and other related literature can be found in the companion text.

Parts I and II cover the infants' relations with caregivers and the infants' relations with peers. The first of these, on caregiver-infant relations, includes a description of the infant's beginning sociability, an analysis of the earliest face-to-face interactions between mothers and infants, and an account of the critical emotional attachment that develops between caregiver and infant. The second, on infant-peer relations, includes one classic and one recent study of the remarkably intimate and mutual relations that are possible between infant peers. Part III, the "individuality" group, consists of an influential account of early temperament and its consequences for personality development, and an important essay that draws links between the infant-caregiver attachment relation and the infant's formation of a stable, coherent personal identity.

In the three parts dealing with childhood, there are again two devoted to social relations with adults and peers, and one to the development of individuality. Part IV includes four important accounts of the processes by which adults influence their children's development: child-rearing style, modeling, modulation of rewards and punishments, and attribution of responsibility. The fifth paper is a documentation of the possible effects of divorce: an increasingly common family circumstance for children and adolescents in our culture. Part V focuses on play, childhood friendships, and the social-developmental consequences of these. One essay describes the properties of children's social play, another describes the nature of early friendships, and the remaining two show how children's peer relations can serve as the training ground for cooperative and empathetic behavior. Finally, Part VI brings together accounts of children's personality development and self-conception, and of sex-role differentiation.

In the final portion of the book, the articles of Part VII focus on social and moral development in adolescence, and those of Part VIII on the formation and consolidation of a personal identity during the adolescent years. The former group of readings contains a psychiatrist's timeless description of intimate peer relations in the early teens, a sociologist's analysis of adolescent cliques and crowds, and a well-known developmental account of moral growth in the adolescent years. The latter group contains a long and thorough discussion of adolescent identity struggles (now the standard source on this topic in the clinical and developmental literature), an analysis of the personal uses to which adolescents put certain peer interactions, and a description of some unique identity-related issues that face adolescent women. Although there is much in this latter essay that is speculative, I considered it a necessary addition, since so much of the literature on adolescent individuality has been based on observations of male youth. This imbalance is only beginning to be redressed in current research.

The scientific study of social and personality development is even younger than psychology itself, but the papers presented in this volume indicate how far we have come in a relatively short span of time. We have gained a palpable sense of the infant's inherent sociability and the infant's rich social life, and we can trace the roots of personality development to early social relations and temperamental dispositions. We know much about the properties of children's peer relations and their significance for the child's further growth. We have identified some of the processes through which adults exert their enormous influence upon children's social development, and we have a sense of what can go wrong when adult-child relations break down. We know a great deal about the personal opportunities, challenges, and hazards of adolescence, and can recognize early signposts towards optimal psychosocial functioning in late adolescence and adulthood. These particular discoveries have largely been made and confirmed since the last World War, a brief moment indeed from the perspective of the history of science. It is hoped that this volume will convey to the reader the qualities of dynamism and excitement that currently characterize this productive area of inquiry. Although much of the story of social and personality development has yet to be told, we have by now enough of an outline to form some basic understanding, and to be captivated by the search for further information. The best outcome to be hoped for from this collection of readings is that it inspire some readers to join the search.

For help with preparation of this manuscript, I wish to thank Wendy Praisner and Bobbi Karman. Don Fusting, my editor at Norton, has been greatly supportive of both this and the textbook project, and has offered me valuable advice concerning the selections. While sharing this material with me, many students at Clark have provided me with candid and thoughtful reactions; these reactions have guided my selections as well as my interpretive comments.

W.D.
1982

Social and Personality Development

Essays on the Growth of the Child

Part I

Infant Relations with Caregivers

ONE of the first jobs of science is to dispel longstanding myths. Among developmental psychology's most important contributions is the challenging of the old myth that infants are born mute, unknowing, passive recipients of adult administrations. Scientists' careful observations of the infant's earliest social engagements have revealed that, far from being socially inert or even inept, the infant at birth is well adapted to its social environment, soon begins participating in social interactions and relationships, and rapidly acquires an extensive array of social capabilities.

Of course it is critical to note that most infants are fortunate enough to be part of a responsive social environment, usually in the form of an attentive caregiver. Because of this, being "well-adapted" in the infant's social world means primarily being able to engage the attentiveness of an already willing adult, and reacting positively to the adult's care and communication. For the baby, therefore, the main task is to fit in to the caregiver-child unit. This does not require anything approaching the social competence of the adult partner in the unit, but does call for an ability to make certain initiatives as well as to signal a vital social receptivity.

Daniel Stern's paper offers us a catalogue of the social "tools" that enable the young infant to participate effectively in the caregiver-child relation. Some of these behavioral tools seem so rudimentary that, without the scientist's perspective, they might be dismissed as lacking in social significance. For example, there is the infant's gaze, the head movement, and the "cry face." When viewed by a naive observer, these primitive activities may seem like little more than meaningless movements or random expressions of affect. Yet each of these simple behaviors serves to draw the caregiver into interaction with the infant. Gazing and moving the head helps the infant establish eye contact with the caregiver, an important precursor to communication. Expressions of distress like crying and facial grimaces signal an infant's need for the attending adult. Because the infant depends upon the caregiver for both survival and social interaction, these rudimentary behaviors are an essential part of an infant's incipient adaptiveness to the world. Through them the infant plays an active part in its relations with caregiving adults.

Stern points to a number of features in the infant's inherent "design" that dispose the infant towards social interaction with the caregiver. The infant's gaze focuses naturally on objects about eight inches away, just the distance of the caregiver's face during feeding and holding. By three months or so infants show particular interest in visual configurations with facelike features. At about the same time, the infant is able to move its head in a manner that is "enormously appealing" to its caregiver, who invariably interprets such a movement as "an affectively positive act of approach." In the space of a few months, the infant smiles in response to social stimulation, another signal that certainly has strong social appeal for adults. Before long, smiles even become "instrumental" in nature, produced *in order to* evoke positive results from others. Crying, too, is a behavior that compels adults to engage in social interaction with the infant. Though certainly present at birth, crying, like many other behaviors, becomes increasingly purposive after a few months of life.

Stern's description of the infant's early social "tools" may not be complete. Other observers are adding all the time to the list, although many of these additions are still speculative. The following early tendencies and behaviors have been cited as predisposing infants toward human interaction: grasping, cooing, babbling, preference for the smell of mother's milk, preference for the sounds of human voices, and bodily movements synchronized to the rhythms of human language. Current research is testing these and yet other supplements to Stern's list. Whether or not all of these should be confirmed, there is no question by now that the infant makes a weighty contribution to its own social life.

What is the precise nature of this social life? Brazelton and Tronick offer us a qualitative analysis of the infant's early interactions with its primary caregiver, in most cases the mother. The authors describe the smooth, gradual cycles of attentiveness and withdrawal of attention between infant and mother, punctuated by smiling, vocalizing, touching, and facial gestures. Mother and child follow one another's behavior in a reciprocal pattern of interaction that the authors characterize as one of "mutual feedback." The roles of the two participants are complementary though distinct. The mother establishes the "regulatory base" for the interaction, monitoring and organizing the infant's social initiative and reactions. As the infant develops within the context of this relationship, the infant increasingly acquires the ability to monitor its own behavior and to control the sequence and rhythm of its social behavior. In this manner, self-regulation is one personal outcome of the infant's participation in the finely tuned reciprocal interactions with its caregiver.

For this and many other reasons, it is impossible to overstate the profound consequences for the infant of the caregiver-child relation. Mary Ainsworth's research on attachment has illuminated the critical emotional implications that follow from different types of caregiver-infant relations. Ainsworth describes three patterns of attachment, each with a distinct quality of affect between caregiver and child. One attachment pattern is the use of the caregiver as a secure base from which to explore the world. This is characteristic of babies whom Ainsworth designates "Group B." Group A babies, in contrast, avoid or ignore the caregiver during times of stress; and Group C babies are often ambivalent, sometimes clinging and sometimes resisting contact or interaction. The latter two groups of babies are considered insecurely attached. Ainsworth describes an ingenious cumulative stress situation (the "strange situation") that she designed to assess the quality of a one-year-old's attachment to its primary caregiver. She then cites research linking the quality of attachment as assessed by the strange situation to the mother's behavior in the home, demonstrating that the types of face-to-face interactions that infants experience have much to do with whether or not they will be securely attached. Further, Ainsworth believes that the quality of an infant's attachment in the first year has important developmental consequences later in life. She refers to a number of prospective studies that have assessed children's attachments at one year and have then followed the children's social and personal growth in subsequent childhood years. Securely attached infants, in contrast with anxiously attached ones, tend to become socially well adapted in childhood peer relations, curious and enthusiastic about exploring the environment, positive in their emotional expression, cooperative, self-directed, and persistent. They seem to carry with them the confidence that emanates from the security of their early attachment to a responsive caregiver.

The more we observe infant social life and its later consequences, the more we gain respect for the importance of the social relationships and events that infants experience early in life. Research has shown how prepared infants are for social interaction and how deeply dependent they are upon the responsiveness of others in their social environment. The articles in this section capture key aspects of the infant's early sociability, and suggest the multiple contributions of this beginning sociability to the individual's lifelong social and personal development.

1

The Infant's Repertoire
Daniel Stern

The infant comes into the world bringing formidable capabilities to establish human relatedness. Immediately he is a partner in shaping his first and foremost relationships. His social equipment, though extraordinary, is obviously immature. However, the notion of immaturity carries some excess baggage that gets in our way. The label "immature" cannot be a green light to dismiss a behavior until its more mature version arrives; nor can it be an invitation to focus on the developmental process itself—that mysterious series of transformations into maturity. Ultimately any human being is simply what he is at the moment we find him. The behaviors of a three-month-old are totally mature and fully accomplished three-month-old behaviors. The same is true at two years, ten years, twenty-one years. You can draw the line where you wish, depending on what human capabilities are of particular interest or under scrutiny.

In taking this relativistic position I do not mean to minimize the forceful reality of development and growth. But where the interaction between two people, and how it works and fits, is of primary interest, the degree of maturity of either partner's contribution to the interaction becomes a secondary issue. Even more important, though a mother well understands, intellectually, that her infant is immature, and often prays he will grow up faster, she cannot enter into a full spontaneous relationship with him unless

Reprinted by permission of the publishers from *The First Relationship* by Daniel Stern, Cambridge, Mass.: Harvard University Press. Copyright 1977 by Daniel Stern.

all that is put aside emotionally. Like any other important person in her life, he is what he is, interacting with what he has, at the moment he is encountered.

What then are the infant's social "tools," the perceptual and motor abilities that lead and permit him to engage in social interchanges? My list will not be comprehensive and will not catalogue all that an infant can do and perceive. Instead it will emphasize only those events that bear on the establishment of human relatedness, communication, and emotional exchanges during social interactions in the first six months of life, when the infant is so sharply focused on the human stimulus world that his primary caregiver provides.

Gaze

What is interesting for an infant to look at? It was only a little over a decade ago that the importance of gaze as a cardinal social and bonding behavior began to be appreciated. At birth, the visual motor system (looking at and seeing) comes immediately into operation. The newborn cannot only see but arrives with reflexes that allow him to follow and fixate upon an object. Without any previous experience he can follow a moving object with his eyes and head and can hold his gaze on it. This is easily demonstrated in most alert newborns. Many of them, within minutes of birth, will alertly follow with their eyes and head an object passed across their visual field. No learning is necessary. But what do they see? There is an all-important difference between looking and seeing, as there is between listening and hearing.

Is the newborn immediately inundated with a chaotic and overwhelming world? A world where there is light and dark and angles and lines and patterns but no meaningful objects, no way to know where one thing leaves off and another begins, no way to distinguish the human from the inanimate. Such a "world" can exist. In the 1920s the surgeon, M. von Senden, came up with some fascinating findings. Von Senden had the rare opportunity to remove cataracts surgically from the eyes of adults who had been blind since birth because of them but who otherwise had perfectly good visual systems. The results were astounding. The patients were given sight for the first time but could not see. Most of them "saw" quite well but found the visual world confusing, nonsensical, and a painful sensory experience. Many wished to be blind again. Only slowly did the objects in the visual world begin to conform to, and at the same time alter, their previois conceptions, schemas that had been built up with their other senses over the years of blindness. A comfortable "fit" came gradually.[1]

Why is it not this way for the newborn? First, and most obviously, the baby does not arrive into life with preformed notions of the world's objects. It is all new. There are no preconceptions or established systems of things to clash against his visual sensations. Thus, there can be no confusion in the sense of disorienting discrepancies or painful reappraisals. He is endowed with the tendency to seek out stimulation—and he is organized so that he will tend to order his experiences into progressively larger, more complex, and more encompassing hierarchies. Such is his nature. So long as the stimuli do not overwhelm him, he goes about his momentous task with intensity and pleasure. So rather than having to reorganize his object world as did Von Senden's patients, he has the more extraordinary, yet less encumbered, task of having to create anew the entire object world. Each infant has to create pictures within his own mind of the world of objects and people.

This may sound like the now discarded view of the infant arriving into the world as a blank page to be written on by his experiences with life. This is neither my view nor the case. The infant arrives with an array of innately determined perceptual predilections, motor patterns, cognitive or thinking tendencies, and abilities for emotional expressiveness and perhaps recognition. Nonetheless, for the line of inquiry we are now pursuing, none of these innate "orderings" of the world are of enough specificity or fixity to make the newborn encounter the dissonance or confusion described in the newly sighted patients.

The infant can readily be overwhelmed by excessive stimulation. However, he is "designed" so that he occupies a niche in nature with his mother which tends to strike a balance between protecting him from excessive stimuli and at the same time assuring his exposure to enough stimulation from the visual world. One of his first "design features" assuring this balance is that the infant can only focus well on objects about eight inches away. He cannot clearly see objects much farther away or much closer. They get out of focus and presumably become fuzzy. So, right away, the newborn's sharp visual world is restricted to a perimeter of roughly eight or so inches. A strong light from a good distance does make an infant turn away, but he will generally be unaffected by most other visual events outside of this focus range.

For the first several weeks after birth, the majority of the baby's awake alert time is spent in and around feeding and somewhat less in diapering or bathing. What will he see? It turns out that when the infant is in the normal breast- or bottle-feeding position his eyes are almost exactly eight inches from his mother's eyes (if she is facing him).[2] We have found that, during feeding, mothers spend about 70 percent of the time facing and looking at their infants. Accordingly, what he is most likely to look at and see is his mother's face, especially her eyes. (Several earlier theories assumed that the first and most important object the infant sees is the breast. This is certainly not correct since during suckling the breast is too close to be in focus.) Thus the arrangement of anatomy, normal positioning, and visual competence dictated by natural design all point to the mother's face as an initial focal point of importance for the infant's early construction of his salient visual world, and a starting point for the formation of his early human relatedness.

A second line of evidence also indicates the importance of gaze in early human relatedness. Ahrens and Spitz noted that infants of about three months showed more interest and smiled more at faces presented to them full face front, compared to profiles, or to other objects.[3] The essence of these observations was distilled into the following experiment. Infants were presented with drawings of a variety of forms, including faces and other objects. They seemed to prefer a simple two-dimensional line for the drawing of a face. Furthermore, the crucial facial features that accounted for the preference were two eyelike, large dots correctly placed within a larger oval.

These findings suggested to many workers that the infant was born with an innate preference for the human face—or at least some of its features.

An innate predilection for a specific visual configuration is no small matter. It implies that some scheme or "picture" of a human face is encoded in our genes, reflected in our nervous systems, and ultimately expresses itself in our behavior without any previous specific learning experiences. A productive controversy was launched, and the issue at stake boiled down to this question: Was it the specific configuration of the face, the face gestalt, that was so interesting to infants, or was it any visual stimulus of the same size containing the same amount of angularity, light and shade contrast, complexity of pattern, curvilinearity, and so on. Through the ingenious early work of Fantz and others, it had become possible to find out fairly exactly what infants were drawn to gaze at.[4]

For a while some experiments leaned to one side of this nature versus nurture controversy, and others tilted the opposite way. The studies of Friedman and Haaf and Bell resolved the issue by carefully controlling the various separate elements of the stimulus, such as complexity and shade contrast.[5] They found that what the infant preferred was not the face configuration itself, but rather any visual stimulus that contained certain qualities and quantities of the stimulus elements mentioned, whether or not this combination of elements came in the configuration of a face or something else. From one point of view, the distinction is quite important because of its implications. Practically, however, the distinction is moot: of all the visual objects in the universe that the average infant is likely to encounter in the "average expectable environment," the human face comes about as close as anything will come to providing just the right combination of captivating stimulus elements. Furthermore, its special interest is founded on a biological basis by virtue of the infant's innate bias for certain kinds and amounts of stimulation. The situation is something like innateness "once removed." Other studies have shown that the sharp angles provided by the corners of the eyes as well as the light-dark contrast of pupil and eye white (sclera) and of eyebrow and skin are especially fascinating to the infant. From the very beginning, then, the infant is "designed" to find the human face fascinating, and the mother is led to attract as much interest as possible to her already "interesting" face.

A change in gaze.   At some point around the sixth week, the infant's visual motor system achieves a developmental landmark that often catapults the social interaction with mother onto a new level. What happens is subtle. The infant simply becomes capable of visually fixating his mother's eyes and holding the fixation with eye widening and eye brightening.[6] As for the mother, she experiences for the first time the very certain impression that the infant is really looking at *her*, even more, *into* her eyes. The effect of this can be dramatic. The mother may experience that she and the baby are finally "connected." Perhaps for the first time, or at least more completely than before, the mother feels that the baby is a fully responsive human being and they are engaged in a real relationship. Most often mothers cannot identify the change. At best, the more observant say that the infant looks at her differently. In any event, beginning about this time the mother's behavior becomes markedly more social—vocally, facially, and in all the other ways mentioned before. Truly social play interactions involving both partners now begin in earnest.

Consequences of the early maturation of gaze.   By the end of the third month, another developmental milestone is reached. The visual motor system has become essentially mature. First of all, his visual world is no longer limited to an eight-inch "bubble." The infant's focal distance has a range almost as extensive as adults. The infant can track the mother as she leaves, approaches, and moves about the room. His communicative network is thus vastly extended.

There are other striking aspects of this precocity. To appreciate them fully, it is necessary to review briefly what is involved in gazing, or the workings of the visual motor system. Gazing involves two quite different things: sight, one of the senses; and a motor act, movement of the eyes and usually the head also, to pursue or hold the visual target. These two functions working together provide visual perception with a unique feature. You can turn sight off or on at will. By closing the eyes, or simply turning the eyes away or down, the target object disappears. It can also be made to "reappear." In comparison, the ears have no earlids, and tuning out sound is not so simple as turning on or off sight. So clearly, gaze has an unusual feature as a mode for dealing with the external world.

By the end of the third month, the infant is about as good as an adult in rapidly moving his eyes to pursue an object or hold a fixation, and he is equally capable of quickly accommodating his eyes to bring objects into focus. This developmental landmark is extraordinary when contrasted with the immaturity of most of his other systems of communication and the regulation of interpersonal contact, for instance, speech, gesture, locomotion, manipulation of objects. (The infant's control over two other motor systems is quite mature by this point: sucking and head movements. We shall consider head movements below, but sucking itself never achieves a full or enduring status as a communicative system.)

The vagaries of man's developmental timetable, which ordains the early maturation of the visual motor system, result in a striking situation. The dyadic gazing interaction between mother and infant involves the interplay between two humans with essentially equal control and use of the same modality. It should be recalled that one member of the pair is only 3 to 4 months old. It is little wonder that early gazing behaviors have attracted more and more attention.

By the end of the third month the infant's mature motor control of gaze direction gives him essentially complete control over what he will see. His perceptual input becomes largely of his own choosing. He can veto or censor or titrate the amount and kind of visual stimulation he takes in from what is available in the outside world. When the outside stimulation is another human being, the infant is in the position to help regulate the degree or level of relatedness and to influence the flow of interpersonal behaviors. He becomes a true partner.

The shift to objects.   Toward the end of the first half year of life, the infant's love affair with the human face and voice and touch is partially replaced by a consuming interest in objects to reach for, grasp, and manipulate. This turn in interest is made possible by the last developmental landmark that will concern us here: the infant's hand-eye coordination, which has now come of age.

Once this happens, the mother-infant interaction becomes quite different. Their play interactions become more a triadic affair among mother, infant, and object. Different behaviors with different goals come into being. The human caregiver is now in the wings rather than at center stage of the infant's attention during the object-play sessions that now dominate his alert waking day. Presumably, the developmental "work" accomplished during the earlier phase—learning the basics of the nature of human beings—is largely over, and the next phase of learning the nature of object things is ushered in. The caregiver remains essential of course during this phase too, but not in the same capacity.

Head behaviors.   How a head is held or postured or how it is moved can be potent social signals among adults. The same is no less true for infants. I mentioned before that motor control of the head matures roughly in step with the precocious maturation of the visual motor system. It is almost impossible to consider gaze behaviors without considering at the same time head movements (as distinct from eye movements). The head and eyes generally move together, but not always and not always to the same degree. Head movements and gaze shifts are generally coordinated, although each adds a separate and different communicative impact to the jointly performed behaviors. In considering these coordinated behaviors it is necessary to hold in mind two different experiences: the infant as performer and the caregiver as recipient.

Starting from the infant's side, there are three main head positions—gaze directions relative to the mother's face.[7] In the central position the infant is gazing at the mother's face and his face is directly facing hers or only slightly turned away to either side. The infant views the mother with foveal vision. The fovea is that functionally central part of the retina where form and pattern perception are possible, and the infant thus sees the exact configuration of facial features presented by the mother. The next position is the peripheral. The infant is not looking directly at the mother but can "see" her out of the "corner" of his eye. His head is turned anywhere from 15 degrees to almost 90 degrees away from mother. He no longer has foveal vision and cannot make out the configuration of her facial features, but he does have peripheral vision of her face. Form perception is lost, but perception of motion, speed, and direction is retained. So in this very common position the infant can monitor the mother's head movements and changes in her facial expression. These also involve motion—even though the qualitative nature of the facial change may be lost. Accordingly, he has not lost contact and can perceive and react to her.[8] The third position is total loss of visual contact. This is generally achieved by the baby's turning his head past 90 degrees away or lowering it, or some combination of both. In this position, form perception and motion perception are both lost.

These three main positions can be broken down into finer gradations, but the central point is that in each different position the infant has a different sensory (visual) and motor (head position) experience relative to the caregiver. So each position provides the infant with a different sensori-motor "experience" of being with his mother which is under his control.

From the mother's side, the nature and degree of the infant's gaze direction and head turning are of great importance as a signal. First there is the vital issue of whether or not the baby is looking into the mother's eyes. If the baby is and also is directly facing her, that is one thing. If, however, he is looking at her but has turned his head slightly away, say 10–15 degrees, that is another matter. Gazing "sideways" has the character of an equivocal or ambivalent signal. It contains the contradictory components of contact with the eyes and aversion or flight with the head. With infants under six months (compared to adults), it is an unstable position that rapidly gets resolved one way or the other, into full facing with eye contact or further head aversion with loss of eye contact.

Turning the head away to the side is almost invariably interpreted as a signal of aversion or flight. (We shall later encounter a notable exception or variant where it is a gleeful invitation to the mother to chase.) In any event, face aversion can be considered part of an innate avoidance pattern which the newborn shows when an object looms toward his face. The face aversion we are dealing with here is a later avatar of that reflex pressed into a social function. The signal function such a pattern serves depends on its fullness of display which, in this case, is easily measured in degree and speed of aversion. The further and faster the infant averts his face the more the mother will assume he does not like something. This applies to a visual stimulus such as her face, as well as to a spoonful of some hated food.

The gaze and face aversions involved in peripheral monitoring are not complete avoidance or flight actions. They are akin to "intention movements" that reflect and signal the internal motivational state of the infant, and still allow him to view and react to the mother's movements, thus maintaining interactive commerce with her. The completed flight pattern would involve a full turning away with loss of all visual contact. This generally marks the termination of the interactive episode or play period.

Head lowering is another effective avoidance behavior. It appears to achieve a more definitive, if temporary, cut-off of the interaction than does face aversion to the side. This action immediately breaks all visual contact while side aversions maintain the peripheral monitoring. Head lowering is a promising area for more research. How early, for instance, does head lowering evolve into later forms of surrender, giving up, signing off, and such? We certainly often enough see infants lower their heads and go limp after they have given up fighting off overstimulation.

We have already seen that some infant head movements appear to belong to approach patterns. Bringing the head forward especially while tilting the face up is enormously appealing to mothers and is invariably interpreted as an affectively positive act of approach.

As early as the third to fourth month of life, then, the infant is capable of the clear performance of mixed or ambivalent head behaviors: he takes, so to speak, an element from one motivational pattern, and another element from a second and conflicting pattern, to produce a conglomerate behavior with a third and separate meaning of its own. For instance, when an infant breaks gaze and averts his face partially (say 45 degrees) but raises his head and tilts his face up, it is generally treated by the mother as a holding action. The mother keeps performing and trying to get the infant's full attention, reading his behavior almost as an invitation for greater efforts on her part. If, on the other hand, an infant breaks gaze and averts his face in exactly the same way, but lowers instead of raises his head and face, it is generally interpreted as a temporary cut-off. The mother will stop performing and resume only after changing her approach strategy.

Facial Expressions

Charles Darwin was one of the first observers of animals to recognize that the survival of highly social species could depend as much on their ability to communicate with one another as on their anatomical equipment for fighting or flight. Since he was also the first to see clearly man's evolutionary relationship to other social animals, he concluded that man, too, had to be equipped with the ability to send and receive important social cues bearing on survival. It was then only a short leap to ask how man acquired these species-specific expressive signals. Were these behaviors inborn and part of the evolutionary process as were anatomical features, or were they all learned? This question led Darwin to the far-reaching insight that the observation of the human newborn's expressive behavior provided a window into what was innate in man. Charlesworth and Kreutzer have beautifully summarized Darwin's findings as well as the hundred years of research in this area which have followed his groundbreaking but until recently neglected book.[9] They conclude that Darwin's essential findings hold up remarkably well. Specifically, Darwin concluded that the facial expressions of the basic emotions of pleasure, displeasure, anger, fear, joy, sorrow, and disgust were either present at birth or, when they appeared a few months later, reflected the unfolding of innate tendencies that were little influenced by socialization. He was less certain about the role of socialization for the more complex emotions.

More recent observers have been impressed with the large number of facial expressions newborns can make which appear to be identical to expressions seen on the faces of adults, expressions such as intense visual interest; cunning and wisdom; wry humor; complicated contortions of disgust or rejection; quizzical frowns and serene smiles. It should be stressed, however, that no one suggests that with such expressions the newborn experiences anything at all, let alone internal feelings comparable to those generally associated with the expressions in adults.

Although these early expressions, which are certainly reflexive, require much more rigorous study and categorization, nonetheless their mere presence is provocative. First, regarding "innateness," the presence of these expressions lends strong evidence to the notion that the infant is born with a surprising degree of facial neuromuscular maturity and, furthermore, that the movement of facial muscles is partly integrated at birth into recognizable configurations that later in life will become meaningful social cues.

The second issue regarding these early expressions relates to individual differences between newborns. Any individual differences in facial neuromuscular integration from the beginning may help stamp the nature of ensuing relationships. A singular study bears on this point.[10] Bennett carefully watched the routine morning activities of newborn nursery nurses and their charges. He noted that most infants were quickly character-typed by the nurses, who rapidly and fairly unanimously dubbed one infant as a lover boy, naughty but lovable, and another as a "simple nice girl, not sexy or flirtatious," and so on. The nature of the nurses' interplay with each infant was strongly colored by how they saw his or her personality.

Even if these observations are a simple case of "adultomorphizing" on the nurses' part (an important event in itself because it is so ubiquitous), the nurses' fantasies are not woven out of whole cloth. What are the individual cues that provide the seeds of the fantasies? Bennett remarks on differences in each infant related to rhythms of wakefulness, arousal, and alertness. He also stressed attention to differences in facial expression during alertness as an important cue for this common kind of early personality typing.

The smile.   During the first two weeks of life smiles are seen during dreaming sleep (also called irregular or rapid eye movement—REM sleep) and during drowsiness. They are rarely seen when the infant is awake and alert with his eyes open. Some of these smiles are fleeting, some prolonged, some are asymmetrical and quite wry-looking, where only one corner of the mouth goes up, and others are beatific. They appear to bear no relationship to anything going on in the external world and are solely the reflection of cycles of neurophysiological excitation and discharges within the brain, unrelated to gas bubbles or any other part of the body except the brain's intrinsic activity. It has been called endogenous smiling because of its internal origin and its unrelatedness to anything external.[11] They have also been called reflexive.

At sometime between six weeks and three months, depending on the study, the smile becomes exogenous, elicited by external events. Different sights and sounds will now reliably elicit a smile. However, among all the external stimuli once again it is the stimuli of a human face, the human gaze, a high-pitched voice, and tickling which are now the more predictable elicitors of the smile. Thus, in becoming exogenous, the smile becomes predominantly a social smile. Still the morphology of the smile does not change, although what triggers it does.

Beginning around the third month, the smile takes another developmental leap and becomes an instrumental behavior. By instrumental we mean simply that the infant will now produce the smile in order to get a response from someone, such as a return smile from mother or a word from her. The smile itself, however, still looks the same.

The last developmental advance is that around the fourth month the smile comes under sufficiently smooth and coordinated performance that it can begin to be performed simultaneously along with a part or parts of other facial expressions; more complex expressions emerge, such as a smile performed with a slight frown. More study is needed here to determine when expressions from different motivational patterns begin to integrate to form more complex and often ambivalent expressions.

These stages in the development in the smile would be impossible without the parallel advances in the infant's perceptual and cognitive abilities that permit the same old smile to appear under different conditions, in response to different stimuli, and in the service of different functions.

Why do we believe these transformations to be largely the unfolding of innate tendencies? The remarkable similarity in course and timetable for infants raised in very different environmental and social conditions lends some weight to the argument. Even more convincing are the studies of blind children who have had no visual opportunity to see or imitate smiles or receive visual reinforcement or feedback for their smiles. Until four to six months their smiles are relatively normal compared to sighted children and follow the same developmental stages and timetable. However, beginning around the fourth to sixth month the blind children begin to show a dampening or muting of facial expressiveness in general, so that the display of their smiles is less dazzling and captivating. This suggests that after an initial epoch of the unfolding of innate tendencies (under the impact of average experiences), some visual feedback or reinforcement appears to be necessary to maintain the fullest range of display of the smile behavior.

To summarize this developmental history: the smile moves from a reflexive activity (internally triggered) to a social response (externally elicited by human and other stimulation) to an instrumental behavior (produced to elicit social responses from others) to a sufficiently coordinated behavior to combine with other facial expressions. This general course, though probably the most common for facial expressions, is certainly not the same for all expressive behaviors. Unlike the smile, the laugh is not present at birth and does not appear to go through an endogenous phase. It appears first as a response to external stimuli somewhere between the fourth and eighth month. At first, from four to six months it is most easily elicited by tactile stimulation, such as tickling. From seven to nine months auditory events become more effective, and from ten to twelve months it is most readily triggered by visual agents.[12] Still like the smile, its form changes little from its first appearance throughout the rest of life. It is present in the blind and has been reported in feral children brought up by animals. Early on, it too becomes an instrumental behavior.

Displeasure. The cry face, with or without a cry, is the most dramatic and unequivocal expression of displeasure. The cry face, however, should be considered an end-point behavior, the last step, so to speak, in a patterned sequence of distinct facial expressions denoting increasing displeasure. The entire sequence of progressing expressions is roughly: first the face "sobers"; then a frown begins to form and deepens as the brows knit more; then the eyes begin to close partially as the upper cheeks raise and become flushed; the lower lip quivers and then the lips are retracted (pulled back) as the mouth opens; next the corners of the mouth turn down and the full cry face is achieved. Fuss noises may occur early on in the sequence, but it is only toward the end that the characteristic catches in breathing occur and the actual cry bursts out along with the cry face. The infant can, of course, stop at any point along the way within this sequence. The degree of displeasure will be interpreted from how far along in the patterned sequence he went. Several points along the way correspond to separate recognizable facial expressions: sobering, frowning, grimacing.

Each of these separate expressions, as well as the entire patterned sequence, follows a developmental course similar to that of the smile. These expressions are present at birth as reflexive activities, especially during sleep, and change very little in morphology throughout our lives. They become exogenous, externally elicited, behaviors earlier than the smile, and some observers believe that the instrumental use of the cry can be seen as early as three weeks of age. In any event, by the third month of life each of these expressions and the entire sequence to which they belong are ready and working as social and instrumental behaviors to help the infant conduct and regulate his half of the interaction with mother.

Pulling Things Together

I have discussed gazing, head movements, and facial expressions separately. Though we can write about or study each of these behaviors separately, in real life they belong together and are generally performed together. What is more, their simultaneous performance is integrated into behavioral "packages." These packages are the units of ongoing behavior which function as communicative units. For instance, in response to a disturbing stimulus, an infant may simultaneously break gaze and, while averting his face to the side, frown and grimace and emit a fuss sound. The simultaneous performance of these five behaviors is not something that the infant has to learn to coordinate. Instead, the particular integration itself is innately organized and reflects the unfolding of inborn tendencies toward organized actions. In ethological terms, each of the five separate behaviors can be considered an innate motor pattern. Similarly, their integrated performance can be considered an innate motor pattern of a higher order.

An example from the more complex realm of delight may help to fill in this notion. When we talk of a captivating infant smile, it is probable that much more is going on than just a full smile. The infant moves his head forward and tilts up his face, but without breaking gaze, as if he is trying to lift his head and face toward the person who elicited the smile. At the same time, body tension will noticeably increase as may limb movements, which may include a poorly coordinated effort to reach toward the person with his arms. The hands will open and close rhythmically. A gurgle may accompany these other acts. Once again, this entire specific integration of behaviors is unlearned.

There are three points to be made about these packages or units of ongoing behavior. The first I have already made, that these integrated units are as innately determined as their component parts are, and they undergo a developmental course mainly influenced by innate tendencies and organizational changes with only a small contribution from processes of learning.

The second point is that these packages appear to operate as functional units of communication within the flow of ongoing behavior. These integrated innate motor patterns are for the mother (or any average adult) the crucial stimulus which, once received and processed, lead her to act in a specific way. In animals, we would call the integrated infant behaviors innate releasers. Referring back to the smile, if the same smile were performed with the same increase in body tension and limb movement, but without the attempted head raising and face tilting and arm reaching, the impact of the communication would be significantly different. The adult would have inferred the same thorough delight on the infant's part, but the infant would have been viewed as a passive observer rather than as an active being moving toward the source of the delightful stimulation. The point, of course, is that the specific configuration of the integrated package of behaviors is perceived as a gestalt and is understood as such. We do not yet know to what extent mothers or other adults are themselves predisposed innately to perceive, comprehend, and react to these packages. The majority of our research has focused on the potency of the separate elements rather than on their action as an integrated whole.

The third point about these integrated units of behavior is that they may also be units in larger sequences that make up the major motivational themes of approach, pleasure, avoidance, and so on. The progression of units of ongoing behavior we have seen, from face sobering through several progressing units to the full cry face, described the displeasure behavioral pattern. We assume that these sequential patterns, as well as the series of units that make them up, are also largely determined by innate factors.

Very clearly then, by three months at least, the infant is well equipped with a large repertoire of behaviors to engage and disengage his caregivers. All of his behaviors—the simple motor patterns; the more complex combinations of these simple patterns into integrated units; and the patterned sequences of these units—have a strong innate predisposition. In addition, they have also been subject to the shaping process of learning during the early months of their emergence.

By the time we observe this very social infant toward the latter part of his first half year, his social capabilities are indeed formidable. He is fully ready to engage in that first phase of learning about and interacting with the human world. During these first six months he and his mother, utilizing their separate repertoires of behavior, have evolved their own interactive style and their own interactive fit as a pair.

NOTES

1. M. von Senden, *Space and Sight,* trans. P. Heath (Glencoe, Ill.: Free Press, 1960). A discussion of Von Senden's work can be found in R. A. Spitz and W. G. Coblinger, *The First Year of Life* (New York: International Universities Press, 1966).
2. K. S. Robson, "The Role of Eye to Eye Contact in Maternal-Infant Attachment," *Journal of Child Psychology and Psychiatry,* 1967, *8,* 13–25.
3. R. Ahrens, "Beitrag zur Entwicklung des Physiognomie-und Mimikerkennens," *Z. Exp. Angew. Psychol.,* 1954, *2,* 412–454. R. A. Spitz and K. M. Wolf, "The Smiling Response: A Contribution to the Ontogenesis of Social Relations," *Genet. Psychol. Monogr.,* 1946, *34,* 57–125.
4. R. L. Fantz, "Visual Experience in Infants: Decreased Attention to Familiar Patterns Relative to Novel Ones," *Science,* 1964, *146,* 668–670.
5. D. Freedman, "Smiling in Blind Infants and the Issue of Innate vs. Acquired," *Journal of Child Psychology and Psychiatry,* 1964, *5,* 171–184. R. A. Haaf and R. Q. Bell, "A Facial Dimension in Visual Discrimination by Human Infants," *Child Development,* 1967, *38,* 893–899.
6. P. H. Wolff, "Observations on the Early Development of Smiling." In B. M. Foss, ed., *Determinants of Infant Behavior,* vol. 2 (New York: Wiley, 1963).
7. B. Beebe and D. Stern, "Engagement-Disengagement and Early Object Experiences." In N. Freedman and S. Grand, eds., *Communicative Structures and Psychic Structures* (New York: Plenum, 1977, forthcoming).
8. D. Stern, "Mother and Infant at Play: The Dyadic Interaction Involving Facial, Vocal and

Gaze Behaviors." In M. Lewis and L. Rosenblum, eds., *The Effect of the Infant on Its Caregiver* (New York: Wiley, 1974).

9. W. R. Charlesworth and M. Kreutzer, "Facial Expressions of Infants and Children." In P. Ekman, ed., *Darwin and Facial Expression* (New York: Academic Press, 1973).

10. S. L. Bennett, "Infant-Caretaker Interactions," *Journal of the American Academy of Child Psychiatry,* 1971, *10,* 321–335.

11. R. Emde, T. Gaensbauer, and R. Harmon, "Emotional Expression in Infancy: A Biobehavioral Study," *Psychological Issues Monograph Series,* 1976, *10,* 1, No. 37.

12. L. A. Sroufe and E. Waters, "The Ontogenesis of Smiling and Laughter: A Perspective on the Organization of Development in Infancy," *Psychological Review,* 1976, *83,* 173–189.

2

Preverbal Communication between Mothers and Infants
T. Berry Brazelton and Edward Tronick

Human infancy offers both infant and parents a period of interdependency more prolonged than that of most other mammals. Such a prolonged period provides the base for handing on from one generation to the next the assurance of increased individuality—among cultures, among families, and among the individuals in each family. In addition, it allows for the learning of complex tasks which are more or less unique but certainly richly refined in the human—a rich repertoire of skilled behavior and of specifically human communication, verbal and nonverbal. Prolonged infancy provides the opportunity both for the learning of these skills and for the growth of a sense of competence. This latter comes from the realization that goals, whether innate or acquired, may be successfully achieved through action coupled with sensorimotor feedback. The learning of the skills comes about in several different ways: 1. by testing and practicing alone, 2. by practice and experimentation reinforced at appropriate times by those around him, 3. by careful observation and direct imitation of the actions of behavior of others, and 4. by identification with others, in which the "quality" as well as the match of the others' actions are understood and reproduced. Thus, the human infant has both the time and the affective and cognitive information necessary to acquire the skills needed to cope with the complexity of human society.

The limitations on these acquisitions and thus on his ultimate development can arise from two sources: directly from the infant when his capacity for development is impaired, as it is in a baby with a sensory defect or with brain damage; or from the environment in which he is being nurtured. Since at least three of the four means of acquiring skilled behavior and communication are directly dependent on "others," the richness of his ultimate capacities may be highly correlated with the quality of his interaction with his caregiving environment. Thus, the two sources for potential limitation become difficult to separate, especially since his chances for optimal development are enhanced when he is rewarding to his caretakers and part of his reward value is dependent on his intactness.

From the infant's standpoint, a nurturing environment will provide not only necessary nutrients and control systems (heat, protection, and so on) but also a protective and rewarding envelope while he is learning about himself and his world. Since Bruner (1972) has demonstrated that the acquisition of knowledge is anchored in systems which are open for new information and equipped with feedback loops that produce the realization of having reached a goal, our work has been toward understanding this system within the environment's protective envelope.

In our work with Bruner at the Center for Cognitive Studies from 1966 to 1970, we first became aware of the system of nonverbal behaviors with which the infant signaled his interactions with both objects and people. At that time, Bruner (1972), Trevarthen (1977), and Bower (1971) were studying the acquisition of early reaching behavior. Their work was demonstrating how early (in the first weeks) an infant's attention to an object in "reach space" (ten to twelve inches in front of him in the midline) captured all of his behavior. Not only did he have an observable, predictable "hooked" state of attention as the object was brought into this space, but also his whole body responded in an appropriate and predictable fashion as he attended to the object.

The infant stared fixedly at the object with wide eyes, fixating on it for as long as two minutes without disruption of gaze or of attention (by six weeks). His expression was fixed, the muscles of his face tense, with eyes staring and mouth and lips protruding toward the object. This static, fixed look of attention was interspersed with little jerks of facial muscles. His tongue jerked out toward the object and then withdrew rapidly. Occasional short bursts of effortful vocalizing toward the object occurred. During these long periods of attention, the eyes blinked occasionally in single, isolated blinks. The body was set in a tense, immobilized sitting position, with the object at his midline. When the object was moved to one side or the other, the infant tended to shift his body appropriately, so it was kept at his midline. His shoulders hunched as if he were about to "pounce." Extremities were fixed, flexed at elbow and knee, and fingers and toes were aimed toward the object. Hands were semiflexed or tightly flexed, but fingers and toes repeatedly jerked out to point at the object. Jerky swipes of an arm or of a leg in the direction of the object occurred from time to time as the period of intense attention was maintained. In this interaction with an object, his attention seemed "hooked," and all his motor behavior alternated between the long, fixed periods of tense absorption and short bursts of jerky, excited movement in the direction of the object. He seemed to hold down any interfering behavior which might break into this prolonged state of attention.

Striking in all of this was the intent, prolonged state of attention, during which tension gradually built up in all segments of his body until abrupt disruption seemed the inevitable and necessary relief for him. This behavior was most striking by twelve to sixteen weeks. It could also be observed as early as four weeks of age, long before a reach could be achieved.

Additionally we have observed the cardio-respiratory involvement of infants who had congenital cardiac defects and whose circulatory balance was precarious. As they get "hooked" on and interact with an object in reach space, their breathing becomes deeper and more labored, their cardiac balance more precarious, cyanosis deepens until attention to the object is decreased momentarily, and their color returns. The return of attention to the object brings on a repetition of the same cycle of "hooked" attention, increasing autonomic imbalance, and recovery as the baby turns away briefly. From these observations it is clear that an infant's attention to an object involves behavioral, neuromotor, and autonomic systems in a predictable alternating increase and decrease in the deployment of attention and nonattention, designed to protect an immature and easily overloaded cardio-respiratory balance.

The contrast of the infant's behavior and attention when he interacted with his mother and when he attended to an object was clear even as early as four weeks of age. Indeed we felt we could see brief episodes of these two contrasting modes of behavior and attention as early as two to three weeks.

A striking way of illustrating the behaviors of the mother and the child, as well as the interaction of the two, is to present them in graphic form (from Brazelton, Koslowski, and Main 1974). To illustrate, figures 1 to 4 are graphs drawn from interaction periods. Time is measured along the horizontal axis; the number of behaviors, along the vertical axis. Curves drawn above the horizontal line indicate that the person whose behavior the curve represents was looking *at* his partner. Curves drawn below the line indicate that he was looking *away*. Solid lines represent the mother's behavior; broken lines, the baby's. Thus, a deep, broken line below the horizontal line indicates that the baby was looking away while engaging in several behaviors.

As reflected in Figure 1, the mother looks at the baby after he turns to her. As they look at each other, she adds behaviors, smiling, vocalizing, touching his hand, and holding his leg, to accelerate their interaction. He responds by increasing the number of his own behaviors (smiling, vocalizing, and cycling his arms and legs) until the peak at X. At this point he begins to decrease his behaviors and gradually cuts down on them toward the end of their interaction. She follows his lead by decreasing her behaviors more rapidly and ends her part of the cycle by looking away just before he does. Figure 2 shows a baby starting a cycle by looking at his mother. She follows by looking at him and adding four more behaviors in rapid succession— touching him, smiling, talking, and nodding her head. He watches her, vocalizes, smiles back, cycles briefly, and then begins to decrease his responses and turns away at *a*. She stops smiling as he begins to turn away but rapidly adds facial gestures to try to recapture his interest. She continues to talk, touch him, nod her head, and make facial gestures until *b*. At this point she stops the gestures but begins to pat him. At *c* she stops talking briefly and stops nodding at him. At *d* she makes hand gestures in addition to her facial

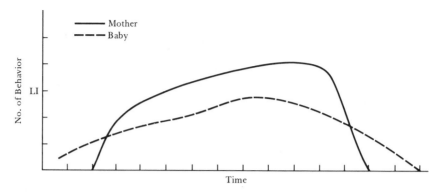

FIGURE 1 Number of behaviors added in period of sixteen-second looking interaction. Baby looking (LI: looking intent).

From Brazelton, T. B., Koslowski, B., Main, M. 1974. The origins of reciprocity: The early
mother-infant interaction. In *The effect of the infant on its caregiver,* ed. M. Lewis and L. A.
Rosenblum, vol. 1. Figures 1–4 reprinted by permission of John Wiley & Sons.

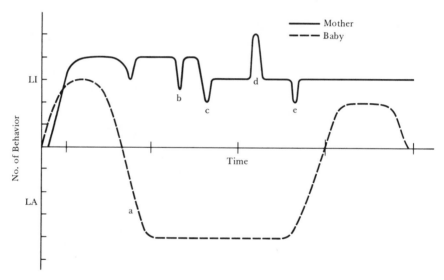

FIGURE 2 Number of behaviors added in a five-second period of interaction (LI: looking interest; LA: looking away).

grimaces but stops them both thereafter. At *e* she stops vocalizing, and he
begins to return to look at her. He vocalizes briefly and then looks away again
when her activity continues.

In Figure 3 the mother and infant are looking at each other; she is
vocalizing, and he is smiling. As she increases her activity by patting him, he
turns away. She begins to nod at him at *a*, and he begins to look at the curtain
across the room. She tries to quiet him down at *b* and again at *c*. After a
period of less activity from her, he begins to turn to her at *d*. As he returns to
look at her, she begins to build up the interaction by smiling and vocalizing;
eventually at *e* she pats him. At this he begins to turn away again.

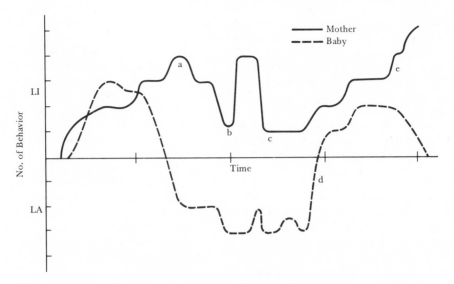

FIGURE 3 Number of behaviors added in a four-second interaction.

In Figure 4 the mother and baby are looking at each other, smiling, and vocalizing together. The baby begins to cycle and reach out to her. At *a* he begins to turn away from her. She responds by looking down at her hands and she stops her activity briefly. This brings him back to look at her at *c*. Her smiling, vocalizing, and leaning toward him bring a smiling response from him. In addition, his arms and legs cycle and he coos contentedly as he watches her. As he turns away she first adds another behavior and gestures. He, however, adds to his activities—ignoring her reminders—and turns away from her. She gradually cuts out all her activity and by *e* she looks away

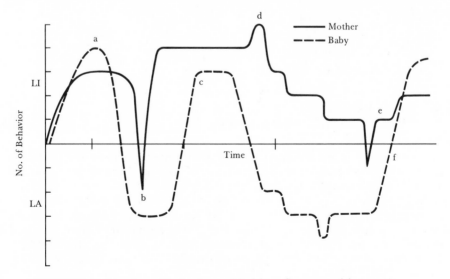

FIGURE 4 Number of behaviors added in a five-second interaction.

from him. Immediately afterward he begins to look back to her, and the cycle of looking at each other begins again at *f*.

Of course the expectancy engendered in an interaction with a static object, as opposed to a responsive person, must be very different (Piaget 1953, 1959). But what surprised us was how early this expectancy seemed to be reflected in the infant's behavior and use of attention. When the infant was interacting with his mother, there seemed to be a constant cycle of attention (A), followed by withdrawal of attention (W)—the cycle being used by each partner as he approached and then withdrew and waited for a response from the other participant. In each of these "states" (A and W) we found there were predicted behaviors and the use of them in clusters predicted the timing of a response of the other. Single behaviors were less predictive. But in order to predict and understand which cluster of behaviors will produce an ongoing sequence of attention, one must first understand the "state" of affective attention which has been captured and is expressed by each member of the dyad. In other words, the strength of the dyadic interaction dominates the meaning of each member's behavior. If the mother responds in one way, their interactional energy builds up (A), if another, the infant may turn away (W). The same holds true of her response to his behavior. The effect of clustering and of sequencing takes over in assessing the value of particular behaviors, and in the same way the dyadic nature of interaction supersedes the importance of an individual member's clusters and sequences.

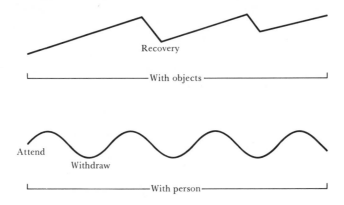

FIGURE 5   Homeostasis in attention.

The power of the interaction in shaping behavior can be seen at many levels. Using looking and not looking at the mother as measures of attention-nonattention, in a minute's interaction there was an average of 4.4 cycles of such attention and apparent nonattention. Not only were the spans of attention and of looking away of shorter duration than they had been with objects, but they were obviously smoother as the attention built up, reached its peak, and then diminished gradually with the mother. Both the build-up as well as the decrease in attention were gradual and were usually smoothly paced.

Mother's Role

In this setting, the most important role of the adult interactant seemed to be that of helping the infant to form a regulatory base for his immature physiological and motor reactions.

The most important rule for maintaining an interaction seemed to be that a mother develop a sensitivity to her infant's capacity for attention and his need for withdrawal—partial or complete—after a period of attention to her. Short cycles of attention and nonattention seemed to underlie all periods of prolonged interaction. Although we thought we were observing continuous attention to her, on the part of the infant, the stop-frame analysis uncovered the cyclical nature of the infant's looking and not-looking in our laboratory setting. Looking away behavior reflects the need of each infant to maintain some control over the amount of stimulation he can take in during such intense periods of interaction. This is a homeostatic model, similar to the type of model that underlies all the physiological reactions of the neonate, and it seems to apply to the immature organism's capacity to attend to messages in a communication system.

In the visual system it was apparent that this model was pertinent. Unless the mother responded appropriately to these variations in his behavior, it appeared to us that his span of attention did not increase, and the quality of his attention was less than optimal. For example, in the case of two similarly tense, overactive infants, the mothers responded very differently. One mother responded with increased activity and stimulation to her baby's turning away; another maintained a steady level of activity which gradually modulated her baby's overreactivity. The end result was powerfully in favor of the latter dyad. This latter baby was more responsive, and for longer periods, as our study progressed. Although this effect could have been based on characteristics of the baby that we were not able to analyze, we felt that the quality of communication changed in this pair. However, the linear tenseness of the first dyad remained throughout the twenty weeks of observation. This baby had learned "rules" about managing his own needs in the face of an insensitive mother. He had learned to turn away and stay away, to decrease his receptivity to information from her. This must be necessary for him in order to maintain a physiological and psychological homeostasis in the face of her insensitivity. These two parallel cases demonstrate that a mother's behavior must be not only reinforcing and contingent upon the infant's behavior, but also adjusted to and supportive of the infant's capacity to receive and utilize stimuli. This, then, becomes the first rule each must learn from the other.

As another example, one of our mothers was particularly striking in the way she released her demands as the infant decreased his attention to her. She sat back in her chair smiling softly, reducing other activities such as vocalizing and moving, waiting for him to return. When he did look back, she began slowly to add behavior on behavior, as if she were feeling out how much he could master. She also sensed his need to reciprocate. She vocalized, then waited for his response. When she smiled, she waited until he smiled before she began to build up her own smiling again. Her moving in close to him was paced sensitively to coincide with his body cycling, and if he became excited or jerky in his movement she subsided back into her chair.

We felt she was outstanding in her sensitivity to the importance of reciprocity in this interaction. She provided an atmosphere that led to longer periods of interaction. She seemed to teach him an expectancy of more than just stimuli from her in the guise of her sensitivity to his needs and his cues. As she allowed for these, she seemed to be teaching him how to expand his own ability to attend to stimulation, for "long-term intention" as well as "long-term interaction." Thus her role took on deeper significance as she not only established the climate for communication but also gave him the experience in pacing himself in order to attend to the environment.

Although this may look as if it were "unlearned" behavior in some mothers, its absence in other mothers may demonstrate the fact that it can be a kind of rule learning. The individuality of each member of the dyad determines the flexibility in the number of rules necessary and sets the limits on the variability within each rule that still allow the goal to be achieved.

Another rule is that the mother use her periods of interaction to "model" more and more complex routines for the baby. She times the complexity of her models to his stage of development. For example, in the early weeks imitation of his activity is limited and enlarged upon by her. This must serve as a feedback mechanism for him (Bruner 1972)—one that enlarges upon his awareness for his behavior. He becomes aware of his action, visualizes her imitation of it, and reproduces it for himself again. As he does so, he has the opportunity to add on to it, either by serendipity or by modeling his behavior to match her enlarged version. Either way, he increases its scope. The timing of imitative reinforcement and her sensitivity to his capacity for attention and learning must depend on her having learned this "rule" about him—his capacity to accept her feedback and to use it as a method for further learning.

This interdependence of rhythms seemed to be at the root of their "attachment" as well as communication. When the balance was sympathetic to the needs of each member of the dyad, there was a sense of rhythmic interaction which an observer sensed as "positive." When the balance was not equalized, and one member was out of phase with the other, there seemed to be a "negative" quality in the entire interaction. Sander says that "each new thrust of activity in the growing infant requires a new period of interactional adjustment with the caretaking environment to reach stable coordination on the bases of new changes" (1965, p. 330). The smoothness with which these dyads made such adjustments reflected the depth of their attachment and probably contributed a further opportunity for each to learn about the other member. Certainly, the strength of the interdependence of the dyad seemed to be more powerful in shaping each member's behavior than did any other force—such as the individual member's style or wish of the moment.

A mother's behavior in a period of interaction might be summarized by five kinds of functions she serves for the infant:

1. Reduction of interfering activity.
2. Setting the stage for a period of interaction by bringing him to a more alert, receptive state.
3. Creating an atmosphere of expectancy for further interaction by her behavior.

4. Acceleration of his attention to receive and send messages.
5. Allowing for reciprocity with sensitivity to his signals, giving him time to respond with his own behavior, as well as time to digest and recover from the activation her cues establish.

The learning of these rules of interaction additionally becomes a system in which the mother learns not only about the infant, but also about herself. As she adapts to her infant, she learns a kind of self-mastery necessary for mothering as well.

The Infant's Role

The infant is equipped with reflex behavioral responses which are organized in rather primitive patterns at birth. He soon organizes them into more complex patterns of behavior which serve his goals for organization at a time when he is still prone to a costly disorganization of neuromotor and physiological systems. Thus, he is set up to learn about himself and his environment, for as he achieves each of these goals his feedback systems give him a double message: "Goal accomplished; now go on." In this way, each time he achieves a state of homeostatic control, he is fueled to go on to the next stage of disruption and reconstitution—a familiar model for energizing a developing system. We use Robert White's (1959) "sense of competence" as our idea for fueling the system from within. We also believe that the infant's quest for social stimuli is in response to his need for fueling from the world outside. As he achieves a homeostatic state, and as he responds to a disruptive stimulus, the reward for each of these states of homeostasis and disruption is thus reinforced by internal and external events. Hence, he starts out with the behaviorally identifiable mechanisms of a bimodal system—1. of attaining a state of homeostasis and a sense of achievement from within; and 2. the ability to incorporate signals from the world around him, fueling him from without. He is set up with behavioral pathways for providing both of these for himself—for adaptation to his new world, even in the neonatal period. Since very little fueling from within or without may be necessary to "set" these patterns and press him onward, they are quickly organized and reproduced over and over until they are efficient, incorporated, and can be utilized as the base for building later patterns.

With this model of a bimodal system which provides an increased availability to the outside world, one can then incorporate Sander's (1965) ideas of early entrainment of biobehavioral rhythms, Condon and Sander's (1974) proposals that the infant's movements match the rhythms of the adult's voice, Meltzoff and Moore's (1977) work on imitation of tongue protrusion in a three-week old, and Bower's (1971) observations on early reaching behavior to an attractive object in the first weeks of life. As each of these responsive behaviors to external stimuli contributes to a realization that he has "done it"—controlled himself in order to reach out for and respond appropriately to an external stimulus or toward an adult—his achievement encourages him to further forms of engagement. The engagement or entrainment involves the two feedback systems of internal control and external responsiveness. Thus, he can learn most about himself by responding to the world around him. This explains the observable drive on the part of the neonate to capture and interact with an adult and his "need" for social interaction.

The infant's feedback system is adaptive to stress and change and to a built-in self-regulatory goal. The immature organism with its vulnerability to being overloaded must be in constant homeostatic regulation—the physiological and psychological. Handling input becomes a major goal for the infant, rather than a demanding or a destructive one. Such a system can handle disruption either by negative and stressful or by positive and attractive stimuli; but the organizing aspect of both is seen in the amount of growth of the system. Since positive stimuli permit growth and homeostasis with less cost, one can predict the value of a sensitive environmental feedback for the immature organism; just as one can predict with a more constantly stressful environment that there will be an attempt at precocious mastery; and finally, if the adult member or members are insensitive to the needs of the immature member of the dyad or triad, an extensive fixation or even breakdown in the system may occur. If disruption or fixation does not occur, then stress can provide a learning paradigm for handling the stress and then recovering (Als et al. 1979a). Either way there is disruption of the old balance, but in one there is the feedback which results from the successful closing of a homeostatic cycle, with the infant thereby being readied for the next task in development.

The first task for a newborn as Als (1978) has pointed out is control over the physiological system, particularly breathing, heart rate, and temperature control. For preterm and at-risk newborns, this control is more difficult to achieve than it is for healthy full-term newborns. While control over these basic physiological demands is being achieved, the newborn begins to establish organization and differentiation of the motor system, effecting the range, smoothness, and complexity of movement. The next major agendum is the attainment of a stable organization of his states of consciousness. First, the infant will have to differentiate six states, from deep sleep to intense crying, and begin to manage transitions between these states. Achieving control over transitions between states demands an integration of the control over the physiological and motoric systems and the states of consciousness. The adult caregiver can play the role of organizer (Sander 1965) and can begin to expand certain states, e.g., the quiet, alert state, as well as the duration and quality of sleep rates. In addition, the caregiver can help regulate the transitions between states for the infant.

As the state organization becomes differentiated and begins to be regulated, usually in the course of the first month, the next newly emerging expansion is that of the increasing differentiation of the alert state (Als, in press; Als, Tronic, and Brazelton, in press, a). Hence, the infant's social capacities begin to unfold. His ability to communicate becomes increasingly sophisticated. The repertoire of facial expressions, vocalizations, cries, gestures, and postures in interaction with a social partner begin to expand. He can now use his well-modulated state organization to regulate social interactions. This, in turn, leads into the fourth state when the infant can be the leader on the signal giver. When he can seek out social cues, when he can establish games, initiate them and terminate them, when he can use toys as a bridge for communication and play with others, he is equipped to take voluntary control over his environment. This is bound to strengthen his own feelings of competence.

We first began to see the value of such a conceptual base when we were developing the Brazelton (1973) *Neonatal Behavioral Assessment Scale.* The concept underlying the assessment is that the neonate can defend himself from negative stimuli, can control interfering autonomic and motoric responses in order to attend to important external stimuli, and can reach out for and utilize stimulation from his environment necessary for his species-specific motor, emotional, social, and cognitive development. Using the baby's own control over his states of consciousness, the examiner attempts to bring the baby from sleep to wakefulness and even to crying and back to sleep again as he assesses the neonate's capacity to respond to and elicit social responses from the environment. In a twenty-minute assessment, an examiner can begin to feel a neonate's strengths in shaping those around him. The newborn responds clearly and differently to appealing and negative intrusive stimuli. Both kinds of stimulation provide some form of organization, but as one handles him and sees him achieve an alert state, using the examiner's cues, and as he then maintains a clearly alert state, one begins to realize how much a part of his organization the nurturing "other" can and must be. We work to achieve the infant's "best performance" on a series of responses to various stimuli—to voice, to face, to handling and cuddling, to the rattle, and to a red ball. As the infant becomes excited and responsive, one can see his increased and increasing sense of mastery and involvement with the adult examiner. His states of consciousness become the matrix for all his reactions; as he responds to individual stimuli and as he moves from state to state, one can see and feel him respond to the stimulus, regain his balance, then move on to respond to the next stimulus.

As one plays with a newborn, one realizes that the newborn is indeed displaying a marvelous capacity to regulate his internal physiological responses by the mechanisms of internal homeostatic control or "state" control. The newborn's "awareness" of this capacity becomes a first basis for internalizing his capacity to control himself and his environment, as well as a base for the next steps. We believe that these observations might lend perspective to Hartmann's (1958) idea of precursors of ego development.

In following the infant's interactions through the first four months of life, we were able to discern successive stages of disruption, progress, and the reachievement of homeostasis (Als et al. 1979a; Als in press). Throughout, the infant learns about himself, and the mother's self-awareness increases as she participates in helping him achieve the goals of each of these stages. These then become a rich base for the infant's affective and cognitive development, as well as his awareness of himself—developmental accomplishments which might be equated with early ego development.

Figure 6 shows the more detailed, second-by-second analysis of the interactions of an infant boy and his mother at 25 days, 46 days, 68 days and 92 days (Als et al. 1979b; Als in press; Als et al. in press). The infant's behavior is represented on the lower part of each subgraph; the mother's behavior, on the top part of each subgraph. The partners' displays are graphed in mirror images of one another, presenting six states of interaction for each participant. The states are scaled to range from displays strongly directed away from the interaction, such as protest, avoid, and avert,

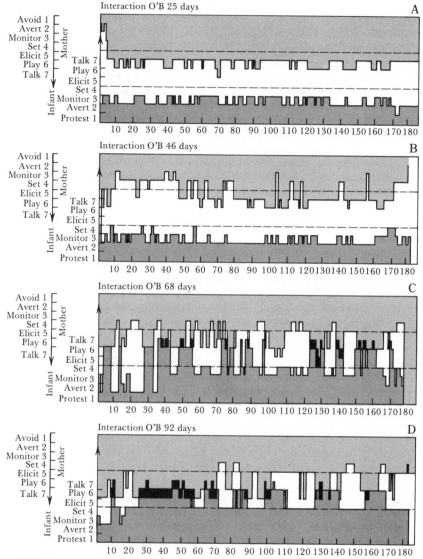

FIGURE 6   "Social Interaction: Matrix for the Development of Behavioral Organization. Some Thoughts Towards a Dynamic
Process Model."

From H. Als. In *New Directions for Child Development: Social Interaction and Communications in
Infancy*, no. 4, ed. Ina C. Uzgiris (San Francisco: Jossey-Bass, 1979). Reprinted by permission of
the publisher.

through displays mildly directed toward the interaction, such as monitor and
set, to displays strongly directed toward the interaction, such as play and talk.
The closer the partners' respective positions to one another are on the
graph, the more in heightened synchrony they are with one another; the
farther away from one another on the graph their respective positions are,
the more interactively distant they are from one another.

At twenty-five days, the infant observed moves mainly from cautious monitoring back to averting, then attempts to monitor again.

By forty-six days (about six weeks), the infant can repeatedly maintain a quiet, brightly alert, oriented state, labeled "set," toward the mother in this situation, and the newly emerging coo and play phase is beginning to be apparent in the initial sally. The mother's range has also widened by six weeks. She moves from intermittent averting, via monitoring, to eliciting and playing. The urgency of continuous prompting and organization exhibited in the tight cycling between eliciting and playing of the earlier interaction is no longer as intense. The infant has become more flexible, and the mother can leave some of the self-modulation up to him.

By sixty-eight days (about two months), the infant's organization has become increasingly differentiated, moving initially between protest and play, and then, from 35 seconds on, between the phases motor, set, play, and talk, until the very end, when he averts again. The repeated cycling through play and talk indicates the full emergence of the new differentiation of his alert state. He is now capable of engaging in interaction with a rich repertoire, integrating smiling and cooing, and he repeatedly achieves an amplitude of affective organization not previously attained. The mother simultaneously expands his peaks, and they achieve a high level of affective interlocking. She spends more time in set than before, indicating her expectant readiness for play and increasing ability to let him take the lead.

By three months (about ninety-two days), this new achievement of differentiation has become more solidified, as is indicated in the prolonged play episodes of the infant and the new baseline at set. The mother's new base is also at set with prolonged cycles through play and talk, indicating her confidence in the infant's self-regulation.

Figure 6 as Als (in press; Als et al. in press) describes the infant's homeostatic curve has literally moved up by two phases, from averting and monitoring at twenty-five days, with its peaks at set by forty-six days, to its base at set and its peaks at play and talk by three months. The wave lengths of the curve have also considerably increased, pointing to the smooth reintegration of the recent differentiation of both partners, now ready for new expansion of an increasingly solidifying base. This system thus gives us a way of documenting and quantifying the progress of early infant development within the matrix of social interaction.

In these interactions the mutual feedback is apparent. As Als (in press; Als et al. 1979a; Als et al. in press) has pointed out, once the infant is oriented to the parent, the parent expands the affective and attentional ambiance to maintain the infant's state. The infant begins to reciprocate with his ways of interaction. The parent maintains this interaction and gradually expands it to include the next achievement, such as, early on, the mere maintenance of alertness, then the achievement of reaching out to sound. Once the new achievement has occurred—for instance, the infant has smiled or cooed—the parent acknowledges the achievement profusely, leaving time for the infant to recognize his achievement and to integrate it into his current structure of competence. The expansion of the child's competence thus requires the sensitive gauging of the affective base necessary and the appropriate timing of the next step. It is a process of balancing support with challenge. It requires the parents' willingness to risk stressing the system when in balance and dealing with the resultant disorganization. When the limits are exceeded and disorganization results, the parent has to maintain perspective on the process and go back to that level of interaction that the child can currently manage. Once back on base, the expansion process can begin again. The levels of interaction are thus passed through over and over again.

The environment potentiates the newborn's increasing differentiation by offering him a controlling kind of organization from the outside which, because it is adapted to his level of development, provides him with appropriate feedback. This differentiation is further enhanced by a recognition of his capacity to reach out for and to shut off social stimuli. This same capacity, in turn, results in growing complexity of the interactional channels and structures and provides increasing opportunities for the individual system to become more differentiated. Given such a flexible system, the infant's individuality is continuously fitted to and shaped by that of the adult. Our model is that of a feedback system of increasing complexity, a system embedded in and catalyzed by the interaction with others.

We have come to realize a fact that must have been evident to others already, that the nurturing adult who provides the "envelope" learns as much about him or herself as does the baby. The very acts of nurturing become an inner feedback system all its own. Successful nurturance which produces rewarding responses in the infant adds further to this self-realization. And the learning about oneself as a parent can be conceptualized in developmental stages which are parallel to and dependent upon those of the infant.

In summary, this model of development is a powerful one for understanding the reciprocal bonds that are set up between parent and infant. The feedback model allows for flexibility, disruption, and reorganization. Within its envelope of reciprocal interaction, one can conceive of a rich matrix of different modalities for communication, individualized for each pair and critically dependent on the contribution of each member of the dyad or triad. There is no reason that each system cannot be shaped in different ways by the preferred modalities for interaction of each of its participants, but each *must* be sensitive and ready to adjust to the other member in the envelope. And at each stage of development, the envelope will be different—richer, we would hope.

This work was supported by grants from the Robert Wood Johnson Foundation, the Carnegie Foundation, and the William T. Grant Foundation—NIMH (#MH14887). The authors wish to thank Dr. Heideliese Als for her participation in this chapter and the work behind it, especially for her elegant contributions expressed in the Four Stages of Development of Mother and Infant. Drs. Barbara Koslowski and Mary Main contributed to much of the earlier work cited here.

REFERENCES

ALS, H. Assessing an assessment: conceptual consideration, methodological issues, and a perspective on the future of the neonatal behavioral assessment scale. In A. J. Sameroff (Ed.), *Organization and stability of newborn behavior: A commentary on the Brazelton neonatal behavior assessment scale.* Monographs of the Society for Research in Child Development, 1978, 177, 14–29.

————. Social interaction: Matrix for the development of behavioral organization. Some thoughts towards a dynamic process model. In Ina C. Uzgiris (Ed.), *Social interaction and communications in infancy: New directions for child development,* vol. 4, San Francisco: Jossey Bass Publishers, in press.

ALS, H., TRONICK, E., AND BRAZELTON, T. B. Stages of early behavioral organization: The study of a sighted infant and of a blind infant in interaction with their mothers. In T. B. Field, S. Goldberg, D. Stern, and A. Sostek (Eds.), *High risk infants and children: Adult and peer interactions.* New York: Grune & Stratton, in press (a).

————. Affective reciprocity and the development of autonomy: The study of a blind infant. *Journal of American Academy of Child Psychiatry,* in press (b).

————. (1979b) Analysis of face to face interaction in infant-adult dyads. In M. E. Lamb, S. J. Suomi, and G. R. Stephenson (Eds.), *Social Interaction Analysis: Methodological Issues.* The University of Wisconsin Press, 1979, 33–76.

BOWER, T. G. The object in the world of the infant. *Scientific American,* 1971, 225, 30–38.

BRAZELTON, T. B. *Neonatal assessment scale.* Clinics in Developmental Medicine, Monograph 50. London: William Heinemann; Philadelphia: J. B. Lippincott, 1973.

BRAZELTON, T. B., KOSLOWSKI, B. AND MAIN, M. The origins of reciprocity: The early mother-infant interaction. In M. Lewis and L. A. Rosenblum (Eds.), *The effect of the infant on its caregiver.* New York: Wiley, Interscience, 1974, 49–77.

BRUNER, J. AND KOSLOWSKI, B. Preadaptation in initial visually guided reaching. *Perception,* 1972, 1, 3–14.

CONDON, W. S. AND SANDER, L. W. Neonate movement is synchronized with adult speech: Interactional participation and language acquisition. *Science,* 1974, 183, 99–101.

CONNOLLY, K. J., AND BRUNER, J. S. *The growth of competence.* London: Academic Press, 1974.

HARTMANN, H. *Ego psychology and the problem of adaptation.* New York: International University Press, 1958.

MELTZOFF, A. N. AND MOORE, M. K. Imitation of facial and manual gestures by human neonates. *Science,* 1977, 198, 75–78.

PIAGET, J. *The origins of intelligence in the child.* London: Routledge, 1953.

————. *The child's construction of reality.* London: Routledge, 1955.

SANDER, L. W. Regulation and organization in the early infant caregiver system. In R. Robinson (Ed.), *Brain and early behavior.* London: Academic Press, 1965, 1–74.

TREVARTHEN, C. Descriptive analyses of infant communicative behavior. In H. R. Schaffer (Ed.), *Studies in mother-infant interaction.* New York: Academic Press, 1977.

WHITE, R. W. Motivation reconsidered: The concept of competence. *Psychological Review,* 1959, 66, 297–333.

3

Infant-Mother Attachment
Mary D. Salter Ainsworth

Bowlby's (1969) ethological-evolutionary attachment theory implies that it is an essential part of the ground plan of the human species—as well as that of many other species—for an infant to become attached to a mother figure. This figure need not be the natural mother but can be anyone who plays the role of principal caregiver. This ground plan is fulfilled, except under extraordinary circumstances when the baby experiences too little interaction with any one caregiver to support the formation of an attachment. The literature on maternal deprivation describes some of these circumstances, but it cannot be reviewed here, except to note that research has not yet specified an acceptable minimum amount of interaction required for attachment formation.

However, there have been substantial recent advances in the areas of individual differences in the way attachment behavior becomes organized, differential experiences associated with the various attachment patterns, and the value of such patterns in forecasting subsequent development. These advances have been much aided by a standardized laboratory situation that was devised to supplement a naturalistic, longitudinal investigation of the development of infant-mother attachment in the first year of life. This *strange situation,* as we entitled it, has proved to be an excellent basis for the assessment of such attachment in 1-year-olds (Ainsworth, Blehar, Waters, and Wall 1978).

The assessment procedure consists of classification according to the pattern of behavior shown in the strange situation, particularly in the episodes of reunion after separation. Eight patterns were identified, but I shall deal here only with the three main groups into which they fell—Groups A, B, and C. To summarize, Group B babies use their mothers as a secure base from which to explore in the preseparation episodes; their attachment behavior is greatly intensified by the separation episodes so that exploration diminishes and distress is likely; and in the reunion episodes they seek contact with, proximity to, or at least interaction with their mothers. Group C babies tend to show some signs of anxiety even in the preseparation episodes; they are intensely distressed by separation; and in the reunion episodes they are ambivalent with the mother, seeking close contact with her and yet resisting contact or interaction. Group A babies, in sharp contrast, rarely cry in the separation episodes and, in the reunion episodes, avoid the mother, either mingling proximity-seeking and avoidant behaviors or ignoring her altogether.

Comparison of Strange-Situation Behavior and Behavior Elsewhere

Groups A, B, and C in our longitudinal sample were compared in regard to their behavior at home during the first year. Stayton and Ainsworth (1973) had identified a security-anxiety dimension in a factor analysis of fourth-quarter infant behavior. Group B infants were identified as securely attached because they significantly more often displayed behaviors characteristic of the secure pole of this dimension, whereas both of the other groups were identified as anxious because their behaviors were characteristic of the anxious pole. A second dimension was clearly related to close bodily contact, and this was important in distinguishing Group A babies from those in the other two groups, in that Group A babies behaved less positively to being held and yet more negatively to being put down. The groups were also distinguished by two behaviors not included in the factor analysis— cooperativeness and anger. Group B babies were more cooperative and less angry than either A or C babies; Group A babies were even more angry than those in Group C. Clearly, something went awry in the physical-contact interaction Group A babies had with their mothers, and as I explain below, I believe it is this that makes them especially prone to anger.

Ainsworth et al. (1978) reviewed findings of other investigators who had compared A-B-C groups of 1-year-olds in terms of their behavior elsewhere. Their findings regarding socioemotional behavior support the summary just cited, and in addition three investigations using cognitive measures found an advantage in favor of the securely attached.

Comparison of Infant Strange-Situation Behavior
with Maternal Home Behavior

Mothers of the securely attached (Group B) babies were, throughout the first year, more sensitively responsive to infant signals than were the mothers of the two anxiously attached groups, in terms of a variety of measures spanning all of the most common contexts for mother-infant interaction (Ainsworth et al. 1978). Such responsiveness, I suggest, enables an infant to form expectations, primitive at first, that moderate his or her responses to events, both internal and environmental. Gradually, such an infant constructs an inner representation—or "working model" (Bowlby 1969)—of his or her mother as generally accessible and responsive to him or her. Therein lies his or her security. In contrast, babies whose mothers have disregarded their signals, or have responded to them belatedly or in a grossly inappropriate fashion, have no basis for believing the mother to be accessible and responsive; consequently they are anxious, not knowing what to expect of her.

In regard to interaction in close bodily contact, the most striking finding is that the mothers of avoidant (Group A) babies all evinced a deep-seated aversion to it, whereas none of the other mothers did. In addition they were more rejecting, more often angry, and yet more restricted in the expression of affect than were Group B or C mothers. Main (e.g., in press) and Ainsworth et al. (1978) have presented a theoretical account of the dynamics of interaction of avoidant babies and their rejecting mothers. This emphasizes the acute approach-avoidance conflict experienced by these infants when their attachment behavior is activated at high intensity—a conflict stemming from painful rebuff consequent upon seeking close bodily contact. Avoidance is viewed as a defensive maneuver, lessening the anxiety and anger experienced in the conflict situation and enabling the baby nevertheless to remain within a tolerable range of proximity to the mother.

Findings and interpretations such as these raise the issue of direction of effects. To what extent is the pattern of attachment of a baby attributable to the mother's behavior throughout the first year, and to what extent is it attributable to built-in differences in potential and temperament? I have considered this problem elsewhere (Ainsworth 1979) and have concluded that in our sample of normal babies there is a strong case to be made for differences in attachment quality being attributable to maternal behavior. Two studies, however (Connell 1976; Waters, Vaughn, and Egeland in press), have suggested that Group C babies may as newborns be constitutionally "difficult." Particularly if the mother's personality or life situation makes it hard for her to be sensitively responsive to infant cues, such a baby seems indeed likely to form an attachment relationship of anxious quality.

Contexts of Mother-Infant Interaction

Of the various contexts in which mother-infant interaction commonly takes place, the face-to-face situation has been the focus of most recent research. By many (e.g., Walters and Parke 1965), interaction mediated by distance receptors and behaviors has been judged especially important in the establishment of human relationships. Microanalytic studies, based on frame-by-frame analysis of film records, show clearly that maternal sensitivity to infant behavioral cues is essential for successful pacing of face-to-face interaction (e.g., Brazelton, Koslowski, and Main 1974; Stern 1974). Telling evidence of the role of vision, both in the infant's development of attachment to the mother and in the mother's responsiveness to the infant, comes from Fraiberg's (1977) longitudinal study of blind infants.

So persuasive have been the studies of interaction involving distance receptors that interaction involving close bodily contact has been largely ignored. The evolutionary perspective of attachment theory attributes focal importance to bodily contact. Other primate species rely on the maintenance of close mother-infant contact as crucial for infant survival. Societies of hunter-gatherers, living much as the earliest humans did, are conspicuous for very much more mother-infant contact than are western societies (e.g., Konner 1976). Blurton Jones (1972) presented evidence suggesting that humans evolved as a species in which infants are carried by the mother and are fed at frequent intervals, rather than as a species in which infants are left for long periods, are cached in a safe place, and are fed but infrequently. Bowlby (1969) pointed out that when attachment behavior is intensely activated it is close bodily contact that is specifically required. Indeed, Bell and Ainsworth (1972) found that even with the white, middle-class mothers of their sample, the most frequent and the most effective response to an infant's crying throughout the first year was to pick up the baby. A recent analysis of our longitudinal findings (Blehar, Ainsworth, and Main[1]) suggests that mother-infant interaction relevant to close bodily contact is at least as important a context of interaction as face-to-face is, perhaps especially in the first few months of life. Within the limits represented by our sample, however, we found that it was *how* the mother holds her baby rather than *how much* she holds him or her that affects the way in which attachment develops.

In recent years the feeding situation has been neglected as a context for mother-infant interaction, except insofar as it is viewed as a setting for purely social, face-to-face interaction. Earlier, mother's gratification or frustration of infant was of interest to both psychoanalytically oriented and social-learning research, on the assumption that a mother's gratification or frustration of infant instinctual drives, or her role as a secondary reinforcer, determined the nature of the baby's tie to her. Such research yielded no evidence that methods of feeding significantly affected the course of infant development, although these negative findings seem almost certainly to reflect methodological deficiencies (Caldwell 1964). In contrast, we have found that sensitive maternal responsiveness to infant signals relevant to feeding is closely related to the security or anxiety of attachment that eventually develops (Ainsworth and Bell 1969). Indeed, this analysis seemed to redefine the meaning of "demand" feeding—letting infant behavioral cues determine not only when feeding is begun but also when it is terminated, how the pacing of feeding proceeds, and how new foods are introduced.

Our findings do not permit us to attribute overriding importance to any one context of mother-infant interaction. Whether the context is feeding, close bodily contact, face-to-face interaction, or indeed the situation defined by the infant's crying, mother-infant interaction provides the baby with opportunity to build up expectations of the mother and, eventually, a working model of her as more or less accessible and responsive. Indeed, our findings suggest that a mother who is sensitively responsive to signals in one context tends also to be responsive to signals in other contexts.

Practical Implications for Intervention

What I have so far summarized about research findings pertaining both to contexts of interaction and to qualitative differences in infant-mother attachment has implications for parenting education, for intervention by professionals to help a mother to achieve better interaction with her baby, and for the practices to substitute caregivers. I cannot go into detail here— and indeed such detail would need to be based on much fuller reports of the relevant research than I am able to include here. Among the intervention programs with which I am familiar, some parent-child development centers have reported success in the application of our research findings in improving and sustaining the rate of development of very young children through improving the quality of mother-infant interaction (e.g., Andrews, Blumenthal, Bache, and Wiener[2]). Furthermore, the expert clinical interventions of Fraiberg and her associates with families at risk have focused on increasing maternal responsiveness to infant behavioral cues (e.g., Shapiro, Fraiberg, and Adelson 1976). It may be that such intervention, although obviously expensive, provides the most effective mode of helping dyads in which the difficulty stems from deep-seated difficulties in the mother's personality, such as the aversion to bodily contact characteristic of our Group A mothers.

Using the Mother as a Secure Base from Which to Explore

Attachment theory conceives of the behavioral system serving attachment as only one of several important systems, each with its own activators, terminators, predictable outcomes, and functions. During the prolonged period of human infancy, when the protective function of attachment is especially important, its interplay with exploratory behavior is noteworthy. The function of exploration is learning about the environment—which is particularly important in a species possessing much potential for adaptation to a wide range of environments. Attachment and exploration support each other. When attachment behavior is intensely activated, a baby tends to seek proximity/contact rather than exploring; when attachment behavior is at low intensity a baby is free to respond to the pull of novelty. The presence of an attachment figure, particularly one who is believed to be accessible and responsive, leaves the baby open to stimulation that may activate exploration.

Nevertheless, it is often believed that somehow attachment may interfere with the development of independence. Our studies provide no support for such a belief. For example, Blehar et al. (see Note 1) found that babies who respond positively to close bodily contact with their mothers also tend to respond positively to being put down again and to move off into independent exploratory play. Fostering the growth of secure attachment facilitates rather than hampers the growth of healthy self-reliance (Bowlby 1973).

Response to Separation from Attachment Figures

Schaffer (1971) suggested that the crucial criterion for whether a baby has become attached to a specific figure is that he or she does not consider this figure interchangeable with any other figure. Thus, for an infant to protest the mother's departure or continued absence is a dependable criterion for attachment (Schaffer and Callender 1959). This does not imply that protest is an invariable response to separation from an attachment figure under all circumstances; the context of the separation influences the likelihood and intensity of protest. Thus there is ample evidence, which cannot be cited here, that protest is unlikely to occur, at least initially, in the case of voluntary separations, when the infant willingly leaves the mother in order to explore elsewhere. Protest is less likely to occur if the baby is left with another attachment figure than if he or she is left with an unfamiliar person or alone. Being left in an unfamiliar environment is more distressing than comparable separations in the familiar environment of the home—in which many infants are able to build up expectations that reassure them of mother's accessibility and responsiveness even though she may be absent. Changes attributable to developmental processes affect separation protest in complex ways. Further research will undoubtedly be able to account for these shifts in terms of progressive cognitive achievements.

Major separations of days, months, or even years must be distinguished from the very brief separations, lasting only minutes, that have been studied most intensively both in the laboratory and at home. Securely attached infants may be able to tolerate very brief separations with equanimity, yet they are likely to be distressed in major separations, especially when cared for by unfamiliar persons in unfamiliar environments. Even so, Robertson and Robertson (1971) showed that sensitive substitute parenting can do much to mute separation distress and avert the more serious consequences of major separations.

Despite a steady increase in our understanding of the complexities of response to and effects of separation from attachment figures in infancy and early childhood, it is difficult to suggest clear-cut guidelines for parents and others responsible for infant and child care. So much depends on the circumstances under which separation takes place, on the degree to which the separation environment can substitute satisfactorily for home and parents, on the child's stage of development and previous experience, and on the nature of his or her relationship with attachment figures. No wonder that the issue of the separations implicit in day care is controversial. Further research is clearly needed. Meanwhile, it would seem wise for parents—if they have a choice—to move cautiously rather than plunging into substitute-care arrangements with a blithe assumption that all is bound to go well.

Other Attachment Figures

Many have interpreted Bowlby's attachment theory as claiming that an infant can become attached to only one person—the mother. This is a mistaken interpretation. There are, however, three implications of attachment theory relevant to the issue of "multiple" attachments. First, as reported by Ainsworth (1967) and Schaffer and Emerson (1964), infants are highly selective in their choices of attachment figures from among the various persons familiar to them. No infant has been observed to have many attachment figures. Second, not all social relationships may be identified as attachments. Harlow (1971) distinguished between the infant-mother and peer-peer affectional systems, although under certain circumstances peers may become attachment figures in the absence of anyone more appropriate (see, e.g., Freud and Dann 1951; Harlow 1963). Third, the fact that a baby may have several attachment figures does not imply that they are all equally important. Bowlby (1969) suggested that they are not—that there is a principal attachment figure, usually the principal caregiver, and one or more secondary figures. Thus a hierarchy is implied. A baby may both enjoy and derive security from all of his or her attachment figures but, under certain circumstances (e.g., illness, fatigue, stress), is likely to show a clear preference among them.

In recent years there has been a surge of interest in the father as an attachment figure. . . . Relatively lacking is research into attachments to caregivers other than parents. Do babies become attached to their regular babysitters or to caregivers in day-care centers? Studies by Fleener (1973), Farran and Ramey (1977), and Ricciuti (1974) have suggested that they may but that the preference is nevertheless for the mother figure. Fox (1977) compared the mother and the *metapelet* as providers of security to kibbutz-reared infants in a strange situation, but surely much more research is needed into the behavior of infants and young children toward caregivers as attachment figures in the substitute-care environment.

Consequences of Attachment

A number of investigators, including Main (1973)[3] Matas, Arend, and Sroufe (1978), and Waters, Wittman, and Sroufe (in press), having assessed the quality of 1-year-olds' attachment, having followed the children through to ascertain whether this assessment bears a significant relationship to later behavioral measures in the second, third, or even sixth year of life. We (Ainsworth et al. 1978) have reviewed these investigations in some detail; only a brief summary can be given here.

In comparison with anxiously attached infants, those who are securely attached as 1-year-olds are later more cooperative with and affectively more positive as well as less aggressive and/or avoidant toward their mothers and other less familiar adults. Later on, they emerge as more competent and more sympathetic in interaction with peers. In free-play situations they have longer bouts of exploration and display more intense exploratory interest, and in problem-solving situations they are more enthusiastic, more persistent, and better able to elicit and accept their mothers' help. They are more curious, more self-directed, more ego-resilient—and they usually tend to achieve better scores on both developmental tests and measures of language development. Some studies also reported differences between the two groups of anxiously attached infants, with the avoidant ones (Group A) continuing to be more aggressive, noncompliant, and avoidant, and the ambivalent ones (Group C) emerging as more easily frustrated, less persistent, and generally less competent.

Conclusion

It is clear that the nature of an infant's attachment to his or her mother as a 1-year-old is related both to earlier interaction with the mother and to various aspects of later development. The implication is that the way in which the infant organizes his or her behavior toward the mother affects the way in which he or she organizes behavior toward other aspects of the environment, both animate and inanimate. This organization provides a core of continuity in development despite changes that come with developmental acquisitions, both cognitive and socio-emotional.

This is not to insist that the organization of attachment is fixed in the first year of life and is insensitive to marked changes in maternal behavior or to relevant life events occurring later on. Nor is it implied that attachments to figures other than the mother are unimportant as supplementing or compensating for anxieties in infant-mother attachment—although too little is yet known about how various attachments relate together to influence the way in which infants organize their perception of and approach to the world. Despite the need for further research, however, the yield of findings to date provides relevant leads for policies, education in parenting, and intervention procedures intended to further the welfare of infants and young children.

NOTES

1. Blehar, M. C., Ainsworth, M. D. S., and Main, M. *Mother-infant interaction relevant to close bodily contact.* Monograph in preparation, 1979.
2. Andrews, S. R., Blumenthal, J. B., Bache, W. L., III, and Wiener, G. *Fourth year report: New Orleans Parent-Child Development Center.* Unpublished document, March 1975. (Available from Susan R. Andrews, 6917 Glenn Street, Metairie, Louisiana 70003).
3. Main, M., and Londerville, S. B. *Compliance and aggression in toddlerhood: Precursors and correlates.* Paper in preparation, 1979.

REFERENCES

AINSWORTH, M. D. S. *Infancy in Uganda: Infant care and the growth of love.* Baltimore, Md.: Johns Hopkins Press, 1967.

AINSWORTH, M. D. S. Attachment as related to mother-infant interaction. In J. S. Rosenblatt, R. A. Hinde, C. Beer, and M. Busnel (Eds.), *Advances in the study of behavior* (Vol. 9). New York: Academic Press, 1979.

AINSWORTH, M. D. S., AND BELL, S. M. Some contemporary patterns of mother-infant interaction in the feeding situation. In A. Ambrose (Ed.), *Stimulation in early infancy.* London: Academic Press, 1969.

AINSWORTH, M. D. S., BLEHAR, M. C., WATERS, E., AND WALL, S. *Patterns of attachment: A psychological study of the strange situation.* Hillsdale, N.J.: Erlbaum, 1978.

BELL, S. M., AND AINSWORTH, M. D. S. Infant crying and maternal responsiveness. *Child Development,* 1972, *43,* 1171–1190.

BLURTON JONES, N. G. Comparative aspects of mother-child contact. In N. G. Blurton Jones (Ed.), *Ethological studies of child behavior.* London: Cambridge University Press, 1972.

BOWLBY, J. *Attachment and loss: Vol. 1. Attachment.* New York: Basic Books, 1969.

BOWLBY, J. *Attachment and loss: Vol. 2. Separation: Anxiety and anger.* New York: Basic Books, 1973.

BRAZELTON, T. B., KOSLOWSKI, B., AND MAIN, M. The origins of reciprocity: The early mother-infant interaction. In M. Lewis and L. A. Rosenblum (Eds.), *The effect of the infant on its caregiver.* New York: Wiley, 1971.

CALDWELL, B. M. The effects of infant care. In M. L. Hoffman and L. W. Hoffman (Eds.), *Review of child development research* (Vol. 1). New York: Russell Sage Foundation, 1964.

CONNELL, D. B. *Individual differences in attachment: An investigation into stability, implications, and relationships to the structure of early language development.* Unpublished doctoral dissertation, Syracuse University, 1976.

FARRAN, D. C., AND RAMEY, C. T. Infant day care and attachment behavior toward mother and teachers. *Child Development,* 1977, *48,* 1112–1116.

FLEENER, D. E. Experimental production of infant-maternal attachment behaviors. *Proceedings of the 81st Annual Convention of the American Psychological Association,* 1973, *8,* 57–58. (Summary)

FOX, N. Attachment of kibbutz infants to mother, *Child Development,* 1977, *48,* 1228–1239.

FRAIBERG, S. *Insights from the blind.* New York: Basic Books, 1977.

FREUD, A., AND DANN, S. An experiment in group up-bringing. *Psychoanalytic Study of the Child,* 1951, *6,* 127–168.

HARLOW, H. F. The maternal affectional system. In B. M. Foss (Ed.), *Determinants of infant behaviour* (Vol. 2). New York: Wiley, 1963.

HARLOW, H. F. *Learning to love.* San Francisco: Albion, 1971.

KONNER, M. J. Maternal care, infant behavior, and development among the !Kung. In R. B. Lee and I. DeVore (Eds.), *Kalabari hunter-gatherers.* Cambridge, Mass.: Harvard University Press, 1976.

MAIN, M. *Exploration, play, and level of cognitive functioning as related to child-mother attachment.* Unpublished doctoral dissertation, Johns Hopkins University, 1973.

MAIN, M. Avoidance in the service of proximity. In K. Immelmann, G. Barlow, M. Main, and L. Petrinovich (Eds.), *Behavioral development: The Bielefeld Interdisciplinary Project.* New York: Cambridge University Press, in press.

MATAS, L., AREND, R.A., AND SROUFE, L. A. Continuity of adaptation in the second year. The relationship between quality of attachment and later competence. *Child Development,* 1978, *49,* 547–556.

RICCIUTI, H. N. Fear and the development of social attachments in the first year of life. In M. Lewis and L. A. Rosenblum (Eds.), *The origins of fear.* New York: Wiley, 1974.

ROBERTSON, J., AND ROBERTSON, J. Young children in brief separation: A fresh look. *Psychoanalytic Study of the Child,* 1971, *26,* 264–315.

SCHAFFER, H. R. *The growth of sociability.* London: Penguin Books, 1971.

SCHAFFER, H. R., AND CALLENDER, W. M. Psychological effects of hospitalization in infancy. *Pediatrics,* 1959, *25,* 528–539.

SCHAFFER, H. R., AND EMERSON, P. E. The development of social attachments in infancy. *Monographs of the Society for Research in Child Development,* 1964, *3* (Serial No. 94).

SHAPIRO, V., FRAIBERG, S., AND ADELSON, E. Infant-parent psychotherapy on behalf of a child in a critical nutritional state. *Psychoanalytic Study of the Child,* 1976, *31,* 464–491.

STAYTON, D. J., AND AINSWORTH, M. D. S. Individual differences in infant responses to brief, everyday separations as related to other infant and maternal behaviors. *Developmental Psychology,* 1973, *9,* 226–235.

STERN, D. N. Mother and infant at play: The dyadic interaction involving facial, vocal, and gaze behaviors. In M. Lewis and I. A. Rosenblum (Eds.), *The effect of the infant on its caregiver.* New York: Wiley, 1974.

WALTERS, R. H., AND PARKE, R. D. The role of the distance receptors in the development of social responsiveness. In L. P. Lipsitt and C. C. Spiker (Eds.), *Advances in child development and behavior.* New York: Academic Press, 1965.

WATERS, E., VAUGHN, B. E., AND EGELAND, B. R. Individual differences in infant-mother attachment relationships at age one: Antecedents in neonatal behavior in an urban economically disadvantaged sample. *Child Development,* in press.

WATERS, E., WITTMAN, J., AND SROUFE, L. A. Attachment, positive affect, and competence in the peer group: Two studies in construct validation. *Child Development,* in press.

Part II

Infant Peer Relations

INFANTS normally do not spend much time with one another. Except in the unusual case of twins, most families are spaced so that children are at least a year apart in age. This means that most families have no more than one infant in them at any time, and those that do generally have infants that are at least a year apart in age, a wide difference early in life. Unless parents make special efforts to arrange peer play sessions for their infants, or unless the infant is enrolled in early daycare or similar programs, the infant will likely interact almost exclusively with older persons.

Because of this, it is not easy to glean from everyday life a sense of the infant's potential for peer engagement. How responsive are infants to other infants? Could an infant possibly profit from interacting with peers? If so, are any of the potential benefits of infant-infant relations similar to the benefits that follow from the infant-caregiver relation, or might infant-infant relations have a different set of developmental consequences? These are questions of great interest for our understanding of children's social development. But they are not easily answered by observations of typical family life, since infant relations have never been common throughout human history.

On this topic, consequently, studies of unusual or artificially manipulated circumstances are particularly valuable. An example of the former is Anna Freud's and Sophie Dann's unique document of a naturally occurring "experiment in group upbringing." An example of the latter is Carol Eckerman's and Judith Whatley's laboratory experiment on the outcome of arranging peer interactions between infants as young as ten months. Both of these studies provide us with rare glimpses into the social-developmental possibilities of infant peer relations.

Freud and Dann provide an account of six orphans who were placed in Sister Sophie Dann's care when they were three years of age. These children had been together since they were young infants. In fact, they had been the only stable companions in each other's lives. Their parents had been killed in the Nazi purges, and otherwise they had been exposed only to a series of transient adult caregivers in hospitals and concentration camps. Thus Freud and Dann were witnesses to a highly unusual case of infants who had had more consistent access to other infants than to dependable adult figures. The nature of these infants' social relations and personal characteristics at age three offers us special insight into the possible developmental implications of intense early peer relations.

It is noteworthy, though perhaps not surprising, that the six orphans had by age three developed close, intimate relations with one another, marked by emotional dependence, positive affect, and an "in-group" sense of loyalty. As far as I know, there is no comparable evidence of such early intimacy between peers in the psychological literature. This is certainly an indication that infants and young children are capable of sustaining productive interactions with one another long before they normally have the opportunity to do so in typical childhood circumstances. It is perhaps also not surprising that these six orphans initially expressed much antipathy towards the adults that attempted to care for them at age three. With each other they acted in a caring and sympathetic manner demonstrating an astonishing lack of jealousy or rivalry, whereas with adults they showed strong and uncontrolled aggression.

What is surprising, given this abnormal pattern of peer and adult relations, is how relatively undisturbed these war orphans turned out to be. Before too long they were able to establish positive attachments to their adult caregivers, and adapted well cognitively and linguistically to their new context. They learned their new language (English) quickly, assumed their share of responsibilities in their new home, and in many ways proved themselves to be bright and active children. There were some lingering personal deficits, such as the children's hypersensitivity, restlessness, and lack of self-control. But by and large these children had survived a tumultuous infancy psychologically unimpaired. Freud and Dann infer that they were able to do so because of the social and emotional relations that they had established with one another during infancy. If so, this is a remarkable testament to the potential of infant peer relations.

The Freud and Dann study not only suggests that early peer relations can offer children a sustaining sense of intimacy, but also indicates that even intense early peer relations may be different in quality early in adult-child relations. This became evident both in observations of the children's conduct with one another as in observations of the children's first positive initiatives towards adults. The children were accustomed to treating one another as equals, sharing and taking turns with one another, expecting and giving assistance to each other, and behaving with a sense of mutual consideration towards one another. During their first positive encounters with adults, the children approached the adults with an identical sense of equality and reciprocal expectation. This struck Freud and Dann as unusual, since adult child relations normally are based more on a sense of adult-directed care and child-centered dependence. The spirit of equal reciprocity with which the six orphans conducted their social affairs arose from their extensive early peer experience, and highlights one possible difference between peer and adult relations during childhood. As we shall see in the studies of childhood, some psychologists believe that because these two types of social relations are qualitatively distinct, they lead to different sorts of developmental outcomes.

Freud and Dann note that in their observations of this unique event, they did not have the luxury of arranging systematic scientific procedures. Real life has none of the neatness or control of a laboratory experiment. The Eckerman and Whatley study is a laboratory test of the infant's capacity for responding to peers. Although the methods of investigation differed greatly from the Freud and Dann study, Eckerman and Whatley's results bear a similar message. Infants in the first year of life can be highly responsive to infant age-mates if given the chance. Toys can act as a catalyst for infant peer engagement, as a number of their studies have also found. But even without toys, infants show interest and positive affect towards one another. They seem to take particular pleasure in imitating one another, although other types of contacts and communications were also frequent. Eckerman and Whatley's scientific manipulations add an important confirmation to our beginning recognition of infant peer possibilities.

At the present time, research on infant and toddler peer relations is burgeoning, thanks to the efforts of the authors represented in this book, as well as to those of other researchers like Edward Mueller. This has been one of the unexplored terrains in the world of social and personality development, and the prospects are exciting for opening it still further.

4

An Experiment
in Group Upbringing
Anna Freud and Sophie Dann

Introduction

The experiment to which the following notes refer is not the outcome of an artificial and deliberate laboratory setup but of a combination of fateful outside circumstances. The six young children who are involved in it are German-Jewish orphans, victims of the Hitler regime, whose parents, soon after their birth, were deported to Poland and killed in the gas chambers. During their first year of life, the children's experiences differed; they were handed on from one refuge to another, until they arrived individually, at ages varying from approximately six to twelve months, in the concentration camp of Tereszin.[1] There they became inmates of the Ward for Motherless Children, were conscientiously cared for and medically supervised, within the limits of the current restrictions of food and living space. They had no toys and their only facility for outdoor life was a bare yard. The Ward was staffed by nurses and helpers, themselves inmates of the concentration camp and, as such, undernourished and overworked. Since Tereszin was a transit camp, deportations were frequent. Approximately two to three years after arrival, in the spring of 1945, when liberated by the Russians, the six children, with others, were taken to a Czech castle where they were given special care and were lavishly fed. After one month's stay, the 6 were

Reprinted from *The Psychoanalytic Study of the Child*, vol. 6, edited by Eissler, Freud, Hartmann, and Kris. Copyright 1951 by International Universities Press. Used with permission.

included in a transport of 300 other children and adolescents, all of them survivors from concentration camps, the first of 1000 children for whom the British Home Office had granted permits of entry. They were flown to England in bombers and arrived in August 1945 in a carefully set-up reception camp in Windermere, Westmoreland,[2] where they remained for two months. When this reception camp was cleared and the older children distributed to various hostels and training places, it was thought wise to leave the six youngest together, to remove them from the commotion which is inseparable from the life of a large children's community and to provide them with peaceful, quiet surroundings where, for a year at least, they could adapt themselves gradually to a new country, a new language, and the altered circumstances of their lives.

This ambitious plan was realized through the combined efforts of a number of people. A friend of the former Hampstead Nurseries, Mrs. Ralph Clarke, wife of the Member of Parliament for East Grinstead, Sussex, gave the children a year's tenancy of a country house with field and adjoining woodland, "Bulldogs Bank" in West Hoathly, Sussex, containing two bedrooms for the children, with adjoining bathrooms, a large day nursery, the necessary staff rooms, a veranda running the whole length of the house and a sun terrace.

The Foster Parents' Plan for War Children, Inc., New York, who had sponsored the Hampstead Nurseries during the war years 1940–1945, took the six children into their plan and adopted Bulldogs Bank as one of their colonies. They provided the necessary equipment as well as the financial upkeep.

The new Nursery was staffed by Sisters Sophie and Gertrud Dann, formerly the head nurses of the Baby Department and Junior Nursery Department of the Hampstead Nurseries respectively. A young assistant, Miss Maureen Wolfison, who had accompanied the children from Windermere was replaced after several weeks by Miss Judith Gaulton, a relief worker. Cooking and housework was shared between the staff, with occasional outside help.

The children arrived in Bulldogs Bank on October 15, 1945. The personal data of the six, so far as they could be ascertained, follow on page 46.[3]

Meager as these scraps of information are, they establish certain relevant facts concerning the early history of this group of children:

- (i) that four of them (Ruth, Leah, Miriam, Peter) lost their mothers at birth or immediately afterward; one (Paul) before the age of twelve months, one (John) at an unspecified date;
- (ii) that after the loss of their mothers all the children wandered for some time from one place to another, with several complete changes of adult environment. (Bulldogs Bank was the sixth station in life for Peter, the fifth for Miriam, etc. John's and Leah's and Paul's wanderings before arrival in Tereszin are not recorded.);
- (iii) that none of the children had known any other circumstances of life than those of a group setting. They were ignorant of the meaning of a "family";
- (iv) that none of the children had experience of normal life outside a camp or big institution.[4]

Name	Date and Place of Birth	Family History	Age at Arrival in Tereszin	Age at Arrival in BULLDOGS BANK
John	18.12.1941 Vienna	Orthodox Jewish working-class parents. Deported to Poland and killed.	Presumably under 12 months	3 years 10 months
Ruth	21.4.1942 Vienna	Parents, a brother of 7 and a sister of 4 years were deported and killed when Ruth was a few months old. She was cared for in a Jewish Nursery in Vienna, sent to Tereszin with the Nursery.	Several months	3 years 6 months
Leah	23.4.1942 Berlin	Leah and a brother were illegitimate, hidden from birth. Fate of mother and brother unknown. Brother presumed killed.	Several months	3 years 5 months Arrived 6 weeks after the others, owing to a ringworm infection.
Paul	21.5.1942 Berlin	Unknown	12 months	3 years 5 months
Miriam	18.8.1942 Berlin	Upper middle-class family. Father died in concentration camp, mother went insane, was cared for first in a mental hospital in Vienna, later in a mental ward in Tereszin where she died.	6 months	3 years 2 months
Peter	22.10.1942	Parents deported and killed when Peter was a few days old. Child was found abandoned in public park, cared for first in a convent, later, when found to be Jewish, was taken to the Jewish hospital in Berlin, then brought to Tereszin.	Under 12 months	3 years

Behavior toward Adults on Arrival

On leaving the reception camp in Windermere, the children reacted badly to the renewed change in their surroundings. They showed no pleasure in the arrangements which had been made for them and behaved in a wild, restless, and uncontrollably noisy manner. During the first days after arrival they destroyed all the toys and damaged much of the furniture.

Toward the staff they behaved either with cold indifference or with active hostility, making no exception for the young assistant Maureen who had accompanied them from Windermere and was their only link with the immediate past. At times they ignored the adults so completely that they would not look up when one of them entered the room. They would turn to an adult when in some immediate need, but treat the same person as nonexistent once more when the need was fulfilled. In anger, they would hit the adults, bite or spit. Above all, they would shout, scream, and use bad language. Their speech, at the time, was German with an admixture of Czech words, and a gradual increase of English words. In a good mood, they called the staff members indiscriminately *Tante* (auntie), as they had done in Tereszin; in bad moods this changed to *blöde Tante* (silly, stupid auntie). Their favorite swearword was *blöder Ochs* (the equivalent of "stupid fool"), a German term which they retained longer than any other.

Group Reactions

Clinging to the Group

The children's positive feelings were centered exclusively in their own group. It was evident that they cared greatly for each other and not at all for anybody or anything else. They had no other wish than to be together and became upset when they were separated from each other, even for short moments. No child would consent to remain upstairs while the others were downstairs, or vice versa, and no child would be taken for a walk or on an errand without the others. If anything of the kind happened, the single child would constantly ask for the other children while the group would fret for the missing child.

This insistence on being inseparable made it impossible in the beginning to treat the children as individuals or to vary their lives according to their special needs. Ruth, for instance, did not like going for walks, while the others greatly preferred walks to indoor play. But it was very difficult to induce the others to go out and let Ruth stay at home. One day, they actually left without her, but kept asking for her until, after approximately twenty minutes, John could bear it no longer and turned back to fetch her. The others joined him, they all returned home, greeted Ruth as if they had been separated for a long time and then took her for a walk, paying a great deal of special attention to her.

It was equally difficult to carry out measures for the children's health, so far as they did not apply to everybody. When the children arrived, they were in fairly good physical condition, though somewhat pale, flabby, with protruding stomachs and dry, stringy hair, cuts and scratches on their skin tending to go septic. All the children were given codliver oil and other vitamins which were taken easily and liked by everybody. But it was nearly impossible to keep individual children in bed for small ailments, or for instance to give Miriam and Peter, who needed it, an afternoon nap while the others had no wish to rest. Sometimes those two children would fall asleep exhaustedly in the middle of the noise made by the others. At night, all children were restless sleepers, Ruth being unable to fall asleep, Paul and

Peter waking up in the night crying. Whoever was awake, naturally disturbed the sleep of the others. The upset about separation was so great that, finally, children with colds were no longer kept upstairs. The only child who was in bed once, for two days with a slight bronchitis, was Paul. Another time three children had to be isolated for several days with stomatitis. The only other child in need of individual physical treatment was Leah. She had a bad squint, her eyes were treated daily but the operation was postponed for six months to give her time for better adjustment to a renewed separation.

Inability to be separated from the group showed up most glaringly in those instances where individual children were singled out for a special treat, a situation for which children crave under normal circumstances. Paul, for example, cried for the other children when he was taken as the only one for a ride in the pony cart, although at other times such rides were a special thrill to him as well as to the others. On another, later, occasion the whole group of children was invited to visit another nursery in the neighborhood. Since the car was not large enough to take everybody, Paul and Miriam were taken earlier by bus. The other four, in the car, inquired constantly about them and could not enjoy the trip nor the pleasures prepared for them, until they were reunited.

Type of Group Formation

When together, the children were a closely knit group of members with equal status, no child assuming leadership for any length of time, but each one exerting a strong influence on the others by virtue of individual qualities, peculiarities, or by the mere fact of belonging. At the beginning, John, as the oldest, seemed to be the undisputed leader at mealtimes. He only needed to push away his plate, for everybody else to cease eating. Peter, though the youngest, was the most imaginative of all and assumed leadership in games, which he would invent and organize. Miriam too played a major role, in a peculiar way. She was a pretty, plump child, with ginger hair, freckles and a ready smile. She behaved toward the other children as if she were a superior being, and let herself be served and spoiled by them as a matter of course. She would sometimes smile at the boys in return for their services, while accepting Leah's helpfulness toward herself without acknowledgment. But she, too, did not guide or govern the group. The position was rather that she needed a special kind of attention to be paid to her and that the other children sensed this need and did their best to fulfill it. The following are some recorded examples of this interplay between Miriam and the group:

November 1945.—Miriam, on a walk, has found a tiny pink flower, carries it in her hand but loses it soon. She calls out "flower!" and John and Paul hurry to pick it up for her, a difficult task since they wear thick gloves. Miriam drops the flower again and again, never makes an attempt to pick it up herself, merely calls "flower!" and the boys hurry to find it.

March 1946.—From the beginning Miriam liked to sit in comfortable chairs. In the winter she would drag such a chair to the fireplace, put her feet on the fire guard and play in that position. When outdoor life began again, Miriam had a chair in the sandbox. She even helped weed the garden while sitting in a chair. But it did not happen often that she had to fetch a chair herself, usually the other children carried it into the garden for her. One day, Miriam and Paul played in the sandbox after supper. Suddenly Paul appears in the house to fetch Miriam's chair. When told that the evening was too cold already for outdoor play and that they had better both come in, he merely looks bewildered and says: "But Miriam wants chair, open door quickly."

May 1946.—Miriam drops her towel, turns around and says: "Pick it up, somebody." Leah picks it up for her.

July 1946.—Miriam enters the kitchen, calls out: "Chair for Miriam, quickly." She looks indignant when she sees no child in the kitchen and nobody to obey her orders. She does not fetch the chair herself but goes out again.

August 1946.—Ruth is found in Miriam's bed in the morning and is asked to get up. Miriam replies instead of Ruth: "Oh no, she much better stays here. She has to wait to fasten Miriam's buttons."

August 1946.—Miriam bangs her hand on the table and says to John: "Can't you be quiet when I want to talk?" John stops talking.

The children's sensitiveness to each other's attitudes and feelings was equally striking where Leah was concerned. Leah was the only backward child among the six, of slow, lower average intelligence, with no outstanding qualities to give her a special status in the group. As mentioned before, Leah's arrival in Bulldogs Bank was delayed for six weeks owing to a ringworm infection. During this period the five other children had made their first adaptation to the new place, had learned some English, had established some contact with the staff and dropped some of their former restlessness. With Leah's coming, the whole group, in identification with her, behaved once more as if they were all newcomers. They used the impersonal *Tante* again instead of first names for the members of staff. They reverted to talking German only, shouted and screamed and were again out of control. This regression lasted approximately a week, evidently for the length of time which Leah herself needed to feel more comfortable in her new surroundings.

Positive Relations with the Group. Absence of Envy, Jealousy, Rivalry, Competition

The children's unusual emotional dependence on each other was borne out further by the almost complete absence of jealousy, rivalry and competition, such as normally develop between brothers and sisters or in a group of contemporaries who come from normal families. There was no occasion to urge the children to "take turns"; they did it spontaneously since they were eager that everybody should have his share. Since the adults played no part in their emotional lives at the time, they did not compete with each other for favors or for recognition. They did not tell on each other and they stood up for each other automatically whenever they felt that a member of the group was unjustly treated or otherwise threatened by an outsider. They were extremely considerate of each other's feelings. They did not grudge each other their possessions (with one exception to be mentioned later), on the contrary lending them to each other with pleasure. When one of them received a present from a shopkeeper, they demanded the same for each of the other children, even in their absence. On walks they were concerned for each other's safety in traffic, looked after children who lagged behind, helped each other over ditches, turned aside branches for each other to clear the passage in the woods, and carried each other's coats. In the nursery they picked up each other's toys. After they had learned to play, they assisted each other silently in building and admired each other's productions. At meal-times handing food to the neighbor was of greater importance than eating oneself.

Behavior of this kind was the rule, not the exception. The following examples merely serve the purpose of illustration and are in no way out-standing. They are chosen at random from the first seven months of the children's stay in Bulldogs Bank:

> *October 1945.*—John, daydreaming while walking nearly bumps into a passing child. Paul immediately sides with him and shouts at the passer-by: "Blöder Ochs, meine John, blöder Ochs Du!" [Stupid fool, my John, you stupid fool!"]

> *November 1945.*—John refuses to get up in the morning, lies in his bed, screams and kicks. Ruth brings his clothes and asks: "Willst Du anziehen?" ["Don't you want to put them on?"] Miriam offers him her doll with a very sweet smile. John calms down at once and gets up.

> *November 1945.*—John cries when there is no cake left for a second helping for him. Ruth and Miriam offer him what is left of their portions. While John eats their pieces of cake, they pet him and comment contentedly on what they have given him.

> *November 1945.*—The children are taken to Mrs. Clarke's house to hear music. Peter lags behind. When the children enter the drive, they shout "musica" in anticipation and excitement and begin to hurry. But Paul stops himself, goes back to Peter, tells him "musica" and arrives with him at the house.

> *November 1945.*—Paul shares his piece of chocolate with the others, or gives it to them altogether.

> *December 1945.*—Paul has a plate full of cake crumbs. When he begins to eat them, the other children want them too. Paul gives the two biggest crumbs to Miriam, the three middle-sized ones to the other children, and eats the smallest one himself.

> *December 1945.*—Leah runs into the inn, climbs on the counter and walks up and down there to the annoyance of the inn-keeper. She is sent home from the walk and Ruth goes back with her, both looking as if they were enjoying a special treat.

> *December 1945.*—Paul loses his gloves during a walk. John gives him his own gloves, and never complains that his hands are cold.

> *December 1945.*—Miriam throws a ball which hits Sister Sophie[5] in the face and makes her eye water. Miriam looks bewildered. Paul who is busy with the other children, pushing furniture, leaves them, looks at Sister Sophie, then at Miriam, says: "Blöder Ochs, Sophie" ["Stupid fool, Sophie"] and tries to comfort

Miriam with a toy. When she does not take it, he repeats: "Blöder Ochs, Sophie," and returns to the other children.

December 1945.—During a walk, Miriam lags behind, singing: "Miriam coming, Miriam coming." When nobody stops or pays any attention to her, her song becomes more and more ill-tempered: "Miriam com-i-i-i-ng!" All at once, the boys notice her being left alone, and hurry back to her. John and Peter lead her forward, Paul brings up the rear, all four children singing together: "Miriam coming!"

January 1946.—A visitor gives sweets to the children in the kitchen. Peter and Leah immediately demand a sweet for Miriam who is alone in the nursery.

January 1946.—Maureen takes the children and a pram to the station to collect a big parcel. Paul, who has some trouble with urination on this particular day, begins to cry. Maureen offers him a seat in the pram and explains to the other children that Paul does not feel well. They are full of sympathy. Peter walks beside Paul, petting him all the way home (about half an hour). When the children pass the baker's shop, the baker gives a bun to each child. While Paul eats his own bun, each one of the others gives him an additional piece of theirs. John gives him more than half of his.

March 1946.—Sister Gertrud opens a door and knocks it against John who stands behind it. When she enters the room next time, Ruth and Peter throw bricks at her and shout: "You naughty boy hit John!"

March 1946.—John has a temper tantrum when a ladybird, which he has caught, flies away. Leah hurries to him, strokes his hair, picks up his basket and all the carrots which he dropped out. She carries both John's and her own full baskets on the way home.

March 1946.—A dog approaches the children who are terrified. Ruth, though badly frightened herself, walks bravely to Peter who is screaming and gives him her toy rabbit to comfort him. She comforts John next by lending him her necklace.

March 1946.—Paul receives a parcel with clothes, toys and sweets from his American foster parents, a new experience in the children's lives. The excitement is great but there is no sign of envy. The children help to unpack, hold whatever Paul gives them to hold, welcome what he gives them as presents but accept the fact that he is, and remains, the owner of most of the contents of the parcel.

When other parcels arrive later for other children, the same scene of thrill and pleasure repeats itself each time.[6] There is no insistence on collective ownership.

April 1946.—On the beach in Brighton, Ruth throws pebbles into the water. Peter is afraid of waves and does not dare to approach them. In spite of his fear, he suddenly rushes to Ruth, calls out: "Water coming, water coming," and drags her back to safety.

May 1946.—When Miriam has bitten Leah several times at supper, she is asked to take her place to another part of the terrace, so that Leah can eat in peace. She does it quietly and begins eating over there, smiling cheerfully at the other children. Soon Peter drags his chair and plate to Miriam; John, Paul and Ruth follow. Finally Leah is left with Sister Sophie at the supper table.

May 1946.—A ladybird is found by the children, sitting on a nettle. John wants to have it but is warned that the nettle will sting. Shortly afterward John appears with the ladybird and Paul reports beaming with pride: "Ich [I] step on stinging nettle for John and and and John got the ladybird and stinging nettle did not hurt and Paul step on it for John."

Discrimination between Group Members. Antipathies and Friendships

Although the positive reactions of the children extended to all members of the group, individual preferences or their opposite were not lacking. There was a certain discrimination against Leah on the part of the other girls, as the following recordings indicate:

February 1946.—When Miriam cries, Leah runs immediately to comfort her, although Miriam each time screams: "Not Leah," and then accepts comfort from the other children.

April 1946.—Ruth is very helpful toward Leah, looks after her on walks and helps her to dress and undress. But her behavior indicates that these actions are duties, imposed by Leah's comparative clumsiness, rather than acts of friendship.

There were, further, close and intimate friendships between individual children, as for example between Paul and Miriam.

October 1945.—On his first evening in Bulldogs Bank, Paul goes to bed, saying with a deep sigh: "My Miriam."

October 1945.—Paul is very fond of Miriam. He gives her toys and serves her at mealtimes. Sometimes he takes her doll, walks with it round the room and returns it to her.

October 1945.—The children hear a cock crowing and ask what it is. When told that it is a cock, John says: "Meine cock" ["My cock"]. Paul says immediately: "Is Miriam's cock."

October 1945.—Paul loves eating corn flakes. He has just started eating when Miriam—who is not sitting next to him—drops her spoon. Paul at once stops eating and picks up the spoon for her before continuing.

November 1945.—Miriam has pushed her spoon under the American cloth which covers the table and cannot get it out again. She sits in front of her pudding waiting to get her spoon back. The others try to retrieve it for her but fail. Paul, who tries harder than anybody else, finally leaves the table and fetches Sister Sophie, crying despairingly: "Sophie, spoon!" He shouts with excitement when Sister Sophie manages to retrieve the spoon and hands it to Miriam.

November 1945.—On her third day in Bulldogs Bank, Miriam has been given a doll from which she became inseparable in day- and nighttime. No other child was allowed to touch it except Paul who sometimes took it for a walk round the room.

On November 11, Miriam gives the doll to Paul when saying good night and goes to sleep without it.

On November 12, she gives him the doll again in the evening but later cries in her bed. Paul, who has the doll in bed with him, gets up and calls through the closed door: "Miriam, dolly!" Miriam gets her doll and Paul goes to sleep without it.

December 1945.—After having had Miriam's doll for a few evenings and twice for a whole night, Paul takes it as his own possession. Now he is inseparable from the doll as Miriam has been before. The children call it now "Paul's dolly."

January 1946.—Miriam is isolated because of stomatitis. Paul waves to her from the door as often as possible. He has been asleep for some time when he wakes up and cries: "Ich mach wave die Miriam." He calms down and falls asleep again after being taken to wave to Miriam.

Aggressive Reactions within the Group

With the exception of one child the children did not hurt or attack each other in the first months. The only aggressiveness to which they gave vent within the group was verbal. They quarreled endlessly at mealtimes and on walks, mostly without any visible provocation. The following is a sample of these word battles, as they raged between October and January:

December 1945.—
　　John: "Is hot."
　　Ruth: "Is nicht [not] hot."
　　John: "Is hot."
　　Ruth (shouting): "Is nis hot."
　　John (triumphantly): "Is hot."
　　Paul: "Is nis hot, blöder Ochs" ["stupid fool"].
　　John: "Blöder Ochs, Paul."
　　Paul: "Nicht blöder Ochs Paul, blöder Ochs John."
　　John (shouting): "Blöder Ochs, Paul!"
　　John shouts so loud that the other children begin to laugh; he joins in the laugh.

The disputes ended sometimes in a general uproar, sometimes in a concerted attack on any adult who had tried to interfere and appease the quarrel; mostly the quarrel merely petered out when some new event distracted the children's attention.

After the children had entered into more normal emotional relationships with the adults and had become more independent of each other, word battles diminished and were replaced to some degree by the fights normal for this age. This second phase lasted approximately from January to July, when the relations between the children became peaceful again on a new basis.

The only child whose reactions did not fit in with the general behavior of the group was Ruth. She behaved like the others so far as being inseparable from the group was concerned, did not want to be left alone and worried about absent children. She also did her share of comforting others or of helping Leah, the latter especially after Leah began to call her "my Ruth." But apart from these reactions, she was moved by feelings of envy, jealousy and competition, which were lacking in the other children and which made her actions stand out as isolated instances of maliciousness or spitefulness. In this connection it is interesting to remember that Ruth is the only child among the group who has a recorded history of passionate attachment to a mother substitute.[7] The evidence is not sufficient to establish with certainty that it is this past mother relationship which prevented her from merging completely with the group, and which aroused normal sibling rivalry in her. On the other hand, the difference between her and the other children's behavior together with the difference in their emotional histories seems too striking to be a mere coincidence.

The following are instances of Ruth's negative behavior in the group. Between October and January these instances were daily events. They lessened considerably after she had formed a new attachment to Sister Gertrud and they disappeared almost altogether after June.

> *October 1945.*—The children collect acorns in their small baskets. Ruth stands, sucking her fingers and crying for acorns. Every now and then she picks up one that is pointed out to her. Sister Gertrud helps her by filling her basket with acorns. Ruth is pleased.

> Soon afterward Peter stumbles and, falling, knocks against Ruth by mistake. She reacts with fury, hits Peter, empties her basket, and seeing it empty stares at it with a puzzled expression. Suddenly her face shows a triumphant, unpleasant grin, she seizes Miriam's basket and empties the contents into her own. She tries to do the same with John's but he defends himself in time and pulls Ruth's hair. Paul, who has watched the fight, joins in to defend John. Peter cries and looks for protection near Sister Gertrud.

> The children quiet down again and continue to collect, Ruth, with a cross expression on her face, helping herself occasionally from the baskets of the others. All at once Paul appears, empties his own basket into that of Ruth and says with a happy smile: "Alle für Ruth; ich find viele, viele, ganz, ganz alleine." ["All for Ruth; I find many, many, all by myself."] Ruth continues to lose her acorns, either on purpose or by mistake and to help herself from the other baskets.

> *October 1945.*—Ruth hurts other children secretly, by kicking or pinching them underneath the table.

> *October 1945.*—Ruth takes other children's toys, shows a very pleased, triumphant expression.

> *October 1945.*—Peter has to wear a bonnet to protect the bandage where he has cut his head. Ruth takes off his bonnet repeatedly.

> *November 1945.*—Peter gets soap in his eyes at bathtime and cries. Ruth watches him. When he has almost ceased crying, her watchful expression changes suddenly to a malicious one. She snatches the piece of soap and tries to put it into Peter's eye.

> *November 1945.*—Ruth takes Paul's plate away while he is eating.

> *November 1945.*—Ruth interferes with whatever the children do.

November 1945.—Each child receives a sweet. Ruth keeps hers until the others have finished eating theirs. Then she offers her sweet to one child after the other, withdrawing it as soon as the child touches it. Repeats this for twenty minutes and again later until the children stop paying attention to her.

November 1945.—Paul and Peter have fun at lunch by pretending to bite each other. When they stop, Ruth encourages them to continue and while they do so, she eats Peter's lunch with her fingers, although her own plate is still full.

November 1945.—Ruth does not enjoy her Chanuka presents. She wants what the others have.

December 1945.—A lady brings toys for the children. Ruth, again, wants the presents of the others.

December 1945.—Ruth breaks everybody's colored pencils.

January 1946.—Ruth kicks Peter under the table. This had not happened for some time.

January 1946.—Ruth has a bad spell of aggression again. Annoys and hurts the other children, bites John.

January 1946.—John, Miriam and Peter are isolated with stomatitis. Ruth cannot stand the extra care given to them and takes out her jealousy on Paul and Leah by hitting and biting them. Her aggressiveness ceases again when the patients recover.

March 1946.—Ruth pushes over what Peter builds and annoys other children.

May 1946.—Ruth cries for her doll which Peter has taken and refuses to return. Leah takes it from Peter and hands it back to Ruth. Ruth, with a malicious expression, gives it once more to Peter and immediately begins to cry for it.

May 1946.—The children pick flowers which grow behind high nettles. They are warned to avoid being stung. John continues but moves and picks carefully. After a while he cries out as he gets stung: "Die Ruth, die Ruth push." Ruth stands behind him, pushing him into the nettles with a malicious expression on her face.

August 1946.—Paul receives a gift parcel from America. Ruth is very jealous and rather irritable during the day. When in bed in the evening, she demands to go to the lavatory with every expression of urgency. In the bathroom she snatches Paul's new toy which he has left lying near the tub, and tries to break it. When prevented from doing so she returns to bed sulkily.

Aggressiveness toward the Adults

As reported above, the children behaved with strong and uncontrolled aggression toward the adults from their arrival. This aggression was impersonal in its character, not directed against any individual and not to be taken as a sign of interest in the adult world. The children merely reacted defensively against an environment which they experienced as strange, hostile and interfering.

On arrival it was striking that the form of aggressive expression used by the children was far below that normal for their age. They used biting as a weapon, in the manner in which toddlers use it between eighteen and twenty-four months. Biting reached its peak with Peter, who would bite anybody and on all occasions when angry; it was least pronounced with Leah who showed very little aggression altogether. For several weeks John and Ruth would spit at the adults, Ruth also spitting on the table, on plates, on toys, looking at the adults in defiance. Similarly, Peter, when defying the staff, urinated into the brick box, on the slide, into the toy scullery, or wetted his knickers.

After a few weeks, the children hit and smacked the adults when angry. This happened especially on walks where they resented the restrictions imposed on them in traffic.

Shouting and noisy behavior was used deliberately as an outlet for aggression against the adults, even though the children themselves disliked the noise.

Toward spring these very infantile modes of aggressiveness gave way to the usual verbal aggressions used by the children between three and four years. Instead of hitting out, the child would threaten to do so, or would say: "Naughty boy, I make noise at you," and then shout at the top of their voices. Other threats used by the children were: "Doggy bite you." Paul once used: "Froggy bite you." After a visit to Brighton in April, where Peter had been frightened of the waves, a new threat was used by them: "You go in a water." They sometimes tried to find a water so as to carry out the threat.

From the summer 1946 onward, the children used phrases copied from the adults to express disapproval: "I am not pleased with you."

The following samples of aggressive behavior are chosen from a multitude of examples of similar or identical nature during the first three months.

October 1945.—Mrs. X from the village returns the clean laundry. Both John and Peter spit at her when she enters the nursery.

October 1945.—A painter works in the nursery with a high ladder. Peter, who climbs on the ladder, is lifted down by Sister Gertrud. He spits at her and shouts: "Blöde Tante, blöder Ochs!" ["Stupid auntie, stupid fool."]

October 1945.—The painter asks John not to touch the wet paint. John spits at him, shouting: "Blöder Ochs!"

October 1945.—John hits Mrs. Clarke repeatedly.

November 1945.—Paul has eaten cabbage on two occasions but refuses it on a third. When asked by Sister Sophie to taste it at least, he shouts his usual "Blöder Ochs." When she does not react, he approaches her and says insistently: "Blöder Ochs, Sophie."

November 1945.—Paul does not like the sweet given by Sister Sophie in the evening, but does not ask for a different one. He wakes up in the night and without seeing Sister Sophie says: "Blöde Sophie." He says it again when waking up in the morning.

November 1945.—Sister Gertrud polishes shoes and tells Ruth not to play with the shoe polish. Ruth spits at her, throws the box with polish down the stairs and runs through the house, shouting: "Blöder Ochs, Gertrud."

First Positive Relations with the Adults

The children's first positive approaches to the adults were made on the basis of their group feelings and differed in quality from the usual demanding, possessive behavior which young children show toward their mothers or mother substitutes. The children began to insist that the members of the staff should have their turn or share; they became sensitive to their feelings, identified with their needs, and considerate of their comfort. They wanted to help the adults with their occupations and, in return, expected to be helped by them. They disliked it when any member of staff was absent and wanted to know where the adults had been and what they had done during their absence. In short, they ceased to regard the adults as outsiders, included them in their group and, as the examples show, began to treat them in some ways as they treated each other.

Sharing with the Adults

Christmas 1945.—The children are invited to a Christmas party in Mrs. Clarke's house. They receive their presents with great excitement. They are equally thrilled when they are handed presents for the staff, they call out: "For Gertrud," "For Sophie" with great pleasure, and run back to Mrs. Clarke to fetch more presents for them.

December 1945.—When Mrs. Clarke, who has been visiting, leaves, Ruth demands to be kissed. Then all the children have to be kissed. Then John and Ruth call out: "Kiss for Sophie."

December 1945.—The children are given sweets in the shop and demand a "sweet for Sophie." After leaving the shop, they want to make sure that she has received the sweet. Sister Sophie opens her mouth for inspection and, in so doing, loses her sweet. The children are as upset as if they had lost one of their own sweets. John offers his but Sister Sophie suggests that she can wait to get another on returning home. When they reach home after an hour's walk with many distracting events, Peter runs immediately to the box of sweets to fetch one for Sophie.

Considerateness for the Adults

November 1945.—When the children are told that one of the staff has a day off and can sleep longer in the morning, they try to be quiet. If one or the other forgets, the others shout: "You quiet. Gertrud fast asleep."

November 1945.—Sister Sophie has told the children that the doctor has forbidden her to lift heavy weights. Paul asks: "Not too heavy?," whenever he sees her with a tray or bucket.

May 1946.—Leah, though a noisy child, tries hard to keep quiet when her Judith is tired.

Equality with the Adults. Helpfulness

December 1945.—The children become keen on fetching from the kitchen what is needed. They carry logs, set chairs and tables. They help to dress and undress themselves and to tidy up.

January 1946.—Ruth sees a woman with a shopping bag in the street. She approaches her and takes one handle silently to help carrying it.

April 1946.—The children are alone in the nursery after breakfast. Ruth and Peter each take a broom and sweep up the rubbish. When Sister Sophie enters, they call to her: "We tidy up nicely."

May 1946.—Miriam begins to help Sister Sophie in the kitchen when the latter is called away. When she returns Miriam has dried four big dishes, twelve bowls, sixteen spoons and has placed them tidily on a tray.

On a similar occasion Miriam is found on a chair in front of the sink, her arms up to the elbows in soapy water, with most of the washing-up done.

May 1946.—Peter sweeps the rubbish into the dustpan, wants to hang pan and broom in the broom cupboard, but cannot reach the hook. He calls: "You better help Peter, grownup toys too high."

June 1946.—The children have their busiest time after supper, while one of them is having the first bath. One helps in the kitchen, one tidies up the nursery, one the sandpit, one the push toys, one sets chairs and tables for "tomorrow morning breakfast." They enjoy doing this work alone and then call out: "You come, I show you!"

August 1946.—The children help Sister Sophie to pull dry lavender blossoms off the stems. Peter says: "You pleased we help you with the lavender. You not play alone."

Sensitiveness to Adults. Identification

March 1946.—Ruth and John lag far behind on a walk. When they reach the others eventually, Peter calls to them: "You naughty boys, you dragging behind; Sophie calling and calling and calling. You not coming. Sophie cross and sad!" Then he turns to Sister Sophie and says in a low voice: "You still cross and sad?" When she nods, he repeats his speech.

May 1946.—While the children are picking bluebells, Sister Sophie listens intently to the calling of birds. Paul suddenly puts his hand into hers and says: "You cross with everybody?" Though she assures him that she is not cross, merely absent-minded, he leaves his hand in hers to comfort her.

Second Phase of Positive Relations to Adults. Personal Relationships

Several weeks after arrival in Bulldogs Bank the first signs of individual personal attachments to adults appeared, alongside with and superimposed on the relationships based on community feelings. These new attachments had many of the qualities which are well known from the relationship of young children to their mothers or mother substitutes. Attitudes such as possessiveness, the wish to be owned, exclusive clinging, appeared, but they lacked the intensity and inexorability which is one of the main characteristics of the emotional life at that age. During the year's stay at Bulldogs Bank these ties of the children to the adults in no way reached the strength of their ties to each other. The children went, as it were, through the motions and attitudes of mother relationships, but without the full libidinal cathexis of the objects whom they had chosen for the purpose.

Examples of Owning and Being Owned

Miriam was the first to say "Meine Sophie, my Sophie" at the end of October.

Peter, the youngest, was the next to show a personal attachment. At the end of November he cried on several occasions when Sister Gertrud left the room. He began to say: "Meine Gertrud" and shortly afterward called himself "Gertrud's Peter." He picked flowers for her and liked her to bathe him. But his attachment was in no way exclusive and he did not mind being with somebody else. He was fond of Sister Sophie too and disliked her going away.

Ruth very soon afterward showed a first preference for Mrs. Clarke. She began showing pleasure in seeing her, kissed her once spontaneously and said on another occasion: "Is bin [I am] Mrs. Clarke's Ruth."

Leah was a clinging child who made advances to every visitor and even to people passing in the street. She became attached to the assistant Judith, would hold her hand on walks, picked flowers for her and sang sometimes all day long: "My Judith bathes me all the time!" But the apparent warmth of this relationship was belied by the fact that she continued to attach herself to every stranger.

John called the young assistant "his" Maureen. His attachment showed more warmth than those of the others but was broken again, unluckily, by Maureen's leaving.

Examples of Conflicting Relationships

Several children had considerable difficulties in choosing their mother substitutes, their positive feelings wavering uncertainly between the adult figures. John, after being left by Maureen, attached himself to Sister Gertrud, and shortly afterward became fond of Sister Sophie. Neither relationship was exclusive or very passionate and consequently he seemed to have no difficulties in maintaining both simultaneously. In contrast to this, Miriam, who was attached equally to Sisters Sophie and Gertrud, suffered badly from the consequent conflict of feeling. She lived in a constant state of tension without finding relief and satisfaction in her relationships. During Sister Sophie's absence, she "wrote" and dictated long letters to her and she was full of happiness on Sister Sophie's return. But the preference for Sister Sophie, which seemed established at the time, gave way once more to a preference for Sister Gertrud in the course of a few weeks.

Examples of Resentment of Separations

Even though the children's attachments to their mother substitutes took second place in their emotional lives, they deeply resented the absences or the leaving of adults.[8]

> *January 1946.*—Sister Sophie has left the house together with Mrs. Clarke. When she returns a few hours later, Peter refuses to say good night to her. He turns to the other side and says: "You go, you go to a Mrs. Clarke."

> *March 1946.*—When Sister Sophie returned to Bulldogs Bank after an absence of two months, Peter refused to let her do anything for him for a week, would not even take bread or sweets from her. Whenever she left the house, he asked: "You go in a London?"
> He regained his affection for her through a process of identification with her interests. Five weeks after her return the children played that they took a bus ride to London. When asked what they wanted to do there, Peter said "Go in a Miss X's[9] house." Peter saying: "Miss X all better?" From then onward, he called the patient "Peter's Miss X," cuddled and kissed Sister Sophie and held her hand on walks although the children usually preferred to walk on their own.

> *April 1946.*—After Maureen's departure, John did not show immediately how much he missed her, though he said occasionally "my Maureen" and showed some aggressiveness toward the other children. He looked very forlorn and depressed, but gave no distinct sign what was the matter with him until twelve days after Maureen's departure. On that day he sat in his bed in the morning, did not want to dress himself, and when asked whether he wanted to be dressed, he began to cry "my Maureen." At lunch time he pulled his curls into his face as Maureen used to do sometimes. He did the same again in the evening. The following day he carried a stick while walking and hit trees, flowers, and children alternately.
> During the next four weeks he showed many disturbances, took away other children's toys, and hurt the children in other ways. . . .

Conclusion

"Experiments" of this kind, which are provided by fate, lack the satisfying neatness and circumspection of an artificial setup. It is difficult, or impossible, to distinguish the action of the variables from each other, as is demonstrated in our case by the intermingled effects of three main factors: the absence of a mother or parent relationship; the abundance of community influence; and the reduced amount of gratification of all needs, from the oral stage onward. It is, of course, impossible to vary the experiment. In our case, further, it proved impossible to obtain knowledge of all the factors which have influenced development. There remained dark periods in the life of each child, and guesswork, conclusions and inferences had to be used to fill the gaps.

Under such circumstances, no claim to exactitude can be made for the material which is presented here and it offers no basis for statistical considerations. Though an experiment staged by fate, in the sense that it accentuates the action of certain factors in the child's life (demonstrated through their absence or their exaggerated presence), it has little or nothing to offer to the experimental psychologist. What it helps to do is to create impressions which either confirm or refute the analyst's assumptions concerning infantile development—impressions which can be tested and in their turn confirmed or rejected in detailed analytic work with single individuals.

According to the results of child analysis and reconstruction from the analyses of adults, the child's relationship to his brothers and sisters is subordinated to his relationship to the parents, is, in fact, a function of it. Siblings are normally accessories to the parents, the relations to them being governed by attitudes of rivalry, envy, jealousy, and competition for the love of the parents. Aggression, which is inhibited toward the parents, is expressed freely toward brothers and sisters, sexual wishes, which cannot become manifest in the oedipal relationship, are lived out, passively or actively, with elder or younger brothers and sisters. The underlying relationship with siblings is thus a negative one (dating from infancy when all siblings were merely rivals for the mother's love), with an overlay of positive feelings when siblings are used for the discharge of libidinal trends deflected from the parents. Where the relations between the children of one family become finally manifestly positive, they do so according to the principles of group formation, on the basis of their common identification with the parents. The rival brother is tolerated as belonging to the mother; in special cases[10] the rival brother even becomes an object of identification as the mother's favorite. The child's first approach to the idea of justice is made· during these developments of the brother-sister relationship, when the claim to be favored oneself is changed to the demand that no one should be favored, i.e., that there should be equal rights for everybody. Since contemporaries outside the family are treated like the siblings, these first relationships to the brothers and sisters become important factors in determining the individual's social attitudes.

It is well in line with these views when our material shows that the relations of the Bulldogs Bank children to each other were totally different from ordinary sibling attitudes. The children were without parents in the fullest sense of the word, i.e., not merely orphaned at the time of observation, but most of them without an early mother or father image in their unconscious minds to which their earliest libidinal strivings might have been attached. Consequently, their companions of the same age were their real love objects and their libidinal relations with them of a direct nature, not merely the products of laborious reaction formation and defenses against hostility. This explains why the feelings of the six children toward each other show a warmth and spontaneity which is unheard of in ordinary relations between young contemporaries.

It merely bears out this theory to find that attachments to a mother figure in single instances disturb these positive relations, such as in Ruth's case. Or when John, in his mourning for Maureen, turned against his companions and began to hurt them. In these instances the positive libidinal attachment was directed toward the adult; the other children were thereby changed from the position of friends and love objects to that of enemies and rivals.

When working with the children of the Hampstead Nurseries (3), one of the authors has described certain attitudes of helpfulness, co-operation, identification and friendship which appeared in a group of toddlers (between fifteen months and two and one half years of age) who had been temporarily deprived of their mothers' care. The six Bulldogs Bank children, as the observations prove, show these attitudes in excess, the quantitative difference between them and the Hampstead Nursery group corresponding to the difference between total and partial absence of a parent relationship.

The high degree of identification with each other's needs is known from one other relationship in early years, that of identical twins to each other. In a recent study of the subject Dorothy Burlingham (1) demonstrates the emotional importance of twins to each other, the way in which the twin is treated as an extension of the self, cathected with narcissistic as well as object love. Identification with the twin prospers on the basis of common needs, common anxieties, common wishes, in short, on the similar reactions of two beings of the same age living in close proximity under the same external conditions. While in the case of twins the twin relationship conflicts with and has to adapt itself to the parent relationship, the attitude to the companion within our age group of orphans reigned supreme.

That the children were able to attach their libido to their companions and the group as such, bypassing as it were the parent relationship which is the normal way to social attitudes, deserves interest in relation to certain analytic assumptions. In recent analytic work the experiences of the first year of life, the importance of the relationship to the mother during the oral phase and the linking of these experiences with the beginnings of ego development have assumed great significance. Explorations in these directions have led to the belief, held by many authors, that every disturbance of the mother relationship during this vital phase is invariably a pathogenic factor of specific value. Grave defects in ego development, lack or loss of speech in the first years, withdrawnness, apathy, self-destructive attitudes, psychotic manifestations, have all be ascribed to the so-called "rejection" by the mother, a comprehensive term which includes every disturbance within the mother relationship from loss of the mother through death, permanent or temporary separation, cruel or neglectful treatment, down to lack of understanding, ambivalence, preoccupation or lack of warmth on the mother's part.

The six Bulldogs Bank children are, without doubt, "rejected" infants in this sense of the term. They were deprived of mother love, oral satisfactions, stability in their relationships and their surroundings. They were passed from one hand to another during their first year, lived in an age group instead of a family during their second and third year, and were uprooted again three times during their fourth year. A description of the anomalies which this fate produced in their emotional life and of the retardations in certain ego attitudes[11] is contained in the material. The children were hypersensitive, restless, aggressive, difficult to handle. They showed a heightened autoerotism and some of them the beginning of neurotic symptoms. But they were neither deficient, delinquent nor psychotic. They had found an alternative placement for their libido and, on the strength of this, had mastered some of their anxieties, and developed social attitudes. That they were able to acquire a new language in the midst of their upheavals, bears witness to a basically unharmed contact with their environment.

The authors hope that further contact with these children, or those of similar experience, will give indications as to how such emotional anomalies of early life influence the shaping of the oedipus phase, superego development, adolescence and the chances for a normal adult love life.

NOTES

1. Theresienstadt in Moravia.
2. The camp was organized and directed by Mr. Oscar Friedmann, now an associate member of the British Psycho-Analytic Society, and Miss Alice Goldberger, former superintendent in the Hampstead Nurseries.
3. Nothing has been changed for the purpose of publication except the children's names. According to a Nazi rule, all Jewish children had to bear names out of the Old Testament. These have been replaced here by another set of biblical names.

    On immigration the official register of the children contained nothing beyond their names, birth-dates and birthplaces. Some additional information concerning the six Bulldogs Bank children was supplied later by letter by Mrs. Martha Wenger, herself a concentration camp victim who had been in charge of the children in the Ward for Motherless Children in Tereszin.
4. An attachment to a mother substitute is recorded of one child only. Martha Wenger, in the letter mentioned above, writes concerning Ruth: "Ruth was passionately attached to me and maltreated me accordingly. When somebody else had night duty with the children, she slept soundly; when it was me, she would stay awake, cry, and force me to sit with her." No similar relationships are mentioned with regard to the other children. Martha Wenger refers to John as "well liked by everybody" and to Peter as "endearing himself to everybody with his gay fearless, naughty ways." For the rest she says: "I can very well understand that the Tereszin children have been very difficult on arrival, and are still difficult to handle. There is something wrong with each of them, difficulties which would have been straightened out if they had had a normal life. In Tereszin everybody tried to work as little as possible to make up for the lack of proper nourishment. In the Ward of Motherless Children there was always too much work and too few people to help me. Besides looking after the children we had to see to their clothes, etc., which took time. We looked after the bodily welfare of the children as well as possible, kept them free of vermin for three years, and we fed them as well as was possible under the circumstances. But it was not possible to attend to their other needs. Actually, we did not have the time to play with them. . . ."
5. For convenience, Sister Sophie Dann, though the author of these notes, is referred to in the third person.
6. With one exception to be recorded later.
7. Miss Alice Goldberger reports that Ruth made an immediate attachment to her in the reception camp in Windermere after she had sat at her bed the first night and comforted her by playing a little mouth organ. From then onward Ruth had danced for her, clung to her whenever she met her, etc.—a behavior shown by none of the other children.
8. Sister Sophie had leave of absence during January and February to nurse a patient in London. Maureen left Bulldogs Bank in April 1946.
9. Sister Sophie's patient.
10. —which lead later to homosexual attitudes—
11. —though much of these have been ascribed to the additional material deprivations—

REFERENCES

BURLINGHAM, D. T. *Twins*, Imago Publ. Co., London, 1951.

DANZIGER, L. AND FRANKL, L. "Zum Problem der Funktionsreifung," *Ztsch f. Kinderforschung*, XLIII, 1934.

FREUD, A. AND BURLINGHAM, D. *Infants Without Families*, Int. Univ. Press, New York, 1944.

GREENACRE, P. "Infant Reactions to Restraint," in *Personality*, edited by Clyde Kluckhohn and Henry A. Murray. A. Knopf, New York, 1948.

WERNER, H. *Comparative Psychology of Mental Development*, Follet, Chicago, 1948.

5

Toys and Social Interaction between Infant Peers
Carol O. Eckerman and Judith L. Whatley

Claims that infants fail to react in any social manner to one another prior to about 2 years of age are being challenged. The claims have been based mainly upon a handful of studies, most over 4 decades old, and most with institutionalized children (Bridges 1933; Bühler 1930; Maudry and Nekula 1939). A reexamination of the early descriptive studies yields evidence of many more seemingly social interactions between infant peers than the summary statements then and later often acknowledged. Further, recent studies of infants together have extended the earlier findings to infants reared at home (Eckerman, Whatley, and Kutz 1975) and have begun to describe factors that affect the ways young peers interact (see Lewis and Rosenblum 1975).

The question remains, however, of how social the behaviors described as occurring between infant peers are. The settings used to observe infants together typically include inanimate play materials; and the most prominent peer-related behaviors reported are those that involve both the peer and a toy. Infant peers have been described as synchronously contacting the same objects, taking toys from one another, struggling over toys, duplicating one another's actions with toys, working together on a common task with toys, and engaging in rudimentary games in which each infant repeatedly acts

From C. O. Eckerman and J. L. Whatley, "Toys and Social Interaction between Infant Peers," *Child Development* 48 (1977): 1645–56. Copyright 1977 by The Society for Research in Child Development. Reprinted by permission of The Society for Research in Child Development, Inc.

upon play material in turn (Eckerman et al. 1975; Ross and Goldman, in press). All such behaviors can be construed as reactions not to the peer but rather to the movements of the toys the peer produces. The infant may be interested in and responding solely to the inanimate spectacle a peer's actions create; the fact that this spectacle is created by a peer, or any social being, may be irrelevant. Similarly, touching the peer and looking, smiling, vocalizing, or gesturing toward him may be reactions more to the changing sights and sounds of toys than to the peer himself.

To assess whether infants are attracted and responsive to the person and behavior of another infant, the present study manipulated the availability of objects commonly thought of as toys. The behaviors seen when unfamiliar peers met in a setting devoid of toys were contrasted with those seen in the customary play setting. It was reasoned that the behaviors directed toward the peer in the setting devoid of toys could be attributed more readily to the appearance and behavior of the peer per se. Infants approaching 1 year of age as well as infants approaching 2 years of age were studied to assess whether younger infants responded more to the inanimate aspects of the setting than to the social aspects and the older infants more to the social aspects.

Prior attempts to assess the role of toys in peer interaction have been limited. In Maudry and Nekula's classic study (1939) the rapid changing of toy materials (every 3 min), the absence of a summary of behavior by the different toy conditions, and the reliance upon such molar measures as positive and negative social behavior preclude firm conclusions regarding the effects of toys. Similarly, the absence of any detailed examination of social interaction involving toys raises questions about the conclusion of Ramey, Finkelstein, and O'Brien (1976) that toys impede social interaction.

Despite the paucity of empirical information, toys often have been assigned a central role in the early development of interaction between peers. At least two such views have been proposed for infants about 1 year of age. The first claims that toys are more attractive and attention-eliciting than infant peers; hence, toys preclude the possibility of any truly social interaction occurring between such young peers (Maudry and Nekula 1939). The second view proposes that an infant's characteristic ways of acting upon toys set the stage for the emergence of peer interaction; peer interaction is a natural by-product of two infants acting individually in similar ways upon the same play materials (Mueller and Lucas 1975). Common to both views is the claim that interest in play materials precedes interest in the peer, a claim that contrasts sharply with current views about the infant's attraction to adults (Schaffer 1971).

Toys may play a singular role in the emergence of peer interaction; but the recurrent emphasis upon toys in peer interaction in contrast to infant-adult interaction may result instead from the fact that the interactions of young peers typically have been assessed only in settings containing toys, whereas their interactions with adults have been assessed in a wider variety of settings. By contrasting peer interaction in the presence and absence of toys, the present study provides a starting point for evaluating claims about the central importance of toys in either prompting or precluding peer interaction.

Pairs of *unacquainted*, like-aged infants were brought together for an extended period of play either in the presence or absence of toys. Mothers accompanied the infants and responded simply to their overtures without directing their activities. Half the pairs were 10–12 months of age, an age marked by the emergence of proficient locomotion and extensive exploration of an inanimate environment (Rheingold and Eckerman 1969); half were 22–24 months of age, an age marked, according to all the researchers cited, by some truly social interaction between peers.

Method

Subjects. Forty-four pairs of like-aged children participated in the study; half were between 10 and 12 months of age and half between 22 and 24 months. At each age, half the pairs were assigned to the toys condition and half to the no-toys condition. Potential subjects were chosen on the basis of age alone from a population of white infants born and residing in an industrial and university city of moderate size (Durham, North Carolina). Mothers of potential subjects were informed by phone of the study; over 80% agreed to participate. Pairs of subjects were scheduled according to random permutations of the four conditions resulting from the two ages studied and the two experimental treatments (toys condition, no-toys condition).

The educational levels of the parents of all four groups were similar. Most fathers had completed college degrees, although the range in years of education was from 10 to 22 years (mean = 17); most mothers had had some college, although the range of 11–20 years of education (mean = 15) was considerable. The two groups of subjects at each age level were similar in the composition of their families, but the older groups contained more children with siblings (48% vs. 30%). Less than 10% of the subjects received as much as 50% of their daytime care outside the family. The average age of the younger groups was 11.6 months (range = 10.6–12.0); that for the older groups was 23.3 months (range = 22.2–24.0).

The subjects were paired on the basis of age and a common convenient time to participate in the study. The resulting pairs were composed in 13 instances of two males, in 11 instances of two females, and in the remaining 20 instances of a male and female. The average difference in the ages of the members of a pair was less than 2 weeks.

The data of five additional pairs were not included in the study. Two mothers of children in the younger no-toys condition failed to follow instructions by repeatedly directing their children's actions; one child in the same condition was unable to locomote through even a few feet; and two children cried, forcing an early termination of the study. One 11-month-old child in the no-toys condition cried at his mother from the start of the session; another 23-month-old child in the toys condition cried while looking at the peer.

Study setting. The study took place in a large room (6.6 × 3.9 m) furnished only with a rug, a circular children's table, a few pictures on the walls beyond the children's reach, and two floor cushions marking the mothers' positions. The cushions were along one end of the room approximately 3 m apart, and the children's table was near the opposite end. In the toys condition, three multipieced toys were also present: three 9-cm vinyl cubes decorated with pictures and letters, a bus with removable pegmen, and a set of five nesting/stacking boxes. The boxes and bus were placed on the floor midway between the mothers' positions and the table; the cubes were arranged on the table within easy reach of the children. A one-way window behind the table provided visual access to the study room; a microphone in the center of the ceiling, auditory access.

Procedure. Each child and mother were escorted to a reception room where they met the other child and mother and the female experimenter. The children were left free to play with the few toys in the room or to sit on their mothers' laps while the experimenter instructed the mothers in their role. The mothers were asked to talk with one another and to allow their children to do as they wished; they could respond with a few words or a smile to the children's overtures, but they were not to initiate interaction with them or direct their activities except if it became necessary to intervene to prevent physical harm.

The experimenter escorted the subjects and mothers into the study room and directed the mothers to their positions on the floor. When the experimenter left the room, closing the door behind her, the 16-min session began. Following the study, the experimenter obtained from the mothers information about the child and his family.

Response measures. The primary goal was to describe in behavioral detail how each child acted upon and reacted to his peer. Two observers behind the one-way window systematically sampled each child's behavior by focusing upon a single child at a time (focus child) and shifting their focus from one child to the other at the end of each 1 min of observation. On paper ruled into 10-sec intervals the observers continuously recorded the occurrence of predefined behaviors by the focus child. They focused simultaneously upon the same child but recorded different behaviors. An auditory signal marked the 10-sec intervals. Both children were observed as much as possible, and several of the behaviors coded describe how the focus child's behavior relates to that of his peer.[1]

With these procedures, 23 behaviors related to the presence or activities of the peer were distinguished and coded, as well as 12 other behaviors indexing the child's responsiveness to the adults present and to the total study setting. The peer-related behaviors were those developed in a prior study of infant peers (Eckerman et al. 1975) with a few additions and revisions. Table 1 lists these behaviors and shows how they were grouped into conceptual categories for this study.

The categories watch, in proximity, same play material, and different play material are state measures, estimating basic relationships between the focus child and his peer. Watch (visual regard of the peer or his activities) indexed visual attention. In proximity (being within 2 feet of some part of the peer's body) was a new measure added to assess correspondence in the infants' location in space. Same play material (contacting the same toy as the peer or manipulating the same room fixture as the peer) and different play material (contacting a different toy or manipulating a different room fixture than the peer) were used to assess correspondence in the infants' choice of play materials. Each state had to last at least 3 continuous sec in order to be coded, and only the presence or absence of this state was noted for each

Table 1 Peer-related activities in the presence and absence of toys

| | *Mean Frequency* | | | | *Significance Level* | | |
| | *10–12 Months* | | *22–24 Months* | | | | |
Response Measure	*No Toys*	*Toys*	*No Toys*	*Toys*	*Toys(T)*	*Age(A)*	*T×A*
State measures:							
Watch	49.9	45.1	52.6	45.1	N.S.	N.S.	N.S.
In proximity	43.0	34.1	34.8	28.9	N.S.	N.S.	N.S.
Same play material	4.6	16.8	7.9	13.5	**	N.S.	N.S.
Toys	...	15.2	...	11.0	...	...	...
Room fixtures	4.6	1.7	7.9	2.6	...	...	...
Different play material	12.9	41.4	13.0	55.5	***	*	*
Toys	...	38.7	...	51.4	...	...	...
Room fixtures	12.9	2.7	13.0	5.0	...	...	...
Peer-directed behaviors:							
Distal social signals	8.6	3.5	15.2	7.0	**	*	N.S.
Smile/laugh	3.3	1.3	8.0	2.2	**	N.S.	N.S.
Fuss/cry	.4	0	0	0	...	...	...
Vocalize	5.1	2.0	6.4	4.7	N.S.	N.S.	N.S.
Gesture	1.9	.6	3.1	.8	**	N.S.	N.S.
Show object	0	.3	0	.2	...	...	...
Physical contact	8.3	2.2	7.2	1.6	***	N.S.	N.S.
Touch	8.0	2.2	5.7	1.4	***	N.S.	N.S.
Strike	.6	0	1.9	.3	**	*	N.S.
Toy exchanges	...	5.7	...	4.4	...	N.S.	...
Offer	...	1.1	...	1.1	...	N.S.	...
Accept	...	1.3	...	.5	...	...	...
Take over	...	.6	...	.1	...	...	...
Take	...	1.2	...	1.1	...	N.S.	...
Resist	...	.6	...	.9	...	...	...
Relinquish	...	.9	...	.6	...	...	...
Struggle	...	.2	...	.3	...	...	...
Duplicate action	2.3	.7	5.8	1.1	***	*	N.S.
Alternate action	.3	.5	4.6	.9	N.S.	N.S.	N.S.
Same action	.3	0	4.6	.4	...	...	...
Different actions	0	.5	0	.6	...	...	...
Summary measures:							
No peer-related activity	30.9	34.8	30.1	41.1	*	N.S.	N.S.
Some peer-directed behavior	16.8	11.2	25.7	13.4	**	N.S.	N.S.
Single acts	10.3	8.3	13.9	9.7	N.S.	N.S.	N.S.
Multiple acts	6.2	2.4	7.1	2.7	**	N.S.	N.S.

Note.—Frequency expressed as percentage of the 96 10-sec periods in which the response measure occurred.
* $p < .05$.
** $p < .01$.
*** $p < .001$.

10-sec period of recording. Different play material was coded only if same play material did not occur in the period.

The remaining peer-related behaviors are discrete behaviors directed by the focus child toward his peer; and, with the exception of alternate action, each occurrence of these behaviors was coded. The criteria for judging these behaviors to be peer directed were accompanying visual regard of the peer, in rare instances the use of the peer's name without visual regard, and for some of the toy exchanges and for duplicate action the appearance of the behavior as a fairly immediate reaction to discrete actions by the peer. Each of these behaviors was thought to have the potential of prompting subsequent reciprocal interaction with the peer.

Smile, laugh, fuss, cry, vocalize, gesture, show object, touch, strike, offer, accept, take over, take, and struggle were defined exactly as in the prior study (Eckerman et al. 1975). Resist (protect or physically resist peer's taking an object) and relinquish (release toy peer takes without protest) were added to the behaviors characterizing exchanges or attempted exchanges of objects between peers. Duplicate action (watch a discrete and distinctive act by the peer and perform the same act within 10 sec) replaced the term imitate in order to avoid the multiple connotations of the latter term. A new category, alternate action, subsumed most of the phenomena originally classified as coordinate play; the defining feature was repeated alternation between the two children in directing behaviors toward one another. Alternate action was coded as soon as the focus child emitted his second peer-directed behavior in such a sequence and continued to be coded for each 10-sec period in which this pattern continued. Two types of alternate action were distinguished: same action, in which the child's behavior took the same form as his peer's, and different actions, in which he directed a different, but related, behavior toward his peer (e.g., accept in response to peer's offer). Most of the actions comprising alternate action were distinctive motor actions, such as jumping, climbing upon the table, or patting; but when the action was one of the behaviors included in distal social signals, physical contact, or toy exchanges it was coded both as alternate action and as the particular form of action. Duplicate action was not coded for behaviors coded as alternate same action. Alternate action estimated the occurrence of reciprocal interaction between the peers.

Additional behaviors provided a context for the peer-related activities. Fussing (fretting sounds) and crying (loud continuous wailing) not directed toward the peer estimated the distress engendered by the study setting as a whole. Contact mother (hugging on physical contact for at least 3 continuous sec), proximity to mother (being within 2 feet of some part of the mother for at least 3 continuous sec without physical contact), and play with mother (offering her a toy, taking a toy from her, or simultaneously contacting a toy or room object and the mother for at least 3 continuous sec) estimated responsiveness to the mother. The same behaviors directed toward the peer's mother estimated responsiveness to an unfamiliar adult.

Each measure was summed across the two children of a pair and across the 16-min session, and the pair was the unit of replication for all data analyses.

Repeated assessments of interobserver agreement and training in the coding system were provided by a second trial of 8-min duration. Procedures for the second trial were identical with those of the study proper except that new toys were available for all pairs and the two observers coded the same set of behaviors. Which of the two sets of behaviors they coded was randomly determined for each pair. The new toys (provided to end the session pleasantly for all children) provided a strong test of interobserver agreement;

with toys there were a greater number and diversity of behaviors coded and the infrequency of several behaviors difficult to judge (e.g., smile, laugh, vocalize) placed a premium upon agreeing about each instance. Interobserver agreement was computed separately for each behavior and each pair of subjects by dividing the smaller of the two observers' scores by the larger and multiplying by 100. Median agreement scores were 95% or above for 25 of the behaviors and 88% or above for all but two. The lower scores for relinquish and strike seemed related to their infrequent occurrence; there was disagreement on more than one instance of these behaviors for only one pair of subjects. In addition, videotapes were taken of the sessions to be used by the observers along with their on-the-spot coding records in the training of new observers. Knowing that the coding record was to be aligned against repeated viewings of a videotape would seem to hold the same potential for increasing precision in the coding as knowing that another observer was simultaneously coding the same set of behaviors (Reid 1970).

Results

General reaction to the study setting. The study setting had at least four salient features: the unfamiliar peer, the mother, the unfamiliar adult (the peer's mother), and the inanimate aspects of the room (both room fixtures and toys). To gain an overview of the infants' reactions to the study setting, the frequency with which the infants engaged in any coded behavior involving each of these four features was examined (see Figure 1). At both ages, behaviors related to the peer and mother were frequent and those related to the adult infrequent regardless of whether toys were present or not. Behaviors related to inanimate features were frequent when toys were present and relatively infrequent in their absence. Since the behaviors coded differed for the peer, the adults, and the inanimate features, more precise comparisons across the social and nonsocial objects are not warranted. A multivariate analysis of variance performed on the four composite frequencies documented that changes in behavior with both toy condition, $F(4,37) = 42.53, p < .001$, and age, $F(4,37) = 4.22, p < .01$, were reliable, as well as the interaction between toy condition and age, $F(4,37) = 5.99, p < .001$. How behavior changed with the availability of toys and the infants' ages will be described in subsequent sections.

The incidence of fussing and crying estimates the distress or discomfort associated with the study setting. Only eight of the 44 pairs of infants fussed or cried at all, and these pairs were distributed between both toy conditions and both ages. Further, fussing or crying occurred during no more than four of the 96 periods for any pair. The frequency of smiling to the peer greatly exceeded that of all fussing and crying for each group (see Table 1).

Peer-related behaviors in the presence and absence of toys. How frequently the infants of each age engaged in the different peer-related behaviors in the presence of toys versus their absence is summarized in Table 1. To facilitate comparisons across behaviors, frequencies are given as the percentage of the 96 10-sec observation periods in which the behavior occurred. Most prominent for each age and toy condition were the states of watching the peer and being in his near proximity. Contacting the same play material as the peer occurred less than half as often and accounted for less than one-third of the

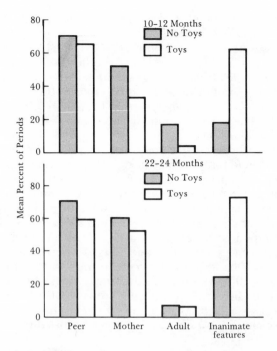

FIGURE 1 Reaction to the total study setting expressed as the frequency with which behaviors occurred involving each of its salient aspects.

total contact of play material. Distal social signals were the most frequent of the peer-directed behaviors that did not require toys, followed by physical contact, duplicate action, and finally alternate action. Less than 5% of the periods were characterized by both children repeatedly directing behaviors at one another in alternation (reciprocal interaction).

The basic contrast of how the peers interacted when they met either with or without toys rests upon the six categories of peer-related behaviors that are customarily thought of as social and that can occur both in the presence and absence of toys. Each such category—watch, in proximity, distal social signals, physical contact, duplicate action, and alternate action—was observed more often when peers met without toys. The contrast was marked for the peer-directed behaviors. Without toys, the peers of both ages directed over twice as many distal social signals at one another and contacted each other and duplicated each other's actions over three times more often; and at the older age they also alternated their actions five times more often. A multivariate analysis of variance on these six categories of behaviors indicated reliable changes in behavior with both toy condition, $F(6,35) = 4.82$, $p < .001$, and age, $F(6,35) = 3.91$, $p < .01$. There was no evidence, however, that the effect of the toy condition differed for the two ages.

Univariate analyses of variance were performed subsequently on each of the six categories of behaviors and within each category on those behaviors shown by at least half the pairs at one or both ages (see Table 1). No reliable differences were found for the states of watching the peer or being in his near proximity. In the absence of toys, the infants more frequently directed distal social signals at each other, $F(1,40) = 9.49, p < .01$, contacted each other, $F(1,40) = 17.29, p < .001$, and duplicated each other's actions, $F(1,40) = 12.70, p < .001$. Smiles, laughs, and gestures contributed most to the increased frequency of distal social signals in the absence of toys—smile/laugh, $F(1,40) = 7.57, p < .01$, and gesture, $F(1,40) = 7.58, p < .01$. Vocal signals were more frequent without toys but not reliably so; and fussing, crying, or showing an object to the peer rarely occurred. Both touches and strikes contributed to the greater frequency of physical contact in the absence of toys—touch, $F(1,40) = 16.20, p < .001$, and strike, $F(1,40) = 9.51, p < .01$—but touching comprised over 70% of the contact.

The older infants, in contrast with the younger ones, more frequently directed distal social signals at each other, $F(1,40) = 5.44, p < .05$, and duplicated each other's actions, $F(1,40) = 5.14, p < .05$. None of the individual behaviors grouped under distal social signals differed reliably with age, although the differences in smiles and laughs approached significance, $F(1,40) = 3.83, p < .06$. Strikes also occurred more often at the older age, $F(1,40) = 5.20, p < .05$, even though the total amount of physical contact with the peer did not differ. Despite the differences in the frequency of a few behaviors at the two ages, there was no evidence that the basic contrast between behaviors in the presence and absence of toys differed for the two ages.

As already documented, duplications of the peer's actions were reliably more frequent both in the absence of toys and at the older age. Eleven of the 22 pairs meeting with toys and 14 of the pairs without toys duplicated each other's actions, producing a total of 113 separate instances of duplicated acts. Table 2 describes the motor activity and what, if any, inanimate objects were involved in the duplicated acts. The observers' records always noted what objects were involved and whether the duplicated act was a verbalization, a touch or strike of the peer, or some other motor action. Combining the observers' records with a review of the videotapes yielded an extended description of 90% of the duplications. Videotaping difficulties or the infants' positions in the room precluded precisely characterizing 11 of the duplications known to involve room fixtures.

Over half of the duplications (55%) involved such room fixtures as the radiator, walls, rug, or table; and the actions engaged in with these fixtures were such commonplace ones as patting, rubbing, fingering, climbing and sitting upon, and opening and closing. Also frequently duplicated were acts involving the peer alone (42%). In duplication of one another, the infants touched, rubbed, patted, or hit one another (23%); pointed toward, clapped hands, or shook their hands at one another (4%); swung their legs from side to side, followed one another, changed from walking to crawling, or raced across the room (9%); and occasionally repeated such a distinctive verbalization as "no jumping" (5%). Only rarely did they duplicate each other's actions with toys (4%).

Repeated alternations of actions between the peers were infrequent except when the older infants met in the setting devoid of toys. Then four of the 11 pairs engaged in at least one episode of alternate action, and one pair spent 29% of the session (or almost 5 min) in such activities. Over 80% of the instances of alternate action took the form of each child performing the same action in alternation while attending to the other child. They "took turns" in shaking hands at one another; patting or kicking the table, radiators, and walls; resting their heads upon the table; following each other; climbing up and down on the table; and running and throwing themselves into one mother's lap. The few occurrences of alternate different actions took the form of repeated sequences of offer and accept or of one child's rushes at the other being met with laughter.

Although toys reduced the frequency of several types of peer-related behavior, they provided further or new opportunities for other types of social interaction. The infants of both ages offered toys to one another, accepted offered toys, moved to contact toys put down less than 3 sec earlier by the peer, took toys from the peer when they were not offered, resisted such attempts to take their toys or relinquished their toys to the peer without protest, struggled over the possession of toys, and showed toys to one another (see Table 1). Although each of these behaviors with peers and toys occurred infrequently, some form of exchange or attempted exchange of a toy occurred an average of six times for the younger peers and four times for the older peers. None of the individual behaviors, nor the composite exchange category, differed reliably with age. At both ages, the smooth exchange of objects (offer, accept, take over, relinquish) outnumbered the exchanges marked by protest or struggling.

Table 2 Frequency of duplication of acts of peer

	10–12 Months		22–24 Months	
Actions Duplicated	*No Toys*	*Toys*	*No Toys*	*Toys*
Actions with toys	. . .	0	. . .	4
Place pegs in bus	. . .	0	. . .	2
Place pegs in box	. . .	0	. . .	1
Pat block	. . .	0	. . .	1
Actions with room fixtures	12	7	37	6
Pat	10	3	11	2
Rub/run hand along	0	0	3	0
Finger	2	2	0	1
Stand, sit, climb on table	0	0	9	1
Open/close radiator doors	0	0	2	0
Kick radiator	0	0	1	0
Turn door knob	0	0	2	0
Look in mirror	0	0	2	0
Unknown	0	2	7	2
Actions of peer alone	13	1	31	2
Verbalize	0	0	6	0
Contact peer	10	1	13	2
Gesture to peer	1	0	2	0
Clap hands	1	0	0	0
Shake hands	0	0	1	0
Swing legs	0	0	1	0
Crawl	1	0	2	0
Race	0	0	5	0
Follow peer	0	0	1	0

The presence of toys also led to more occasions when both infants were simultaneously contacting the same object, $F(1,40) = 11.60, p < .01$, as well as more occasions when they were contacting different objects, $F(1,40) = 150.33, p < .001$. The older infants also were in the state of different play material more often than those younger, $F(1,40) = 6.01, p < .05$. Same play material, however, did not comprise a greater proportion of the total periods of object manipulation either when toys were present or for the younger infants.

In summary, whether toys were present or not, the peers of both ages watched and stayed near one another often. The presence of toys, however, altered the frequency of a number of further interactions between the peers and provided new opportunities for interaction. With toys, the peers of both ages spent more time in simultaneous manipulation of the same objects, and they exchanged and showed toys between themselves. Without toys, the infants of both ages more frequently smiled and gestured to one another, contacted each other, and duplicated each other's actions; and, although the difference was not reliable, the older infants more frequently engaged in reciprocal social interaction.

Collapsing across all the peer-related activities and all the peer-directed behaviors provides a further summary (see Table 1, Summary measures). Without toys, there were fewer periods in which no peer-related activity occurred, $F(1,40) = 4.96, p < .05$, and more periods with at least one discrete peer-directed behavior, $F(1,40) = 8.48, p < .01$. When the periods with some peer-directed behavior were subdivided into those with but a single such act and those with two or more acts of the same or different form, a reliable difference between toy conditions appeared only in the frequency of periods with multiple peer-directed acts, $F(1,40) = 9.93, p < .01$. No reliable differences in these summary measures were found for the two ages, and the infants' ages did not interact with the effects produced by the toys. Thus, the presence or absence of toys prompted a greater change in the frequency of peer-directed behaviors than did a difference in age of 12 months.

Adult-related behaviors in the presence or absence of toys. Three measures were examined for each adult: the number of periods the infant was near the adult (any of the adult-related behaviors coded in this study), the number of periods with physical contact of the adult (alone, not in conjunction with other objects), and the number of periods of play with the adult (offering her a toy, taking a toy, or sustained simultaneous contact of the adult and a toy or room fixture). As shown in Table 3, regardless of the toy condition, each of

Table 3 Percentage of periods with behaviors involving adults

Behavior	10–12 Months		22–24 Months	
	No Toys	*Toys*	*No Toys*	*Toys*
Near mother	51.7	33.2	59.9	51.9
Contact	22.7	16.5	32.2	16.0
Play with	. . .	4.6	. . .	10.4
Near adult	16.0	4.4	7.2	6.6
Contact	1.6	.2	.5	.3
Play with	. . .	.3	. . .	.5

these classes of behavior was directed markedly more often toward the mother than toward the unfamiliar adult. In fact, each of the 44 pairs of infants had more proximity to and contact with the mother than the unfamiliar female; and each of the 22 pairs who engaged an adult in play did so more often with the mother.

The presence of toys, however, altered how the infants interacted with both their mother and their peer's mother. Univariate analyses of variance examined how the toy condition and the infant's age affected the proximity and contact measures for the mother and the proximity measures for the adult. The frequent zero scores for the remaining measures prompted the use of Fisher exact probability tests for examining changes in the number of pairs showing the behavior. When toys were not available, the infants were more often near the mother, $F(1,40) = 3.85$, $p < .06$, and more often in contact with her, $F(1,40) = 4.63$, $p < .05$. The presence of toys, however, resulted in reliably more pairs of each age engaging their mothers in play ($p < .05$, two-tailed). Over two-thirds of this play took the form of simultaneously contacting the mother and a toy. Ten of the older pairs also offered her toys, but only three of the younger pairs did so; and two of the older pairs meeting without toys managed to offer a shoe to their mothers. The older infants were more often near the mother, $F(1,40) = 4.02$, $p < .05$, but age did not alter reliably the effect of the toy condition.

Contacting the unfamiliar adult and playing with her were rare events. Contacting her was somewhat more frequent without toys, but not reliably so. Playing with her occurred only when toys were available and for only two of the pairs at each age. With proximity to the unfamiliar adult there was a reliable interaction between toy condition and age, $F(1,40) = 11.79$, $p < .001$. The older infants were near the adult almost as often in the presence of toys as in their absence; but at the younger age, being near the adult occurred almost four times more often when toys were not present.

Discussion

Infant peers, 1 or 2 years of age, engaged more frequently in several forms of social interaction when in an empty room rather than one containing a few simple toys. Without toys, the unfamiliar peers directed more behaviors at one another; they more often smiled and gestured toward one another, touched and hit one another, and duplicated each other's actions. Yet with toys, the peers showed toys to one another and exchanged them and engaged in more synchronous contact with the same play material. Although the older peers directed more distal social signals toward one another and duplicated each other's actions more than the younger peers, the age of the infants did not alter how toys affected their social interactions. Further, toys altered the infants' interactions with adults—both mothers and unfamiliar females—and peers in similar ways. When toys were available, social interactions involving the toys occurred; without toys, the infants more often contacted or stayed near other persons.

The results document that infants as young as 10 months of age are attentive and responsive to unfamiliar like-aged children. Clearly the behaviors with peers that occurred reliably more often in the absence of toys cannot be construed as reactions to the movements of toys. Instead, they appear as reactions to the person and behavior of the peer himself and, in this sense, they are social behaviors. The smiling and gesturing toward the peer and the showing and offering of toys to him suggests too that the infants treated the peer more like people (adults) than like toys. Even the physical contact made with the peer rarely resembled the sustained manipulation of toys; more often the pokes, pats, rubs, and hits resembled those directed in play toward the mother. Examining which actions of a peer were duplicated also further substantiated the infants' social responsiveness to peers. The infants watched each other as often when toys were present as when they were not; and although they frequently contacted the same play material as the peer, they rarely duplicated what they observed the peer do with the toys. Instead, they duplicated the peer's routine manipulation of room fixtures or his social contacts, gestures, and gross motor movements. It is tempting to speculate that the import of these actions lies less in the actions themselves and more in the peer's performance of actions like those of the observing infant.

Infants approaching 1 year of age were as responsive to the social versus nonsocial aspects of the novel play setting as infants approaching 2 years of age. The findings provide no support for claims of a shift during the second year of life from a focus upon toys to a focus upon the peer (Maudry and Nekula 1939; Mueller and Lucas 1975). The frequency with which the infants directed social signals at one another and duplicated each other's actions increased with age and reciprocal social interaction was more often seen, but the basic contrast between peer interactions in the presence or absence of novel play materials did not change.

The question now turns from whether infants are socially responsive to one another to whether toys facilitate or inhibit this social responsiveness. This latter question, however, is unprofitable since a convincing formula for combining the frequencies of different peer-related behaviors into a composite social responsiveness score is lacking. Does an offer of a toy to the peer equal two smiles, or 1 period of same play a vocalization? More promising are attempts to understand the complex interplay between an infant's exploration of his inanimate world and his social interactions. Toys, or inanimate features, appear often as vehicles for social interactions. They allow infants, like adults, to exchange objects and show them to one another; and they facilitate side-by-side play with the same materials. At the same time, the presence and actions of other social beings may influence the ways in which the infant explores his inanimate world. And further, the nature of a peer's actions upon objects may be a major source of his attraction to the infant, facilitating diverse forms of social interaction. If the infant is viewed as a single individual who is responsive to both the animate and inanimate features of his world, then any major change in these features, whether by introducing another person or salient inanimate objects, should be expected to alter how he behaves.

How toys bring about reductions in certain types of peer interaction and not others, however, remains a viable question. Physical contact with the peer may decrease because toys provide additional and competing objects for manipulation. Touching and hitting the peer may have been replaced by manipulating a toy beside him, just as the presence of a novel toy has been shown to produce decreased contact with the mother accompanied by extensive manipulation of the toy near her (Rheingold and Eckerman 1969). The decreased smiling and gesturing to the peer is problematical given that the infants watched one another as often when toys were present as not. What was being watched, however, may have differed. Without toys, infants may have more often looked at each other's faces, prompting social signals; with toys, they may have watched each other's actions with toys. Or smiling and gesturing may have been the most readily available behaviors for initiating peer interactions in a setting without toys, whereas offers of toys or demonstrations of actions with toys may have served this function when toys were available. The rarity of duplications involving the toys was unexpected; age-appropriate actions with novel materials would seem prime candidates for duplication if the infants were exploring the inanimate consequences of their actions. The routine and peer-centered nature of many of the actions duplicated suggests instead a social function for these duplications. Duplication is an option available to an infant for reacting to almost any activity of a peer and an option that may function to continue interaction. The most frequent form of reciprocal social interaction between the peers consisted of each child duplicating the preceding act of the peer repeatedly and in turn. If there is a paucity of other learned action-reaction sequences (e.g., offer a toy—accept or take a toy—resist), duplicating each other's actions may predominate as a way of generalizing social interaction. Documentation of such speculations, or others, awaits the detailed analysis of how infants initiate and sustain interactions with one another.

The issue of whether the infant's developing exploration of inanimate objects plays a special role in his development of responsiveness to peers (Mueller and Lucas 1975) remains problematical. The infant's ways of acting upon his inanimate world may be a major source of his attractiveness to other infants, but the same may hold true for the infant's responsiveness to adults during similar periods of his life. Similarly, many forms of social interaction, both with adults and peers, revolve around inanimate objects. The present study offers only the suggestive findings that the infants' reactions to adults as well as to the peer changed in similar ways when novel toys were present and the affirmation that by 10 months of age peers are potent stimuli for the infant.

In addition to documenting that infants are responsive to one another, the present findings underscore the situational specificity of infant social behavior. Behavior related to each potential social partner—unfamiliar peer, unfamiliar adult, and mother—was altered by the simple addition of three toys to the room in which the encounter took place. The changes produced were often marked. The older infants, for example, contacted their mothers only half as much when toys were available, and they smiled and gestured to the peer less than one-third as often. In fact, the presence or absence of toys prompted greater differences in some of the peer-related activities assessed here than did 12 months of development. An examination of each peer-directed behavior for which a reliable main effect of age was obtained shows that these behaviors were more frequent for the younger children meeting without toys than for the older children meeting with toys. Conclusions about infants' social responsiveness based on observing infants in one of these inanimate contexts might well have differed from those based upon the other inanimate context. An understanding of encounters between infant peers, as well as those between infants and adults, clearly should be pursued within multiple contexts.

Further evidence for the influence of the inanimate context upon peer-related behaviors can be found by comparing the present findings for infants meeting with toys to those of an earlier study in which infants also met with toys (Eckerman et al. 1975). The same peer-related behaviors were observed in both studies and with similar relative frequencies. However, the changes with age in the frequency of peer interactions involving toys received only partial replication. Duplication of a peer's activity and reciprocal interaction increased with age similarly in both studies, but exchanges of toys (particularly struggles) and synchronous contact of the same play material did not. The major factor thought responsible for the conflicting findings is the presence in the prior study of duplicates of each toy. Duplicates of the toys would seem to facilitate simultaneous play with similar objects, but what of the various forms of exchanging objects? Informal observations provide only the answer that with duplicate toys infants were often seen contacting one of the duplicate toys and offering their particular version to the peer or attempting to exchange the peer's particular toy for their own. Without duplicates, the infants often seemed to tacitly acknowledge each other's possession of the toy in hand and move to take a toy only after the peer had released it. The absence of duplicate play materials clearly alters the task demands involved in playing together with similar objects, exchanging objects, and duplicating or coordinating actions with objects; and study of this aspect of the setting for interaction between infants may provide new insights into the social skills mastered during infancy.

By affirming that infants from at least 10 months of age are socially responsive to one another, the present work generates a flood of further questions. To what aspects of another infant's appearance and behavior is the young infant responsive? How does he respond to these aspects, and how do these responses alter his experience? How do the relevant aspects of social stimulation provided by a peer compare with those provided by adults or older children? What may be the consequences for the infant's experience of growing up with adults as the customary social partner rather than also with other children—either peers, siblings, or older friends? Obtaining answers to each question will be a difficult adventure, but one of central import to our understanding of infant sociability and the origins of interpersonal influence.

This research was supported by a Duke University Research Council grant to author Eckerman and a postdoctoral award (NIMH grant 13112) to author Whatley. We thank William McDonald, Marilyn Prince, and Stephanie Weisband for their aid in data analysis.

NOTES

1. The method of coding was a compromise, pragmatically achieved. Recording on the spot, simultaneously, and in behavioral detail how each child acted upon and reacted to one another proved unattainable with the observers available. The possibility of repeated codings from video-tapes of the sessions was explored; but facial expressions, the person vocalizing, and the targets of visual regard, facial expressions, sounds, and gestures could

not be resolved adequately. It was decided to code on the spot to maximize resolution of the child's behavior, to record the behavior of a single child at a time so that an observer could distinguish up to 20 different behaviors of that child, and to have two observers focus simultaneously upon the same child but code different sets of behavior to achieve an even finer-grained analysis of the individual child's behavior.

REFERENCES

BRIDGES, K. M. B. A study of social development in early infancy. *Child Development*, 1933, *4*, 36–49.

BÜHLER, C. *The first year of life*. New York: John Day, 1930.

ECKERMAN, C. O.; WHATLEY, J. L.; AND KUTZ, S.L. Growth of social play with peers during the second year of life. *Developmental Psychology*, 1975, *11*, 42–49.

LEWIS, M., AND ROSENBLUM, L. A. (Eds.), *Friendship and peer relations*. New York: Wiley, 1975.

MAUDRY, M., AND NEKULA, M. Social relations between children of the same age during the first two years of life. *Journal of Genetic Psychology*, 1939, *54*, 193–215.

MUELLER, E., AND LUCAS, T. A developmental analysis of peer interaction among toddlers. In M. Lewis and L. A. Rosenblum (Eds.), *Friendship and peer relations*. New York: Wiley, 1975.

RAMEY, C. T.; FINKELSTEIN, N. W.; AND O'BRIEN, C. Toys and infant behavior in the first year of life. *Journal of Genetic Psychology*, 1976, *129*, 341–342.

REID, J. B. Reliability assessment of observation data: a possible methodological problem. *Child Development*, 1970, *41*, 1143–1150.

RHEINGOLD, H. L., AND ECKERMAN, C. O. The infant's free entry into a new environment. *Journal of Experimental Child Psychology*, 1969, *8*, 271–283.

ROSS, H. S., AND GOLDMAN, B. D. Establishing new social relations in infancy. In T. Alloway, L. Krames, and P. Pliner (Eds.), *Advances in communication and affect*. Vol. 4. New York: Plenum, in press.

SCHAFFER, H. R. *The growth of sociability*. Harmondsworth, Middlesex: Penguin, 1971.

Part III

The Development of Individuality in Infants

FREUD'S famous comment that one's character is mostly formed by age five was certainly an exaggeration of the case, but there is good reason to believe that important dimensions of personality do emerge very early in life and remain stable throughout the childhood and adolescent years. The readings that follow identify some of the dimensions that are already apparent during infancy. They also suggest the developmental processes responsible for the formation of these early personality characteristics.

Thomas and Chess focus on the contribution of the child's temperament. According to Thomas and Chess's research, infants as young as two months differ from one another in their temperamental characteristics. The authors have identified nine dimensions, ranging from activity level to persistence, that define what they call the "behavioral profile" of an infant. This profile is the basis, they believe, for the infant's emerging individuality. The authors have also explained how certain patterns of these nine dimensions predominate in the children that they have studied. In particular, a majority of infants can be described by three basic patterns: the easy child, the difficult child, and the slow-to-warm-up child. According to results from Thomas and Chess's New York Longitudinal Study, these patterns remain stable for years of childhood. Far more of the difficult than the easy infants developed behavioral problems during their school years.

The Thomas and Chess research on infant temperamental differences has been enormously influential, but it has also been roundly criticized on methodological grounds. Questions have been raised about the validity of parental interviews as the main measure of infant temperament. The authors have countered that "independent checks by trained observers established that the descriptions of the children's behavior supplied by the parents in these interviews could be accepted as reliable and significant." Still, this controversy will probably not be resolved until research using observational techniques confirms the existence and stability of the temperamental dispositions that Thomas and Chess have identified. Solid information about this issue may be available soon, since infant temperament is currently a lively research topic in developmental psychology.

In their article, Thomas and Chess are careful to stress their belief that temperament alone does not determine personality. They do not negate the role of the child's social context, in particular the parents' influence. Temperament, they write, can be modified and even transformed through a critical set of experiences as the child grows. But the authors add the proviso that children themselves help shape the nature of their own social environments. In this article, Thomas and Chess show how a child's temperament can affect the child's interactions with a parent, which in turn affects the child's personality development. Thus, despite the nativist thrust of their research on the infant's "own" temperamental style of responding to the environment, the authors are careful to maintain an overall theoretical position that asserts the interaction between temperament and social experience.

L. Alan Sroufe's account of early personality development is even more assertedly interactionist in tone and substance. Sroufe, like Thomas and Chess, maintains that there are important continuities in a child's behavior over time. This is what Sroufe means when he writes that "the child is a coherent person." But Sroufe believes that these continuities arise not from factors *within* the child, but rather from patterns of *interaction* between the child and others. Patterns of interaction that are adaptive at one age will lead to patterns of interaction that are adaptive in later years: this is the notion of developmental continuity.

Sroufe's particular focus is the attachment relation in infancy and its subsequent developmental consequences in later years. Attachment, of course, is a relation to which both the caregiver and infant contribute. The interaction between the two determines the quality of the relation. Ainsworth's three patterns of attachment—Group A, Group B, and Group C—offer a means of assessing the quality of attachment relations between individual caregiver-infant pairs in terms of the adaptiveness of the relation. The Group B pattern of secure attachment is clearly the most adaptive in infancy, since it enables the infant to use its caregiver as a secure base for exploration. Sroufe's point is that the adaptiveness of this early relation enables one to predict the adaptiveness of the child's later social relations with peers and adults. He cites an impressive array of recent studies that confirm his point.

There are two distinctive features in Sroufe's treatment of individuality and personality. First, as noted above, Sroufe portrays the child as establishing an individual personality in the context of certain key social relationships, beginning with attachment to the caregiver in infancy. If the relationships change in quality, the child changes with them. In moving in and out of these key relationships, the child discovers a unique sense of self that endures over time, providing personality continuity from one period of life to the next. This personal continuity may be modified by new and different experience in relationships, but whether it changes or remains stable, it does so in a coherent manner.

The second distinctive feature of Sroufe's position is his treatment of the continuity notion itself. By continuity in individual development, Sroufe does not mean that the individual's behavior remains identical over time. As he notes, an infant's vigorous nursing does not predict aggression later in childhood, nor does clinging in infancy lead to clinging in the childhood years. The meaning of these behaviors changes as the child enters new phases of life and must deal with new social challenges. Behavior that is adaptive during one phase of life (like the infant's clinging) may become maladaptive in later years. Sroufe, therefore, assesses individual continuity only in relation to the individual's adaptation to the social world at different ages. Adaptiveness in infancy—as determined by secure caregiver-child attachments—therefore predicts adaptiveness in the preschool years, even though here adaptiveness may mean competent peer relations rather than the same type of secure attachment measured earlier. This is a developmental approach, since it recognizes that continuity in an individual is provided by developmental changes that build upon another, and not by a repetition of the identical behavior patterns throughout life. Behavior becomes reorganized in the course of development, and therefore may seem discontinuous to the naive observer. But these reorganizations bear a developmental relation to one another, and therein lies the true continuity.

Individual differences in personality development are in many ways the focal point of psychology as a discipline, since it is here that we must look for an answer to why people are the way they are. The infant years already provide a firm beginning to the formation of distinct individual characteristics that have enduring consequences for the self. In later sections, we shall see the contributions of childhood and adolescence to this process.

6

Temperament and Parent-Child Interaction

Alexander Thomas and Stella Chess

All psychological theories, no matter how they differ from each other, agree in emphasizing the crucial significance of the parents or parent surrogates for the child's development in the early years of life. This is the period in which the young child masters the initial demands for socialization within the family. The establishment of regular sleep and feeding patterns, toilet-training, mastery of self-feeding and dressing, acceptance of family rules and prohibitions, response to masturbatory experiences, the emergence and growth of interpersonal relations with parents, sibs and other significant members of the family group—these are the areas in which consonance or dissonance between infant and environment is elaborated.

In all these areas it is primarily the parents or parent substitutes who make the demands and communicate environmental expectations, establish and implement routines, mediate the infant's relationships with the outside world. The parents may or may not get guidance and assistance from others—grandparents, baby nurses, pediatricians, or child-care profession-als. In any event they are generally held responsible for the kind of patterns of socialization developed by the infant and preschool child.

In the preschool years the development of peer group relations becomes an increasingly important issue. Here, too, it is the parents who are usually most directly influential in helping or hindering the course of the

Reprinted with permission from *Temperament and Development*, by Alexander Thomas and Stella Chess, Brunner/Mazel, 1977, pp. 66–81.

youngster's mastery, whether or not the child is involved in nursery school or day care center experiences. As the youngster grows older, new and increasingly more complex developmental issues emerge, such as formal learning, incorporation of socio-cultural values and standards, and adolescent group adaptations. The role of the parent becomes progressively less dominant, and the parents' influence is more and more shared with and modified by teachers, other important adults in the child's life, peer groups, and community organizations.

A similar evolution over time is evident in the contribution made by the child's own characteristics to the developmental process. The infant's behavior patterns are relatively simple, and variations in cognitive and perceptual levels and expression of special skills are uncomplicated in most normal infants. Motivations are only beginning to develop, and psychodynamic mechanisms are not structured as yet. In this infancy period, temperamental traits and their contribution to the child's development are relatively easy to identify.

As the child grows older, environmental demands, expectations and opportunities become increasingly more complex, elaborate and varied; at the same time the child's own attributes increase in complexity, as perception, cognition, motivations, psychodynamic mechanisms, special skills and talents are developed and crystallized. The role of temperament remains important, sometimes even decisive, but increasingly more complicated to isolate for analysis, as the child's behavior patterns become more and more complex in their determination and expression.

General Aspects of Parent-Child Interaction

Central to the consideration of the parent-child relationship is that each influences the other from the beginning in a constantly evolving process of interaction. The infant is not a *homunculus,* as previous centuries had it, in which his final adult psychological structure was present within him at birth, and in which development consisted of the maturation and unfolding of these fixed inherent characteristics. In this simplistic constitutional view, the parents and other child caretakers could enforce specific modifications of behavior and ideas by discipline and persuasion but were not the primary shapers of the child's personality.

Neither is the infant a *tabula rasa,* as recent theories might indicate, a clean slate on which the family and society can inscribe any pattern and outcome at will. It seems amusing to think of John Watson's behaviorist assertion of 50 years ago, "Give me a dozen healthy infants, well-formed, and my own specified world to bring them up in, and I'll guarantee to take any one at random and train him to become any type of specialist I might select—doctor, lawyer, artist, merchant-chief, and yes, even beggarman and thief, regardless of his talents, penchants, abilities, vocations, and race of his ancestors."[1] In actual practice, this view dominated the thinking of most mental health professionals until very recently, dressed up though it may have been in the professional and sophisticated language of one theory or another.

In truth, of course, the infant is neither a *homunculus* nor a *tabula rasa,* either in his psychological or biological development.[2] The influence of the infant's biochemical and physiological characteristics, temperamental traits and cognitive and perceptual attributes is determined by the opportunities, constraints and demands of the family and society. Conversely and simultaneously, the influence of the family and society is shaped by the quality and degree of its consonance or dissonance with the infant's capacities and style of functioning. Furthermore, this reciprocal interaction is not a static process. It is a constantly evolving dynamic, as the child and family and society change over time.

Recent research on the infancy period has documented dramatically the active participation of the infant, even in the newborn state, in this interactive process. The young baby's perceptual, behavioral and cognitive capacities are developed to an extent not imagined by students of development even 10 years ago.[3] The newborn infant not only responds actively to stimulation from the mother but initiates communication with vocalizations, facial expressions and body movements. Rutter summarizes this research in three generalizations.

> First, it is evident that, although limited in many ways, the young infant has a surprisingly sophisticated response to his environment and quite substantial learning skills. Second, these skills and capacities have a marked influence on the process of parent-child interaction. In many instances it is the baby who shows initiative and the parent who responds by following. Third, even in the early months of life there are striking temperamental differences between infants which influence both their response to the environment and also how other people react to them.[4]

As indicated above, in the infancy period temperament and parental attitudes and practices play a major role in the child-environment interaction. The effect of the child's specific temperament on the parent can take many directions, depending on the latter's personality structure, goals and expectations for the child, and on socio-economic opportunities and constraints. The effect of the parent's attitudes and practices on the child can also be varied, depending on the latter's specific style of response and adaptation.

In the remainder of this chapter, these generalizations will be documented by a number of specific examples and contingencies. While numerous, these illustrations will in no way exhaust the myriad ways in which this mutual influence can take place. The relationship between parent and young child is so fundamental and so complex that it is impossible in any single discussion to exhaust all its possible manifestations, even in this one area of the child's temperament and its role in parent-child interaction. Our hope is that the specific examples cited are sufficient in their variety and quantity to document adequately the fundamental thesis of a constantly active and evolving reciprocal process between parent and the child's temperament.

Effect of Child's Temperament on Parent

It is a static mechanical concept to assume that a parent's attitudes and behavior toward the child are fixed and determined by pre-existing fully formed parental personality patterns and psychodynamic defenses and conflicts. Any adult or child, unless suffering from serious mental illness, has the capacity and flexibility to respond differentially and selectively to the wide range of external situations and people which make up his life. In each specific instance the response is shaped by some aspect of the individual's personality structure, but, in the absence of serious mental illness, this structure is not homogeneous, global or insensitive to the nature of external reality.

A child's specific temperamental traits can affect the parent's attitudes and behavior in many ways, and this has been clearly evident in many families in our various longitudinal studies. The anterospective nature of the data has made it possible to identify temporal relationships between the child's temperament and parental functioning, and the differential responses of parents to their children with different temperamental patterns. This was usually most dramatically evident in those instances where the parent's reaction was antagonistic or anxious, but was also obvious and important in the many instances where the parent responded favorably to the child's individual characteristics.

In the infancy period, parental responses are most frequently and strongly influenced by whether the infant has the temperamental constellation of the Easy or Difficult Child. This determines whether management routines proceed smoothly or with turmoil, and whether the landmarks of early socialization (regular sleep and feeding schedules, toilet-training, adaptation to family living patterns, etc.) are achieved quickly with initial efforts or after prolonged trial and error. If the mother believes the middle-class conventional wisdom that the course of the infant's development is determined primarily by her maternal attitudes, motivations and needs, an Easy Child will reassure her that she is an adequate, healthy and loving mother. She will be delighted with her child who has given her this opportunity to prove herself and may even feel superior to those other mothers who are struggling painfully with their Difficult Children. If the father has the same standards he will reinforce his wife's judgments and perhaps even gain an unrealistic estimate of her psychological assets. Unfortunately, this outcome is not always an unmixed blessing to the mother. As in any case where self-esteem is built on the evidence of one specific achievement, the mother can become vulnerable and easily threatened by any failure of her Easy Child to adapt quickly and smoothly to every new situation and demand.

The parents of an Easy Child may be pleased and even grateful that they have to exert relatively little effort, time and attention to the child's care. This may have a positive effect on the parent-child relationship, stimulating the expansion and growth of parental love and affection, and in turn enhancing the child's sense of being wanted and loved. In other instances, however, the needs of the Easy Child may be ignored because he adapts so quickly and fusses so little. The parents may concentrate their efforts and attention on another child with special needs or problems, such as physical handicaps or cognitive lags. In such cases, the Easy Child may very well react with feelings of rejection, with all the deleterious psychological consequences that such a reaction may bring. It may also happen, even if infrequently, that a parent, with his or her special value system, may be displeased if the youngster has the Easy Child characteristics of quick adaptability or mild mood expressiveness. Thus, one father was highly critical of his daughter's easy adaptability because in his eyes she was "a pushover," someone who wouldn't fight for what she wanted.

By contrast, the parents can hardly ignore a Difficult Child. The special child-care demands made by such an infant can in general create three types of parental responses, depending on the parents' personality structures and the socio-cultural pressures of their group. The parents may feel threatened and anxious because they feel that the turmoil and difficulties of care expose their inadequacy as parents. They may believe they are unconsciously rejecting their child, or unloving, or just plain inept as caretakers. Or the parents may blame the infant and resent the extra burdens and demands he puts on them. Finally, the parents may be intimidated by the infant's frequent loud screaming and "resistance" to training procedures.

In all these cases, whether the parents are threatened, resentful or intimidated, they can hardly provide the patient, gradual and repeated exposures to new situations and demands that such a child requires to make a positive adaptation. They are more likely to pressure, appease, punish, or vacillate, all the time communicating a host of negative feelings to the infant, such as hostility, impatience or bewilderment. This only leads to intensification of the infant's negative mood expressions and difficulties in adaptation. A vicious cycle is created, leading to behavior disorder development. It is then all too easy for the mental health professional or pediatrician to incorrectly identify the parents' unhealthy attitudes and behavior as the sole cause of the disorder.

Occasionally, a parent may respond positively to the temperament of the Difficult Child. One parent, the father of a child with one of the most extreme Difficult Child patterns in the NYLS, took pride and pleasure in his infant's vigor and "lustiness." He was also aware that after the initial storm and turmoil that accompanied the exposure to any new situation, his son gradually adapted positively and energetically. Because of his positive attitude and patience, he was able to be very supportive to his wife, who felt anxious and guilty over the child's behavior pattern. As a consequence, this youngster did not develop a behavior disorder.

In fact, most parents of Difficult Children with behavior disorders responded positively once they understood that their child's temperament existed independently of their own attitudes and functioning, and that a specific management approach was required. Basically, this resulted from the reassurance that their patient efforts would finally be rewarded by a change in adaptation by the child, who would then function on a level congenial to their own value system. Because of this, parent guidance in the cases of Difficult Children with behavior problems was as successful as in the Easy Child clinical sample.

Gregg, in her Infant Accident Study, postulated that some mothers with difficult infants might perceive these children as "evil" or "mean" and be more likely to subject them to abuse. Also, child-abusing mothers might perceive their children as more difficult than they actually were.[5] Her clinical study, in which mothers' temperamental ratings were compared with those obtained by the pediatrician's direct observation, suggested that both possibilities might be true. In addition, she found that babies who showed neglect, chronic illness or failure to thrive were, as a group, less active, less intense and bland in mood. She could not decide, from her data, whether she was tapping poor physical and mental status or temperamental characteristics.

Other temperamental traits can, of course, initiate inappropriate parental reactions to their infants. For example, Carey has found that sleep disturbance in infants with night waking is significantly correlated with low sensory threshold.[6] He points out that if the mother is automatically held responsible for this sleep problem she may develop "anxiety, anger or feelings of helplessness" which may be, in reality, "the result rather than the cause of the baby's waking."

In the preschool years the temperamental constellation of the Easy or Difficult Child can continue to affect the parents' responses as new demands for adaptation and self-mastery arise. In addition, these new demands and expectations, combined with the child's ever expanding range of activities and capabilities, enhance the significance of other temperamental attributes in the developmental process. Here, too, as in the earlier period, temperament can affect the parents' attitudes and behavior toward the child.

For example, the highly active young child, once he is walking and running, can present special problems of management, especially in an urban environment. He is more apt to get burned and bruised, to break things, to dart out into the street in front of an oncoming car and to interfere unintentionally with the activities and comforts of others than is the child with a moderate or low activity level. Some parents can enjoy the liveliness of a highly active child. Others become resentful, overwhelmed or anxious at the more vigilant attention such a youngster demands. They may also interpret lack of compliance with demands for unrealistic restraint of motor activity as deliberate disobedience, especially if their other children respond easily to similar requests. If this leads the parents to scold or punish the highly active child for each infraction of the rules, the youngster may decide there is no point in trying to please his parents and that he might just as well ignore or resist their wishes altogether. He may then, in fact, become disobedient.

By contrast, the low activity child may be a convenient member of the household. He does not require special vigilance and his slow movements will interfere very little with the activities of other family members. Parental impatience and displeasure may develop, however, when the child's slowness in finishing meals or getting dressed interferes with the family's schedule. The parents may also compare him unfavorably to their other more active children, and even interpret the slow motor activity as evidence of inferior intellectual ability.

A highly distractible child may facilitate management during infancy. Such a child's resistance to being held still while being dressed or diapered can easily be countered by offering him a toy or other distraction. The crawling infant's attention can be quickly diverted from a potentially dangerous activity, such as poking at an electrical socket. As the child grows older, however, this quality of easy distractibility becomes less convenient, especially if combined with low persistence and attention span. These characteristics interfere with the goal of quick and complete task completion, a demand which is made increasingly on the growing child, especially in middle-class families. The parental response to these traits is frequently crucial for the child's developmental course. If the parents understand that the distractibility is not motivated by a desire to avoid the completion of a task and that the child is not deficient in "a sense of responsibility," they can avoid a derogatory or punitive attitude. They can then accept with good humor and patience the frequent "forgetting" to finish a task and appreciate the high level of general alertness and awareness of the nuances of other people's behavior and feelings such distractible children frequently show. Other parents, to the contrary, interpret the typical behavior of the distractible child as reflecting conscious disobedience, laziness or lack of willpower and responsibility. These derogatory judgments lead to excessive pressure on the child, hypercritical and punitive attitudes, and foster a pathological child-parent interaction which may produce increasing malfunction and symptomatology in the child.

Parental response to high persistence in the preschool child can be influenced greatly by the selectivity of his interests and activities and by coexisting temperamental traits. If the youngster's persistence is focused on areas which the parents value highly, this will gain parental approval and more than counterbalance the inconvenience and annoyance that result when the child's attention cannot be turned easily. The child who resists coming for meals, getting dressed or going to bed because he is absorbed in putting a puzzle together, trying to learn to read, or practicing an athletic skill will meet parental tolerance and even encouragement if the parents approve of these activities and goals. If, however, the child focuses on activities which may be unsafe, or interests which appear unimportant or unproductive, then his persistence may be interpreted as nagging, stubbornness or inconsiderateness.

The persistent preschool youngster is likely to suffer many frustration reactions as he struggles intently to master difficult new activities and tasks, and attempts are made to call him away to meals or bedtime. If his mood expression is mild, these frustrations will typically be expressed in a way which is likely to be acceptable to the family. If, however, his mood expression is intense, there may be storms, loud protests, and even tantrums which may tax or overwhelm the parents. Patience and tolerance with the persistent child are also easier if he has a low activity level and sits quietly or moves slowly as he is absorbed in his pursuits. If, however, he has a high activity level which annoys or interferes with other people, this trait in combination with his persistence may easily create serious dissonances with parental expectations and demands.

Finally, the typical behavior of the Slow-To-Warm-Up Child usually creates few if any issues in infancy, but may begin to do so in the preschool period. As an infant he may react negatively to the bath, to new foods, to strangers, as does the Difficult Child. But inasmuch as the Slow-To-Warm-Up Child expresses his withdrawal reactions mildly and quietly, it is usually easy for the parents to tolerate them and wait patiently until the infant finally makes a positive adaptation. But this tolerance and patience are harder for the parents to maintain when the withdrawal reactions begin to occur in an area which has high priority in their value system. Thus, the middle-class parents in the NYLS were uniformly unconcerned if time was required to persuade the infant to accept various foods. But many of them became deeply concerned when this same child, two or three years later, showed similar negative reactions to a new nursery school or preschool play group. For these parents, the development of a varied and regular diet ranked low in the scale of their hierarchies of goals and standards for the child. By contrast, the ability to make quick and positive interpersonal relations ranked very high.

For the parents who understood the initial social withdrawal reactions of their Slow-To-Warm-Up Child as part of his normal behavioral style of functioning, a willingness to wait and give the youngster time to make a final positive adaptation was exhibited. For the parents who saw the initial negative reaction as "timidity or anxiety," such patience was much more difficult to achieve. Some of them pressured the child to adapt quickly and actively to the new group, which usually resulted in an intensification of the child's withdrawal response, increased parental pressure and the initiation of a snowballing pathogenic parent-child interaction. Other parents were similarly threatened by the slow-to-warm-up social behavior but responded with overprotectiveness, trying to shield the youngster from these demanding new situations. As a result, the child was denied the opportunity for frequent exposure to new situations that he needed in order to achieve a positive adaptation, and tended to develop only a constricted range of activities and interests.

In the school years, each child's developmental course was increasingly affected by the school setting and peer groups. Parental influences, though not as dominant as in the infancy and preschool periods, continued to be important. Patterns of parent-child interaction established in these earlier years were sometimes reinforced by the child's school functioning. This occurred especially when the child's temperament made the adaptation to formal learning demands slow or stressful, as we will discuss in a later chapter on school functioning. In many other families the increasingly complex and varied aspects of the older child's psychological functioning made for significant shifts in parental attitudes and behavior. In these instances the child's temperament was only one of a number of interacting factors in influencing the course of the parent-child relationship.

As a final comment on the effect of the child's temperament on the parent, it is our impression that this was not determined in any uniform way by congruence or lack of congruence of parent and child characteristics. In some instances it was difficult for parents to understand a child with temperamental traits different from their own. Thus, in one family the parents were both lively, expressive and predominantly cheerful individuals. Their oldest child, Dorothy, had a low activity level and frequent negative mood reactions of low intensity. The parents grew to feel that their daughter was disinterested in most activities because of her slow movements and negative mood and that they did not know what she wanted because her needs were expressed with such mild intensity. They became increasingly impatient with Dorothy, failed to recognize the cues she gave as to her desires, and labeled her as "fussy" and "whiney."

Another mother, by contrast, was concerned over her daughter Kaye's pattern of quiet easy adaptability. The mother felt she herself had been this type of child and had been pressured by her parents into patterns of adaptation which were not in her own best interests. She was therefore determined that her own daughter would not suffer a similar fate. The mother's child-care practices were consequently guided by the determination to keep demands on Kaye to a minimum and allow her to develop "spontaneously." As a result the youngster had difficulties with any situation demanding specific task performances. This was evident by age three years in her response to psychometric testing and became a serious impediment to academic achievement.

As a general rule, the nature of the parents' response to the child's temperament was determined not so much by the degree of congruence with their own personality characteristics as by consonance with their goals, standards and values. In discussing parent-child interactions, this is indicated throughout this volume. It is sharply demonstrated by our analysis of the outcome of parent guidance in the NYLS clinical cases. As reported in our previous volume, the need for the parents to know and respect their child's temperament was a major element in our approach to parent guidance. To implement this respect for the child's temperament, specific advice was given to eliminate inappropriate and harmful attitudes and practices and to substitute practices which were consonant with the child's behavioral style. Where indicated, and where possible, parents were advised to change other excessively stressful demands in the environment, whether at home, in the school setting, or elsewhere.

In the majority of the 42 clinical cases tabulated,[7] parent guidance was successful in varying degrees in each temperamental pattern group, with the exception of the distractible, non-persistent group where parent guidance was a failure in four out of four cases. In other children, whether easy, difficult, slow-to-warm-up, persistent, or with high or low activity level, most parents responded positively to the assurance that appropriate behavior on their part would lead to final adaptive patterns on the child's part which would be consonant with the family's standards and goals. For the distractible and non-persistent children, however, the parents had to accept the judgment that the child might never pursue a difficult task doggedly, might always lack persistence, and might always have problems in carrying through a responsibility from beginning to end in one sustained effort. For these middle-class and largely professional parents, this judgment appeared to run counter to their own deep commitments to disciplined work and persistence in the face of obstacles which had shaped their lives and careers. To them, a youngster without these virtues "lacked character," was "irresponsible" or "lazy." Repeated discussions with the parents uniformly failed to change these judgments. It is of interest that all four clinical cases with distractible characteristics were boys. The parents of both sexes considered these traits to be especially objectionable in boys, reflecting the sexist values of our society for male achievement.

Effect of Parent on Child

In contrast to the importance of the child's temperament in influencing the parent, especially in the early childhood years, the parent's influence on the child at all ages is compounded of many factors. The discussion above has emphasized the significant role played by the parent's values, standards and goals. The professional literature over a number of decades has considered this issue as well as a number of others. Psychological and psychodynamic characteristics have been emphasized. The contrast for the course of the child's development between favorable parental attitudes such as love, tenderness, acceptance and empathy, and noxious attitudes such as rejection, overprotection, and ambivalence or anxiety in the parental role have been documented. . . . Our quarrel with the formulations arises when they assume an all or nothing character, when they are credited with exclusive significance in determining the child's psychological development. Similarly, these concepts can be criticized when the parental attributes are reified and given a global dimension. It is insufficient and inaccurate to characterize a parent in an overall, diffuse way as "rejecting," "overprotective," "insecure," etc. A parent may be unsympathetic and antagonistic to certain of the child's characteristics and accepting and approving of others; overprotective and restrictive of some of the child's activities but not of others; insecure and unsure in specific areas of child-care responsibilities and self-confident and assured in others.

An interesting question concerns the possibility that the effective communication of the parents' attitudes to the child may be influenced by their own temperamental characteristics. For example, is it possible that a parent may have tender, empathetic feelings toward the child, and yet communicate these attitudes inadequately because of his or her own traits of low intensity of mood expression and frequent or predominant reactions of negative mood? Or may a parent's own characteristics of high persistence and low distractibility result in frequent oblivion to important cues from the child? Unfortunately, we have no data on which to base even impressions as to the significance, if any, of this issue. It remains a fruitful, if complex, project for future investigation.

Recent years have also witnessed an increasing emphasis on sociocultural influences on the child's development, either as mediated through the family or directly through the child's life and experiences outside the family group. We ourselves consider these influences as significant, and even decisive in many cases. We have explored the issues by mounting a longitudinal study of a cohort with major sociocultural differences from the NYLS sample. This is the study of children coming from Puerto Rican working-class families. Thus far, cross-cultural analyses of our data have revealed significant differences between the two samples in the age of incidence and types of symptoms in those with behavior disorders,[8] in their response to the demand for task performance in cognitive evaluation,[9] and in their response to the examiner in a psychometric test situation.[10] These findings have been clearly related to sociocultural differences between the two populations.

Thus, parental attitudes and practices may affect the child's developmental course, depending on the child's temperament and other attributes and the degree of consonance or dissonance between parental demands and expectations and the child's temperament and capacities. This is clearly seen in the early years in the child's ability to respond positively to the specific child-care practices of the parents. An approach to the child as a *tabula rasa* results in the assumption "that each child will react in the same way to any specific approach by the parent, whether in feeding, toilet-training, discipline or any other area of functioning. A child-care practice which has a favorable effect on some children is assumed to be desirable for all; a practice which has unfavorable effects on some children is considered undesirable for all. Where a particular child-care practice appears to have varying effects on different children, explanations for these deviations tend to be given in terms of the presence of counteracting influences in the mother, father, or sibling relationship."[11]

This approach, criticized by us 20 years ago, unfortunately still is believed by many parents and professionals. Such an approach has several unfortunate consequences. The child who cannot respond to a currently favored categorical rule becomes at risk for the development of behavior disorder. The mother whose child does not respond favorably and smoothly to the prescribed rule is held culpable because of postulated ineptitude, disinterest or hostility to the child.[12] The inevitable finding that all children do not respond positively to the prescribed child-care regime initiates a swing of the pendulum and a search for a new, universally applicable set of rules. It indeed appears difficult for many mental health professionals, though easier for parents, baby nurses and pediatricians, to accept the fact that babies respond differently and that no single set of prescriptions can be desirable for all infants.

It is clear that the exhortations "treat your child as an individual," and "respect the uniqueness of your child" become clichés and slogans unless given content and substance. And this content demands that the child-care expert and adviser be fully aware of the phenomenon of temperamental individuality, the different types of temperamental characteristics, and the manner in which such temperamental individuality shapes the infant's responses to specific child-care practices.

NOTES

1. J. B. Watson, *Behaviorism* (New York: W. W. Norton, 1924).
2. T. Dobzhansky, *Mankind Evolving* (New Haven: Yale University Press, 1962).
3. R. Lewin, ed., *Child Alive* (London: Temple Smith, 1975).
4. M. Rutter, "A Child's Life," *Child Alive, op. cit.*, p. 208.
5. G. Gregg, "Clinical Experience with Efforts to Define Individual Differences in Temperament," *Individual Differences in Children*, ed., J. Westman (New York: John Wiley and Sons, 1973), pp. 306–322.
6. W. B. Carey, "Night Waking and Temperament in Infancy," *J. Pediatrics*, 84:756–758 (1974).
7. A. Thomas, S. Chess and H. G. Birch, *Temperament and Behavior Disorders in Children* (New York: New York University Press, 1968), pp. 198–201.
8. A. Thomas, S. Chess, J. Sillen and O. Mendez, "Cross-cultural Study of Behavior in Children with Special Vulnerabilities to Stress," *Life History Research in Psychopathology, Vol. III*, eds., D. F. Ricks, A. Thomas and M. Roff (Minneapolis: University of Minnesota Press, 1974), pp. 53–67.
9. M. Hertzig, H. G. Birch, A. Thomas and O. A. Mendez, "Class and Ethnic Differences in the Responsiveness of Preschool Children to Cognitive Demands," *Monographs of the Society for Research in Child Development*, 33:1–69 (1968).
10. A. Thomas, M. E. Hertzig, I. Dryman and P. Fernandez, "Examiner Effect in I.Q. Testing of Puerto Rican Working-Class Children," *Am. J. Orthopsychiatr.*, 41:5 (1971).
11. S. Chess and A. Thomas, "Characteristics of the Individual Child's Behavioral Responses to the Environment," *Am. J. Orthopsychiatr.*, 24:791–802 (1959).
12. S. Chess, "Mal de Mère," *Am. J. Orthopsychiatr.*, 34:613–614 (1964).

7

The Coherence of Individual Development: Early Care, Attachment, and Subsequent Developmental Issues

L. Alan Sroufe

The idea that the child is a coherent person, that despite changes he or she remains in important ways the same individual, has been a powerful force in developmental psychology. In many ways it spurred the emergence of our field, and it moves us forward still. For if the child is a coherent person and individual development a coherent process, and if conditions can be specified that promote psychologically healthy or unhealthy development, then there are powerful implications not only for behavioral scientists but for our entire society. If, for example, one's feelings of self-worth and personal power (efficacy), one's expectations concerning people, and one's capacity for empathic involvement with others are strongly influenced by early experience, then we cannot hesitate to examine fully our public policies in these times of rapid social change. Type and extent of out-of-home care become more than purely economic matters. Teenage pregnancy, chemical dependency, child physical or sexual abuse, and other signs of family dysfunction become matters of urgent national concern. It becomes clear that nothing is more important than understanding the shaping of the child.

Only recently, however, has continuity in individual development proved empirically demonstrable. This was despite the fact that such an assumption is central in prominent developmental theories and despite the

From L. Alan Sroufe, "The Coherence of Individual Development," *American Psychologist* 34 (1979):834–41. Copyright 1979 by the American Psychological Association. Reprinted by permission of the publisher and author.

fact that intuition and personal experience testified daily to the coherence of the individual. Research, so it seemed, previously suggested that such continuity was an illusion. But it was the research that was wrong, not the idea of continuity.

One problem in past research on continuity concerned errors of measurement. Measuring behavioral continuity in the developing child is difficult because behaviors that are beyond the capacity of the younger infant are added rapidly to the repertoire, old behaviors take on new meanings, and behavior becomes organized in increasingly complex ways. Its meaning varies with behavioral and situational context. Therefore, behavior of children must be assessed extensively across situations or in especially salient situations. Counting frequencies of particular behaviors in a single observational session or examining performance on a single task cannot yield stable individual differences any more than can performance on a single item from an intelligence test (Epstein 1979). Unless measurements are stable, individuals cannot reveal their continuities.

Another problem in research on continuity is conceptual. Psychological development is characterized not by mere additions but by transformations and epigenesis. Infants are not merely small children. Therefore, one cannot find continuity by simply measuring the same behavior over time. Clingy overdependency, for example, is one form of maladaptation in the preschool years. Such dependency is the norm in infancy. Recent studies have shown that infants who, when threatened or distressed, actively seek physical contact, mold, cling, and derive comfort from such contact with the caregiver (i.e., are effectively dependent) are more effectively autonomous as toddlers and more competent as preschoolers (Arend, Gove, and Sroufe in press; Main 1977; Matas, Arend and Sroufe 1978; Waters, Wippman, and Sroufe in press). Likewise, aggression in childhood would not likely be predicted from vigorous nursing.

One solution to the problem of continuity in individual development lies in seeking qualitative similarities in patterns of behavior over time, rather than behavioral identities. In this view, children play active roles in seeking solutions to a series of developmental issues. Assessments focus on how well the child is meeting developmental challenges, on the quality of the child's adaptation. It is at this level of abstraction that continuity can be demonstrated. Behavior does change lawfully, but the person remains the same. Such an approach does not mean less emphasis on observable behavior but more emphasis on the meaning and organization of behavior and on affective constructs underlying that organization.

Principles for a Theory of Individual Development

The theory proposed is not really new. It is a synthesis of several powerful viewpoints—revised psychoanalytic theory, ethological-evolutionary theory, and cognitive developmental theory (e.g., Breger 1974). The following features distinguish this eclectic perspective.

1. *A focus on adaptation.* At the individual level, adaptation refers to children's active engagement of the environment, fitting and shaping them-

selves to that environment and effecting changes in the environment to satisfy needs. The child does not merely react to environmental events but seeks stimulation and selects and organizes behavior in terms of his or her own goals.

2. *A view of the person as a coherent whole.* There is a hierarchy of goals, and there is a coordination of different aspects of the persons functioning with respect to those goals. There is a logic and coherence to the person that can only be seen in looking at total functioning. A child may not behave the same way in different situations, but behavior is coherent across situations. For example, an infant on one occasion may be distressed by separation. Upon reunion, she may seek physical contact, maintain contact, and be readily comforted by it. On another occasion, perhaps because she is older, in better health, or more familiar with the surroundings, the same infant is not distressed. Here it is predicted (and has been confirmed) that she will not seek physical contact but will actively greet and initiate interaction with the caregiver (smile, show a toy, etc.). A common experience, a coherent personality, underlies these two behavior patterns. It is the same individual, as shown by the active initiation of contact or interaction and by the role of her relationship with the caregiver in mediating affective response. But the reunion occurs in two different contexts; thus, different behaviors result. It is predictable that the infant who is happy to see the caregiver when the former is not distressed is effective in achieving comforting when he or she is distressed. As another example, the child who can be spontaneous and expressive when the situation permits, but characteristically purposeful and deliberate when circumstances require, is not viewed as inconsistent but as coherent (Block and Block in press).

3. *A central role for affective constructs and emotion.* Affect plays a key role in the organization of behavior (Sroufe 1979). Central in the current view is a motivational duality: security in the familiar, yet attraction to the unfamiliar. Thus, in confronting novelty, curiosity and wariness (retreat to the familiar) are both activated. As an opportunistic species, exploration of the new has adaptive advantage, but novel events may also pose unknown hazards. Curiosity must be tempered by the capacity to delay, but wariness must not submerge curiosity entirely.

4. *A focus on individual differences.* The nature of this balance between exploration and wariness is an important dimension of individual differences; some children are unduly timid in the face of novelty, others characteristically deal with new situations impulsively, and still others show little involvement. A closely related aspect of individual differences concerns effectiveness in managing tension or arousal. Given development, continuity of specific behaviors over time is unlikely. But individual children may show continuity in their ability to modulate arousal and to maintain organized behavior in the face of excitation (novelty, complexity, ambiguity). Children may not be characterized by specific behaviors they exhibit, but they may be characterized by their degree of involvement in the face of environmental challenges and opportunities and by the way in which their behavior is organized in meeting such confrontations. Groups of children may be defined in terms of patterns of behavior, rather than by frequencies of any particular behavior.[1] Likewise, important individual differences in caregiving will be revealed by examining the caregiver's role in helping the

child learn to manage tension and experience joy in mastery. These differences will be reflected more generally in the pattern of care and in the quality
of the infant-caregiver relationship, not in any particular child-rearing practice (e.g., breast vs. bottle feeding).

5. *Development as a series of reorganizations.* Development does not proceed in a linear, incremental manner. Not only are capacities added, there
are changes in behavioral organization. Through such change the infant is
transformed, being qualitatively different in the way it views and transacts
with the world. Periods of reorganization can be defined, with consequent
changes in focal developmental issues. Assessment of individual differences
should address these changing issues.

The Child as Active Participant in Its Own Experience

To understand the coherence of individual adaptation, viewing children as active participants in their own experience is essential. At least by the
second half year, the infant's reaction to events is subjective; it is determined
by evaluative processes within the infant, as well as by objective information.
Individual infants and children differ in their tendencies to see events as
opportunities or threats, in their threshold for threat, in their capacity to
maintain organized behavior in the face of arousal (novelty, complexity),
and in their ability to derive security from the presence of the caregiver.
More generally, children vary in their abilities to draw on personal and
environmental resources in the face of a challenge.

Normative studies of infant development illustrate the role of subjective
factors in behavior. The same event can produce strikingly different reactions depending on its context. For example, mother putting on a mask
uniformly elicits smiling and laughter in a playful home context. In the
laboratory, however, following a separation experience, the same masked
approach produces almost no smiling. Some infants become distressed,
especially if a masked stranger approached first. With groups of subjects,
any reaction can be produced by varying familiarization time, setting, sequence of events, and availability of the caregiver (Sroufe, Waters, and
Matas 1974).

The reactions cannot be due to novelty *per se*. The event is novel in every
case (and less so following the stranger). Nor can the reaction be due simply
to amount of arousal. High levels of arousal are required for laughter as well
as distress. And even if one fully calms an infant following separation (he
returns to play and autonomic levels recover), the negative effect of the
separation is still produced when mother subsequently puts on the mask.
Apparently the infant's threshold for threat (the amount of arousal tolerable) has been altered. On the other hand, in the playful home context, the
most arousing play (e.g., mother bouncing the infant) rarely leads to distress.
No fixed amount of arousal automatically leads to distress. Infants can stay
engaged and affectively positive, even purposefully repeat the event, when
highly aroused.

Individual children elicit different reactions from the environment;
they also differentially seek, filter, interpret, and evaluate experience. The
infant who cannot separate from mother to explore the novel playroom and

the preschooler who isolates himself from peers are not having the same experience as the more positively engaged child. Once constitution and early experience have interacted to produce the emergent personality, the child is an active force in his or her own development. As Adler wrote, the child is the artist as well as the painting. Personality develops from a foundation, increasing in organizational complexity, differentiating from early general modes of engaging the environment. Later reorganizations are elaborations and transformations of this foundation. It is for this reason that quality of early experience, especially of significant relationships, is of fundamental importance in healthy development.

Early Developmental Issues for Child and Caregiver

To trace the course of healthy development we must be able to assess qualitative differences in functioning among children at different points in time, from early environmental transactions within the caregiver-infant relationship to later functioning outside the home. In this task it is useful to view development as organized around a series of issues. Learning to manage tension and active exploration have already been mentioned; other issues are also important. A working scheme is presented in Table 1. Parallels between this sequence and those of Piaget, Sander, and Spitz have been described previously (Sroufe 1977, 1978, 1979). These issues are not viewed as tasks to be passed or failed, never to be faced again. All but the first, in fact, are lifetime psychological issues. The issues form a sequence, however, ascendant during various phases of early development and laying the groundwork for approaching subsequent issues. At the same time, preceding issues are continually reworked in facing later issues. As Erikson (1963) suggested, early trust provides the foundation for autonomy, but trust is also deepened by the clarity, firmness, and support the parents provide in the autonomy phase.

The scheme can be illustrated by considering the issue for the second half year, the formation of an effective, secure attachment relationship. During this period the infant's behavior becomes focused on and organized around the caregiver. Separation protest, retreating to the caregiver when

Table 1 Issues in early development

Phase	Age in months	Issue	Role for caregiver
1	0–3	Physiological regulation	Smooth routines
2	3–6	Management of tension	Sensitive, cooperative interaction
3	6–12	Establishing an effective attachment relationship	Responsive availability
4	12–18	Exploration and mastery	Secure base
5	18–30	Individuation (autonomy)	Firm support
6	30–54	Management of impulses, sex role identification, peer relations	Clear roles and values, flexible self-control

distressed, and immediate greeting reactions appear. The infant has assumed a more mutual, fully reciprocal role in interaction with the caregiver.

Attachment, of course, has its roots in earlier infancy: It is a product of caregiver-infant interaction. The infant secure in his or her attachment has experienced the caregiver as a reliable source of comforting, as responsive to his or her signals, and as available and sensitive. The infant has learned that stimulation in the context of the caregiver will generally not be overwhelming and that when arousal threatens to exceed the infant's organizational capacity, the caregiver will intervene (Ainsworth 1979).

In psychoanalytic theory the caregiver's role in relieving tension was emphasized. My view emphasizes the caregiver's role in helping the infant maintain organized behavior in the face of novelty-produced excitation. In part through face-to-face play, in which the caregiver continually varies facial expression, voice tone, and movements, the infant learns to deal with novelty and complexity within a familiar context. As the caregiver engages, relaxes, then reengages the infant (all in response to the infant's signals) the infant learns to maintain organized behavior in the face of increasingly high levels of arousal (Brazelton, Kowslowski and Main 1974; Stern 1974). There is security in that which is familiar. The attachment relationship, based on reliable patterns of caregiver interaction, represents familiarity the infant can take into new situations, especially as the relationship is increasingly internalized.

Attachment has its roots in early interaction; it also lays the foundation for subsequent development. A central issue for the 12–18-month-old infant (Phase 4) is exploration and mastery of the environment. The child secure in its attachment is able to use the caregiver as a base for this exploration. The mere presence of the caregiver provides sufficient security in a novel setting to promote active exploration. This psychological availability of the caregiver during exploration and later problem solving deepens the security of attachment and helps a new mode of psychological contact to evolve. The infant can be comforted by a glance across the room or by a word. At the same time, infants can affectively share their play, smiling, showing toys to the caregiver, and so forth. The infant and caregiver can remain in psychological contact, even when at a physical distance (Sroufe 1977).

Just as the quality of attachment influences the infant's exploratory competence, these early adaptations in turn influence the quality of autonomous functioning in the toddler period (Matas, Arend, and Sroufe 1978). The child who has developed mastery skills, the capacity for affective involvement, and a sense of confidence within the caregiver-infant relationship will be more enthusiastic, persistent and effective in facing environmental challenges on its own. Later, given continued support by the caregiver, this child will be confident, skilled, and positive in dealing with peers and other tasks of the preschool period (Arend et al. in press; Sroufe 1978). In successfully approaching each issue the child is acquiring capacities needed for further effective adaptation, as is illustrated below.

Continuity of Individual Adaptation

When early childhood is viewed in terms of a series of organizational issues, the pursuit of the person means assessing how well the child is functioning with respect to each issue. Assessment situations, procedures, and behavioral domains tapped may be vastly different at different developmental periods; still, the prediction remains: The quality of the child's earlier adaptation will influence its adaptation with respect to subsequent issues.

We began our research on the coherence of individual adaptation with the study of infant-caregiver attachment. Ainsworth (e.g., Ainsworth, Blehar, Waters, and Wall 1978) had provided a scheme in which attachment is viewed in terms of its balance with exploration. When stress is minimal, the securely attached child (Group B) can separate readily from the caregiver to explore. When distressed, however, by a brief separation, for example, the securely attached infant actively seeks and maintains contact until comforted, which promotes a return to play. Under other circumstances, or when the infant is older, a brief separation from the caregiver may not produce distress, especially if the baby is not left alone. If not upset, secure infants are nonetheless active in reestablishing contact, although as noted above, the contact is interactive rather than physical.

Ainsworth described two other major patterns of attachment. One group (Group A) is characterized by avoidance of the caregiver upon reunion, ignoring, looking away, turning away, or abortive approach. Such avoidance was especially striking during a second reunion, when stress was presumed to be greater. Thus, although this infant can separate readily from its caregiver, it fails to seek contact under circumstances of need, which interferes with the return to active exploration. Another group (Group C) is characterized by poverty of exploration and an inability to be settled upon reunion. This group may mix contact seeking with interaction resistance (squirming to get down, kicking, hitting, batting away offered toys) or may merely continue to cry and fuss despite attempts at comforting. (For details, see Ainsworth et al. 1978; Sroufe and Waters 1977.) These patterns have been predicted by maternal behavior as early as 6–15 weeks of life.

Everett Waters showed that in a middle-class sample these three patterns of attachment were stable across a six-month period; 48 of 50 suburban infants classified as belonging to Group A, B, or C at 12 months were similarly classified by independent coders at 18 months ($p < .001$; Sroufe and Waters 1977; Waters 1978). This stability occurred despite the fact that the period spanned is a time of great behavioral change. Frequencies and durations of particular discrete behaviors (proximity seeking, smiling, vocalizing) were not stable, but the quality of the attachment, the effectiveness in support of exploration, remained similar. Individual babies cried less or more, sought more or less contact, showed a toy to mother one time, brought a toy another time, but in some way the overall pattern of behavior indicative of a secure attachment relationship was revealed on both occasions. Likewise, avoidant infants may have exhibited different particular behaviors on reunion (e.g., crawling away on one occasion, looking away and ignoring on another), but scaled scores on avoidance were stable across the 6-month period ($r = .61, p < .001$). Infants in Group C were difficult to settle on both occasions.

We do not view these differences in attachment in terms of temperament, but as emergent patterns of personality organization. First, securely attached children may be hypoactive or hyperactive, cuddly or noncuddly, slow to warm up or not. They may cry a lot or a little. They have in common the capacity to use the caregiver as a secure base for exploration and to actively initiate contact upon reunion. Second, they show the same behaviors as do the anxiously attached children, but in different contexts. They may, for example, squirm and otherwise resist contact with the stranger during separation but not with mother on reunion. They may pay little or no attention to the mother at times prior to separation but not on reunion. Third, the behaviors of securely attached children predict to quite different behavioral domains in later years. Finally, under some circumstances these patterns of behavior are subject to change.

If these individual differences do reflect emerging personality, they should forecast later functioning. To examine consequences of these patterns of attachment, we followed up on 48 infants who were observed in a problem-solving situation when they were 2 years old. This situation was appropriate for assessing movement toward autonomous functioning (Phase 5) because some of the problems were within the child's capacity and others were quite challenging (e.g., weighting down a lever with a block to raise candy from a Plexiglas box), requiring the child to fall back on the caregiver's assistance. As toddlers, securely attached infants were more enthusiastic, more persistent, and exhibited more positive affect. They complied with maternal suggestions more, ignored less, and showed less oppositional behavior. In various ways temperamental and IQ factors were ruled out as explanations for these differences (Matas et al. 1978). Main (1977) has reported similar findings.

In a subsequent study (with Gove, Egeland, and Deinard) we found that securely attached infants showed a particular pattern of behavior across tasks. When they came to the more challenging lever problem, they maintained their involvement but sought more help. They increased their compliance and decreased their opposition. Their mothers, in turn, maintained a high level of support and offered more directives. Infants in Group C (the resistant, difficult-to-settle group), on the other hand, fell apart completely. They became increasingly oppositional, highly frustrated, angry and distressed, even though they did increase their help seeking. Their mothers increased their directives, but the quality of their assistance decreased markedly. Infants in Group A (avoidant) and their mothers were best characterized as low on involvement throughout. Unlike Groups B and C they made little adjustment to the harder problem.

To illustrate that these patterns of adaptation have further developmental consequences for the child (away from the mother), we conducted two other studies. In the first (using data gathered by Wanda Bronson), Everett Waters and I found that quality of attachment at 15 months was related to independent Q-sort descriptions of the children in nursery school at age 3½ years. Securely attached children were later described as peer leaders, socially involved, attracting the attention of others, curious, and actively engaged in their surroundings. Overall differences between securely and insecurely attached infants in "peer competence" and "personal competence" were highly significant, and these differences were not due to IQ (Waters et al. in press).

In a more recent study we linked our work on attachment to the Blocks' important work on two dimensions of personality organization—ego control and ego resiliency (Block and Block in press). *Ego control* refers to the degree of control the child maintains over impulses, wishes, and desires. Over-controlled children are rigid, unable to be spontaneous; undercontrolled children cannot delay gratification, control impulses, or behave purposefully. *Ego resiliency* refers to flexibility of controls. The resilient child can plan and delay when circumstances require but can also exhibit spontaneity, enthusiasm, and curiosity, letting up controls appropriately. Although assessment procedures vary with age, as an organizational approach would suggest, the Blocks have presented striking evidence for stable individual differences on these dimensions from 3½ to 7½ years, in both laboratory and observational situations (Block and Block in press). They have begun tying these individual differences to patterns of care and are currently following up on their children at age 11 years. They will also assess them at age 14.

We were able to obtain follow-up measures on 26 children from our original attachment study at age 5 years (Arend et al. in press), using a subset of the Blocks' laboratory measures (e.g., Banta's curiosity box, level of aspiration, social problem solving, Lowenfeld mosaics, motor inhibition) and their observational technique. As was predicted and theoretically required, children who earlier were securely attached were independently described by their teachers as highly resilient. Items typically placed in the "most characteristic" category included "resourceful in initiating activities," "curious and exploring," and "self-reliant, confident." (Least characteristic items included "inhibited and constricted," "tends to disengage under stress," and "becomes anxious when the environment is unpredictable.") They were also described as moderate on control, neither over- nor undercontrolled. Infants classified in Groups A (avoidant) and C (resistant) were significantly lower on resiliency, with those in Group A tending to be overcontrolled, and those in Group C undercontrolled. Such patterns of over- and undercontrol already appeared incipient in the earlier attachment assessments and in our toddler data and were in fact predicted by the Blocks. The composite laboratory data also showed the securely attached infants to be significantly higher on resiliency (laboratory battery composite and teacher Q-sort resiliency scores correlated .46, $p < .01$).

What began as a competent caregiver-infant pair led to a flexible, resourceful child. Our attachment assessments predicted later functioning more powerfully than had any previously used measures, including standardized infant tests. A focus on developmentally salient issues enables assessment that taps the core of early competence. Such predictability is not due to the inherently higher IQ of the securely attached infant or, apparently, to inborn differences in temperament, though such differences likely have important influences on behavior.

Continuity and Change in Adaptation

Demonstrating coherence in individual development does not rest on continuity alone. Change may be comprehended as well. In a current research project (with Byron Egeland, Amos Deinard, and Brian Vaughn) we are following a large sample of poor children from birth to 4½ years. In contrast with our middle-class samples, these children experience noticeably fluctuating environmental circumstances, with life situations changing markedly both toward and away from stability. There are changes in residency, parents' job status, health, substitute care, parents' drug dependency, and perhaps most important, living group membership. People move out and they move in. Separations are common.

These fluctuating circumstances appear linked to the child's quality of adaptation. There is still significant stability in this sample, but there is considerable change, too. For example, whereas 48 of 50 (96%) middle-class infants had the same attachment classifications at 12 and 18 months, only 62 of 100 poor children were classified similarly. Most important, changes in the quality of attachment were related to changing life events. Mothers of infants changing from an insecure (Groups A and C) to a secure (Group B) attachment relationship reported a significantly greater reduction in stressful life events than did mothers of infants changing in the other direction (Vaughn, Waters, Egeland, and Sroufe in press). These life-event-related changes provide clear evidence that the individual differences we assess are not simply differences in temperament or socio-emotional *g*. Even though changing, the development of these infants is coherent, their pattern of adaptation comprehensible. Nor do these findings suggest that all continuity resides in the environment. All children are vulnerable to stress, but further research may show that some children are more stress resistant and better able to rebound following periods of stress. This would be consistent with a view of the child as an active participant in his or her own development.

Conclusion

In these times of rapid social change, understanding the nature of the developing child is essential for the well-being and perhaps the survival of our society. A beginning has been made toward this understanding. Many questions about the shaping of the person remain to be answered, but they no longer appear to be unanswerable. The quality and importance of the child's early relationships can be assessed. The quality of the child's functioning in facing challenges and in establishing peer relations can be assessed. Questions concerning the impact of substitute care (of varying amounts and quality), alternative lifestyles, and changing social support systems can all be addressed.

There is reason to doubt that children are infinitely resilient, even given the flexibility of our species. Our biology may not be able to adapt to any and all changes in societal conditions proceeding at any rate. What children experience, early and later, makes a difference. We cannot assume that early experiences will somehow be canceled out by later experience. Lasting consequences of early inadequate experience may be subtle and complex, taking the form of increased vulnerability to certain kinds of stress, for example, or becoming manifest only when the individual attempts to establish intimate adult relationships or engage in parenting. But there will be consequences.

To be sure, children have inborn differences in certain behavior characteristics. These characteristics probably influence how we behave toward them (as should be the case if our care is sensitive and responsive). But we shape the persons they are. It is their birthright that the environment to which they must adapt is one that promotes healthy psychological development. It is our obligation to understand the nature of that development.

NOTES

1. Block (1971) has discussed how lawful relationships among variables can be found for subsets of subjects which do not characterize the whole sample. This is basic to the definition of a type.

REFERENCES

AINSWORTH, M. D. S. Infant-mother attachment. *American Psychologist,* 1979, *34,* 932–937.

AINSWORTH, M. D. S., BLEHAR, M. C., WATERS, E., AND WALL, S. *Patterns of attachment.* Hillsdale, N.J.: Erlbaum, 1978.

AREND, R. A., GOVE, F. L., AND SROUFE, L. A. Continuity of early adaptation: From attachment in infancy to ego-resiliency and curiosity at age 5. *Child Development,* in press.

BLOCK, J. *Lives through time.* Berkeley, Calif.: Bancroft Books, 1971.

BLOCK, J. H., AND BLOCK, J. The role of ego-control and ego-resiliency in the organization of behavior. In W. A. Collins (Ed.), *Minnesota Symposia on Child Psychology* (Vol. 11). Hillsdale, N.J.: Erlbaum, in press.

BRAZELTON, T. B., KOWSLOWSKI, B., AND MAIN, M. The origins of reciprocity: The early mother-infant interaction. In M. Lewis and L. Rosenblum (Eds.), *The effect of the infant on its caregiver.* New York: Wiley, 1974.

BREGER, L. *From instinct to identity.* Englewood Cliffs, N.J.: Prentice-Hall, 1974.

EPSTEIN, S. The stability of behavior: I. On predicting most of the people much of the time. *Journal of Personality and Social Psychology,* 1979, *37,* 1097–1126.

ERIKSON, E. H. *Childhood and society* (2nd ed.). New York: Norton, 1963.

MAIN, M. Analysis of a peculiar form of reunion behavior seen in some day-care children: Its history and sequelae in children who are home-reared. In R. Webb (Ed.), *Social development in childhood: Daycare programs and research.* Baltimore, Md.: Johns Hopkins University Press, 1977.

MATAS, L., AREND, R. A., AND SROUFE, L. A. Continuity of adaptation in the second year: The relationship between quality of attachment and later competence. *Child Development,* 1978, *49,* 547–556.

SROUFE, L. A. *Knowing and enjoying your baby.* Englewood Cliffs, N.J.: Prentice-Hall, 1977.

SROUFE, L. A. Attachment and the roots of competence. *Human Nature,* October, 1978, pp. 50–59.

SROUFE, L. A. Socioemotional development. In J. Osofsky (Ed.), *Handbook of infant development.* New York: Wiley, 1979.

SROUFE, L. A., AND WATERS, E. Attachment as an organizational construct. *Child Development,* 1977, *48,* 1184–1199.

SROUFE, L. A., WATERS, E., AND MATAS, L. Contextual determinants of infant affective response. In M. Lewis and L. Rosenblum (Eds.), *The origins of fear.* New York: Wiley, 1974.

STERN, D. The goal and functions of mother-infant play. *Journal of the American Academy of Child Psychiatry,* 1974, *13,* 402–421.

VAUGHN, B., WATERS, E., EGELAND, B., AND SROUFE, L. A. Individual differences in infant-mother attachment at 12 and 18 months: Stability and change in families under stress. *Child Development,* in press.

WATERS, E. The reliability and stability of individual differences in infant-mother attachment. *Child Development,* 1978, *49,* 483–494.

WATERS, E., WIPPMAN, J., AND SROUFE, L. A. Attachment, positive affect, and competence in the peer group: Two studies in construct validation. *Child Development,* in press.

Part IV

Adult-Child Relations and Socialization

OUT of the intensely affectionate caregiver-infant relation grows an adult-child relation marked by the child's love, respect, and obedience for the adult. Throughout the childhood years, adults continue to be children's main source of protection, nurturance, and guidance. Adults play a particularly critical role in children's socialization: they are the primary representatives of the culture's standards and rules. It is the adult world, through family, school, church, and other societal institutions, that transmits the values and constraints of the social order to the child.

This transmission of culture need not be accomplished harshly or against the will of the child. As the Ainsworth and Sroufe articles on infancy note, children who are securely attached to adults are generally easily compliant with adults. They willingly seek and accept rather than resist adult instruction. Socialization, therefore, does not necessarily imply a process in which powerful adults force their standards on recalcitrant children. Although certainly this does happen in many instances, it is only one of many ways in which adults can influence children. Some of the less forceful ways may actually be more effective in the long run, as several authors represented here suggest.

The readings in this section were chosen to reveal the major adult-child socialization processes identified by contemporary child-development research. These processes are comprised of the techniques used by adults to influence children and, at the same time, of the social-psychological mechanisms through which children receive and react to such influence.

Some of the authors represented here place the socialization enterprise mainly within the context of the family, the institution that for most children provides the predominant socializing contact with the adult world. Alfred Baldwin's classic study of democracy in the home is an early example of this family focus. Other authors describe socialization as a general process that occurs both within and beyond the family as the child participates in various culture-transmitting adult-child interactions.

Diana Baumrind's focus is on the parent-child relation, especially with regard to the parent's style of exercising authority. Baumrind distinguishes three authority patterns: authoritative, authoritarian, and permissive. She links the authoritative pattern in particular to the development of "instrumental competence" in children. Instrumental competence is a cluster of adaptive traits that includes social responsibility, independence, vitality, and an orientation towards achievement. Authoritative parents tend to have children who score high on all measures of instrumental competence, and who behave cooperatively with their parents and with friendliness towards their peers. Both authoritarian and permissive parents, on the other hand, tend to have children who are low in instrumental competence, and who show a lack of self-control.

It is interesting that two seemingly opposite child-rearing patterns—authoritarian and permissive—are associated with similar deficits in children's adaptive behavior. Baumrind believes that this is because both authoritarian and permissive parents shield their children from stress, the former through hampering their children's initiative and the latter through permitting their children to avoid the consequences of their actions. These two patterns of child-rearing, though drastically different in quality, both result in a growth-stunting overprotectiveness. In contrast, authoritative child-rearing imposes realistic demands on children and provides clear communication about the rationale behind these demands. In this way, authoritative child-rearing encourages children to cope with pressure, to assume responsibility, and to tolerate life's disappointments.

There are some differences between the correlates of authoritarian and permissive child-rearing, such as the greater vitality and more positive needs of children raised in permissive homes. But Baumrind's conclusions strongly favor the authoritative mode over each of these, and suggest that it is girls in particular who may suffer the effects of nonauthoritative parenting. This is because, she writes, "the affiliative and cooperative orientation of girls increases their receptivity to the influence of socializing agents." Baumrind's findings indicate that, of the three child-rearing patterns, authoritarian child-rearing is most responsible for inculcating instrumental *in*competence in girls, because it encourages them to develop a mode of passive dependency. Boys may be less vulnerable in the long run to this type of influence because of external supports for self-reliance and assertiveness in the social system. But, in general, Baumrind's belief is that all children thrive best when exposed to a consistent pattern of authoritative parent-child relations, complete with disciplinary techniques that are firm, clearly communicated, and fairly enforced.

What are the psychological mechanisms through which adults manage to exert their influence over children's behavior? The "Bobo Doll" study of Bandura, Ross, and Ross is a classic demonstration of one such mechanism:

imitation through observation. In this study, the authors showed that children who observed an adult beating up a Bobo doll were later more likely themselves to beat up the doll than were children who were exposed to a nonaggressive adult model and performed their own, nonimitative aggressive acts towards the doll as well. In contrast, children who watched an adult who behaved in a quiet, subdued manner were even less likely to act aggressively than control-group children who watched nothing at all. These results left little doubt that children were influenced by what they saw.

The imitative learning process proposed by Bandura and his associates is direct, but it is by no means simple. In subsequent writings, Bandura has explicated at least four distinct component processes that must be invoked to explain imitative learning through observation. These components include: attentional processes that account for the child's initial apprehension of the model's behavior; retention processes that account for interpretation and mental storage of the model's behavior; motor reproduction processes that account for the physical carrying out of the imitative act itself; and motivational processes that account for the child's urge to imitate the model at any time subsequent to the initial observation. Bandura's theoretical model has been used not only to explain socialization within the parent-child relation, but also to analyze the effects of television and other media on children's behavior. Many developmentalists, however, have wondered whether the model can account for novelty or recalcitrance in children's social behavior. Others have doubted whether observational learning processes in themselves are enough to account for long-term changes in children's behavior.

Mark Lepper's research program addresses the issue of how adults may exert an enduring socializing influence on children. The combined results of Lepper's studies suggest that the most effective means of changing a child's behavior in a long-term sense is guidance applied with just enough coercion or reward to induce the child to engage in the new behavior, but not so much that the child finds the coercion or reward to be the most memorable part of the experience. In other words, adult rewards and punishments must be "minimally sufficient" to alter the child's behavior without being more salient in themselves than the behavioral standards that the adult is trying to promote. "Subtle" social influence techniques that emphasize reasoning and persuasion are therefore more permanently effective than heavy-handed assertions of adult power, mainly because in the subtler techniques children are more likely to adopt the new standards as their own rather than merely behave out of deference to external punishment or reward. Internalization of standards proceeds best when social control conditions allow children to focus their attention on the standards themselves rather than on the social controls.

Lepper's model can explain the findings of socialization studies like those of Baumrind. In terms of Lepper's model, authoritative parents provide optimal conditions for their children to internalize socially responsible behavioral standards because these parents combine judicious amounts of control with reasoning and argument. In contrast, the power-assertive authoritarian mode of parenting fosters temporary compliance rather than permanent attitude change. Permissive parenting fails to provide children with even the minimal controls necessary to induce new behavior in the first place. For these reasons, children of both authoritarian and permissive parents are alike in their difficulties with self-control and social responsibility.

Carol Dweck and Therese Goetz explicate the attribution process, another social-psychological mechanism through which children may be influenced by adult-induced controls and rewards. Dweck and Goetz focus on a deleterious outcome of the attribution process, the fostering of learned helplessness. Studies by Dweck and her colleagues have shown that children who see their failure on an insurmountable task as a lack of ability lose the will to persevere even when a new, surmountable task is introduced. In contrast, children who attribute their failure to a lack of effort persevere on the new task. Further studies have indicated that "helpless" children can be trained to become more mastery-oriented by inducing them to attribute their failures to effort deficits rather than ability deficits. Unfortunately, it seems that in real life teachers and other adults often do just the opposite, thereby engendering a sense of passivity and inefficacy in young children. Even more unfortunately, this naturally occurring training in helplessness has a systematic sex-linked bias. According to Dweck's research, teachers are far more likely to transmit helplessness-inducing messages to girls than to boys. The authors speculate that this is because girls are generally perceived as trying hard to begin with, so that their failures are rarely attributed to a lack of motivation. Ironically, boys receive harsher criticism for their supposed lack of effort, but this criticism has less insidious effects, since it leaves the boys feeling in control of their success or failure rather than helpless and ineffectual. The Dweck and Goetz article demonstrates that children's socialization experiences can have effects that are unintended and even unrecognized by the adult socializers.

E. Mavis Hetherington's important work on divorce reminds us that adults and children normally interact within *families,* which constitute systems with special properties of their own. When this system is disrupted, the adult-child relation is altered in critical ways. Sometimes the change is for the good and sometimes for the ill, depending upon family circumstances before and after the divorce. But the important message is that no member or dyad within the family unit exists in a vacuum, and the state of the family as a collective has fundamental consequences for the relations between any of its members. For this and many other reasons, adult-child influence does not occur in a linear, one-way causal path. Not only does the child have its own influence on the adult, but the system of family relationships itself has a powerful impact on all of its members.

8

Socialization and the Parent-Child Relationship

Alfred L. Baldwin

To those who deal with parents, it often seems that by the time a theory has been put into actual practice by parents, it is no longer accepted. We often wish that some of the publicized methods had been tested in real life situations before being advocated so strongly. While it is true that practice may lag a generation or two behind theories of child development, there is a section of the culture, an *avant garde*, which is much quicker to learn about and adopt the newer scientific opinions. There are intellectual parents who experiment with such methods as self-demand schedule, raising babies in boxes, release of repressions in play or the use of group decisions in determining family policy within a few years of the time the ideas were first discussed in scientific literature. This intellectual section of our culture thus provides an experimental proving ground which we should exploit as fully as possible to observe impartially the actual consequences of modern scientific theories of child development. It is the purpose of this report to explore some of the consequences of "democracy in the home" upon the personality development of young children.

It is well to recognize the limitations of this proving ground as an experimental test of the applicability of various theories. The intellectual culture is certainly no random sample of the culture as a whole. Therefore,

From A. L. Baldwin, "Socialization and the Parent-Child Relationship," *Child Development* 19 (1948): 127–36. Copyright 1948 by The Society for Research in Child Development, Inc. Reprinted by permission of The Society for Research in Child Development, Inc.[1]

the methods of raising children practiced by these people are inevitably colored by the fact that they have a high verbal intelligence; they put a high value on rationality and intellectuality; and they substitute "progressive principles" for the traditional middle-class values without markedly reducing the compulsiveness of their adherence to these principles.

The research which I shall discuss is based upon the observations of preschool children in the experimental nursery school conducted by the Fels Research Institute. Each child of preschool age attends this nursery school for a month each year during which time he is rated upon a battery of child behavior variables. Concurrently, he is visited in his home every 6 months by an independent investigator who rates the impact of the home environment upon the child in terms of a battery of Parent Behavior Ratings. The sample used in the present study is a group of 67 children, who were observed at the approximate age of 4 years both in the free play group and in the home.

Figure 1 is a diagram showing the interrelationships among the various child behavior variables. The variables have been so placed upon the sheet that those which are highly correlated are close to each other spatially. A group of variables whose members are highly intercorrelated with each other form, for the purposes of this report, a syndrome. The members of the various syndromes are indicated in the diagram by a line which extends from the variables at one border of the cluster through all the variables in the cluster to the variable at the other side. The end points of a cluster are indicated by a heavy dot at the end of the line. It will be seen that many syndromes overlap. In some cases these overlapping clusters will on further examination be combined into a single larger one. In other cases the overlapping variables have very different significance in the two syndromes. For example, aggressiveness and competitiveness take on a particular flavor in the cluster composed of *aggressiveness, competitiveness, leadership* and *curiosity.* In the cluster composed of *aggressiveness, competitiveness, cruelty, quarrelsomeness* and *resistance,* the same two variables have quite a different meaning.

There is evidence for a general factor in this battery of variables, a factor which might be called activeness, or maturity, or good nursery school behavior. The bottom of the diagram tends to represent the socially positive aspects of activity; the top represents the more rebellious and uncontrolled aspects of activity. The right side of the diagram includes variables which describe inter-*personal* relationships; the variables at the left are more impersonal. With this orientation to the battery of child behavior variables, we can proceed to analysis of the consequences of freedom and permissiveness on the one hand, and restrictiveness and pressure on the other.

When the variables in the Parent Behavior Rating Scales, used in the appraisal of the home environment, are factor analyzed, two of the factors which are closely related to this problem are democracy and control. Democracy is characterized by a high level of verbal contact between parent and child, appearing as consultation about policy decisions, as explanation of reasons for the family rules, and as verbal explanation in response to the child's curiosity. Accompanying this flow of verbal communication is a lack of arbitrariness about decisions and a general permissiveness plus restraint on emotionality. The second factor, control, is correlated with the first. It emphasizes the existence of restrictions upon behavior which are clearly conveyed to the child, although not necessarily arrived at democratically. Another characteristic of control is the lack of friction over disciplinary

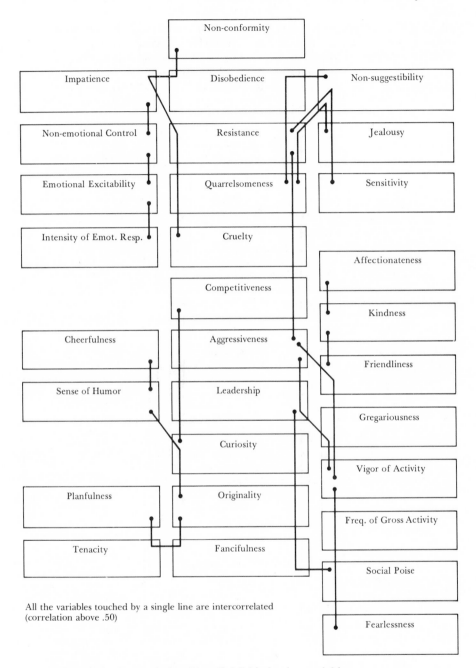

All the variables touched by a single line are intercorrelated
(correlation above .50)

FIGURE 1 Interrelationship of child behavior variables.

decisions. This lack of disagreement might stem from various characteristics, prohibitions on talking back, easy conformity by child, or the determination of the policy by mutual agreement. These two factors are correlated; most democratic homes are not uncontrolled.

If the consequences of these two factors on the child's behavior in nursery school are analyzed together, i.e. if the effects of democracy are studied, keeping control constant, and the effects of control are studied, with democracy kept constant, the following results are obtained:

Democracy tends to have two sorts of effects upon the child's behavior as illustrated in Figure 2. It tends to accentuate by a statistically significant

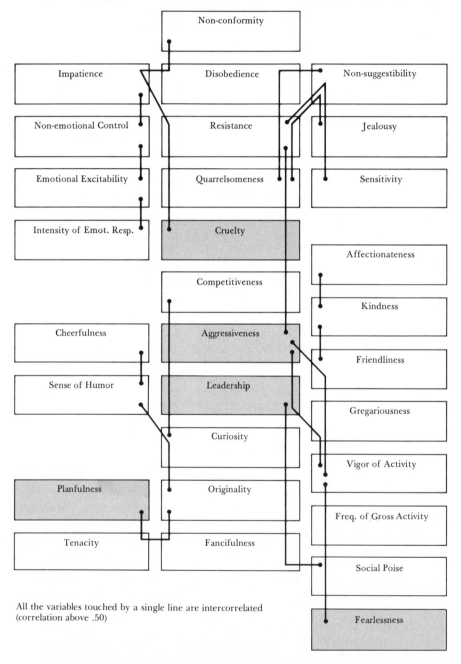

All the variables touched by a single line are intercorrelated (correlation above .50)

FIGURE 2 Democracy increases the shaded variables.

amount the variables which are shaded in the diagram. It seems generally to raise the activity level and to produce an aggressive, fearless, planful child, likely to be a leader in the nursery school situation, but who is also more cruel than the average child of his age. These are the statistically significant effects; other variables on which the differences are almost significant are *curiosity, non-conformity* and *disobedience.*

Control has not only more significant effects as shown in Figure 3 but they are in the opposite direction. It tends to decrease *quarrelsomeness, negativism* and *disobedience* but at the same time to decrease *aggressiveness, planfulness, tenacity,* and *fearlessness.*

Occurring together, control and lack of democracy produce very marked effects in a large number of variables, as shown in Figure 4. The combination produces a quiet, well-behaved, non-resistant child who is at the same time socially unaggressive and restricted in his curiosity, originality and fancifulness. The opposite picture of high democracy and low control produces opposite effects, but very few of the variables are significant.

Thus far, the results generally confirm most of our impressions of the effect of freedom and restrictiveness upon socialization. Socialization by definition demands the development of contradictory aspects of the personality. Conformity to cultural demands is not easily obtained without robbing the child of that personal integrity which gives him a mind of his own and which supports him in his attempts to satisfy his curiosity and to carry out his ideas and phantasies in his dealing with the real world. Authoritarian control seems to do just that; it obtains conformity but at the expense of personal freedom in areas which are not intended to be restricted. Democracy runs the risk of producing too little conformity to cultural demands; but as actually practiced in the Fels families, it seems to be accompanied by sufficient control to avoid the more serious consequences of this risk.

A third aspect of the home environment, its general activity level, is closely related to these problems of socialization. The active home is characterized by a high level of interaction between the parent and the child. In different homes this interaction takes different forms: In some it appears as a well ordered schedule; in others as a continuous flow of criticism and suggestion; in others as child-centeredness of the home activities; in still others as special training and acceleratory attempts. But if active homes of all varieties are compared with inactive homes as shown in Figure 5, it appears that activity in the home generally raises the child's level of activity in nursery school, and again it raises both the rebellious non-conforming aspects as well as the socially positive aspects. Activity and democracy have similar effects, but it is possible to differentiate between them. Activity in the home seems to affect the variables describing personal relations rather than curiosity and planfulness which are increased in the democratic home. Activity also differs from democracy in affecting the emotionality variables.

The exact relationship between activity and democracy is revealed by a study of their interaction. There are in this sample about the same number of democratic inactive homes and democratic active ones. These two groups show some rather marked differences. That is, activity is an important factor affecting the child's behavior in democratic homes while in non-democratic homes, activity plays a less important role. Figure 6 shows the effect of activity in democratic homes. The shaded variables are those which are significantly greater in democratic active homes than in democratic inactive homes: *aggressiveness, competitiveness, quarrelsomeness* and *resistance,* plus *curiosity* on the one side, and on the other *emotional excitability, intensity of emotional response* and *impatience. Cruelty* too is almost significantly greater.

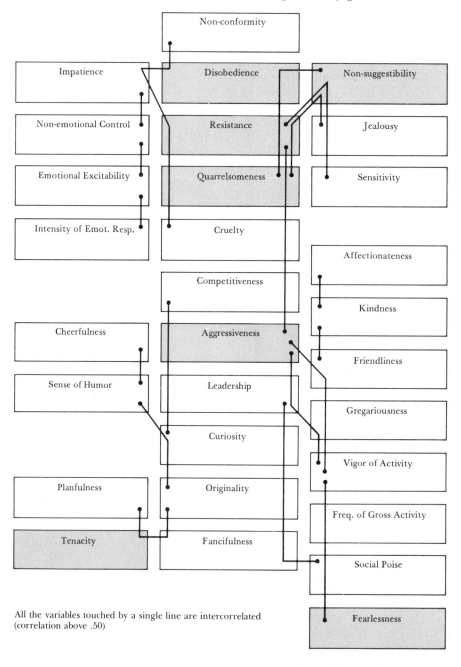

All the variables touched by a single line are intercorrelated (correlation above .50)

FIGURE 3   Control decreases the shaded variables.

These findings indicate the advisability of attempting to discriminate among the various kinds of democratic homes. In the inactive democratic homes there is, by comparison with the active homes, more detachment of parent and child; democracy is more casual and less ideological; the level of

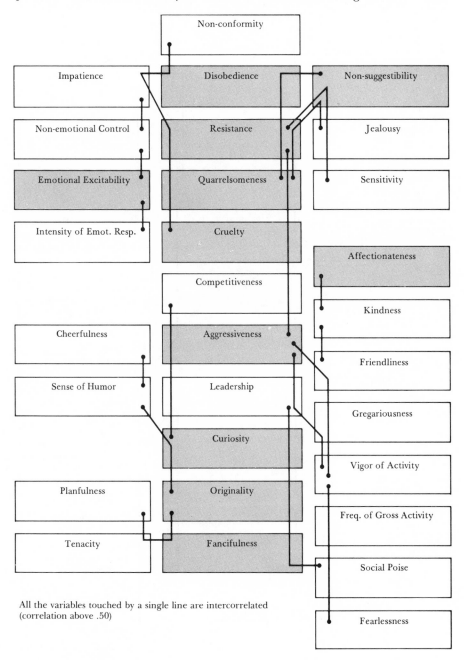

All the variables touched by a single line are intercorrelated (correlation above .50)

FIGURE 4 High control combined with low democracy lowers the shaded variables.

verbal interchange which characterizes democratic homes is more lethargic and spasmodic; there is more *laissez-faire* and less leadership. In this type of home the effects of democracy are less marked than in a home where there is a high level of interaction. That such a condition would result in a less active

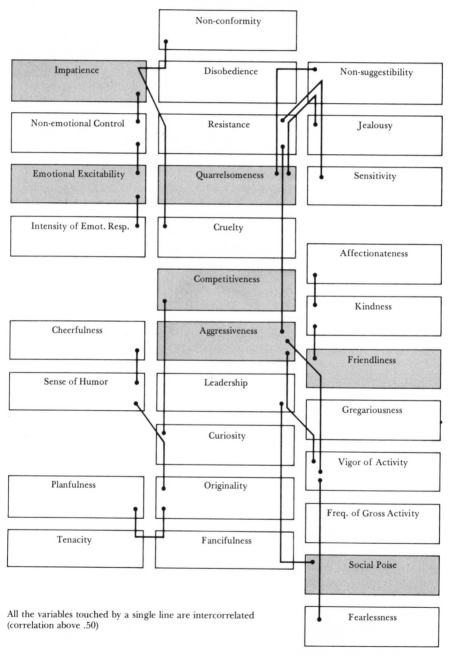

All the variables touched by a single line are intercorrelated (correlation above .50)

FIGURE 5 Activity in the home increases the shaded variables.

approach to the world is reasonable. Hereditary factors probably play a role, but in addition, an unresponsive environment can certainly stultify active expressiveness and aggressiveness toward the world. The child requires not only freedom but response and encouragement if his wishes and his emo-

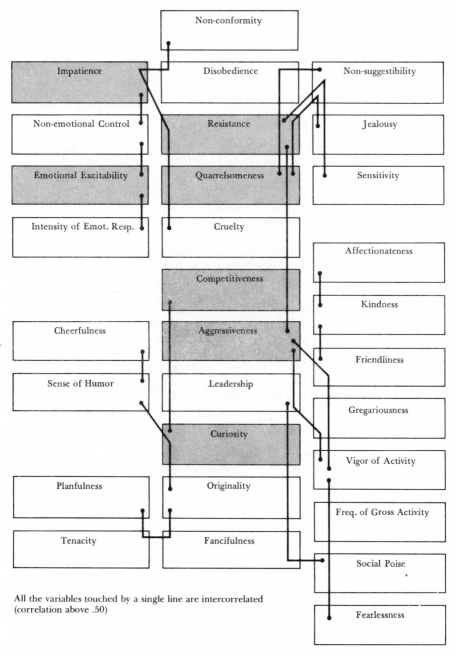

All the variables touched by a single line are intercorrelated (correlation above .50)

FIGURE 6 High activity in democratic homes increases the shaded variables.

tions are to be expressed actively, particularly in his relations to people.

These findings suggest that the predominant effect of parent behavior upon the socialization of the preschool child is to raise or lower his willingness and ability to behave actively toward his environment. Freedom and permissiveness in the home by not punishing his active explorations and his aggressive reactions to frustrations, permits the child to become active, outgoing and spontaneous. Freedom alone does not, however, actively encourage the development of spontaneity; a high level of interaction between the parent and child is required to push the child into activity, particularly of the interpersonal variety. The child's expressiveness must be elicited by the parent's spontaneous expression of warmth and emotionality, and the child's attempts to establish emotional contacts with other people must be greeted with warmth and reciprocation, if he is to develop the pattern of habitual expressiveness.

This activity level of the child seems a prerequisite for socialization, but it is obviously not the whole picture. A high level of activity is accompanied, during the preschool years, by non-conformity and rebelliousness. At this early age, the child responds to stimulation in a generalized and undifferentiated manner, not as yet discriminating between the social and the anti-social forms of activity. The active child, by predisposition or environmental encouragement, is able to express his hostility, but by the age of four he has not, generally speaking, learned how to manage it. The inactive child does not have the same problem of management of hostility; for him the problem is an intrapersonal one which cannot be adequately investigated by this sort of a statistical analysis of overt behavior. The inactive child's problem, on the overt level, is that of achieving a satisfactory degree of social interaction. The important question from a practical point of view might be stated as follows, "Which of these various patterns of preschool behavior is most likely to lead to a healthy adjustment?" We in child development seem at present to believe that spontaneity, even if it involves rebelliousness, is a sign of good preschool adjustment. Whether that belief is true, true in some cases, or untrue, must be discovered by further research.

NOTES

1. Paper presented at a general meeting of the Society for Research in Child Development held in Chicago, Ill., December 27, 1947.

9

Socialization and Instrumental Competence in Young Children
Diana Baumrind

For the past 10 years I have been studying parent-child relations, focusing upon the effects of parental authority on the behavior of preschool children. In three separate but related studies, data on children were obtained from three months of observation in the nursery school and in a special testing situation; data on parents were obtained during two home observations, followed by an interview with each parent.

In the first study, three groups of nursery school children were identified in order that the child-rearing practices of their parents could be contrasted. The findings of that study (Baumrind 1967) can be summarized as follows:

1. Parents of the children who were the most self-reliant, self-controlled, explorative, and content were themselves controlling and demanding; but they were also warm, rational, and receptive to the child's communication. This unique combination of high control and positive encouragement of the child's autonomous and independent strivings can be called *authoritative* parental behavior.

2. Parents of children who, relative to the others, were discontent, withdrawn, and distrustful, were themselves detached and control-

ling, and somewhat less warm than other parents. These may be called *authoritarian* parents.

3. Parents, of the least self-reliant, explorative, and self-controlled children were themselves non-controlling, nondemanding, and relatively warm. These can be called *permissive* parents.

A second study, of an additional 95 nursery school children and their parents, also supported the position that "authoritative control can achieve responsible conformity with group standards without loss of individual autonomy or self-assertiveness" (Baumrind 1966, p. 905). In a third investigation (Baumrind 1971a), patterns of parental authority were defined so that they would differ from each other as did the authoritarian, authoritative, and permissive combinations which emerged from the first study.

Patterns of Parental Authority

Each of these three authority patterns is described in detail below, followed by the subpatterns that have emerged empirically from the most recent study. The capitalized items refer to specific clusters obtained in the analysis of the parent behavior ratings.

The *authoritarian* parent[1] attempts:

> to shape, control and evaluate the behavior and attitudes of the child in accordance with a set of standard of conduct, usually an absolute standard, theologically motivated and formulated by a higher authority. She values obedience as a virtue and favors punitive, forceful measures to curb self-will at points where the child's actions or beliefs conflict with what she thinks is right conduct. She believes in inculcating such instrumental values as respect for authority, respect for work, and respect for the preservation of order and traditional structure. She does not encourage verbal give and take, believing that the child should accept her word for what is right (Baumrind 1968, p. 261).

Two subpatterns in our newest study correspond to this description; they differ only in the degree of acceptance shown the child. One subpattern identifies families who were Authoritarian but Not Rejecting. They were high in Firm Enforcement, low in Encourages Independence and Individuality, low in Passive-Acceptance, and low in Promotes Nonconformity. The second subpattern contained families who met all the criteria for the first subpattern except that they scored high on the cluster called Rejecting.

The *authoritative* parent, by contrast with the above, attempts:

> to direct the child's activities but in a rational issue-oriented manner. She encourages verbal give and take, and shares with the child the reasoning behind her policy. She values both expressive and instrumental attributes, both autonomous self-will and disciplined conformity. Therefore, she exerts firm control at points of parent-child divergence, but does not hem the child in with restrictions. She recognizes her own special rights as an adult, but also the child's individual interests and special ways. The authoritative parent affirms the child's present qualities, but also sets standards for future conduct. She uses reason as well as power to achieve her objectives. She does not base her decisions on group consensus or the individual child's desires; but also, does not regard herself as infallible, or divinely inspired (Baumrind 1968, p. 261).

Two subpatterns corresponded to this description, differing only in the parents' attitudes towards normative values. One subpattern contained families who were Authoritative and Conforming. Like the Authoritarian parents described above, these parents had high scores in Passive-Acceptance. However, they also had high scores in Encouraging Independence and Individuality. The second subpattern contained parents who met the criteria for the first subpattern, but who also scored high in Promotes Nonconformity.

The *permissive* parent attempts:

> to behave in a nonpunitive, acceptant and affirmative manner towards the child's impulses, desires, and actions. She consults with him about policy decisions and gives explanations for family rules. She makes few demands for household responsibility and orderly behavior. She presents herself to the child as a resource for him to use as he wishes, not as an active agent responsible for shaping or altering his ongoing or future behavior. She allows the child to regulate his own activities as much as possible, avoids the exercise of control, and does not encourage him to obey externally defined standards. She attempts to use reason but not overt power to accomplish her ends (Baumrind 1968, p. 256).

We were able to locate three subpatterns reflecting the different facets of this prototypic permissiveness. One subpattern, called Nonconforming, typified families who were nonconforming but who were not extremely lax in discipline and who did demand high performance in some areas. The second subpattern, called Permissive, contained families who were characterized by lax discipline and few demands, but who did not stress nonconformity. The third subpattern contained families who were both conforming and lax in their discipline and demands; hence, they are referred to as Permissive-Nonconforming.

Instrumental Competence

Instrumental Competence refers to behavior which is socially responsible and independent. Behavior which is friendly rather than hostile to peers, cooperative rather than resistive with adults, achievement rather than nonachievement-oriented, dominant rather than submissive, and purposive rather than aimless, is here defined as instrumentally competent. Middle-class parents clearly value instrumentally competent behavior. When such parents were asked to rank those attributes that they valued and devalued in children, the most valued ones were assertiveness, friendliness, independence, and obedience, and those least valued were aggression, avoidance, and dependency (Emmerich and Smoller 1964). Note that the positively valued attributes promote successful achievement in United States society and, in fact, probably have survival value for the individual in any subculture or society.

There are people who feel that, even in the United States, those qualities which define instrumental competence are losing their survival value in favor of qualities which may be called *Expressive Competence*. The author does not agree. Proponents of competence defined in terms of expressive, rather than instrumental, attributes, value feelings more than reason, good thoughts more than effective actions, "being" more than "doing" or "becoming," spontaneity more than planfulness, and relating intimately to others more than working effectively with others. At present, however, there is no evidence that emphasis on expressive competence, at the expense of instrumental competence, fits people to function effectively over the long run as members of any community. This is not to say that expressive competence is not essential for effective functioning in work as well as in love, and for both men and women. Man, like other animals, experiences and gains valid information about reality by means of both noncognitive and cognitive processes. Affectivity deepens man's knowledge of his environment; tenderness and receptivity enhance the character and effectiveness of any human being. But instrumental competence is and will continue to be an essential component of self-esteem and self-fulfillment.

One subdimension of instrumental competence, here designated *Responsible vs. Irresponsible,* pertains to the following three facets of behavior, each of which is related to the others:

(a) *Achievement-oriented vs. Nonachievement-oriented.* This attribute refers to the willingness to persevere when frustration is encountered, to set one's own goals high, and to meet the demands of others in a cognitive situation as opposed to withdrawal when faced with frustration and unwillingness to comply with the teaching or testing instructions of an examiner or teacher. Among older children, achievement-orientation becomes subject to autogenic motivation and is more closely related to measures of independence than to measures of social responsibility. But in the young child, measures of cognitive motivation are highly correlated with willingness to cooperate with adults, especially for boys. Thus, in my study, resistiveness towards adults was highly negatively correlated with achievement-oriented behavior in boys, but not for girls. Other investigators (Crandall, Orleans, Preston, and Rabson 1958; Haggard 1969) have also found that compliance with adult values and demands characterizes young children who display high achievement efforts.

(b) *Friendly vs. Hostile Behavior Towards Peers.* This refers to nurturant, kind, altruistic behavior displayed toward agemates as opposed to bullying, insulting, selfish behavior.

(c) *Cooperative vs. Resistive Behavior Towards Adults.* This refers to trustworthy, responsible, facilitative behavior as opposed to devious, impetuous, obstructive actions.

A second dimension of child social behavior can be designated *Independent vs. Suggestible.* It pertains to the following three related facets of behavior:

(a) *Domineering vs. Tractable Behavior.* This attribute consists of bold, aggressive, demanding behavior as opposed to timid, nonintrusive, undemanding behavior.

(b) *Dominant vs. Submissive Behavior.* This category refers to individual initiative and leadership in contrast to suggestible, following behavior.

(c) *Purposive vs. Aimless Behavior.* This refers to confident, charismatic, self-propelled activity vs. disoriented, normative, goalless behavior.

The present review is limited to a discussion of instrumental competence and associated antecedent parental practices and is most applicable to the behavior of young children rather than adolescents. Several ancillary topics will be mentioned, but not discussed in depth, including:

The Relation of IQ to Instrumental Competence

My own work and that of others indicate that, in our present society, children with high IQs are most likely to be achievement-oriented and self-motivated. The correlations between IQ and measures of purposiveness, dominance, achievement-orientation, and independence are very high even by ages three and four. In my study Stanford-Binet IQ tests were administered to 122 preschool boys and girls as part of an investigation of current patterns of parental authority and their effects on the behavior of preschool children. White children with IQs of at least 96 were grouped within sex on the basis of IQ to form five continuous groups for both boys and girls. Groups were compared on child behavior and parent socialization practices. Higher and lower IQ groups differed significantly from each other on measures of social responsibility and independence, notably with regard to clusters designated Achievement Oriented and Independence.[2]

The Relation of Moral Development and Conscience to Instrumental Competence

This area of research, exemplified by some of the work of Aronfreed, Kohlberg, Mussen, and Piaget, is of special importance with older age groups and will be covered tangentially when the antededents of social responsibility are explored.

The Relation of Will to Instrumental Competence

This topic, which overlaps with the previous one, has received very little direct attention during the past 30 years. In the present review, this area is discussed to some extent along with antecedents of independence.

The Antecedents of Creative or Scientific Genius

Socialization practices which lead to competence are not the same as those associated with the development of high creativity or scientific genius. Most studies, such as those by Roe (1952) and Eiduson (1962), suggest that men of genius are frequently reared differently from other superior individuals. It has been found, for example, that as children men of genius often had little contact with their fathers, or their fathers died when they were young; they often led lonely, although cognitively enriched, existences. Such rearing cannot be recommended, however, since it is unlikely that the effects on most children, even those with superior ability, will be to produce genius or highly effective functioning.

The Development of Instrumental Competence in Disadvantaged Families

The assumption cannot be made that the same factors relate to competence in disadvantaged families as in advantaged families. The effect of a single parental characteristic is altered substantially by the pattern of variables of which it is a part. Similarly, the effect of a given pattern of parental variables may be altered by the larger social context in which the family operates. The relations discussed here are most relevant for white middle-class families and may not always hold for disadvantaged families. In my study of current patterns of parental authority and their effects on the behavior of preschool children, the data for the 16 black children and their families were analyzed separately, since it was assumed that the effect of a given pattern of parental variables would be altered by the larger social context in which the family operates. The major conclusion from this exploratory analysis was that if black families are viewed by white norms they appear deviant, and yet, judged by the same norms, their so-called authoritarian methods seem to produce self-assertive, independent girls.

Development of Instrumental Incompetence in Girls

Rapid social changes are taking place in the United States which are providing equal opportunity for socially disadvantaged groups. If the socially disadvantaged group is one whose members are discouraged from fully developing their potentialities for achieving status and leadership in economic, academic, and political affairs, women qualify as such a group.

There is little evidence that women are biologically inferior to men in intellectual endowment, academic potential, social responsibility, or capacity for independence. Constitutional differences in certain areas may exist, but they do not directly generate differences in areas such as those mentioned. The only cognitive functions in which females have been shown consistently to perform less well than males are spatial relations and visualization. We really do not know to what extent the clearly inferior position women occupy in United States society today should be attributed to constitutional factors. The evidence, however, is overwhelming that socialization experiences contribute greatly to a condition of instrumental *incompetence* among women. It follows that if these conditions were altered, women could more nearly fulfill their occupational and intellectual potential. The interested reader should refer to Maccoby's excellent "Classified Summary of Research in Sex Differences" (1966, pp. 323–51).

Few Women Enter Scientific Fields and Very Few of These Achieve Eminence

According to the President's Commission on the Status of Women in 1963, the proportion of women to men obtaining advanced degrees is actually dropping. Yet there is little convincing evidence that females are constitutionally incapable of contributing significantly to science. Girls obtain better grades in elementary school than boys, and perform equally to boys on standard achievement tests, including tests of mathematical reasoning. By the high school years, however, boys score considerably higher than girls on the mathematical portion of the *Scholastic Aptitude Test* (Rossi 1969).

It is interesting to note that a high positive relation between IQ and later occupational levels holds for males, but does not hold for females (Terman and Oden 1947). According to one study of high school physics students, girls scored higher on understanding scientific processes, while boys scored higher on a test of physics achievement (Walberg 1969). As Rossi has argued:

> If we want more women to enter science, not only as teachers of science but as scientists, some quite basic changes must take place in the way girls are reared. If girls are to develop the analytic and mathematical abilities science requires, parents and teachers must encourage them in independence and self-reliance instead of pleasing feminine submission; stimulate and reward girls' efforts to satisfy their curiosity about the world as they do those of boys; encourage in girls not unthinking conformity but alert intelligence that asks why and rejects the easy answer (Rossi 1969, p. 483).

Femininity and Being Female Is Socially Devalued

Both sexes rate men as more worthwhile than women (e.g., McKee and Sherriffs 1957). While boys of all ages show a strong preference for masculine roles, girls do not show a similar preference for feminine roles, and indeed, at certain ages, many girls as well as boys show a strong preference for masculine roles (Brown 1958). In general, both men and women express a preference for having male children. (Dinitz, Dynes, and Clarke 1954). Masculine status is so to be preferred to feminine status that girls may adopt tomboy attributes and be admired for doing so, but boys who adopt feminine attributes are despised as sissies. Feminine identification in males (excluding feminine qualities such as tenderness, expressiveness, and playfulness) is clearly related to maladjustment. But even in females, intense feminine identification may more strongly characterize maladjusted than adjusted women (Heilbrun 1965). Concern about population control will only further accelerate the devaluation of household activities performed by women and decrease the self-esteem of women solely engaged in such activities.

Intellectual Achievement and Self-assertive Independent Strivings in Women Are Equated with Loss of Femininity by Men and Women Alike

Women, as well as men, oppose the idea of placing women in high-status jobs (Keniston and Keniston 1964). One researcher (Horner 1968) thinks that women's higher test anxiety reflects the conflict between women's motivation to achieve and their motivation to fail. She feels that women and girls who are motivated to fail feel ambivalent about success because intellectual achievement is equated with loss of femininity by socializing agents and eventually by the female herself.

Generally, Parents Have Higher Achievement Expectations for Boys than They Do for Girls

Boys are more frequently expected to go to college and to have careers (Aberle and Naegele 1952). The pressure towards responsibility, obedience, and nurturance for girls, and towards achievement and independence for boys which characterizes United States society also characterizes other societies, thus further reinforcing the effect of differential expectations for boys and girls (Barry, Bacon, and Child 1957). In the United States, girls of nursery school age are not less achievement-oriented or independent than boys. By adolescence, however, most girls are highly aware of, and concerned about, social disapproval for so-called masculine pursuits. They move toward conformity with societal expectations that, relative to males, they should be nonachievement-oriented and dependent.

Girls and Women Consistently Show a Greater Need for Affiliation than Do Boys and Men

The greater nurturance toward peers and cooperation with adults shown by girls is demonstrable as early as the preschool years. In general, females are more suggestible, conforming, and likely to rely on others for guidance and support. Thus, females are particularly susceptible to social influences, and these influences generally define femininity to include such attributes as social responsibility, supportiveness, submissiveness, and low achievement striving.

There are complex and subtle differences in the behavior of boys and girls from birth onward, and in the treatment of boys and girls by their caretaking adults. These differential treatments are sometimes difficult to identify because, when the observer knows the sex of the parent or child, an automatic adjustment is made which tends to standardize judgments about the two sexes. By the time boys enter nursery school, they are more resistant to adult authority and aggressive with peers. Thus, a major socialization task for preschool boys consists of developing social responsibility. While preschool girls (in my investigations) are neither lacking in achievement-orientation nor in independence, the focal socialization task for them seems to consist of maintaining purposive, dominant, and independent behavior. Without active intervention by socializing agents, the cultural stereotype is likely to augment girls' already well-developed sense of cooperation with authority and eventually discourage their independent strivings towards achievement and eminence. As will be noted later, there is reason to believe that the socialization practices which facilitate the development of instrumental competence in *both* girls and boys have the following attributes: (a) they place a premium on self-assertiveness but not on anticonformity; (b) they emphasize high achievement and self-control but not social conformity; (c) they occur within a context of firm discipline and rationality with neither excessive restrictiveness nor overacceptance. For a more complete discussion of changes in socialization practices which might produce greater competence in girls, see the author's paper entitled "From each woman in accord with her ability" (Baumrind 1972a).

Socialization Practices Related to Responsible vs. Irresponsible Behavior

The reader will recall that I defined Responsible vs. Irresponsible Behavior in terms of Friendliness vs. Hostility Towards Peers, Cooperation vs. Resistance Towards Adults, and High vs. Low Achievement Orientation. Socialization seems to have a clearer impact upon the development of social responsibility in boys than in girls, probably because girls vary less in this particular attribute. In my own work, parents who were authoritative and relatively conforming, as compared with parents who were permissive or authoritarian, tended to have children who were more friendly, cooperative, and achievement-oriented. This was especially true for boys. Nonconformity in parents was not necessarily associated with resistant and hostile behavior in children. Neither did firm control and high maturity demands produce rebelliousness. In fact, it has generally been found that close supervision, high demands for obedience and personal neatness, and pressure upon the child to share in household responsibilities are associated with responsible behavior rather than with chronic rebelliousness. The condition most conducive to antisocial aggression, because it most effectively rewards such behavior, is probably one in which the parent is punitive and arbitrary in his demands, but inconsistent in responding to the child's disobedience.

Findings from several studies suggest that parental demands provoke rebelliousness only when the parent both restricts autonomy of action and does not use rational methods of control. For example, Pikas (1961), in a survey of 656 Swedish adolescents, showed that differences in the child's acceptance of parental authority depended upon the reason for the parental directive. Authority based on rational concern for the child's welfare was accepted well by the child, but arbitrary, domineering, or exploitative authority was rejected. Pikas' results are supported by Middleton and Snell (1963) who found that discipline regarded by the child as either very strict or very permissive was associated with rebellion against the parents' political views. Finally, Elder (1963), working with adolescents' reports concerning their parents, found that conformity to parental rules typified subjects who saw their parents as having ultimate control (but who gave the child leeway in making decisions) and who also provided explanations for rules.

Several generalizations and hypotheses can be drawn from this literature and from the results of my own work concerning the relations of specific parental practices to the development of social responsibility in young children. The following list is based on the assumption that it is more meaningful to talk about the effects of *patterns* of parental authority than to talk about the effects of single parental variables.

1. *The modeling of socially responsible behavior facilitates the development of social responsibility in young children, and more so if the model is seen by the child as having control over desired resources and as being concerned with the child's welfare.*

The adult who subordinates his impulses enough to conform with social regulations and is himself charitable and generous will have his example followed by the child. The adult who is self-indulgent and lacking in charity will have his example followed even if he should preach generous, cooperative behavior. Studies by Mischel and Liebert (1966) and Rosenhan, Frederick and Burrowes (1968) suggest that models who behave self-indulgently produce similar behavior in children and these effects are even more extensive than direct reward for self-indulgent behavior. Further, when the adult preaches what he does not practice, the child is more likely to do what the adult practices. This is true even when the model preaches unfriendly or uncooperative behavior but behaves toward the child in an opposite manner. To the extent that the model for socially responsible behavior is perceived as having high social status (Bandura, Ross, and Ross 1963), the model will be most effective in inducing responsible behavior.

In our studies, both authoritative and authoritarian parents demanded socially responsible behavior and also differentially rewarded it. As compared to authoritative parents, however, authoritarian parents permitted their own needs to take precedence over those of the child, became inaccessible when displeased, assumed a stance of personal infallibility, and in other ways showed themselves often to be more concerned with their own ideas than with the child's welfare. Thus, they did not exemplify prosocial behavior, although they did preach it. Authoritative parents, on the other hand, both preached and practiced prosocial behavior and their children were significantly more responsible than the children of authoritarian parents. In this regard, it is interesting that nonconforming parents who were highly individualistic and professed anticonforming ideas had children who were more socially responsible than otherwise. The boys were achievement-oriented and the girls were notably cooperative. These parents were themselves rather pacific, gentle people who were highly responsive to the child's needs even at the cost of their own; thus, they modeled but did not preach prosocial behavior.

2. *Firm enforcement policies, in which desired behavior is positively reinforced and deviant behavior is negatively reinforced, facilitate the development of socially responsible behavior, provided that the parent desires that the child behave in a responsible manner.*

The use of reinforcement techniques serves to establish the potency of the reinforcing agent and, in the mind of the young child, to legitimate his authority. The use of negative sanctions can be a clear statement to the child that rules are there to be followed and that to disobey is to break a known rule. Among other things, punishment provides the child with information. As Spence (1966) found, nonreaction by adults is sometimes interpreted by children as signifying a correct response. Siegel and Kohn (1959) found that nonreaction by an adult when the child was behaving aggressively resulted in an increased incidence of such acts. By virtue of his or her role as an authority, the sheer presence of parents when the child misbehaves cannot help but affect the future occurrence of such behavior. Disapproval should reduce such actions, while approval or nonreaction to such behavior should increase them.

In our studies, permissive parents avoided the use of negative sanctions, did not demand mannerly behavior or reward self-help, did not enforce their directives by exerting force or influence, avoided confrontation when the child disobeyed, and did not choose or did not know how to use reinforcement techniques. Their sons, by comparison with the sons of authoritative parents, were clearly lacking in prosocial and achievement-oriented behavior.

3. *Nonrejecting parents are more potent models and reinforcing agents than rejecting parents; thus, nonrejection should be associated with socially responsible behavior in children provided that the parents value and reinforce such behavior.*

It should be noted that this hypothesis refers to nonrejecting parents and is not stated in terms of passive-acceptance. Thus, it is expected that nonrejecting parental behavior, but not unconditionally acceptant behavior, is associated with socially responsible behavior in children. As Bronfenbrenner pointed out about adolescents, "It is the presence of rejection rather than the lack of a high degree of warmth which is inimical to the development of responsibility in both sexes" (1961, p. 254). As already indicated, in our study authoritarian parents were more rejecting and punitive, and less devoted to the child's welfare than were authoritative parents; their sons were also less socially responsible.

4. *Parents who are fair, and who use reason to legitimate their directives, are more potent models and reinforcing agents than parents who do not encourage independence or verbal exchange.*

Let us consider the interacting effects of punishment and the use of reasoning on the behavior of children. From research it appears that an accompanying verbal rationale nullifies the special effectiveness of immediate punishment, and also of relatively intense punishment (Parke 1969). Thus, by symbolically reinstating the deviant act, explaining the reason for punishment, and telling the child exactly what he should do, the parent obviates the need for intense or instantaneous punishment. Immediate, intense punishment may have undesirable side effects, in that the child is conditioned through fear to avoid deviant behavior, and is not helped to control himself consciously and willfully. Also, instantaneous, intense punishment produces high anxiety which may interfere with performance, and in addition may increase the likelihood that the child will avoid the noxious agent. This reduces that agent's future effectiveness as a model or reinforcing agent. Finally, achieving behavioral conformity by conditioning fails to provide the child with information about cause and effect relations which he can then transfer to similar situations. This is not to say that use of reasoning alone, without negative sanctions, is as effective as the use of both. Negative sanctions give operational meaning to the consequences signified by reasons and to rules themselves.

Authoritarian parents, as compared to authoritative parents, are relatively unsuccessful in producing socially responsible behavior. According to this hypothesis, the reason is that authoritarian parents fail to encourage verbal exchange and infrequently accompany punishment with reasons rather than that they use negative sanctions and are firm disciplinarians.

Socialization Practices Related to Independent vs. Suggestible Behavior

The reader will recall that Independent vs. Suggestible Behavior was defined with reference to: (a) Domineering vs. Tractable Behavior, (b) Dominance vs. Submission, (c) Purposive vs. Aimless Activity, and (d) Independence vs. Suggestibility. Parent behavior seems to have a clearer effect upon the development of independence in girls than in boys, probably because preschool boys vary less in independence.

In my own work, independence in girls was clearly associated with authoritative upbringing (whether conforming or nonconforming). For boys, nonconforming parent behavior and, to a lesser extent, authoritative upbringing were associated with independence. By independence we do not mean anticonformity. "Pure anticonformity, like pure conformity, is pure dependence behavior" (Willis 1968, p. 263). Anticonforming behavior, like negativistic behavior, consists of doing anything but what is prescribed by social norms. Independence is the ability to disregard known standards of conduct or normative expectations in making decisions. Nonconformity in parents may not be associated in my study with independence in girls (although it was in boys) because females are especially susceptible to normative expectations. One can hypothesize that girls must be trained to act independently of these expectations, rather than to conform or to anticonform to them.

It was once assumed that firm control and high maturity demands lead to passivity and dependence in young children. The preponderance of evidence contradicts this. Rather, it would appear that many children react to parental power by resisting, rather than by being cowed. The same parent variables which increase the probability that the child will use the parent as a model should increase the likelihood that firm control will result in assertive behavior. For example, the controlling parent who is warm, understanding, and supportive of autonomy should generate less passivity (as well as less rebelliousness) than the controlling parent who is cold and restrictive. This should be the case because of the kinds of behavior reinforced, the traits modeled, and the relative effectiveness of the parent as a model.

Several generalizations and hypotheses can be offered concerning the relations between parental practices and the development of independence in young children:

1. *Early environmental stimulation facilitates the development of independence in young children.*

It took the knowledge gained from compensatory programs for culturally disadvantaged children to counteract the erroneous counsel from some experts to avoid too much cognitive stimulation of the young child. Those Head Start programs which succeed best (Hunt 1968) are those characterized by stress on the development of cognitive skills, linguistic ability, motivational concern for achievement, and rudimentary numerical skills. There is reason to believe that middle-class children also profit from such early stimulation and enrichment of the environment. Fowler (1962) pointed out, even prior to the development of compensatory programs, that concern about the dangers of premature cognitive training and an overemphasis on personality development had delayed inordinately the recognition that the ability to talk, read, and compute increase the child's self-respect and independent functioning.

Avoidance of anxiety and self-assertion are reciprocally inhibiting responses to threat or frustration. Girls, in particular, are shielded from stress and overstimulation, which probably serves to increase preferences for avoidant rather than offensive responses to aggression or threat. By exposing a child to stress or to physical, social, and intellectual demands, he or she becomes more resistant to stress and learns that offensive reactions to aggression and frustration are frequently rewarding. In our studies, as the hypothesis would predict, parents who provided the most enriched environment, namely the nonconforming and the authoritative parents, had the most dominant and purposive children. These parents, by comparison with the others studied, set high standards of excellence, invoked cognitive insight, provided an intellectually stimulating atmosphere, were themselves rated as being differentiated and individualistic, and made high educational demands upon the child.

2. *Parental passive-acceptance and overprotection inhibits the development of independence.*

Passive-acceptant and overprotective parents shield children from stress and, for the reasons discussed above, inhibit the development of assertiveness and frustration tolerance. Also, parental anxiety about stress to which the child is exposed may serve to increase the child's anxiety. Further, willingness to rescue the child offers him an easy alternative to self-mastery. Demanding and non-protective parents, by contrast, permit the child to extricate himself from stressful situations and place a high value on tolerance of frustration and courage.

According to many investigators (e.g., McClelland, Atkinson, Clark, and Lowell 1963), healthy infants are by inclination explorative, curious, and stress-seeking. Infantile feelings of pleasure, originally experienced after mild changes in sensory stimulation, become associated with these early efforts at independent mastery. The child anticipates pleasure upon achieving a higher level of skill, and the pleasure derived from successfully performing a somewhat risky task encourages him to seek out such tasks.

Rosen and D'Andrade (1959) found that high achievement motivation, a motivation akin to stress-seeking, was facilitated both by high maternal warmth when the child pleased the parent and high maternal hostility and rejection when the child was displeasing. Hoffman et al. (1960), found that mothers of achieving boys were more coercive than those who performed poorly, and it has also been found (Crandall, Dewey, Katkovsky, and Preston 1964) that mothers of achieving girls were relatively nonnurturant. Kagan and Moss (1962) reported that achieving adult women had mothers who in early childhood were unaffectionate, "pushy," and not protective. Also, Baumrind and Black (1967) found paternal punitiveness to be associated positively with independence in girls. Finally, in a recent study (Baumrind 1971), there were indications for girls that parental nonacceptance was positively related to independence. That is, the most independent girls had parents who were either not passive-acceptant or were rejecting.

Authoritarian control and permissive noncontrol both may shield the child from the opportunity to engage in vigorous interaction with people. Demands which cannot be met, refusals to help, and unrealistically high standards may curb commerce with the environment. Placing few demands on the child, suppression of conflict, and low standards may understimulate him. In either case, he fails to achieve the knowledge and experience required to desensitize him to the anxiety associated with nonconformity.

3. *Self-assertiveness and self-confidence in the parent, expressed by an individual style and by the moderate use of power-oriented techniques of discipline, will be associated with independence in the young child.*

The self-assertive, self-confident parent provides a model of similar behavior for the child. Also, the parent who uses power-oriented rather than love-oriented techniques of discipline achieves compliance through means other than guilt. Power-oriented techniques can achieve behavioral conformity without premature internalization by the child of parental standards. It may be that the child is, in fact, more free to formulate his own standards of conduct if techniques of discipline are used which stimulate resistiveness or anger rather than fear of guilt. The use of techniques which do not stimulate conformity through guilt may be especially important for girls. The belief in one's own power and the assumption of responsibility for one's own intellectual successes and failures are important predictors of independent effort and intellectual achievement (Crandall, Katkovsky, and Crandall 1965). This sense of self-responsibility in children seems to be associated with power-oriented techniques of discipline with critical attitudes on the part of the adult towards the child, provided that the parent is also concerned with developing the child's autonomy and encourages independent and individual behavior.

In my study, both the authoritative and the nonconforming parents were self-confident, clear as well as flexible in their child-rearing attitudes, and willing to express angry feelings openly. Together with relatively firm enforcement and nonrejection, these indices signified patterns of parental authority in which guilt-producing techniques of discipline were avoided. The sons of nonconforming parents and the daughters of authoritative parents were both extremely independent.

4. *Firm control can be associated with independence in the child, provided that the control is not restrictive of the child's opportunities to experiment and to make decisions within the limits defined.*

There is no logical reason why parents' enforcing directives and demands cannot be accompanied by regard for the child's opinions, willingness to gratify his wishes, and instruction in the effective use of power. A policy of firm enforcement may be used as a means by which the child can achieve a high level of instrumental competence and eventual independence. The controlling, demanding parent can train the child to tolerate increasingly intense and prolonged frustration; to broaden his base of adult support to include neighbors, teachers, and others; to assess critically his own successes and failures and to take responsibility for both; to develop standards of moral conduct; and to relinquish the special privileges of childhood in return for the rights of adolescence.

It is important to distinguish between the effects on the child of restrictive control and of firm control. *Restrictive control* refers to the use of extensive proscriptions and prescriptions, covering many areas of the child's life; they limit his autonomy to try out his skills in these areas. By *firm control* is meant firm enforcement of rules, effective resistance against the child's demands, and guidance of the child by regime and intervention. Firm control does not imply large numbers of rules or intrusive direction of the child's activities.

Becker (1964) has summarized the effects on child behavior of restrictive vs. permissiveness and warmth vs. hostility. He reported that warm-

restrictive parents tended to have passive, well-socialized children. This author (Baumrind 1967) found, however, that warm-*controlling* (by contrast with warm-*restrictive*) parents were not paired with passive children, but rather with responsible, assertive, self-reliant children. Parents of these children enforced directives and resisted the child's demands, but were not restrictive. Early control, unlike restrictiveness, apparently does not lead to "fearful, dependent and submissive behaviors, a dulling of intellectual striving, and inhibited hostility," as Becker indicated was true of restrictive parents (1964, p. 197).

5. *Substantial reliance upon reinforcement techniques to obtain behavioral conformity, unaccompanied by use of reason, should lead to dependent behavior.*

To the extent that the parent uses verbal cues judiciously, she increases the child's ability to discriminate, differentiate, and generalize. According to Luria (1960) and Vygotsky (1962), the child's ability to "order" his own behavior is based upon verbal instruction from the adult which, when heeded and obeyed, permits eventual *cognitive* control by the child of his own behavior. Thus, when the adult legitimizes power, labels actions clearly as praiseworthy, explains rules and encourages vigorous verbal give and take, obedience is not likely to be achieved at the cost of passive dependence. Otherwise, it may well be.

It is self-defeating to attempt to shape, by extrinsic reinforcement, behavior which by its nature is autogenic. As already mentioned, the healthy infant is explorative and curious, and seems to enjoy mild stress. Although independent mastery can be accelerated if the parent broadens the child's experiences and makes certain reasonable demands upon him, the parent must take care not to substitute extrinsic reward and social approval for the intrinsic pleasure associated with mastery of the environment. Perhaps the unwillingness of the authoritative parents in my study to rely solely upon reinforcement techniques contributed substantially to the relatively purposive, dominant behavior shown by their children, especially by their daughters.

6. *Parental values which stress individuality, self-expression, initiative, divergent thinking, and aggressiveness will facilitate the development of independence in the child, provided that these qualities in the parent are not accompanied by lax and inconsistent discipline and unwillingness to make demands upon the child.*

It is important that adults use their power in a functional rather than an interpersonal context. The emphasis should be on the task to be done and the rule to be followed rather than upon the special status of the powerful adult. By focusing upon the task to be accomplished, the adult's actions can serve as an example for the child rather than as a suppressor of his independence. Firm discipline for both boys and girls must be in the service of training for achievement and independence, if such discipline is not to facilitate the development of an overconforming, passive life style.

In our study, independence was clearly a function of nonconforming but nonindulgent parental attitudes and behavior, for boys. For girls, however, nonconforming parental patterns were associated with independence only when the parents were also authoritative. The parents in these groups tended to encourage their children to ask for, even to demand, what they desired. They themselves acquiesced in the face of such demands provided that the demands were not at variance with parental policy. Thus, the children of these parents were positively reinforced for autonomous self-expression. In contrast to these results, the authoritarian parents did not value willfulness in the child and the permissive parents were clearly ambivalent about rewarding such behavior. Further, the permissive parents did not differentiate between mature or praiseworthy demands by the child and regressive or deviant demands. These permissive parents instead would accede to the child's demands until patience was exhausted; punishment, sometimes very harsh, would then ensue.

Conclusions

Girls in Western society are in many ways systematically socialized for instrumental incompetence. The affiliative and cooperative orientation of girls increases their receptivity to the influence of socializing agents. This influence, in turn, is often used by socializing agents to inculcate passivity, dependence, conformity, and sociability in young females at the expense of independent pursuit of success and scholarship. In my studies, parents designated as authoritative had the most achievement-oriented and independent daughters. However, permissive parents whose control was lax, who did not inhibit tomboy behavior, and who did not seek to produce sex-role conformity in girls had daughters who were nearly as achievement-oriented and independent.

The following adult practices and attitudes seem to facilitate the development of socially responsible and independent behavior in both boys and girls:

1. Modeling by the adult of behavior which is both socially responsible and self-assertive, especially if the adult is seen as powerful by the child and as eager to use the material and interpersonal resources which he has control on the child's behalf.
2. Firm enforcement policies in which the adult makes effective use of reinforcement principles in order to reward socially responsible behavior and to punish deviant behavior, but in which demands are accompanied by explanations, and sanctions are accompanied by reasons consistent with a set of principles followed in practice as well as preached by the parent.
3. Nonrejecting but not overprotective or passive-acceptant parental attitudes in which the parent's interest in the child is abiding and, in the preschool years, intense; and where approval is conditional upon the child's behavior.
4. High demands for achievement and for conformity with parental policy, accompanied by receptivity to the child's rational demands and willingness to offer the child wide latitude for independent judgment.
5. Providing the child with a complex and stimulating environment

offering challenge and excitement as well as security and rest, where divergent as well as convergent thinking is encouraged.

These practices and attitudes do not reflect a happy compromise between authoritarian and permissive practices. Rather, they reflect a synthesis and balancing of strongly opposing forces of tradition and innovation, divergence and convergence, accommodation and assimilation, cooperation and autonomous expression, tolerance and principled intractability.

NOTES

1. In order to avoid confusion, when I speak of the parent I will use the pronoun "she," and when I speak of the child, I will use the pronoun "he," although, unless otherwise specified, the statement applies to both sexes equally.
2. A paper entitled "The relationship of cognitive ability as measured by IQ tests to interpersonal competence: educational implications" (1971, in preparation) discusses this area in full. In that paper social implications of IQ as a predictor of adult achievement, interpersonal competence, and level of moral development, are discussed. The possible effects of different types of educational environment on achievement, in particular "discovery" vs. direct training methods, and ability groups vs. integrated classrooms, are explored. The importance of evaluating current programs in which the classroom is integrated (e.g., Berkeley) is emphasized.

REFERENCES

ABERLE, D. F. AND NAEGELE, K. D. Middle-class fathers' occupational role and attitudes toward children. *Am. J. Orthopsychiat.*, 1952, *22*, 366–378.

BANDURA, A., ROSS, D. AND ROSS, S. A. A comparative test of the status envy, social power, and the secondary-reinforcement theories of identificatory learning. *J. Abnorm. Soc. Psychol.*, 1963, *67*, 527–534.

BARRY, H., BACON, J. K. AND CHILD, I. L. A cross-cultural survey of some sex differences in socialization. *J. Abnorm. Soc. Psychol.*, 1957, 327–332.

BAUMRIND, D. Effects of authoritative parental control on child behavior. *Child Develpm.*, 1966, *37*, 887–907.

———. Child care practices anteceding three patterns of preschool behavior. *Genet. Psychol. Monogr.*, 1967, *75*, 43–88.

———. Authoritarian vs. authoritative parental control. *Adolescence*, 1968, *3*, 255–272.

———. Current patterns of parental authority. *Develpm. Psychol. Monogr.*, 1971, *4(I)*, 1–102.

———. From each woman in accord with her ability. *School Rev.*, Feb. 1972, in press. (a)

———. An exploratory study of socialization effects on black children: Some black-white comparisons. *Child Develpm.*, 1971, in press. (b)

BAUMRIND, D. AND BLACK, A. E. Socialization practices associated with dimensions of competence in preschool boys and girls. *Child Develpm.*, 1967, *38*, 291–327.

BECKER, W. C. Consequences of different kinds of parental discipline. In M. L. Hoffman and L. W. Hoffman (Eds.), *Review of Child Development Research*, Vol. 1. New York: Russell Sage Foundation, 1964, pp. 169–208.

BRONFENBRENNER, U. Some familial antecedents of responsibility and leadership in adolescents. In L. Petrullo and B. M. Bass (Eds.), *Leadership and Interpersonal Behavior*. New York: Holt, Rinehart & Winston, 1961, pp. 239–271.

BROWN, D. Sex role development in a changing culture. *Psychol. Bull.*, 1958, *55*, 232–242.

CRANDALL, V., DEWEY, R., KATKOVSKY, W. AND PRESTON, A. Parents' attitudes and behaviors and grade school children's academic achievements. *J. Genet. Psychol.*, 1964, *104*, 53–66.

CRANDALL, V., KATKOVSKY, W. AND CRANDALL, V. J. Children's beliefs in their own control of reinforcements in intellectual-academic achievement situations. *Child Develpm.*, 1965, *36*, 91–109.

CRANDALL, V., ORLEANS, S., PRESTON, A. AND RABSON, A. The development of social compliance in young children. *Child Develpm.*, 1958, *29*, 429–443.

DINITZ, S., DYNES, R. R. AND CLARKE, A. C. Preferences for male or female children: Traditional or affectional. *Marriage & Family Living*, 1954, *16*, 128–130.

EIDUSON, B. T. *Scientists, Their Psychological World.* New York: Basic Books, 1962.

ELDER, G. H. Parental power legitimation and its effect on the adolescent. *Sociometry*, 1963, *26*, 50–65.

EMMERICH, W. AND SMOLLER, F. The role patterning of parental norms. *Sociometry*, 1964, *27*, 382–390.

FOWLER, W. Cognitive learning in infancy and early childhood. *Psycho. Bull*, 1962, *59*, 116–152.

HAGGARD, E. A. Socialization, personality, and academic achievement in gifted children. In B. C. Rosen, H. J. Crockett and C. Z. Nunn (Eds.), *Achievement in American Society.* Cambridge, Mass.: Schenkman Publishing, 1969, pp. 85–94.

HEILBRUN, A. B. Sex differences in identification learning. *J. Genet. Psychol.*, 1965, *106*, 185–193.

HOFFMAN, L., ROSEN, S. AND LIPPITT, R. Parental coerciveness, child autonomy, and child's role at school. *Sociometry*, 1960, *23*, 15–22.

HORNER, M. S. Sex differences in achievement motivation and performance in competitive situations. Unpubl. doctoral dissertation, Univ. of Michigan, 1968.

HUNT, J. MCV. Toward the prevention of incompetence. In J. W. Carter, Jr. (Ed.), *Research Contributions from Psychology to Community Mental Health.* New York: Behavioral Publications, 1968.

KAGAN, J. AND MOSS, H. A. *Birth to Maturity: A Study in Psychological Development.* New York: John Wiley, 1962.

KENISTON, E. AND KENISTON, K. An American anachronism: the image of women and work. *Am. Scholar*, 1964, *33*, 355–375.

LURIA, A. R. Experimental analysis of the development of voluntary action in children. In *The Central Nervous System and Behavior.* Bethesda, Md.: U.S. Dept. of Health, Education, and Welfare, National Institute of Health, 1960, pp. 529–535.

MACCOBY, E. E. (Ed.). *The Development of Sex Differences.* Stanford, Calif.: Stanford Univ. Press, 1966.

MCCLELLAND, D., ATKINSON, J., CLARK, R. AND LOWELL, D. *The Achievement Motive.* New York: Appleton-Century-Crofts, 1963.

MCKEE, J. P. AND SHERRIFFS, A. C. The differential evaluation of males and females. *J. Pers.*, 1957, *25*, 356–371.

MIDDLETON, R. AND SNELL, P. Political expression of adolescent rebellion. *Am. J. Sociol.*, 1963, *68*, 527–535.

MISCHEL, W. AND LIEBERT, R. M. Effects of discrepancies between observed and imposed reward criteria on their acquisition and transmission. *J. Pers. Soc. Psychol.*, 1966, *3*, 45–53.

PARKE, R. D. Some effects of punishment on children's behavior. *Young Children*, 1969, *24*, 224–240.

PIKAS, A. Children's attitudes toward rational versus inhibiting parental authority. *J. Abnorm. Soci. Psychol.*, 1961, *62*, 315–321.

ROE, A. *The Making of a Scientist.* New York: Dodd, Mead, 1952.

ROSEN, B. C. AND D'ANDRADE, R. The psychological origins of achievement motivation. *Sociometry*, 1959, *22*, 185–218.

ROSENHAN, D. L., FREDERICK, F. AND BURROWES, A. Preaching and practicing: Effects of channel discrepancy on norm internalization. *Child Develpm.*, 1968, *39*, 291–302.

ROSSI, A. Women in science: why so few? In B. C. Rosen, H. J. Crockett, C. Z. Nunn (eds.), *Achievement in American Society.* Cambridge, Mass.: Schenkman Publishing, 1969, pp. 470–486.

SIEGEL, A. E. AND KOHN, L. G. Permissiveness, permission, and aggression: The effects of adult presence or absence on aggression in children's play. *Child Develpm.*, 1959, *36*, 131–141.

SPENCE, J. T. Verbal-discrimination performance as a function of instruction and verbal reinforcement combination in normal and retarded children. *Child Develpm.*, 1966, *37*, 269–281.

TERMAN, L. M. AND ODEN, H. H. *The Gifted Child Grows Up.* Stanford, Calif.: Stanford Univ. Press, 1947.

VYGOTSKY, L. S. *Thought and Language.* Cambridge, Mass.: M. I. T. Press, 1962.

WALBERG, H. J. Physics, femininity, and creativity. *Develpm. Psychol.*, 1969, *1*, 47–54.

WILLIS, R. H. Conformity, independence, and anticonformity. In L. S. Wrightsman, Jr. (Ed.), *Contemporary Issues in Social Psychology.* Belmont, Calif.: Brooks/Cole Publishing, 1968, pp. 258–272.

10

Transmission of Aggression through Imitation of Aggressive Models

Albert Bandura, Dorothea Ross, and Sheila A. Ross

A previous study, designed to account for the phenomenon of identification in terms of incidental learning, demonstrated that children readily imitated behavior exhibited by an adult model in the presence of the model (Bandura and Huston 1961). A series of experiments by Blake (1958) and others (Grosser, Polansky, and Lippitt 1951; Rosenblith, 1959; Schachter and Hall 1952) have likewise shown that mere observation of responses of a model has a facilitating effect on subjects' reactions in the immediate social influence setting.

While these studies provide convincing evidence for the influence and control exerted on others by the behavior of a model, a more crucial test of imitative learning involves the generalization of imitative response patterns to new settings in which the model is absent.

In the experiment reported in this paper children were exposed to aggressive and nonaggressive adult models and were then tested for amount of imitative learning in a new situation in the absence of the model. According to the prediction, subjects exposed to aggressive models would reproduce aggressive acts resembling those of their models and would differ in this respect from both subjects who observed nonaggressive models and

From A. Bandura, D. Ross, and S. A. Ross, Transmission of Aggression through Imitation of Aggressive Models, *Journal of Abnormal and Social Psychology* 63 (1961):575–82. Copyright 1961 by the American Psychological Association. Reprinted by permission of the publisher and author.[1]

from those who had no prior exposure to any models. This hypothesis assumed that subjects had learned imitative habits as a result of prior reinforcement, and these tendencies would generalize to some extent to adult experimenters (Miller and Dollard 1941).

It was further predicted that observation of subdued nonaggressive models would have a generalized inhibiting effect on the subjects' subsequent behavior, and this effect would be reflected in a difference between the nonaggressive and the control groups, with subjects in the latter group displaying significantly more aggression.

Hypotheses were also advanced concerning the influence of the sex of model and sex of subjects on imitation. Fauls and Smith (1956) have shown that preschool children perceive their parents as having distinct preferences regarding sex appropriate modes of behavior for their children. Their findings, as well as informal observation, suggest that parents reward imitation of sex appropriate behavior and discourage or punish sex inappropriate imitative responses, e.g., a male child is unlikely to receive much reward for performing female appropriate activities, such as cooking, or for adopting other aspects of the maternal role, but these same behaviors are typically welcomed if performed by females. As a result of differing reinforcement histories, tendencies to imitate male and female models thus acquire differential habit strength. One would expect, on this basis, subjects to imitate the behavior of a same-sex model to a greater degree than a model of the opposite sex.

Since aggression, however, is a highly masculine-typed behavior, boys should be more predisposed than girls toward imitating aggression, the difference being most marked for subjects exposed to the male aggressive model.

Method

Subjects

The subjects were 36 boys and 36 girls enrolled in the Stanford University Nursery School. They ranged in age from 37 to 69 months, with a mean age of 52 months.

Two adults, a male and a female, served in the role of model, and one female experimenter conducted the study for all 72 children.

Experimental Design

Subjects were divided into eight experimental groups of six subjects each and a control group consisting of 24 subjects. Half the experimental subjects were exposed to aggressive models and half were exposed to models that were subdued and nonaggressive in their behavior. These groups were further subdivided into male and female subjects. Half the subjects in the aggressive and nonaggressive conditions observed same-sex models, while the remaining subjects in each group viewed models of the opposite sex. The control group had no prior exposure to the adult models and was tested only in the generalization situation.

It seemed reasonable to expect that the subjects' level of aggressiveness would be positively related to the readiness with which they imitated aggressive modes of behavior. Therefore, in order to increase the precision of treatment comparisons, subjects in the experimental and control groups were matched individually on the basis of ratings of their aggressive behavior in social interactions in the nursery school.

The subjects were rated on four five-point rating scales by the experimenter and a nursery school teacher, both of whom were well acquainted with the children. These scales measured the extent to which subjects displayed physical aggression, verbal aggression, aggression toward inanimate objects, and aggressive inhibition. The latter scale, which dealt with the subjects' tendency to inhibit aggressive reactions in the face of high instigation, provided a measure of aggression anxiety.

Fifty-one subjects were rated independently by both judges so as to permit an assessment of interrater agreement. The reliability of the composite aggression score, estimated by means of the Pearson product-moment correlation, was .89.

The composite score was obtained by summing the ratings on the four aggression scales; on the basis of these scores, subjects were arranged in triplets and assigned at random to one of two treatment conditions or to the control group.

Experimental Conditions

In the first step in the procedure subjects were brought individually by the experimenter to the experimental room and the model who was in the hallway outside the room, was invited by the experimenter to come and join in the game. The experimenter then escorted the subject to one corner of the room, which was structured as the subject's play area. After seating the child at a small table, the experimenter demonstrated how the subject could design pictures with potato prints and picture stickers provided. The potato prints included a variety of geometrical forms; the stickers were attractive multicolor pictures of animals, flowers, and western figures to be pasted on a pastoral scene. These activities were selected since they had been established, by previous studies in the nursery school, as having high interest value for the children.

After having settled the subject in his corner, the experimenter escorted the model to the opposite corner of the room which contained a small table and chair, a tinker toy set, a mallet, and a 5-foot inflated Bobo doll. The experimenter explained that these were the materials provided for the model to play with and, after the model was seated, the experimenter left the experimental room.

With subjects in the *nonaggressive condition*, the model assembled the tinker toys in a quiet subdued manner totally ignoring the Bobo doll.

In contrast, with subjects in the *aggressive condition*, the model began by assembling the tinker toys but after approximately a minute had elapsed, the model turned to the Bobo doll and spent the remainder of the period aggressing toward it.

Imitative learning can be clearly demonstrated if a model performs sufficiently novel patterns of responses which are unlikely to occur independently of the observation of the behavior of a model and if a subject reproduces these behaviors in substantially identical form. For this reason, in addition to punching the Bobo doll, a response that is likely to be performed by children independently of a demonstration, the model exhibited distinctive aggressive acts which were to be scored as imitative responses. The model laid Bobo on its side, sat on it and punched it repeatedly in the nose. The model then raised the Bobo doll, picked up the mallet and struck the doll on the head. Following the mallet aggression, the model tossed the doll up in the air aggressively and kicked it about the room. This sequence of physically aggressive acts was repeated approximately three times, interspersed with verbally aggressive responses such as, "Sock him in the nose. . . ," "Hit him down . . . ," "Throw him in the air . . . ," "Kick him . . . ," "Pow . . . ," and two nonaggressive comments, "He keeps coming back for more" and "He sure is a tough fella."

Thus in the exposure situation, subjects were provided with a diverting task which occupied their attention while at the same time insured observation of the model's behavior in the absence of any instructions to observe or to learn the responses in question. Since subjects could not perform the model's aggressive behavior, any learning that occurred was purely on an observational or covert basis.

At the end of 10 minutes, the experimenter entered the room, informed the subject that he would now go to another game room, and bid the model goodbye.

Aggression Arousal

Subjects were tested for the amount of imitative learning in a different experimental room that was set off from the main nursery school building. The two experimental situations were thus clearly differentiated; in fact, many subjects were under the impression that they were no longer on the nursery school grounds.

Prior to the test for imitation, however, all subjects, experimental and control, were subjected to mild aggression arousal to insure that they were under some degree of instigation to aggression. The arousal experience was included for two main reasons. In the first place, observation of aggressive behavior exhibited by others tends to reduce the probability of aggression on the part of the observer (Rosenbaum and deCharms 1960). Consequently, subjects in the aggressive condition, in relation both to the nonaggressive and control groups, would be under weaker instigation following exposure to the models. Second, if subjects in the nonaggressive condition expressed little aggression in the face of appropriate instigation, the presence of an inhibitory process would seem to be indicated.

Following the exposure experience, therefore, the experimenter brought the subject to an anteroom that contained these relatively attractive toys: a fire engine, a locomotive, a jet fighter plane, a cable car, a colorful spinning top, and a doll set complete with wardrobe, doll carriage, and baby crib. The experimenter explained that the toys were for the subject to play with but, as soon as the subject became sufficiently involved with the play material (usually in about 2 minutes), the experimenter remarked that these were her very best toys, that she did not let just anyone play with them, and that she had decided to reserve these toys for the other children. However, the subject could play with any of the toys that were in the next room. The experimenter and the subject then entered the adjoining experimental room.

It was necessary for the experimenter to remain in the room during the experimental session; otherwise a number of the children would either refuse to remain alone or would leave before the termination of the session. However, in order to minimize any influence her presence might have on the subject's behavior, the experimenter remained as inconspicuous as possible by busying herself with paper work at a desk in the far corner of the room and avoiding any interaction with the child.

Test for Delayed Imitation

The experimental room contained a variety of toys including some that could be used in imitative or nonimitative aggression, and others that tended to elicit predominantly nonaggressive forms of behavior. The aggressive toys included a 3-foot Bobo doll, a mallet and peg board, two dart guns, and a tether ball with a face painted on it which hung from the ceiling. The nonaggressive toys, on the other hand, included a tea set, crayons and coloring paper, a ball, two dolls, three bears, cars and trucks, and plastic farm animals.

In order to eliminate any variation in behavior due to mere placement of the toys in the room, the play material was arranged in a fixed order for each of the sessions.

The subject spent 20 minutes in this experimental room during which time his behavior was rated in terms of predetermined response categories by judges who observed the session through a one-way mirror in an adjoining observation room. The 20-minute session was divided into 5-second intervals by means of an electric interval timer, thus yielding a total number of 240 response units for each subject.

The male model scored the experimental sessions for all 72 children. Except for the cases in which he served as model, he did not have knowledge of the subjects' group assignments. In order to provide an estimate of interscorer agreement, the performances of half the subjects were also scored independently by a second observer. Thus one or the other of the two observers usually had no knowledge of the conditions to which the subjects were assigned. Since, however, all but two of the subjects in the aggressive condition performed the models' novel aggressive responses while subjects in the other conditions only rarely exhibited such reactions, subjects who were exposed to the aggressive models could be readily identified through their distinctive behavior.

The responses scored involved highly specific concrete classes of behavior and yielded high interscorer reliabilities, the product-moment coefficients being in the .90s.

Response Measures

Three measures of imitation were obtained:

Imitation of physical aggression: This category included acts of striking the Bobo doll with the mallet, sitting on the doll and punching it in the nose, kicking the doll, and tossing it in the air.

Imitative verbal aggression: Subject repeats the phrases, "Sock him," "Hit him down," "Kick him," "Throw him in the air," or "Pow."

Imitative nonaggressive verbal responses: Subject repeats, "He keeps coming back for more," or "He sure is a tough fella."

During the pretest, a number of the subjects imitated the essential components of the model's behavior but did not perform the complete act, or they directed the imitative aggressive response to some object other than the Bobo doll. Two responses of this type were therefore scored and were interpreted as partially imitative behavior.

Mallet aggression: Subject strikes objects other than the Bobo doll aggressively with the mallet.

Sits on Bobo doll: Subject lays the Bobo doll on its side and sits on it, but does not aggress toward it.

The following additional nonimitative aggressive responses were scored:

Punches Bobo doll: Subject strikes, slaps, or pushes the doll aggressively.

Nonimitative physical and verbal aggression: This category included physically aggressive acts directed toward objects other than the Bobo doll and any hostile remarks except for those in the verbal imitation category; e.g., "Shoot the Bobo," "Cut him," "Stupid ball," "Knock over people," "Horses fighting, biting."

Aggressive gun play: Subject shoots darts or aims the guns and fires imaginary shots at objects in the room.

Ratings were also made of the number of behavior units in which subjects played nonaggressively or sat quietly and did not play with any of the material at all.

Results

Complete Imitation of Models' Behavior

Subjects in the aggression condition reproduced a good deal of physical and verbal aggressive behavior resembling that of the models, and their mean scores differed markedly from those of subjects in the nonaggressive and control groups who exhibited virtually no imitative aggression (see Table 1).

Since there were only a few scores for subjects in the nonaggressive and control conditions (approximately 70% of the subjects had zero scores), and the assumption of homogeneity of variance could not be made, the Friedman two-way analysis of variance by ranks was employed to test the significance of the obtained differences.

The prediction that exposure of subjects to aggressive models increases the probability of aggressive behavior is clearly confirmed (see Table 2). The main effect of treatment conditions is highly significant both for physical and verbal imitative aggression. Comparison of pairs of scores by the sign test shows that the obtained over-all differences were due almost entirely to the aggression displayed by subjects who had been exposed to the aggressive models. Their scores were significantly higher than those of either the nonaggressive or control groups, which did not differ from each other (Table 2).

Table 1 Mean aggression scores for experimental and control subjects

| | Experimental groups | | | | |
| | Aggressive | | Nonaggressive | | |
Response category	F Model	M Model	F Model	M Model	Control groups
Imitative physical aggression					
Female subjects	5.5	7.2	2.5	0.0	1.2
Male subjects	12.4	25.8	0.2	1.5	2.0
Imitative verbal aggression					
Female subjects	13.7	2.0	0.3	0.0	0.7
Male subjects	4.3	12.7	1.1	0.0	1.7
Mallet aggression					
Female subjects	17.2	18.7	0.5	0.5	13.1
Male subjects	15.5	28.8	18.7	6.7	13.5
Punches Bobo doll					
Female subjects	6.3	16.5	5.8	4.3	11.7
Male subjects	18.9	11.9	15.6	14.8	15.7
Nonimitative aggression					
Female subjects	21.3	8.4	7.2	1.4	6.1
Male subjects	16.2	36.7	26.1	22.3	24.6
Aggressive gun play					
Female subjects	1.8	4.5	2.6	2.5	3.7
Male subjects	7.3	15.9	8.9	16.7	14.3

Imitation was not confined to the model's aggressive responses. Approximately one-third of the subjects in the aggressive condition also repeated the model's nonaggressive verbal responses while none of the subjects in either the nonaggressive or control groups made such remarks. This difference, tested by means of the Cochran Q test, was significant well beyond the .001 level (Table 2).

Partial Imitation of Models' Behavior

Differences in the predicted direction were also obtained on the two measures of partial imitation.

Analysis of variance of scores based on the subjects' use of the mallet aggressively toward objects other than the Bobo doll reveals that treatment conditions are a statistically significant source of variation (Table 2). In addition, individual sign tests show that both the aggressive and the control groups, relative to subjects in the nonaggressive condition, produced significantly more mallet aggression, the difference being particularly marked with regard to female subjects. Girls who observed nonaggressive models performed a mean number of 0.5 mallet aggression responses as compared to mean values of 18.0 and 13.1 for girls in the aggressive and control groups, respectively.

Although subjects who observed aggressive models performed more mallet aggression ($M = 20.0$) than their controls ($M = 13.3$), the difference was not statistically significant.

With respect to the partially imitative response of sitting on the Bobo

Table 2 Significance of the differences between experimental and control groups in the expression of aggression

Response category	X^2_r	Q	p	Comparison of pairs of treatment conditions		
				Aggressive vs. Nonaggressive p	Aggressive vs. Control p	Nonaggressive vs. Control p
Imitative responses						
Physical aggression	27.17		<.001	<.001	<.001	.09
Verbal aggression	9.17		<.02	.004	.048	.09
Nonaggressive verbal responses		17.50	<.001	.004	.004	ns
Partial imitation						
Mallet aggression	11.06		<.01	.026	ns	.005
Sits on Bobo		13.44	<.01	.018	.059	ns
Nonmitative aggression						
Punches Bobo doll	2.87		ns			
Physical and verbal	8.96		<.02	.026	ns	ns
Aggressive gun play	2.75		ns		ns	

doll, the over-all group differences were significant beyond the .01 level (Table 2). Comparison of pairs of scores by the sign test procedure reveals that subjects in the aggressive group reproduced this aspect of the models' behavior to a greater extent than did the nonaggressive (p = .018) or the control (p = .059) subjects. The latter two groups, on the other hand, did not differ from each other.

Nonimitative Aggression

Analyses of variance of the remaining aggression measures (Table 2) show that treatment conditions did not influence the extent to which subjects engaged in aggressive gun play or punched the Bobo doll. The effect of conditions is highly significant (X^2r = 8.96, p < .02), however, in the case of the subjects' expression of nonimitative physical and verbal aggression. Further comparison of treatment pairs reveals that the main source of the over-all difference was the aggressive and nonaggressive groups which differed significantly from each other (Table 2), with subjects exposed to the aggressive models displaying the greater amount of aggression.

Influence of Sex of Model and Sex of Subjects on Imitation

The hypothesis that boys are more prone than girls to imitate aggression exhibited by a model was only partially confirmed. t tests computed for subjects in the aggressive condition reveal that boys reproduced more imitative physical aggression than girls (t = 2.50, p < .01). The groups do not differ, however, in their imitation of verbal aggression.

The use of nonparametric tests, necessitated by the extremely skewed distributions of scores for subjects in the nonaggressive and control conditions, preclude an over-all test of the influence of sex of model per se, and of the various interactions between the main effects. Inspection of the means presented in Table 1 for subjects in the aggression condition, however, clearly suggests the possibility of a Sex × Model interaction. This interaction effect is much more consistent and pronounced for the male model than for the female model. Male subjects, for example, exhibited more physical (t = 2.07, p < .05) and verbal imitative aggression (t = 2.51, p < .05), more nonimitative aggression (t = 3.15, p < .025), and engaged in significantly more aggressive gun play (t = 2.12, p < .05) following exposure to the aggressive male model than the female subjects. In contrast, girls exposed to the female model performed considerably more imitative verbal aggression and more nonimitative aggression than did the boys (Table 1). The variances, however, were equally large and with only a small N in each cell the mean differences did not reach statistical significance.

Data for the nonaggressive and control subjects provide additional suggestive evidence that the behavior of the male model exerted a greater influence than the female model on the subjects' behavior in the generalization situation.

It will be recalled that, except for the greater amount of mallet aggression exhibited by the control subjects, no significant differences were obtained between the nonaggressive and control groups. The data indicate, however, that the absence of significant differences between these two groups was due primarily to the fact that subjects exposed to the nonaggressive female model did not differ from the controls on any of the measures of aggression. With respect to the male model, on the other hand, the differences between the groups are striking. Comparison of the sets of scores by means of the sign test reveals that, in relation to the control group, subjects exposed to the nonaggressive male model performed significantly less imitative physical aggression ($p = .06$), less imitative verbal aggression ($p = .002$), less mallet aggression ($p = .003$), less nonimitative physical and verbal aggression ($p = .03$), and they were less inclined to punch the Bobo doll ($p = .07$).

While the comparison of the subgroups, when some of the over-all tests do not reach statistical significance, is likely to capitalize on chance differences, nevertheless the consistency of the findings adds support to the interpretation in terms of influence by the model.

Nonaggressive Behavior

With the exception of expected sex differences, Lindquist (1956) Type III analyses of variance of the nonaggressive response scores yielded few significant differences.

Female subjects spent more time than boys playing with dolls ($p < .001$), with the tea set ($p < .001$), and coloring ($p < .05$). The boys, on the other hand, devoted significantly more time than the girls to exploratory play with the guns ($p < .01$). No sex differences were found in respect to the subjects' use of the other stimulus objects, i.e., farm animals, cars, or tether ball.

Treatment conditions did produce significant differences on two measures of nonaggressive behavior that are worth mentioning. Subjects in the nonaggressive condition engaged in significantly more nonaggressive play with dolls than either subjects in the aggressive group ($t = 2.67, p < .02$), or in the control group ($t = 2.57, p < .02$).

Even more noteworthy is the finding that subjects who observed nonaggressive models spent more than twice as much time as subjects in aggressive condition ($t = 3.07, p < .01$) in simply sitting quietly without handling any of the play material.

Discussion

Much current research on social learning is focused on the shaping of new behavior through rewarding and punishing consequences. Unless responses are emitted, however, they cannot be influenced. The results of this study provide strong evidence that observation of cues produced by the behavior of others is one effective means of eliciting certain forms of responses for which the original probability is very low or zero. Indeed, social imitation may hasten or short-cut the acquisition of new behaviors without the necessity of reinforcing successive approximations as suggested by Skinner (1953).

Thus subjects given an opportunity to observe aggressive models later reproduced a good deal of physical and verbal aggression (as well as nonaggressive responses) substantially identical with that of the model. In contrast, subjects who were exposed to nonaggressive models and those who had no previous exposure to any models only rarely performed such responses.

To the extent that observation of adult models displaying aggression communicates permissiveness for aggressive behavior, such exposure may serve to weaken inhibitory responses and thereby to increase the probability of aggressive reactions to subsequent frustrations. The fact, however, that subjects expressed their aggression in ways that clearly resembled the novel patterns exhibited by the models provides striking evidence for the occurrence of learning by imitation.

In the procedure employed by Miller and Dollard (1941) for establishing imitative behavior, adult or peer models performed discrimination responses following which they were consistently rewarded, and the subjects were similarly reinforced whenever they matched the leaders' choice responses. While these experiments have been widely accepted as demonstrations of learning by means of imitation, in fact, they simply involve a special case of discrimination learning in which the behavior of others serves as discriminative stimuli for responses that are already part of the subject's repertoire. Auditory or visual environmental cues could easily have been substituted for the social stimuli to facilitate the discrimination learning. In contrast, the process of imitation studied in the present experiment differed in several important respects from the one investigated by Miller and Dollard in that subjects learned to combine fractional responses into relatively complex novel patterns solely by observing the performance of social models without any opportunity to perform the models' behavior in the exposure setting, and without any reinforcers delivered either to the models or to the observers.

An adequate theory of the mechanisms underlying imitative learning is lacking. The explanations that have been offered (Logan, Olmsted, Rosner, Schwartz, and Stevens 1955; Macoby 1959) assume that the imitator performs the model's responses covertly. If it can be assumed additionally that rewards and punishments are self-administered in conjunction with the covert responses, the process of imitative learning could be accounted for in terms of the same principles that govern instrumental trial-and-error learning. In the early stages of the developmental process, however, the range of component responses in the organism's repertoire is probably increased through a process of classical conditioning (Bandura and Huston 1961; Mowrer 1950).

The data provide some evidence that the male model influenced the subjects' behavior outside the exposure setting to a greater extent than was true for the female model. In the analyses of the Sex × Model interactions, for example, only the comparisons involving the male model yielded significant differences. Similarly, subjects exposed to the nonaggressive male model performed less aggressive behavior than the controls, whereas comparisons involving the female model were consistently nonsignificant.

In a study of learning by imitation, Rosenblith (1959) has likewise found male experimenters more effective than females in influencing children's behavior. Rosenblith advanced the tentative explanation that the school setting may involve some social deprivation in respect to adult males which, in turn, enhances the male's reward value.

The trends in the data yielded by the present study suggest an alternative explanation. In the case of a highly masculine-typed behavior such as physical aggression, there is a tendency for both male and female subjects to imitate the male model to a greater degree than the female model. On the other hand, in the case of verbal aggression, which is less clearly sex linked, the greatest amount of imitation occurs in relation to the same-sex model. These trends together with the finding that boys in relation to girls are in general more imitative of physical aggression but do not differ in imitation of verbal aggression, suggest that subjects may be differentially affected by the sex of the model but that predictions must take into account the degree to which the behavior in question is sex-typed.

The preceding discussion has assumed that maleness-femaleness rather than some other personal characteristics of the particular models involved, is the significant variable—an assumption that cannot be tested directly with the data at hand. It was clearly evident, however, particularly from boys' spontaneous remarks about the display of aggression by the female model, that some subjects at least were responding in terms of a sex discrimination and their prior learning about what is sex appropriate behavior (e.g., "Who is that lady. That's not the way for a lady to behave. Ladies are supposed to act like ladies. . . ." "You should have seen what that girl did in there. She was just acting like a man. I never saw a girl act like that before. She was punching and fighting but no swearing."). Aggression by the male model, on the other hand, was more likely to be seen as appropriate and approved by both the boys ("Al's a good socker, he beat up Bobo. I want to sock like Al.") and the girls ("That man is a strong fighter, he punched and punched and he could hit Bobo right down to the floor and if Bobo got up he said, 'Punch your nose.' He's a good fighter like Daddy.").

The finding that subjects exposed to the quiet models were more inhibited and unresponsive than subjects in the aggressive condition, together with the obtained difference on the aggression measures, suggests that exposure to inhibited models not only decreases the probability of occurrence of aggressive behavior but also generally restricts the range of behavior emitted by the subjects.

"Identification with aggressor" (Freud 1946) or "defensive identification" (Mowrer 1950), whereby a person presumably transforms himself from object to agent of aggression by adopting the attributes of an aggressive threatening model so as to allay anxiety, is widely accepted as an explanation of the imitative learning of aggression.

The development of aggressive modes of response by children of aggressively punitive adults, however, may simply reflect object displacement without involving any such mechanism of defensive identification. In studies of child training antecedents of aggressively antisocial adolescents (Bandura and Walters 1959) and of young hyperaggressive boys (Bandura 1960), the parents were found to be nonpermissive and punitive of aggression directed toward themselves. On the other hand, they actively encouraged and reinforced their sons' aggression toward persons outside the home. This pattern of differential reinforcement of aggressive behavior served to inhibit the boys' aggression toward the original instigators and fostered the displacement of aggression toward objects and situations eliciting much weaker inhibitory responses.

Moreover, the findings from an earlier study (Bandura and Huston

1961), in which children imitated to an equal degree aggression exhibited by a nurturant and a non-nurturant model, together with the results of the present experiment in which subjects readily imitated aggressive models who were more or less neutral figures suggest that mere observation of aggression, regardless of the quality of the model-subject relationship, is a sufficient condition for producing imitative aggression in children. A comparative study of the subjects' imitation of aggressive models who are feared, who are liked and esteemed, or who are essentially neutral figures would throw some light on whether or not a more parsimonious theory than the one involved in "identification with the aggressor" can explain the modeling process.

Summary

Twenty-four preschool children were assigned to each of three conditions. One experimental group observed aggressive adult models; a second observed inhibited nonaggressive models; while subjects in a control group had no prior exposure to the models. Half the subjects in the experimental conditions observed same-sex models and half viewed models of the opposite sex. Subjects were then tested for the amount of imitative as well as nonimitative aggression performed in a new situation in the absence of the models.

Comparison of the subjects' behavior in the generalization situation revealed that subjects exposed to aggressive models reproduced a good deal of aggression resembling that of the models, and that their mean scores differed markedly from those of subjects in the nonaggressive and control groups. Subjects in the aggressive condition also exhibited significantly more partially imitative and nonimitative aggressive behavior and were generally less inhibited in their behavior than subjects in the nonaggressive condition.

Imitation was found to be differentially influenced by the sex of the model with boys showing more aggression than girls following exposure to the male model, the difference being particularly marked on highly masculine-typed behavior.

Subjects who observed the nonaggressive models, especially the subdued male model, were generally less aggressive than their controls.

The implications of the findings based on this experiment and related studies for the psychoanalytic theory of identification with the aggressor were discussed.

The authors wish to express their appreciation to Edith Dowley, Director, and Patricia Rowe, Head Teacher, Stanford University Nursery School for their assistance throughout this study.

NOTES

1. This investigation was supported by Research Grant M–4398 from the National Institute of Health, United States Public Health Service.

REFERENCES

BANDURA, A. Relationship of family patterns to child behavior disorders. Progress Report, 1960. Stanford University, Project No. M-1734, United States Public Health Service.

BANDURA, A., AND HUSTON, ALETHA C. Identification as a process of incidental learning. *J. Abnorm. Soc. Psychol.*, 1961, *63*, 311–318.

BANDURA, A., AND WALTERS, R. H. *Adolescent aggression.* New York: Ronald, 1959.

BLAKE, R. R. The other person in the situation. In R. Tagiuri and L. Petrullo (Eds.), *Person perception and interpersonal behavior.* Stanford, Calif.: Stanford Univer. Press, 1958, pp. 229–242.

FAULS, LYDIA B., AND SMITH, W. D. Sex-role learning of five-year olds. *J. Genet. Psychol.*, 1956, *89*, 105–117.

FREUD, ANNA. *The ego and the mechanisms of defense.* New York: International Univer. Press, 1946.

GROSSER, D., POLANSKY, N., AND LIPPITT, R. A laboratory study of behavior contagion. *Hum. Relat.*, 1951, *4*, 115–142.

LINDQUIST, E. F. *Design and analysis of experiments.* Boston: Houghton Mifflin, 1956.

LOGAN, F., OLMSTED, O. L., ROSNER, B. S., SCHWARTZ, R. D., AND STEVENS, C. M. *Behavior theory and social science.* New Haven: Yale Univer. Press, 1955.

MACCOBY, ELEANOR E. Role-taking in childhood and its consequences for social learning. *Child Develpm.*, 1959, *30*, 239–252.

MILLER, N. E., AND DOLLARD, J. *Social learning and imitation.* New Haven: Yale Univer. Press, 1941.

MOWRER, O. H. (Ed.) Identification: A link between learning theory and psychotherapy. In, *Learning theory and personality dynamics.* New York: Ronald, 1950, pp. 69–94.

ROSENBAUM, M. E., AND DECHARMS, R. Direct and vicarious reduction of hostility. *J. Abnorm. Soc. Psychol.*, 1960, *60*, 105–111.

ROSENBLITH, JUDY F. Learning by imitation in kindergarten children. *Child Develpm.*, 1959, *30*, 69–80.

SCHACHTER, S., AND HALL, R. Group-derived restraints and audience persuasion. *Hum. Relat.*, 1952, *5*, 397–406.

SKINNER, B. F. *Science and human behavior.* New York: Macmillan, 1953.

11

Intrinsic and Extrinsic Motivation in Children: Detrimental Effects of Superfluous Social Controls

Mark R. Lepper

My goal in this chapter is to present an overview of a research program concerned with the effectiveness of different techniques of social control in influencing a person's behavior in subsequent situations in which salient extrinsic controls are minimal. In particular, I wish to examine some of the conditions under which initially successful, but functionally unnecessary, social-control techniques—involving the use of rewards, threats of punishment, and other forms of extrinsic constraint—may sometimes have detrimental effects on subsequent behavior in settings in which such external constraints are no longer salient.

My more specific aims are several: First, I wish to describe briefly a set of studies concerned with the effects of threats of punishment on children's "internalization" of adult prohibitions and their behavior in subsequent situations in the absence of further prohibitions. Second, I wish to consider in greater detail more recent research concerned with the effects of extrinsic rewards on children's subsequent intrinsic interest in the activities for which rewards had been previously offered. Both lines of investigation, I wish to suggest, provide evidence that the use of unnecessarily powerful techniques of social control to achieve initial compliance with an adult request may lead to lessened later internalization or subsequent intrinsic interest.

From M. R. Lepper, "Intrinsic and Extrinsic Motivation in Children: Detrimental Effects of Superfluous Social Controls," in *Aspects of the Development of Competence: The Minnesota Symposia on Child Psychology*, vol. 14, ed. W. A. Collins (Hillsdale, N.J.: Lawrence Erlbaum Associates, 1981). Reprinted by permission of the publisher and author.

After sketching out these two lines of research, I wish to place this research in a broader context—to make clear that the phenomena examined in these studies are only a small (though, I think, an interesting) part of the larger picture of the ways in which social-influence attempts may affect subsequent behavior and the factors that determine the effects of extrinsic incentives on subsequent behavior. Finally, I wish to conclude with some speculations on potential differences in the dynamics of the effects of rewards and punishments and possible implications of this work for traditional issues in the study of the socialization process.

Internalization versus Compliance: The Effects of Threats of Punishment on Children's Internalization of Adult Prohibitions

There is, of course, a long history in social and developmental psychology to the distinction between compliance and internalization, and to the underlying premise that techniques that are most effective in eliciting immediate "compliance" with some request or command will not always be those most likely to produce "internalized" changes in attitudes or values that would affect behavior in subsequent situations where one's actions are no longer under the immediate control of the stimuli that produced initial compliance. In social psychology, this distinction appears first in experimental work in Lewin's group-dynamics laboratory—in demonstrations, for example, that children's groups run by dictatorial and authoritarian leaders will be more productive and less overtly aggressive, as long as the leader is present, but less productive and more aggressive than other sorts of groups as soon as the leader exercising this power is absent (Lewin, Lipsitt, and White 1939). Over the years, comparable distinctions have also appeared in the study of conformity and attitude change (Hovland, Janis, and Kelley 1953; Kelman 1958, 1961), dissonance theory (Aronson 1969; Festinger 1957), and attribution and self-perception processes (Bem 1967, 1972; Kelley 1967, 1973). In developmental psychology, similar issues have been a persistent focus of investigations concerned with children's internalization of adult values—standards that permit children to inhibit antisocial behavior (Sears, Whiting, Nowlis, and Sears 1953) and promote their acquisition of moral standards (Hoffman 1970, 1975) or prosocial behavior patterns (Rosenhan 1969; Staub 1978, 1979). Yet, despite its central theoretical significance, this problem has received surprisingly little empirical investigation.

The "Insufficient-Justification" Paradigm

My own concern with generalized effects of social controls derived initially from an interest in a now-classic series of studies in social psychology that examined the effects of more and less severe threats of punishment used to induce children to comply with an initial adult prohibition of a particular activity on children's later evaluation of that previously prohibited activity and their later behavior in similar settings in which further prohibitions were lacking. Let us begin with a consideration of this work.

The paradigmatic study in this area, by Aronson and Carlsmith (1963), can be summarized simply. Preschool children were first asked to rank a number of desirable toys in terms of their relative attractiveness. Then, under a suitable pretext, the experimenter indicated that he would need to leave the child alone briefly. During that period, the experimenter continued, the child would be free to play with all of the toys, except one particularly attractive toy that he or she was not to touch. For half the children, this initial prohibition was accompanied by a relatively "mild" threat of punishment for disobedience—the experimenter indicated that he would be annoyed if the child were to play with the forbidden toy in his absence. For other children, this prohibition was accompanied by a much more severe threat—the experimenter indicated that he would be very angry and might tell the child's teacher, or leave the school, if the child transgressed. Importantly, by means of careful pretesting, the mild-threat procedure was selected to be sufficient, though barely so, to induce all children to comply with the prohibition. Hence, the severe-threat procedure added yet further, but functionally superfluous, justification for not playing with the forbidden toy. At the end of the temptation period, during which all children did, indeed, comply with the prohibition, children's personal preferences for the different toys were then reassessed. The study showed that children who had resisted the temptation to play with the forbidden toy under mild threat of punishment were significantly more likely to devalue or derogate that toy than children in the severe-threat condition.

Within a dissonance framework, these preferences were conceptualized as a function of the amount of justification provided by the two threat manipulations for the child to refrain from engaging in an activity he or she would normally have enjoyed—a response that was otherwise inconsistent with the child's prior attitudes. When the child is provided with compelling external justification for not playing with this attractive toy, as in the severe-threat conditions, he or she should experience little dissonance about the decision to comply with the adult's request; when the external justification is minimal and psychologically "insufficient" (Aronson 1969), dissonance will be produced. One way of reducing this dissonance, the theory suggested, would be to decide that the activity is itself not worth undertaking—to bring one's private attitudes into line with one's overt behavior. These findings were of particular interest, of course, because they appeared to contradict a simplistic associationistic view that the pairing of an activity with a more powerful threat of punishment would increase subsequent compliance with the prohibition of that activity. The results presupposed an active and cognitive, rather than a passive and automatic, response to temptation.

At the time I became interested in this work, considerable further research had already been conducted using this basic "forbidden-toy" paradigm. These studies both attested to the strength and persistence of these effects over time (e.g., Freedman 1965; Pepitone, McCauley, and Hammond 1967; Turner and Wright 1965) and demonstrated that children's subsequent behavior, as well as their reported attitudes, towards the previously forbidden activity was influenced by the strength of the prior prohibition. In the most impressive of these follow-up studies, Freedman (1965) showed significant increases in avoidance of the prohibited toy among mild-threat subjects some 6 weeks later, when these children were tested by another adult in a very different setting in which they were only inadvertently confronted with an opportunity to play with any or all of the toys they had previously encountered. Increased avoidance of the toy was not apparent, however, under either mild- or severe-threat conditions when the children had been kept under close surveillance by the experimenter during the initial "temptation period." These data suggested that it was the experience of resisting temptation under conditions of minimal justification, and not the specific content of the two threats of punishment, that led to later devaluation and continued avoidance of the activity in the absence of further constraints.

These impressive behavioral consequences, obtained in a different setting weeks after the initial experimental sessions, suggested that these studies might have significant implications for our understanding of children's internalization of attitudes and values. Yet, this work seemed to provide little evidence concerning the processes presumed to underlie such effects; it was to this general issue that our initial studies were addressed.

Cognitive Processes in the "Forbidden-Toy" Situation

In the first of these, Mark Zanna, Bob Abelson, and I (Lepper, Zanna, and Abelson 1970) posed a relatively straightforward question. If the devaluation of the forbidden activity in these prior studies were the result of an active process of justification of one's behavior during the temptation period, should not the effects of external justification provided to induce initial compliance differ from the effects of identical justifications provided to the child only after the temptation period? Indeed, if children in the mild-threat condition were motivated to reduce the dissonance aroused by their own behavior during the temptation period, might subsequent justifications for their actions, provided only after the fact, not prove functionally irrelevant to their later attitudes and actions?

To address these issues experimentally, kindergarten children were presented with a typical forbidden-toy procedure, in which they were asked not to play with an attractive toy during the experimenter's absence under either a relatively mild or a more severe threat of punishment for transgression. Then, to provide further justification consistent with a decision not to transgress, experimental subjects were provided with "consensus" information concerning their behavior (Kelley 1967)—that is, they were told that other children in similar situations had all complied with the experimenter's requests not to play with particular toys. For half the subjects, this consensual justification was provided before the temptation period; for the other half, exactly the same information was provided immediately after the temptation period. Control subjects received no such information. Subsequently, children's evaluations of the toys they had encountered were assessed by a second, "blind" experimenter.

The results of this procedure appear in Figure 1 and provide relatively compelling evidence that the processes underlying derogation of the forbidden activity do indeed occur during the temptation period. The control conditions to the left of the Figure establish a difference between mild- and severe-threat conditions in the absence of consensus information, paralleling the results of previous studies. The experimental conditions beside them indicate that when consensual justification was added to the threat manipu-

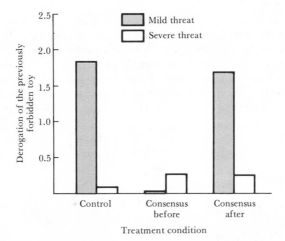

FIGURE 1 Mean derogation of the previously forbidden toy, by conditions.

Data from M. R. Lepper, M. P. Zanna, and R. P. Abelson, "Cognitive Irreversibility in a Dissonance-Reduction Situation," *Journal of Personality and Social Psychology* 16 (1970):191–98. Reprinted by permission of the author.

lation prior to the temptation period, this additional justification was sufficient to prevent devaluation of the forbidden activity under mild threat; but, this same information, if provided after the temptation period, seemed to have little effect on subjects' attitudes towards the activity.

Having established that the processes underlying derogation in this setting seem to occur during the temptation interval, we were led to ask how these processes might be examined more directly. Suppose, for example, that the child's attention could be drawn explicitly to the salient ingredients of this conflictful situation—the attractive forbidden toy and the fact that the child was not playing with this toy. If, by such a procedure, children could be induced to perform more "cognitive work"—to think more about the dilemma presented—one might expect derogation of the forbidden activity to be further enhanced. In two studies designed to examine this proposition, we attempted to draw the child's attention to this basic conflict (Carlsmith, Ebbesen, Lepper, Zanna, Joncas, and Abelson 1969). In one, this attention manipulation took the form of a "janitor" who appeared in the experimental room unexpectedly during the temptation period, ostensibly to retrieve a chair from the room for one of the teachers. As he did so, the janitor excused himself for interrupting the child and indicated casually to the child that he or she had a nice bunch of toys. In the forced-attention condition, however, the janitor also added, conversationally, the critical question: "How come you're not playing with this (i.e., the forbidden) toy?" In a conceptual replication of this first study, salience was manipulated rather differently. The forbidden toy was placed on a table by the experimenter, next to a "defective lamp," and, for half the subjects, this lamp began to buzz and flicker on and off during the temptation period, illuminating the forbidden toy and drawing the child's attention to it.

The results of these two studies were quite comparable, though not precisely in accord with our expectations, and are presented in Figure 2. Whereas our expectation had been that increasing salience of the forbidden toy would enhance derogation for mild-threat subjects, who should presumably experience the situation as dissonance provoking, we had not expected that this manipulation would affect the responses of severe-threat subjects. As Figure 2 clearly indicates, however, derogation of the forbidden activity was increased by this procedure in both the mild- and severe-threat conditions.

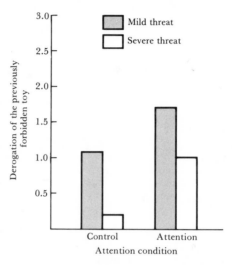

FIGURE 2   Mean derogation of the previously forbidden toy, by conditions, Experiments 1 and 2 combined.

Data from J. M. Carlsmith, E. B. Ebbesen, M. R. Lepper, M. P. Zanna, A. J. Joncas, and R. P. Abelson, "Dissonance Reduction Following Forced Attention to the Dissonance," *Proceedings of the 77th Annual Convention of the American Psychological Association* 4 (1969):321–22. Reprinted by permission of the author.

With the wisdom of hindsight, however, it seemed to us that perhaps these unanticipated results were not completely inconsistent with our basic formulation. Perhaps by making salient the forbidden toy, without at the same time restating the threatened punishment that would follow if the child were to transgress, we had simply magnified the dissonance produced in this situation for all subjects. By this account, the forced-attention manipulation should have differential effects as a function of the threat manipulation only if the level of initial threat were also made salient at the time the child's attention is drawn to the forbidden toy. In this case, a salience manipulation should magnify the effects of dissonance only within the mild-threat condition.

To examine this argument, one further study was conducted (Zanna, Lepper, and Abelson 1973). As before, children were asked not to play with one of a set of attractive toys under either mild or severe threat of punishment. In this study, however, as the experimenter delivered the prohibition against playing with the forbidden toy, he placed a large sticker on the side of the toy facing the child, as a "reminder" to the child that this was the toy he or she was not to play with, and restated the critical threat manipulation. Subsequently, during the temptation period, our familiar janitor entered the room, retrieved an extra chair, and commented on the toys. For half the subjects, however, the janitor casually added the critical question: "How come this (i.e., the forbidden) toy is up here on the table?" Following the temptation period, children's relative preferences for the various toys were again assessed by a second experimenter.

The results of this experiment—in which the procedure employed to call the child's attention to the forbidden toy was explicitly designed to remind the child simultaneously of the threat delivered at the time the toy had been forbidden—appear in Figure 3. In this case, our manipulation of subjects' attention had quite different effects within the two threat conditions. For subjects in the mild-threat conditions, derogation of the forbidden toy was increased; for subjects in the severe-threat conditions, a nonsignificant trend in the opposite direction was observed.

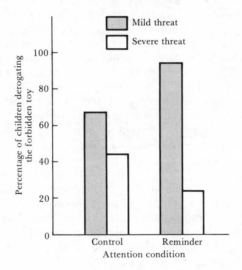

FIGURE 3   Percentage of children derogating the forbidden toy, by conditions.

Data from M. P. Zanna, M. R. Lepper, and R. P. Abelson, "Attentional Mechanisms in Children's Devaluation of a Forbidden Activity in a Forced-Compliance Situation," *Journal of Personality and Social Psychology* 28 (1973):355–59. Reprinted by permission of the author.

Taken together, these studies suggested to us that the devaluation of a previously forbidden activity observed so consistently in this paradigm was the result of an active cognitive process that served to justify the child's own resolution not to play with the prohibited activity under conditions of minimal external pressure. Additional justification provided following the temptation period appeared to have no effects on the devaluation process, and manipulations designed to focus the child's attention during this period on either the forbidden activity itself or the activity and the threat of punishment that accompanied its prohibition appeared to influence children's responses in a systematic fashion, consistent with our basic hypotheses.

Producing Internalization of More General Values

At the same time, more informal observations over the course of these studies also suggested the possibility of an even more general effect of exposure to the "insufficient" justification provided the children in the mild-threat conditions of these studies. Under mild-, but not severe-, threat conditions, a number of children spontaneously volunteered to the second experimenter, following the temptation period, comments suggesting that they had been "good" boys or girls—e.g., that they had not played with the forbidden toy, that they had done just what the other man asked, or that they had done things "just right." Such seemingly self-congratulatory responses, of course, may have many potential meanings. The possibility that interested us most, however, was that these responses represented an alternative or additional means of justifying or explaining one's resistance to temptation in the absence of salient external constraints. Clearly, the conflict involved in resisting temptation is less if one decides the forbidden activity is not very attractive. Perhaps a decision that it is really important to obey adult requests or that the ability to resist temptation reflects something good about oneself may similarly reduce the conflict the child experiences in this situation.

Such a possibility seemed reminiscent of one account offered by Freedman and Fraser (1966) to explain the unexpected cross-situational generality of what they termed the "foot-in-the-door" effect—an increase in subsequent compliance with a large request produced following prior compliance with a much smaller request. In their study, housewives were asked first to comply with a seemingly trivial request, either to place a small placard in their window or to sign a relatively innocuous petition, on one of two rather (at the time) noncontroversial issues—promoting auto safety or saving the California redwoods. Virtually all subjects complied. Several weeks later, these same subjects were contacted by a different individual and were all asked to comply with a much larger request—to place a 6' × 12' hand-painted and rather ugly billboard reading "Drive Safely" on their lawns for the next few weeks. Compared to subjects who had not been originally contacted with an initial smaller request, all of the prior-compliance conditions showed significant increases in the likelihood of agreeing to this second request. Most striking was the fact that even those subjects who had initially complied with a smaller request on a different issue showed increased compliance with this later request: Virtually half of the subjects asked to sign a petition to keep California beautiful subsequently agreed to have the safe driving billboard placed on their lawn. Perhaps, Freedman and Fraser speculated, compliance with the initial request may have led subjects to view themselves as more altruistic or public spirited or to see such campaigns as generally more significant and important.

Might not a similar process be involved in children's reactions to the forbidden-toy paradigm under conditions of mild threats of punishment? The key question, clearly, was whether exposure to this situation would have effects on their later behavior in different, though conceptually related, situations involving adherence to adult standards in the absence of salient external coercion. Such effects would have important implications for understanding the development of internalized standards and controls.

To examine these generalized consequences of initial compliance elicited under varying levels of initial justification required an experimental procedure in which children were seen in two ostensibly unrelated experimental sessions (Lepper 1973). The first of these sessions involved the same basic paradigm as our previous studies. Second-grade children were asked not to play with a particular, highly attractive toy under the threat of either a mild or a severe punishment for transgression, with predictable results. Relative to the severe-threat conditions, mild-threat subjects were significantly more likely to rate the specific previously forbidden toy as less inherently attractive following the temptation period, as in prior experiments. To permit us, in addition, to assess the later effects of both threat procedures relative to an appropriate baseline, a no-prohibition control condition was added to the design.

Several weeks later, these same children were seen in a second experimental session, conducted by a different and ostensibly unrelated experimenter in a different part of the school. In this second session, children were presented with another common, but quite distinct, test of resistance to temptation.

Specifically, children were asked to play a bowling game, presented as a test of skill, but in which their scores were actually programmed in advance. The children were asked, and shown how, to keep score for themselves and were informed that if they obtained a sufficiently high score on the game, they would be allowed to choose a reward for themselves from among a collection of attractive small prizes—e.g., dolls, flashlights, toy cars, etc.—and were then left alone to play the game in the experimenter's absence. The score each child obtained, however, fell just short of that required to win a prize; hence, children could obtain the reward only by falsifying their actual scores at the game.

In contrast to the first session, in which great care was taken to ensure that all children would be able to resist temptation, this second situation was intentionally designed, after substantial pretesting, to elicit transgression from roughly half of the children—through the use of quite attractive rewards for transgression and the creation of a setting in which children believed that the experimenter would have no possible way of knowing how they had actually performed in her absence. The prizes offered, moreover, were deliberately chosen to be quite different from the toys employed in the initial session to ensure that any differences in behavior in this second session were not some simple function of a differential attractiveness of the rewards across conditions.

This procedure, then, allowed us to examine the effects of prior compliance with an adult prohibition, in the face of either minimal or unnecessarily powerful external pressures, on subsequent resistance to temptation in a very different context in which children were confronted with the opportunity to transgress in the face of minimal external pressures with little probability of detection. The data from this second session are presented in Figure 4, and provide some evidence consistent with our analysis. There is, specifically, a highly significant difference in subsequent resistance to temptation between the mild-threat and severe-threat conditions. Not only were mild-threat subjects more likely to show derogation of the particular toy that had been previously forbidden; they behaved more "honestly" in a different temptation situation several weeks later, as well. Comparisons of both ex-

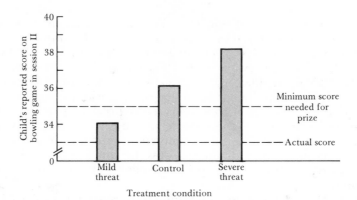

FIGURE 4   Mean scores reported by children playing the bowling game
in Session II, by condition.

Data from M. R. Lepper, "Dissonance, Self-Perception, and Honesty in Children," *Journal of Personality and Social Psychology* 25 (1973):65–74. Reprinted by permission of the author.

perimental conditions to the no-prohibition control condition, moreover, suggested an active effect of both treatments; children who had initially complied under mild-threat conditions proved more likely to resist temptation in this later setting, whereas children who had initially complied under severe-threat conditions tended to be less likely to resist this subsequent temptation.[1]

Prior compliance with an adult prohibition, it seemed, may breed later internalization of that specific prohibition and perhaps some more general values concerning compliance, but only when the external pressure used to promote initial compliance is relatively minimal. The same behavior elicited through the use of unnecessary powerful external pressures, by contrast, seemed counterproductive; if anything, it produced an opposite effect. . . .

The "Overjustification" Paradigm

More generally, this view suggested that the use of unnecessarily powerful or salient techniques of social control—even of a seemingly benign sort, such as the addition of attractive rewards contingent upon engagement in a task of inherent interest—in order to induce an individual to engage in an activity of initial interest may, in effect, undermine that individual's later interest in the activity per se, when extrinsic rewards and constraints are no longer salient. Colloquially, we were suggesting that the use of functionally superfluous extrinsic incentives may turn *play*—that is, something that is seen as enjoyable in its own right—into *work*—that is, something that is seen as worth undertaking only when it will lead to some attractive extrinsic goal.

Our basic hypothesis was the following: If a child were led to view his or her engagement in an activity of initial intrinsic interest as an explicit means to some ulterior goal, his or her subsequent interest in the activity, in the later absence of further extrinsic pressures, may be decreased. In order to emphasize the conceptual parallel between this line of work and our prior research on insufficient justification, we termed this proposition the "over-justification" hypothesis.

To examine this proposition experimentally requires several critical ingredients that we attempted to incorporate into our initial study in this area (Lepper, Greene, and Nisbett 1973). It requires, first, an operational definition of intrinsic interest. For this purpose, we turned to the Bing Nursery School, a laboratory preschool facility, located on the Stanford University campus, that seemed to provide a nearly ideal setting for examining children's intrinsic interest in various activities. First, the structure of the program at the school was, by intention, child-centered, with large blocks of time devoted explicitly to "free-play" periods in which children were encouraged to choose freely among a wide variety of interesting and enjoyable activities. Second, it was possible in this school to ask teachers to set out, as a part of the children's regular classroom program, particular target activities without intrusion into the classroom by research personnel; we could then observe children's responses to these activities without their knowing their behavior was being monitored. Under these conditions, we were willing to infer that children's choices among activities reflected their relative intrinsic interest in those activities. Thus, on the basis of covert baseline observations of children's choices in the classroom, we selected as subjects for our study only those children who had shown initial intrinsic interest in a target activity.

To examine the hypothesis that inducing subjects to engage in an activity of initial interest as an explicit means to the attainment of extrinsic reward should adversely affect later interest in the activity also necessitated a comparison between subjects who had engaged in the target activity in order to obtain a reward and others who had engaged in the activity and had received the same reward, but who should not perceive their behavior as having been instrumentally governed. To accomplish this, our subjects were escorted individually to a different setting in which they were asked to engage in our target activity under one of three conditions. In the Expected-Award condition, children were first shown an extrinsic reward—a "Good Player" certificate—and were asked if they wished to engage in the target activity in order to obtain this reward. Our intent, obviously, was to make salient to the children in this group the instrumentality of their actions as a means of obtaining the proffered reward. In a second, Unexpected-Award, condition, children were simply asked if they would be willing to engage in the target activity without any means of an extrinsic reward. Unexpectedly, after having finished with the activity, these subjects were presented with the same reward and the same feedback as our Expected-Award subjects. This procedure provided a control for task engagement and receipt of reward without producing conditions likely to promote a perception of one's activity as having been directed towards obtaining the reward. Finally, in a third, Control, condition, children were simply asked to engage in the same activity without promise or receipt of a reward. These children received the same feedback as children in the other conditions, but no tangible reward.

Our hypothesis predicted decreased subsequent intrinsic interest in later situations where extrinsic constraints were no longer salient among children who had contracted to engage in the activity in order to obtain the reward, relative to the two other groups. Hence, several weeks following the individual experimental sessions, we again observed unobtrusively the amount of time each child chose to spend with the target activity in the classroom setting. The results of this procedure, presented in Figure 5, appear to support our basic contention. Children in the Expected-Award condition showed significantly less interest in the activity in the classroom following the experimental sessions than they had during baseline period; indeed, they spent only half as much time during the posttest sessions as they had during baseline, whereas subjects in the remaining two conditions showed no significant change in interest from baseline levels. Corresponding between-groups comparisons of subsequent intrinsic interest revealed significant differences between the Expected-Award condition and both the Unexpected-Award and Control conditions.

Conceptually, these findings concerning the detrimental effects of "overly sufficient" justification parallel the results of our earlier work on "insufficient" justification. In contrast to these earlier findings that went largely unnoticed outside of social psychology, the reaction to this first overjustification study and comparable early results obtained with older subject populations by other investigators (Deci 1971; Kruglanski, Friedman, and Zeevi 1971) has been extensive and extraordinarily varied. Although in our initial presentation of these results, we noted a number of theoretical limitations of our findings and cautioned against "overgeneralization"—indicating, in fact, (Lepper et al. 1973) that "certainly there is nothing in the present line of reasoning or the present data to suggest that contracting to engage in an activity for an intrinsic reward will

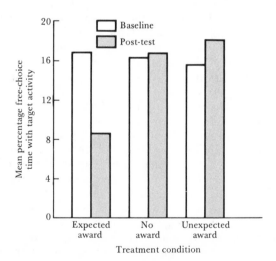

FIGURE 5 Mean intrinsic interest in the target activity during baseline and postexperimental observations in children's classrooms, by condition.

Data from M. R. Lepper, D. Greene, and R. E. Nisbett, "Undermining Children's Intrinsic Interest with Extrinsic Rewards: A Test of the Overjustification Hypothesis," *Journal of Personality and Social Psychology* 28 (1973): 129–37. Reprinted by permission of the author.

always, or even usually, result in a decrement in intrinsic interest in the activity [p. 135]"—extravagant claims concerning these studies have been offered on both sides of the issue. Extreme proponents of the underlying model have extrapolated far beyond the available evidence to argue, in general, against the use of systematic reward programs to modify behavior. Extreme opponents, on the other hand, have argued not only that this work is fundamentally incorrect, but also that it stands in the way of the use of effective procedures for alleviating human suffering through the application of tested behavioral principles.

Both these extreme cases are, I believe, overstated (cf. Lepper and Greene 1978a, 1978c). There are clearly settings in which the use of tangible rewards is appropriate and commendable, and other settings in which their use may be inappropriate. To evaluate this question more fully, let us examine the research literature that has developed in this area over the last several years in some detail and consider the central issues this research has addressed. Several of these issues may be seen as the result of attempts to assess the relevance of alternative models for understanding the processes underlying the appearance of undermining effects; all deal, in one fashion or another, with the conditions under which such detrimental effects are likely to occur and the conditions under which extrinsic rewards are alternatively likely to enhance or maintain subsequent interest.

Variations in Reward Contingency

Consider first the role of the contingency imposed between the receipt of extrinsic rewards and engagement in the experimental activity. In an attributional account, decreases in subsequent intrinsic interest are hypothesized to result from the perceived instrumentality of one's behavior as a means to some extrinsic goal. There are, however, a variety of other models that imply somewhat different accounts of these effects. Perhaps these decreases are a simple function of the linking of the target activity with a reward usually associated with tasks or activities of little interest value. Alternatively, children could have found it distracting, frustrating, or otherwise aversive simply to have to wait during the experimental sessions before they would receive the proffered reward. From these accounts, one might expect comparable decreases in subsequent intrinsic interest even if the reward were not specifically contingent upon task performance. There are, by now, a number of studies that speak to these issues. They suggest, I believe, two general conclusions.

Salience of instrumentality. There is, first, considerable evidence of the importance of perceived instrumentality to the demonstration of subsequent detrimental effects of extrinsic rewards. It is, for instance, a reasonably consistent finding that extrinsic rewards that are not anticipated at the time the activity is undertaken will not produce detrimental effects on subsequent interest (e.g., Enzle and Ross 1978; Greene and Lepper 1974; Lepper and Greene 1975; Lepper, Sagotsky, and Greene 1980; W. F. Smith 1976). Indeed, the one study in which objectively unexpected rewards have been shown to produce subsequent decrements in interest (Kruglanski, Alon, and Lewis 1972) is one in which an explicit attempt was made to

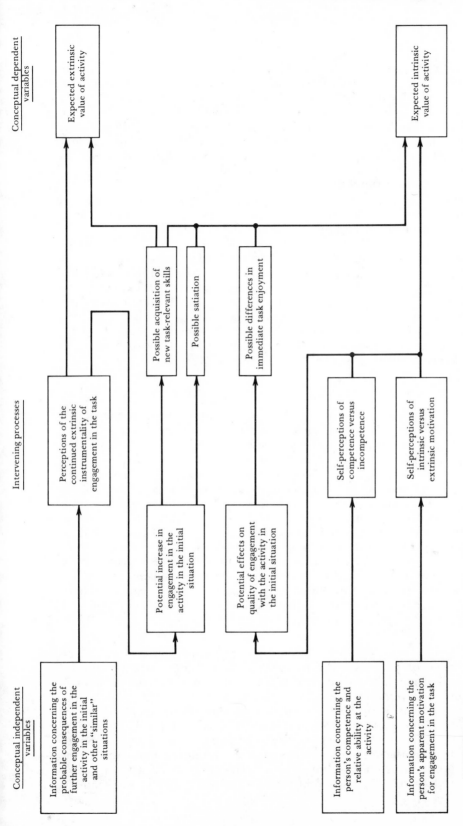

Conceptual independent variables

Conceptual dependent variables

Intervening processes

FIGURE 6 A conceptual analysis of the effects of reinforcement procedures on subsequent expected extrinsic and intrinsic incentive values associated with an activity.

From M. R. Lepper, and D. Greene, "Overjustification Research and Beyond: Toward a Means-Ends Analysis of Intrinsic and Extrinsic Motivation," in *The Hidden Costs of Reward*, ed. M. R. Lepper and D. Greene (Hillsdale, N.J.: Lawrence Erlbaum Associates, 1978). Reprinted by permission of the publisher and author.

deceive children into believing that the reward *had* been mentioned at the time they undertook the target activities, and even within this study, detrimental effects appear to have occurred only for those children who accepted this deliberate deception. Hence, these effects seem not to depend simply on the linkage of the activity with some reward typically associated with tasks of little inherent value. . . .

Understanding Social Constraints: Some Developmental Issues

Before turning to my final concern with an integration of these two experimental literatures on the effects of superfluous extrinsic constraints on internalization and later intrinsic interest, let me turn briefly to the question of how children come to understand the implicit meaning of social-control attempts. Obviously, I am asserting that children as young as 4 and 5 seem to respond to manipulations of perceived constraint in ways that parallel the responses of much older children and even adult subjects faced with comparable situations. This assumption raises some obvious questions about how children come to understand the social meaning of offers of rewards or threats of punishment.

Indeed, one can phrase the question as a paradox. Implicit in the attributional analysis of these findings is the presumed use of a "discounting" principle (cf. Kelley 1973)—the notion that the imposition of salient extrinsic constraints on one's actions typically implies that the action in question is one that would not be performed in the absence of such constraints. In abstract terms, the principle can be shown to govern the inferences adult subjects and older children will make when asked to infer the motivational state of another person undertaking an activity either in the face of or the absence of external constraints; they will infer that the other is less intrinsically motivated if the activity is undertaken in order to obtain a reward than if the activity is undertaken seemingly for its own sake. Several studies, however, suggest that young children typically do not employ such an inferential principle in drawing conclusions about the motives of others (Karniol and Ross 1976; Shultz, Butkowsky, Pearce, and Shanfield 1975; M. C. Smith 1975); in fact, they may sometimes employ an opposite, "additive" principle.

In part, the young child's lack of sophistication in the use of attributional principles in these person-perception tasks may stem from methodological difficulties inherent in the use of hypothetical and verbal materials. Children confronted with identical social situations presented in a more concrete and vivid fashion will typically respond in a more sophisticated fashion (e.g., Chandler, Greenspan and Barenboim 1973; Shultz and Butkowsky 1977). More importantly, however, I suspect that these studies and the traditional self-perception analysis have put the cart before the horse. Thus, it is from their own experiences with social control and constraint that children eventually develop inferential principles that permit them to make systematic inferences about the motives of others, rather than the reverse. Hence, as in other work on social cognition (cf. Hoffman 1976; Piaget 1932; Wells and Shultz 1978), we might expect children to behave in a more adult fashion when they are themselves involved in a concrete situation than when they are asked to take the role of another and make inferences about the motives or intentions of that other person.

How, then, might children come to understand the social meaning of extrinsic constraints? Let me sketch out a speculative analysis of this process (cf. Lepper and Greene 1978c). Soon after children acquire the capacity to "get into mischief," they become the target of an increasing variety of constraints placed on their actions by adult socializing agents (cf. Minton, Kagan, and Levine 1971). To prevent children from injuring themselves or others or doing damage to property, parents quickly begin to apply extrinsic contingencies designed to control and modify children's behavior. The child is, at various times, begged, threatened, cajoled, or bribed to induce compliance with adult demands (Carlsmith, Lepper, and Landauer 1974). As particular interaction patterns are repeated, the child begins to abstract not only the common elements that define "approved" versus "disapproved" behavior patterns, but also the elements that signal social-control attempts. Presumably, at first, children's understanding of social-control techniques will vary in sophistication as a function of their familiarity with particular social situations and the ease with which new situations can be assimilated to more familiar social schemas. Only as the child's inventory of social experiences is expanded will he or she begin to employ more abstract distinctions (e.g., between work and play or bribes and bonuses) that adults may use to describe experiences of social constraint.

That children's social reasoning abilities and the meaning they extract from social interactions may develop as successively more abstract generalizations from initially concrete social schemas seems intuitively reasonable. It is also consistent with recent theoretical formulations concerning the representation of social knowledge (Abelson 1976, 1978; Schank and Abelson 1977) in terms of "scripts"—that is, organized and coherent event sequences anticipated in the presence of particular situational cues, reflecting an individual's expectations concerning apparent regularities in his or her social environment. In this model (Lepper and Greene 1978c), relatively hypothetical or categorical scripts (e.g., "When someone offers me an extrinsic reward for doing something, the chances are that that something is boring or unpleasant.") are derived by abstraction of common features from sets of relatively more concrete "episodic" scripts (e.g., "When mom tells me I can't have my dessert until I clean my plate, what's left on my plate is usually yuckky."). Assimilation of novel situations to familiar social scripts on the basis of a small number of salient cues, moreover, has been shown to have profound effects on subjects' interpretations of and reactions to social influence attempts (Abelson 1976; Carlsmith et al. 1974; Langer 1978; Langer and Abelson 1972).

This line of reasoning is consistent, as well, with our preliminary attempts to interview preschool children about their perceptions of social constraints. When asked to make inferences about their own behavior or that of others in a variety of social situations, these children did not appear to judge the motivational state of others (or, usually, themselves) in terms of any generalized "discounting" principle; there were, however, some familiar situations in which children's social inferences appeared to follow such an inferential script. To examine one of the more pervasive of these situations, 16 preschoolers were asked to imagine that Johnny's mother had brought home two new foods for dinner. When these subjects were told that Johnny's mother had said that he had to eat his "hule" in order to have his "hupe," or vice versa, every subject appeared to understand the social message implied by the imposition of this contingency. All but four confidently asserted that Johnny would prefer the second food; the remaining four each gave reasons for the opposite choice that nevertheless indicated an understanding of the underlying script. One child, for example, indicated that Johnny would prefer the first food because the second food "probably has refined sugar in it, and that's real bad for you." Control subjects told simply that Johnny's mother had given Johnny first one and then the other food showed no systematic preferences.

These results encouraged us to examine children's reactions to the imposition of a more general means—end script on their own actions, and their inferences about the attitudes of others placed in a similar setting (Lepper, Sagotsky, Dafoe, and Greene 1980). In the self-perception version of this study, then, children were presented with two initially, and equally, attractive activities. Subjects in the means-end condition were asked if they would like to play with the "end" and, when they had assented, were told that they could win a chance to do so only by first playing with the "means." Control subjects were simply shown the two activities and asked to engage in one of the activities first and the other second, but without the imposition of any contingency between the two. Subsequently, we obtained independent, unobtrusive measures of children's intrinsic interest in each of these activities in their classrooms in the absence of further constraints. The results are presented in Figure 7, which illustrates that the imposition of this nominal

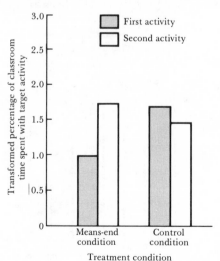

FIGURE 7   Mean intrinsic interest in the two experimental activities, during postexperimental classroom observations, by condition.

Data from M. R. Lepper, G. Sagotsky, J. L. Dafoe, and D. Greene, "Consequences of Superfluous Social Constraints: Effects on Young Children's Social Inferences and Subsequent Intrinsic Interest," *Journal of Personality and Social Psychology* 42 (1982): 51–65. Reprinted by permission of the author.

contingency led to decreased interest in the activity presented as a means of obtaining a chance to play with the other activity.

In the corresponding social-perception version of this study, different children were presented with narrated slide show presentations of versions of the two conditions of the preceding study and were asked to make predictions concerning how much the child in the slide show would subsequently like each of the two activities. The results on children's inferences about the protagonist's attitudes towards the two activities, as a function of their presentation in either a means-end or first-second relationship, are illustrated in Figure 8. These findings, clearly, parallel those reported in Figure 7, and suggest that children in this situation are employing some principle that reflects at least a rudimentary understanding of the social meaning of the imposition of a contingency on one's choices. Despite their systematic responses to specific questions about the protagonist's preferences, however, very few subjects seemed able to give a cogent explanation of their answers. Their inferences, in short, appeared to reflect an intuitive understanding of the social meaning of this situation, rather than some systematic analysis of social-control processes.

These findings, then, give us reason to suspect that children may have some knowledge, even at a relatively early age, of the implicit message of constraint that the imposition of a contingency may convey. However, it seems likely that there may be important developmental changes in children's responses to social-control attempts resulting from an increased ability to distinguish among the social contexts in which rewards may be employed. I have already noted the data suggesting that young children seem not to be responsive to information that rewards may convey concern-

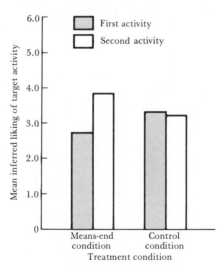

FIGURE 8 Mean inferred liking by the protagonist of the two experimental activities, by condition.

Data from M. R. Lepper, G. Sagotsky, J. L. Dafoe, and D. Greene, "Consequences of Superfluous Social Constraints: Effects on Young Children's Social Inferences and Subsequent Intrinsic Interest," *Journal of Personality and Social Psychology* 42 (1982):51–65. Reprinted by permission of the author.

ing their competence or incompetence at an activity, relative to other children (Boggiano and Ruble 1979). Other changes in our perception of the appropriateness of rewards as a function of the context in which they are offered may also vary with age. As one example, adults frequently appear to employ a "lesser-of-several-evils" principle in cases in which one is committed by external forces to some general goal, but is permitted a choice among several means for achieving that common end. If, under such circumstances, we believe ourselves to have had the luxury of choosing the most attractive, or least noxious, means of attaining that goal, we are, I suspect, less likely to show decreases in subsequent interest in that activity. With children, precisely the opposite effect seems to occur. In one study (Greene et al. 1976), children choosing the activities for which they were to receive rewards showed greater decreases in later interest than those for whom the activities were simply assigned. Perhaps more generally, one might expect our reactions to external social controls to come to depend, with increased experience and cognitive maturity, in a much more differentiated fashion on our perceptions of the relevant social norms, potential alternatives, or presumed motives of the agent of control in particular settings (cf. Lepper and Gilovich in press).

The Effects of Superfluous Social Controls: Implications and Speculations

I have now summarized two basic lines of research involving the effects of threats of punishment on the subsequent internalization of adult prohibitions and the effects of extrinsic rewards on subsequent intrinsic interest. In this final section, I wish to bring together these two trains of thought, to consider some of the salient similarities and differences between these two paradigms, and to speculate a bit on the relationship of this research program to traditional issues in the study of socialization processes.

Parallels and Contrasts: The Minimum-Sufficiency Principle

Let me begin with a naive statement of the common ground between these two literatures—what we might call the *minimal-sufficiency principle* of social control (cf. Lepper in press). Presumably, by now, the parallels are clear. In both cases, the use of seemingly less powerful techniques of social control to induce initial compliance with a request has proved more effective, under certain conditions, in producing subsequent behavior in accord with the presumed intent of the initial attempt at social control, in the later absence of further controls and the agent who administered them. Conversely, the use of unnecessarily powerful, functionally superfluous social-control procedures in both cases appears to decrease later internal controls when external constraints are subsequently minimized. In the forbidden-toy paradigm, unnecessarily powerful threats of punishment are less likely to produce subsequent adherence to the previous prohibition, or related but more implicit prohibitions, in the later absence of further explicit threats. In the overjustification paradigm, unnecessarily powerful extrinsic rewards are less likely to produce subsequent engagement in the previously rewarded activity in the later absence of further explicit rewards. Both sorts of effects are amenable to similar theoretical interpretations; both appear to respond in similar fashion to comparable manipulations involving attentional focus, timing of justification, and so forth.

Obviously, however, there are some contrasts between these two research programs. Perhaps the most salient, as should be apparent from the preceding reviews, involves the relative complexity of the processes that appear to define the limiting conditions under which each of these phenomena will occur. An analysis of the reasons underlying the greater complexity involved in the study of the effects of extrinsic rewards on subsequent intrinsic interest may prove informative and deserves further attention.

There are two obvious sources of potential divergence between the two paradigms. The first involves the historically significant theoretical distinction between social-influence attempts employed to induce the child to engage in explicitly counterattitudinal, and presumably dissonance-arousing, behavior, as in the forbidden-toy situation, and those employed to produce behavior that is not overtly inconsistent with one's previous attitudes, as in the overjustification case. The second involves two more procedural sorts of distinctions between these two paradigms: differences in the nature of the social-control technique employed—that is, promise of reward versus threat of punishment—and differences in the behavior that is the target of control—that is, producing active engagement in some activity versus inhibiting a tendency to engage in some activity.

Taking into account both sets of factors leads to a threefold classification of the circumstances in which social-control processes may take place: involving (1) the use of either promise of reward or threat of punishment; (2) either inducing an overt action or inhibiting that action; and (3) a target action that is initially either "attractive" or "unattractive" to the subject. In this schematic categorization, the two paradigms considered here represent only two of eight possible sets of conditions to which a minimal sufficiency principle might be applied.[2]

Space limitations preclude extended consideration of this classification scheme, but two salient features of this categorization deserve mention. On the one hand, this analysis provides one way of looking at the contexts in which rewards and punishments may be employed that illustrates clearly the limitations of the current literature. Although there is no necessary reason for the association, for example, some cells in this table seem quite unlikely in everyday life. We are much more likely, for instance, to threaten children with punishment than to offer them rewards to induce them to refrain from engaging in attractive, but socially undesirable, activities. Other combinations, including the overjustification case (i.e., promising a child a reward to induce engagement in an activity he or she would undertake anyway), seem to represent cases that are more likely to be created unintentionally than intentionally (Lepper and Dafoe 1979; Lepper and Greene 1978a). Still other cases that seem more highly representative of the situations in which promises of rewards and threats of punishment are commonly used—e.g., to induce children to engage in activities of little initial interest or activities that are inherently aversive—have received virtually no experimental attention. A very specialized version of this case, involving the effects of payments offered for espousing a counterattitudinal position on subsequent attitudes, has received extensive study (e.g., Calder, Ross, and Insko 1973; Collins and

Hoyt 1972; Zanna and Cooper 1976). But, the effects of variations in the coerciveness of contingencies for inducing children to comply with adult requests to perform particular tasks (Landauer, Carlsmith, and Lepper 1970) on their later compliance with related requests when incentive conditions are constant has not been studied. Looking at the literature in this way may serve to clarify some of the directions in which further research might be profitably pursued in contexts that have clearer implications for the socialization process (cf. Lepper in press).

A second heuristic function of this analysis is that it provides a tool for examining the features of our two basic paradigms that may contribute to their differential conceptual complexity. In this sense, each of the dimensions of this classification suggests distinctions that may determine the range of additional factors—beyond perceptions of instrumentality and constraint common to all cases—that may influence subsequent behavior. Thus, issues concerning the possible effects of constraint on the quality of performance, the potential acquisition of additional skills or knowledge through increased task engagement, or the role of perceived competence seem particularly relevant when the target behavior in question involves active engagement in an activity. However, these same factors seem largely irrelevant to social-control attempts that involve the inhibition of activity. In the forbidden-toy paradigm, for instance, once compliance has been obtained, it is hard to imagine what measures of quality of performance of skill acquisition might look like. Indeed, the role of increased task engagement, even within those cells where active compliance is sought, should vary considerably as a function of the nature of the activity involved—whether the task is of high initial interest, is of potential intrinsic interest once certain proficiency levels have been attained, or is inherently dull and boring. Perhaps less obviously, even within otherwise comparable conditions, there seem to be some interesting asymetries inherent in the ways in which we typically use rewards and punishments, although there is, again, no necessary reason why this should be the case. Threats of punishment seem much less frequently tied to performance criteria than promises of reward; hence, variations in perceived competence may be relatively unimportant in the former case, but potentially critical in the latter. Attention to differences of this sort, and more generally to the phenomenologically distinct situations created by our typical uses of rewards and punishments (Lewin 1935), may help clarify the relative complexity of different cases within this larger matrix of possibilities.[3]

Implications for the Socialization Process

Much research, then, is still needed to examine the more general applicability of the minimal sufficiency principle and its relevance to the socialization process. Nonetheless, I wish to speculate for a moment on the possible relevance of this analysis to broader questions concerning the conditions that promote internalization of adult values that have been a source of continuing interest to students of the socialization process.

Is there any evidence within the socialization literature to suggest that seemingly less powerful techniques of social control may prove ultimately more effective in promoting subsequent internalization of the behaviors that were the target of these controls? Let us consider, first, the area in developmental psychology in which the study of internalization has its longest legacy—the study of the development of moral values and behavior. For many years, investigators in this area have been interested in the subsequent effects of variations in the child-rearing techniques that parents use at home to teach moral values and the inhibition of "immoral" behaviors on children's later behavior in other settings in which they are no longer under their parents' surveillance or direct control. The results of this search for the antecedents of subsequent internalized controls, as illustrated most recently in the elegant work of Hoffman and his colleagues (Hoffman 1970, 1975; Hoffman and Saltzstein 1967; cf. also Sears, Maccoby, and Levin 1957) suggest an inverse relationship between salience of external control and later internalization that parallels our earlier speculations.

Distinguishing between three types of disciplinary techniques that parents might employ—power assertion, love withdrawal, and induction—Hoffman finds that those techniques one would expect to be most likely to lead the child to view compliance with the parents' requests at home as extrinsically motivated are the least effective in producing subsequent internalization of parental values. Parents' use of overt power-assertive techniques, involving the heavy-handed use of physical punishment, withdrawal of tangible rewards and privileges, and so on, correlates negatively with subsequent moral behavior in situations outside the home, whereas the use of induction and reasoning, the least clearly coercive of Hoffman's categories, shows consistent positive correlations with positive internalization of moral standards and behavior.

Other related findings in different contexts suggest a similar set of conclusions. For example, Baumrind's informative studies (e.g., 1971, 1973) on patterns of child-rearing practices and their association with indices of social responsibility and social competence outside the home provide a similar picture. In these studies, children of authoritarian parents who favor the use of highly "forceful" and "punitive" measures to elicit compliance from the child at home appear less well socialized outside of the home on a variety of measures than children of authoritative parents who were, in turn, more likely to use less power-oriented means of control and more reasoning with their children. Findings on the effects of power-oriented techniques of punishment for aggression in the home on later aggressive behavior in other settings provide analogous results (cf. Dienstbier, Hillman, Lehnhoff, Hillman, and Valkenaar 1975).

In addition to these large-scale correlational projects, other experimental research has shown that the overt labeling of a child's compliance with an adult request as either intrinsically or extrinsically motivated may have substantial effects on the child's later behavior in settings in which he or she is no longer under the direct control of the person administering the initial request (Dienstbier et al. 1975; Grusec in press; Grusec, Kuczynski, Rushton, and Simutis 1978; Miller, Brickman, and Bolen 1975). Inducing the child to think of his or her behavior—whether resistance to temptation (Dienstbier et al. 1975), altruism (Grusec in press; Grusec et al. 1978), or cleaning up the schoolyard (Miller et al. 1975)—in internal, rather than external terms, made it more likely that the child would show subsequent behavior in accord with the intent of the initial request in the later absence of further explicit controls.

Obviously, there are many factors that contribute to the differential effectiveness of various parental practices, and the correlational findings reported in this area are overdetermined (Dienstbier et al. 1975; Hoffman 1970, 1975). The convergence of results obtained in these studies, the labeling literature, and the research I have reviewed, however, suggests that the minimal sufficiency principle may be implicated in the socialization process (cf. Lepper in press). To close this chapter, let us consider two more general implications of this analysis.

Successful Versus Unsuccessful Social-Control Attempts

The first point to be made about the minimal sufficiency principle is that it suggests an active positive effect of the use of social-control techniques that are successful at producing compliance—when compliance would not otherwise be obtained—if those techniques are not so overly salient or patently coercive as to lead the child to view his or her behavior entirely as a response to those external pressures (e.g., Lepper 1973). Hence, this proposition is not an argument for "permissiveness" or a lack of social controls by parents and is not inconsistent with data indicating that children of parents favoring a completely permissive approach to child-rearing fare less well than those reared by authoritative parents employing firm, but not extreme, control techniques (Baumrind 1971, 1973).

At the same time, this analysis also suggests that a complementary negative effect on later internalization or intrinsic motivation should be the result of social-control attempts that are unsuccessful (i.e., that fail to produce initial compliance). Thus, the child who feels under external pressure to behave in a particular way but resists that pressure would be predicted to view his or her failure to comply in internal terms, and should be more likely to do so the greater the pressure applied, unsuccessfully, to induce initial compliance. The child in the forbidden-toy situation, for example, who yields to temptation despite a threat of punishment for transgression should be likely to find the previously forbidden activity more attractive and should be less likely to resist temptation in future situations than a child never exposed to a request not to engage in the activity. The more powerful the threat of punishment the child has chosen to disregard in this setting, the greater this effect should be (Lepper in press; Mills 1958).

This formulation, therefore, implies that parents and other socializing agents must frequently walk a fine line. The difference between a barely sufficient, successful attempt at social control and a barely insufficient and unsuccessful attempt is, in terms of the parent's behavior, a small one. The difference between these two cases in terms of their subsequent effects on the child's behavior, by contrast, is theoretically enormous. Whereas the former case may result in enhanced internalization and responsiveness to further requests, the latter case may produce decreased internalization and increased resistance to further social-influence attempts. To the extent that the behavior of permissive parents may involve as much the use of insufficiently powerful and ineffective social-control techniques as a complete absence of attempts at control, the potentially detrimental effects of such practices may be increased.

Salience Versus Subtlety of Social-Control Attempts

Second, within the domain of successful social-control procedures, sufficient to elicit initial compliance from the child, an attributional account suggests that there may be important differences in the general salience and coerciveness of different sorts of social-control techniques. These differences, and the consequent differences in the likelihood that particular techniques will produce perceptions of one's actions as extrinsically motivated, ought then to determine the effects of these procedures on subsequent internalization and later behavior in unconstrained settings.

Most of the literature I have discussed, for example, deals with the subsequent effects of tangible rewards and threats of punishment presented in an explicit contingent, and typically contractual, fashion. In this research, these procedures were chosen because they represent the case in which children are most likely to view their behavior as extrinsically governed. Both in other traditions of laboratory research and in everyday life, however, we are often exposed to social-influence techniques that may be equally effective in modifying our behavior, but do not produce the same perceptions of external constraint. Consider, for example, the large literatures documenting the effectiveness of various modeling techniques (Bandura 1971, 1977) or the use of contingent social reinforcement or approval (Kazdin 1975) as means of producing dramatic changes in children's behavior. My suspicion is that, despite their demonstrable effectiveness in producing functional control over behavior, both of these techniques would be less likely to lead children to view their behavior as extrinsically constrained than the use of tangible rewards and punishments. I believe that we learn early on to think about immediate palpable rewards and punishments as reasons for our actions (e.g., "I did it for the money," or "I did it to avoid a spanking."), but that we are less likely to view our actions in comparable instrumental terms when the stimulus to our actions is some prior model or even diffuse social approval. Control in the former case seems to demand a response; in the latter case, the control technique seems more suggestive than demanding. If this were so, one might predict that less phenomenologically coercive techniques of this sort would be less likely to produce subsequent negative effects and more likely to produce positive effects on subsequent behavior in the later absence of further constraint (cf. Grusec in press; Lepper, Sagotsky, and Mailer 1975; Rosenhan 1969).

Similar considerations may also apply in the case of more delayed and diffuse, as opposed to immediate and highly palpable, goals or incentives. Often, we encourage children to engage in particular activities because they will be ultimately instrumental to long-term goals that may be many years away. The power of such distant goals to provoke continuing perceptions of one's actions as instrumentally directed is, I suspect, much less than the power of more immediate goals to do so. There may be a world of difference between doing your schoolwork in order to win the $5.00 Dad pays for each "A" on your report card and doing the same work because success will eventually enable you to go to the college or pursue the career of your choice.

Finally, there may be similar elements involved in the difference between self-imposed versus externally imposed standards and contingency systems. In recent years, we have seen the growth of a large literature investigating the use of techniques for training children to impose contingencies on their own actions (Bandura 1976; Mahoney 1974, 1977)—a trend that seems based in part on the assumption that changes in behavior produced through techniques that involve the subject as an active participant in the social-control process will be more likely to produce generalization of those changes in behavior to other settings in which salient extrinsic constraints are absent. Although good comparative evidence is lacking, the existing data in support of this argument (e.g., Brownell et al. 1977; Drabman, Spitalnik, and O'Leary 1973; Turkewitz, O'Leary, and Ironsmith 1975; Weiner and Dubanoski 1975) can be viewed in attributional terms, as a function of the relative likelihood of perceptions of external constraint generated by these two techniques (cf. Lepper, Sagosky, and Greene in preparation). For most of these speculations, there is no compelling comparative evidence at the moment; my goal in presenting them is to raise issues that deserve further study.

In closing, I should note that these ideas are not entirely without precedent. Nearly 300 years ago, John Locke proposed a similar thesis in his book of advice to parents and teachers (Locke 1693):

> *Rewards*, I grant, and *Punishments* must be proposed to Children if we intend to work upon them. The Mistake, I imagine, is that those that are generally made use of, are *ill chosen*. The Pains and Pleasures of the Body are, I think, of ill consequence, when made the Rewards and Punishments, whereby Men would prevail on their Children: For as I said before, they serve but to increase and strengthen those Inclinations which 'tis our business to subdue and master. [p. 55].

The principal alternatives Locke proposed to the use of immediate tangible rewards and punishments involved teaching the child to be responsive to the model and social approval of the parent and to view his or her actions in terms of long-term goals that extend beyond particular current situations. Perhaps, at this point, it is time to investigate the utility of his admonitions experimentally.

Preparation of this chapter was supported, in part, by Research Grant HD-MH-09814 from the National Institute of Child Health and Human Development. The report was written during the author's term as a Fellow at the Center for Advanced Study in the Behavioral Sciences, Stanford, California, and financial support for this fellowship from National Science Foundation Grant BNS 78-24671 and the Spencer Foundation is gratefully acknowledged. John Condry and Thomas Gilovich also deserve thanks for their helpful comments on an earlier draft of this chapter.

NOTES

1. For purposes of presentation, these data are collapsed across a second factor—a procedure designed to minimize, for some subjects, initial derogation of the specific forbidden activity—because this variation had no effect on subsequent resistance to temptation (cf. Lepper 1973 for further details).

2. I am indebted to Merrill Carlsmith, Gregory Northcraft, and Richard Nisbett for suggesting, independently, the utility of considering various parts of this classification scheme systematically. I should also note that even this categorization is itself an oversimplification. In any more comprehensive analysis, for example, one would probably wish to distinguish—within the cells in which active task engagement is the goal—between the use of task-contingent versus performance-contingent incentives.
3. Thus, it is worth noting that there may be other important differences between the use of rewards and punishments that are not included in the foregoing analysis. Clearly, in socialization contexts, the two procedures provide quite different social models to the child, and may thereby have different effects on specific classes of behaviors such as interpersonal aggression. It may also be the case, although the scaling problems are considerable, that punishment will generally produce more intense emotional responses and feelings of coercion than equivalently powerful reward procedures.

REFERENCES

ABELSON, R.P. Script processing in attitude formation and decision-making. In J. S. Carroll and J. W. Payne (Eds.), *Cognition and social behavior.* Hillsdale, N.J.: Lawrence Erlbaum Associates, 1976.

ABELSON, R. P. *Scripts.* Unpublished manuscript, Yale University, 1978.

AMABILE, T. M. Effects of external evaluation on artistic creativity. *Journal of Personality and Social Psychology,* 1979, *37,* 221–233.

AMABILE, T. M., DEJONG, W., AND LEPPER, M. R. Effects of externally-imposed deadlines on subsequent intrinsic motivation. *Journal of Personality and Social Psychology,* 1976, *34,* 92–98.

ANDERSON, R., MANOOGIAN, S. T., AND REZNICK, J. S. The undermining and enhancing of intrinsic motivation in preschool children. *Journal of Personality and Social Psychology,* 1976, *34,* 915–922.

ARONSON, E. The theory of cognitive dissonance: A current perspective. In L. Berkowitz (Ed.), *Advances in experimental social psychology* (Vol. 4). New York: Academic Press, 1969.

ARONSON, E., AND CARLSMITH, J. M. The effect of the severity of threat on the devaluation of forbidden behavior. *Journal of Abnormal and Social Psychology,* 1963, *66,* 584–588.

BANDURA, A. Vicarious and self-reinforcement processes. In R. Glaser (Ed.), *The nature of reinforcement.* New York: Academic Press, 1971.

BANDURA, A. Self-reinforcement: Theoretical and methodological considerations. *Behaviorism,* 1976, *4,* 135–155.

BANDURA, A. *Social learning theory.* Englewood Cliffs, N.J.: Prentice-Hall, 1977.

BAR-TAL, D. Attributional analysis of achievement related behavior. *Review of Educational Research,* 1978, *48,* 259–271.

BAUMRIND, D. Current patterns of parental authority. *Developmental Psychology Monographs,* 1971, *4*(Whole No. 1).

BAUMRIND, D. The development of instrumental competence through socialization. In A. Pick (Ed.), *Minnesota symposium on child psychology* (Vol. 7). Minneapolis: University of Minnesota Press, 1973.

BEM, D. J. Self-perception: An alternative interpretation of cognitive dissonance phenomena. *Psychological Review,* 1967, *74,* 183–200.

BEM, D. J. Self-perception theory. In L. Berkowitz (Ed.), *Advances in experimental social psychology* (Vol. 6). New York: Academic Press, 1972.

BLACKWELL, L. *Student choice in curriculum, feelings of control and causality, and academic motivation and performance.* Unpublished doctoral dissertation, Stanford University, 1974.

BLANCK, P. D., REIS, H. T., AND JACKSON, L. *The effects of verbal reinforcement on intrinsic motivation.* Unpublished manuscript, University of Rochester, 1979.

BOGGIANO, A. K., AND RUBLE, D. N. Perception of competence and overjustification effect: A developmental study. *Journal of Personality and Social Psychology,* 1979, *37,* 1462–1468.

BROWNELL, K., COLLETTI, G., ERNSER-HERSHFIELD, R., HERSHFIELD, S. M., AND WILSON, G. T. Self-control in school children: Stringency and leniency in self-determined and externally-imposed performance standards. *Behavior Therapy,* 1977, *8,* 442–455.

CALDER, B. J., ROSS, M., AND INSKO, C. A. Attitude change and attitude attribution: Effects of incentive, choice, and consequences. *Journal of Personality and Social Psychology,* 1973, *25,* 84–89.

CALDER, B. J., AND STAW, B. M. Self-perception of intrinsic and extrinsic motivation. *Journal of Personality and Social Psychology*, 1975, *31*, 599–605.

CARLSMITH, J. M., EBBESEN, E. B., LEPPER, M. R., ZANNA, M. P., JONCAS, A. J., AND ABELSON, R. P. Dissonance reduction following forced attention to the dissonance. *Proceedings of the 77th Annual Convention of the American Psychological Association*, 1969, *4*, 321–322.

CARLSMITH, J. M., LEPPER, M. R., AND LANDAUER, T. K. Children's obedience to adult requests: Interactive effects of anxiety arousal and apparent punitiveness of the adult. *Journal of Personality and Social Psychology*, 1974, *30*, 822–828.

CHANDLER, M. J., GREENSPAN, S., AND BARENBOIM, C. Judgments of intentionality in response to videotaped and verbally presented moral dilemmas: The medium is the message. *Child Development*, 1973, *44*, 315–320.

COLLINS, B. E., AND HOYT, M. F. Personal responsibility-for-consequences: An integration and extension of the "forced compliance" literature. *Journal of Experimental Social Psychology*, 1972, *8*, 558–593.

COLVIN, R. H. Imposed extrinsic reward in an elementary school setting: Effects on free-operant rates and choices. (Doctoral dissertation, Southern Illinois University, 1971.) *Dissertation Abstracts International*, 1972, *32*, 5034–A.

CONDRY, J. C. Enemies of exploration: Self-initiated versus other-initiated learning. *Journal of Personality and Social Psychology*, 1977, *35*, 459–477.

CONDRY, J., AND CHAMBERS, J. C. Intrinsic motivation and the process of learning. In M. R. Lepper and D. Greene (Eds.), *The hidden costs of reward*. Hillsdale, N.J.: Lawerence Erlbaum Associates, 1978.

DAVIDSON, P., AND BUCHER, B. Intrinsic interest and extrinsic reward: The effects of a continuing token program on continuing nonconstrained preference. *Behavior Therapy*, 1978, *9*, 222–234.

DECI, E. L. Effects of externally mediated rewards on intrinsic motivation. *Journal of Personality and Social Psychology*, 1971, *18*, 105–115.

DECI, E. L. The effects of contingent and non-contingent rewards and controls on intrinsic motivation. *Organizational Behavior and Human Performance*, 1972, *8*, 217–229. (a)

DECI, E. L. Intrinsic motivation, extrinsic reinforcement, and inequity. *Journal of Personality and Social Psychology*, 1972, *22*, 113–120. (b)

DECI, E. L. *Intrinsic motivation*. New York: Plenum, 1975.

DIENSTBIER, R. A., HILLMAN, D., LEHNHOFF, J., HILLMAN, J., AND VALKENAAR, M. C. An emotion-attribution approach to moral behavior: Interfacing cognitive and avoidance theories of moral development. *Psychological Review*, 1975, *82*, 299–315.

DOLLINGER, S. J., AND THELEN, M. H. Overjustification and children's intrinsic motivation: Comparative effects of four rewards. *Journal of Personality and Social Psychology*, 1978, *36*, 1259–1269.

DRABMAN, R. S., SPITALNIK, R., AND O'LEARY, K. D. Teaching self-control to disruptive children. *Journal of Abnormal Psychology*, 1973, *82*, 10–16.

EASTERBROOK, J. A. The effect of emotion on cue utilization and organization of behavior. *Psychological Review*, 1959, *66*, 183–201.

ENZLE, M. E., AND ROSS, J. M. Increasing and decreasing intrinsic interest with contingent rewards: A test of cognitive evaluation theory. *Journal of Experimental Social Psychology*, 1978, *14*, 588–597.

ESTES, W. K. Reinforcement in human behavior. *American Scientist*, 1972, *60*, 723–729.

FARR, J. L. Task characteristics, reward contingency, and intrinsic motivation. *Organizational Behavior and Human Performance*, 1976, *16*, 294–307.

FAZIO, R. H., ZANNA, M. P., AND COOPER, J. Dissonance vs. self-perception: An integrative view of each theory's proper domain of application. *Journal of Experimental Social Psychology*, 1977, *5*, 464–479.

FEINGOLD, B. D., AND MAHONEY, M. J. Reinforcement effects on intrinsic interest: Undermining the overjustification hypothesis. *Behavior Theory*, 1975, *6*, 367–377.

FESTINGER, L. *A theory of cognitive dissonance*. Stanford, Calif.: Stanford University Press, 1957.

FREEDMAN, J. L. Long-term behavioral effects of cognitive dissonance. *Journal of Experimental Social Psychology*, 1965, *1*, 145–155.

FREEDMAN, J. L., AND FRASER, S. C. Compliance without pressure: The foot-in-the-door technique. *Journal of Personality and Social Psychology*, 1966, *4*, 195–202.

GARBARINO, J. The impact of anticipated rewards on cross-age tutoring. *Journal of Personality and Social Psychology*, 1975, *32*, 421–428.

GREENE, D., AND LEPPER, M. R. Effects of extrinsic rewards on children's subsequent intrinsic interest. *Child Development*, 1974, *45*, 1141–1145.

GREENE, D., STERNBERG, B., AND LEPPER, M. R. Overjustification in a token economy. *Journal of Personality and Social Psychology,* 1976, *34,* 1219–1234.

GREENWALD, A. G. On the inconclusiveness of "crucial" cognitive tests of dissonance versus self-perception theories. *Journal of Experimental Social Psychology,* 1975, *11,* 490–499.

GRUSEC, J. E. Training altruistic dispositions: A cognitive analysis. To appear in T. E. Higgins, D. N. Ruble, and W. W. Hartup (Eds.). *Social cognition and social behavior: A developmental perspective.* San Francisco: Jossey-Bass, in press.

GRUSEC, J. E., KUCZYNSKI, L., RUSHTON, J. P., AND SIMUTIS, Z. M. Modeling, direct instruction, and attributions: Effects on altruism. *Developmental Psychology,* 1978, *14,* 51–57.

HAMNER, W. C., AND FOSTER, L. W. Are intrinsic and extrinsic rewards additive: A test of Deci's cognitive evaluation theory of task motivation. *Organizational Behavior and Human Performance,* 1975, *14,* 398–415.

HARACKIEWICZ, J. M. The effects of reward contingency and performance feedback on intrinsic motivation. *Journal of Personality and Social Psychology,* 1979, *37,* 1352–1361.

HARTER, S. Effectance motivation reconsidered: Toward a developmental model. *Human Development,* 1978, *21,* 34–64. (a)

HARTER, S. Pleasure derived from challenge and the effects of receiving grades on children's difficulty level choices. *Child Development,* 1978, *49,* 788–799. (b)

HOFFMAN, M. L. Moral development. In P. Mussen (Ed.), *Carmichael's handbook of child psychology* (Vol. 2). New York: Wiley, 1970.

HOFFMAN, M. L. Moral internalization, parental power, and the nature of parent-child interaction. *Developmental Psychology,* 1975, *11,* 228–239.

HOFFMAN, M. L. Empathy, role-taking, guilt, and the development of altruistic motives. In T. Lickona (Ed.), *Moral development and behavior.* New York: Holt, Rinehart, and Winston, 1976.

HOFFMAN, M. L., AND SALTZSTEIN, H. D. Parent discipline and the child's moral development. *Journal of Personality and Social Psychology,* 1967, *5,* 45–57.

HOLT, J. *How children fail.* New York: Dell, 1964.

HOVLAND, C. I., JANIS, I. L., AND KELLEY, H. H. *Communication and persuasion.* New Haven: Yale University Press, 1953.

JOHNSON, E. J., GREENE, D., AND CARROLL, J. S. *Overjustification and reasons: A test of the means-end analysis.* Unpublished manuscript, Carnegie-Mellon University, 1979.

KARNIOL, R., AND ROSS, M. The development of causal attributions in social perception. *Journal of Personality and Social Psychology,* 1976, *34,* 455–464.

KARNIOL, R., AND ROSS, M. The effect of performance-relevant and performance-irrelevant rewards on children's intrinsic motivation. *Child Development,* 1977, *48,* 482–487.

KAZDIN, A. E. *Behavior modification in applied settings.* Homewood, Ill.: Dorsey Press, 1975.

KAZDIN, A. E., AND BOOTZIN, R. R. The token economy: An evaluative review. *Journal of Applied Behavior Analysis,* 1972, *5,* 343–372.

KELLEY, H. H. Attribution theory in social psychology. In D. Levine (Ed.), *Nebraska symposium on motivation* (Vol. 15). Lincoln: University of Nebraska Press, 1967.

KELLEY, H. H. The processes of causal attribution. *American Psychologist,* 1973, *28,* 107–128.

KELMAN, H. C. Compliance, identification, and internalization: Three processes of opinion change. *Journal of Conflict Resolution,* 1958, *2,* 51–60.

KELMAN, H. C. Processes of attitude change. *Public Opinion Quarterly,* 1961, *25,* 57–78.

KRUGLANSKI, A. W. Endogenous attribution and intrinsic motivation. In M. R. Lepper and D. Greene (Eds.), *The hidden costs of reward.* Hillsdale, N.J.: Lawrence Erlbaum Associates, 1978.

KRUGLANSKI, A. W., ALON, S., AND LEWIS, T. Retrospective misattribution and task enjoyment. *Journal of Experimental Social Psychology,* 1972, *8,* 493–501.

KRUGLANSKI, A. W., FRIEDMAN, I., AND ZEEVI, G. The effects of extrinsic incentives on some qualitative aspects of task performance. *Journal of Personality,* 1971, *39,* 606–617.

KRUGLANSKI, A. W., STEIN, C., AND RITER, A. Contingencies of exogenous reward and task performance: On the "minimax" principle in instrumental behavior. *Journal of Applied Social Psychology,* 1977, *7,* 141–148.

LANDAUER, T. K., CARLSMITH, J. M., AND LEPPER, M. R. Experimental analysis of the factors determining obedience of four-year-old children to adult females. *Child Development,* 1970, *41,* 601–611.

LANGER, E. J. Rethinking the role of thought in social interaction. In J. H. Harvey, W. J. Ickes, and R. F. Kidd (Eds.), *New directions in attribution research* (Vol. 2). Hillsdale, N.J.: Lawrence Erlbaum Associates, 1978.

LANGER, E. J., AND ABELSON, R. P. The semantics of asking a favor: How to succeed in getting help without really dying. *Journal of Personality and Social Psychology*, 1972, *24*, 26–32.

LEPPER, M. R. Dissonance, self-perception, and honesty in children. *Journal of Personality and Social Psychology*, 1973, *25*, 65–74.

LEPPER, M. R. Social control processes, attributions of motivation, and the internalization of social values. To appear in T. E. Higgins, D. N. Ruble, and W. W. Hartup (Eds.), *Social cognition and social behavior: A developmental perspective.* San Francisco: Jossey-Bass, in press.

LEPPER, M. R., AND DAFOE, J. Incentives, constraints, and motivation in the classroom: An attributional analysis. In I. Frieze, D. Bar-Tal, and J. Carroll (Eds.), *Attribution theory: Applications to social problems.* San Francisco: Jossey-Bass, 1979.

LEPPER, M. R., AND GILOVICH, T. J. The multiple functions of reward: A social-developmental perspective. To appear in S. S. Brehm, S. M. Kassin, and F. X. Gibbons (Eds.), *Developmental social psychology.* New York: Oxford University Press, in press.

LEPPER, M. R., GILOVICH, T., AND REST, G. Detrimental effects of extrinsic rewards on immediate task performance vs. subsequent intrinsic interest. Research in progress, 1980.

LEPPER, M. R., AND GREENE, D. Turning play into work: Effects of adult surveillance and extrinsic rewards on children's intrinsic motivation. *Journal of Personality and Social Psychology*, 1975, *31*, 479–486.

LEPPER, M. R., AND GREENE, D. On understanding "overjustification": A reply to Reiss and Sushinsky. *Journal of Personality and Social Psychology*, 1976, *33*, 23–35.

LEPPER, M. R., AND GREENE, D. Divergent approaches to the study of rewards. In M. R. Lepper and D. Greene (Eds.), *The hidden costs of reward.* Hillsdale, N.J.: Lawrence Erlbaum Associates, 1978. (a)

LEPPER, M. R., AND GREENE, D. (Eds.), *The hidden costs of reward.* Hillsdale, N.J.: Lawrence Erlbaum Associates, 1978. (b)

LEPPER, M. R., AND GREENE, D. Overjustification research and beyond: Toward a means-ends analysis of intrinsic and extrinsic motivation. In M. R. Lepper and D. Greene (Eds.), *The hidden costs of reward.* Hillsdale, N.J.: Lawrence Erlbaum Associates, 1978. (c)

LEPPER, M. R., GREENE, D., AND NISBETT, R. E. Undermining children's intrinsic interest with extrinsic rewards: A test of the overjustification hypothesis. *Journal of Personality and Social Psychology*, 1973, *28*, 129–137.

LEPPER, M. R., SAGOTSKY, G., DAFOE, J., AND GREENE, D. *Consequences of superfluous social constraints: Effects on young children's social inferences and subsequent intrinsic interest.* Unpublished manuscript, Stanford University, 1980.

LEPPER, M. R., SAGOTSKY, G., AND GREENE, D. *Overjustification effects following multiple-trial reinforcement procedures: Experimental evidence concerning the assessment of intrinsic interest.* Unpublished manuscript, Stanford University, 1980.

LEPPER, M. R., SAGOTSKY, G., AND GREENE, D. *Effects of choice and self-imposed vs. externally-imposed contingencies on children's subsequent intrinsic motivation.* In preparation, 1980.

LEPPER, M. R., SAGOTSKY, G., AND MAILER, J. Generalization and persistence of effects of exposure to self-reinforcement models. *Child Development*, 1975, *46*, 618–630.

LEPPER, M. R., ZANNA, M. P., AND ABELSON, R. P. Cognitive irreversibility in a dissonance-reduction situation. *Journal of Personality and Social Psychology*, 1970, *16*, 191–198.

LEWIN, K. The psychological situations of reward and punishment. In K. Lewin (Ed.), *A dynamic theory of personality.* New York: McGraw-Hill, 1935.

LEWIN, K., LIPSITT, R., AND WHITE, R. Patterns of aggressive behavior in experimentally created "social climates." *Journal of Social Psychology*, 1939, *10*, 271–299.

LOCKE, J. *Some thoughts concerning education.* London: A. and J. Churchill, 1693.

LOVELAND, K. K., AND OLLEY, J. G. The effect of external reward on interest and quality of task performance in children of high and low intrinsic motivation. *Child Development*, 1979, *50*, 1207–1210.

MCCULLERS, J. C. Issues in learning and motivation. In M. R. Lepper and D. Greene (Eds.), *The hidden costs of reward.* Hillsdale, N.J.: Lawrence Erlbaum Associates, 1978.

MCGRAW, K. O. The detrimental effects of reward on performance: A literature review and a prediction model. In M. R. Lepper and D. Greene (Eds.), *The hidden costs of reward.* Hillsdale, N.J.: Lawrence Erlbaum Associates, 1978.

MCGRAW, K. O., AND MCCULLERS, J. C. Evidence of a detrimental effect of extrinsic incentives on breaking a mental set. *Journal of Experimental Social Psychology*, 1979, *15*, 285–294.

MCLOYD, V. C. The effects of extrinsic rewards of differential value on high and low intrinsic interest. *Child Development*, 1979, *50*, 1010–1019.

MAHONEY, M. J. *Cognition and behavior modification.* Cambridge: Ballinger, 1974.

MAHONEY, M. J. Reflections on the cognitive-learning trend in psychotherapy. *American Psychologist,* 1977, *32,* 5–13.

MILLER, R. L., BRICKMAN, P., AND BOLEN, D. Attribution versus persuasion as a means for modifying behavior. *Journal of Personality and Social Psychology,* 1975, *31,* 430–441.

MILLS, J. Changes in moral attitudes following temptation. *Journal of Personality,* 1958, *26,* 517–531.

MINTON, C., KAGAN, J., AND LEVINE, J. A. Maternal control and obedience in the two-year-old. *Child Development,* 1971, *42,* 1873–1894.

O'LEARY, K. D. The operant and social psychology of token systems. In A. C. Catania and T. A. Brigham (Eds.), *Handbook of applied behavior analysis.* New York: Irvington, 1978.

O'LEARY, K. D., AND DRABMAN, R. Token reinforcement programs in the classroom: A review. *Psychological Bulletin,* 1971, *75,* 379–398.

PEPITONE, A. MCCAULEY, C., AND HAMMOND, P. Change in attractiveness of forbidden toys as a function of severity of threat. *Journal of Experimental Social Psychology,* 1967, *3,* 221–229.

PIAGET, J. *The moral judgment of the child.* London: Kegan Paul, 1932.

PINDER, C. C. Additivity versus nonadditivity of intrinsic and extrinsic incentives: Implications for work motivation, performance, and attitudes. *Journal of Applied Psychology,* 1976, *61,* 693–700.

PITTMAN, T. S., COOPER, E. E., AND SMITH, T. W. Attribution of causality and the overjustification effect. *Personality and Social Psychology Bulletin,* 1977, *3,* 280–283.

PITTMAN, T. S., DAVEY, M. E., ALAFAT, K. A., WETHERILL, K. V., AND WIRSUL, N. A. Informational vs. controlling verbal rewards, levels of surveillance, and intrinsic motivation. *Personality and Social Psychology Bulletin,* in press.

REISS, S., AND SUSHINSKY, L. W. Oversimplification, competing responses, and the acquisition of intrinsic interest. *Journal of Personality and Social Psychology,* 1975, *31,* 1116–1125.

ROSENHAN, D. Some origins of concern for others. In P. A. Mussen, J. Langer, and M. Covington (Eds.), *Trends and issues in developmental psychology.* New York: Holt, Rinehart, and Winston, 1969.

ROSS, M. Salience of reward and intrinsic motivation. *Journal of Personality and Social Psychology,* 1975, *32,* 245–254.

ROSS, M., KARNIOL, R., AND ROTHSTEIN, M. Reward contingency and intrinsic motivation in children: A test of the delay of gratification hypothesis. *Journal of Personality and Social Psychology,* 1976, *33,* 442–447.

SCHANK, R., AND ABELSON, R. P. *Scripts, plans, goals, and understanding.* Hillsdale, N.J.: Lawrence Erlbaum Associates, 1977.

SEARS, R. R., MACCOBY, E. E., AND LEVIN, H. *Patterns of child rearing.* Evanston, Ill.: Row, Peterson and Co., 1957.

SEARS, R. R., WHITING, J. W. M., NOWLIS, V., AND SEARS, P. S. Some childrearing antecedents of aggression and dependency in young children. *Genetic Psychology Monographs,* 1953, *47,* 135–234.

SHAPIRA, Z. Expectancy determinants of intrinsically motivated behavior. *Journal of Personality and Social Psychology,* 1976, *34,* 1235–1244.

SHULTZ, T. R., AND BUTKOWSKY, I. Young children's use of the scheme for multiple sufficient causes in the attribution of real and hypothetical behavior. *Child Development,* 1977, *48,* 464–469.

SHULTZ, T. R., BUTKOWSKY, I., PEARCE, J. W., AND SHANFIELD, H. Development of schemes for the attribution of multiple psychological causes. *Developmental Psychology,* 1975, *11,* 502–510.

SIMON, H. A. Motivational and emotional controls of cognition. *Psychological Review,* 1967, *74,* 29–39.

SMITH, M. C. Children's use of the multiple sufficient cause schema in social perception. *Journal of Personality and Social Psychology,* 1975, *32,* 737–747.

SMITH, W. F. *The effects of social and monetary rewards on intrinsic motivation.* Unpublished doctoral dissertation, Cornell University, 1976.

SMITH, T. W., AND PITTMAN, T. S. Reward, distraction, and the overjustification effect. *Journal of Personality and Social Psychology,* 1978, *36,* 565–572.

SPENCE, K. W. *Behavior theory and conditioning.* New Haven, Yale University Press, 1956.

STAUB, E. *Positive social behavior and morality* (Vol. 1). New York: Academic Press, 1978.

STAUB, E. *Positive social behavior and morality* (Vol. 2). New York: Academic Press, 1979.

SWANN, W. B., JR., AND PITTMAN, T. S. Initiating play activity of children: The moderating influence of verbal cues on intrinsic motivation. *Child Development,* 1977, *48,* 1125–1132.

TURKEWITZ, H., O'LEARY, K. D., AND IRONSMITH, M. Producing generalization of appropriate behavior through self-control. *Journal of Consulting and Clinical Psychology,* 1975, *43,* 577–583.

TURNER, E. A., AND WRIGHT, J. Effects of severity of threat and perceived availability on the attractiveness of objects. *Journal of Personality and Social Psychology*, 1965, *2*, 128–132.

VASTA, R. On token rewards and real dangers: A look at the data. *Behavior Modification*, in press.

VASTA, R., ANDREWS, D. E., MCLAUGHLIN, A. M., STIRPE, L. A., AND COMFORT, C. Reinforcement effects on intrinsic interest: A classroom analog. *Journal of School Psychology*, 1978, *16*, 161–166.

VASTA, R., AND STIRPE, L. A. Reinforcement effects on three measures of children's interest in math. *Behavior Modification*, 1979, *3*, 223–244.

WEINER, B. *Theories of motivation: From mechanism to cognition.* Chicago: Markham, 1972.

WEINER, B. (Ed.). *Achievement motivation and attribution theory.* Morristown, N.J.: General Learning Press, 1974.

12

Attributions and Learned Helplessness

Carol S. Dweck and Therese E. Goetz

Learned helplessness in achievement situations exists when an individual perceives the termination of failure to be independent of his responses. This perception of failure as insurmountable is associated with attributions of failure to invariant factors, such as a lack of ability, and is accompanied by seriously impaired performance. In contrast, mastery-oriented behavior—increased persistence or improved performance in the face of failure—tends to be associated with attributions of failure to variable factors, particularly to a lack of effort. One would think that persistence following failure would be related to one's level of ability or to one's history of success in that area. Yet our research with children has shown that, compared to achievement cognitions, these variables are relatively poor predictors of response to failure.

In this chapter we examine the role of attributions in determining the response to failure of learned helpless and mastery-oriented children. First we review research that establishes the link between attributions and reactions to failure and that documents the nature of the performance change occasioned by failure. Next we explore the generality of individual differences in helplessness, specifically sex differences, and present findings that indicate how these individual differences develop. In addition, we show how attributions can mediate the generalization of failure effects to novel

From Carol Dweck and Therese Goetz, "Attributions and Learned Helplessness," in *New Direction in Attribution Research*, vol. 2, ed. J. Harvey, W. Ickes, and R. Kidd, pp. 157–79 (Hillsdale, N.J.: Lawrence Erlbaum Associates, 1978). Reprinted by permission of the publisher and author.

achievement and academic situations and demonstrate how this phenomenon can account for individual differences in particular academic areas such as sex differences in verbal and mathematical achievement. We then describe current research on the applicability of this learned helplessness analysis, developed in intellectual-achievement failure situations, to children's responses to failure in social situations. Finally, we present evidence that helpless and mastery-oriented children differ not only in the attributions they report when asked, but also in less structured situations, in the timing of their achievement-related cognitions and, indeed, in the role played by causal attributions.

Attributions, Helplessness, and Response to Failure

Learned helplessness was first investigated systematically in animals by Seligman and Maier (1967), who found that subjects who were pretreated with unavoidable, inescapable shock in one situation subsequently failed to avoid or escape from shock in a different situation in which control animals readily learned the avoidance contingency. In contrast to the normal animals, whose behavior following shock was characterized by intense activity, these animals tolerated extreme amounts of shock passively. Few attempts were made to prevent its recurrence. Even with forced exposure to the contingency between responding and shock termination, many trials were required before all of the animals began responding reliably on their own (Seligman, Maier, and Geer 1968). The authors proposed that the animals exposed to prior, inescapable shock learned that the probability of shock termination given a response was equal to the probability of shock termination given no response—or, that shock termination and responding were independent. In other words, in the same way that organisms can learn about contingencies, they can learn about the absence of contingencies. Moreoever, this learning can generalize to similar situations, seriously decreasing the probability of attempting instrumental responses and therefore of recognizing the presence of a contingency when one in fact exists.

Analogous divergent behavioral patterns are apparent when children are confronted with failure in intellectual problem-solving situations. Some children tend actively to pursue alternative solutions when they encounter failure, often to a greater extent than prior to failure. The performance of others, however, undergoes marked deterioration, with some children becoming literally incapable of solving the identical problems they solved with relative ease only shortly before. Our first question, then, was whether this behavioral parallel between the experimental animals in the Seligman and Maier studies and the children in problem-solving situations is accompanied by parallel cognitions. Do children who tend to give up in the face of failure tend to see the remedy as beyond their control, to see the probability of success following failure as negligible whether they respond or not? To answer this question, a study was conducted (Dweck and Reppucci 1973) in which a series of problems was administered to children by two experimenters, one of whom gave soluble problems, the other insoluble ones.[1] Problems from the success and the failure experimenters were randomly interspersed. After a number of trials, however, the failure experimenter began to administer soluble problems, ones that were virtually identical to some that had been administered by the success experimenter earlier. A surprisingly large number of children failed to solve these problems, despite the fact that they were motivated to solve as many problems as they possibly could (they earned tokens, redeemable for highly attractive prizes, for correct solutions), despite the fact that they had solved similar problems from the success experimenter, and despite the fact that they continued to show a rather large practice effect on problems administered by the success experimenter.

On the basis of their performance on the soluble problems from the failure experimenter compared to the analogous problems from the success experimenter, the children were split at the median into two groups: those who failed to solve the problems or who showed the greatest increases in solution times versus those who tended to maintain or improve their performance. It should be emphasized that these two groups had not differed on initial performance. If anything, among the females, those who subsequently showed the most deterioration had shown superior performance under success. What did distinguish the two groups were their attributional patterns, that is, their characteristic ways of explaining their intellectual academic successes and failures (see Weiner 1972, 1974).

Children's attributions were assessed by means of the Intellectual Achievement Responsibility Scale (Crandall, Katkovsky, and Crandall 1965), a forced-choice attribution questionnaire in which achievement situations with positive and negative outcomes are depicted and the child selects the one of two alternatives that best describes how he would explain that outcome. One of the alternatives always presents an external factor as the cause of the success or failure, whereas the other alternative presents an internal factor, either one's ability or one's effort, as the cause.

We found that children who persisted in the face of failure placed significantly more emphasis on motivational factors as determinants of outcomes. Attributions of failure to lack of motivation imply that failure is surmountable through effort, a factor that is generally perceived to be under the control of the individual. Children whose performance deteriorated tended more than persistent children to place the blame for their failures on largely uncontrollable external factors rather than effort. When they did take responsibility for failures, they were relatively more likely than the persistent children to blame their lack of ability. Both attributions to external factors and attributions to lack of ability imply that failure is difficult to overcome, particularly within a given situation where transformations in, say, the teacher's attitude or in one's aptitude are highly unlikely. This pattern of helpless attributions—minimizing the role of effort—was more characteristic of girls than boys.

Given that helpless children emphasize the unchangeable nature of failure and deemphasize the role of effort in overcoming failure, it is not surprising that their performance suffers. But terms like "decreased persistence," "reduced effort," or "impaired performance" can encompass a multitude of behaviors. What then is the precise nature of the performance decrement that takes place when failure occurs? We know that helpless children do not merely slow down and take greater care, since their error rate, as well as their response latency, increases with failure. Do they simply withdraw when failure occurs and begin to respond randomly? Do they at first attempt sophisticated alternative solutions but abandon them more quickly than the more persistent children? Do they, under the pressure, slip a notch or two to less mature problem-solving strategies that are easier to execute but less efficient and less likely to yield correct answers? Or, does the sophistication of their strategies undergo a gradual erosion as they experience successive failures until they become incapable of problem solving? By the same token, one might ask what accounts for the often improved performance of mastery-oriented children following failure. Again, citing an undifferentiated construct like "effort" is somewhat unsatisfying as an explanation. After all, one would hardly expect a knotty intellectual problem to yield to the same kind of exertion as a demanding physical task. Clearly, "heightened effort" must be broadened to include alterations in task strategy in addition to increases in speed, concentration, force, and the like.

In order to examine the precise nature of the performance change exhibited by helpless and mastery-oriented children under failure, children were given a task that allowed us to monitor moment-to-moment changes in their problem-solving strategies (Diener and Dweck in press, Study I). Children, categorized as helpless or mastery-oriented on the basis of their tendency to neglect or emphasize effort as a determinant of failure, were first trained on eight soluble discrimination-learning problems. For each problem they were shown pictures on cards, two at a time, that differed in three respects: the shape of the form depicted (e.g., circle or triangle), the color of the form (e.g., red or green), and the symbol that appeared in the center of the form (e.g., star or dot). One of the six stimulus values (e.g., red) was correct for the whole problem, and the child's task was to discover which one by utilizing the feedback ("correct" or "wrong") that was provided. On the first training problem feedback was given after every choice, but by the seventh problem children received feedback only after every fourth response. From the child's choices in the block of four trials before feedback was given, we could infer his hypothesis. From the sequence of hypotheses over blocks of trials, we could infer his problem-solving strategy. Strategies could be ordered in terms of maturity, the most sophisticated being the one that on the average yields the solution most quickly and the least sophisticated being one that can never lead to problem solution and that is exhibited most often by the youngest children.

All children in the study were able to employ problem-solving strategies that were successful in reaching the correct solutions on the training problems. On all measures of performance on the training problems—sophistication of strategy, trials to criterion on each problem, number of hints required to reach criterion on the training problems, efficiency of feedback utilization—helpless and mastery-oriented children were virtually identical.

When children reached criterion on the eighth training problem, four insoluble test problems were administered. In essence, every fourth trial the child was told that his choice was incorrect. (The number of trials administered on the test problems was limited, so that the feedback could conceivably be veridical.) Changes in problem-solving strategy over the four failure problems were monitored. The mastery-oriented children not only were able to maintain the sophistication of the problem-solving strategy they had displayed earlier, but, to our surprise, an appreciable proportion (26.3%) of them actually began using even more mature strategies—those typical of older children. It would appear that in response to the limited number of trials they were now allowed, they attempted and perfected a more advanced form of problem solving than they appeared capable of before failure. Helpless children, in contrast, showed a steady regression in strategy across the failure problems. By the second trial, 37.9% had already abandoned strategies that could lead to solution, and by the fourth trial, 68.9% were failing to show any sign of a useful strategy. Of these, two-thirds showed the repeated choice of a single stimulus value regardless of feedback and one-third showed alternating choice of the left and right stimulus, regardless of its nature. Although some girls displayed a sudden dramatic decline in strategy use near the beginning, most of the children displayed a more gradual regression over the course of the failure trials. None showed any evidence of attempting more sophisticated strategies.

After the test problems, children were asked to generate attributions for their failures: "Why do you think you had trouble with these problems?" Over half of the helpless children cited a lack of ability (e.g., "I'm not smart enough") as the cause. None of the mastery-oriented children offered this explanation. Instead they tended to cite effort and other potentially surmountable factors. Again, despite the equivalent initial proficiency and successes of the helpless and mastery-oriented children, the cognitions they entertained about their failures differed and their performance over failure trials became progressively divergent. In fact, by the time helpless children made their postfailure attributions to lack of ability, they could perhaps find evidence for this in their performance on the later trials.

Thus helplessness, the perception of failure as uncontrollable, does indeed predict responses to failure. But does it cause them? If so, we reasoned, then it should be possible to alter children's responses to failure by altering their attributions for failure (Dweck 1975). Specifically, helpless children taught to attribute their failures to a lack of effort—as mastery-oriented children do—should become more able to cope with failure effectively. To test this possibility, a number of extremely helpless children were identified and were assigned to one of two relatively long-term treatment procedures. All of the children showed the attributional pattern indicative of helplessness on the Intellectual Achievement Responsibility Scale, and, on a questionnaire that directly pitted attributions of failure to lack of effort against attributions of failure to lack of ability, all showed a strong tendency to endorse the lack of ability alternative. Moreover, every one evidenced severely impaired performance following the occurrence of failure, with some being unable to recover baseline performance for several days after a relatively mild failure experience.

In order to assess precisely the effects of failure on the problem-solving performance of the helpless children before and after treatment, stable baselines of speed and accuracy were established on math problems. When the baseline performance had stabilized, failure trials were interpolated between the sets of problems the children had been solving daily. The decrease in the speed and accuracy on the problems that followed the failure problems (compared to the identical problems on the previous day) was used as the index of the disruptive effects of failure.

Following this assessment of their reactions to failure, the children were given one of two treatment procedures in a different situation. Half of the children received only success experiences in the treatment situation, a procedure recommended by advocates of what might be called the "deprivation theory" of maladaptive responses to failure. This position holds that poor reactions to failure stem from a lack of confidence in one's abilities, which in turn stems from a scarcity of success experiences in a given area. If such children, then, could be supplied with the missing success, their confidence would rise and would bolster them against the negative effects of failure. Indeed, there is evidence to suggest that reported expectations of success are correlated with persistence in the face of failure (e.g., Battle 1965; Feather 1966). Moreover, the treatment was one that highlighted the contingency between the child's efforts and his successes.

The other half of the children received attribution retraining. Although here, too, success predominated, several failure trials were programmed each day. On the occasions when failure occurred the child's actual performance was compared to criterion performance and the failure was explicitly attributed by the experimenter to a lack of effort. Thus the children in this group received direct instruction in how to interpret the causes of their failures. Both treatments were carried out for 25 daily sessions. At the middle and the end of training, children were returned to the original situation, and the effects of failure on their performance were again assessed.

By the middle of training, all of the children in the attribution retraining condition showed improvement in their response to failure, although all still showed some impairment when their postfailure performance was compared to that of the previous, prefailure day. However, by the end of training, none of the children showed any appreciable impairment, and unexpectedly most of them showed improvement in performance as a result of failure. According to the investigator (Dweck), who tended to eavesdrop during the testing, several of the children, upon encountering failure, were heard to mutter such things as "I missed that one. That means I have to try harder." In addition, when the effort versus ability attribution measure was readministered by an individual unconnected with the study, children in the attribution retraining treatment showed significant increases in their tendency to emphasize effort over ability as a determinant of failure.

The children in the success-only treatment, as well as the proponents of the "deprivation model," fared far more poorly. This group showed no improvement on the midtraining and posttraining failure tests and no change on the attribution measures. Some of the children even showed a tendency to react somewhat more adversely to failure than they had before the start of this treatment. (Of course, children in this group were subsequently given attribution retraining.) Thus even though the performance of these children had been showing steady improvement during training and during the nonfailure days of testing, failure remained a cue for continued failure, and they remained incapable of dealing with it competently. Just as level of proficiency did not predict mastery-oriented responses to failure, a history of success did not do so either. In contrast, intervention at the level of failure attributions can essentially eliminate the deleterious effects of failure.

Why does prior mastery fail to predict future mastery attempts? Why is success not enough? To begin to answer this question, we turn to the issue of how helplessness develops.

The Development of Helplessness

We have studied the development of helplessness in the context of sex differences in children's attributions for and responses to failure—a context in which an intriguing paradox exists. It is often assumed that girls learn to blame their abilities for failure because teachers and other adults view them as less competent than boys and somehow convey this to them. This seems to be far from the case. If anything, in grade school it is the girls who are receiving the information that they are the ones who possess the ability; hence, the paradox.[2]

Girls, on the average, are far more successful than boys in the academic arena during the elementary school years. They receive consistently higher grades (e.g., McCandless, Roberts, and Starnes 1972) and regularly outscore boys on tests of reading achievement (see Asher and Markel 1974). In addition, they receive less criticism from teachers (see Brophy and Good 1974) and are, in fact, more highly regarded by teachers on almost every conceivable dimension: skills, motivation, personal characteristics, conduct, and more (Coopersmith 1967; Digman 1963; Stevenson, Hale, Klein, and Miller 1968). One would hardly call this discrimination against females. What is more, girls themselves think that teachers believe them to be smarter, that teachers believe they work harder, and that teachers like girls better (Dweck, Goetz, and Strauss 1977).

Yet despite this record of success and this largely benign environment, girls show far greater evidence of helplessness than boys when they receive failure feedback from adult evaluators. Girls place less emphasis than boys on motivational factors as determinants of failure and are more likely than boys to attribute failure feedback to a lack of ability (Dweck and Reppucci 1973; Nicholls 1975). In line with this, they are also more likely than boys to show decreased persistence or impaired performance when failure occurs, when the threat of failure is present, or when the evaluative pressure on a difficult task is increased (Butterfield 1965; Crandall and Rabson 1960; Dweck and Gilliard 1975; Nicholls 1975; Veroff 1969). This occurs even on tasks at which girls have demonstrated their ability or have even outperformed boys.

Boys, in spite of their poorer grades and the greater criticism they receive, and despite the lower esteem in which they are held by teachers, respond quite differently to failure feedback from adults. They tend to attribute it to controllable or variable factors. In line with this, they tend to confront failure with improved performance or increased persistence and to seek out tasks that present a challenge. Boys have also been found to credit success to their abilities more readily than girls (Nicholls 1975).

Some have argued that this differential response to failure stems from boys' and girls' discrepant socialization histories (e.g., Barry, Bacon, and Child 1957; Crandall 1963; Veroff 1969). Boys, it is said, have been trained to be independent and to formulate their own standards of excellence against which to judge the adequacy of their performance. Thus, this line of reasoning continues, when a boy receives negative feedback, he can accept it or reject it depending on how it matches his own assessment. Girls, however, are believed not to develop independent standards and therefore to remain more dependent upon external evaluation. They consequently look to the feedback of others to assess their performance and evaluate their abilities.

If this position were correct, one would expect the typical sex differences in responses to failure to have wide generality. For example, although the research showing the sex differences has always been conducted with adult evaluators, one would expect the difference to remain relatively constant regardless of who delivered the feedback. Boys' internal standards, after all, should withstand variations of this sort. Yet we know that in the late grade-school years, peers become increasingly important to boys as sources of evaluative feedback (Bronfenbrenner 1967; Hollander and Marcia 1970). Perhaps, then, boys do not view adult criticism as indicative of their abilities, but would view such feedback from peers as reflecting their level of competence.

In research designed to test this hypothesis (Dweck and Bush 1976), children attempted several trials of a task and received failure feedback from either a male or female, adult or peer evaluator. As in past research, when feedback was provided by an adult evaluator, particularly a female adult, girls showed greater helplessness than boys; they were more likely to attribute their failures to a lack of ability and to show impaired performance in the face of failure. Interestingly, there was a tendency for boys to blame the female adult evaluator more than girls did and for those who did so to show impaired performance. However, most boys attributed their failures to a lack of effort and persisted under failure. With peer evaluators (and particularly the male peer), the pattern was essentially reversed. Boys were the ones who saw the failure feedback as indicative of their abilities and the ones whose performance suffered. In fact, boys receiving negative feedback from male peers showed the most impairment of any group. Girls in this condition tended to ascribe the feedback to a lack of effort and to show significant improvement in their performance under failure.

These findings suggest that it is not boys' and girls' general socialization histories that determine response to failure, but rather their specific histories with particular agents. This, in turn, implies that in order to learn how feedback acquires different meanings for the two sexes, one should analyze the pattern of evaluative feedback they experience from the various evaluators. Because adults are the major evaluators in all academic environments, this analysis was undertaken in grade-school classrooms and the findings were then corroborated in a laboratory experiment (Dweck, Davidson, Nelson, and Enna, in press).

Of particular interest were the ways in which negative feedback was used—how much it was used compared to positive feedback, what it was typically used for, the specificity with which it was used—and the attributions teachers made for children's intellectual failures. It would be expected, for example, that negative feedback from an evaluator who is typically more negative than positive, whose feedback typically refers to nonintellectual aspects of behavior, whose criticism is used diffusely for a wide variety of referents, and who attributes failure to lack of motivation, would *not* be interpreted as indicating a lack of ability. It would be expected that negative feedback from an agent who is generally positive, who uses feedback quite specifically to refer to intellectually inadequate aspects of performance, and who does not attribute failure to a lack of effort, would more readily be attributed to a lack of ability. These, basically, were the patterns hypothesized to occur for boys and girls in the classroom.

Trained observers coded every instance of evaluative feedback given by fourth- and fifth-grade teachers to their students during academic subjects. The observers noted whether the feedback was positive or negative and recorded the class of behavior for which the feedback was given—either conduct, nonintellectual aspects of academic work (e.g., neatness), or intellectual aspects of academic work (e.g., correctness of answer). Observers also noted when teachers made explicit attributions for children's successes or failures.

The results have helped to resolve the paradox of how the more favorable treatment of girls can lead to their denigration of their competence, to helplessness, and to lessened ability to cope with failure. They also show how boys can learn to discount failures or see them as unrelated to their abilities. But first a brief indication of ways in which girls and boys did not differ. They did not differ in the absolute amount of feedback for *intellectual aspects of work* (i.e., average per boy and average per girl within classroom) or the portion of this feedback that was positive, negative, or absent. Therefore, sex differences do not appear to be related to the amount or proportion of success and failure feedback for intellectual performance.

However, when one looks at the feedback in general and at the feedback for intellectual quality of work within the context of all feedback, striking sex differences become apparent. First, negative feedback to boys was, overall, far more frequent. Since negative outcomes that are in accord with environmental forces can plausibly be attributed to them (see Enzle, Hansen, and Lowe 1975; Kelley 1971), boys may attribute failure feedback to the teacher's attitude. Second, negative feedback was used in a more diffuse and a more ambiguous fashion vis-à-vis the intellectual quality of boys' work. Past research has clearly shown that feedback used in a nonspecific manner to refer to a wide variety of nonintellectual behaviors comes to lose its meaning as an assessment of the intellectual quality of the child's work (Cairns 1970; Eisenberger, Kaplan, and Singer 1974; Warren and Cairns 1972). In fact, negative feedback for boys was used *more often* for conduct and nonintellectual aspects of work than it was for the intellectual quality of their academic performance (67.5% and 32.5%, respectively).

One might argue that although conduct feedback may convey to the child something about the teacher's values or attitudes toward him or her, such feedback can easily be discriminated from feedback for work-related matters and would not seriously affect the information value of feedback addressed to the child's work. In contrast, intellectual and nonintellectual aspects of work occur simultaneously and if feedback is typically used for both, then the basis for the feedback or its referent on any given occasion is more likely to be ambiguous. However, even if conduct is excluded from the analysis and we look only at work-related feedback, still 45.6% of the feedback for boys' work referred to intellectually irrelevant aspects of their performance. That means that almost half of the criticism that boys got for their work had nothing to do with its intellectual adequacy. Instead this feedback referred to such things as neatness, instruction-following, and style of response delivery—"form" rather than "content." Finally, looking at the explicit attributions teachers made for children's intellectual failures, we find that teachers attributed boys' failures to lack of motivation eight times more often than they did girls'. In short, when boys are given failure feedback by adults they can easily view it as reflecting something about the evaluators' attitude toward them or as being based on an assessment of some nonintellectual aspect of their work. When they do see it as referring to the intellectual quality of their work, they can attribute the failure to a lack of motivation.

In striking contrast, girls received relatively little negative feedback for conduct, and the vast majority (88.2%) of the negative feedback they received for their work referred specifically to its intellectual aspects. Thus, since the teacher is generally positive toward girls (they also got more praise than boys), they are less apt to see criticism as reflecting a negative attitude toward them. Second, since feedback is used for them in a very specific fashion for intellectual aspects of work, girls are not as likely to see the assessment as being based on an evaluation of nonintellectual qualities. Finally, since teachers view girls as highly motivated and girls themselves concur in this assessment, they cannot attribute their failures to a lack of motivation. They may have little choice but to view the negative feedback as an objective evaluation of their work and to attribute their intellectual failures to a lack of ability.

Thus the two sexes differ widely in the degree to which negative feedback serves as a valid indicant of the intellectual ability displayed in their academic performance. The results for positive feedback, although not as striking, were essentially the opposite. For work-related praise, 93.8% was contingent upon the intellectual quality of work for boys, but only 80.9% for girls, suggesting that positive evaluation for boys may be more indicative of competence than it is for girls.

These patterns of negative and positive feedback to the two sexes were both consistent across classrooms and rather general across children within classrooms. Are teachers simply reacting to the different behavior of the two sexes, or are they instead reacting differentially to similar behavior from the two sexes? The answer is probably a bit of both. Although it is clear that boys are often more disruptive, less neat in their work, and less motivated to perform well in the elementary school years, there is also some evidence that they tend to be scolded more often and more severely than girls for similar transgressions (Etaugh and Harlow 1973).

In terms of trying to understand how the use of negative feedback determines its meaning for boys and girls, however, this question may not be critical. We have shown (Dweck et al. in press) that any child exposed to the contingencies that boys and girls are exposed to in the classroom will interpret the feedback accordingly. These contingencies can serve as direct and powerful causes of children's attributions. We have taken the "teacher-girl" and the "teacher-boy" contingencies of negative feedback that we observed in the classroom and have programmed them in an experimental situation.

Specifically, on an initial anagram task with mixed success and failure trials, children received negative feedback that either: (1) referred exclusively to the correctness of their answers (like girls in the classroom), or (2) referred sometimes to correctness and sometimes to neatness (like boys in the classroom). There were two teacher-girl groups—one matched to the teacher-boy group on number of intellectual (correctness) criticisms and the other matched on total number of criticisms. All children next performed a second task (a digit-symbol substitution task) at which they failed on the initial trials and received standardized feedback from the same experimenter. They were then given a written question that asked them to attribute the failure feedback on this second task to one of the three factors described: ability, effort, or the experimenter.

As predicted, most of the children in the teacher-boy condition (75%) did *not* view the failure feedback on the second task as reflecting a lack of ability. Instead, insufficient effort was the alternative that was most frequently endorsed. Although an attempt was made to assure the children of the anonymity of their choices, only two of the 60 children in the study cited the evaluator as the cause of the failure. However, both of these children were in the teacher-boy condition.

In sharp contrast, children in both the teacher-girl conditions overwhelmingly interpreted the failure feedback they received as indicating a lack of ability. Only 25% of these children ascribed their failures to a lack of effort. There were no differences between male and female subjects in their attribution choices in any of the conditions.

These findings clearly indicate that regardless of sex, children who receive failure feedback that is solution-specific (and for which no alternative explanation is provided) are far more likely to regard subsequent failure feedback from that agent as indicative of their ability than are children who receive failure feedback that is often solution-irrelevant. It appears then that the pattern of feedback observed in the classroom for teacher-boy versus teacher-girl interactions can have direct effects on children's interpretations of their failures.

The Generalization of Helplessness

What are the implications of these individual differences in attributions for the generalization of failure experiences to new situations? To the extent that one's perceived cause of failure remains in effect in a new situation, then one will view past outcomes as predictive of future ones (cf. Brickman, Linsenmeier, and McCareins 1976). In this way, an individual's causal attributions might serve as mediators of failure effects from one situation to others involving new tasks or new evaluators.

For girls, attributions of failure to a lack of ability on a task or in an academic area imply that when presented with a similar task in the future, the past outcome is relevant to subsequent ones and, in this case, would presage a poor future. To the extent that one encounters similar academic subjects throughout school, girls' earlier condemnations of their ability will continue to be applicable. Thus girls' attributions of failure to ability may discourage continued "testing" of the environment in future grades both because similar tasks may mediate generalization of the effects of past failures and because it is unpleasant to conclude that one lacks ability despite renewed effort.

For boys, however, although blaming the teachers' attitudes or biases may impair motivation and performance in the immediate situation, by blaming the evaluator they can maintain their belief in their ability to succeed. Therefore, when the agent changes, as when they are promoted to the next grade or attend a new school, they can discount their past failures and can approach the situation with renewed effort. Thus boys' attributions of past failures to the agent may encourage testing of the environment when the agent changes. Moreover, attributions of past failures to a lack of effort imply that when in the future one cares to succeed one can at that time begin to apply oneself.

When one considers success feedback, the picture becomes even clearer. To the extent that girls' successes are not viewed by them as indicative of their ability but are attributed to the beneficence of the agent or to intellectually irrelevant aspects of their work, then past successes should not be seen by them as predictive of future success with a new agent. For boys, however, past successes have been achieved despite an "inhibitory" environmental force (Kelley 1971)—the teacher—and are therefore more apt to be chalked up to their abilities. Thus in new school situations with a new teacher, boys will see their successes more than their failures as indicative of ability and as predictive of future performance.

This analysis—postulating attributions as mediators of the effects of past outcomes—provides a mechanism with which to explain the commonly found sex differences in expectancy of success. Crandall (1969) presents a good deal of evidence that girls underestimate their chances for success relative to what their past performance in similar situations would warrant. Boys, on the other hand, are more likely to overestimate their chances of future success relative to their past accomplishments. For example, girls have been found to predict lower grades for themselves than boys do for themselves, even when they have received equal or higher grades than boys in the past. This effect does not appear to be due to sex typing or social desirability of responses. It is plausible to assume that in formulating an expectancy, one will focus on those past outcomes that are most indicative of what is likely to occur in the situation at hand. If boys focus on their successes and girls on their failures, this would yield overestimation and underestimation, respectively. In fact, Crandall presents data to suggest that when feedback is mixed or inconsistent, girls tend to weight the negative aspects and boys the positive.

This analysis further predicts that the sex discrepancy in achievement expectancies would be maximal at the beginning of a school year, when the subject matter (ability areas) remain roughly constant but the teacher (evaluator) has changed. Under these circumstances one would expect boys' expectancies to rise dramatically, but girls' perhaps to decline. However, as the year progresses and both boys and girls learn that this year's teacher is similar to last year's—for example, in attitudes, criteria, grading practices, and feedback patterns—the gap in expectancy should diminish.

Two studies were designed to investigate the hypothesis that sex differences in attributions mediate the generalization of prior failure experiences to new situations. Essentially, one would predict that no change in the situation or changes in factors perceived to be irrelevant to past failures should lead to persistence of failure effects, whereas changes in factors that are viewed as causes of failure should encourage recovery from failure.

In the first laboratory study, children worked on a task (on which both neatness and accuracy were said to be important) and received failure feedback from an adult female experimenter after each of the first four trials. Expectancy of success was monitored prior to each trial. For the fifth trial, children experienced one of four conditions: a new task, a new evaluator, both a new task and a new evaluator, or no change from the previous four trials.[3] The recovery of the child's expectancy on the fifth trial served as the index of the perceived relevance of the change to his future outcomes. This procedure is analogous to that employed in studies of habituation, in which a stimulus is repeatedly presented until the response to it has diminished. The original stimulus and the novel stimulus are then administered during testing. The magnitude of the recovery of the response reflects the perceived novelty of the testing stimulus.

In the present study, it was predicted that changes in only those factors to which boys and girls attribute their failures would promote a recovery of expectancy by creating the perception of the situation as a new one. Specifically, since boys tend to attribute failure to teacher-like agents more than girls do, it was expected that boys' expectancies would recover significantly more than girls' when the evaluator was changed. This prediction was confirmed. Not only did girls show no recovery, but their expectancies declined from Trial 4 to Trial 5 much as they did in the condition in which nothing was altered.

Since girls tend to attribute their failures to a lack of ability more than boys do, it was predicted that their expectancies would recover more than boys' when a new task was introduced. The perception of oneself as lacking ability should no longer be valid if the task on which one failed has been eliminated—provided that the ability one blamed was task-specific. Boys' recovery should be limited by the continued presence of the same evaluator. The results indicated that although both sexes recovered significantly in this condition, girls by no means regained their initial level of confidence and in fact did not recover any more than boys did. More striking, however, was our finding that even when both the evaluator and the task were varied—making it a largely new situation—girls' expectancies did not show complete recovery. Boys', naturally, did.

Of course it is possible that girls were simply more reluctant to state high expectancies again given the fate of their original predictions. However, these findings suggest that perhaps failure feedback leads girls to consider themselves lacking in an intellectual ability that goes beyond the particular task at hand. In this way, they may be transferring a failure experience from one domain to another by applying a general label to their perceived deficit. It is interesting to note that we started with a situation in which boys and girls confronted a new task with equivalent expectancies and ended with a situation in which boys and girls confronted a new task with the typical sex difference in expectancy.

The second study tested the hypothesis that sex differences in academic achievement expectancies would be maximal at the beginning of a school year at which time the ability areas remain similar but the evaluator is different. Prior to the first and second report cards of the year, over 300 fourth-, fifth-, and sixth-grade children were given questionnaires that assessed how well they expected to do on their upcoming report cards. Although girls had received significantly higher grades than boys on their final report cards the previous year, girls predicted significantly poorer performance for themselves than boys predicted for themselves on their first report cards. Needless to say, girls then received higher grades on their first (and second) report cards. By the second report card the gap had closed, but girls still did not give higher predictions than boys, which is what accurate estimates from both would yield.

The results from these studies provide strong support for the view that individual differences in attributions result in differences in the generalization of failure effects. The results also suggest that failure effects may have more of a long-term and cumulative effect for girls than for boys and provide a way of understanding why, despite their early advantage, girls begin to lag behind boys in many achievement areas later on. Even more interesting is the fact that this analysis can account for the development of differential performance by the two sexes in different subject areas.

It has long been a source of curiosity that although girls fairly typically have outperformed boys on tests of verbal achievement, starting at around the junior high or early high school years boys begin to outscore girls on tests of mathematical achievement (Maccoby and Jacklin 1974). If one analyzes the characteristics of math versus verbal skills as they are acquired over the school years and considers this in conjunction with responses to and generalization of failure experiences, an explanation for the emerging achievement differences becomes clear (although, of course, it does not rule out other potential contributing factors). Once the basic verbal skills—reading, spelling, vocabulary—are acquired, increments in difficulty are gradual. Never again, or rarely, is the child confronted in school with a new unit that puts him at a complete loss or for which a totally new set of concepts and skills must be mastered. Learning to read a new word or to spell it or define it involves fundamentally the same process one has gone through before with old words. New learning is, in a sense, assimilated into a larger, pre-existing body of knowledge.

With math, however, a new unit may involve totally new concepts, the relevance of which to past learning may not be immediately, or ever, clear. New units in math often involve quantum leaps as from arithmetic to algebra to geometry to calculus and so on. For a young child even the links between addition and multiplication or between multiplication and division may not be readily apparent. This characteristic of the acquisition of mathematical skills provides numerous opportunities for initial failures and, if one is so inclined, for concluding that one lacks ability. To the extent that one blames a lack of general mathematical ability, the effects of the failures may generalize to all future tasks subsumed under the label "math," resulting in: (1) lowered persistence in the face of difficulties, which are inevitably encountered even by those accomplished in mathematics; (2) avoidance of math courses when that option becomes possible; and (3) perhaps interference with new learning, which in math often requires sustained attention and the maintenance of systematic problem-solving strategies, both of which are hampered by helplessness. Thus, it may be the case that two children who start out with equivalent skills and equivalent "aptitude" in elementary school end up with divergent skills later on. This possibility—that differential achievement can be accounted for by how well the nature of skill acquisition coincides with attributional tendencies—is currently under investigation (by Carol Dweck and Barbara Licht).

Although this research has focused on sex differences in helplessness, the variable "sex," like many demographic variables, simply serves as a convenient way of summarizing a particular learning history. In this case the histories of the two sexes favor different attributional tendencies. However, there are important within-sex differences in these tendencies and one would expect the relationships elaborated here to apply to these individual differences as well.

In the same vein, most of the research to date relating perceptions of causality to responses to outcomes has focused on intellectual achievement situations; yet similar relationships should hold for situations involving social interaction.

Helplessness and Social Interactions

In the same way that intellectual failures can be met with a variety of responses, so, too, can social rejection. One may attempt a variety of strategies designed to reverse the rejection, or one may respond with behavior that represents a marked deterioration from the previous interaction. For instance, a normally socially facile person may withdraw or resort to hostile retaliatory measures. Do attributions guide selection of coping patterns in social situations in the same way that they appear to in academic-intellectual ones?

The importance of this question is highlighted when it is viewed in the context of past work on children's interpersonal coping and peer relationships. Most previous investigations have virtually ignored the role of perceptions of control and have concentrated instead on cognitive and social skills, with the assumption that problems in coping must be primarily a result of deficits in these skills (Allen, Hart, Buell, Harris, and Wolf 1964; Baer and Wolf 1970; Keller and Carlson 1974; O'Connor 1969, 1972; Spivack and Shure 1974). Yet those programs that have focused on skill or overt behavior alone have not reliably promoted or maintained effective peer relationships (see Gottman 1977). The most effective programs have been the ones that appear to be teaching the contingency between the child's actions and the social outcomes he experiences (see Gottman, Gonso, and Schuler 1976; Oden and Asher 1977).

Focusing on perception of control over aversive outcomes brings to the fore a number of important possibilities not addressed by earlier approaches. Past researchers have considered only rejected and isolated children, implicitly assuming the more popular ones to be free of potentially serious problems in interpersonal coping. However, just as learned helplessness in achievement situations appears to be unrelated to competence, responses to negative social outcomes may be relatively unrelated to social skills; popular as well as unpopular individuals may have coping problems. For instance, some popular children may interpret their few experiences with social rebuff as indications of permanent rejection not open to change by their actions, paralleling the instance of the "A" student who attributes a low grade to a lack of ability despite all previous evidence to the contrary. Moreover, it may be that some individuals are isolated *not* because they lack social skills or the knowledge of appropriate behavior, but because they fear or have experienced social rejection and view it as insurmountable.

We are currently conducting an investigation to establish the relationship between perceptions of control and causal attributions for rejection.[4] In order to tap causal attributions for social rejection, we have developed a questionnaire depicting a series of hypothetical social situations in which children are either rejected or accepted by same-sex peers. Responses to this measure are being related to responses in a situation in which each child must cope with potential social rejection by a peer of the same sex. In this way, we can determine whether causal attributions that imply difficulty in surmounting rejection are in fact associated with deterioration of social behavior in the face of rejection.

In the questionnaire, children are presented with an instance of rejection and are asked to evaluate a list of reasons the rejection may have occurred. Both the situations and their causes were selected as the most representative of those generated by children in the course of extensive interviews. For example: "Suppose you move into a new neighborhood. A girl you meet does not like you very much. Why would this happen to you?" The reasons include such factors as personal ineptitude, a characteristic of the rejector, chance, misunderstandings, and a mutual mismatch of temperaments or preferences.

Just as failure attributions to some factors, like effort, imply surmountability, so too do rejection attributions to misunderstanding. Similarly, attributing rejection to one's lack of ability (e.g., "It happened because it's hard for me to make friends") implies a relatively enduring outcome, as would an ability attribution for academic failure. Blaming the rejector for interpersonal rejection has the same implications as blaming the evaluator for academic failure. Given the parallel implications of interpersonal and intellectual attributions, one would also expect parallel reactions and generalization effects.

The data from over 100 children tested thus far indicate that individuals differ in consistent ways from one another in the causes to which they ascribe social rejection. In order to test the hypothesized relationships between attributions and responses to rejection, a method of sampling each child's interpersonal strategies both before and after social rejection has been devised. Children try out for a pen pal club by communicating a sample getting-to-know-you letter (conveying the "kind of person" they are) to a peer evaluator. The experimenter then relays to the child the evaluator's decision—in this case, not to admit the child into the club. To assess the effect the evaluation has on subsequent responses, the child is told he has a chance to try again, to send another message to the same evaluator.[5] After a short wait, enthusiastic acceptance is relayed to the child, and his home address is recorded to place on file for the club (which has actually been set up for this project).

These communications are currently being rated by trained, independent judges along a number of dimensions designed to reflect the child's strategy for attaining acceptance and to reveal alterations in strategy across situations. As with the attribution measure, the data thus far indicate that there are striking differences in strategies for coping with interpersonal rejection. Responses range from mastery-oriented patterns, with more and different strategies used after rejection, to complete withdrawal—about 10% of the children could not come up with a second message to the rejecting evaluator, even after gentle prodding and prompting. Only after the experimenter explicitly attributed the rejection to an idiosyncracy of the committee member would these children produce a message for a different evaluator, which enabled us to provide acceptance feedback.

The initial data indicate that those children who either gave up or were extremely reluctant to send a message to the rejecting committee member also favored attributions that emphasized the insurmountability of rejection. Those children who were notable for their self-confident responses to the rejection and thoughtful approaches to their second communication emphasized the role of surmountable factors like misunderstandings. Thus, preliminary analysis of the attribution and coping measures suggests that individual differences in attribution are indeed systematically related to responses following rejection in the predicted ways.

Helplessness and the Occurrence of Attributions

Researchers in the area of attributions assume that following some discrete event, such as the delivery of evaluative feedback, an attribution is always made (see Dweck and Gilliard 1975). Individual differences are assumed to occur only in the nature of the attribution that is made at that point. However, we have recently completed research that shows there are also clear individual differences in the timing or occurrence of causal attributions when the situation is less structured (Diener and Dweck in press).

When attributions were measured at a prespecified time—either on a preexperimental attribution questionnaire or on a task-specific, postfailure attribution probe—we obtained the typical helpless versus mastery-oriented differences in attributions and task persistence. However, when children's spontaneous, ongoing reports of achievement-cognitions were monitored, we found that attributions were made primarily by helpless children and not by mastery-oriented ones. In this research, described in part earlier, children were trained to criterion on a discrimination-learning task. Following the training problems, failure feedback ("wrong") was begun, and chances in problem-solving strategies were tracked. As noted above, helpless children showed a steady decline in the sophistication of the strategies they employed, whereas nearly all of the mastery-oriented children maintained their strategies and a number even began using more mature strategies than they had before. These results were replicated in a second study, which was identical in all respects but one: prior to the seventh training trial, children were requested to verbalize what they were thinking, if anything, while performing the task. The instructions gave them license to report anything—from justification for their stimulus selection to plans for their lunch. This procedure allowed us to monitor differences in not only the nature of particular achievement-related cognitions but also in the presence, the timing, and the relative frequency of various cognitions.

All children verbalized freely; and, prior to failure, the verbalizations of the helpless and mastery-oriented children were virtually identical. Almost all of the statements pertained to task strategy and almost none reflected achievement-related cognitions. Following the onset of failure, however, a dramatic shift took place. Both groups of children began to report many more achievement cognitions, but what they emphasized differed markedly. The helpless children rather quickly began to make attributions for their failures, attributing them to a lack or loss of ability, and to express negative affect about the task. The mastery-oriented children, in contrast, did not make attributions for failure. Instead they engaged in self-instruction and self-monitoring designed to bring about success. They continued to express a positive prognosis for future outcomes (e.g., "One more guess and I'll have it") and to express positive affect toward the task (e.g., "I love a challenge"). It would appear that despite the feedback of the experimenter, the mastery-oriented children did not consider themselves to have failed. They were making mistakes, to be sure, but they seemed certain that with the proper concentration and strategy they could get back on the track. Thus they dwelled on prescription rather than diagnosis, remedy rather than cause.

One might argue that although mastery-oriented children did not verbalize effort attributions, they were implied by their self-instructions. However, the few attributions that were explicitly verbalized did not seem to fall into any one category. Moreover, when one considers the nature of the task, it is clear that identifying the cause of failure is in this case irrelevant to achieving success. Whether the cause is thought to be insufficient effort, bad luck, increased task difficulty, or lower ability than previously believed, the remedy still would be sustained concentration and the use of sophisticated strategies.

This observed difference in the tendency of helpless and mastery-oriented children to attend to the cause of failure raises a number of interesting questions. Would the mastery-oriented children have attended to the causes of failure sooner if a diagnosis were necessary for the prescription of a remedy? Or, is there among them a subset of children who are too "action oriented" to analyze causal factors systematically? Although helpless children readily concede that they have failed soon after negative feedback begins, at what point do mastery-oriented children define themselves as having failed, when do they attribute, and at what point do they consider terminating their efforts? Are there those among the mastery-oriented who suffer from what may be termed the "Nixon syndrome"—unusually prolonged persistence designed to forestall the admission of failure (cf. Bulman and Brickman 1976)? For such children, as for helpless children, failure may have highly negative connotations for their competence; yet rather than surrender to it prematurely, they persist past the point of diminishing returns in the belief that, as expressed by Richard Nixon, "You're never a failure until you give up."

In short, in past research, experimenters have typically at a predetermined point defined failure for the subject and asked him to make a causal attribution. The current results suggest that there are also important differences in the timing or even the occurrence of attributions. The implications of these differences have yet to be explored.

NOTES

1. In this and in subsequent studies the participants were late grade-school-age children (grades four to six). Throughout the research great care was taken to ensure that every child left the experimental situation feeling that his performance had been commendable. For example, in a typical study following the failure trials, children were given mastery experiences, were assured that they had conquered a difficult task more quickly than most, and were told they had done so well there was no need to complete the remaining problems. Thus the procedure incorporated what is essentially persistence training.
2. This is not to deny that later in their academic careers girls may indeed encounter these attitudes.
3. Pilot work has ensured that both tasks employed elicited identical mean initial expectancies, that boys and girls did not differ in their initial expectancies, and that ability, effort, and evaluator attributions for failure were all perceived as plausible candidates.
4. This research is the second author's dissertation.
5. A test for generalization to a new evaluator is also included.

REFERENCES

ALLEN, K. E., HART, B., BUELL, J. S., HARRIS, F. R., AND WOLF, M. M. Effects of social reinforcement of isolate behavior of a nursery school child. *Child Development*, 1964, *35*, 511–518.

ASHER, S. R., AND MARKEL, R. A. Sex differences in comprehension of high- and low-interest material. *Journal of Educational Psychology*, 1971, *66*, 680–687.

BAER, D. M., AND WOLF, M. M. Recent examples of behavior modification in pre-school settings. In C. Neuringer and J. L. Michael (Eds.), *Behavior modification in a clinical psychology*. New York: Appleton-Century-Crofts, 1970.

BARRY, H., BACON, M. C., AND CHILD, I. L. A cross-cultural survey of some sex differences in socialization. *Journal of Abnormal and Social Psychology*, 1957, *55*, 327–332.

BATTLE, E. Motivational determinants of academic task persistence. *Journal of Personality and Social Psychology*, 1965, *2*, 209–218.

BRICKMAN, P., LINSENMEIER, J. A. W., AND MCCAREINS, A. Performance enhancement by relevant success and irrelevant failure. *Journal of Personality and Social Psychology*, 1976, *33*, 149–160.

BRONFENBRENNER, U. Response to pressure from peers versus adults among Soviet and American school children. *International Journal of Psychology*, 1967, *2*, 199–207.

BROPHY, J. E., AND GOOD, T. L. *Teacher-student relationships*. New York: Holt, 1974.

BULMAN, R. J., AND BRICKMAN, P. *When not all problems are soluble, does it still help to expect success?* Unpublished manuscript, 1976.

BUTTERFIELD, E. C. The role of competence motivation in interrupted task recall and repetition choice. *Journal of Experimental Child Psychology*, 1965, *2*, 354–370.

CAIRNS, R. B. Meaning and attention as determinants of social reinforcer effectiveness. *Child Development*, 1970, *41*, 1067–1082.

COOPERSMITH, S. *The antecedents of self-esteem*. San Francisco: Freeman, 1967.

CRANDALL, V. C. Sex differences in expectancy of intellectual and academic reinforcement. In C. P. Smith (Ed.), *Achievement-related motives in children*. New York: Russell Sage Foundation, 1969.

CRANDALL, V. C., KATKOVSKY, W., AND CRANDALL, V. J. Children's beliefs in their own control of reinforcements in intellectual-academic situations. *Child Development*, 1965, *36*, 91–109.

CRANDALL, V. J. Achievement. In H. W. Stevenson (Ed.), *Child Psychology*. The sixty-second yearbook of the National Society for the Study of Education. Chicago: NSSE, 1963.

CRANDALL, V. J., AND RABSON, A. Children's repetition choices in an intellectual achievement situation following success and failure. *Journal of Genetic Psychology*, 1960, *97*, 161–168.

DIENER, C. I., AND DWECK, C. S. An analysis of learned helplessness: Continuous changes in performance, strategy, and achievement cognitions following failure. *Journal of Personality and Social Psychology*, in press.

DIGMAN, J. M. Principal dimensions of child personality as inferred from teachers' judgments. *Child Development*, 1963, *34*, 43–60.

DWECK, C. S. The role of expectations and attributions in the alleviation of learned helplessness. *Journal of Personality and Social Psychology*, 1975, *31*, 674–685.

DWECK, C. S., AND BUSH, E. S. Sex differences in learned helplessness: (1) Differential debilitation with peer and adult evaluators. *Developmental Psychology*, 1976, *12*, 147–156.

DWECK, C. S., DAVIDSON, W., NELSON, S., AND ENNA, B. *Sex differences in learned helplessness: (II) The contingencies of evaluative feedback in the classroom and (III) An experimental analysis. Developmental Psychology*, in press.

DWECK, C. S., AND GILLIARD, D. Expectancy statements as determinants of reactions to failure: Sex differences in persistence and expectancy change. *Journal of Personality and Social Psychology*, 1975, *32*, 1077–1084.

DWECK, C. S., GOETZ, T. E., AND STRAUSS, N. *Sex differences in learned helplessness: (IV) An experimental and naturalistic study of failure generalization and its mediators.* Unpublished manuscript, 1977.

DWECK, C. S., AND REPPUCCI, N. D. Learned helplessness and reinforcement responsibility in children. *Journal of Personality and Social Psychology*, 1973, *25*, 109–116.

EISENBERGER, R., KAPLAN, R. M., AND SINGER, R. D. Decremental and nondecremental effects of noncontingent social approval. *Journal of Personality and Social Psychology*, 1974, *30*, 716–722.

ENZLE, M. E., HANSEN, R. D., AND LOWE, C. A. Causal attributions in the mixed-motive game: Effects of facilitory and inhibitory environmental forces. *Journal of Personality and Social Psychology*, 1975, *31*, 50–54.

ETAUGH, C., AND HARLOW, H. *School attitudes and performance of elementary school children as related to teacher's sex and behavior.* Paper presented at the meeting of the Society for Research in Child Development, Philadelphia, March 1973.

FEATHER, N. T. Effects of prior success and failure on expectations of success and subsequent performance. *Journal of Personality and Social Psychology*, 1966, *3*, 287–298.

GOTTMAN, J. M. The effects of modeling film on social isolation in preschool children: A methodological investigation. *Journal of Abnormal Child Psychology*, in press.

GOTTMAN, J., GONSO, J., AND SCHULER, P. Teaching social skills to isolated children. *Journal of Abnormal Child Psychology*, 1976, *4*(2), 179–197.

HOLLANDER, E. P., AND MARCIA, J. E. Parental determinants of peer-orientation and self-orientation among preadolescents. *Developmental Psychology*, 1970, *2*, 292–302.

KELLER, M. F., AND CARLSON, P. M. The use of symbols modeling to promote social skills in preschool children with low levels of social responsiveness. *Child Development*, 1974, *45*, 912–919.

KELLEY, H. H. *Attribution in social interaction.* Morristown, N.J.: General Learning Press, 1971.

MACCOBY, E. E., AND JACKLIN, C. N. *The psychology of sex differences.* Stanford, Calif.: Stanford University Press, 1974.

MCCANDLESS, B., ROBERTS, A., AND STARNES, T. Teachers' marks, achievement test scores, and aptitude relations with respect to social class, race, and sex. *Journal of Educational Psychology*, 1972, *63*, 153–159.

NICHOLLS, J. G. Causal attributions and other achievement-related cognitions: Effects of task outcomes, attainment value, and sex. *Journal of Personality and Social Psychology*, 1975, *31*, 379–389.

O'CONNOR, R. D. Modification of social withdrawal through symbolic modeling. *Journal of Applied Behavior Analysis*, 1969, *2*, 15–22.

O'CONNOR, R. D. Relative efficacy of modeling, shaping, and the combined procedures for modification of social withdrawal. *Journal of Abnormal Psychology*, 1972, *79*, 327–334.

ODEN, S. L., AND ASHER, S. R. Coaching children in social skills for friendship-making. *Child Development*, 1977, *48*, 495–506.

SELIGMAN, M. E. P., AND MAIER, S. F. Failure to escape traumatic shock. *Journal of Experimental Psychology*, 1967, *74*, 1–9.

SELIGMAN, M. E. P., MAIER, S. F., AND GEER, J. The alleviation of learned helplessness in the dog. *Journal of Abnormal and Social Psychology*, 1968, *73*, 256–262.

SPIVAK, G., AND SHURE, M. B. *Social adjustment of young children.* San Francisco: Jossey-Bass, 1974.

STEVENSON, H. W., HALE, G. A., KLEIN, R. E., AND MILLER, L. K. Interrelations and correlates in children's learning and problem solving. *Monographs of the Society for Research in Child Development*, 1968, *33* (7, Serial No. 123).

VEROFF, J. Social comparison and the development of achievement motivation. In C. P. Smith (Ed.), *Achievement-related motives in children.* New York: Russell Sage, 1969.

WARREN, V. L., AND CAIRNS, R. B. Social reinforcement mediation: An outcome of frequency or ambiguity. *Journal of Experimental Child Psychology*, 1972, *13*, 249–260.

WEINER, B. *Theories of motivation.* Chicago: Markham, 1972.

WEINER, B. *Achievement motivation and attribution theory.* Morristown, N.J.: General Learning Press, 1974.

13

Divorce: A Child's Perspective
E. Mavis Hetherington

The rate of divorce in the United States, particularly of divorce involving those who have children, has increased dramatically since 1965. It is estimated that 40% of the current marriages of young adults will end in divorce and that 40%–50% of children born in the 1970s will spend some time living in a single-parent family. The average length of time spent by children in a single-parent home as a result of marital disruption is about six years. The majority of these children reside with their mothers, with only 10% living with their fathers even though this proportion has tripled since 1960. Living with the father is most likely to occur with school-aged rather than preschool children (Glick and Norton 1978).

This article first presents an overview of the course of divorce and its potential impact on children and then uses research findings as a basis for describing the process of divorce as it is experienced by the child. Since the research on single-parent families headed by fathers is meager and since after divorce most children live in a single-parent family headed by the mother, the article focuses primarily on children in this family situation.

The Course of Divorce

In studying the impact of divorce on children, much confusion has resulted from viewing divorce as a single event rather than a sequence of

From E. Mavis Hetherington, "Divorce: A Child's Perspective," *American Psychologist* 34 (1979):851–58. Copyright 1979 by the American Psychological Association. Reprinted by permission of the publisher and author.

experiences involving a transition in the lives of children. This transition involves a shift from the family situation before divorce to the disequilibrium and disorganization associated with separation and divorce, through a period when family members are experimenting with a variety of coping mechanisms, some successful and some unsuccessful, for dealing with their new situation. This is followed by the reorganization and eventual attainment of a new pattern of equilibrium in a single-parent household. For most children, within five years of the divorce there is also a later period of reentry into a two-parent family involving a stepparent, which necessitates further alterations in family functioning. The point at which we tap into the sequence of events and changing processes associated with divorce will modify our view of the adjustment of the child and the factors which influence that adjustment. Although divorce may be the best solution to a destructive family relationship and may offer the child an escape from one set of stresses and the opportunity for personal growth, almost all children experience the transition of divorce as painful. Even children who later are able to recognize that the divorce had constructive outcomes initially undergo considerable emotional distress with family dissolution. The children's most common early responses to divorce are anger, fear, depression, and guilt. It is usually not until after the first year following divorce that tension reduction and an increased sense of well-being begin to emerge.

A crisis model of divorce may be most appropriate in conceptualizing the short-term effects of divorce on children. In the period during and immediately following divorce the child may be responding to changes in his or her life situation—the loss of a parent, the marital discord and family disorganization that usually precede and accompany separation, the alterations in parent-child relations that may be associated with temporary distress and emotional neediness of family members, and other real or fantasized threats to the well-being of the child that are elicited by the uncertainty of the situation. In this period, therefore, stresses associated with conflict, loss, change, and uncertainty may be the critical factors.

The research evidence suggests that most children can cope with and adapt to the short-term crisis of divorce within a few years. However, if the crisis is compounded by multiple stresses and continued adversity, developmental disruptions may occur. The longer term adjustment of the child is related to more sustained or concurrent conditions associated with the quality of life in a household headed by a single parent—alterations in support systems, the increased salience of the custodial parent, the lack of availability of the noncustodial parent, the presence of one less significant adult in the household to participate in decision making, to serve as a model or disciplinarian, or to assume responsibility for household tasks and child care, and finally, changes in family functioning related to continued stresses associated with practical problems of living, such as altered economic resources.

Variability in Response to Divorce

In considering how the child experiences and responds to divorce and to life in a single-parent household, investigators are beginning to examine the interplay among situational factors, stresses, and support systems. However, even when these factors are comparable, wide variability in the quality and intensity of responses and the adaptation of children to divorce remains. Some children exhibit severe or sustained disruptions in development, others seem to sail through a turbulent divorce and stressful aftermath and emerge as competent, well-functioning individuals. Although there is increasing interest in the relative vulnerability or invulnerability of children to psycho-social stress (Garmezy 1975; Rutter in press-b), this issue has not been systematically explored in relation to divorce. It seems likely that temperamental variables, the past experience of the child, and the child's developmental status all contribute to individual differences in coping with divorce. There also have been some provocative findings suggesting that boys are more vulnerable to the adverse effects of divorce than are girls, although the reasons for this difference have yet to be clarified.

Temperament and the Response to Divorce

Temperamentally difficult children have been found to be less adaptable to change and more vulnerable to adversity (Chess, Thomas, and Birch 1968; Graham, Rutter, and George 1973; Rutter in press-a) than are temperamentally easy children. The difficult child is more likely to be the elicitor and the target of aversive responses by the parent, whereas the temperamentally easy child is not only less likely to be the recipient of criticism, displaced anger, and anxiety but also is more able to cope with it when it hits. Children who have histories of maladjustment preceding the divorce are more likely to respond with long-lasting emotional disturbance following divorce (Kelly, see note 1). This, of course, could be attributable either to temperamental factors or to a history of pathogenic environmental factors.

Cumulative Stress and the Response to Divorce

Rutter (in press-b) reported that when children experience only a single stress it carries no appreciable psychiatric risk. However, when children who have been exposed to chronic stress or several concurrent stresses must deal with family discord the adverse effects increase multiplicatively. The effects of stresses in the family also are compounded by those in the larger social milieu. Extrafamilial factors such as stresses and supports in other social institutions or networks, the quality of housing, neighborhoods, child care, the need for the mother to work, economic status, and geographic mobility will moderate or potentiate stresses associated with divorce (Colletta 1978; Hodges, Wechsler, and Ballantine).[2] Finally, transactional effects may occur in cases where divorce may actually increase the probability of occurrence of another stressor. This is most apparent in the stresses associated with the downward economic movement that frequently follows divorce and makes raising children and maintaining a household more difficult (Bane 1976; Brandwein, Brown, and Fox 1974; Kriesberg 1970; Winston and Forsher 1971).

Developmental Status and the Response to Divorce

The adaptation of the child will also vary with his or her developmental status. The limited cognitive and social competencies of the young child, the young child's dependency on parents and more exclusive restriction to the home will be associated with different responses and coping strategies from those of the more mature and self-sufficient older child or adolescent who operates in a variety of social milieus. Note that I am saying the experience of divorce will differ qualitatively for children of varying ages rather than that the trauma will be more or less intense. The young child is less able accurately to appraise the divorce situation, the motives and feelings of his or her parents, his or her own role in the divorce, and the array of possible outcomes. Thus the young child is likely to be more self-blaming in interpreting the cause of divorce and to distort grossly perceptions of the parents' emotions, needs, and behavior, as well as the prospects of reconciliation or total abandonment (Tessman 1978; Wallerstein and Kelly 1974, 1975). Although most adolescents experience considerable initial pain and anger when their parents divorce, when the immediate trauma of divorce is over, they are more able accurately to assign responsibility for the divorce, to resolve loyalty conflicts, and to assess and cope with economic and other practical exigencies (Wallerstein and Kelly 1974, 1975). It should be noted that this is often accompanied by premature, sometimes destructive disengagement from the family and an increased future orientation. However, if the home situation is particularly painful adolescents more than younger children do have the option to disengage and seek gratification elsewhere, such as in the neighborhood, peer group, or school.

Sex Differences in Responses to Divorce

The impact of marital discord and divorce is more pervasive and enduring for boys than for girls (Hetherington, Cox, and Cox 1978 in press; Porter and O'Leary in press; Rutter in press-a; Tuckman and Regan 1966; Hetherington et al.[3]; Wallerstein).[4] Disturbances in social and emotional development in girls have largely disappeared two years after the divorce, although they may reemerge at adolescence in the form of disruptions in heterosexual relations (Hetherington 1972). Although boys improve markedly in coping and adjustment in the two years after divorce, many continue to show developmental deviations. Boys from divorced families, in contrast with girls from divorced families and children from nuclear families, show a higher rate of behavior disorders and problems in interpersonal relations in the home and in the school with teachers and peers. Although especially in young children both boys and girls show an increase in dependent help-seeking and affection-seeking overtures following divorce, boys are more likely also to show more sustained noncompliant, aggressive behavior in the home (Hetherington et al., 1978, in press, see note 3).

Why should this be the case? It has been suggested that loss of a father is more stressful for boys than for girls. It also may be that the greater aggressiveness frequently observed in boys and the greater assertiveness in the culturally prescribed male role necessitates the use of firmer, more consistent discipline practices in the control of boys than of girls. Boys in both nuclear and divorced families are less compliant than girls, and children are less compliant to mothers than fathers (Hetherington et al. 1978). It also could be argued that it is more essential for boys to have a male model to imitate who exhibits mature self-controlled ethical behavior or that the image of greater power and authority vested in the father is more critical in controlling boys, who are culturally predisposed to be more aggressive.

Although these factors may all be important, recent divorce studies suggest that these sex differences may involve a more complex set of mediators. Boys are more likely to be exposed to parental battles (Wallerstein see note 4) and to confront inconsistency, negative sanctions, and opposition from parents, particularly from mothers, following divorce. In addition, boys receive less positive support and nurturance and are viewed more negatively by mothers, teachers, and peers in the period immediately following divorce than are girls (Hetherington et al. 1978, in press; Santrock 1975; Santrock and Trace 1978; Hetherington et al., see note 3). Divorced mothers of boys report feeling more stress and depression than do divorced mothers of girls (Colletta 1978; Hetherington et al. 1978). Boys thus may be exposed to more stress, frustration, and aggression and have fewer available supports.

The Child's Changed Life Experiences Following Divorce

Keeping in mind the many factors that contribute to the wide variability in the responses of children to divorce, let us examine the changes in the child's experiences associated with divorce. Some of these changes are related to alterations in economic status and practical problems of living, others involve changes in family functioning, and still others are associated with social networks external to the family.

Economic Changes and Practical Problems of Living

Some of the most prevalent stresses confronting children of divorce are those associated with downward economic mobility. Poor parents and those with unstable incomes are more likely to divorce (Brandwein et al. 1974; Ross and Sawhill 1975), and divorce is associated with a marked drop in income. This is in part attributable to the fact that less than one third of ex-husbands contribute to the support of their families (Kriesberg 1970; Winston and Forsher 1971). Moreover, many divorced women do not have the education, job skills, or experience to permit them to obtain a well-paying position or to pay for high-quality child care. Divorced mothers are more likely to have low-paying part-time jobs or positions of short duration. For the child this results in erratic, sometimes inadequate provisions for child care and, if the mother feels forced to work, in a dissatisfied, resentful mother.

If the divorced mother wishes to work and adequate provisions are made for child care and household management, maternal employment may have positive effects on the mother and no adverse effects on the children. However, if the mother begins to work at the time of divorce or shortly thereafter, the preschool child seems to experience the double loss of both parents, which is reflected in a higher rate of behavior disorders (Hetherington et al. 1978). In addition, maternal employment may add to the task overload experienced when a single parent is attempting to cope with the tasks ordinarily performed by two parents in a nuclear family. It has been suggested that as the divorced mother struggles to distribute her energies across the many demands placed on her, the child may be maternally deprived rather than paternally deprived (Brandwein et al. 1974). This is sometimes associated with what one mother termed a "chaotic lifestyle," where family roles and responsibilities are not well delineated and many routine chores do not get accomplished. Children of many divorced parents receive less adult attention and are more likely to have erratic meals and bedtimes and to be late for school (Hetherington et al. 1978).

The downward economic mobility of families headed by a divorced mother also involves a lower standard of living and relocation. Following divorce, families are likely to shift to more modest housing in poorer neighborhoods, and their greater social isolation may be exacerbated by moving (Marsden 1969; Pearlin and Johnson 1977). For the child, such moves not only involve losses of friends, neighbors, and a familiar educational system, but also may be associated with living in an area with high delinquency rates, risks to personal safety, few recreational facilities, and inadequate schools. For children involved in family dissolution, such moves represent further unraveling of the skein of their lives at a time when continuity of support systems and the environment can play an ameliorative role (Tessman 1978).

Changes in Parent-Child Relations

Many changes in family interaction are associated with divorce and living in a single-parent family. In early studies the role of the loss or relative unavailability of the father was emphasized. More recently, family conflict, the increased salience of the custodial mother, changes in mother-child interaction and in the life circumstances of the single-parent family have been the focus of attention.

Conflict. A high degree of discord characterizes family relations in the period surrounding divorce. The conflict between parents often enmeshes the child in controversy. Children are exposed to parental quarreling, mutual denigration and recrimination, and are placed in a situation of conflicting loyalties, with one parent frequently attempting to coerce or persuade children to form hostile alliances against the other parent. This results in demands for a decision to reject one parent which children are unprepared or unable to make. The vast majority of children wish to maintain relations with both parents. Conflict also gives children the opportunity to play one parent against the other and in some children develops exploitative manipulative skills (Tessman 1978; Wallerstein, see note 4). The behavior of some children actively escalates conflict between divorced parents and between parents and stepparents following remarriage.

The frequent mutual demeaning and criticism of divorcing parents leads to dissonance, questioning, and often precipitous revision and deidealization of children's perceptions of their parents (Hetherington 1972; Tessman 1978; Wallerstein, see note 4). When the mother is hostile and critical of the father, the child begins to view the father in a more ambivalent or negative manner and as a less acceptable role model. For young boys this is associated with disruption in sex typing (Hetherington et al. note 3). For girls it may be associated with disruptions in heterosexual relations at adolescence (Hetherington 1972). Elementary-school-aged children and adolescents in particular are concerned with their parents' morality and competence. Perhaps because of their own awakening sexuality, preadolescents and adolescents are particularly distressed by an increased awareness of their parents as sex objects, first when both parents are dating and then when parents remarry (Wallerstein and Kelly 1974). Younger children are most anxious about the mother's ability to cope with family conflicts and stresses and her emotional condition following divorce, because of their precarious dependence on the single parent (Wallerstein, see note 4).

Research findings are consistent in showing that children in single-parent families function more adequately than children in conflict-ridden nuclear families (Rutter in press-b; Hetherington et al., see note 3). The eventual escape from conflict may be one of the most positive outcomes of divorce for children. However, family conflict does not decline but escalates in the year following divorce (Hetherington et al. 1978; Kelly, see note 1; Hetherington et al., see note 3; Wallerstein, see note 4). During this period children in divorced families, particularly boys, show more problems than do children in discordant nuclear families.

Father absence. In the current eagerness to demonstrate that single-parent families headed by mothers can provide a salutary environment for raising children and that the presence of fathers is not essential for normal development in children, there has been a tendency to overlook the contribution of fathers to family functioning. In trying to escape from the earlier narrowly biased view emphasizing father absence as the cause of any obtained developmental differences between children from single-parent and nuclear families, the pendulum may have swung too far in the other direction. Fathers may have a relatively unique contribution to make to family functioning and the development of the child. In the single-parent home some of the father's functions may be taken over by the mother or by other people, social institutions, relatives, siblings, a stepfather, friends, neighbors, a housekeeper, day-care centers, and schools. However, the roles the alternative support systems play may be qualitatively different from those of an involved accessible father (Pederson, Rubenstein, and Yarrow in press).

Some of the roles fathers play in parenting are indirect and serve to support the mother in her parenting role; others impact more directly on the child. The father in a nuclear family indirectly supports the mother in her maternal role in a number of ways—with economic aid, with assistance and relief in household tasks and child rearing, and with emotional support and encouragement and appreciation of her performance as a mother. In addition, an intimate relation in which the mother is valued and cherished contributes to her feelings of self-esteem, happiness, and competence, which influence her relationship with her children (Hetherington et al. 1978).

The father also may play a more direct and active role in shaping the child's behavior as an agent of socialization, by discipline, direct tuition, or acting as a model. In a single-parent family there is only one parent to serve those functions. The single parent or even two adults of the same sex offer the child a more restricted array of positive characteristics to model than do two parents (Pederson et al. in press). A mother and father are likely to exhibit wider ranging interests, skills, and attributes than a single parent. In addition, the father with his image of greater power and authority may be more effective in controlling children's behavior and in serving as backup authority for the mother's discipline.

Finally, one parent can serve as a protective buffer between the other parent and the child in a nuclear family. In a nuclear family a loving, competent, or well-adjusted parent can help counteract the effects of a rejecting, incompetent, emotionally unstable parent. In a single-parent family headed by a mother, the father is not present to mitigate any deleterious behaviors of the custodial parent in day-to-day living experiences (Hetherington et al., see note 3). Thus, the constructive and pathogenic behaviors of the mother are funneled more directly onto the child, and the quality of the mother-child relationship will be more directly reflected in the adjustment of the child than it is in a nuclear family.

Divorced fathers and their children. A finding that should be of some concern to those making custody recommendations is that there is little continuity between the quality of pre- and post-separation parent-child interaction, particularly for fathers (Hetherington et al. 1976; Kelly, see note 1). This discontinuity is another factor contributing to the sense of unpredictability in the child's situation. Some intensely attached fathers find intermittent fathering painful and withdraw from their children. On the other hand, a substantial number of fathers report that their relationship with their children improves after divorce, and many fathers, previously relatively uninvolved, become competent and concerned parents.

The parents' response to divorce and the quality of the child's relationship with both parents immediately after divorce has a substantial effect on the child's coping and adjustment (Hetherington et al. 1976; Kelly, see note 1). In the first year after divorce, parents are preoccupied with their own depression, anger, or emotional needs and are unable to respond sensitively to the wants of the child. During this period divorced parents tend to be inconsistent, less affectionate, and lacking in control over their children (Hetherington et al. 1978). However, they recover markedly in the second year after divorce.

Although in the early months following divorce fathers are having as much or even more contact with children as they did preceding the divorce, most divorced fathers rapidly become less available to their children. Fathers are more likely to maintain frequent contact with their sons than with their daughters (Hess and Camara in press). Most children wish to maintain contact with the father, and in preschool children, mourning for the father and fantasies of reconciliation may continue for several years (Hetherington et al. 1978; Tessman 1978; Wallerstein and Kelly 1975). Unless the father is extremely poorly adjusted or immature, or the child is exposed to conflict between the parents, frequent availability of the father is associated with positive adjustment and social relations, especially in boys (Hess and Camara in press; Hetherington et al. 1978, see note 3; Wallerstein, see note 4). A continued mutually supportive relationship and involvement of the father with the child is the most effective support system for divorced women in their parenting role and for their children. The recommendation that has been made that the custodial parent have the right to eliminate visitation by the noncustodial parent, if he or she views it as adverse to the child's well-being, seems likely to discourage parents from working out their differences and runs counter to the available research findings.

Divorced mothers and their children. With time, the custodial parent in single-parent families becomes increasingly salient in the development of the child (Hetherington et al., see note 3). Fathers who maintain frequent contact and involvement with their children have more impact on the child's development than do fathers whose contacts are relatively infrequent or who are relatively detached. However, even highly involved noncustodial fathers are less influential than the custodial mother in many facets of the child's personality and social and cognitive development. The well-being of the divorced mother and the quality of mother-child relations thus become central to the adjustment of the child. However, this is not a one-way street, since the mother's sense of competence, self-esteem, and happiness is modified by the behavior of her children, particularly her sons. The mother who must cope with too many young children or with acting-out, noncompliant behavior in sons becomes increasingly distressed and inept in her parenting. Divorced adults have more health and emotional problems, even after the initial crisis period of divorce, than do married adults (Bloom, Asher, and White 1978). This suggests that the child may be coping with a mother who is not only confronting many stresses but who may be physically and psychologically less able to deal with adversity.

In most divorcing families there is a period in the first year after divorce when mothers become depressed, self-involved, erratic, less supportive, and more ineffectually authoritarian in dealing with their children. Divorced mothers and their sons are particularly likely to get involved in an escalating cycle of mutual coercion. As was noted above, parenting improves dramatically in the second year after divorce; however, problems in parent-child relations continue to be found more often between divorced mothers and children, especially sons, than between mothers and children in nuclear families.

Different aspects of the divorced mother's relationship with her children are important with children of different ages. With preschool children, organization of the home and authoritative control, accompanied by nurturance and maturity demands, seem to be particularly important in the adjustment of the child. Young children have more difficulty than older children in exerting self-control and ordering their changing lives and thus require more external control and structure in times of stress and transition (Hetherington et al., see note 3). On the other hand, divorced mothers of older children and adolescents are more likely to rely on their children for emotional support and for assistance with practical problems of daily life. The children are asked to fulfill some of the functions of the departed father. There is great pressure for elementary-school-aged children and adolescents to function in a mature, autonomous manner at an early age. Weiss (see note 5) described the phenomenon of great self-sufficiency and growing up faster in one-parent families. If the mother is not making excessive or inappropriate demands for emotional sustenance, her greater openness about concerns and plans can lead to a companionate relationship between her and her children. However, being pushed toward early independence and the assumption of adult responsibilities leads to feelings of being overwhelmed by unsolvable problems, incompetence, and resentment about lack of support and unavailability of mothers, and to precocious sexual concerns in some school-aged children and adolescents (Kelly, see note 1; Wallerstein, see note 4).

Extrafamilial Support Systems

Willard Hartup (in press) discussed how little we know about extrafamilial social and affectional systems and the relationships among familial and extrafamilial systems. This is nowhere more apparent than in the area of divorce, where the focus of study largely has been confined to parent-child relations and where the emphasis has been on supports for the divorced parents rather than for the children. Even the role of siblings and the extended family as support systems for children going through family disruption has received only cursory examination. The research thus far indicates that extended family and community services play a more active role as support systems for low-income than for moderate-income families (Colletta 1978; Spicer and Hampe 1975). With preschool children, family relations are prepotent in the adjustment of the child. Disruptions in family functioning are associated with maladaptive behaviors both in the home and in other social situations (Hess and Camara in press; Wallerstein and Kelly 1975; Hetherington et al., see note 3).

With older children, although the disruptive effects of divorce may flood over into other relations in the period immediately surrounding divorce, they are more rapidly able to circumscribe these effects. Older children are frequently able to confine their stress within the family arena and to use peers and schools as sources of information, satisfaction, and support (Hetherington et al. in press; Wallerstein, see note 4). The validation of self-worth, competence, and personal control are important functions served by peers, and positive school and neighborhood environments are to some extent able to attenuate the effects of stressful family relations (Hess and Camara in press; Hetherington et al. in press; Rutter in press-b; Wallerstein, see note 4; Hetherington et al., see note 3).

Summary

The best statistical prognostications suggest that an increasing number of children are going to experience their parents' divorce and life in a single-parent family. A conflict-ridden intact family is more deleterious to family members than is a stable home in which parents are divorced. An inaccessible, rejecting, or hostile parent in a nuclear family is more detrimental to the development of the child than is the absence of a parent. Divorce is often a positive solution to destructive family functioning; however, most children experience divorce as a difficult transition, and life in a single-parent family can be viewed as a high-risk situation for parents and children. This is not to say that single-parent families cannot or do not serve as effective settings for the development of competent, stable, happy children, but the additional stresses and the lack of support systems confronted by divorced families impose additional burdens on their members.

Most research has viewed the single-parent family as a pathogenic family and has failed to focus on how positive family functioning and support systems can facilitate the development of social, emotional, and intellectual competence in children in single-parent families. Neither the gloom-and-doom approach nor the political stance of refusing to recognize that many single-parent families headed by mothers have problems other than financial difficulties is likely to be productive. We need more research and applied programs oriented toward the identification and facilitation of patterns of family functioning, as well as support systems that help families to cope with changes and stress associated with divorce and that help to make single-parent families the basis of a satisfying and fulfilling life-style.

NOTES

1. Kelly, J. B. *Children and parents in the midst of divorce: Major factors contributing to differential response.* Paper presented at the National Institute of Mental Health Conference on Divorce, Washington, D.C., February 1978.
2. Hodges, F. H., Wechsler, R. C., and Ballantine, C. *Divorce and the preschool child: Cumulative stress.* Paper presented at the meeting of the American Psychological Association, Toronto, August 1978.
3. Hetherington, E. M., Cox, M., and Cox, R. *Family interactions and the social, emotional and cognitive development of children following divorce.* Paper presented at the Johnson and Johnson Symposium on the Family: Setting Priorities, Washington, D.C., 1978.
4. Wallerstein, J. S. *Children and parents 18 months after parental separation: Factors related to differential outcome.* Paper presented at the National Institute of Mental Health Conference on Divorce, Washington, D.C., February 1978.
5. Weiss, R. *Single-parent households as settings for growing up.* Paper presented at the National Institute of Mental Health Conference on Divorce, Washington, D.C., February 1978.

REFERENCES

BANE, M. J. Marital disruption and the lives of children. *Journal of Social Issues*, 1976, *32*, 103–117.

BLOOM, B. L., ASHER, S. J., AND WHITE, S. W. Marital disruption as a stressor: A review and analysis. *Psychological Bulletin*, 1978, *85*, 867–894.

BRANDWEIN, R. A., BROWN, C. A., AND FOX, E. M. Women and children last: The social situation of divorced mothers and their families. *Journal of Marriage and the Family*, 1974, *36*, 498–514.

CHESS, S., THOMAS, A., AND BIRCH, H. O. Behavioral problems revisited. In S. Chess and H. Birch (Eds.), *Annual progress in child psychiatry and child development.* New York: Brunner/Mazel, 1968.

COLLETTA, N. D. *Divorced mothers at two income levels: Stress, support and child-rearing practices.* Unpublished thesis, Cornell University, 1978.

GARMEZY, N. The experimental study of children vulnerable to psychopathology. In A. Davids (Ed.), *Child personality and psychopathology* (Vol. 2). New York: Wiley, 1975.

GLICK, P. G., AND NORTON, A. J. Marrying, divorcing and living together in the U.S. today. *Population Bulletin*, 1978, *32*, 3–38.

GRAHAM, P., RUTTER, M., AND GEORGE, S. Temperamental characteristics as predictors of behavior disorders in children. *American Journal of Orthopsychiatry.* 1973, *43*, 328–399.

HARTUP, W. Two social worlds: Family relations and peer relations. In M. Rutter (Ed.), *Scientific foundations of developmental psychiatry.* London: Heinemann Medical, in press.

HESS, R. D., AND CAMARA, K. A. Post-divorce family relations as mediating factors in the consequences of divorce for children. *Journal of Social Issues*, in press.

HETHERINGTON, E. M. Effects of father absence on personality development in adolescent daughters. *Developmental Psychology*, 1972, 7, 313–326.

HETHERINGTON, E. M., COX, M., AND COX, R. Divorced fathers. *Family Coordinator*, 1976, *25*, 417–428.

HETHERINGTON, E. M., COX, M., AND COX, R. The aftermath of divorce. In J. H. Stevens, Jr., and M. Matthews (Eds.), *Mother-child, father-child relations.* Washington, D.C.: National Association for the Education of Young Children, 1978.

HETHERINGTON, E. M., COX, M., AND COX, R. Play and social interaction in children following divorce. *Journal of Social Issues*, in press.

KRIESBERG, L. *Mothers in poverty: A study of fatherless families.* Chicago: Aldine, 1970.

MARSDEN, D. *Mothers alone: Poverty and the fatherless family.* London: Allen Lane the Penguin Press, 1969.

PEARLIN, L. I., AND JOHNSON, J. S. Marital status, life strains, and depression. *American Sociological Review*, 1977, *42*, 704–715.

PEDERSEN, F. A., RUBENSTEIN, J., AND YARROW, L. J. Infant development in father-absent families. *Journal of Genetic Psychology*, in press.

PORTER, G., AND O'LEARY, D. K. Marital discord and child behavior problems. *Journal of Abnormal Child Psychology*, in press.

ROSS, H. L., AND SAWHILL, I. V. *Time of transition: The growth of families headed by women.* Washington, D.C.: Urban Institute, 1975.

RUTTER, M. Maternal deprivation 1972–1978: New findings, new concepts, new approaches. *Child Development*, in press. (a)

RUTTER, M. Protective factors in children's responses to stress and disadvantage. In M. W. Kent and J. E. Rolf (Eds.), *Primary prevention of psychopathology: Vol. 3. Promoting social competence and coping in children*. Hanover, N.H.: University Press of New England, in press. (b)

SANTROCK, J. W. Father absence, perceived maternal behavior and moral development in boys. *Child Development*, 1975, *46*, 753–757.

SANTROCK, J. W., AND TRACE, R. L. Effect of children's family structure status on the development of stereotypes by children. *Journal of Educational Psychology*, 1978, *70*, 754–757.

SPICER, J., AND HAMPE, G. Kinship interaction after divorce. *Journal of Marriage and the Family*, 1975, *28*, 113–119.

TESSMAN, L. H. *Children of parting parents*. New York: Aronson, 1978.

TUCKMAN, J., AND REGAN, P. A. Intactness of the home and behavioral problems in children. *Journal of Child Psychology and Psychiatry*, 1966, *7*, 225–233.

WALLERSTEIN, J. S., AND KELLY, J. B. The effects of parental divorce: The adolescent experience. In A. Koupernik (Ed.), *The child in his family: Children at a psychiatric risk* (Vol. 3). New York: Wiley, 1974.

WALLERSTEIN, J. S., AND KELLY, J. B. The effects of parental divorce: Experiences in the preschool child. *Journal of the American Academy of Child Psychiatry*, 1975, *14*, 600–616.

WEISS, R. *Marital separation*. New York: Basic Books, 1975.

WINSTON, M. P., AND FORSHER, T. *Nonsupport of legitimate children by affluent fathers as a cause of poverty and welfare dependence*. New York: Rand Corporation, 1971.

Part V

Children's Peer Relations

DURING infancy the possibility of peer interaction may remain for many children an untapped potential, but during childhood the peer relation becomes for most a central part of social life. While relations with adults still dominate the child's social world, a gradual shift in the relative significance of peers to adults has begun and will continue through the adolescent years.

Willard Hartup in his article points out that peer interaction for the child is not a "superficial luxury" to be experienced or not for the fun of it. Like adult-child relations, peer experience is, as Hartup writes, "a necessity in childhood socialization." Hartup's discussion identifies a number of ways in which peer interaction contributes to the social and personality development of children. Among these are the child's moral development, the child's emotional stability, the child's intellectual growth, and the child's willingness to engage the environment in an active and adventuresome manner. A lack of sociability with peers, maintains Hartup, is one of the critical indicators of disturbances in the child's development. Creating opportunities for peer engagement can be a highly effective means of remediating behavioral difficulties and facilitating positive social and emotional growth.

As Hartup also points out, the phenomenon of social play is largely a peer activity during childhood. Catherine Garvey's analysis of 158 social play episodes among preschoolers reveals some key properties of peer play in early childhood. First, children while playing with peers distinguish play from reality, as is demonstrated by children in exchanges such as "Really?"

217

. . . "No, just pretend." Second, during social play children abstract rules of social interaction, in particular the rule of turn-taking. This is demonstrated by children who spontaneously give turn-taking directives to one another, such as "You go next," or "Do it again." Third, children engaged in social play develop and vary a theme collaboratively. As Garvey writes, "Any episode of social play entails the exercise of *shared imagination.*" It is as if children simultaneously act as playwrights and actors in the creation and performance of a narrative script.

In the course of multiple peer engagements like social play, children begin to establish continuing relations with each other. These relations endure over time and build up their own set of expectations and rules. The archetypical social relation between peers is friendship. Friendship is a relationship based upon affection ("liking" one another); it serves to provide its participants with companionship and mutual support. Only recently have developmental psychologists realized the extent to which young children are capable of initiating and maintaining stable friendships with their peers.

Zick Rubin reviews some of the informative recent research on children's friendships. One outcome of this research is a description of how children's understanding of friendship changes in the course of development. Preschoolers commonly view friendship as a set of shared activities between playmates who like each other and who often spend time together. Later in childhood develops the notion that friends help and cooperate with one another. By early adolescence, friendship is seen as a relationship based upon intimacy and loyal commitment. Friends share exclusive secrets with one another, stick with each other through fair and foul weather alike, respect and accept one another's idiosyncrasies, and enjoy common interests. Thus the developmental progression of children's views of friendship is from a relationship characterized by frequent shared activity to a relationship characterized by long-term commitment and a sense of knowing someone (and being known by someone) in an especially intimate way. Rubin notes that not all children develop along this progression at the same ages, and that there is only an uncertain relation between a child's understanding of the friendship relation and the child's behavior with peers. Still, the child's changing conceptions of friendship no doubt reflect fundamental advances in the child's ability to form and maintain social relations with peers.

Many psychologists believe that a major contributor to a child's ability to conduct positive social relations is a sense of empathy. An empathic response is one that is similar or compatible with another's feelings. It is likely that a child's shared feelings of happiness for another's joy motivates the child to create the conditions for the other's joy through prosocial acts, just as a child's shared feelings of unhappiness for another's distress motivates the child to alleviate that distress through acts of kindness and aid.

Martin Hoffman describes the development of empathy in the child and shows how this growing capacity facilitates the child's interpersonal relations with peers. During infancy, the child feels discomfort when faced with another's distress, but this is a global feeling that does not precisely distinguish the discomforts of self and other. At about age two, the child begins to make this distinction by locating the true source of distress in the other. The child can then make a realistic assessment of the other's needs and respond appropriately by coming to the other's aid. Sometime between the ages of six and nine, according to Hoffman, the child increasingly becomes aware of self and other as persons with continuing identities that go beyond the behavior of self and other in the immediate situation. Consequently, the child becomes concerned about the general condition of persons rather than only about situationally induced distress. The child still retains the ability to empathize with another's pains and pleasures of the moment, but now is more sensitive to the "general plight" of life's chronic victims. These include particularly the poor, the handicapped, and the socially outcast. This new sensitivity opens the way for a concerted effort to aid those less fortunate than oneself.

Peer relations offer children opportunities to interact with persons who are truly their equals. In the course of such interactions, children experience genuine mutuality and cooperation. They learn to give and expect kindness, consideration, and loyalty; and they discover the consequences of fair and unfair behavior. Further, the special intimacy of the peer friendship enables close friends to reveal innermost secrets to one another while remaining confident of each other's acceptance and trust. For these reasons, children's peer relations are at the heart of their social, moral, and personal development, and many psychiatrists believe early friendships to be an important contributor to future mental health.

14

Peer Interaction and the Behavioral Development of the Individual Child

Willard W. Hartup

Experience with peers is commonly assumed to make numerous contributions to child development. Such experiences are believed to provide a context for sex-role learning, the internalization of moral values, the socialization of aggression, and the development of cognitive skills. The research literature, however, contains relatively little hard data concerning the functional contributions of peer interaction to the development of the individual child. There is little evidence that the give-and-take occurring during peer interaction actually determines the moral restructuring that occurs in middle childhood, as Piaget (1932) suggested; there is no direct evidence that rough-and-tumble play contributes to the effectiveness with which the human child copes with aggressive affect (Harlow 1969); and the contributions of peer attachments to social and intellectual development are largely unspecified.

Nevertheless, the purpose of this paper is to argue that peer interaction is an essential component of the individual child's development. Experience with peers is not a superficial luxury to be enjoyed by some children and not by others, but is a necessity in childhood socialization. And among the most sensitive indicators of difficulties in development are failure by the child to engage in the activities of the peer culture and failure to occupy a relatively comfortable place within it.

From E. Schopler and R. J. Reichler, eds., *Psychopathology and Child Development: Deviations and Treatment* (New York: Plenum Press, 1976). Reprinted by permission of the publisher and author.

Two issues provide the basis for this discussion: a) the thesis that peer interactions are essential to the normal development of children; and b) the contention that intervention in children's peer relations can appropriately alter the general course of behavioral development.

Peer Relations and the Individual Child's Development

Attachment and Sociability. Recent research confirms that during the third and fourth years of life there is a decrease in the frequency with which the child seeks proximity with the mother (Maccoby and Feldman 1972), an increase in the frequency of attention-seeking and the seeking of approval relative to the frequency with which the child seeks affection (Heathers 1955), and a change in the objects toward whom social overtures are made—specifically, there is an increase in the frequency of contact with peers (Heathers 1955). Peer attachments become even more characteristic of the child's social life during middle childhood.

The bonds which children establish with agemates are dissimilar to the earlier bonds which are forged between mother and child (Maccoby and Masters 1970). First, children employ different behaviors to express affection to agemates and to adults. They follow one another around, giving attention and help to each other, but rarely express verbal affection to agemates, hug one another, or cling to each other. Moreover, children do not seem to be disturbed by the absence of a specific child even though the absence of specific adults may give rise to anxiety and distress.[1] Second, the conditions which elicit attachment activity differ according to whether the available attachment object is an adult or another child. For example, fear tends to elicit running to the teacher rather than fleeing to one's peers. Third, the behavior of adults toward children differs qualitatively from the behavior of one child toward another. Adults do not engage in sustained periods of playful behavior with children; rather, they assume roles as onlookers or supervisors of children's playful activities. In fact, play appears to emerge in the human repertoire almost completely within the context of peer interaction.[2] This fact casts further doubt on the assumption that the parent-child and child-child social systems are manifestations of unitary "attachment" orientation.

What developmental benefits does the child derive from peer attachments? What are the correlates and/or consequences of sociability with agemates? What attitudes and orientations typify the child who is *not* involved in easy-going social activities with peers? To my mind, the best evidence (although not the only evidence) bearing on this problem is to be found in Bronson's (1966) analysis of the data from the Berkeley Guidance Study. Among three "central" behavioral orientations emerging in her analysis, the clearest way a bi-polar dimension labeled *reserved-somber-shy/ expressive-gay-socially easy.* Across each of four age periods, covering the ages from 5 through 16 years, this orientation (social reservedness) in boys was associated with: a) an inward-looking social orientation, b) high anxiety, and c) low activity. In later childhood, the correlates of reservedness also came to include: a) vulnerability, b) lack of dominance, c) nonadventuresomeness, and d) instability. In other words, lack of sociability in boys was correlated with discomfort, anxiety, and a general unwillingness to engage the environment.

The correlates of social reservedness among girls were not substantially different. The associations between sociability and vulnerability, level of activity, and caution were significant across all four age periods, and a correlation with passivity tended to increase over time. Note that the cluster of traits which surrounds low sociability may be indicative of behavior which is in greater accord with social stereotypes among the girls than among the boys. In general, though, the findings suggest that failure to be involved with one's peers is accompanied by a lower level of instrumental competence (Baumrind 1972) and higher anxiety than is the condition of high peer involvement. Other research provides a composite picture of the socially *rejected* child which is very much like the composite picture of the socially *inactive* child: he is neither outgoing nor friendly; he is either very high or very low in self-esteem; he is particularly dependent on adults for emotional support; he is anxious and inappropriately aggressive (Hartup 1970).

Although the foregoing findings are relatively firm, interpretation of them is difficult. Everything we know concerning the developmental consequences of peer involvement is based on correlational data. It is not clear, therefore, that peer involvement is instrumental in producing an outgoing, active, non-anxious, assertive posture toward the world, or whether a reverse interpretation is to be preferred. More than likely, some set of external influences is responsible for this whole configuration of traits, i.e., for both sociability and its correlates. But what might such external influences be? Clearly, biological factors may be operative as well as social influences. Individual differences in sociability stabilize early, such differences are not closely associated with child rearing practices (Bronson 1966) and these characteristics possess moderate heritabilities (Scarr 1969). Thus, the origins of the linkage between general personal-social effectiveness and the presence or absence of effective peer relations remain obscure. It is important, however, for both theoreticians and practitioners to know that this linkage exists and to know that it characterizes child behavior across a variety of samples, times, and circumstances.

Aggression.   Scattered evidence suggests that children master their aggressive impulses within the context of the peer culture rather than within the context of the family, the milieu of television, or the culture of the school. Nonhuman primate studies demonstrate rather convincingly that peer contact during late infancy and the juvenile stage produces two effects on the individual: a) he acquires a repertoire of effective aggressive behaviors, and b) he acquires mechanisms for coping with the affective outcomes of aggressive interaction (Harlow 1969). In fact, socialization seems to require both rough-and-tumble play and experiences in which rough play escalates into aggression, and de-escalates into playful interaction (Hamburg and Van Lawick-Goodall 1974). Field studies suggest that such experiences are readily available to the young in all primate species, including *Homo sapiens*, although opportunities are greater for males than for females (Jay 1968; Hartup 1974).

Whether parents can produce such a marked impact on the development of aggression is doubtful. The rough-and-tumble experiences necessary for aggressive socialization seem to be incompatible with the demands for maternal bonding because, for all primate species, some tie to the mother must be maintained after the time when socialization of aggression is begun. Fathers may contribute significantly to aggression learning, both because they provide frequent and effective displays of aggressive behavior with their children and because bonding to the father is "looser," more "secondary," and less constraining than is bonding with the mother. Selected studies support this: research on father absence shows that boys from such homes are less aggressive than boys in father present homes (Hetherington and Deur 1972). Nevertheless, whether fathers alone could effectively socialize their children's aggression—even their male children— remains doubtful. The father's social role in Western culture requires him to spend most of his time outside the family and, even in close-knit family cultures, paternal contacts with the young child are insufficient to produce all of the learning required for the successful modulation of aggressive behavior.

Thus, nature seems to have prepared for human socialization in such a way that child-child relations are more important contributors to the successful control of aggressive motivation than parent-child relations. Patterson and his associates (Patterson, Littman, and Bricker 1967; Patterson and Cobb 1971) have confirmed convincingly the various ways in which reinforcement for both aggression and yielding to aggression are provided within the context of peer interactions.

According to this line of reasoning, children who show generalized hostility and unusual modes of aggressive behavior, or children who are unusually timid in the presence of aggressive attack may be lacking exposure to certain kinds of contacts with peers, i.e., rough-and-tumble play. In other words, peer contacts which never allow for aggressive display or which allow only for successful aggression (never for unsuccessful aggression) may be precursors of malfunctioning in the aggression system. Clearly, this hypothesis is plausible when applied to boys, although it is more tenuous for girls. Traditional socialization produces women who are ineffectively prepared for exposure to aggressive instigating events (except perhaps, for threats to their children). Women are notably more anxious and passive than men when exposed to aggressive instigation, and this sex difference may be greater than is good for the future of the species. In any event, if women are to assume social roles more like those of men, and men are to assume roles more like those of women, some manipulation of early peer experiences is necessary. Opportunities for early exposure to rough-and-tumble play must be as equal for males and for females as opportunities for exposure to other normative behaviors.

Sex.   If parents were to be given sole responsibility for the socialization of sexuality, *Homo sapiens* would not survive. With due respect to the efforts of modern sex educators, we must recognize that the parent-child relationship is no better suited to the task of socializing sex than to the task of socializing aggression. Evolution has established the incest taboo (Lindzey 1967), a taboo which is so pervasive that interaction with agemates is virtually the only opportunity available to the child in which he may engage in the trial and error, the modeling, and the information gathering that ultimately produce his sexual life style.

There can be little doubt that sexual attitudes and the basic sexual repertoire are shaped primarily by contacts with other children. Kinsey (1948) said: "Children are the most frequent agents for the transmission of the sexual mores. Adults serve in that capacity only to a smaller extent. This will not surprise sociologists and anthropologists, for they are aware of the great amount of imitative adult activity which enters into the play of children, the world around. In this activity, play though it may be, children are severe, highly critical, and vindictive in their punishment of a child who does not do it 'this way,' or 'that way.' Even before there has been any attempt at overt sex play, the child may have acquired a considerable schooling on matters of sex. Much of this comes so early that the adult has no memory of where his attitudes were acquired (p. 445)." These comments are repeated, nearly word for word, in the records of those many investigators who have observed the various non-human primate species in the field (Jay 1968).

Of course, the child's earliest identification of itself as male or female and the earliest manifestations of sex-typed behavior patterns derive from interactions with its parents. Parents are known to respond differentially to boys and to girls from infancy onward (Rothbart and Maccoby 1966), and the sex-typed outcomes of parent-child interaction have been discussed extensively in the child development literature (e.g., Lynn 1969). Nevertheless, there is strong evidence that the peer culture supports and extends the process of sex-typing beginning in the earliest preschool years. Sex is the overriding polarizer in peer group formation in all primate species from the point of earliest contact (Hartup 1975). Sex is a more powerful determinant of "who plays with whom" than age, race, social class, intelligence, or any other demographic factor with the possible exception of propinquity. And clearly, this sex cleavage is instrumental in transmitting normative sex-role standards to the child. How else to account for the vast number of sex differences that have been observed in the social activities of children (e.g., aggression) beginning with the preschool years?

Another vivid demonstration of the power of the peer culture in early sex-typing is contained in a series of experiments by Kobasigawa (1968). With kindergarten children, he found that: a) exposure to peer models who inhibited playing with inappropriate-sex toys enhanced the observer's self-control over inappropriate responses; b) exposure to models demonstrating alternative activities to sex-inappropriate responses also reduced inappropriate sex-typed activity; c) exposure to peer models who displayed sex-inappropriate behavior had disinhibitory effects on the observer, although the amount of the disinhibition depended on the sex of the model in relation to the sex of the child—that is, boys disinhibited inappropriate sex behavior only when the model was a boy while the sex of the model made relatively little difference in amount of disinhibition for girls. Similar results have been found in other modeling work: for example, aggressive peer models enhance aggression in young children, but more effectively if the model is a boy than if the model is a girl (Hicks 1967).

Do these findings imply that aberrant and inadequate sexual behaviors derive from aberrant and/or inadequate contacts with the peer culture? My knowledge of life history research in sexual pathology is very limited, but my impression is that most such pathologies derive from some combination of early hangups with parents and hangups with peers. Peer modeling, in other words, seldom accounts for all of the variance in criminally violent or aberrant sexual behavior. Even so, Roff (1966) has shown that a history of poor peer relations is more characteristic of certain kinds of homosexual males than comparison groups of heterosexual males; case studies show with considerable frequency that persons committing crimes of sexual assault have histories of peer rejection and social isolation.

Moral Development. According to Piaget (1932), both the quantity and the quality of social participation are related to the child's moral development. Moral understanding is assumed to derive partly from the amount of social interaction in which the child participates and partly from his centrality in the peer group. During early childhood, the child's behavior reflects an "objective" moral orientation (i.e., he believes that rules are immutable and the power of adults is absolute). Adoption of a "subjective" moral orientation requires some opportunity to view moral rules as changeable products of group consensus. For this purpose, social give-and-take is required. Such opportunity is not common in the child's experiences with his parents and teachers because social systems such as the family and the school are structured in authoritarian terms. Only in rare instances is there sufficient reciprocity in adult-child interaction to facilitate the disequilibration which is necessary to form a mature moral orientation. The peer group, on the other hand, is seldom organized along authoritarian dimensions and possesses the inherent characteristics for furthering moral development.

Precious little data exist to support the thesis that the *amount* of agemate contact is associated with advanced moral development. Keasey (1971) has recently published a study, however, based on 144 preadolescents, in which he found that children who belonged to relatively many clubs and social organizations had higher moral judgment scores than children belonging to few organized groups. These results, which were somewhat stronger for boys than for girls, stand alone in revealing a correlation between amount of social participation with peers and advances in moral functioning.

Evidence is more profuse concerning the association between the *quality* of a child's peer contacts and the level of his moral reasoning. Keasey (1971) also reported that self-reports of leadership functions, peer ratings of leadership and friendship nominations, and teacher ratings of leadership and popularity were all positively related to level of moral judgment as assessed by Kohlberg's (1958) techniques. Irwin (1967) was unable to demonstrate consistent relations between popularity and measures of moral understanding within several groups of nursery school children, either because the samples were too homogeneous or because the period in question is too early for the relation between acceptance and morality to be reflected in a systematic manner. Other data, though, support Keasey's findings: Gold (1962) reported that peer leaders have "more socially integrative" ideologies than non leaders; Porteus and Johnson (1955) showed that acceptance was related to good moral judgment as perceived by peers; Campbell and Yarrow (1961) found that popular children, as compared to less popular children, made more extensive use of subtle inferences concerning the causes of other children's behavior; and Klaus (1959) found that accepted children tend to emphasize being neat and tidy, being a good sport, and being able to take a joke in their descriptions of classmates. Each of these diverse findings suggests that popularity is linked with effectively internalized social norms. Studies of peer group leaders also show them to be actively and appropriately sociable.

Once again, there is difficulty in interpreting the findings. Existence of a significant correlation between the extent of social participation and level of moral functioning does not prove that the latter derives from the former. Membership in clubs may facilitate change in the structuring of moral understanding but higher levels of moral understanding may also be prerequisite to membership in large numbers of social clubs. Children may choose friends and teachers may nominate children as popular who can demonstrate advanced levels of moral understanding; on the other hand, popularity itself may enhance the child's level of moral reasoning. Another possibility is that the linkages cited here exist partly because estimates of moral understanding and estimates of popularity are both modestly related to intelligence.

Thus, the basic hypothesis that peer interaction contributes to advances in moral development remains unproven. The available evidence is consistent with this hypothesis, to be sure, but only controlled manipulation of the child's social experiences with agemates can provide adequate causal evidence. Needless to say, such manipulations are very hard to produce.

Are children who have successful peer relations more overtly honest and upright than children who are loners and/or who are rejected by their peers? Some of the previously-cited evidence is suggestive of such a state of affairs, although additional evidence is not extensive. In one early investigation, Roff (1961) found that in a sample of servicemen, all of whom were former patients in a child guidance clinic, those receiving bad conduct discharges were significantly more likely to have been rated by their childhood counselors as having poor peer adjustment than those with successful service records. These data are important for two reasons: a) they demonstrate a linkage between peer adjustment and moral behavior; and b) the relation is a predictive one—childhood failure in peer relations was correlated with bad conduct discharge rates in adulthood. In a more recent study (Roff and Sells 1968), a significant relation was demonstrated between peer acceptance-rejection during middle childhood and delinquency during early adolescence. Among upper lower-class and middle-class children, there was a dramatically higher delinquency rate among children who were not accepted by their peers than among those who were. Among the very lowest social class subjects, however, a different pattern held—both highly accepted and highly rejected boys had higher delinquency rates than those who were moderately accepted by their peers. Examination of individual case records indicated that the nature of the delinquency and the adequacy of the child's personality adjustment differed between the chosen and nonchosen lower class groups—in fact, there is every reason to expect that, among the subjects from the lowest social strata, ultimate adjustment of the peer accepted delinquent group will be better than the nonaccepted delinquent subjects. Thus far, path analysis techniques have not been applied to Roff's data, so that some question still remains concerning the relative primacy of delinquent activity and the poor peer relations. But the data point to peer interaction as one source of the individual's willingness to live according to accepted social standards.

Other research, dealing with the problem in a different manner, suggests that peer pressures can move child behavior both in the direction of socially accepted and socially nonaccepted norms. Such pressures are directly revealed in the studies of spontaneous peer groups published by the Sherifs (1964) and more indirectly in Kandel's (1973) study of peer influences in relation to drug use among adolescents.[3] Indirect peer influences on moral behavior are also shown in a set of studies by Shelton and Hill (1969) in which it was found that children were more likely to falsify their scores in a laboratory game if they expected that their peers would be informed about their performance than if information about the subject's performance was to be kept secret.

Anxiety and Emotional Disturbance. Evidence can be found in at least twenty studies to show that a child's general emotional adjustment is related to his popularity (Hartup 1970). Assessment of adjustment in these studies has been accomplished with devices as various as the TAT, on the one hand, and observations of school adjustment, on the other. The data consistently show that, in samples of children who are functioning within the normal range, degree of maladjustment is inversely related to degree of social acceptance. In addition to the studies with normal samples, work with institutionalized populations shows that popularity in disturbed groups is also inversely related to relative degree of maladjustment (Davids and Parenti 1958). Sheer quantity of social participation has not been studied in relation to general personality adjustment, although one suspects that such a relation exists.

Some fifteen years ago, a spate of studies was published concerning the relation between a more specific affective component, anxiety, and social acceptance. In general there tends to be a low negative correlation between anxiety, as measured by the *Children's Manifest Anxiety Scale,* and sociometric status (e.g., McCandless, Castaneda, and Palermo 1956) although, once again, we know very little about the relation between amount of social participation and anxiety.

The major predictive studies of the relation between childhood peer status and adult emotional adjustment have been completed by Roff (1963) within the context of his follow-up investigations of the adult status of boys who, as children, were seen in child guidance clinics. Within these samples, poor peer relations in childhood have been predictive of both neurotic disturbance and psychotic episodes of a variety of types.

Once again, the evidence relating affective disturbance and peer relations is correlational and invites an interpretation suggesting that rejection leads to anxiety, lowered self-esteem, and hostility which, in turn, lead to further rejection. A simple uni-directional interpretation does not seem plausible. However, in spite of the fact that explanatory hypotheses do not receive clear support from this research, there is no evidence which contradicts the basic hypothesis that peer relations are of pivotal importance in personality development (Roff, Sells, and Golden 1972).

Intellectual Development. The contributions of peer relations to intellectual development are difficult to specify. There seems to be no evidence that sociability is related to IQ, either in younger or older children. Parten (1932) found a small positive correlation between cooperative participation and IQ ($r = .33$) but an even larger correlation was obtained between parallel play and IQ ($r = .62$). On the other hand, amount of social participation appears to be neither markedly greater or less among gifted children than among children of average IQ (Terman and Oden 1947), and moderately retarded children are not notably less sociable than children of greater intellectual ability. Brighter children occupy more central positions in the peer culture, being of higher sociometric status than less bright children (Roff, Sells, and Golden 1972) and of higher social effectance (Hartup 1970), but competence in social relations does not bear a consistent relation to IQ. At least one study (Lurie, Newburger, Rosenthal, and Outcalt 1941) shows an inverse relation between measured intelligence and social maturity. Thus, it is difficult to make a case for the hypothesis that social participation is related to mental abilities (as measured by IQ tests) in any systematic way.

The evidence is also conflicting concerning the relation between sociability and achievement; much depends on the parameters of achievement and social behavior being measured. For example, Van den Munckhof (1970) reported a correlation of .42 between sociability and performance on the *Nijmegen School Achievement Test* for a sample of 454 Dutch school children, a finding which was replicated with a second sample including 91 handicapped young girls. On the other hand, Crandall (1970) found that both men and women who spend large amounts of time in academic achievement efforts had early childhood histories of alienation from their peers.

Several studies indicate that peer affiliations can either reward or punish academic performance, depending on the values of the peer group. An inverse correlation has sometimes been found between studiousness and popularity (Coleman 1961) but opposite findings have also been obtained (Hartup 1970). Thus, at the moment, there is no strong evidence that either sheer amount of social participation or the centrality of the child's position in the peer group has a consistent bearing on achievement behavior.

The status of Piaget's (1926) hypothesis that peer interaction is the primary mechanism for overcoming childhood egocentrism is also uncertain. Most of the research based on this hypothesis has involved the study of correlations between measured popularity, on the one hand, and measures of role-taking ability or referential communication, on the other hand. Using this paradigm, Rubin (1972) found that popular kindergarten and second grade children had low scores on a measure of communicative egocentrism as compared to their nonpopular peers. Finley, French, and Cowan (1973), however, reported that they were unable to generate any significant relations between popularity and three different measures of egocentrism in two different samples of elementary school children. And finally, Rardin and Moan (1971) reported very, very weak relations between popularity and classification and conservation abilities among kindergarten and first grade children.

Thus, the evidence does not support the Piagetian thesis that the peer group is the primary locus of social "decentration." Of course, certain questions may be raised concerning the adequacy of the research strategies which have been used to explore the interface between peer relations and cognitive development. Co-variation of individual differences within age groups should not be expected to reveal the functional contribution of social experience to the restructuring of mental abilities. Also, popularity may not be the most appropriate index of social participation for studying this problem. Although popular children are more sociable than nonpopular children (McCandless and Marshall 1957), the relation between amount of social experience and cognitive change should be explored more directly.

Thus, the contribution of peer relations to intellectual development is unclear. Neither general nor specific cognitive abilities appear to be consistently related to either the quantity or quality of a child's contact with the peer culture. Whether such social experiences represent unimportant contributions to mental development or whether our research strategies have been defective remains an open question. But no claim can be made, on the basis of present data, to the effect that large portions of variance in children's intellectual competencies derive from their commerce with agemates.

Improving Children's Peer Relations

Calculated attempts to improve children's peer relations have been successful since the first behavior modification experiments (Jack 1934; Page 1936; Chittenden 1942). These early studies included the invention of protocols which utilized out-of-class training experiences in modifying assertive and dominance behaviors. The protocols, which made liberal use of contingent social reinforcement, modeling, and verbal instructions, represent excellent examples of efficient supplemental socialization experiences for young children. The procedures were clearly explicated, and the outcomes were documented with respect to both short-term and somewhat longer-term effects. More recent studies, such as those by Harris, Wolf, and Baer (1967), demonstrate how contingencies of adult attention can be used within the classroom itself to being about increased peer contacts from isolated, socially-incompetent children. Although most of these studies have included follow-up checks which were conducted weeks or months later and which demonstrate the lastingness of the induced effects, long-term follow-up studies are rare. This deficit can be cited as a critical gap in this literature.

Other ways of modifying children's social competencies consist of manipulating the context in which peer interaction occurs. One contextual element which can be used to modify the individual child's behavior is feedback from the peer group itself. Thus, Wahler (1967) picked five nursery school children, established baseline rates for a number of different response classes (e.g., cooperation, social overtures, and social speech), and then instructed the peer groqp to behave toward the target children with different contingencies than were ordinarily used. Two outcomes of this experiment should be mentioned: a) the children's peers were able to use attention selectively, thus demonstrating the feasibility of programming peer interaction; and b) behavior change in the selected response class occurred during the experimental phase for each of the five subjects. Other studies (e.g., Patterson and Brodsky 1966) have described instances in which the peer group has been used to modify more deviant behaviors than in the Wahler experiment.

Group leaders can manipulate the context of peer interaction in a variety of other ways. The classic studies of group atmosphere, in which social behavior was determined by leadership style, are pertinent to this discussion (e.g., Lewin, Lippitt, and White 1938). So are the studies of the effects of superordinate goals on intergroup conflict and cooperation (Sherif, Harvey, White, Hood, and Sherif 1961).

Simply manipulating the composition of the peer group apparently has therapeutic potential. For example, there is the possibility that interaction with nonagemates provides a more sanguine context for the development of social competence by low competent children than does interaction with children who are similar in age. Suomi and Harlow (1972) reported that the untoward effects of prolonged isolation on the social development of rhesus monkeys is effectively reversed by a carefully managed program of contact between the isolated monkey and other monkeys who are appreciably *younger* in age. The data indicate that such a program of social rehabilitation is more effective than contact with agemates. Similarly, human children who are not especially competent in social situations may be assisted by opportunities to interact with younger children. Indeed, this idea seems implicit in the strategies commonly employed by nursery school and kindergarten teachers. Two practices are typical: a) at the beginning of the school year, socially incompetent children are frequently assigned to classes of younger rather than older children, and b) subgroups are used within a classroom in which less skilled children are placed in contact with younger (but not inept) peers. These procedures undoubtedly maximize the less competent child's chances of obtaining positive feedback for prosocial activity while, at the same time, chances of social punishment are minimized.

Conclusion

Access to agemates, acceptance by them, and constructive interactions with them are among the necessities of child development. The sensitive student of child behavior has a variety of avenues available to maximize the input of peer relations to the development of the individual child. Ensuring each child the opportunity for productive intercourse with peers is not an easy task, but such experiences are the child's inalienable right.

This paper was completed with assistance from Grant No. 5–P01–05027, National Institute of Child Health and Human Development.

NOTES

1. A possible exception to this statement is the mild depression that is sometimes reported when younger children are separated from their siblings.
2. Just why adults do not engage in long periods of play with their children is something of a mystery. From a psychological viewpoint, it is probably not possible for an adult to regress cognitively to a degree sufficient to permit sustained, child-like play. From an evolutionary

viewpoint, it is probably not conducive to species survival for adult members of a troupe to spend large blocks of time playing with their offspring instead of hunting and gathering. The fact remains, however, that play occurs primarily in the context of peer interaction rather than in interaction with adults.
3. A significant concordance between friends in incidence of drug use does not, of course, reveal which comes first—the use of drugs or contact with drug-using friends.

REFERENCES

BAUMRIND, D. Socialization and instrumental competence in young children. In W. W. Hartup (Ed.), *The young child: Reviews of research*, Vol. 2. Washington, D.C.: National Association for the Education of Young Children, 1972, pp. 202–224.

BRONSON, W. C. Central orientations: A study of behavior organization from childhood to adolescence. *Child Development*, 1966, *37*, 125–155.

CAMPBELL, J. D., AND YARROW, M. R. Perceptual and behavioral correlates of social effectiveness. *Sociometry*, 1961, *24*, 1–20.

CHITTENDEN, G. E. An experimental study in measuring and modifying assertive behavior in young children. *Monographs for the Society for Research in Child Development*, 1942, 7, No. 1.

COLEMAN, J. S. *The adolescent society*. Glencoe, Ill.: Free Press, 1961.

CRANDALL, V. C., AND BATTLE, E. S. The antecedents and adult correlates of academic and intellectual achievement effort. In J. P. Hill (Ed.), *Minnesota symposia on child psychology*, Vol. 4. Minneapolis: University of Minnesota Press, 1970, pp. 36–93.

DAVIDS, A., AND PARENTI, A. N. Time orientation and interpersonal relations of emotionally disturbed and normal children. *Journal of Abnormal and Social Psychology*, 1958, *57*, 299–305.

FINLEY, G. F., FRENCH, D., AND COWAN, P. A. Egocentrism and popularity. XIVth Interamerican Congress of Psychology. Sao Paulo, Brazil, April, 1973.

GOLD, H. A. The importance of ideology in sociometric evaluation of leadership. *Group Psychotherapy*, 1962, *15*, 224–230.

HAMBURG, D. A., AND VAN LAWICK-GOODALL, J. Factors facilitating development of aggressive behavior in chimpanzees and humans. In W. W. Hartup and J. de Wit (Eds.), *Determinants and Origins of Aggression*. The Hague: Mouton (1974).

HARLOW, H. F. Age-mate or peer affectional system. In D. S. Lehrman, R. A. Hinde, and E. Shaw (Eds.), *Advances in the study of behavior*. Vol. 2. New York: Academic Press, 1969, pp. 333–383.

HARRIS, F. R., WOLF, M. M., AND BAER, D. M. Effects of adult social reinforcement on child behavior. In W. W. Hartup and N. L. Smothergill (Eds.), *The young child: Reviews of research*. Washington, D.C.: National Association for the Education of Young Children, 1967, pp. 13–26.

HARTUP, W. W. Peer interaction and social organization. In P. H. Mussen (Ed.), *Carmichael's manual of child psychology*. Vol. 2. New York: John Wiley, 1970, pp. 361–456.

HARTUP, W. W. Violence in development: The functions of aggression in childhood. *American Psychologist*, 1974, *29*, 336–341.

HARTUP, W. W. Cross-age vs. same age peer interaction: Ethological and cross-cultural perspectives. In V. L. Allen (Ed.), *Interage-interaction in children: Theory and research on the helping relationship*. Madison, Wisconsin: University of Wisconsin Press, 1975.

HEATHERS, G. Emotional dependence and independence in nursery school play. *Journal of Genetic Psychology*, 1955, *87*, 37–57.

HETHERINGTON, M., AND DEUR, J. The effects of father absence on child development. In W. W. Hartup (Ed.), *The young child: Reviews of research*, Vol. 2. Washington, D.C.: National Association for the Education of Young Children, 1972, pp. 303–319.

HICKS, D. J. Imitation and retention of film-mediated aggressive peer and adult models. *Journal of Personality and Social Psychology*, 1965, *2*, 97–100.

IRWIN, D. M. Peer acceptance related to the young child's concept of justice. Unpublished bachelor's thesis, University of Minnesota, 1967.

JACK, L. M. An experimental study of ascendant behavior in preschool children. *University of Iowa Studies in Child Welfare*, 1934, *9*, No. 3.

JAY, P. (Ed.) *Primates: Studies in adaptation and variability*. New York: Holt, Rinehart, and Winston. 1968.

KANDEL, D. Adolescent marijuana use: Role of parents and peers. *Science*, 1973, *181*, 1067–1070.

KEASEY, C. B. Social participation as a factor in the moral development of preadolescents. *Developmental Psychology*, 1971, *5*, 216–220.

KINSEY, A. C., POMEROY, W. B., AND MARTIN, C. E. *Sexual behavior in the human male.* Philadelphia: W. B. Saunders, 1948.

KLAUS, R. A. Interrelationships of attributes that accepted and rejected children ascribe to their peers. Unpublished doctoral dissertation, George Peabody College for Teachers, 1959.

KOBASIGAWA, A. Inhibitory and disinhibitory effects of models on sex-inappropriate behavior in children. *Psychologia*, 1968, *11*, 86–96.

KOHLBERG, L. The development of modes of moral thinking and choice in the years ten to sixteen. Unpublished doctoral dissertation, University of Chicago, 1958.

LEWIN, K., LIPPITT, R., AND WHITE, R. K. Patterns of aggressive behavior in experimentally created "social climates." *Journal of Social Psychology*, 1938, *10*, 271–299.

LINDZEY, G. Some remarks concerning incest, the incest taboo, and psychoanalytic theory. *American Psychologist*, 1967, *22*, 1051–1059.

LURIE, L. A., NEWBURGER, M., ROSENTHAL, F. M., AND OUTCALT, L. C. Intelligence quotient and social quotient. *American Journal of Orthopsychiatry*, 1941, *11*, 111–117.

LYNN, D. B. *Parental and sex role identification: A theoretical formulation.* Berkeley: McCutchan, 1969.

MACCOBY, E. E., AND FELDMAN, S. S. Mother-attachment and stranger-reactions in the third year of life. *Monographs of the Society for Research in Child Development*, 1972, *37* (No. 146).

MACCOBY, E. E., AND MASTERS, J. C. Attachment and dependency. In P. H. Mussen (Ed.), *Carmichael's manual of child psychology.* Vol. 2. New York: Wiley, 1970, pp. 73–157.

MCCANDLESS, B. R., CASTANEDA, A., AND PALERMO, D. S. Anxiety in children and social status. *Child Development*, 1956, *27*, 385–391.

MCCANDLESS, B. R., AND MARSHALL, H. R. A picture sociometric technique for preschool children and its relation to teacher judgments of friendship. *Child Development*, 1957, *28*, 139–148.

PAGE, M. L. The modification of ascendant behavior in preschool children. *University of Iowa Studies in Child Welfare*, 1936, *12*, No. 3.

PARTEN, M. B. Social participation among preschool children. *Journal of Abnormal and Social Psychology*, 1932–1933, *27*, 243–269.

PATTERSON, G. R., AND BRODSKY, G. A behavior modification program for a child with multiple problem behavior. *Journal of Child Psychology and Psychiatry*, 1966, *7*, 277–295.

PATTERSON, G. R., AND COBB, J. A. A dyadic analysis of "aggressive" behavior. In J. P. Hill (Ed.), *Minnesota symposia on child psychology*, Vol. 5. Minneapolis: University of Minnesota Press, 1971.

PATTERSON, G. R., LITTMAN, R. A., AND BRICKER, W. Assertive behavior in children: A step toward a theory of aggression. *Monographs of the Society for Research in Child Development*, 1967, *32*, No. 113.

PIAGET, J. *The language and thought of the child.* New York: Harcourt, Brace, 1926.

PIAGET, J. *The moral judgment of the child.* Glencoe, Ill.: Free Press, 1932.

PORTEUS, B. D., AND JOHNSON, R. C. Children's responses to two measures of conscience development and their relation to sociometric nomination. *Child Development*, 1965, *36*, 703–711.

RARDIN, D. R., AND MOAN, C. E. Peer interaction and cognitive development. *Child Development*, 1971, *42*, 1685–1699.

ROFF, M. Childhood social interactions and young adult bad conduct. *Journal of Abnormal and Social Psychology*, 1961, *63*, 333–337.

ROFF, M. Childhood social interaction and young adult psychosis. *Journal of Clinical Psychology*, 1963, *19*, 152–157.

ROFF, M. Some childhood and adolescent characteristics of adult homosexuals. U.S. Army Medical Research and Development Command, Report No. 66-5, May, 1966.

ROFF, M., AND SELLS, S. B. Juvenile delinquency in relation to peer acceptance-rejection and socioeconomic status. *Psychology in the Schools*, 1968, *5*, 3–18.

ROFF, M., SELLS, S. B., AND GOLDEN, M. M. *Social adjustment and personality development in children.* Minneapolis: University of Minnesota Press, 1972.

ROTHBART, M. K., AND MACCOBY, E. E. Parents' differential reactions to sons and daughters. *Journal of Personality and Social Psychology*, 1966, *4*, 237–243.

RUBIN, K. H. Relationship between egocentric communication and popularity among peers. *Developmental Psychology*, 1972, *7*, 364.

SCARR, S. Social introversion-extraversion as a heritable response. *Child Development*, 1969, *40*, 823–832.

SHELTON, J., AND HILL, J. P. Effects on cheating of achievement anxiety and knowledge of peer performance. *Developmental Psychology*, 1969, *1*, 449–455.

SHERIF, M., HARVEY, O. J., WHITE, B. J., HOOD, W. R., AND SHERIF, C. W. *Intergroup conflict and cooperation: The robbers cave experiment.* Norman: University of Oklahoma Press, 1961.

SHERIF, M., AND SHERIF, C. W. *Reference groups.* New York: Harper and Row, 1964.

SUOMI, S. J., AND HARLOW, H. F. Social rehabilitation of isolate-reared monkeys. *Developmental Psychology*, 1972, *6*, 487–496.

TERMAN, L. M., AND ODEN, M. H. *Genetic studies of genius, Vol. IV: The gifted child grows up: Twenty-five years' follow-up of a superior group.* Stanford, Calif.: Stanford University Press, 1947.

VAN DEN MUNCKHOF, H. C. P. Sociable interaktie en cognitieve ontwikkeling bij kleuters. Niet-gepubliceerde doctoraalscriptie ontwikkelingspsychologie, Universiteit Nijmegen, 1970.

WAHLER, R. G. Child-child interactions in five field settings: Some experimental analyses. *Journal of Experimental Child Psychology*, 1967, *5*, 278–293.

15

Some Properties of Social Play

Catherine Garvey

The extensive literature on children's play, although arising from a number of diverse theoretical orientations, reflects a major concern with the functions of play in the child's individual cognitive, physical, or psychosocial development. Empirical studies which have dealt with play as social behavior have examined the role of age, sex, and ethnic identity in determining choice of play activities or partner or have treated settings as independent variables affecting physical or psychological features of play (Herron and Sutton-Smith 1971). However, even those studies that have examined play in a social context have failed to ask how the interaction is carried out or what kinds of skills are involved in play interchanges. It is the purpose of this paper to describe the structure of spontaneous episodes of dyadic play and to suggest some of the basic competencies which underlie social play activity.

It is useful to distinguish four possible states which may obtain when two children are alone together: social nonplay, e.g., both may collaborate to repair a broken toy; nonsocial nonplay, e.g., one or both may independently explore an object; nonsocial play, e.g., one or both may engage in an independent imaginative activity, as when one child irons the laundry and the other builds a wall with blocks; and social play, e.g., both are mutually engaged in a housekeeping activity such as cooking and eating dinner or are driving the toy car to a family vacation. This paper will examine some properties of the state of social play, analyzing first the structures underlying

Reprinted from Catherine Garvey, "Some Properties of Social Play," *Merrill-Palmer Quarterly* 20, no. 3 (1974), by permission of the Wayne State University Press.

the rhythmic, repetitive behaviors which we will call ritual play and then tracing the same structures in less stylized play episodes.

Social play is defined here as a state of engagement in which the successive, nonliteral behaviors of one partner are contingent on the nonliteral behaviors of the other partner. Viewed from the standpoint of either partner, this means leaving interstices in one's behaviors for the other's acts and modifying one's successive behaviors as a result of the other's acts. Nonliteral behavior is not necessarily not serious—for play can be a serious business—but it is abstract in the sense that the primary purpose of a given behavior is reduced to a meaning component, and its reinterpreted function in the chain of activity becomes primary. Applying these two criteria (alternating, contingent behaviors and nonliteralness of those behaviors) we can contrast a very simple example of social play with a type of engagement which we would wish to exclude from this category. Two children stand close together in a playroom near a wooden car which both want to ride. One shoves the other who immediately shoves back, and simultaneous shoving occurs until one child is displaced from the area of a car. The behaviors are immediate, not spaced; neither child waits for the other to complete a behavior. The same setting can result in social play. Both children stand near the car and one shoves the other, the second shoves back and waits, the first repeats the above and waits for the other to shove in turn. Neither child is displaced for the shoving is nonliteral. Aggressive and defensive gestures identify the type of meaning of the play but this meaning is not primary; the reinterpreted function (marked by giggles or smiles) is that of moves or turns in a mock-challenge. The play episode may end with both children getting on the car or with both forgetting the car in the excitement of the contact established in the interaction.

Various markers can indicate nonliteralness, as Bateson (1956) pointed out in his discussion of the boundary signals that mark a transition to a state of play. Attenuation or exaggeration of the gestures that in nonplay would have their primary form, as well as laughter, smiles or giggles, can mark the fact that a behavior is to be interpreted nonliterally. Alternating behaviors reflect the fact that in play, rules obtain, that is, that there are "turns," assigned roles, and a mutual set of expectations as to what constitutes the particular format of the activity.

Procedures

The data on which these observations are based consisted of 36 15–20 minute videotaped play sessions. Children came in groups of three to the laboratory accompanied by their nursery school teacher. Each child formed a dyad with each of the two other members of the group. All members of the group were previously acquainted from nursery school. The children in 12 dyads fell into a younger age group (3½ to 4⅓ years); 12 into a middle group (4½ to 5 years); and 12 into an older age group (5 to 5½ years). In all there were 21 girls and 15 boys, all from middle-class and, predominately, professional families. A dyad was left alone in a well-furnished playroom where they were observed through one-way mirrors. The membership of the dyad was changed at the end of approximately 15 minutes. The third child was occupied with a series of identification tasks presented by an adult in another room. The videotapes were transcribed. A number of features of the interactions have been reported elsewhere (Garvey and Hogan 1973; Greif 1973). It can be mentioned here that episodes of focused interaction were frequent (an average of 66% of each session was spent in mutual engagement) and that there was a good deal of talk in each session (the average density of speech was one utterance every four seconds).

There are obvious dangers in inferring the meaning or intent of children's behavior from their speech. Three procedural safeguards were adopted to reduce the possibility of overinterpreting or misinterpreting the meaning of the children's verbal and nonverbal gestures. First, if an event (verbal or nonverbal behavior of one child) was to be accepted as evidence of awareness or of competence in making a distinction among modes of behavior or as evidence of recognition of an obligation in an interaction, that event was required to be nonunique. That is, the event must have occurred in a similar context in more than one dyad. This requirement reduces the danger of generalizing from idiosyncratic behavior. Second, in interpreting the meaning of lexical terms or expressions, both the verbal and nonverbal context of events were taken into account. For example, in the text the meaning of "pretend" was opposed to the meaning of "really" or "real"; that is, the meaning was defined contrastively. Further, in the instances cited, consistently different behaviors accompanied the use of these terms. Positive associations as well as oppositions in the immediate context of the event contribute to the interpretation of meaning as, for example, the collocations that contribute to an understanding of the role concept "doctor" in one episode in which doctor, baby, sick, medicine, and checkup were joined.

A third safeguard was the use of the children's own reactions to interpret the significance of an event. The immediate consequence of an event was included as evidence of the meaning of that event. For example, an assertion can be interpreted as an intended joke when the partner laughs and then is joined in laughter by the first speaker.

Using the criteria of nonliteralness and alternating contingent behaviors as well as observing the procedural safeguards, two investigators independently identified social play episodes in the corpus. Interjudge agreement on the identification of episodes of social play was 80%, and only episodes on which the investigators agreed were used in the subsequent analysis. From these episodes the ritual play sequences were selected and classified according to the formats described below.

The ritual interactions, composed of repetitive, rhythmic exchanges were clearly and redundantly marked for the characteristics of social play. Alternating, contingent behaviors were closely integrated in time, and exaggerated intonation, distorted rhythms, and broad or extreme gestures marked the nonliteralness of the activity. Thus, the investigators were able to concur on the selection of all ritual sequences.

Analysis of Social Play Formats

Recurring patterns of interaction were observed in the play episodes of the dyads. The clearest examples of these patterns were found in the ritual play sequences, and we will examine these first. The structure of the interpersonal behaviors can be described in terms of the rules governing alternation of participation (turns), the substantive and formal relations of the alternating behaviors, and the manner in which sequences are built up (rounds).

Interactions may be analyzed as composed of *turns* at acting. A turn is the contribution (verbal and/or nonverbal) of one participant in the interchange. The content of the second participant's turn may be the same as or different from that of the first participant. If different, the difference may be paradigmatic (a member of the same class) or syntagmatic (a member of a different class, one which has some linear or sequential relation to the first class). Using the conventions of indicating first speaker or actor as X, second speaker or actor as Y and of identifying the content of a turn by capital letters with subscript p = paradigmatic difference and s = syntagmatic difference, the basic patterns of turns can be illustrated.

Turn Patterns	X's Turn	Y's Turn
1. A-A	Bye, mommy.	Bye, mommy.
2. A-B_p	Bye, mommy.	Bye, daddy.
3. A-B_s	You're a nut.	No, I'm not.
4. A-B_s	I have to go to work.	You're already at work.
C_s	No, I'm not.	

In the first pattern, the rule is that all features of the second turn must be identical; relevant features appear to include rhythm, intonation, and volume. In the second pattern such features also appear to be maintained in the second turn, but the latter substitutes some component—here another term of address. The third pattern employs a sequential relation. The example is an assertion followed by a counterassertion.

The first three patterns exemplify a *symmetrical* distribution of turns. A more complex pattern is constructed of *asymmetrical* turns, which is illustrated in pattern 4.

Each of the patterns forms a *round*, which is a repeatable unit of interaction. A round may be repeated intact (R_i) or may be modified (R_m).[1] Returning to the patterns of turns, some of the ways in which sequences are constructed can be illustrated in two-round episodes.

Turn Pattern, Round Type	X's Turn	Y's Turn
1, R_i	Bye, mommy.	Bye, mommy.
	Bye, mommy.	Bye, mommy.
2, R_i	Bye, mommy.	Bye, daddy.
	Bye, mommy.	Bye, daddy.
2, R_m	Hello, my name is Mr. Donkey.	Hello, my name is Mr. Elephant.
	Hello, my name is Mr. Tiger	Hello, my name is Mr. Lion.
4, R_m	I have to go to work.	You're already at work.
	No, I'm not.	
	I have to go to school.	You're already at school.
	No, I'm not.	

4, R_i I'll be the dragon and
you be St. George that
killed him.

                     (shoots the dragon, X)

(falls dead)

                     Now I'll be the dragon.

(shoots Y, the dragon)

                     Do it again, I'm not dead.

(shoots again)

                     (falls dead)

In a sequence of rounds, role assignment may be symmetrical, as in the first four examples above, or asymmetrical as in the last one, where roles are reversed at the beginning of the second round. The second round begins with "Now I'll be the dragon." (Nonverbal acts are enclosed in parentheses, and events are numbered sequentially.)

The turn patterns and round types were grouped into formats which identify the structure of many of the play episodes observed. The formats, ranked in order of increasing complexity, are as follows:

	Turn Pattern	Round Type
Format 1:	1	R_i
2a:	1	R_m
2b:	2 or 3	R_i
3:	2 or 3	R_m
4:	4	R_i or R_m

Format 1 is, of course, symmetrical in respect to role alternation in rounds. Formats 3 and 4 may be symmetrical or asymmetrical. Format 2 occurred in the present corpus predominately in symmetrical form.

The 36 dyads produced 158 clearly identified episodes of social play, which were distributed among the groups as follows: younger, 44; middle, 58; older, 56. Of these episodes, 74 were instances of ritual play. No child failed to participate in at least one episode of ritual play. The distribution of the ritual play episodes among the four play formats is presented in Table 1.[2] A fifth category included in Table 1 is that of mixed formats, which includes temporally cohesive sequences with a single theme which utilized successively two or more basic formats.

Table 1 Ritual play episodes of two or more rounds

Format	1	2(a&b)	3	4	Mixed	Total Episodes	Average # Rounds per Episode
Younger Group[a]	5	14	3	2	2	26	3.8
Middle Group[a]	2	6	12	3	2	25	2.5
Older Group[a]	1	7	8	4	3	23	2.2
Total Episodes in Each Format	8	27	23	9	7	74	

[a]N = 12 dyads.

Table 1 indicates that ritual play episodes occurred in all age groups. It is clear that for this sample of children ritual play episodes were still a frequent type of interaction even among the older dyads. Further, the results suggest that the relative complexity of the formats as ranked corresponds to some degree to the increasing age of the three groups, although all age groups employed both simpler and more complex formats.

The final column of Table 1 indicates that younger dyads repeated the rounds of such episodes more extensively than older dyads. While the older dyads did not tend to repeat rounds more than twice the younger dyads repeated rounds on the average 3.8 times. On two occasions, younger dyads continued the sequence for 10 or more rounds.

Although this discussion has concentrated on the alternating, contingent behaviors of ritual interchanges, it is necessary to recall that such play episodes are characterized, not only by the successive and contingent behaviors described above, but by the quality of nonliteralness. Thus, in the corpus from which these patterns have been abstracted, each episode is marked, often redundantly, as nonliteral. For example, in the "Bye, mommy" episodes, which occurred primarily in R_i sequences, the utterances were chanted. Further, the literal leave-taking meaning was subordinated to rhythmic echoing—neither child left or turned away. In the St. George episode, nonliteralness was marked by explicit preparatory role assignment, "I'll be, you be." That episode also illustrates another feature of the sequences, which is that a turn or round can be interrupted for clarification of rules or discussion of procedures and then resumed at the point where the break occurred. This feature appears to support the observation that play can be conducted seriously; that is, the actions must be performed in a certain way and must accomplish their intended outcome—in the St. George episode, that of effectively killing the dragon.

Abilities Underlying Social Play

Certain abilities must be postulated to account for the structures of play described above. We will discuss these abilities which are required to conduct ritual play episodes but will extend the discussion to include the nonrepetitive episodes of social play.

1. Reality-Play Distinction

First, both participants must recognize that a state of social play obtains. In order to play with another, one must have a firm grasp of reality. Since the task of explicating what is meant by "reality," either in the sense of Piagetian cognitive theory or in the sense of phenomenologists such as Peter Berger or Peter Winch, would take us too far afield, we can restate that condition: in order to play, one must have a grasp of what is not play—of what is and is not "for real." Although the mode of behavior we intuitively identify as play may itself be primarily assimilative (Piaget 1951), that is, rather than accommodating itself to perceived (or absolute) reality it transforms and absorbs its object to previously held perceptions, the necessity of moving into or out of the mode requires the distinction between play and other activities. The children we observed gave ample evidence of making this distinction. One kind of evidence that the children were able to make this distinction is their use of the terms "really" and "pretend." In relation to the use of speech content, it is important to note that, following Vygotsky (1962), we do not contend that word meanings of lexical items are, either in reference or connotation, identical with the word meanings that the lexical items might have for an adult. Nor is it necessary to the argument to specify the word meanings of the items to be used as evidence. What is necessary is that the meanings be used contrastively in the children's speech and that the contrast is symmetric and nonunique. Example (1) illustrates the use of these terms.

Reality-play distinction

Example 1

(X sits on a 3-legged stool that has a magnifying glass in its center)
X. I've got to go to the potty.

Y. (turns to him) Really?

X. (grins)
No, pretend.

Y. (smiles and watches X)

Since the state of play entails a suspension of literalness, the reality-play distinction appears to be essential to interpreting the partner's gesture in terms of its primary meaning or its nonliteral meaning. In social play the possibility of interaction requires mutual consent to and recognition of the state of play. Play is a delicate state which must be actively sustained. Knowledge of whether the state obtains or not is an important factor in interpreting another's behavior and in responding to his behavior. Evidence of this claim is the fact that participants often check on the state in order to determine the appropriate response. In another dyad, the statement, "I've got to go to the potty," was followed by the partner's comment, "So do I," and both children immediately headed for the door. In Example 1, some cue (X's sitting on the magnifying stool, his expression, or both) led Y to check on the meaning of X's announcement, and the information that Y received led to his subsequent response. Often the state of play was explicitly bounded. The most frequent markers opening a state of play were "pretend," e.g., "Pretend you called me on the telephone"; or explicit role assignment, e.g., "I'll be the mommy and you be the daddy, OK?" The state might end by tacit, mutual consent, or its termination might be explicitly marked, e.g., "I'm not playing anymore."

Bateson (1956) has suggested that the multiple coding characteristic of objects and relations in the play state contributes to the child's exploring and learning of the effects of situational context on the classification of sorts and categories of behavior. The reality-play distinctions as made by the children themselves may be viewed as manipulations of categories and contexts, as explorations of the "fit" of behaviors to changing definitions of situations. Whatever the cognitive functions served by these explorations, the important point is that the distinction was often tested, even among the younger dyads. It appeared to be a relevant factor in the attitude or alignment taken, not only to objects, but to the behavior of the partner, whose definition of the situation is critical to the continuing interchange.

2. Abstraction of Rules

Winch (1958) has pointed out that it is only possible to talk of rule-governed behavior when one can predict what will be done next and can recognize an error in procedure. According to these criteria, the children, often explicitly, gave evidence of awareness of the fact that their social play depended on mutually accepted rules of procedure. Inspection of the videotapes produces the impression that play requires more structuring and management by the dyad than does nonplay. It is necessary to make a distinction here between basic general rules for interaction and specific or local strictures applicable to a limited context. The most basic general rule which holds across both verbal and nonverbal interaction is that of reciprocity. Explicit encoding of this rule often took the form of "taking turns," but implicit conformity to the rule was clearly apparent in the alternation of turns and their integration into rounds as exemplified in the play formats. Violations of the reciprocity rule were frequently challenged by invoking the rule; for example, "You go next." Since this basic rule underlies much adult conversation, it will be useful to trace the probably simpler forms of that rule in children's play, and we will attempt to describe a portion of its development in a later section of this paper.

The point to be made here is that the explicit invocation of a rule under similar conditions across a number of different situations indicates the ability to abstract that rule from the varied and often complex activities which it structures. It further suggests an ability to perceive actions in terms of socially distributed entities such as turns or, more complex than turns, rounds, for it is these entities rather than utterances which are apportioned to speakers in play and in conversation. An illustration of an interaction that reflects this ability follows in Example 2.

Round referenced as unit of interaction

Example 2

(X and Y conduct a game that consists of X discovering a stuffed snake, Y sharing the discovery, X playing the straight man, and Y expressing fear.)

X. (holds up snake)

                                        Y. (draws back in alarm)
                                              What's that?

X. It's a snake!
   (laughs at Y's exaggerated fear)

                                          Y. Do it again.

X. (holds up snake)

In Y's request "it" refers to the whole round. The round was then repeated exactly as before. (Example 2, which shows asymmetrical turn structure but lacks role reversal, is classified as Format 4.)

The operation of local strictures in specific situations reveals both the orderliness and the credibility that children attribute to play episodes. One type of stricture applicable to role-centered states of play is that role behaviors and role attributes must remain consistent throughout the episode. If one partner departs from the jointly created image of the pretend state, the other partner has the right to correct him. The negligent partner usually accepts the correction as in Example 3.

Operation of local strictures in specific situations

Example 3

(X, preparing to speak on telephone, addresses Y)

X. Pretend you're sick.

        Y. OK.

X. (speaks into phone)
Hey, Dr. Wren, do you got any
medicine?

        Y. Yes, I have some medicine.

X. (to Y)
No, you aren't the doctor,
remember?

        Y. OK.

X. (speaks into phone)
I need some medicine for the kids.
Bye.
(turns to Y)
He hasn't got any medicine.

        Y. No? Oh, dear.

Y was corrected by X for misinterpreting his role. Y then accepted the correction and returned to role acceptable behavior.

Vygotsky pointed out that there is no such thing as play without rules, though in the case of spontaneous imaginative play these rules need not be laid down in advance. Vygotsky stated, "Only actions which fit these rules are acceptable to the play situation [1967, p. 9]." In addition to basic rules for interaction, some of which we have discussed (e.g., turn-apportionment rules), there are rules which are based on concepts of what behaviors and attitudes are appropriate to the particular role or activity represented in the play episode. Such local strictures are sometimes explicitly stated as normative guidelines. For example, in a role-playing episode, a boy told a girl, "Take that [holster] off. Girls don't wear things like that." Often the children's concepts of role appropriate behaviors were reflected in the selection of actions and objects for the cooperatively created situation. For example, in several mixed sex dyads, the girl expressed fear of a large, stuffed snake. The boy reassured her and fearlessly killed the snake while the girl watched. Both general procedural rules and rules guiding behavior in particular situations are essential to the conduct of social play.

3. Theme and Variation

Related to the ability to recognize and abstract the format of the play state is the ability to jointly construct the theme of the activity and to develop it in a manner consonant with the jointly held image of the state. Any episode of social play entails the exercise of *shared* imagination and the shared development of the image of the episode. An example of joint development of a theme by two boys is found in Example 4. It is clear that neither child has alone determined the course of this episode, since although X initiated it, Y contributed to its development by adopting the role of little boy, rejecting the coffee, and asking for milk. This move was then accepted by X, who had not explicitly identified himself as mother or father, but now addressed Y as "Kid." The move led to further integrated activity, that is, going to get the milk.

Joint development of a theme

Example 4

(X is busy cooking at the stove; Y watches)

X. OK, dinner is ready. Now what do
   you want for dinner?
   (turns to Y)

                      Y. Well . . . (indecisively)

X. Hot beef?

                      Y. OK, hot beef.

X. Coffee, too?

                      Y. No, I'm the little boy. I'll have some
   milk.

X. OK, you can eat now.

                      Y. (moves closer to stove)

X. Kid, we're going to get some milk
   from the store. Come on in the
   dunebuggy.

                      Y. OK, I'm in the dunebuggy.

(Dunebuggy is a small toy car; X pushes it and Y moves beside it)

While objects are freely transformed, for example, stool to milk carton, to conform to the needs of the episode, consistency is maintained in respect to motives and appropriate actions for the roles adopted. The little boy drinks milk, not coffee; milk must be fetched; and as they started to take the milk home, X, taking into account Y's little boy role, assured him that the milk was not too heavy for him to carry. A large number of cases of concern with motives and with role consonant behaviors contrasted with an equally large number of cases of a cavalier freedom with the identity of objects, which could be whatever they needed to be for the purposes of the pretend game. This fact suggests greater person-centered than object-centered concern in children of the ages observed. It is, perhaps, this person-centered concern which, in part, enabled the children to so efficiently express and perceive the often subtle cues necessary to the flexible and often rapid development of the themes of pretend play.

To summarize the discussion thus far, we have proposed that young children distinguish between play and nonplay modes of interaction. We have suggested some of the competencies that underlie the observed play episodes. And we have suggested some procedures for using the data of spontaneous speech to examine the nature of children's play. We will now turn to a further discussion of increasingly complex interaction structures.

Interaction Structures

We have suggested that taking turns implies an ability to identify a unit of social interaction, the turn or the round. In "doing the same thing" as in a simple imitation of another's act one must be able to abstract the critical features of the act as well as its function in the structure or format of the interaction (Guillaume 1971). The simplest forms of ritual play involve alternating repetitions as in Format 1 where the round composed of two turns can be repeated in virtually identical form a number of times. Non-verbal parallels were frequently observed. For example, one child threw a curtain into the air, smiled, and waited while the other threw his curtain up. The round was repeated, with laughter accompanying each turn. Slightly more elaborate versions occur with identical turns when each round intro-duces a change of content as in Format 2a or when the content of the turns differs but each person repeats the content of his own previous turn in successive rounds, as in Format 2b. A still more complex format is achieved when the content of each turn in each successive round is modified as in Format 3. This last type can exhibit considerable sophistication in use of words and syntax while still retaining the feature of constant intonation over each lexically varied event. A sophisticated example of the progressive modification of turns is in Example 5, a Format 3 type.

Progressive modification of turns

Example 5

(X and Y, an older dyad, are discussing their feelings about the play room)

X. Don't you wish we could get out of this place?

Y. Yeah, 'cause it has yucky things.

X. Yeah.

Y. 'Cause it's fishy too, 'cause it has fishes.

X. And it's snakey too 'cause it has snakes. And it's beary too 'cause it has bears.

Y. And it's hatty too 'cause it has hats.

X. Where's the hats?

(This ends the game.)

Although X slipped in a double play at his turn, the intonation of the four variant sentences was the same, and each production was greeted with an appreciative smile. X's last utterance was a serious request for informa-tion. Its rapid tempo contrasted sharply with the measured rhythm of the ritual. A still more complex format can be achieved when a round is com-posed of asymmetrically distributed turns, as in Format 4. In this type, as in previously described formats, the turns may be verbal or nonverbal. In Example 6 only Y's turn was a verbal one.

We can only speculate about the beginnings of the basic interaction structures which were already skillfully manipulated by the younger dyads.

Progressive modification of turns asymmetrically distributed

Example 6

(X puts a toy car under the magnifying glass in the stool)

> Y. (looks in the glass)
> That's the biggest car I ever saw!
> (with exaggerated surprise)

X. (looks in glass and laughs)

(fetches a hat and places it under
glass, looking expectantly at Y)

> Y. That's the biggest hat I ever saw!

However, it is worth describing a spontaneous incident recently witnessed, one which would not be likely to occur in a situation in which a mother was aware that she was being observed. A mother holding the hand of a toddler (about 18 months old) strolled down a dock at a marina, both looking down into the water from time to time. The child asked by hand gesture and verbal gesture for a plastic tennis racket the mother was holding. She gave it to him saying, "Don't drop it." They turned at the end of the dock, the child swinging the racket. He said, "Ducks all gone." [There were two ducks which had been swimming around the dock and which they had probably seen earlier.] She said, "Yes, ducks all gone." Then he said, as they strolled back, "All gone," and she replied, "All gone." They passed out of hearing, half-chanting at least six rounds of "All gone ducks" in virtually identical rhythm. The child initiated the modification each time. Another mother to whom this incident was described recognized the type of episode and volunteered the information that she had been embarrassed once or twice when she realized that someone was watching while she had been absorbed in a similar game with her own child.

The basic formats of these social play episodes form patterns of interaction from which the ritual aspects can be abstracted. Example 7 of a conversational exchange free of ritual features is taken from an older dyad.

Progressive modification of turns

Example 7

(X and Y have just been left alone in the playroom)

X. (looks at Y)

Hey, we have to be all by ourselves.
But there's a good thing. I know
how to be.

> Y. (approaches X)
> But there's a good thing. I won't cry
> when someone leaves me alone.
> Well, when I was little I always cried
> when someone left me alone. Once
> mommy and daddy both left and I
> cried and cried, and I've been so
> lonesome.

X. (attends story and nods)

The first turn is echoed and elaborated in the second turn. Y produced her variant of the act produced by X, and X appeared to recognize, just as Y did, that they were doing the same thing. A shift in content (perhaps only a minimal one) would produce an exchange virtually indistinguishable from an episode in an adult associative conversation. Sacks (1967) pointed out that "doing the same thing" in adult conversation provides a way of tacitly acknowledging the intent of the speaker's gesture by advancing and elaborating the meaning of that gesture.

Of course, many conversational and interactional structures which reflect turn taking are based on doing a complementary thing, rather than the same thing. But providing an appropriate complementary, or syntagmatic, response requires that the first gesture be correctly interpreted. Gordon and Lakoff (1971) have described how in adult speech the alternative forms of indirect requests for action are interpreted as requests, for the interpretation determines the appropriate response. For example, if the interrogative utterance "Can you open the door?" were interpreted as a request for information the response, "Yes, I can," would be appropriate; if it were interpreted as a request for action, then opening the door, with or without a verbal accompaniment, would be an appropriate response. Utterances in children's conversations, which are interpreted as requests for action, their contexts, and responses are examined by Garvey (1973). Example 8 shows two exchanges composed of another type of request and its conventionalized complementary response; the request was encoded in two different ways before being correctly interpreted.

Progressive modification of turns: syntagmatic response

Example 8

(X and Y are talking while X, who is "Mom," sets the table)

X. Why do brother and sister always laugh at me?

                Y. I don't know.

X. Every once a week they go out playing and start laughing at me.

                Y. I know, um, that's an awful thing.

(same dyad, same roles and activities, a few seconds later)

X. How come our house is so dirty? Brother and sister have to make it dirty?

                Y. What?

X. Brother and sister have to make my whole nice room dirty.

                Y. I know, that's a horrible thing to do too.

Y's commiserative responses to X's complaints reveal that at least X's second utterance in each episode was interpreted as a request for sympathy. Y's final responses were instances of a conventionally appropriate complementary response (rather than an instance of doing the same thing). In the first segment of Example 8 it appears that X recoded his first message because Y's first answer, "I don't know," did not provide the requested response. In both cases, X appeared to be satisfied with the final response. The request for a sympathetic response occurs frequently in social play among the older dyads. Although free of the rhythmic features characteristic of ritual play, exchanges of this type were marked by the somewhat exaggerated intonation associated with pretend and role play. We suggest that the ritual play formats which employ syntagmatically varied turns and round modifications provide a basis for the acquisition of these more specialized conversational exchange types.

Summary and Conclusions

Three abilities were proposed to underlie social play: the ability to distinguish play and nonplay states, the ability to abstract the organizing rule from its specific or local representation, and the ability to identify a theme of the interaction and contribute to its development. The behaviors from which these abilities were inferred were mutually adaptive behaviors. All dyads gave evidence of jointly recognizing that a state of play was in force, that rules for interaction were mutually binding, and that the thematic content of the interaction was subject to modification by both parties. Evidence of such recognition was just as compelling in arguments as in more harmonious interactions. The episodes of social play interaction discussed here contrasted sharply with the episodes of independent or isolated activity, which, of course, also occurred. Further, episodes of social nonplay occurred frequently, often centered on discussions about where the teacher or the third child was, or of favorite television programs.

The structured play formats were presented as basic interaction formats on which more complex formats can be built and in which more substantively varied content can be expressed. But what might actually sustain the practice, or repetition, of these social formats? Why engage so often in the work of meshing or interrelating behaviors instead of simply singing, chanting, or performing some rhythmically satisfying monologue or individual game? It is reasonable to postulate that an intrinsically satisfying feature of social play, which is present for each participant, is the feature of control. Observations of the apparent satisfaction obtained in manipulating features of the physical environment or, differently stated, of the effectiveness of successful manipulation in maintaining behavior have been made of infant behavior (Millar 1968, Chapter 4). Rapidly accumulating evidence on the sensitivity of young children to features of the human environment suggests that they would be ready and willing, perhaps before they were able, to attempt control of the human environment and derive satisfaction from successful control of another's behavior. In the performances of ritual play such control is precise and knowledge of its success is immediate; furthermore, the satisfaction derived is mutual, since each party is instrumental in eliciting and maintaining the responsive behavior of the other. The analogy of the acquisition of basic social interaction patterns with the modularization of physical action patterns in the development of complex skills as described by Bruner (1971) is more than a suggestive metaphor.

We have presented a brief description of some relatively simple interaction formats which were observed in both verbal and nonverbal forms. These formats were shown to be based on a principle of reciprocity, turn-taking, which shows two major types—doing the same thing and doing a complementary thing. The practice of these formats was most extensive in episodes of social play, and the simpler formats were frequently accompanied by ritual features.

Research leading to this study was supported by Research Grant #1 RO1 MH 23883-01 from the Public Health Service, National Institutes of Mental Health; and by Grant #GS-31636 from the National Science Foundation. The author is grateful to Edward Mueller for comments on an earlier version of the paper and to Rita Berndt for her assistance in the identification and classification of play episodes.

NOTES

1. Round modification also may be analyzed as paradigmatic or syntagmatic, but this distinction will not be made in the present discussion.
2. Two points should be made in respect to the figures in Table 1. First, we have no basis for comparison of these frequencies with other subject samples on such parameters as age, social class, or setting. Second, although a round in any play episode is potentially repeatable, we do not know what conditions influence the children to produce a ritual sequence, to choose another course of interaction, or to end the state of play.

REFERENCES

BATESON, G. The message "This is play." In B. Schaffner (Ed.), *Group processes*. New York: Macy Foundation, 1956.
BRUNER, J. S. The growth and structure of skill. In K. J. Connolly (Ed.), *Motor skills in infancy*. London: Academic Press, 1971.
GARVEY, C. Direct and indirect requests in children's communication. Unpublished manuscript. The Johns Hopkins University, 1973.
GARVEY, C. AND HOGAN, R. Social speech and social interaction: Egocentrism revisited. *Child Development*, 1973, Vol. 44, 562–568.
GORDON, D. AND LAKOFF, G. Conversational postulates. *Papers from the Seventh Regional Meeting of the Chicago Linguistics Society*, 1971, 63–84.
GREIF, E. B. A study of role playing in preschool children. Unpublished doctoral dissertation, The Johns Hopkins University, 1973.
GUILLAUME, P. *Imitation in children*. Chicago: The University of Chicago Press, 1971.
HERRON, R. E. AND SUTTON-SMITH, B. *Child's play*. New York: Wiley and Sons: 1971.
MILLAR, S. *The psychology of play*. Baltimore: Penguin Books, 1968.
PIAGET, J. *Play, dreams, and imitation in childhood*. New York: W. W. Norton, 1951.
SACKS, H. Unpublished lecture notes. The University of California at Irvine, 1967.
VYGOTSKY, L. *Thought and language*. Cambridge, Mass.: M.I.T. Press, 1962.
VYGOTSKY, L. Play and its role in the mental development of the child. Soviet Psychology, 1967, Vol. 5(3), 6–18.
WINCH, P. *The idea of a social science*. London: Routledge and Kegan Paul, 1958.

16

What Is a Friend?

Zick Rubin

We're friends now because we know each other's names.—Tony, age three and a half

Friends don't snatch or act snobby, and they don't argue or disagree. If you're nice to them, they'll be nice to you.—Julie, age eight

A friend is someone that you can share secrets with at 3 in the morning with Clearasil on your face.—Deborah, age thirteen

The friendship we have in mind is characterized by mutual trust; it permits a fairly free expression of emotion; it allows the shedding of privacies (although not inappropriately); it can absorb, within limits, conflict between the pair; it involves the discussion of personally crucial themes, it provides occasions to enrich and enlarge the self through the encounter of differences.—Elizabeth Douvan and Joseph Adelson, adults

As these statements illustrate,[1] people have widely differing notions of what a friend is and of the nature of friendship. In his second week at nursery school, three-year-old Dwayne plays with Eddie for the first time and minutes later runs around the yard shouting, "We're friends!"

Reprinted by permission of the publishers from *Children's Friendships* by Zick Rubin, Cambridge, Mass.: Harvard University Press. Copyright 1980 by Zick Rubin.

Thirteen-year-old Deborah, in contrast, might spend months getting to know a classmate, gradually extending the range and intimacy of their conversations, before deciding that their relationship merits the label of friendship. Some observers may conclude that young children's notions of friendship are so different from the conceptions held by older children, adolescents, and adults that it is misleading to consider them as variations of the same concept. From this point of view, when preschoolers talk about their friends, they are really referring to their playmates, which is a rather different sort of thing. My own view is that the use of the word "friend" by children of different ages nicely reflects the common functions of peer relationships for people of all ages. Both three-year-old Dwayne and thirteen-year-old Deborah are referring to nonfamilial relationships which are likely to foster a feeling of belonging and a sense of identity; it seems quite appropriate that they choose to use the same word. It is clear, however, that the ways in which people reason about friendship change over the course of childhood. Moreover, there appear to be some basic consistencies among people in the nature of this change.

The most systematic research on children's understandings of friendship is being conducted by Robert Selman and his colleagues at the Harvard Graduate School of Education. Selman has patterned both his theoretical approach and his research style on the model of the Swiss psychologist Jean Piaget. He follows Piaget in taking as his central concern the progressively developing mental structures that characterize children's social thought. He also follows Piaget in his method of documenting these mental structures— the clinical interview, in which the interviewer probes deeply and resourcefully to capture the child's own understanding of her social world. Selman has adopted this procedure to assess the "friendship awareness" of both normal and emotionally disturbed children, from early childhood through adolescence.[2] On the basis of this work, it is possible for us to identify two sharply contrasting stages of children's conceptions of friendship.

The young child, from about age three to five, characteristically views friends as "momentary physical playmates"—whomever one is playing with at a particular time. Children at this stage do not have a clear conception of an enduring relationship that exists apart from specific encounters. Young children may in fact *have* enduring relationships with others, but they typically conceive of them only in terms of momentary interaction. In addition, children at this stage reflect only on the physical attributes and activities of playmates, rather than on psychological attributes such as personal needs, interests, or traits. In contrast, the older child—by age eleven or twelve— comes to view close friendships as involving "intimate and mutual sharing." Children at this later stage regard friendship as a relationship that takes shape over a period of time. Friends are seen as providers of intimacy and support. The child realizes that, to achieve these ends, close friends need to be psychologically compatible—to share interests and to have mutually agreeable personalities.

To gain a fuller understanding of the contrast between these two stages of reasoning about friendship, let us compare the ways in which younger and older children reflect upon certain central issues: what sorts of people make good friends, how friendships are formed, and the nature of closeness and intimacy.

What sorts of people make good friends? For the young child who views friendship in terms of momentary interactions, the most important qualification for friendship is physical accessibility. When asked what sort of person makes a good friend, preschoolers are likely to provide such answers as "Someone who plays a lot" or "Someone who lives in Watertown."[3] Young children are also likely to focus on specific physical actions. Steven tells me, for example, that Craig is his friend because "he doesn't take things away from me." Conversely, Jake is not his friend because "he takes things away from me." For children at this level, moreover, one's own desires may be seen as a sufficient basis for friendship. When you ask a young child why a certain other child is his friend, the most common reply is "Because I like him." Attempts to probe more deeply are likely to frustrate both the researcher and the child:

ZR: Why is Caleb your friend?
Tony: Because I like him.
ZR: And why do you like him?
Tony: Because he's my friend.
ZR: And why is he your friend?
Tony (speaking each word distinctly, with a tone of mild disgust at the interviewer's obvious denseness): Because . . . I . . . choosed . . . him . . . for . . . my . . . friend.

Children at this stage do not make reference to psychological attributes of friends; at most, they will resort to such stereotypical descriptions as "she's nice" or "he's mean."

Older children are aware of other sorts of qualifications for friendship. Instead of focusing on physical accessibility, they are likely to emphasize the need for psychological compatibility. One aspect of this rapport is the sharing of outlooks and interests. When asked why Jimmy was his friend, thirteen-year-old Jack explained: "We like the same kinds of things. We speak the same language."[4] Children at this level of social awareness also realize that compatibility is not to be equated with similarity. "Good friends sort of fit together," thirteen-year-old Alan said. "They don't have to be exactly alike, but if one is strong in something the other can be weak and he may be good at something else."[5]

How are friendships formed? For children who view friendship in terms of momentary physical interaction, the way to form a friendship is simply to play with the other child. When asked how one should go about making friends, younger children are likely to provide such answers as "Move in next door," "Tell him your name," and "Just go up and ask her to play." From this perspective, the barriers to making friends are physical rather than psychological. A four-year-old interviewed by Selman explained things this way:

Interviewer: Is it easy or hard to make friends?
Child: Hard, because sometimes if you wave to the other person, they might not see you wave, so it's hard to get that friend.
Interviewer: What if they see you?
Child: Then it's easy.[6]

Older children, who view friendships as relationships that continue beyond single encounters, view the process as more complicated. Although they recognize that people may sometimes "hit it off" immediately, these children believe that friendships can best be established gradually, as people find out about one another's traits, interests, and values. "You don't really pick your friends," thirteen-year-old Jack reported. "It just grows on you. You can find out that you can talk to someone, you can tell them your problems, when you understand each other."[7]

The nature of intimacy. For the young child, the question of what constitutes closeness translates into the question of what distinguishes a best friend from other friends. And when such a distinction is made, it is in strictly quantitative terms—whatever you do with a friend, you simply do more of it with a best friend: "If you *always* visit, you're best friends." Preschool children may in fact have best friends with whom they interact in ways that seem qualitatively unique to the adult observer. Nevertheless, children who view friendship in terms of momentary physical interactions seem unable to reflect on the special nature of such friendships.

Children who view friendship as a mutual relationship, in contrast, can reflect specifically on the nature of intimacy. Closeness is defined in terms of the degree of understanding that has been built up between two friends, the extent to which they trust each other with personal thoughts and feelings, and the extent to which they are concerned with one another's welfare. A fifteen-year-old boy put it this way:

> A really tight friendship is when you start to really care about the person. If he gets sick, you kind of start worrying about him—or if he gets hit by a car. An everyday friend, you say, I know that kid, he's all right, and you don't really think much of him. But a close friend you worry about more than yourself. Well, maybe not more, but about the same.[8]

This conception of intimacy between friends is remarkably similar to the ways in which philosophers and psychologists have typically defined love.[9] In his discussion of the friendships of late childhood, Harry Stack Sullivan made this equation explicit: "If you will look very closely at one of your children when he finally finds a chum . . . you will discover something very different in the relationship—namely, that your child begins to develop a new sensitivity to what matters to another person. And this is not in the sense of 'what should I do to get what I want,' but instead 'what should I do to contribute to the happiness or to support the prestige and feeling of worth-whileness of my chum' . . . This change represents the beginning of something very like full-blown psychiatrically defined *love.*"[10]

Along what path do children progress from a view of friendship as a momentary physical interaction to a view of friendship as mutual sharing and intimacy? Is there a sudden flash of social insight, akin to the rapid vocabulary growth of the second year of life or to the height spurt that accompanies puberty? Surely this is not the way it happens. One view of the way it does happen, taken by Selman—with due credit to Piaget—is that social awareness develops in a series of stages, each of which involves a reorganization of mental elements by the child. The two stages of reasoning about friendship that we have examined are labeled "Stage 0" and "Stage 3." To get from Stage 0 to Stage 3, the child progresses through two intermediate stages. In Stage 1, most often characteristic of children between the ages of about six and eight, the child conceives of friendship as "one-way assistance." A friend is a person who does things that please you; accordingly, friends must become aware of one another's likes and dislikes. At this stage, however, there is still no awareness of the reciprocal nature of friendship. This comes at Stage 2, which is most often characteristic of children between the ages of about nine and twelve. For the first time, friendship is understood as a two-way street in which each friend must adapt to the needs of the other. In Stage 2, however, children's awareness of reciprocity remains focused on specific incidents rather than on the friendship itself, as an enduring social relationship. For this reason, Selman labels this the stage of "fairweather cooperation." It is only in the transformation from Stage 2 to Stage 3 that children, by now typically in late childhood or early adolescence, come to reflect on issues of intimacy and mutality in a continuing relationship.

Thus Selman describes a stepladder progression in children's concepts of friendship. Children climb the ladder, stopping to rest for a while at each rung—in part, presumably, to consolidate the new level of interpersonal awareness that they have achieved—before going on. Other researchers, while confirming this general progression, doubt that the stages are as distinct as Selman's scheme suggests. Whether the progression is like ascending a stepladder or a gradually inclining ramp, however, it involves steady movement along three dimensions of social understanding.

First, there is a progression in the child's ability to take other people's point of view, comparable to the broadening of visual perspective-taking ability that takes place in early childhood.[11] Whereas young children assume that everyone else sees physical objects in precisely the same way that they do, they later come to recognize that different people will see a particular object in different ways, depending on their physical vantage point. An analogous progression takes place in the domain of social understanding. At first, children view friendship in a one-sided and egocentric way, solely in terms of what a friend can do for them. A friend is a friend because "I like him" or "He plays with me" or "I want him to be my friend." Only at later stages do children become capable of figuratively standing back and taking the other person's viewpoint ("She doesn't like it when I act too wild") and, still later, a third-person perspective on their relationships, with an appreciation of interlocking needs and provisions ("We share a lot of the same values"). Thus the developing ability to take another person's point of view can be seen as a mark of both cognitive and social maturing.

Second, there is a shift from viewing people only as physical entities to viewing people as psychological entities as well.[12] When younger children are asked to describe their friends or acquaintances, they concentrate on physical attributes and activities: "Andy's got red hair and he always wears cowboy boots." As children grow older they begin to supplement such concrete descriptions with abstract concepts that refer to behavioral dispositions: "He's a big showoff."[13] Children also become increasingly likely to provide their own psychological explanations of other people's behavior, such as "Because he is black he is very defensive" or "She says bad things about other people so you'll be closer to her."[14] Children, like adults, are everyday psychologists, and their psychologizing becomes more sophisticated—even if not always more accurate—over the course of childhood. In accord with these changes, appraisals of the psychological attributes of others become increasingly important aspects of friendship.

Third, children's conceptions of friendship reflect a shift from viewing social relationships as momentary interactions to viewing them as social systems that endure over some period of time. In terms of a distinction suggested by Erving Goffman, young children conceptualize their commerce with others only as *encounters,* whereas older children become able to conceptualize *relationships.*[15] Following a fight, for example, a young child may be quick to shout "We're not friends!" An older child, like this twelve-year-old, takes a longer view:

> You have known your friend so long and loved him so much, and then all of a sudden you are so mad at him, you say, I could just kill you and you still like each other, because you have always been friends and you know in your mind you are going to be friends in a few seconds anyway.[16]

These three developmental progressions have a basic theme in common: there is a shift in focus from the concrete to the abstract—from observable, here-and-now characteristics of people and their behavior to inferred, underlying characteristics. These progressions in social understandings are made possible, in part, by parallel progressions from concrete to abstract reasoning in a child's intellectual development.[17] But intellectual development alone cannot account for the specific content of children's conceptions of friendship. What is it that causes children to transform their notions of friendship from momentary interaction to one-way assistance, from fair-weather cooperation to shared intimacy? One possibility is that it is chiefly a matter of cultural learning, from the models and formulas provided by adults, older children, and the mass media: "You have to share with your friends," "Mommy's talking on the phone to her best friend," "Batman and Superman are Superfriends—they never let each other down." From this standpoint, the child's changing conceptions of friendship are a series of successively closer approximations to the views of friendship held in a particular culture. It must be acknowledged that Selman and other researchers have derived their descriptions from studies of children in Western societies, usually from middle-class backgrounds. We can safely assume that at least some of the details of these progressions tend to be different among children in non-Western cultures—where, for example, friendship may be based to some degree on formalized arrangements such as blood brotherhood.[18] Even within the United States, as we shall see in Chapter 9, there is reason to believe that children from different social backgrounds come to have somewhat different conceptions of friendship.

Without denying the likelihood of such differences. however, most developmental psychologists believe that the principal architect of social understanding is not the child's culture but the child himself. According to this "constructivist" view, as espoused by both Piaget and Sullivan, children work out for themselves what social relationships are all about on the basis of their actual encounters with others. Through their interactions with peers, children discover that other children are similar to them in some respects and different in others. And as children attempt to cooperate with one another, they discover that the coordination of behavior requires an appreciation of the other's capabilities, desires, and values. At first, these "discoveries" remain implicit and unexamined. Gradually, however, children integrate and organize what they have learned, leading to increasingly sophisticated understandings of social relationships. Talking openly about conflicts may be one particularly valuable way to further one's understanding of friendship.

Although the constructivist view is widely held, there is still no systematic research that succeeds in pinning down the ways in which specific experiences lead to transformations in children's social awareness.[19] Even in the absence of such research, however, the constructivist view can help us to make sense out of several observations about children's social understandings that might otherwise be puzzling.

First, the constructivist view helps to make clear that there is no inevitable relation between a child's age and his or her level of interpersonal understanding. Whereas almost all children begin to walk within a limited age range—between about nine and fourteen months—there is much greater variation in the ages at which children begin to reason about friendship at particular levels. Unlike walking, the development of social understanding depends on both developing intellectual skills, which may vary widely among individuals, and on specific social experiences, which vary even more widely. As a result, we should be sure not to rely on chronological age as an unfailing index of children's social understanding.

The constructivist view also helps us to see why there are almost always discrepancies between how children answer questions about friendship and how the same children relate to their friends in practice. For example, young children who characteristically view friendship as momentary physical interactions may still demonstrate an ability to work out compromises that suggests a clear practical awareness of the give-and-take of relationships. "I'll live with you there," one preschool boy told a girl who wanted him to play house again, "but I'll work here, and I'm working now"—and he went on building with blocks.[20] As Piaget emphasizes, "Thought always lags behind action and cooperation has to be practiced for a very long time before it can be brought fully to light by reflective thought."[21]

Finally, the constructivist view accommodates the fact that there are often apparent inconsistencies in children's responses to questions about friendship. My nephew Larry, at age twelve, explained why Mark was his best friend in terms of the sharing of outlooks and interests: "We're both short, we're the same smartness, and we like the same sports." Such awareness of the psychological bases of compatibility is characteristic of Stage 3 reasoning in Selman's scheme. But when I asked Larry what would lead people who were best friends not to be friends any more, he could think only of the possibilities that one of them moved away or transferred to another school, reflecting a physicalistic conception of friendship that is more characteristic of Selman's Stage 0. The notion that friends can grow apart because of changing outlooks or interests did not occur to Larry, who had not yet had much experience with the ending of friendships. Such "inconsistencies" are to be expected, once we recognize that the child's conceptions are derived from interpretations of concrete experiences rather than from logical analysis of friendships in the abstract.

This discussion of children's progression toward increasingly "advanced" conceptions of friendship may seem to imply that, by the time we become adults, we all reason about friendship in thoroughly sophisticated, humane, and logical terms. The conception of friendship by two psychologists that I quoted at the start of this chapter—with its mutual trust, absorption of conflict, and opportunity for self-enrichment—is one definition of this ideal endpoint. It is worthwhile to ask, however, whether most adults typically conceive of friendship in such terms. The fact is that they do not. When adults of varying ages are asked to explain the basis of their close friendships, they mention a wide range of factors, including physical proximity ("Because we're neighbors"), likability ("He is a good companion"), similarity of outlooks ("We have the same interests . . . in religion and the way we look at things"), trust ("She listens and you know it is not going any further"), and reciprocal help and support ("I know that if I ever needed help with anything I could always go to her").[22] The reasoning behind these descriptions runs the gamut from Stage 0 to Stage 3 and beyond. Adults' descriptions of an "ideal close relationship" reflect almost the same range and diversity.

My point is not that adults frequently reason like children about friendship. It is, rather, that people do not in fact progress toward more advanced levels of social awareness in an ever-upward climb toward an ideal endpoint, with each "higher" level, once attained, replacing the lower levels already passed. Instead, as Selman and others have noted, lower stages are not discarded but are built upon and remain available for future use in specific situations. It is interesting to note, in this connection, that both children and adults tend to reason in more sophisticated ways about their deepest friendships and loves than about casual relationships. Indeed, one's view of any close relationship, as it progresses from first meetings to intimacy, may have to go through the very same stages—albeit in a shorter time period—as do conceptions of friendship through the course of childhood.[23]

What, then, is a friend? Philosophers and psychologists can provide their own definitions, but these are not entirely adequate to our purposes. Friendship, in the sense that it matters to us, is what a child makes it out to be. Whether Billy views Sean as "someone I play with in school" or as "someone I can trust—and who can trust me" will inevitably have a major impact on the way in which Billy proceeds to conduct his relationship with Sean. And these conceptions contain important clues about how Billy is likely to navigate relationships with other children as well. If we are interested in understanding a child's friendships, therefore, we must do our best to understand them in the child's own terms.

NOTES

1. From William Damon, *The Social World of the Child* (San Francisco: Jossey-Bass, 1977), pp. 160, 164. Elizabeth Douvan and Joseph Adelson, *The Adolescent Experience* (New York: Wiley, 1966), p. 176.
2. Robert Selman, "Toward a Structural Analysis of Developing Interpersonal Relations Concepts: Research With Normal and Disturbed Preadolescent Boys," in Anne D. Pck, ed., *Minnesota Symposium on Child Psychology*, vol. 10 (Minneapolis: University of Minnesota Press, 1976). Robert Selman and Dan Jaquette, "Stability and Oscillation in Interpersonal Awareness: A Clinical-Developmental Analysis," in Charles B. Keasey, ed., *Nebraska Symposium on Motivation, 1977* (Lincoln: University of Nebraska Press, 1978).
3. Robert Selman and Dan Jaquette, "The Development of Interpersonal Awareness" (working draft of manual, Harvard-Judge Baker Social Reasoning Project, 1977).

4. Damon, *The Social World of the Child,* p. 163.
5. Selman and Jaquette, "The Development of Interpersonal Awareness," p. 132.
6. Selman and Jaquette, "The Development of Interpersonal Awareness," p. 118.
7. Damon, *The Social World of the Child,* p. 164.
8. Selman and Jaquette, "The Development of Interpersonal Awareness," p. 144.
9. See, for example, Zick Rubin, *Liking and Loving: An Invitation to Social Psychology* (New York: Holt, Rinehart and Winston, 1973), chap. 10 ("The Nature of Love").
10. Harry Stack Sullivan, *The Interpersonal Theory of Psychiatry* (New York: Norton, 1953), p. 245.
11. See John H. Flavell, "The Development of Knowledge About Visual Perception," in Keasey, ed., *Nebraska Symposium on Motivation, 1977.*
12. W. J. Livesley and D. B. Bromley, *Person Perception in Childhood and Adolescence* (London: Wiley, 1973).
13. Helaine H. Scarlett, Allan N. Press, and Walter H. Crockett, "Children's Descriptions of Peers: A Wernerian Developmental Analysis," *Child Development,* 1971, *42,* 439–453.
14. Barbara Hollands Peevers and Paul Secord, "Developmental Change in Attribution of Descriptive Concepts to Persons," *Journal of Personality and Social Psychology,* 1973, *27,* 120–128.
15. Erving Goffman, *Encounters* (Indianapolis: Bobbs-Merrill, 1961).
16. Selman and Jaquette, "The Development of Interpersonal Awareness," p. 165.
17. See Thomas J. Berndt, "Relations Between Social Cognition, Nonsocial Cognition, and Social Behavior: The Case of Friendship," in Lee Ross and John H. Flavell, eds., *New Directions in the Study of Social-Cognitive Development,* in press.
18. For description of friendships in non-Western cultures, see, for example, Robert Brain, *Friends and Lovers* (New York: Basic Books, 1976). Yehudi A. Cohen, "Patterns of Friendship," in Cohen, ed., *Social Structure and Personality* (New York: Holt, Rinehart and Winston, 1961).
19. For an impressive beginning along these lines, see William A. Corsaro, "Friendship in the Nursery School: Social Organization in a Peer Environment," in Steven R. Asher and John M. Gottman, eds., *The Development of Children's Friendships* (Cambridge University Press, in press).
20. Katherine H. Read, *The Nursery School,* 6th ed. (Philadelphia: Saunders, 1976), p. 347.
21. Jean Piaget, *The Moral Judgment of the Child* Glencoe, Ill.: Free Press, 1948), p. 56; originally published in 1932.
22. Lawrence Weiss and Marjorie Fiske Lowenthal, "Life Course Perspectives on Friendship," in Lowenthal, Majda Turner, David Chiriboga, et al., *Four Stages of Life* (San Francisco: Jossey-Bass, 1975).
23. For a discussion of the development of adult social relationships that parallels the stages we have been discussing, see George Levinger and J. Diedrick Snoek, *Attraction in Relationship: A New Look at Interpersonal Attraction* (Morristown, N.J.: General Learning Press, 1972).

17

Developmental Synthesis of Affect and Cognition and Its Implications for Altruistic Motivation

Martin L. Hoffman

A type of moral encounter of increasing interest to psychology is that in which an individual witnesses another person in distress. Whether or not the individual attempts to help is presumably the net result of altruistic and egoistic forces. The source of egoistic forces requires no explanation, since they have long been the focus of motivation theories (e.g., Cofer and Appley 1964). The primary objective of this article is to present a developmental theory of altruistic motivation that may provide an integrative framework for ordering the available knowledge about people's reactions to others in distress. The theoretical argument focuses on the contribution of empathy to the motive to help as a function of various facets of cognitive development. A secondary objective, necessary for the first, is to pull together diverse research findings that suggest a certain developmental progression in the child's cognitive construction of others. A third objective, which for purposes of coherence will be presented first, is to present a case for the plausibility of at least a component of the motive to help others in distress that may be independent of the observer's egoistic motive system.

Independent Altruistic Motive

The doctrinaire view in psychology has been that altruism can ultimately be explained in terms of egoistic, self-serving motives. Although
widespread, this assumption remains untested—perhaps a reflection of
Western philosophical thought—with no more empirical support behind it
than the assumption that there is an independent, constitutional basis for the
motive to help others. The issues are complex, and clear support for one
position or the other is unavailable. Several convergent lines of evidence,
however, seem to suggest that the assumption of an independent motive to
help others may be somewhat more reasonable than the assumption that an
egoistic motive base underlies all such behavior.

A first crude line of evidence for an independent motive to help others
is the burgeoning research showing that—contrary newspaper accounts
notwithstanding—people of all ages do tend to offer help, at least when they
are the only witness present and the need is clear (see reviews by Bryan and
London 1970; Krebs 1970; Staub 1974). Furthermore, the percentage of
those who help is quite high. Children 8–10 years of age, for example, were
found to attempt to help others in about half the opportunities to help that
occurred in a naturalistic setting (Severy and Davis 1971). This is consistent
with Staub's (1970, 1971a) findings in a laboratory experiment: Half the
second-to-fourth graders left what they were doing to help a crying child in
the next room—which is particularly interesting in view of the usual restraint
shown by young children in laboratory studies. Although fewer sixth graders offered help in the same situation, half of those who had been given prior
permission to enter the room did so, as did over 90% of a seventh-grade
sample. The findings for adults are sometimes quite dramatic, both in terms
of the frequency and the speed with which the subjects aid the victim. Latané
and Darley (1968) found that 85% of their subjects attempted to help
someone they thought was having an epileptic fit, 90% of them acting within
60 sec. Piliavin and Piliavin (1972) and Piliavin, Rodin and Piliavin (1969)
also found helping response rates of nearly 100%, and median reaction
times of 5 and 10 sec, in two experimental studies in which a subway rider
carrying a cane collapsed on the floor of the train. Clark and Word (1972)
report that all their subjects rushed to help a man they heard fall and cry out
in pain; the average reaction time was less than 9 seconds. The fact that
people normally help when they are the only witness suggests that they are
not acting for purposes of gaining social approval. Furthermore, although
their behavior might reflect an internalized norm of social responsibility
(Berkowitz and Connor 1966), the quick reaction times, which suggest an
element of impulsiveness in the behavior, would seem to argue in favor of a
more basic action tendency triggered by the awareness of another's distress
rather than, or perhaps in addition to, a social responsibility norm.

More convincing support for an independent altruistic motive component may be found in research that relates the observer's egoistic, social, and
emotional needs to his helping behavior. If egoism underlies altruism we
would expect people to be more likely to help others when their own needs
for approval are aroused and unmet. The research findings are exactly the
opposite. People are more apt to help when their approval needs are satis-

fied. For example, children who are popular, emotionally secure, and self-confident are more apt to help than children who lack social approval (Murphy 1937; Staub and Sherk 1970). Children who receive a great deal of affection at home are more likely to help than children who receive little affection (Hoffman 1975; Mussen, Harris, Rutherford, and Keasy 1970; Yarrow 1973). Furthermore, the tendency to help is increased by the experimental arousal of positive moods and feelings of success and decreased by the arousal of such deprived need states as feelings of failure (Berkowitz and Connor 1966; Isen 1970; Isen, Horn, and Rosenhan 1973; Moore, Underwood, and Rosenhan 1973). Perhaps egoistic need fulfillment reduces preoccupation with one's own concerns and thus leaves one more open and responsive to the needs of others. Also pertinent is the evidence that altruistic action may be self-rewarding, that is, the opportunity to terminate an aversive stimulus delivered to another person can serve as a reinforcer for a learned response in the absence of any conventional egoistic reinforcer; furthermore, the latency of the response is reduced when the number of distress cues from the victim is increased (Weiss, Boyer, Lombardo, and Stich 1973). It thus appears that helping is often not a self-serving act, which lends credence to the existence of an altruistic motive system that may operate to some degree independently of the egoistic.

A final argument bears on man's evolution, with which any theory of intrinsic motivation must be in accord. Two lines of evidence are potentially relevant: observation of higher mammals and inferences about human nature based on knowledge of the circumstances in which man evolved. Systematic animal studies have unfortunately not been made, and the evidence for altruism in animals is scanty, anecdotal, and often subject to alternative interpretations (Hebb 1971; Krebs 1970, 1971), although some reasonably clear-cut examples can be found.[1] The theoretical issues bearing on human evolution are too complex to be given full treatment here (see Alexander 1971; Campbell 1972), but a brief summary seems in order. First, there is general agreement among the theorists, based on evidence from fossil remains (bones, tools, weapons), that during most of man's evolutionary history he lived in a highly adverse environment and under constant threat from starvation and predators. He faced his adverse environment not alone but by banding together with others in small nomadic hunting groups. The obviously greater survival value of cooperative and social life over solitary life has led some writers to take the view that natural selection must have favored altruism and other prosocial traits rather than a crude, unbridled egoism alone (e.g., Wynne-Edwards 1962). Others, however, claim this is impossible: Since the unit of reproduction is the individual, natural selection must have favored egoistic traits that maximize the fitness of the individual (e.g., Williams 1966).[2] Both points of view seem to have merit. So does Campbell's (1965) notion that the joint presence of both egoistic and altruistic tendencies would have had the greatest survival value; the varied and multiply contingent nature of the environment makes it seem likely that egoistic behavior was more adaptive at certain times and altruistic behavior at other times.

One obvious solution is to find evidence for some type of prosocial tendency that may also contribute to individual fitness. Such a conception has been advanced by Trivers (1971), who uses a rescue model to show that natural selection had to favor altruistic behavior because of its long-run benefit to the organism performing it. In the model, individual A encounters another person, B, whose life is in danger (e.g., from drowning). It is assumed that (a) the probable cost to A of rescuing B is far less than the gain to B, and (b) there is a high likelihood of a role reversal in the future. Both assumptions seem valid. The first appears to be an accurate portrayal of most such encounters even today; the second is entirely consistent with the known conditions of man's existence during the long period of evolution—small face-to-face groups, long interaction between the same specific others, and frequent exposure to danger. Trivers shows mathematically that if the entire population is sooner or later exposed to the same danger, the two who make the attempt to save the other will be more apt to survive than two who face these dangers on their own. It follows that the tendency to help others in distress is very likely a part of man's biological inheritance, despite the fact that his contemporary social and physical environment differs markedly from that of his remote ancestors and may no longer support one-to-one reciprocity.

Recent research on the limbic system, an ancient part of the brain which humans share with all mammals, offers further support for the evolutionary argument. According to MacLean (1958, 1962, 1967, 1973), the research shows that whereas one part of the limbic system is concerned with feelings, emotions, and behavior that insures self-preservation, another part appears to be involved in expressive and feeling states that are conducive to sociability and preservation of the species. MacLean (1962) concludes that the research suggests that "in the complex organization of the phylogenetically old and new structures under consideration we presumably have a neural ladder for ascending from the most primitive sexual feeling to the highest level of altruistic sentiments" (p. 300).

Although by no means conclusive, the available evidence thus appears to be more in keeping with the conception of independent altruistic and egoistic motive systems than with the view that all altruism derives from egoistic motives. This is not to deny that man is also by nature selfish and aggressive (e.g., Tinbergen 1968) nor that helping others may often be selfishly motivated or fostered by such essentially irrelevant personality characteristics as courage and independence (London 1970). Indeed, as noted earlier, the acquisition of both egoistic and altruistic structures would appear to have been most adaptive in man's evolution. Our argument does suggest, however, that a built-in mechanism for direct mediation of helping behavior is a tenable hypothesis, however fragile it may at times appear in individualistic societies such as our own.

What might this mechanism be? An obvious candidate is man's capacity for empathy. MacLean's research (1973) indicates that the primitive limbic cortex has strong neural connections both with the hypothalamus, which plays a basic role in integrating emotional expression with viscerosomatic behavior, and with the prefrontal cortex, a newer formation of the brain. The prefrontal cortex functions in "helping us to gain insight into the feelings of others . . . [and] receives part of this insight—the capacity to see with feeling—through its connection with the limbic brain" (MacLean 1973, p. 58). In other words, the brain structures required for affective involvement with objects in the external world, including people, were apparently present early in man's evolution. The more recent addition of newer brain structures along with the acquisition of connective neural circuits have made it possible for such affect to be experienced in conjunction with a cognitive, increasingly sophisticated social awareness or insight into others—and all of this appears to be independent of the neural base for egoistic, self-preserving behavior. In brief, the neural basis for a primitive empathy was apparently present early in man's evolution. Empathy could thus have served man and continued to evolve into increasingly complex forms as his brain developed and grew.

The idea that empathy has been defined in many ways, most of which fall into two general rubrics, one pertaining to the cognitive awareness of another person's feelings or thoughts (e.g., Borke 1971; Dymond 1949) and the other to the affective reaction to another's feelings (e.g., Feshbach and Roe 1968; Stotland 1969). The latter conception is used here.

The idea that empathy may provide a motive for altruism is not new. It was suggested two centuries ago by Adam Smith (1759/1948) and David Hume (1751/1957) and has appeared frequently in the recent psychological literature (e.g., Freud 1937; Hoffman 1963, 1970; Hoffman and Saltzstein, see note 4; Isaacs 1933; Piliavin and Piliavin 1972; Stern 1924; Aronfreed and Paskal, see note 3). These writers have typically stressed the affective aspects of empathy, however, and neglected cognitive factors, which "appear to be indispensable to any formulation of emotion" (Schachter and Singer 1962). Since cognition determines how even simple emotions like joy and fear are experienced (Hunt, Cole, and Reis 1958; Ruckmick 1936; Schachter and Singer 1962), we may presume that cognition also determines how one experiences a complex emotion like empathy. The central idea of the theory to be presented here is that since a fully developed empathic reaction is an internal response to cues about the affective states of someone else, the empathic reaction must depend heavily on the actor's cognitive sense of the other as distinct from himself, which undergoes dramatic changes developmentally. The development of a sense of the other will now be examined, followed by a discussion of how this cognitive development interacts with the individual's early empathic responses to lay the basis for altruistic motivation.

Development of a Cognitive Sense of Others

To delineate the broad stages in development of a sense of the other requires bringing together several different strands of research—that pertain to object or person permanence, role taking, and personal identity.

Person Permanence

Person permanence pertains to the awareness of another's existence as a separate physical entity. The young infant apparently lacks this awareness; objects, events, and people are not experienced as distinct from the self. Not until about 6 months, according to Piaget (1954), does the infant organize the fleeting images making up his world into discrete objects and experience them as separate from his own biologically determined sensations. The main empirical evidence comes from studies of object displacement (e.g., Bell 1970; Décarie 1965; Escalona, Corman, Galenson, Schecter, Schecter, Golden, Leoi, and Barax, see note 5; Uzgiris and Hunt, see note 6). If a desired object is hidden behind a screen before the infant's eyes, he loses interest in it as though it no longer existed. By 6 months he removes the screen to get the object, which shows that he can then internally reproduce the image of an object and use the image as a guide to the object. His sense of the object is still limited, however, since it is short lived and the screen's presence is necessary as a sign of the object. We know this because until about 18 months the infant does not seek the object if the experimenter first places it in a container that he then hides behind a screen and brings out empty after releasing the object. At that age the child retrieves an object after a succession of such invisible displacements, indicating that he can then evoke an object's image even where there is nothing in sight to attest to its existence. Piaget sees this as the beginning of object permanence—a stable sense of the separate existence of physical objects even when outside the individual's immediate perceptual field. Recent research by Bell (1970) and Saint-Pierre (see note 7), however, suggests that "person" permanence occurs several months earlier; that is, by 1 year children can retain a mental image of a person.

Although not stressed in the literature, there is evidence that the process of acquiring a sense of the object, hence person permanence, is gradual (Bell 1970; Uzgiris and Hunt, see note 6). Children may also regress to the global level because of fatigue and emotional arousal, which lessen the ability to "utilize available cues" (Easterbrook 1959). Only later may person permanence be expected to become stable enough for self and other to be sharply differentiated throughout the normal course of daily events.

Role Taking

The child's sense of the separate existence of persons is for some time highly limited. Although aware of people's existence as physical entities, he does not yet know that they have inner states of their own, and he tends to attribute to them characteristics that belong to him. Piaget (1932) believes it is not until about 7 or 8 years that this egocentrism begins to give way to the recognition that others have their own perspective. The role-taking research is generally supportive although its emphasis has been heavily cognitive, dealing with the other person's perceptions and thoughts, and ignoring affect.[8] Furthermore, the experimental tasks often require cognitive and verbal skills. For example, the task might involve predicting how objects would look to people in different positions around a room (Flavell 1968; Lovell 1959; Piaget and Inhelder 1948/1967; Selman 1971), selecting appropriate gifts for males and females of different ages (Flavell 1968), or communicating a message to someone whose perspective is lacking in some respect, that is, he is blindfolded, very young, or enters the situation late and consequently lacks certain necessary information (Chandler and Greenspan 1972; Flavell 1968). These skills may mask the child's actual role-taking competence. To estimate how early in life the child can take another's role requires evidence from studies employing cognitively less complex measures. Three recent studies approach this ideal. In two, some of the children as young as 2 years 6 months were able to perform simple visual role-taking tasks (Fishbein, Lewis, and Keiffer 1972; Masangkay, McCluskey, McIntyre, Sims-Knight, Vaughn, and Flavell 1974). In another, 4-year-olds showed that they could take the cognitive and motivational perspective of younger children by using simpler and more attention-getting language (Shatz and Gelman 1973).

It seems likely that even younger children are capable of role taking in highly motivating, natural settings: two examples follow. In one, which the writer observed, Marcy, aged 20 months, was in the playroom of her home and wanted a toy that her sister Sara was playing with. She asked Sara for it, but Sara refused vehemently. Marcy paused, as if reflecting on what to do, and then began to rock on Sara's rocking horse (which Sara never allowed anyone to touch), yelling "Nice horsey! Nice horsey!" and keeping her eyes on Sara all the time. Sara came running angrily, whereupon Marcy immediately ran directly to the toy and grabbed it. Without analyzing the full complexity of Marcy's behavior, it is clear that she deliberately set about to lure her sister away from the toy. Though not yet 2 years, she showed awareness of another's inner states that differed from her own. Although her behavior was more Machiavellian than altruistic, Marcy demonstrated that she could take another's role, even though she probably could not have understood the instructions in a typical role-taking experiment.

In the second incident, Michael, aged 15 months, and his friend Paul were fighting over a toy and Paul started to cry. Michael appeared disturbed and let go, but Paul still cried. Michael paused, then brought his teddy bear to Paul but to no avail. Michael paused again, and then finally succeeded in stopping Paul's crying by fetching Paul's security blanket from an adjoining room. Several aspects of this incident deserve comment. First, it is clear that Michael initially assumed that his own teddy bear, which often comforts him, would also comfort Paul. Second, Paul's continued crying served as negative feedback that led Michael to consider alternatives. Third, Michael's final, successful act has several possible explanations: (a) He simply imitated what he had observed in the past; this is unlikely since his parents were certain he had never seen Paul being comforted with a blanket. (b) He may have remembered seeing another child soothed by a blanket, which reminded him of Paul's blanket (more complex than it first appears, since Paul's blanket was out of Michael's perceptual field at the time). (c) He was somehow able to reason by analogy that Paul would be comforted by something he loved in the same way that Michael loved his own teddy bear. Whatever the correct interpretation, this incident, as well as a strikingly similar one reported by Borke (1972), suggests that a child not yet 1 year and 6 months can, with the most general kind of feedback, assess the specific needs of another person which differed from his own.

If we may generalize tentatively from these two instances, it would appear that role taking in familiar, highly motivating natural settings may precede laboratory role taking by several years. That is, the rudiments of role-taking competence may be present in some children by age 2 years or earlier, although performance varies with the setting and cognitive complexity of the particular task.[9]

Personal Identity

The third broad step in the development of a sense of the other pertains to the view of the other having his own personal identity—his own life circumstances and inner states beyond the immediate situation. This developmental stage has been ignored in the literature. The closest to it is Erikson's (1950) conception of ego identity, which pertains in part to the individual's sense of his own sameness through time. In support of Erikson, it seems reasonable that at some point the child develops the cognitive capacity to integrate his own discrete inner experiences over time and to form a conception of himself as having different feelings and thoughts in different situations but being the same continuous person with his own past, present, and anticipated future. There is little relevant research. Kohlberg (1966) suggests that during the preoperational period (2–7 years) children not only lack the concept of conservation with respect to mass, weight, and number (Piaget 1954) but also with regard to qualitative attributes such as gender. He found, for example, that it is not until 6 or 7 years that children firmly assert that a girl could not be a boy even if she wanted to or even if she played boys' games or wore boys' haircuts or clothes, thus demonstrating a sense of stabilization and continuity regarding gender. There is also evidence that a firm sense of one's own racial identity may not be established until about 7 or 8 years (Proshansky 1966). (Although younger children use racial terms and show racial preferences, their racial conception appears to reflect verbal fluency rather than a stable attainment of racial concepts.) Finally, in a developmental study by Guardo and Bohan (1971), 6- and 7-year-olds recognized their identity as humans and as males or females mainly in terms of their names, physical appearance, and behaviors—which is consistent with the gender and racial identity research. Their sense of self-continuity from past to future was hazy, however, until 8 or 9 years when more covert and personalized differences in feelings and attitudes began to contribute to self-recognition, although even then their names and physical characteristics were the main anchorage points of identity.

It appears, then, that somewhere between 6 and 9 years marks the beginning of the child's emerging sense of his own continuing identity. By early adolescence, this may be expected to expand considerably. Furthermore, once the child can see that his own life has coherence and continuity despite the fact that he reacts differently in different situations, he should soon be able to perceive this in others. He can then not only take their role and assess their reactions in particular situations but also generalize from these and construct a concept of their general life experience. In sum, his awareness that others are coordinate with himself expands to include the notion that they, like him, have their own person identities that go beyond the immediate situation.

To summarize, the research suggests that by about the age of 1 year children are capable of recognizing others as separate physical entities; by about 2–3 years they have a rudimentary awareness that others have inner states independent of their own; and by about 6–9 years they are beginning to be aware that others have their own identities outside the immediate situation.

Development of Altruistic Motives

A theory of altruistic motivation aroused by distress cues from another will now be presented. It is essentially a developmental account of the synthesis of the above three levels of a cognitive sense of the other with the affect experienced when witnessing another person in distress. The sharing of positive emotions like joy and excitement may also contribute to helping behavior, but the connection is probably less direct because the empathic response to another's distress must be presumed to be primarily unpleasant.

Empathic Distress

Empathic distress refers to the involuntary, at times forceful experiencing of another person's painful emotional state. It may be elicited by expressive cues that directly reflect the other's feelings or by other cues that convey the impact of external events on him. The most parsimonious explanation of empathic distress as a learned response in early childhood is the classical conditioning paradigm in which cues of pain or displeasure from another or from his situation evoke associations with the observer's own past pain, resulting in an empathic affective reaction. A simple example is the child who cuts himself, feels the pain, and cries. Later, on seeing another child cut himself and cry, the sight of blood, the sound of the cry, or any other distress cue or aspect of the situation having elements in common with his own prior pain experience can now elicit the unpleasant affect initially associated with that experience.

There is also suggestive evidence for a rudimentary, possibly isomorphic distress response shortly after birth. Thus Simner (1971) reports that 2-day-old infants cried vigorously and intensely at the sound of another infant's cry. He also gives evidence that this was not merely a response to a noxious stimulus; that is, the infants reacted in a more subdued manner to equally loud nonhuman sounds including computer-simulated infant cries. Nor did the subjects' cries appear to be due to imitation, since they appeared to be genuinely upset and agitated by the other's cry (Simner, see note 10). Regardless of the process involved, the resulting co-occurrence of the infant's own cry, his distress, and the other's cry—given the fusion of self and other in the infant's mind—may contribute to his eventually learning that others experience distress just as he does. Simner's finding may thus signify an innate mechanism that contributes to the early learning of empathic distress.

Such an innate mechanism is consistent but not crucial to the present thesis. What is crucial is that conditioning is possible in the early weeks of life (Kessen, Haith, and Salapatek 1970). This together with the inevitable distress experiences in infancy makes it highly likely that humans are capable of experiencing empathic distress long before acquiring a cognitive sense of the other, the early manifestations of which, as already noted, appear at about 1 year or later. For much of the first year at least, then, it follows that distress cues from others probably elicit a global empathic distress response in the infant—presumably a fusion of unpleasant feelings and stimuli from his own body, the dimly perceived "other," and the situation. The infant cannot yet differentiate himself from the other, and there is evidence that he also has difficulty differentiating the other from the other's situation (Burns and Cavey 1957; Deutsch 1974). Consequently, he must often be unclear as to who is experiencing any distress that he witnesses, and he may at times be expected to behave as though what happened to the other person was happening to him. That is, the cues associated with another person's distress evoke an upset state in him, and he may then seek comfort for himself. Consider a colleague's 11-month-old daughter who, on seeing another child fall and cry, first stared at the victim, appearing as though she were about to cry herself, and then put her thumb in her mouth and buried her head in her mother's lap—her typical response when she has hurt herself and seeks comfort.

This appears to be a primitive, involuntary response, that is, a response based mainly on the "pull" of surface cues and minimally on higher cognitive processes, attention, and effort. If the child acts, his motive may in a sense be egoistic: to eliminate discomfort in the "self." It is not entirely egoistic, however, since the "self" at this stage is not in opposition to the other but rather a fusion (self/other/situation) that includes the other. Perhaps the more fundamental reason for viewing this empathic distress as basic in the development of altruistic motivation despite its egoistic components is that it shows that we may involuntarily and forcefully experience emotional states pertinent to another person's situation rather than to our own—that we are built in such a way that our own feelings of distress will often be contingent not on our own but on someone else's misfortune.

Sympathetic Distress and the Role of Cognition

As noted earlier, the meaning of an emotion is determined by appropriate cognitions. Schachter and Singer's (1962) formulation seems pertinent:

> One labels, interprets, and identifies this stirred-up state in terms of the characteristics of the situation and one's apperceptive mass. . . . The cognition, in a sense, exerts a steering function [and] determines whether the state of arousal will be labeled as "anger," "joy," "fear" or whatever. (p. 380)

In like fashion, one's cognitive sense of the other may be presumed to determine the meaning of his affective response to cues about the other's inner states. A major change may therefore be expected when the child begins to discriminate between the stimuli from his own body and those from without, acquiring a sense of the other as separate from himself. When confronted with someone in pain, he now knows that it is the other and not he who is actually in distress. Consequently, it seems reasonable to assume that the earlier empathic distress, a parallel affective response, is gradually transformed into a more reciprocal, sympathetic concern for the victim, here called sympathetic distress. This transformation is hypothesized to occur in three stages, which correspond to the three cognitive levels described earlier.

1. It seems reasonable to suppose that along with the gradual emergence of a sense of the other as distinct from the self, the affective portion of the child's global empathic distress—the feeling of distress and desire for its termination—is extended to the separate self and other that

emerge. Early in this process the child may be only vaguely and momentarily aware of the other as distinct from the self; the image of the other, being transitory, may often slip in and out of focus. Consequently, he probably reacts to another's distress as though his dimly perceived self and other were somehow simultaneously, or alternately, in distress. Consider a child known to the writer whose typical response to his own distress, beginning late in the first year, was to suck his thumb with one hand and pull his ear with the other. At 12 months, on seeing a sad look on his father's face, he proceeded to look sad and suck his thumb, while pulling his father's ear. The co-occurrence of distress in the emerging self and other may be an important factor in the transition from the simple empathic distress, discussed above, to the first stage of sympathetic distress which includes an affective response, awareness of the fact that another person is the victim, and desire to terminate his distress.

The child's response at this stage may continue to have a purely em-pathic component, including the desire to terminate his own distress, and perhaps an element of fear that the undesired event may happen to him. The important thing, however, is that the quasi-egoistic concern for his "own" discomfort gives way, at least in part, to the feeling of concern for another. This is a new addition to the child's repertoire which enables him for the first time to behave in what appears to be a truly altruistic manner, that is, to attempt to relieve the distress of another person who is perceptu-ally distinct from the self. The response of a colleague's 20-month-old son is illustrative. When a visiting friend who was about to leave burst into tears, complaining that her parents were not home (they were away for 2 weeks), his immediate reaction was to look sad, but then he offered her his beloved teddy bear to take home. His parents reminded him that he would miss the teddy if he gave it away, but he insisted—possibly because his sympathetic distress was greater than the anticipated unpleasantness of not having the teddy, which would be indicative of the strong motivational potential of sympathetic distress.

Although the child now knows that the other is a separate physical entity and therefore that the other is the victim, he cannot yet distinguish between his own and the other's inner states (thoughts, perceptions, needs); without thinking about it, he automatically assumes that they are identical to his own. Consequently, although he can sense the other's distress, he does not under-stand what caused it nor does he know the other's needs in the situation (except when they happen to coincide with his own as in the preceding example). This lack of understanding is often evidenced in the child's efforts to help, which consist chiefly of giving the other what he himself finds most comforting. Examples are Michael's initial attempt to placate his friend Paul; the action of another child, 13 months old, who brought his own mother to comfort a crying friend even though the friend's mother was equally avail-able; and still another child who offered his beloved doll to comfort an adult who looked sad.

Despite the limitation of this initial level of sympathetic distress, it is a significant advance; for the first time the child experiences a feeling of concern for the other as distinct from the self, although his actual attempts to help may be misguided due to limited understanding of the nature of the distress and the type of action needed to relieve it.

2. At about 2 years, according to our earlier role-taking discussion, the child has begun to acquire a sense of others not only as physical entities but also as sources of feelings and thoughts in their own right, that is, as persons who have inner states that at times differ from his own, as well as perspectives based on their own needs and interpretations of events. He does not know what their perspectives are, however, and is in general no longer certain that the real world and his perception of it are the same thing.

Perhaps at this point a clarification is in order. Although the role-taking, research stresses development of the capacity to grasp another's perspective when it differs from one's own, this is only to expose the nature of the child's progress away from egocentrism. In real life, the child usually finds the perspective of others is similar to his own, since all children have the same basic nervous system as well as many experiences in common during the long period of socialization. This was true in the earlier example: Although Michael discovered he and Paul had different specific preferences in the situation, his assumption that Paul's basic emotional need was the same as his was confirmed. Thus while moving away from the automatic, egocentric assumption that the other's inner states are identical to his, the child discovers that his feelings resemble the feelings experienced independently by others in similar situations. The other's feelings are independent of his, but not basically different. This must inevitably contribute to a sense of "oneness," which preserves and may even enhance the motivation to alleviate the other's distress which he acquired earlier.

At this second level the child's empathic proclivity continues to direct his attention away from himself and toward others, and he may still have a tendency to attribute his own feelings to the victim. But now, because of the emerging awareness that others have independent inner states, the affect aroused in him by another's distress may be presumed to motivate more active efforts to put himself in the other's place and find the true source of his distress.[11] He is also very likely more aware of the tentative and hypothetical nature of his resulting inferences. Consequently, his motivation to relieve the other's distress is less egocentric and based to a greater degree on veridical assessment of the other's needs, trial and error, and response to corrective feedback. With increased role-taking ability, he can also detect more subtle cues of distress (e.g., those reflecting such inferred inner states as disappointment and longing). These too may then stimulate his concern and motivate efforts to discern the source of the other's discomfort.

3. Despite the obvious progress, the child's response is still confined to the other's immediate distress. This limitation is overcome at the third cognitive level, around 6 to 9 years according to our previous discussion, at which stage the child has an emerging conception of himself and others as continuous persons each with his own history and identity. By early adolescence he is fully aware not only that others feel pleasure and pain in situations but also that these feelings occur in the context of their larger pattern of life experiences. Consequently, although he may continue to react to their situational distress, his concern is intensified when he knows this reflects a chronic condition. That is, being aware that others have inner states and a separate existence beyond the situation enables him to respond not only to their transitory, situation-specific distress but also to what he

imagines to be their general condition. Although the situational may often reflect the general, this is not always true and there at times may be a discrepancy between the two. On these occasions the observer will ordinarily be expected to respond in terms of the general since it is the more inclusive, hence compelling index of the victim's welfare.

This third level, then, consists of the synthesis of empathic distress and a mental representation of the other's general plight—his typical day-to-day level of distress or deprivation, the opportunities available or denied to him, his future prospects, and the like. If this representation falls short of what the observer conceives to be a minimally acceptable standard of well-being (and if the observer's own life circumstances place him substantially above this standard), a sympathetic distress response may be expected, regardless of the other's apparent momentary state.

To summarize, the individual who progresses through these three stages becomes capable of a high level of sympathetic distress. He can process various types of information—that gained through his own empathic reaction, immediate situational cues, and general knowledge about the other's life. He can act out in his mind the emotions and experiences suggested by this information and introspect on all of this. He may thus gain an understanding of the circumstances, feelings, and wishes of the other and have feelings of concern and the wish to help while maintaining the sense that this is a separate person from himself.

With further cognitive development the person may also be able to comprehend the plight not only of an individual but also of an entire group or class of people—such as the economically impoverished, politically oppressed, socially outcast, victims of war, or mentally retarded. Because of his different background, his own specific distress experiences may differ from theirs. All distress experiences may be presumed to have a common affective core, however, and this together with the individual's cognitive capabilities at this age provides the requisites for a generalized empathic distress. (Possible exceptions are people rendered incapable of empathy by their socialization or people whose status in life has permitted only the most superficial contact with less fortunate people; consider as an example Marie Antoinette's apocryphal "Let them eat cake" response to the people who were clamoring for bread.) The synthesis of empathic distress with the perceived plight of an unfortunate group may result in what would seem to be the developmentally most advanced form of sympathetic distress.

Sympathetic Distress as Egoistic or Altruistic Motive

Since sympathetic distress has an empathic component, the act of helping another person should contribute to reduction of the actor's distress as well as that of the other. The question may be asked, does this mean that sympathetic distress is really an egoistic motive? The writer suggests that all motives may prompt action that is potentially gratifying to the actor but this must not obscure certain fundamental differences among them. Sympathetic distress differs from the usual egoistic motives (e.g., sensual pleasure, material gain, social approval, economic success) in three significant ways: It is aroused by distress in another person rather than oneself; a major goal of the ensuing behavior is to help the other, not just oneself; and, the potential for gratification in the observer is contingent on his acting to reduce the other's distress. In brief, the arousal condition, aim of the ensuing action, and basis of gratification in the actor are all dependent on someone else's welfare. It therefore seems appropriate to designate sympathetic distress as an altruistic motive and distinguish it from more directly self-serving, egoistic motives.

Summary of Evidence for the Theory

The attempt will now be made to show that the theoretical model advanced here may provide an integrative framework for ordering existing knowledge on helping and related behavior, as well as generating hypotheses for further research.

Several predications about sympathetic distress and its relation to helping behavior follow from the theory: (a) People should generally respond to another's distress with an affective response as well as a tendency to help. (b) The intensity of the affect and the speed of the helping response should increase with the salience of the pain cues. (c) The affect should tend to subside more quickly when the observer engages in helping behavior than when he does not. First, there is abundant evidence, noted earlier, that people of all ages tend to help. More importantly, affect seems to accompany the helping behavior. That is, witnessing another person in physical pain or failing in a task typically results in an affective reaction as measured physiologically and is usually followed by an overt attempt to help (Berger 1962; Craig and Weinstein 1965; Geer and Jarmecky 1973; Lazarus, Speisman, Mordkoff, and Davison 1962; Murphy 1937; Stotland 1969; Tannenbaum and Gaer 1965; Tomes 1964; Weiss et al. 1973).[12] Second, the intensity of the affect and the speed of the overt response have been found to increase as the number and intensity of distress cues from the victim increase (Geer and Jarmecky 1973; Weiss et al. 1973). And third, there is evidence that the affect continues at a high level of intensity in adult subjects who do not go to the aid of the victim but declines for those who do (Latané and Darley 1970). A similar finding was obtained in Murphy's (1937) classic nursery school study: When children overtly helped others, their affective response diminished; when they did not help, the affect was prolonged.

The theory would also lead to the expectation that young children, even before acquiring the necessary cognitive skills, would nevertheless experience empathic or sympathetic distress, although at times they may do nothing or engage in inappropriate action. Evidence for this can be found in the nursery school observations reported by Bridges (1931) and Murphy (1937) in which the younger children usually reacted to another's distress with a worried, anxious look but did nothing, whereas the older children typically engaged in an overt helpful act. Further evidence is provided by the several anecdotes mentioned earlier in this article describing an affective response followed by an overt act that was clearly designed to help but inappropriate. (Reinforcement and imitation theories might have difficulty explaining these findings, since the child's socialization agents are not often likely to reward or to provide models of inaction or inappropriate action.)

Other findings and their possible relevance to the theory follow: (a) The evidence that helping correlates positively with role-taking ability (Rubin and Schneider 1973) and is increased by role-taking training (Clore and Jeffrey 1972; Staub 1971b) is clearly in keeping with the theory. (b) The evidence, cited earlier, that people are more apt to help another when their emotional needs are satisfied also fits the theory, since sympathetic distress requires the observer to pay attention to the needs of others, which is more apt to happen if he is not preoccupied with his own emotional needs. (c) Since the theory implies a general human readiness to help others in distress, it would lead to the general expectation that little effort is ordinarily required to instigate helping behavior in children. Thus the evidence that helping behavior in children may result from exposure to altruistic models—both experimentally (see review by Bryan and London 1970) and in the home (Rosenhan 1969; Hoffman 1970, 1975) can be readily encompassed by the theory, although it may not be a logical deduction from it. (d) Finally, the assumed synthesis between the affect aroused and the observer's cognitive sense of the other is, as discussed earlier, in agreement with the recent research both on emotions and on the structure of the brain.

The theory thus seems to provide a broad integrative framework that encompasses much of what is known about people's responses to others in distress. A true assessment of the model, however, awaits the test of predictions derived specifically from it. Here are some possible examples. The presumed interaction between empathic distress and cognition suggests that training in role taking, or exposure to information regarding the life condition of others, should be especially effective in producing helping behavior when it directs the subject's attention to feelings and when the subjects are empathic to begin with (although there may be a ceiling effect); and similarly, the arousal of empathic distress should result in more helping in children who are cognitively able to take the other's role than in those who are not. The theory would also predict that certain socialization experiences would enhance the child's naturally developing motivation to help others in distress. For example, altruism should be more prevalent in children whose empathic proclivities have been strengthened by being allowed the normal run of distress experiences, rather than being shielded from them, since this would help provide a broad base for empathic and sympathetic distress in the early years. (We refer here to mild distress experiences that the child can readily resolve on his own or with parental help when necessary; frequent, severe distress may lead to a building up of frustration and subsequent egoistic self-preoccupation that could interfere with the child's sensitivity and openness to the needs of others.) It would also follow from the theory that when a discrepancy exists between the various cues indicating another person's distress (e.g., when the cues indicating the victim's immediate distress are at odds with the available information regarding his general life condition), the observer will ordinarily react in terms of the more inconclusive distress index.

Concluding Remarks

Although the focus of this article has been on sympathetic distress as a motive, the evidence cited suggests that it is typically accompanied by helping behavior. The relation between the arousal of the motive and relevant behavior is not guaranteed, however, any more than it is for other motives. In addition to the strength and developmental level of the motive, which have been stressed here, other factors presumably have an effect. Evidence was cited earlier, for example, which suggests that level of intensity of the distress cues and extent of the observer's well-being may be important considerations. Other factors found to influence the observer's response are the extent to which the observer has the cognitive and coping skills required for appropriate action (Bridges 1931; Murphy 1937; Latané and Darley 1970) and the extent to which the situation points up his individual responsibility to act rather than indicating, for example, that the responsibility is diffused (Geer and Jarmecky 1973; Latané and Darley 1970; Schwartz 1970; Tilker 1970).

In individualistic societies, the motive to help will also often be overridden by more powerful egoistic motives, as evidenced by the negative relation obtained between helping others and competitiveness (Rutherford and Mussen 1968). As noted by Hoffman (1970) and Staub (1970), American middle-class children are often socialized both to help others and to respect authority and follow the rules, but in some situations one cannot do both. Perhaps the best known instance of the way authority attitudes may serve as a deterrent to prosocial behavior is Milgram's (1963) finding that adult males will administer high levels of electric shock on instruction from the experimenter, despite strong feelings of compassion for the victim—a finding that must make us less sanguine about the altruistic potentialities of at least American men. It should be noted, however, that in a partial replication of Milgram's experiment, Tilker (1970) found that when the subject was placed in the role of observer he not only showed an increasing sympathetic distress response as the shock levels were increased but often intervened to stop the experiment, despite the instructions to the contrary and the continuing opposition from the person administering the shock.

The evidence that sympathetic distress may continue when the observer does not act has been cited. We would also expect the observer at times to engage in some sort of defense or cognitive restructuring of the situation so as to justify inaction (e.g., by derogating the victim or seeing him as deserving his fate). There is some evidence that this may happen, at least when it is physically impossible for the observer to help (Chaikin and Darley 1973; Lincoln and Levinger 1972; Stokols and Schopler 1973). Whether this restructuring reduces the observer's distress is not known.

Pending further research, the following relationship between altruistic motives and action seems in keeping with current knowledge: (a) Distress cues from another person trigger the sympathetic distress response in the observer; (b) his initial tendency is to act; (c) if he does not act, he will typically continue to experience sympathetic distress or cognitively restructure the situation to justify inaction.

This article was prepared in conjunction with Grant HD-02258 from the National Institute of Child Health and Human Development. It is an expansion of a paper presented initially at the NICHHD workshop. "The Development of Motivation in Childhood," in Elkridge, Maryland, in 1972.

NOTES

1. A chimpanzee in the wild who discovers a new food source will, before having his own fill, typically call out to the others who immediately join him (Lawick-Goodall, 1968). As for chimpanzee behavior in captivity, Nissen (Nissen and Crawford, 1936) describes a female who, upon seeing Nissen taunt and strike her cagemate, attempted to pull the cagemate to safety; a week later, when Nissen next appeared and the cagemate approached him, she tried strenuously and continuously to pull the cagemate back until Nissen left. Finally, porpoises are known to aid wounded adults and newborn infants whose mothers are unavailable—and also drowning humans—by raising them to the surface for needed air (Kellogg, 1961; McBride, 1940; McBride and Hebb, 1948).
2. It should perhaps be noted that evolutionists do not regard maternal sacrifice or any form of action in the service of a kin's well-being as altruistic, since such action benefits one's own genetic line.
3. Aronfreed, J., and Paskal, V. *Altruism, empathy, and the conditioning of positive affect.* Unpublished manuscript, University of Pennsylvania, 1965.
4. Hoffman, M. L., and Saltzstein, H. D. Parent practices and the development of children's moral orientations. In W. E. Martin (Chair), *Parent behavior and children's personality development: Current project research.* Symposium presented at the meeting of the American Psychological Association, Chicago, September 1960.
5. Escalona, S., Corman, H., Galenson, E., Schecter, D., Schecter, E., Golden, M., Leoi, A., and Barax, E. *Albert Einstein scales of sensori-motor development.* Unpublished manuscript, Department of Psychiatry, Albert Einstein School of Medicine, 1967.
6. Uzgiris, I., and Hunt, J. McV. *Ordinal scales of infant development.* Paper presented at the 18th International Congress of Psychology, Moscow, August 1966.
7. Saint-Pierre, J. *Etude des différences entre la récherché active de la personne humaine et celle de l'object inanimé.* Unpublished master's thesis, University of Montreal, 1962.
8. Research like Borke's (1971, 1973), which seems to show that young children can infer emotional states of others, is plagued by the problem that the subjects may simply be attributing their own emotional reactions to others rather than demonstrating awareness of their independent inner states.
9. The fact that role-taking competence may occur so early in life suggests an interesting analogy with Chomsky's (1965) "language acquisition device." Perhaps children have the capacity to take others' perspectives at an earlier age than usually assumed, and all it takes to be manifested in performance is the appropriate social context, along with the necessary feedback. If so, the years of social interaction often thought to be necessary for role-taking competence may instead serve the function of providing exercise for a preexisting capacity.
10. Simner, M.: Personal communication, 1973.
11. Although this discussion stresses the effect of cognitive role taking, it is also intended to illustrate the importance of empathic distress. That is, in the absence of empathic distress role taking may serve other more egoistic needs.
12. A major exception is Lerner's (Note *13*) finding that adults lowered their esteem of perceived victims. This was, however, apparently due to an empathy-inhibiting set created by the experimental instructions (Aderman and Berkowitz, 1970; Aderman, Brehm, and Katz, 1974; Stotland, 1969).
13. Lerner, M. J. *The effect of a negative outcome on cognitions of responsibility and attraction.* Unpublished manuscript, University of Kentucky, 1968.

REFERENCES

ADERMAN, D., AND BERKOWITZ, L. Obervational set, empathy, and helping. *Journal of Personality and Social Psychology,* 1970, *14,* 141–168.
ADERMAN, D., BREHM, S. S., AND KATZ, L. B. Empathic observation of an innocent victim: The just world revisited. *Journal of Personality and Social Psychology,* 1974, *29,* 342–347.
ALEXANDER, R. D. The search for an evolutionary philosophy of man. *Proceedings of the Royal Society of Melbourne,* 1971, *84,* 99–120.
BELL, S. M. The development of the concept of the object as related to infant-mother attachment. *Child Development,* 1970, *41,* 291–311.
BERGER, S. M. Conditioning through vicarious instigation. *Psychological Review,* 1962, *69,* 450–466.

BERKOWITZ, L., AND CONNOR, W. H. Success, failure and social responsibility. *Journal of Personality and Social Psychology*, 1966, 4, 664–669.

BORKE, H. Interpersonal perception of young children: Ego-centrism or empathy? *Developmental Psychology*, 1971, 5, 263–269.

BORKE, H. Chandler and Greenspan's "Ersatz ego-centrism": A rejoinder. *Developmental Psychology*, 1972, 7, 107–109.

BORKE, H. The development of empathy in Chinese and American children between three and six years of age. *Developmental Psychology*, 1973, 9, 102–108.

BRIDGES, K. M. B. *The social and emotional development of the preschool child.* London: Kegan Paul, 1931.

BRYAN, J. H., AND LONDON, P. Altruistic behavior by children. *Psychological Bulletin*, 1970, 73, 200–211.

BURNS, N., AND CAVEY, L. Age differences in empathic ability among children. *Canadian Journal of Psychology*, 1957, 11, 227–230.

CAMPBELL, D. T. Ethnocentric and other altruistic motives. In D. Levine (Ed.), *Nebraska Symposium on Motivation* (Vol. 13). Lincoln: University of Nebraska Press, 1965.

CAMPBELL, D. T. On the genetics of altruism and the counter-hedonic components in human culture. *The Journal of Social Issues*, 1972, 28, 21–38.

CHAIKIN, A. L., AND DARLEY, J. M. Victim or perpetrator: Defensive attribution of responsibility and the need for order and justice. *Journal of Personality and Social Psychology*, 1973, 25, 268–275.

CHANDLER, M. J., AND GREENSPAN, S. Ersatz egocentrism: A reply to H. Borke. *Developmental Psychology*, 1972, 7, 104–106.

CHOMSKY, N. A. *Aspects of the theory of syntax.* Cambridge: M.I.T. Press, 1965.

CLARK, R. D., AND WORD, L. E. Why don't bystanders help? Because of ambiguity? *Journal of Personality and Social Psychology*, 1972, 24, 392–400.

CLORE, G. L., AND JEFFERY, K. M. Emotional role playing, attitude change, and attraction toward a disabled person. *Journal of Personality and Social Psychology*, 1972, 23, 105–111.

COFER, C., AND APPLEY, M. *Motivation: Theory and research.* New York: Wiley, 1964.

CRAIG, K. D., AND WEINSTEIN, M. S. Conditioning vicarious affective arousal. *Psychological Reports*, 1965, 17, 955–963.

DARLEY, J. M., AND BATSON, C. D. From Jerusalem to Jericho: A study of situational and dispositional variables in helping behavior. *Journal of Personality and Social Psychology*, 1973, 27, 100–108.

DÉCARIE, T. G. *Intelligence and affectivity in early childhood.* New York: International Universities Press, 1965.

DEUTSCH, F. Female preschoolers' perceptions of affective responses and interpersonal behavior in videotaped episodes. *Developmental Psychology*, 1974, 10, 733–740.

DYMOND, R. A scale for the measurement of empathic ability. *Journal of Consulting Psychology*, 1949, 13, 127–133.

EASTERBROOK, J. A. The effect of emotion on cue utilization and the organization of behavior. *Psychological Review*, 1959, 66, 183–201.

ERIKSON, E. H. *Childhood and society.* New York: Norton, 1950.

FESHBACH, N. D., AND ROE, K. Empathy in six and seven year olds. *Child Development*, 1968, 39, 133–145.

FISHBEIN, H. D., LEWIS, S., AND KEIFFER, K. Children's understanding of spatial relations. *Developmental Psychology*, 1972, 7, 21–33.

FLAVELL, J. H. *The development of role-taking and communication skills in children.* New York: Wiley, 1968.

FREUD, A. *Ego and the mechanisms of defense.* London: Hogarth Press, 1937.

GEER, J. H., AND JARMECKY, L. The effect of being responsible for reducing another's pain on subject's response and arousal. *Journal of Personality and Social Psychology*, 1973, 26, 232–237.

GUARDO, C. J., AND BOHAN, J. B. Development of a sense of self-identity in children. *Child Development*, 1971, 42, 1909–1921.

HEBB, D. O. Comment on altruism: The comparative evidence. *Psychological Bulletin*, 1971, 76, 409–410.

HOFFMAN, M. L. Parent discipline and the child's consideration for others. *Child Development*, 1963, 34, 573–588.

HOFFMAN, M. L. Conscience, personality, and socialization techniques. *Human Development*, 1970, 13, 90–126.

HOFFMAN, M. L. Altruistic behavior and the parent-child relationship. *Journal of Personality and Social Psychology*, 1975, 31, 937–943.

HOFFMAN, M. L., AND SALTZSTEIN, H. D. Parent discipline and the child's moral development. *Journal of Personality and Social Psychology*, 1967, 5, 45–57.

HUME, D. *An inquiry concerning the principles of morals.* New York: Liberal Arts Press, 1957. (Originally published, 1751.)

HUNT, J. MCV., COLE, M., AND REIS, H. Situational cues distinguishing anger, joy, and sorrow. *American Journal of Psychology,* 1958, *71,* 136–151.

ISAACS, S. S. *Social development in young children.* London: Routledge, 1933.

ISEN, A. M. Success, failure, and reaction to others: The warm glow of success. *Journal of Personality and Social Psychology,* 1970, *15,* 294–301.

ISEN, A. M., HORN, N., AND ROSENHAN, D. L. Effects of success and failure on children's generosity. *Journal of Personality and Social Psychology,* 1973, *27,* 239–247.

KELLOGG, W. N. *Porpoises and sonar.* Chicago: University of Chicago Press, 1961.

KESSEN, W., HAITH, M. M., AND SALAPAREK, P. H. Infancy. In P. Mussen (Ed.), *Carmichael's manual of child psychology.* New York: Wiley, 1970.

KOHLBERG, L. A cognitive-developmental analysis of children's sex-role concepts and attitudes. In E. Maccoby (Ed.), *The development of sex differences.* Stanford, Calif.: Stanford University Press, 1966.

KREBS, D. L. Altruism: An examination of the concept and a review of the literature. *Psychological Bulletin,* 1970, *73,* 258–303.

KREBS, D. L. Infrahuman altruism. *Psychological Bulletin,* 1971, *76,* 411–414.

LATANÉ, B., AND DARLEY, J. Bystander intervention in emergencies. In J. Macaulay and L. Berkowitz (Eds.), *Altruism and helping behavior.* New York: Academic Press, 1970.

LAWICK-GOODALL, J. V. The behavior of free-living chimpanzees in the Gombe Stream Reserve. *Animal Behavior Monographs,* 1968, *1,* 161–311.

LAZARUS, R. S., SPEISMAN, J. C., MORDKOFF, A. M., AND DAVISON, L. A. A laboratory study of psychological stress produced by a motion picture film. *Psychological Monographs,* 1962, *76* (34, Whole No. 553).

LINCOLN, H., AND LEVINGER, G. Observer's evaluations of the victim and the attacker in an aggressive incident. *Journal of Personality and Social Psychology,* 1972, *22,* 202–210.

LONDON, P. The rescuers: Motivational hypotheses about Christians who saved Jews from the Nazis. In J. Macaulay and L. Berkowitz (Eds.), *Altruism and helping behavior.* New York: Academic Press, 1970.

LOVELL, K. A follow-up of some aspects of the work of Piaget and Inhelder on the child's conception of space. *British Journal of Educational Psychology,* 1959, *29,* 107–117.

MACLEAN, P. D. The limbic system with respect to self-preservation and the preservation of the species. *Journal of Nervous Mental Disease,* 1958, *127,* 1–11.

MACLEAN, P. D. New findings relevant to the evolution of psychosexual functions of the brain. *Journal of Nervous Mental Disease,* 1962, *135,* 289–301.

MACLEAN, P. D. The brain in relation to empathy and medical education. *Journal of Nervous Mental Disease,* 1967, *144,* 374–382.

MACLEAN, P. D. *A triune concept of the brain and behavior.* Toronto, Canada: University of Toronto Press, 1973.

MCBRIDE, A. F. Meet Mister Porpoise. *National History Magazine,* 1940, *45,* 16–29.

MCBRIDE, A. F., AND HEBB, D. O. Behavior of the captive bottle-nose dolphin, *tursiops truncatus. Journal of Comparative Physiological Psychology,* 1948, *41,* 111–123.

MASANGKAY, Z., MCCLUSKEY, K., MCINTYRE, C.; SIMS-KNIGHT, J., VAUGHN, B., AND FLAVELL, J. The early development of inferences about the visual percepts of others. *Child Development,* 1974, *45,* 357–366.

MILGRAM, S. A behavioral study of obedience. *Journal of Abnormal and Social Psychology,* 1963, *67,* 371–378.

MOORE, B. S., UNDERWOOD, B., AND ROSENHAN, D. L. Affect and altruism. *Developmental Psychology,* 1973, *8,* 99–104.

MURPHY, L. B. *Social behavior and child personality.* New York: Columbia University Press, 1937.

MUSSEN, P., HARRIS, S., RUTHERFORD, E., AND KEASEY, C. B. Honesty and altruism among preadolescents. *Developmental Psychology,* 1970, *3,* 169–194.

NISSEN, H. W., AND CRAWFORD, M. P. A preliminary study of food-sharing behavior in young chimpanzees. *Journal of Comparative Psychology,* 1936, *22,* 383–419.

PIAGET, J. *The moral judgment of the child.* New York: Harcourt, Brace, and World, 1932.

PIAGET, J. *The construction of reality in the child.* New York: Basic Books, 1954.

PIAGET, J., AND INHELDER, B. *The child's conception of space.* New York: Norton, 1967. (Originally published, 1948.)

PILIAVIN, I. M., RODIN, J., AND PILIAVIN, J. A. Good samaritanism: An underground phenomenon. *Journal of Personality and Social Psychology,* 1969, *13,* 289–299.

PILIAVIN, J. A., AND PILIAVIN, I. The effect of blood on reactions to a victim. *Journal of Personality and Social Psychology*, 1972, 23, 353–361.

PROSHANSKY, H. M. The development of intergroup attitudes. In L. W. Hoffman and M. L. Hoffman (Eds.). *Review of Child Development Research* (Vol. 2). New York: Russell Sage Foundation, 1966.

ROSENHAN, D. Some origins of concern for others. In P. H. Mussen, J. Langer, and M. Covington (Eds.). *Trends and issues in developmental psychology.* New York: Holt, Rinehart and Winston, 1969.

RUBIN, K. H., AND SCHNEIDER, F. W. The relationship between moral judgment, egocentrism, and altruistic behavior. *Child Development*, 1973, 44, 661–665.

RUCKMICK, C. A. The psychology of fear and emotion. New York: McGraw-Hill, 1936.

RUTHERFORD, E., AND MUSSEN, P. Generosity in nursery school boys. *Child Development*, 1968, 39, 755–765.

SCHACHTER, S., AND SINGER, J. E. Cognitive, social and physiological determinants of emotional state. *Psychological Review*, 1962, 69, 379–399.

SCHWARTZ, S. Moral decision making and behavior. In J. Macaulay and L. Berkowitz (Eds.), *Altruism and helping behavior.* New York: Academic Press, 1970.

SELMAN, R. L. Taking another's perspective: Role-taking development in early childhood. *Child Development*, 1971, 42, 1721–1734.

SEVERY, L. J., AND DAVIS, K. E. Helping behavior among normal and retarded children. *Child Development*, 1971, 42, 1017–1031.

SHATZ, M., AND GELMAN, R. The development of communication skills: Modifications in the speech of young children as a function of listener. *Monographs of the Society for Research in Child Development*, 1973, 38 (5, Serial No. 152).

SIMNER, M. L. Newborn's response to the cry of another infant. *Developmental Psychology*, 1971, 5, 136–150.

SMITH, A. *Moral and political philosophy.* New York: Hafner, 1948. (Originally published, 1759.)

STAUB, E. A child in distress: The influence of age and number of witnesses on children's attempts to help. *Journal of Personality and Social Psychology*, 1970, 14, 130–140.

STAUB, E. Helping a person in distress: The influence of implicit and explicit "rules" of conduct on children and adults. *Journal of Personality and Social Psychology*, 1971, 17, 137–144. (a)

STAUB, E. The use of role-playing and induction in children's learning of helping and sharing behavior. *Child Development*, 1971, 42, 805–816. (b)

STAUB, E. Helping a distressed person. In L. Berkowitz (Ed.), *Advances in experimental social psychology* (Vol. 7). New York: Academic Press, 1974.

STAUB, E., AND SHERK, L. Need for approval, children's sharing behavior, and reciprocity in sharing. *Child Development*, 1970, 41, 243–253.

STERN, W. *Psychology of early childhood up to the sixth year of age.* New York: Holt, 1924.

STOKOLS, D., AND SCHOPLER, J. Reactions to victim under conditions of situational detachment: The effects of responsibility, severity, and expected future interaction. *Journal of Personality and Social Psychology*, 1973, 25, 199–209.

STOTLAND, E. Exploratory investigations of empathy. In L. Berkowitz (Ed.), *Advances in experimental social psychology* (Vol. 4). New York: Academic Press, 1969.

TANNENBAUM, P. H., AND GAER, E. P. Mood changes as a function of stress of protagonist and degree of identification in a film-viewing situation. *Journal of Personality and Social Psychology*, 1965, 2, 612–616.

TILKER, H. A. Socially responsible behavior as a function of observer responsibility and victim feedback. *Journal of Personality and Social Psychology*, 1970, 14, 95–100.

TINBERGEN, N. On war and peace in animals and man: An ethologist's approach to the biology of aggression. *Science*, 1968, 160, 1411–1418.

TOMES, H. The adaption, acquisition, and extinction of empathically mediated emotional responses. *Dissertation Abstracts*, 1964, 24, 3442–3443.

TRIVERS, R. L. The evolution of reciprocal altruism. *Quarterly Review of Biology*, 1971, 46, 35–57.

WEISS, R. F., BOYER, J. L., LOMBARDO, J. P., AND STICH, M. H. Altruistic drive and altruistic reinforcement. *Journal of Personality and Social Psychology*, 1973, 25, 390–400.

WILLIAMS, G. C. *Adaptation and natural selection.* Princeton, N.J.: Princeton University Press, 1966.

WYNNE-EDWARDS, V. C. *Animal dispersion in relation to social behavior.* Edinburgh, Scotland: Oliver and Boyd, 1962.

YARROW, M. R., SCOTT, P. M., AND WAXLER, C. Z. Learning concern for others. *Developmental Psychology*, 1973, 8, 240–260.

Part VI

Individuality and Self in Childhood

As the infancy studies in this collection indicate, a number of individual differences between children emerge soon after birth. Many of these differences are sharpened, modified, or transformed by children's interactions with their particular social environments during the infant and childhood years. Ultimately, even fundamental characteristics like temperament can make a contribution to the child's personality only under the influence of social feedback and interpretation. There is no such thing as a native behavioral disposition unaffected by social contact. Because all children are interacting continually with the social world, there is always an interplay between the child's personality characteristics and the child's social experience.

After infancy, this interplay between personality and social experience extends to many new aspects of a child's behavior. Individual differences between children multiply and become increasingly stabilized, leading to distinct patterns in children's social-interactional tendencies. The readings that follow show how such dimensions of personality as ego-control, ego-resiliency, self-conception, and sexual identity develop in the context of social feedback and come to exert profound influences on children's social lives. Such influences result from the workings of these personality dimensions themselves as well as from the reactions of others in the social world to the child's particular personal characteristics.

Jeanne and Jack Block's article describes the most comprehensive longitudinal study of children's personality development yet attempted in the field of psychology. The Blocks have administered a massive battery of psychological tests and experimental procedures to over one hundred children as these children turned three, four, five, seven, and eleven years of age. In the reading selected here, the Blocks report findings on their subjects' personality growth up to age seven. These findings demonstrate that early individual differences in children's personal dispositions can have longstanding consequences for their social and personal development years later.

The focal constructs in the Blocks' ambitious study are ego-control and ego-resiliency. Ego-control pertains to the child's "expression or containment of impulses, feelings, and desires." A child who overcontrols is inhibited, emotionally withdrawn, and stressful in ambiguous situations. An undercontroller, in contrast, is distractible, highly expressive, and has difficulty delaying gratification. Ego-resiliency pertains to how well one can alter one's level of ego-control in changing life situations. This is an index of resourcefulness. When necessary, a child high in ego-resiliency can be planful and organized; but should spontaneity or originality be called for, the ego-resilient child rises to the occasion by giving up some ego-control and adopting a more impulsive mode.

The Blocks document several developmental continuities related to ego-control and ego-resiliency. Undercontrollers at age three are in later years more "energetic, curious, restless, expressive of impulse . . . [and] less constricted and less relaxed" than more ego-controlled children. Early ego-undercontrol was also associated with later negative social behavior, like teasing, manipulativeness, and aggression. Ego-overcontrol at age three predicted shyness in later years. As for ego-resiliency, children high on this dimension at age three were later "able to recoup after stress, verbally fluent, less anxious, less brittle, less intolerant of ambiguity, and less likely to externalize or become rigidly repetitive or to withdraw under stress." Early ego-resiliency was associated with later positive social behavior like empathy, social responsiveness, and protectiveness. A combination of high ego-control and high ego-resiliency was a particularly adaptive pattern, leading to social ease and self-confidence. In contrast, high ego-control combined with low ego-resiliency proved to be socially and personally maladaptive, leading to anxiety, immobilization, and a lack of confidence in the world by age seven.

The Blocks believe that early individual differences in ego-control and ego-resiliency have roots in the interaction between children's temperamental dispositions and their family environments. Overcontrol is fostered by families that emphasize structure and order, whereas undercontrol is fostered by a conflictual and undemanding family atmosphere. Ego-resilience is fostered by family communication around philosophical and moral issues, and thrives in a home where parents are loving, competent, and patient.

From their awareness of their own personal dispositions and abilities, children construct a conception of self. This conception has many components, both cognitive and affective. Cognitively, a conception of self serves to establish the intellectual basis for a coherent identity: it combines the child's self-awareness with the feedback of others into a sense of what is unique about the child's personal characteristics. Affectively, the self-conception provides the basis for self-evaluation, evoking a sense of pride or shame in one's way of being.

Diane Ruble and her colleagues discuss how social comparison information is used by children in middle childhood to understand and evaluate their own abilities and limitations. Their studies show that, prior to ages seven or eight, children do not normally base their self-conceptions on comparisons between self and other. Rather, they base their self-evaluations on "absolute" standards, like whether or not they can perform an act or complete a task. A major developmental transformation occurs when children begin to draw conclusions about their own performances and abilities in light of *how well* they perform relative to others. At this point, peers become a reference point for self-evaluation, since peers provide information about the relative quality of one's performance as compared with that of others the same age. This, the authors maintain, is an important step in the "self-socialization" process, particularly with regard to a realistic construction of one's sense of self. The research of Ruble and her colleagues suggests that in middle childhood peer interaction and feedback heavily influence children's conceptions of their own individual abilities.

Gender and sex role are sources of individual differences with pervasive social-relational significance all through life. In psychological literature, "gender" usually refers to one's biological endowment, male or female; "sex role" refers to the social and psychological implications of gender. Juanita Williams, in her summary of the literature, points to a number of widespread differences between boys' and girls' social behavior. Among the most frequently observed are the tendency of boys to play rougher than girls, and the tendency of boys to choose boy playmates and girls to do the opposite. These two behavioral differences can be seen in children's free play from early through middle childhood.

Some gender-related differences in children's social behavior have been observed in virtually every culture studied by social scientists. Carolyn Pope Edwards and Beatrice Whiting report research findings that show consistent patterns of sex-role behavior across several widely varying cultures. By middle childhood, girls in all cultures proved to be more nurturant than boys, although in some cultures the differences between boys and girls were sharper than in others. The authors believe that the sex differences themselves are due to the greater propensity of girls to play with and care for younger siblings. This begins as young as three, and paves the way for the development of marked nurturance by middle childhood. Further, cultures vary in the extent to which they encourage girls to take responsibility for the young. In a New England community, for example, young girls interact far less with infants than in African and Mexican communities. This, the authors speculate, is the reason that sex differences in nurturance are sharper in some cultures than in others. The authors make the very strong statement that "different cultural groups can magnify, minimize, or perhaps even eliminate any sex differences in nurturance to the extent that they place boys and girls in the settings that promote the development of nurturant behavior." Whether or not cultural influence could eliminate as pervasive a sex difference as nurturance is a matter of speculation, since no culture has yet been created in a way that would give this proposition an adequate test. But Edwards and Whiting's statement is another reminder of the dynamic interpenetration between social forces and the individual's personal development.

18

The Role of Ego-Control and Ego-Resiliency in the Organization of Behavior

Jeanne H. Block and Jack Block

For what now approaches 30 years, we have been thinking about and investigating the implications of two personality parameters we have chosen to call *ego-control* and *ego-resiliency*. We began while graduate students at Stanford, many eras ago. Reasoning from the constructs as we then understood them, we sought to evaluate their behavioral relevance in a wide range of experimental situations and psychological tests—response extinction in a partial reinforcement context, norm establishment while experiencing movement in an autokinetic situation, performance in the Gottschaldt Embedded Figures Test, reactions to authority, divergent thinking, level of aspiration, reactions to stress, psychological fatigue or satiation, perceptual standards of similarity, ethnocentrism—all administered to the same group of college students. Our dissertation results (J. Block 1950; J. H. Block 1951; J. Block and J. H. Block 1951; J. H. Block and J. Block 1952) were encouraging: In diverse areas of psychology—learning, perception, interpersonal behaviors, attitudes, problem solving—the observed individual differences (often considered then to be no more than "nuisance variance") were frequently, reliably, and lawfully related to the personality constructs we had formulated. Especially powerful as a predictor was a composite variable

From Jeanne H. Block and Jack Block, "The Role of Ego-Control and Ego-Resiliency in the Organization of Behavior," in *Development of Cognition, Affect, and Social Relations: The Minnesota Symposia on Child Psychology*, vol. 13, ed. W. Andrew Collins (Hillsdale, N.J.: Lawrence Erlbaum Associates, 1980), pp. 39–101. Reprinted by permission of the author and publisher.

generated by summing the behaviors of an individual over a variety of phenotypically diverse but conceptually related experimental situations (J. Block 1950, Chapter 10).

In the intervening years at Berkeley, although interrupted often by other, pre-empting priorities, our focus on these theoretical constructs and their behavioral compass has continued. Relationships have been demonstrated, for example, between ego-control and the ability to delay gratification (J. H. Block and Martin 1955), to constructiveness manifested by children under conditions of frustration in a replication of the Barker, Dembo, and Lewin (1941) classical experiment (J. H. Block and Martin 1955), to subjective certainty in the face of ambiguity (J. Block and Petersen 1955), to similarity between self- and ideal-self-perceptions (J. Block and Thomas 1955), and to identification and adjustment (J. Block and Turula 1963). Ego-control and ego-resiliency have coordinated with the first two factors of standard psychological inventories (J. Block 1965), to constellations of political-social-personal values in adulthood (J. Block 1971), and to children's interest in and behavior with fire and other hazardous materials (J. H. Block and J. Block 1975; J. H. Block, J. Block, and W. Folkman 1976; Kafry 1978).

Although these studies generated useful data and extended our understandings, we came to recognize that for many of the intra-individual developmental issues with which we were concerned, a proper longitudinal study was required. Accordingly, in 1968 we initiated a longitudinal study of approximately 130 children we have since individually assessed at the ages of 3, 4, 5, 7, and most recently, at 11 years. During each of the years of assessment, every child was administered a battery of from 26 to 43 (averaging 36) widely ranging experimental procedures, requiring 10 or 11 testing sessions at ages 3 and 4, four or five sessions at ages 5 and 7, and nine sessions at age 11. In addition, we have developed extensive assessment data on the parents of these children and on parent-child interaction styles.

In the planning and implementation of our longitudinal design, we have been guided by a number of conceptual principles, theoretical choices, and methodological values. As the study starts to bear some harvest, this Symposium seems like the time and the place to bring together and to bring out the many kinds of considerations that have shaped the enterprise and, consequently, the findings beginning to emerge.

To begin, we talk of the theoretical decisions we elected to make, of how we mean the concepts of ego-control and ego-resiliency, of how we do not mean those concepts, of why we suggest these concepts may have some advantages in terms of incisiveness, power, and esthetics over a variety of related concepts. We then describe some of the measurement strategies employed and how the concepts were operationalized. The heuristic value of ego-control and ego-resiliency as an organizing rubric for the many kinds of data is then evaluated, followed by some results issuing from our study that are germane to the topic of this Symposium—social-emotional development. Finally, after bringing forward brief mention of our future research plans, we close with two suggestions—one regarding strategies of empiricism, the other regarding scope of conceptualization—that we believe can advance understanding of personality development. Our agenda is long and so we begin.

Some Theoretical Perspectives

Two Meanings of Ego in Psychoanalytic Psychology

The constructs of ego-control and ego-resiliency evolved in an attempt to integrate some of the aspects of psychoanalytic theory, especially as systematized by Fenichel (1945), with the theorizing of Lewin regarding the dynamics of motivational states in the individual (Lewin 1935; 1936; 1938; 1951).

Psychoanalytic theory is centrally concerned with impulse, a primitive notion viewed as energizing the organism. But if the individual is to be adaptively tuned to his psychosocial ecology, impulse must be modulated and monitored, i.e., controlled. In Fenichel's (1945) terms, developmentally there must be "acquisition of tension tolerance [p. 42]." Such impulse control develops over time via the maturation and experientially derived construction of various personality structures. These personality structures, many of which have a strong cognitive component, serve to bring the individual, otherwise bent on maximizing the "pleasure principle," reluctantly under the governance of the pre-emptive "reality principle." The interrelated, sequentially organized set of personality structures, programmed to give priority to avoidance of threats to the viability of the individual but, within that overriding constraint, programmed also to gratify the individual, is what psychoanalytic theory means by the term "ego." Examples of specific "ego-functioning" structures (orientations, implemented by behavioral routines) include delay of gratification, inhibition of aggression, caution in unstructured situations, "experimental action" (i.e., internal cognitive manipulation of anticipated, alternatively possible behaviors so as to foresee consequences) whenever feasible, affective constraints oriented to prevent loss of love, and so on. Common, and essential, to the functioning of each of these specific ego functions is the control of impulse. The cognitive strategems and the experienced context may vary; but in each, impulse is modulated and "ego" is served. It is this common denominator of the various specific ego structures—degree of impulse control and modulation—that we mean by *the construct of ego-control.*

These various specific ego structures (mechanisms, routines, frames) are interrelated and are invoked sequentially. The interrelations and sequencing may be effective or ineffective in maintaining the personality system of the individual within the bounds of psychological viability as the individual responds to and acts upon the flux of experience, facing different contextual demands and different contextual opportunities. Psychological viability for the individual entails a tolerable anxiety level, a tolerable mesh with situational impingements, and a tolerable level of impulse expression. The linkages of the ego structures that keep the personality system within tenable bounds or permit the finding again of psychologically tenable adaptational modes is a second broad, characteristic aspect of ego functioning, which we denote as *the construct of ego-resiliency.*

The constructs of ego-control and ego-resiliency represent abstractions, condensations, simplifications that we believe carry the essential qualities and functions of the psychoanalytic core concept of "ego." For all of the richness, insight, and seriousness of psychoanalytic theory regarding the understanding of personality functioning, it has also been imprecise, overly facile with supposed explanations, and seemingly inaccessible scientifically. The concept of ego has especially come under disparagement as being, in psychoanalytic theory, something akin to homonculus ensconced in the pineal body. In formulating the concepts of ego-control and ego-resiliency, our intention was to respect and to encompass the phenomena that the notion of "ego" was invoked to explain (i.e., motivational control and resourceful adaptation as enduring, structural aspects of personality), but with concepts somewhat less grandiose and certainly more explicitly generative. Toward this end, Lewinian theory seemed especially apt.

In Lewin's effort to formally represent the psychological system of the individual, he posited (1) a system of needs that becomes both more differentiated and more hierarchically integrated in the course of development (cf. Werner's orthogenetic law), and (2) a sensori-motor system mediating between the internal need system and the external environment that also becomes both more differentiated and more integrated during development. Now, the very idea of differentiation (i.e., the separation or articulation of regions) within both the motivational and sensori-motor systems requires the conceptualization of boundaries and boundary-systems that can demarcate or delineate these differentiations. In his model, interposed between the need system (where motivations emanate) and the sensori-motor system (where contexts register and behaviors are forged), there was a boundary system logically positioned to have ego functions. And, in his formulation of the properties of boundaries, Lewin postulated two boundary characteristics that excited us because they could be coordinated with the two broad aspects of ego functioning we had separately conceptualized as ego-control and ego-resiliency.

Formalizing the Construct of Ego-Control

The first property of boundaries Lewin posited was *degree of permeability*, referring to the boundary's capacity to contain or to fail to contain psychological needs or tensions or forces. Lewin suggested that permeability could be assessed by the degree of communication obtaining between systems. Boundaries that were relatively permeable would permit neighboring systems to mutually influence each other. Relatively impermeable boundaries would limit the "spillage" from one system to another. Excessively impermeable boundaries would result in isolation or compartmentalization of psychological subsystems and lack of communication across systems.

The deductive or generative implications of the permeability property of boundaries are several and, stated in Lewinian terms, include:

1. Given permeability, there will be greater communication across systems.
2. Given permeability, there will be greater diffusion of tensions originating in one system to other systems.
3. Given permeability, there will be greater communication between internal systems and the external environment resulting in greater susceptibility to environmental demands and distractions.
4. Given permeability, there will be more direct, immediate, and untransformed manifestations of internal need states in behavior.

It seemed to us that given the behavioral implications of differences in the degree of boundary permeability, the permeability property could be coordinated with the psychoanalytic notion of impulse control. By so doing, the deductive (and when operationalized, predictive) possibiilties of the Lewinian model could be brought to bear on a central aspect of ego functioning.

The construct of ego-control, then, when integrated into the Lewinian framework, relates to boundary permeability-impermeability. When dimensionalized, the underlying continuum at one end identifies what we have termed as *overcontrol:* excessive boundary impermeability resulting in the containment of impulse, delay of gratification, inhibition of action and affect, and insulation from environmental distractors. The opposite end of the continuum identifies what we have termed as *undercontrol:* excessive boundary permeability and its consequences, insufficient modulation of impulse, the inability to delay gratification, immediate and direct expression of motivations and affects, and vulnerability to environmental distractors.

Phrased in somewhat more contemporaneous terms, the concept of ego-control refers to the threshold or operating characteristic of an individual with regard to the expression or containment of impulses, feelings, and desires. Presuming the environmental context is not massively directive and compelling and registers equivalently on all of its experiences, and presuming also that motivational impetus is constant, the ego overcontroller can be expected to have a high modal threshold for response, to be constrained and inhibited, to manifest needs and impulses relatively indirectly, to delay gratification unduly, to show minimal expression of emotion, to tend to be categorical and overly exclusive in processing information, to be perseverative, nondistractible, less exploratory, relatively conforming, with narrow and unchanging interests, to be relatively planful and organized, and to be made uneasy by and therefore avoidant of ambiguous or inconsistent situations. In contrast, the ego undercontroller can be expected to have a low modal threshold for response, to be expressive, spontaneous, to manifest needs and impulses relatively directly into behavior, to tend toward the immediate gratification of desires, to readily manifest feelings and emotional fluctuations, to be overly inclusive in processing information, to have many but relatively short-lived enthusiasms and interests, to be distractible, more ready to explore, less conforming, relatively comfortable with or undiscerning of ambiguity and inconsistency, to manifest actions that cut across conventional categories of response in ways that are (for better or for worse) original, and to live life on an ad hoc, impromptu basis. In this conceptualization, extreme placement at either end of the ego-control continuum implies a constancy in mode of behavior that, given a varying world, can be expected to be adaptively dysfunctional.

Distinguishing Ego-Control From Other Constructs.   The construct of ego-control should not be quickly and casually equated or categorized with other personality variables seemingly or even actually related to it, such as *extraversion-introversion, externalizing-internalizing, acting-out, psychopathy, reflection-impulsivity, delay of gratification, motor inhibition, activity level* (hyperkinesis versus hypokinesis), and the like. We believe that more than conceptual chauvinism prompts this suggestion. On strictly conceptual grounds, important distinctions can and must be made among a variety of personality variables commonly employed, but commonly unanalyzed, by psychologists. Extended consideration of the concepts relatable to ego-control cannot be afforded here; we are reduced to some quick observations and declarations from the armchair.

The concept of *extraversion-introversion* is generally not much more than a vaguely and variously held label and, with the exception of Eysenck's formulation (Eysenck 1967), has not been embedded in a generative system of behavior. Even for Eysenck, the concept has been confounded and changing meaning over the years, being a blend in changing proportions of the components of *sociability* and *impulsivity* (e.g., J. Block 1978; Guilford 1975; Revelle, personal communication, 1976). If it is granted that an individual can be impulsive but not sociable, or sociable but not impulsive, then the inadequacy of the extraversion-introversion concept as commonly conveyed becomes apparent. Historically, the essential meaning of the term extraversion-introversion has reference to the external-internal orientation of the individual to inputs from the world: The extravert was a person perceptually oriented and highly receptive to the impingements of the outer world; the introvert was oriented and receptive to the inner world of thought and fantasy (Jung 1923). Were the concept of extraversion-introversion to revert to its original meaning, this important distinction regarding attentional orientation would be recovered.

The concept of *externalizing-internalizing* is not so frequently invoked as is the concept of extraversion-introversion, but it also is imprecisely specified and without a position in theoretical system. Although the dimension of externalizing-internalizing has been only informally conceptualized, it appears to be concerned with whether need tensions are discharged via external, action modes of expression or whether needs are routed internally into cognitive and visceral channels of discharge. In these terms, the externalizer need not be an undercontroller and the internalizer need not be an overcontroller, because the direction of a motivated response carries no necessary implication regarding the immediateness of, or the controls on, that motivated response. The label of externalizing-internalizing, if employed restrictedly, could usefully refer to the direction of action, allocentric or autocentric (i.e., outer or inner), taken by the individual in responding to the motivations that have gained regnancy.

The notion of *acting-out* is almost invariably misused in personological parlance. Usually, what is meant is "acting-up" and, defined in this sense, acting-out is often equated with undercontrol. However, the distinction between acting-out and undercontrol is fundamental and is well conveyed by Frosch (1977). In acting-out, as conceptualized in psychoanalytic theory, symbolic transformation of motivations are involved. Such transformations often lead to behavior that is related only in convoluted ways to the initial motivation. In undercontrol, on the other hand, motivations are directly expressed and are directly understandable through the behavior manifested. Acting-out, according to its original psychodynamic definition, does not necessarily imply undercontrol. Misunderstanding would be averted if the concept of acting-out were again reserved for behaviors derivative from symbolically-transformed motivations.

The notion of *psychopathy* is often overlapped with the notion of undercontrol. But psychopaths are not necessarily undercontrollers, as a reading of Cleckley (1964) and Smith (1978) will attest. Psychopaths can be planful and premeditated as well as shortsighted and impulsive. Perhaps the defining feature of the psychopath is a failure or inability or an absence of introspection in those contexts where more ordinary individuals have their self-percepts activated. As a result, psychopaths are unable to place themselves affectively in the situations of others and are, therefore, less constrained in the behaviors than are more empathic, introspective individuals. The undercontroller, on the other hand, is not thereby less likely (or more likely) to be introspective; the possibility of introspective undercontrollers and nonintrospective overcontrollers indicates the conceptual necessity of distinguishing between psychopathy and the construct of ego-control.

Reflection-impulsivity is a construct that, at quick glance, appears connectible to overcontrol and undercontrol. The notion of reflection-impulsivity was evolved some years ago by Kagan, Rosman, Day, Albert, and Philips (1964) as a specific explanation for the individual differences observed in response to a "match-to-standard" task. The empirical support for this interpretation of "match-to-standard" performance has come under challenge (e.g., Achenbach and Weisz 1975; Block, Block, and Harrington 1974). The concept itself sometimes has been offered in a restricted form, as having no implications or generalizations beyond affecting performance in "match-to-standard" tasks (Kagan and Messer 1975); to the extent that reflection-impulsivity is construed so narrowly, it loses relevance. Sometimes reflection-impulsivity has been applied with a broader meaning and with assorted implications (Kagan 1966, 1967; Kagan and Kogan 1970, p. 1315), but these implications do not derive from an explicit model and have oscillated over the years. Bothersome, too, is the commitment in the concept of reflection-impulsivity to the positive value of reflection and the negative value of impulsivity. The conceptual possibility that reflection can verge into obsessiveness and indecisiveness and that impulsivity can be linked with spontaneity and creative forms of "inaccuracy" (i.e., rejection of unimportant details, focusing instead on important general features or principles) is not recognized in the concept of reflection-impulsivity as it is in the concept of ego-control.

Delay of gratification and *motor inhibition* are single, isolated personality variables more limited in scope than the construct of ego-control, from which they may be derived but which they, in turn, cannot encompass. In the usual definition and usage of these variables, as with reflection-impulsivity, there is an unacknowledged suggestion that behavior representative of one pole of the dimension (delay of gratification or motor inhibition) is to be preferred over behavior indicative of the other pole (absence of delay of gratification or absence of motor inhibition). The conceptual possibility of excessive delay of gratification or excessive motor inhibition is not generally considered, although this recognition is incorporated in the construct of ego-control (i.e., overcontrol).

The concept of *activity level* is also not equatable with the construct of ego-control. It is probably the case that individuals can be stratified reliably with respect to their general level of activity or psychological energy, their characteristic tempo of "urges and surges." Holding the degree of ego-control constant, the individual high on activity level will *appear* more undercontrolled because there are more, and more frequent, motivations and impulses requiring expression in behavior. The child classified as hyper-kinetic or hyperactive may not have an ego structure characterizable, in absolute terms, as "undercontrolling"; instead, he or she may be besieged by more impulses and motivational demands than his/her ordinary enough personality structure can modulate. The conceptual necessity of distinguish-ing between amount of impulses and the control of impulse requires clear separation of activity level from ego-control.

So much for this necessarily brief effort to connect and to disconnect the construct of ego-control and other concepts more or less related. Much more could, and should, be said on the issues so tersely addressed, but for now it is necessary to go on.

Antecedents of Ego-Control

Although the inborn antecedents of ego-control remain to be specified, it may be anticipated that further research will establish a significant role for genetic and constitutional factors. There are sound ethological reasons for presuming that variations in ego-control will have genetic consequence. The recent volume by Buss and Plomin (1975) on the genetic inheritance of temperament is especially pertinent. Their review and integration of the available evidence, much of it quite relevant to ego-control, is recommended to interested readers.

With respect to experiential antecedents of ego-control, abundant and increasingly clear relationships with socialization practices have been docu-mented (J. Block 1971). One of the developmental tasks of the young child is the learning of impulse control and the regulation of self-expression. For parents, the socialization of the child's primitive impulses is a major goal of child-rearing. Referencing the longitudinal data collected over many years at the Institute of Human Development, we found that overcontrolled adults in their mid-30s tended to come from families earlier and indepen-dently characterized as emphasizing structure, order, and conservative val-ues. Undercontrolled adults tended to come from homes earlier and inde-pendently characterized as conflict-ridden, where the basic values of the parents were discrepant. Less emphasis was placed on socialization of the child in that parents tended to neglect their teaching roles, placed fewer demands for achievement on the child, and required less assumption by the child of personal and familial responsibilities. For a more extended discus-sion of the socialization antecedents of ego-control, the reader is referred to the last chapter of *Lives Through Time* (Block 1971) and to the essay by J. H. Block (1976).

Formalizing the Construct of Ego-Resiliency

In Lewinian terms, ego-resiliency may be coordinated with a second property of boundaries posited by Lewin, the property of *elasticity*. Elasticity refers to the capacity of a boundary to change its characteristic level of permeability-impermeability depending upon impinging psychological forces and to return to its original modal level of permeability after the temporary, accommodation-requiring influence is no longer pressing. In our own conceptualization, ego-resiliency refers to the dynamic capacity of an individual to modify his/her moral level of ego-cont ol, in either direction, as a function of the demand characteristics of the environmental context.

Degree of boundary elasticity, or ego-resiliency, has implication for the individual's adaptive or equilibrative capabilities under conditions of environmental stress, uncertainty, conflict, or disequilibrium. The selective, adaptive organizing aspects of psychoanalytic ego functioning can be subsumed under the concept of ego-resiliency. Ego-resiliency can explain dynamically both "regression in the service of the ego" (Kris 1952) (e.g., as seen in the characteristically overcontrolled individual who is enabled to become ideationally fluid, loose, and even illogical, in certain circumstances such as "brainstorming") and what we term "progression in the service of ego" (e.g., as seen in the characteristically undercontrolled individual who becomes highly organized and even obsessive in certain circumstances, as when psychology graduate students study for their goals). The construct of ego-resiliency relates to Klein's (1954) formulation of "cognitive controls," which are concerned with the mediating, accommodating functions required to regulate drive expression in accordance with situational requirements. It appears to relate closely to the recently offered concept of "mobility" (Witkin and Goodenough 1976), defined as the ability to use both the field-dependent and field-independent modes of adaptation, depending on situational requirements and inner states; to the concept of "competence" (White 1959); and to the concept of coping and coping strategies (Murphy 1957, 1962).

Ego-resiliency, when dimensionalized, is defined at one extreme by resourceful adaptation to changing circumstances and environmental contingencies, analysis of the "goodness of fit" between situational demands and behavioral possibility, and flexible invocation of the available repertoire of problem-solving strategies (problem-solving being defined to include the social and personal domains as well as the cognitive). The opposite end of the ego-resiliency continuum (ego-brittleness) implies little adaptive flexibility, an inability to respond to the dynamic requirements of the situation, a tendency to perseverate or to become disorganized when encountering changed circumstances or when under stress, and a difficulty in recouping after traumatic experiences.

Holding the degree of ego-control constant, the ego-resilient person is resourceful before the strain set by new and yet unmastered situations, manifests more *umweg* solutions when confronted by a barrier, can maintain integrated performance while under stress, is better able to process two or more completing stimuli, is better able to resist sets or illusions, is engaged with the world but not subservient to it, and is capable of both "regressing in the service of the ego" when task requirements favor such an adaptation and, conversely, of becoming adaptively organized and even compulsive when under certain other environmental presses. With degree of ego-control held constant, the ego-unresilient (brittle) person, according to our conceptualization, is generally fixed in his/her established pattern of adaptation, has only a small adaptive margin, is stereotyped in responding to new situations, becomes immobilized, rigidly repetitive, or behaviorally diffuse when under stress, becomes anxious when confronted by competing demands, is relatively unable to resist sets or illusions, is slow to recover after stress, is disquieted by changes in either the personal psychological environment or the larger world, and cannot modify his/her preferred personal tempo in accordance with reality considerations.

Distinguishing Ego-Resiliency from Other Constructs. The construct of ego-resiliency, while related to such concepts as *intelligence, ego strength, competence, coping,* and the like, should not be viewed as the equivalent of any of them.

The concept of *intelligence* is not a unitary one; it means many different things to many different psychologists. Certainly, "intelligence" is not simply what intelligence tests measure! There is a practical or societal utility to "intelligence" tests; but there needs also to be a conceptual justification, an understanding or specification of the various cognitive capacities and processes that, when sequenced and organized, result in what is called "intelligent" behavior. The sequencing and organization of cognitive processes is obviously not unlike the sequencing and organization of ego processes from which we have abstracted the construct of ego-resiliency. The difference is that in ego-resiliency, the sequencing and organization of behavior serves broad and overarching motivational and affectual functions in addition to specific and immediate cognitive ends.

The extent to which intelligent tests, particularly of the omnibus variety (e.g., the Stanford-Binet or WPPSI), get at the crucial sequencing and organizational capacities of an individual is uncertain, arguable, and we judge, little. Omnibus intelligence tests appear to emphasize measurement of various information-processing, memorial, and cognitive elemental abilities necessary for subsequent intelligent behavior, but often do not index intelligent behavior itself. Therefore, there will be an asymmetric relation between performance on most omnibus intelligence tests and a more conceptual definition of intelligent behavior; but there will not be an equivalence.

We may further distinguish between intelligence, conceived in this grander vein, and ego-resiliency by noting that the failures of an individual in certain intelligence-requiring tasks or problems may be due not so much to cognitive or information-processing insufficiencies as they are due to orientational premises or motivational conditions within that individual. A person may be intrinsically cognitively capable, but may be made anxious by unstructured situations, or by unfamiliar adults, or in evaluative contexts, or may be intolerant of ambiguity; for these latter reasons, the person may not confront or become immersed in a cognitive problem that, if only it were faced and examined, would be found to be readily solvable. In this way, ego-resiliency or egobrittleness can have consequential implications for effectively registered intelligence and cannot be viewed as a variable from which intelligence should be "partialled." The direction of partialling can, with justification, well be reversed. So, for this reason also, the constructs of ego-resiliency and of intelligence need to be maintained as separate.

While a popular label in personality and clinical psychology, the concept of *ego strength* has, in our view, been employed so broadly and so nonspecifically as to become little more than a jargonistic term for "adjustment." (In some versions of the concept, there arises the anomaly of excessive "ego strength"!) In our view, the original core meanings of ego strength in psychoanalysis can, when partitioned, essentially be encompassed by the constructs of ego-control and ego-resiliency.

The term *competence* has been so widely applied and so generalized since its introduction by White (1959) that it now frequently requires a modifier: We speak of "social competence" (Anderson and Messick 1974) or "intellectual competence" or "linguistic competence," and so on. Implicit in the use of these qualifiers is the recognition that effective functioning, the core meaning of competence, is defined by criterion behaviors that are context-specific. Not only are the criteria for competence context-specific but, in a pluralistic society, definitions of competence seem to vary also as a function of cultural and subcultural values (Zigler and Trickett 1978). The definition of competence in relativistic, context-specific terms seems to us to limit its usefulness as a theoretically generative variable (J. Block, J. H. Block, Siegelman, and von der Lippe 1971). In contrast, ego-resiliency, conceptually defined as the ability to modify one's behavior in accordance with contextual demands, is a variable applicable across domains and across cultures.

The notion of *coping* (Murphy 1957, 1962) is a broadly used concept, referring sometimes to intrapsychic mechanisms for modulating anxiety and sometimes to externally adaptive behaviors in the face of challenge, frustration, or stress. A broad repertoire of problem-solving or coping strategies is viewed as underlying the general capacity to cope. However, coping often is defined in ways that are not independent of behavioral outcome; that is, behaviors that "work" in negotiating difficult situations are manifestations of coping by definition, thus introducing circularity into the sense and operationalization of the construct. The construct of ego-resiliency, by contrast, is defined in formal terms that entail definite kinds of behaviors in specifiable circumstances.

The preceding discussion indicates, if only briefly, the kinds of arguments that can be advanced to distinguish ego-resiliency from other, related concepts.

Antecedents of Ego-Resiliency

The antecedents of ego-resiliency seem likely to include genetic and constitutional factors. Differences in what may be thought of as resiliency (and, given longitudinal study, may indeed prove to be resiliency) can be observed early in life in the extent and way in which the infant responds to environmental changes, can be comforted, equilibrates physiological responses, and modifies sleep-wake states (Bell, Weller, and Waldrop 1971; Chess, Thomas, and Birch 1959; Sander, Stechler, Julia, and Burns 1970; Sander, Julia, Stechler, and Burns 1972; Thomas, Chess, and Birch 1969). At an entirely conjectural level, ego-oriented psychoanalysts have posited a rudimentary "conflict-free" ego structure with which the infant begins life (Hartmann, Kris, and Loewenstein 1946). To the extent that a predisposition to the occurrence of societally recognized psychopathology is indicative of an absence of ego-resiliency, the evidence that has accrued for a genetic contribution to psychopathology can be interpreted as evidence as well for inborn individual differences in subsequent ego-resiliency (Rosenthal 1970).

Experiential influences on ego-resiliency also appear to be substantial.

Referencing the longitudinal data collected over many years at the Institute of Human Development, we found that individuals we would call ego-resilient tended to come from families earlier and independently characterized as having loving, patient, competent and integrated mothers, free interchange of problems and feelings, sexual compatibility of parents, agreement on values and concern with philosophical and moral issues, among other qualities. Individuals characterizable as ego-brittle tended to come from homes earlier and independently observed to be conflictful, discordant, with neurotic and anxious mothers ambivalent about their maternal role, and without intellectual or philosophical emphasis, among other qualities (Siegelman, J. Block, J. H. Block, and von der Lippe 1970). The work of Robins (1966) is also highly pertinent. For a more extended discussion of the antecedents of ego-resiliency, the reader is referred to the last chapter of *Lives Through Time* (J. Block 1971).

The Longitudinal Study

We had four major goals for our research:

1. to investigate two parameters of personality functioning, ego-control and ego-resiliency, with regard to their developmental course over the childhood years;
2. to explore the relations of ego-control, ego-resiliency, and their interaction, to cognitive functioning, affective differentiation, moral development, and interpersonal behaviors;
3. to identify parental, environmental, and experiential factors associated with differences in ego-control and ego-resiliency; and
4. to assess the predictive utility of these two constructs measured in early childhood for understanding personality characteristics, interests, achievement orientation, attitudes, and adaptations in the preadolescent and adolescent years.

The Sample

The children included in our study were drawn from the two nursery schools constituting the Harold E. Jones Child Study Center at Berkeley over the three year period 1969–71. Extensive individual assessments were conducted at ages 3, 4, 5, and 7; we are currently concluding the assessment at age 11. The numbers of children participating vary by year, ranging from a high of 130 at age 4 to a low at age 7. In the 11-year-old follow-up, children from 110 families are being seen. Given the great mobility characterizing American society, the number of children lost from the study impresses us as low. Earlier analyses of subject loss showed no differential attrition as a function of socioeconomic level or ethnic origin. Following completion of the current assessment, the possible role of differential attrition will again be evaluated.

One of the participating nursery schools is a university laboratory school, administered by the University of California; the second nursery school is a parent cooperative, administered by the Berkeley Public Schools. The two schools, jointly considered, attract children from heterogeneous backgrounds with regard to education, socioeconomic level, and ethnic origin. Although the sample over-represents the middle and upper-middle class, the range of socioeconomic status (SES) is wide. Sixty-one percent of the children are white, 31% are black, and the remaining 8% represent other ethnic groups, primarily Oriental and Chicano.

Both the mothers and the fathers of the children are also included in the study. When their children were 3 years old, the parents each provided descriptions of their child-rearing orientations; when their children were 4 years old, the parents each interacted with their children in a teaching situation; when the children were 6 years old, the mothers were interviewed and completed both self-descriptive and child-descriptive adjective Q-sorts. Currently, additional parental data are being collected.

Some Orienting Principles Underlying the Research

It is important to register some of the underlying orienting and strategic principles shaping the research enterprise. Broadly put, it was our intention to apply a personality assessment model within the context of a prolonged longitudinal investigation that would begin with young children and study them over *multiple time periods* through the years.

Concern for a Broad Assessment of Personality and Cognitive Functioning. Besides our intention to study the *same people* over *multiple time periods*, we were oriented toward the study of *multiple concepts* within each time period. In our view, longitudinal investigators have the responsibility of not being exclusively or narrowly focused on their personal theoretical concerns. Longitudinal studies are yet rare; the unique opportunity they present should be used to advance broad developmental understandings, as well as perhaps partisan theoretical emphases. In addition, then, to assessing the importance of ego-control and ego-resiliency for a wide variety of behaviors, we sought to study many additional and important aspects of psychological functioning at each age level. Table 1 lists the measures used at each assessment period. Various aspects of cognitive functioning—cognitive differentiation, creativity, focal attention, hypothesis-generation, memory—are represented. Additionally, cognitive-style marker variables such as field-dependence, category breadth, and reflection-impulsivity are included. Role-taking, moral reasoning, and prosocial behaviors constitute another measurement category. Affective differentiation—both recognition of affect and generation of responses to affective stimuli—is addressed by several procedures, as is the development of gender-role concepts over the childhood years. Comprehensive personality characterizations of each child provided by nursery school teachers, elementary school teachers, mothers, clinicians, and examiners complete the assessment battery.

Because we shall be traveling the longitudinal road but once and because of recognitions developed in earlier analyses of longitudinal data (J. Block 1971), we have been oriented toward the inclusion (some might say, the overinclusion!) of a wide variety of personality-relevant measures. Yet, inevitably, the broad net cast will still, for many psychological fish, prove inadequate. No longitudinal inquiry will provide the data base to respond to all developmental issues. We can hope only that the scope of our inquiry usefully improves understanding of developmental courses and patterns.

Table 1 Significance levels of group differences on experimental tasks at ages 3, 4, 5, and 7 surrounding ego resiliency, ego control and ego-resiliency/ego-control conjunctions (specified by independent Q-sort descriptions of children at age 3[l])

Experimental Measure	Age 3				Age 4				Age 5				Age 7			
	Sex	UCQ	ResQ	R×C	Sex	UCQ	ResQ	R×C	Sex	UCQ	ResQ	R×C	Sex	UCQ	ResQ	R×C
Ego control indices																
Actometer[a]		.000U[b]		.01R	.03M	.000U										
Delay of gratification																
Candy train		N.S.				N.S.										
Gift delivery		.000O			.08F	.04O										
Accumulation of rewards										.0008O						
DePree delay procedure													.02M			
Exploratory behavior																
Curiosity box–Play delay		.001O	.07B													
Curiosity box–Exploration	.03M	.01U														
Incidental		N.S.														
Question asking	.000M	.002U		.10BU	.04M	.001U										
Inhibition of impulse																
Competing set		.09O				.03O										
Simon Says													.001M			
Resistance to temptation							N.S.									
Goal-setting estimates	.04M	.005U				.09U										
Satiation time			.003B	.04BO		N.S.				N.S.		.06BO				
Planfulness			.03R			.07O		.09RO		N.S.			.009F	N.S.		
Distractability	.000M				.07M											

295

Table 1 *continued*

Experimental Measure	Age 3				Age 4				Age 5				Age 7			
	Sex	UCQ	ResQ	R×C	Sex	UCQ	ResQ	R×C	Sex	UCQ	ResQ	R×C	Sex	UCQ	ResQ	R×C
Percept recognition–Guesses			N.S.													
Barrier intensity		.02U			N.S.	.09U						N.S.				
Motor inhibition–tempo	.10M					N.S.			.008M							
Undercontrol experimental composite		.000U				.000U		.05B	.04M				not yet analyzed			
Undercontrol Q-composite		.000U				.000U			.000U				.000U			
Ego resiliency indices																
Dual focus			.003R	.04RO							N.S.					
Constructiveness under frustration	.01F	.01U	.06R													.03RU
Premature decision making						.02O	.001B									
Level of aspiration																
Achievement average			.02R				.000R									
Discrepancy average			.002B				N.S.									
Percept recognition			.06R				.07R									
PPVT, time/difficulty ratio	not yet analyzed				.09M											
Anticipating consequences															N.S.	
Incidental learning			.06R					.02RU		.04O	.001R	.10R			.09U	.001R
Formation of hypotheses							.007R	.03RO								
Partial reinforcement							.09R									
Object sorting	N.S.					N.S.				.01U		.10RU				
Barrier hypothesis	.005M	.10U								.03U	.002R					

Measure	Reported values
Alternative solutions, barrier	.10RU .05M N.S. .03R
Digit span backwards	.009O .000R .007R .04R
Motor inhibition test	.10O .000R .003R .09O .003R
Resiliency experi-mental composite	not yet analyzed .03R
Resiliency Q-composite	.000R .000R
Cognitive abilities	
Peabody picture vocabulary	.000R .05M .10O .02R
Ravens progressive matrices	.004R .10M .009R .009RU .10M .04U .001R
WPPSI picture completion	.05U
Block Design	.02O .003R
Memory for sentences	.01O
Mazes	.03R .07O .09RO
Information	.10R
Comprehension	.09R
Similarites	.02R
Geometric designs	.07R
Arithmetic	N.S.
Landauer short-term memory	.003RU .05RU
Memory for narrative	.06R .10R .05RU
Conservation tasks	.001R .04R .05RU
Convergent task com-posite	not yet analyzed .02F .000R .002R .03RO
Cognitive styles	
Reflection-impulsivity	.05M
MFF time	.001B .03BU N.S.
MFF error	.001B .10M .01U .009BU

Table 1 *continued*

Experimental Measure	Age 3				Age 4				Age 5				Age 7			
	Sex	UCQ	ResQ	R×C	Sex	UCQ	ResQ	R×C	Sex	UCQ	ResQ	R×C	Sex	UCQ	ResQ	R×C
Field independence																
Embedded figure tests			.07R		.001F		.02R				N.S.				.07R	
Rod and frame						N.S.						.000RO				.03R .02RO
Categorization-breadth																
Object sorting tasks					.01M			.07RU		.01U		.10RU				
Concept evaluation test						N.S.				N.S.				N.S.		
Tinkertoy sorting					.02M		.009B									
Composite breadth							.07B			N.S.		.07RU				
Conceptual style																
Descriptive-analytic		.07O				N.S.				.07U						
Relational-functional		.07U				N.S.				N.S.						
Categorical		N.S.				N.S.				N.S.						
Sex role typing																
Engagement-composite		.000U		.001R		not yet analyzed				not yet analyzed			.001M	not yet analyzed		
Creativity																
Lowenfeld imaginativeness		N.S.				N.S.			.04F	.03U						
Instances									.02F				.02F			
Unusual uses												.08R		not yet analyzed		
Word association														not yet analyzed		
Parallel lines														not yet analyzed		
Social behaviors																
Role-taking tasks	.10F	.00R														
Spatial egocentrism		.06B														
Sharing									.05F	.10B	.01BU	.004R		.05U		

Affective differentiation			
Physiognomic perception		.04R .02RO	N.S.
Differentiation of affect	.04F	N.S.	
Stanford locus of Control-I	N.S.	N.S. .05F	N.S.

Moral development			
Selman moral reasoning		N.S.	
Moral behavior situations			not yet analyzed
Conceptions of "badness"	not yet analyzed	not yet analyzed	

[a] When a particular measure was not administered at a given age, as, for example, the Actometer at ages 5 and 7, the pertinent section of the table has been left blank.

[b] Letters following the significance levels indicate the group favored in the comparison: Male vs. Female, Undercontrolled vs. Overcontrolled; Resilient vs. Brittle.

Concern for Measurement Using Multiple Kinds of Data. Besides study of the same sample with respect to *multiple concepts* over *multiple time periods,* we were oriented further toward the use of *multiple kinds of data.* A principle of personality assessment is to employ personality measures involving fundamentally different kinds of data, then to insist that these various kinds of measures of a given concept converge in their empirical implications.

A useful basis for distinguishing among kinds of psychological data was offered by Cattell (1957, 1973) some years ago, distinctions which we subsequently have slightly modified and relabeled (J. Block 1975, 1977). There are L (for *life*) data, O (for *observer*) data, S (for *self-reported*) data, and T (for *test*) data (the acronym, LOST can serve as a useful mnemonic).

L-data are societal, demographic, nonobserver-based, nonobstrusive, actuarial, indisputably ascertainable indicators or aspects or attributes surrounding the person, manifest in the real, natural, ongoing, everyday world. Some examples of L-data in our sample of children are gender, age, ethnicity, social class, presence of allergy, obesity, absenteeism, school grades, parental divorce, parental disagreement in child-rearing, and so on.

O-data are data derived from observers' evaluations of individuals leading more or less natural lives. Generally, these data take the form of personality ratings, checklists, *Q*-sorts, or diagnoses. O-data depend quintessentially on the use of an observer as an active, filtering, cumulating, weighting, configurating, integrating instrument.

S-data are data derived from the self observations of individuals regarding their behaviors, feelings, attitudes, interests, and characteristics. Self-ratings, responses to personality inventories and questionnaires, and answers to specific interview questions exemplify this kind of data.

T-data are data derived from standardized, objective, more or less artificial test or laboratory situations wherein selected, specific, readily identified or enumerated behaviors, usually but not always unbeknownst to the participating subject, are focused upon as indicators of particular personality variables.

All four of these kinds of data have their unique strengths and weaknesses. L-data are indisputably "real," but L-data often have confounded or obscure meaning. O-data are able to express the "deep structure" of behavior by permitting the integrating and contextualizing observer to recognize when a behavior has a certain significance and when it does not; but O-data can also be unreproduceable and distortion-prone. S-data are quickly gathered and are capable of generating important and nonobvious understandings of the individual; but S-data can also derive from foolish and superficial questions of little relevance to non-S behaviors. T-data are "objective," "hard" data, not dependent on what the individual being studied happens to say or how an observer makes inferences; but T-data can also be pallid, conceptually impoverished laboratory demonstrations lacking pertinence or generalizability. At this stage in the development of psychology as a science, it should now be obvious that *all* of these kinds of data can, separately and by their interrelations, help advance understanding. The wise psychologist will not willingly deprive him/herself of any of these complementary and supplementary ways of investigation.

Each of these sources of data is represented in our assessment battery. Various kinds of L-data have been noted already (e.g., illnesses, accidents, school progress, etc.); at each succeeding assessment, as the subjects have lived longer or experienced more or done more, additional L-indicators are being recorded. O-data are generated during all assessments and include observer's descriptions in nursery schools, in elementary school, observations of free play in a standardized sandbox situation, observations in a modification of Erikson's (1951) play construction situation, examiner descriptions of child functioning in structured test situations, and maternal descriptions of the child. S-data begin to be represented in the age 7 assessment and include self-descriptive adjective Q-sorts, interest expressions, patterns of free-time activities, responses in an interview, and a questionnaire. The heaviest investment in time and energy during each assessment period has gone toward T-data, including both standardized tests (e.g., the Peabody Picture Vocabulary Test, the WPPSI, the Matching Familiar Figures Test, the Rod-and-Frame Test, the Embedded Figures Test, the Concept Evaluation Test) and standardized situational or experiment-based procedures (e.g., delay of gratification (J. H. Block and Martin 1955; DePree 1966), motor inhibition, incidental learning, level of aspiration, sharing, signal detection, distractibility, satiation). Our study is unusual for the range of tests and procedures administered to the same sample of subjects, often over several assessment periods. . . .

Concern for Age-Appropriate Measurement of Psychological Concepts. Longitudinal investigations generally have been simply designed and have had simple intents; it has been thought useful to administer the same procedure several times and then to evaluate, usually via correlational techniques, whether individuals show "continuity" or "change." However, long-term longitudinal research that begins with young children requires a research strategy that neither depends on nor assumes the virtues of readministration of precisely the same procedures over time. At these early developmental levels, the age-appropriateness of many measures is short-lived. To evaluate important, salient aspects of psychological functioning over the childhood and adolescent years, concepts or dimensions have to be operationally indexed by procedures that are age-appropriate. The behavioral manifestation of a concept at one age may be very different from the behavioral manifestation of the same concept at a different age. The conceptual manifestation of a behavior at one age may be very different from the conceptual implication of the same behavior at another age. Because of the changing relations between genotype and phenotype (i.e., behavioral expression) as a function of development, the search for homotypic similarities across age is often not only futile, it is wrong. As Bell et al. (1971) and Waters and Sroufe (1977) have emphasized, developmental psychologists must seek age-appropriate expressions of underlying abilities and personality characteristics. Many failures to find evidence for developmental coherence probably reflect nothing more than a neglect of the necessity of age-appropriate measurement of concepts.

Recognition of this inescapable problem requires the adoption of a measurement strategy that does not depend upon the repetitive application of the same but perhaps meaning-changed procedures to exemplify a concept. Perhaps the only alternative is to use a conceptual domain-sampling approach. The conceptual domain-sampling strategy requires multiple but diverse indicators of a concept, the concept then being represented by some average or total or composite of the multiple indicators. The presumption is that the concept entails a domain of indicators and that composites based upon a good sample of indicators can be expected to be reliable and valid measures of the concept. It also follows that two samples of indicators of a concept need not overlap; the only requirement is that samples decently represent the conceptual domain. It is well known that two intelligence scales, composed of entirely different but intelligence-related items, will correlate highly, even if the two sets of intelligence-sampling items are administered at two widely-separated times. Similarly, it should be possible to develop nonoverlapping sets of experiment-based, concept-related, age-appropriate measures that, when composited, correlate from one age to another. The design of our assessment battery sought to follow this psycho-metric strategy, insofar as feasible, so as to respond to the measurement problem posed by the ever-changing developmental status of children. . . .

The Structure and Logic of the Data Presentation.   There are various ways of organizing our findings for presentation and various considerations to which we must attend. For our purposes here, we have chosen to explore the implications of ego-control and ego-resiliency that override the possible influence of gender, even though our male and female subjects differ often both with respect to level of ego-control and the behavioral quality of their manifestations of ego-control. On another occasion, we expect to consider closely the differential developmental progression of the sexes with regard to ego-functioning. For now, however, to stringently evaluate the functional relevance of ego-control and ego-resiliency, we have elected to assess the envelopmental power of the constructs *after statistically controlling for the effects of gender.* The easy way to achieve this analytical intention is via hierarchical multiple regression analysis, the logic and attractions of which are well conveyed by Cohen and Cohen (1975).

In our many multiple regression analyses of the implications of ego-control and ego-resiliency vis-à-vis our host of "dependent" variables, the variable of gender has always been introduced first, prior to the introduction of the ego-control and ego-resiliency variables. By so doing, insofar as gender is confounded the ego-control and ego-resiliency variables subsequently entered into the multiple regression equation, the role of gender is controlled or "partialled out" in a way logically identical to analysis of covariance. The independent variables, ego-control and ego-resiliency, are then entered into the multiple-regression analysis to evaluate their respective explanatory power for the dependent measure. Finally, the possibility of a significant interaction of ego-control and ego-resiliency with the dependent measure is evaluated by forming a "product variable" from the ego-control and ego-resiliency measures, then entering this constructed variable into the multiple-regression analysis to identify the additional variance contributed by this measure over and beyond the variance already encompassed by ego-control and ego-resiliency (Cohen 1978).

As the primary measures of ego-control and ego-resiliency to be entered as independent variables into this analytical structure, we chose to employ the indices of ego-control and ego-resiliency generated from the earlier described Q-sort composites characterizing the children at the age of 3 years.

Two considerations contributed to this decision: We wished to use ego-control and ego-resiliency measures from the earliest possible time, which meant indices available from the assessment of age 3; and we wanted to use the indices in which we had the greatest faith, which, for us, meant the Q-based indices.

It will be remembered that these Q-descriptions were contributed by three nursery-school teachers, each of whom had observed each child for 3 hours each day, 5 days a week, for several months before offering their independent Q-characterizations. These observers did not "score" the children with respect to our ego variables; rather, they described the children in the terms made available by the Q-language, using the forced-distribution method to bring their language scalings into a commensurate frame of reference. After compositing these comparably offered personality descriptions, these composites were referenced against criterion-definitions of ego-control and ego-resiliency, as described earlier, to generate "scores" for each child.

In our view, the extensive observational base for these descriptions, the methodological advantages of the Q-sort method, the multiplicity and independence of the observers, and the "removed" nature of the derivation of the ego-control and ego-resiliency "scores"—all these considerations taken together—provide us with the best available (and in absolute terms, quite good) measures of ego-control and ego-resiliency. Around these measures, we orient the subsequent multiple regression analyses and reference the strengths and weaknesses, validity and invalidity of other, and later, measures, especially those in the experimental or T-domain.

Relations Between O-Indices of Ego-Control and Ego-Resiliency at Age 3 and T-Data at Ages 3, 4, 5, and 7.   Table 1 presented the currently available experimental or T-domain findings accruing from our several analytical decisions. The extensity of experimental procedures, applied over so long a period to the same subject sample, makes this table unprecedented in developmental psychology.

Some further explanation is helpful for a proper reading and perspective on the reported relationships. Measures have been grouped into various a priori categories; in a number of instances, however, the assignment of a particular measure to a particular category should be understood as arbitrary. Generally, for diverse and usually supportable reasons, particular procedures were administered during only one or two of the four assessment years: Certain procedures appropriate at one or two age levels were deemed inappropriate at earlier or later times; certain procedures were intrinsically unrepeatable, for memorial reasons; certain procedures, after employment, were thought to be weak or weaker than later available procedures; logistical problems when the children entered the public school system restricted testing time and precluded continued use of certain procedures; and, we were sometimes unwise. Also, because of our strategic emphasis on the compositing of concept-relevant experimental measures or "items," a logic that presumes the essential interchangeability of items, we did not feel tied to the usual (and, as we have already noted, sometimes misguided) preoccupation of longitudinal studies, i.e., the application, repeatedly over the years, of seemingly same procedures to the studied sample. When a measure was not administered at a given age, the pertinent section of Table 1 has been left blank. Non-significant relationships and measures not yet analyzed are also noted. Where an independent variable explains significant incremental variance, the probability level and the direction of relationship are indicated. The reader may wish to know that at age 3, ego-control and ego-resiliency are essentially unrelated, correlating −.10. Additionally, at this age level, both are essentially independent of sex (correlations of .07 and −.02 for ego-control and ego-resiliency, respectively). The Peabody Picture Vocabulary Test, considered by some to be a general-purpose intelligence measure, was administered at age 3; it correlates −.01 and .37, respectively, with ego-control and ego-resiliency.

To provide a context for viewing the results presented in Table 1, the percentage of the total number of multiple-regression analyses yielding significant ($p < .05$) results for ego-control, ego-resiliency, and/or their interaction at each age level will be indicated. At age 3, 51% of the multiple-regression analyses issued significant results involving at least one of three independent variables; at age 4, the percentage is 44%; at age 5, the comparable percentage is 50%; and at age 7, 46% of the analyses were significant. These percentages, which are high absolutely, become more impressive when it is recognized that all of these analyses are independent; that the dependent variables derive from the generally less tractable experimental or T-data domain; that 11 nursery-school teachers contributed to the CC Q-descriptions of the children at 3, from which the independent variables for ego-control and ego-resiliency were derived; that 15 different examiners were involved in collecting the experiment-based dependent data; and that the effects of sex have been partialled out prior to testing for the effects of ego-control and ego-resiliency. The results of these analyses demonstrate that the two dimensions of ego functioning with which we are concerned, ego-control and ego-resiliency, can be measured reliably at age 3 and account for significant amounts of variance in both the personality and cognitive realms, both contemporaneously and across a time span of 4 years.

Examining the effects of sex, we find a trend toward increasing sex differences from the preschool years to age 7. The percentage of multiple-regression analyses showing significant sex effects is about the same during the preschool years (16% at age 3; 13% at age 4; and 14% at age 5) but increases markedly to 29% at age 7. This pattern accords well with the evidence for increasing sex differentiation with age noted by J. H. Block (1976) when she categorized the studies cited by Maccoby and Jacklin (1974) according to the age of the subjects.

Not only do sex differences emerge in greater frequency by the age of 7; we find sex effects also in the *pattern* of psychological correlates surrounding particular dimensions. In particular, ego-control in 7-year-olds appears to be manifested quite differently in boys and girls. As a result, the formula for our a priori conceptual, experiment-based ego-control index, which we applied equally to the two sexes, has issued results which do not support our anticipations. Because the analyses were conducted only days before this writing, we have not yet properly explored the reasons for, and implications of, these findings. It seems reasonable to ascribe this disappointment in part to the relative brevity of the assessment conducted at age 7, (only 4 hours). But the experiment-based ego-resiliency composite at age 7 has fared well in both sexes, and so this explanation is not sufficient. We believe the major reason for the breakdown of the ego-control experiment-based composite at age 7 lies in our deficient understanding of the demand quality of the procedures employed, given the diverging developmental progression of the sexes. During the preschool years, our subjects were more children than they were boys and girls; by age 7, however, they need to be recognized as boys and as girls and not viewed, conglomerately, simply as children. Given this belated insight, we expect that we will have to develop separate experiment-based indices of ego-control for males and for females much in the way that different scoring templates already are used for the two sexes when scoring for ego-control in psychological inventories (J. Block 1965).

Although much should be said about the voluminous T-domain results reported in Table 1, only those findings most pertinent to social and affective development are now mentioned. We then go to a richer and more germane source of information about the social-affective realm, additional and later observer data. It should be noted, however, that among the many undiscussed findings in Table 1 some dramatic coherencies across time can be observed, and also some dismaying failures. Of especial interest are some empirical indications that ego-control as tempered by ego-resiliency influences attention-deployment strategies, memory, and ease of memorial access. A full and critical evaluation of the salience of ego-control and ego-resiliency as organizing rubrics for behavior in different domains over time is being delayed until data from the comprehensive assessment now underway of the subjects at age 11 become available.

One consequential aspect of the self-concept is the nature of the premises developed by the child about the self-world relationship. Some children face the world with confidence and the expectation that their behaviors can produce effects in the world (Baumrind 1973; J. H. Block, J. Block, and Harrington 1975; Piaget 1954; Rotter 1966; White 1959), while other children approach the world tentatively, anticipating that their efforts may go unheeded (J. H. Block, J. Block, and Harrington 1975; Harrington, J. H. Block, and J. Block 1978; Hunt 1961). Our T-data suggest that early undercontrol relates to confidence in goal setting (level of aspiration), to active engagement with the experimental tasks presented (engagement composite), to inquisitive, exploratory orientation (Curiosity Box, incidental curiosity), and to active, intense efforts directed at overcoming barriers (barrier tasks). One aspect of the self-concept—and the most salient component of the self-concept in preschoolers, according to Keller, Ford, and Meacham (1978)—relates to action schemata. The set of T-findings surrounding the effects of early undercontrol emphasizes action, engagement, boldness, and assuredness that may, or may not, generally be contextually appropriate.

Role-taking ability has been shown to be importantly related to prosocial behaviors—altruism, empathy, sharing, caring (Krebs and Sturrup 1974; Rubin and Schneider 1973). We find that ego-resiliency as it is manifested at age 3 predicts role-taking ability as reflected by performance on a set of Flavell's role-taking tasks (Flavell 1968) and spatial non-egocentrism as reflected by performance on an adaptation of Piaget and Inhelder's "three-mountain" problem (Piaget and Inhelder 1956). Early ego-resiliency also is found to relate to sharing behavior in an experimental situation designed to elicit altruism (Rutherford and Mussen 1968) and to field independence-dependence (as measured by the Embedded Figures Test and by the Rod-and-Frame Test), a dimension previously shown to have implications in the social domain (Witkin and Goodenough 1977).

Looking at the T-data in the difficult-to-sample affective domain, ego-resiliency assessed at age 3 relates only to scores on the Physiognomic Perception Test at age 5. The Physiognomic Perception Test (Ehrman 1951) measures the consensually referenced accuracy of the subject in matching a word to one of four line drawings (e.g., the word, "anger," vis-à-vis a circle, a line rising from left to right, a square, and a jagged line, this last being the alternative that norms designate as correct).

The T-procedures bearing on the social-affective domain, although of interest, are few in number and lacking in direct pertinence. This should not be surprising since, by their very nature, T-assessment procedures trade off both the richness and the complexity of social experience for the affectively sparser, but also eminently manageable, scores derivable from standardized tests. To gain understanding of social-affective development, it seems likely psychology will have to rely primarily on observer-based data, to which we now turn.

Relations between O-Indices of Ego-Control and Ego-Resiliency at Age 3 and O-Data at Ages 4 and 7.   Following the multiple-regression logic earlier described, it is possible to evaluate the consequentiality of ego-control and ego-resiliency, as assessed when the children were 3 years old by the Under-control and Ego-Resiliency Q-Composites, for the social and affective behaviors characterizing these children at ages 4 and 7, as extensively described in these later years by entirely independent sets of teachers' Q-descriptions.

In the interests of data reduction and to simplify the reporting task, the 100 items in the CC Q-set have been grouped, according to both empirical and conceptual criteria, into 40 homogeneous mini-scales or "superitems," so as to lessen (albeit at some cost) the redundancy among our Q-items. Table 2 reports the results surrounding the superitems at ages 4 and 7, the superitems being classified into large, somewhat arbitrary categories: ego-control, ego-resiliency, orientations on self and the world, social behaviors, social stimulus value, and behavioral symptoms. The relations in Table 2 demonstrate the time-spanning power of the ego-control and ego-resiliency indices developed at age 3 in predicting important aspects of ego, social, and cognitive functioning at ages 4 and 7. At age 4, one year after the initial assessment, ego-control and/or ego-resiliency accounted for significant ($p < .05$) portions of the variance of 90% (36 of 40) of the superitems. Four years after their initial assessment, these two variables measured at age 3 account for significant portions of the variance in 47.5% (19 of 40) of the CC Q-superitems at age 7. The number and, as we shall see, the nature of these relations across time strike us as compelling.

Early-measured ego-control relates to the CC Q-superitems assessed at age 4 and age 7 that we have grouped as related to ego-control in many and conceptually required ways. Children with high scores on the undercontrol index at age 3 were described independently one and, often, 4 years later as: energetic, curious, restless, expressive of impulse, and as less constricted, less compliant, and less relaxed. Clearly, these personality characteristics em-

Table 2 Observation-based findings at ages 4 and 7 surrounding ego-control and ego-resiliency as specified by independent Q-sort descriptions of the children at age 3[a]

California Child Q-Sort "Superitems"	Age 4								Age 7							
	Sex		UCQ_3		$ResQ_3$		$R \times UC$		Sex		UCQ_3		$ResQ_3$		$R \times UC$	
	Raw	MRSig	Raw	MRSig	Raw	MRSig	Raw	MRSig	Raw	MRSig	Raw	MRSig	Raw	MRSig	Raw	MRSig
Ego-control																
Inhibited, constricted			-.63	.000O	-.12	.005B					-.37	.000O	-.27	.006B		
Compliant			-.58	.000O	.28	.04R					-.53	.000O				
Energetic, active			.57	.000U	.09	.03R					.49	.000U	.16	.06R		
Curious, exploring	.22	.04M	.16	.01U	.50	.000R							.18	.09R		
Restless, fidgety	.20	.06M	.35	.007U	-.32	.007B			.35	.002M	.33	.001U			.08	.07BU
Undercontrolling of impulse			.62	.000U	-.39	.001B					.37	.001U				
Calm, relaxed			-.44	.000O	.44	.000R					-.27	.01O	.21	.07R		
Ego-resiliency																
Worrying, anxious			-.14	.03O	-.40	.000B							-.32	.009B		
Recoups, resilient			.14	.01U	.48	.000R							.25	.03R		
Externalizing vulnerability			.35	.001U	-.51	.000B									.28	.10BU
Brittle, fragile margin of integration			.37	.002U	-.49	.000B					.23	.07U				
Intolerant of ambiguity			-.23	.003O	-.39	.000B							-.26	.02B		
Verbal facility			.42	.000R							.28	.01R				
Rigid repetition under stress			-.12	.04O	-.43	.000B										
Withdraws under stress			-.41	.000O	-.15	.02B										

Table 2 *continued*

California Child Q-Sort "Superitems"	Age 4								Age 7							
	Sex		UCQ_3		$ResQ_3$		$R \times UC$		Sex		UCQ_3		$ResQ_3$		$R \times UC$	
	Raw_r	MRSig	Raw_r	MRSig	Raw_r	MRSig	Raw_r	MRSig	Raw_r	MRSig	Raw_r	MRSig	Raw_r	MRSig	Raw_r	MRSig
Orientations on self and world																
Autonomy striving					.47	.000R					not significant					
Likes to compete	.26	.01M	.48	.000U	.54	.000R	.43	.10RU	.19	.09M	.23	.03U	.20	.06R		
Likes to play alone	.31	.003M	−.40	.000O							.24	.02U				
Fantasy orientation	.20	.06M	−.15	.05O					.30	.01M	−.30	.02O				
Negative self-image					−.34	.002B					not significant					
Negative evaluation of others					−.27	.009B					not significant					
Imitates those admired			not significant								not significant					
Behaves in sex-typed ways	−.24	.03F							−.24	.05F			−.21	.10B		
Admits negative feelings			not significant								not significant		−.20	.09B	.20	0.8BU
Social behaviors																
Empathic			−.41	.001O	.51	.000R					−.30	.008O				
Interpersonal reserve			−.57	.000O	−.08	.04B					−.38	.000O	−.18	.06B		
Interpersonal relatedness					.25	.009R					not significant					
Straightforward, open					.34	.003R									−.24	.07RO
Protective of others					.26	.01R					not significant					
Teases			.25	.04U					.21	.09M	.21	.05U				
Manipulative			.44	.000U	−.27	.04B										
Seeks physical contact			.19	.06U							.21	.07U				

Social Stimulus Value

Interesting, arresting	.28 .003U	.21 .01R		.39 .000R
Popular with peers		.35 .001R		not significant
Scapegoated by peers	−.34 .001O		.21 .03RO	−.32 .01O
Attractive	−.24 .02F	.33 .001R		.31 .005R

Behavioral Symptoms

Bodily symptoms		−.38 .000B		not significant
Behavioral mannerisms	−.12 .08O	−.30 .002B		−.18 .10B
Inappropriate affect	.22 .04M −.05 .04O	−.55 .000B		not significant

[a] The reader should note that, in a few multiple regression analyses, an independent variable explains significant incremental variance even though the direct correlation of the independent variable with the dependent variable is clearly not significant. This seeming discrepancy can result as a function of suppressor effects not recognized by the direct correlation.

body the core meaning of the construct of ego-control and testify to its long-term social and affective implications.

Similar support for the implicativeness of early-measured ego-resiliency is provided by the CC *Q*-superitems assessed at ages 4 and 7 that we have classified as relevant to ego-resiliency. Children with high scores on the ego-resiliency index at age 3 were described independently at age 4 as: able to recoup after stress, verbally fluent, less anxious, less brittle, less intolerant of ambiguity, and as less likely to externalize or to become rigidly repetitive or to withdraw under stress. At age 7, the number of relationships is fewer and the correlations of lesser significance; nevertheless, these data continue to underscore the importance and the essential progressive continuity of ego-resiliency.

Before continuing with Table 2, we detour briefly to present some perspective on the reciprocal implications of ego-control and ego-resiliency gained by considering a subset of the CC *Q*-findings. Some of the CC *Q*-superitems significantly related at age 4 to ego-control at age 3 are also related to ego-resiliency as measured at age 3; other CC *Q*-superitems significantly related to ego-control are not related to ego-resiliency, and vice versa. By attending only to the CC *Q*-superitems *conjointly* related to ego-control and ego-resiliency, classifying these items according to the particular pattern of ego-control and ego-resiliency relationships manifested, vivid psychological portrait emerges of the individuals representing each of these patterns. Table 3 presents, in four quadrants, the CC *Q*-superitems at age 4 that were significant ($p < .05$) functions of *both* earlier (age 3) ego-control and also earlier ego-resiliency. The quadrants are identified as: Resilient Undercontrol, Resilient Overcontrol, Brittle Undercontrol, and Brittle Overcontrol.

Table 3 CC *Q*-items significantly associated with the four ego-control/ego-resiliency conjunctions

Resilient Undercontroller	*Resilient Overcontroller*
Energetic, active	Compliant
Curious, exploring	Calm, relaxed
Recoups, resilient	Empathic
Interesting, arresting	
Brittle Undercontroller	*Brittle Overcontroller*
Restless, fidgety	Inhibited, constricted
Undercontrolling of impulse	Worrying, anxious
Externalizing, vulnerable	Intolerant of ambiguity
Brittle, narrow margin of integration	Rigidly repetitive under stress
Manipulative	Interpersonally reserved
	Withdraws under stress
	Manifests inappropriate effect
	Manifests behavioral mannerisms

While the correlation between ego-control and ego-resiliency as measured at age 3 is of zero order ($r = -.10$), the position of an individual child in this two-dimensional psychological space has strong implications for manifestly different patterns of interpersonal functioning. For the undercontrolling child, the presence of ego-resiliency tends to temper the expression of impulse without suppressing spontaneity, engagement, and enthusiasm. For the undercontrolling child with little ego-resiliency, however, impulse is unmodulated and we see a restless, externalizing, impulsive, easily disrupted child, a syndrome that fits more than a little the description of the hyperactive child (Whalen and Henker 1976).

For the overcontrolling child, the presence of ego-resiliency results in a high degree of socialization that fits and feels well, a relative absence of anxiety and intimidation in reacting to and acting on the world. The overcontrolling child with little ego-resiliency appears victimized, immobilized, anxious, overwhelmed by a world apprehended as threatening and unpredictable. There is appreciable evidence of psychopathology in the Brittle Overcontroller, as evidenced by behavioral mannerisms, inappropriate affect, and immobilization when confronted by stress.

Thus, within the individual, the reciprocal interactions of ego-control and ego-resiliency have much consequence for the nature of the perceptual and behavioral premises established, the development of character structure, and the quality of functioning in the interpersonal world.

Returning now to further consideration of Table 2, it may be observed that, with respect to the CC Q-superitems reflecting orientations toward the self and the world, children who were ego-resilient at age 3 were seen as task oriented and as emphasizing of autonomy and independence at age 4, while less resilient children were seen as critical and devaluing of both self and others. Undercontrol at age 3 relates to an emphasis on and pleasure derived from competition, a manifestation of engagement and desire for active mastery also seen in the T-data as salient components of undercontrol. Children who were described at 3 as overcontrolling were seen as enjoying solitary play and oriented toward fantasy at age 4, manifestations of reserve and psychological "distancing."

The CC Q-superitems in the realm of social behaviors also are substantially influenced by early ego-control and ego-resiliency. In general, positive patterns of social interaction (e.g., empathy, protectiveness, relatedness, directness) are associated with early ego-resiliency, while negative interpersonal behaviors (e.g., teasing, manipulativeness) are associated with early undercontrol.

Ego-resiliency as assessed at age 3 has significance for the later-evaluated social stimulus value of 4-year-olds and, to a lesser extent, 7-year-olds. Early ego-resiliency is associated with positive social stimulus value: with being seen as popular, interesting, and physically attractive at age 4. The ability to modify behavior in response to the demand qualities of a situation, a hallmark of ego-resiliency, benefits social interactions where differentiated responsiveness to moods, interests, needs, and sensitivities of others is a necessary condition for communication and relatedness. It is not surprising that the more resourceful, responsive, resilient children evoke positive evaluations and reactions from both adults and peers. Negative reactions in the form of scapegoating and victimization, on the other hand, are elicited by overcontrolling children. One might conjecture that these negative, aggressive behaviors represent extreme attempts by their peers to evoke responses from these inhibited, shy, constrained children.

In summarizing the results from the O-data domain, abundant evidence for behavioral coherencies with regard to ego-control and ego-resiliency across time were found. We also find evidence for the implicativeness of these concepts for interpersonal behaviors, for social evocativeness, for patterns of personal adaptations, and for psychopathology. Not surprisingly, the relationships with the measures of ego-control and ego-resiliency achieved at age 3 are both more robust and more numerous at age 4 than at age 7. Several factors may contribute to this observation. First, the Q-sorts at age 4 are more reliable, since three teachers typically contributed to the CC Q-composites at that age, whereas at age 7, typically only one teacher described each child. A second attenuating factor is that nine teachers were involved in Q-sorting when the children were 4-year-olds, while 67 teachers contributed Q-sort descriptions of the children at age 7. Third, the elementary-school teachers necessarily developed their knowledge of the children in a more restricted context than that available to nursery school teachers who see the children at work, at rest, at play, alone, and with peers. Fourth, and perhaps most critical, children are active, developing creatures; new information, new experiences, and new efforts to integrate information and experiences serve to modify earlier-established orientations on the world and to transform behaviors. Seven-year-olds simply have had more developmental time than 4-year-olds and, for this reason alone, will have evolved further from the way they were at age 3.

Relations between O-Indices of Ego-Control and Ego-Resiliency at Age 3 and S-Data at Age 7. The final sets of data to be presented derive from data in the S-domain, scores obtained from self-descriptions provided by the children at age 7, and the preferences expressed by them for television programs classified into several broad categories.

The children were given a 19-item set of descriptive phrases and asked to "describe the child in this picture," the picture being a color Polaroid picture of the subject placed on a stand to encourage detached evaluation and thus benefit discrimination. The children were instructed to place the cards in one of five clearly labeled categories ranging from "Very Much Like the Boy/Girl in This Picture" to "Not At All Like the Boy/Girl in This Picture." Because of the age of the children, an unforced distribution was used. Following completion of the self-description, the child was asked to use the cards once again to describe the child in the picture in the way his/her classmates would describe him/her. The adjectives selected for the task were pretested for vocabulary level and, as an additional check on understandings, the child was asked to read aloud each word and to indicate any adjectives that had unclear meaning. The adjectives were familiar to and comprehended by the children.

The results of multiple-regression analyses, completed according to the format described earlier, are presented in Table 4.

It is of interest to note that children appear to respond in a more discriminating way when describing themselves according to their construals of their classmates' perceptions of them than when under the self-descriptive instructions. Asking children to consider their classmates' impressions of them requires greater objectivity and appears to have resulted in more candid responses.

Table 4 Self-descriptive items at age 7 significantly associated with ego-control and ego-resiliency as specified by independent Q-sort descriptions of the children at age 3

	Age 7			
Self-Descriptive Q-Items	*Sex*	*UCQ_3*	*$ResQ_3$*	*$R \times UC$*
My classmates say I am helpful	.04F[a]			
My classmates say I am shy	.04F			
My classmates say I worry	.002M			
My classmates say I get mad easily	.03M			
My classmates say I obey	.04F	0.1O		
My classmates say I am neat		0.5O		
I am lazy		.007U		
My classmates say I am lazy		.000U		
I am shy				.03RO
My classmates say I like to be the best				.02BU

[a] Letters following the significance levels indicate the group favored in the comparison: *M*ale vs. *F*emale; *U*ndercontrolled vs. *O*vercontrolled; *R*esilient vs. *B*rittle.

Results of these analyses indicate that children judged as undercontrolled at age 3 say their peers would describe them at age 7 as lazy, less neat, less obedient—adjectives clearly connecting with the conceptual definition of undercontrol. Early-evaluated ego-resiliency does not produce significant results except when conjoined with ego-control. Resilient, overcontrolled children say they are shy, while brittle undercontrolling children indicate their classmates think they like to be the best. The adjective self-descriptions are also sex-differentiating. Girls describe themselves in the peer condition as significantly more helpful, shy, and obedient, while boys in the same condition say these are more worried and more easily angered. These results are attenuated to some degree by our inability to use the forced-choice Q-sort format with children at this age. It is likely that greater discrimination would have resulted if effects due to the operation of response sets could have been lessened.

Early ego-control and ego-resiliency are found to be associated with the television-program preferences of boys and girls at age 7. Children were asked to indicate their favorite television program, and the nominated programs were subsequently grouped into one of nine categories: family situation comedies, educational television, cartoons, children's programs (non-cartoon), game shows, aggressive shows (crime shows and westerns), sports, cultural programs (ballet, music, dramatic theatre), and miscellaneous. The multiple regression analysis strategy earlier-described was applied to the television preference data. Preference for family situation shows was expressed by girls ($p < .007$) and by children seen as both resilient and undercontrolling (ER × EC) at age three ($p < .004$). Aggressive television programs were preferred by boys ($p < .003$) and by children seen as brittle and undercontrolling (ER × EC) at age three ($p < .05$). Cartoon shows (typically Saturday morning cartoon programs) were preferred by children described as brittle and nonresilient at age 3 ($p < .001$). These data are of considerable interest because they suggest that television programs have a differential "pull," depending upon the personality characteristics of the child. Children "at risk" for watching TV programs in which violence and aggression are featured (crime shows and westerns) are those children who, it might be argued, are most likely to be influenced by the program's content.

The findings in the S-domain deriving from self-descriptive adjective *Q*-sorts not only fit well with the results of analyses in the O-domain; they also provide additional support for our conceptualizations of ego-control and ego-resiliency and attest again to the salience of these dimensions over time.

Going Further

The present report, it should be remembered, is an interim and selective accounting of our longitudinal journey; the study continues, and our effort to make sense of our data continues. There is no need now for a discursive discussion. As we have gone along, we have communicated our scientific (and personal) beliefs, preferences, goals, understanding, and puzzlements. Our results have been conveyed and commented upon. We expect this report to be superseded as progress is made on three major analytical themes now being pursued.

Shortly, we will be involved in evaluating the data from the assessment being completed at the preadolescent age of 11 years. (In addition, we are planning for the assessment to be conducted at age 14, when the children are well into adolescence). The host of assessment data soon to be available will abruptly double the length of time spanned by our longitudinal study, from 4 years (age 3 to age 7) to 8 years (from age 3 to age 11). The kind of analyses reported here will be extended to new data, further to evaluate the consequentiality, direct and via transformation, of early character structure for later personality, social behavior, and cognitive status. . . .

A second analytical focus will be on systematically relating the extensive L-, O-, and S-data available regarding the parents to the qualities of their children as evaluated concomitantly and years later. These data already have received some attention, and relationships have begun to emerge that we judge to be exciting and of great implication.

Our third analytical preoccupation, now underway, is an attempt to better understand personality differences and personality similarities by better understanding the psychological demand qualities of the situations in which these differences and similarities are observed. Just as one can scale or order individuals with respect to various personality dimensions, one can scale or order situations with respect to various facets of their "evocativeness." A *Q*-set has been developed and is being applied to describe situations as they would (or should) register on a hypothetical normative individual. By using this *Q*-set to characterize each of the many experimental situations encountered by our subjects in the course of longitudinal study, we expect to be able to then order the situations experienced with regard to various "presses" and "pulls." Subsequently, it may be feasible to perceive, more abstractly and more functionally than before, the nature of the situations that differentially influence the behavior of individuals varying with respect to personality. We are especially keen on the possibility this approach may have for offering a conceptual understanding of the kinds of situations differentially responded to by the sexes.

Plans for future analyses, however, are not the note on which we shall end this long essay. Instead, and at the risk of seeming presumptuous, we wish to suggest two guiding recognitions that the study of personality development might well adopt in its empirical and conceptual future.

There has been disappointment with the empirical results regarding personality development accruing in the scientific literature. Relationships have been weak and inconsistent; lawfulness has been hard to find. In response to these failures of expectation, some psychologists have become disillusioned about the scientific possibilities of the field. Others have sought a larger principle that could underlie the erratic empirical accomplishments to date and have converted the observation of poor lawfulness from one time to another to an assertion of a conceptual viewpoint: There is little implication of character structure at one stage for character structure at a later stage, because situations and environmental contexts change with time. By simply assuming behavior to be largely and directly a function of the operative situational context, a quite sufficient explanation of the observed absence of lawfulness is claimed.

As is now well recognized, this "reconciling" explanation is logically flawed because it depends upon often unrecognized and often unexamined assumptions (e.g., J. Block 1975, 1977; Epstein 1979). Positive assertions predicated only on failures to reject the null hypothesis are difficult to justify seriously. All one needs to do to fail to reject the null hypothesis is to execute research of poor quality and to evaluate research badly. Studies lacking in statistical power, using measures that are invalid or unreliable, and evaluated naively will continue to provide "evidence" for "personality inconsistency." A better examination of the nature and basis of the developmental "discontinuities" that doubtless will be found to exist must first await research that brings to a sufficient point of precision and accuracy the specification of the psychological qualities being studied in individuals over time and over context. The road to improving the quality of our empiricism is long and difficult, but there is good reason to believe psychology can go much further than yet it has. In making this progress, we anticipate that ancient methodological principles, some of which have been incorporated in our longitudinal study, will prove worthwhile.

In the last 15 years or so, the field of developmental psychology has been dominated by issues of cognitive development. The journals record this general emphasis; due homage especially should be paid Piaget for his important contribution to the recognitions won. But, for all the importance and even centrality of cognitive psychology for the understanding of many aspects of behavior, it should also be realized that cognitive psychology, as generally conceived and generally studied, deals with only a small portion of the mental lives, the experience, and the consequently forged behaviors of individuals. The psychological world of the individual is surprisingly seldom occupied by the purely cognitive problems with which psychologists have been prone to concern themselves. Cognition in everyday life is not oriented around such problems as pouring water into containers of different shape or the factors influencing the swing of a pendulum. Paradigmatic and essential to study though such cognitive problems are, they are problems without a social or interpersonal context, placed before an individual presumed to function without passions and without highly personal, often behaviorally preempting affect-optimizing criteria.

Thus, psychological thinking about how cognitive structures are created and transformed has derived primarily from consideration of how children interact with the physical world. In the version of the physical world provided to the child, the child observes a "reality" that is impressively orderly and follows clearly inferable rules. The child can test the nature of this reality by actions, actions that elicit direct, immediate, unequivocal feedback from the world. Further, and for entirely useful reasons, the cognitive problems employed are selected to be distant from the central motivational system of the child so that the "cool" process of cognitive structural development can be perceived most purely, without the intrusive influence of "hot" motivations.

But children live in an interpersonal world as well, a world which, depending on time, place, and person, can be far more central, psychologically, than the physical world. And, they must construct intake, output, and integrational structures for dealing with this interpersonal world. The social world is complex and perhaps ultimately fractious, behaving in ways only fuzzily comprehensible. Efforts by the child to test the nature of the interpersonal reality by acting upon it have erratic or dim results; social feedback is often indirect, delayed (sometimes forever in the interpersonal sphere), and equivocal, permitting only the uneasiness of uncertain inference instead of the pleasure of certain deduction afforded by the physical world. Because there is little or no feedback on the basis of which to build cognitive structures for dealing with the social world, the child must evolve and apply not-so-cognitive structures functional enough or sufficient for the predication of behavior. In doing so, the principles that come into play to govern such structures, construed in the absence of unmistakable, unambiguous feedback, are principles that are less than rational. They include the forms of irrationality called "primary process modes of thought" (Freud 1900/1953), the "cognitive illusions" observed by Tversky and Kahneman (e.g., 1974), and attributional errors in social judgment (e.g., Jones, Kanouse, Kelley, Nisbett, Valins and Weiner 1972), among others.

"Irrational" modes of perception, action, and cognition are due, at least in part, to intrinsic information-processing limitations of the human mind. But also, these intrinsic limitations develop the possibility for individuals to be influenced by strong motivations, pervading fears, and prevailing aspirations. The extent to which and way in which reigning passions will affect development of the not-so-cognitive structures can be expected to be a joint function of the efficacy of the reality-testing available to the developing child and the motivational stresses being endured.

The processes underlying the development of not-so-cognitive structures (premises, orientations, attitudes on the world, deutero-learnings, scripts, and so forth) are, of course, the processes underlying the development of personality or ego structures. Conceived in these terms, the timeliness of extended study of character development becomes apparent; there is promise of a fruitful integration of cognitive and personality psychology. In that integration, reasoning from the relationships reported earlier, we anticipate that concepts very much akin to ego-control and ego-resiliency will be found useful.

The research reported is being supported by a National Institute of Mental Health Research Grant MH 16080 to Jack and Jeanne H. Block and by a

National Institute of Mental Health Research Scientist Award to Jeanne H. Block. The ordering of the authors' names is immaterial; they could as well be reversed. As with other "projects" we have parented and nurtured, we both have contributed, differently but equally. We wish to express our appreciation to the children and their families who continue to participate in our longitudinal study. Much has been asked of them; they have responded with a grace and enthusiasm that we find affirming. We are grateful to the teachers, both at the Harold E. Jones Child Study Center and in the cooperating Bay Area elementary schools who have devoted many hours to completing the Q-sort descriptions upon which our analysis depend heavily. The administrative staff in these schools also have facilitated our research efforts in many ways for which we are thankful. We are deeply appreciative of the research staff, Myrna Walton, Jolinda Taylor, Judy Casaroli, Mark Haarz, Joy Moore, Mimi Rosenn, Rachel Melkman, Suzie Schmookler, Tammy Socher, Jon Feshbach, Elaine Simpson, Marjorie Hayes, Jackie Heumann, and Betty Goodman, whose diligence, sensitivity, and commitment during the process of data collection were essential to the success of our research venture. In addition to participating in data collection, Drs. Anna von der Lippe and Ellen Siegelman importantly contributed to the development of the assessment battery for the 3-year-olds. Finally, we wish to thank our colleague, Professor David Harrington, for the many responsibilities he assumed on this project over the years, participating in data collection, supervising the scoring and coding of the data, managing the complex data bank, and for his many psychological perceptions.

REFERENCES

ACHENBACK, T. M., AND WEISZ, J. R. Impulsivity-reflectivity and cognitive development in preschoolers: A longitudinal analysis of development and trait variance. *Developmental Psychology*, 1975, *11*, 413–414.

AINSWORTH, M. D. S., AND WITTIG, B. A. Attachment and exploratory behavior in one-year-olds in a strange situation. In B. M. Foss (Ed.), *Determinants of infant behavior* IV. London: Methuen, 1969.

ANDERSON, S., AND MESSICK, S. Social competency in young children. *Developmental Psychology*, 1974, *10*, 282–293.

BANTA, T. J. Tests for the evaluation of early childhood education: The Cincinnati Autonomy Test Battery (CATB). In J. Hellmuth (Ed.), *Cognitive studies* (Vol. 1). New York: Brunner/Mazel, 1970.

BARKER, R. G., DEMBO, T., AND LEWIN, K. Frustration and regression: An experiment with young children. *University of Iowa, Studies in Child Welfare*, 1941, *18*, 1–314.

BAUMRIND, D. The development of instrumental competence through socialization. In A. D. Pick (Ed.), *Minnesota symposium on child psychology* (Vol. 7). Minneapolis: University of Minnesota Press, 1973.

BELL, R. Q., WELLER, G. M., AND WALDROP, M. F. Newborn and preschooler: Organization of behavior and relations between periods. *Monographs of The Society for Research in Child Development*, 1971, *36*, 1–2 (Whole No. 142).

BLOCK, J. *An experimental investigation of the construct of ego-control.* Unpublished doctoral dissertation, Stanford University, 1950.

BLOCK, J. *The Q-sort method of personality assessment and psychiatric research.* Springfield, Ill.: C. C. Thomas, 1961.

BLOCK, J. *The challenge of response sets.* New York: Appleton-Century-Crofts, 1965.

BLOCK, J. *Lives through time.* Berkeley, Calif.: Bancroft Books, 1971.

BLOCK, J. *Recognizing the coherence of personality.* Unpublished manuscript, University of California, Berkeley, 1975.

BLOCK, J. Advancing the science of personality: Paradigmatic shift or improving the quality of research? In D. Magnusson and N. S. Endler (Eds.), *Psychology at the crossroads: Current issues in interactional psychology.* Hillsdale, N.J.: Lawrence Erlbaum Associates, 1977.

BLOCK, J. Review of H. J. Eysenck and S. B. G. Eysenck, *The Eysenck Personality Questionnaire.* In O. Buros (Ed.), *The eighth mental measurement yearbook.* Highland Park, N.J.: Gryphon, 1978.

BLOCK, J., AND BLOCK, J. H. An investigation of the relationship between intolerance of ambiguity and egocentrism. *Journal of Personality,* 1951, *19,* 303–311.

BLOCK, J., BLOCK, J. H., AND HARRINGTON, D. M. Some misgivings about the Matching Familiar Figures Test as a measure of reflection-impulsivity. *Developmental Psychology,* 1974, *10,* 611–632.

BLOCK, J., BLOCK, J. H., SIEGELMAN, E., AND VON DER LIPPE, A. Optimal psychological adjustment: Response to Miller's and Brofenbrenner's discussions. *Journal of Consulting and Clinical Psychology,* 1971, *36,* 325–328.

BLOCK, J., AND PETERSON, P. Some personality correlates of confidence, caution, and speed in a decision situation. *Journal of Abnormal and Social Psychology,* 1955, *51,* 34–41.

BLOCK, J., AND THOMAS, H. Is satisfaction with self a measure of adjustment? *Journal of Abnormal and Social Psychology,* 1955, *51,* 254–259.

BLOCK, J., AND TURULA, E. Identification, ego-control and adjustment. *Child Development,* 1963, *34,* 945–953.

BLOCK, J. H. *An experimental study of a topological representation of ego structure.* Unpublished doctoral dissertation, Stanford University, 1951.

BLOCK, J. H. *Familial and environmental factors associated with the development of affective disorders in young children.* Paper presented at the National Institute of Mental Health Conference on Mood and Related Affective States. Washington, D.C., November, 1976. (a)

BLOCK, J. H. Issues, problems, and pitfalls in assessing sex differences: A critical review of the *Psychology of sex differences. Merrill-Palmer Quarterly,* 1976, *22,* 283–308. (b)

BLOCK, J. H., AND BLOCK, J. An interpersonal experiment on reaction to authority. *Human Relations,* 1952, *5,* 91–98.

BLOCK, J. H., AND BLOCK, J. *The California Child Q-Set.* Institute of Human Development, University of California, Berkeley, 1969. (In mimeo)

BLOCK, J. H., AND BLOCK, J. *Fire and young children: A study of attitudes, behaviors, and maternal teaching strategies.* Technical Report for Pacific Southwest Forest and Range Experimental Station, Forest Service, U.S. Department of Agriculture, 1975.

BLOCK, J. H., BLOCK, J., AND FOLKMAN, W. *Fire and children: Learning survival skills.* U.S. Department of Agriculture Forest Service Research Paper, PSW-119, 1976.

BLOCK, J. H., BLOCK, J., AND HARRINGTON, D. *Sex-role and instrumental behavior: A developmental study.* Paper presented at the meeting of The Society for Research in Child Development, Denver, April, 1975.

BLOCK, J. H., AND MARTIN, B. Predicting the behavior of children under frustration. *Journal of Abnormal and Social Psychology,* 1955, *51,* 281–285.

BUSS, A. H., AND PLOMIN, R. *A temperament theory of personality.* New York: Wiley, 1975.

CAMPBELL, D. T., AND FISKE, D. W. Convergent and discriminant validation by the multitrait-multimethod matrix. *Psychological Bulletin,* 1959, *56,* 81–105.

CATTELL, R. B. *Personality and motivation structure and measurement.* New York: World Book Company, 1957.

CATTELL, R. B. *Personality and mood by questionnaire.* San Francisco: Jossey-Bass, 1973.

CHESS, S., THOMAS, A., AND BIRCH, H. Characteristics of the individual child's behavioral response to the environment. *American Journal of Orthopsychiatry,* 1959, *29,* 791–802.

CLECKLEY, H. M. *The mask of sanity* (4th ed.). St. Louis: C. V. Mosby Co., 1964.

COHEN, J. Partialed products *are* interactions; partialed powers *are* curve components. *Psychological Bulletin,* 1978, *85,* 858–866.

COHEN, J., AND COHEN, P. *Applied multiple regression/correlation analysis for the behavioral sciences.* Hillsdale, N.J.: Lawrence Erlbaum Associates, 1975.

DEPREE, S. *Time perspective, frustration-failure and delay of gratification in middle-class and lower-class children from organized and disorganized families.* Unpublished doctoral dissertation, University of Minnesota, 1966.

EHRMAN, D. M. *A preliminary investigation of a new research method.* Unpublished doctoral dissertation, Stanford University, 1951.

EPSTEIN, S. The stability of behavior: I. On predicting most of the people much of the time. *Journal of Personality and Social Psychology,* 1979, in press.

ERIKSON, E. H. Sex differences in the play configurations of preadolescents. *American Journal of Orthopsychiatry*, 1951, *21*, 667–692.

EYSENCK, H. J. *The biological basis of personality.* Springfield, Ill.: C. C. Thomas, 1967.

FENICHEL, O. *The psychoanalytic theory of neurosis.* New York: Norton, 1945.

FLAVELL, J. H. *The development of role-taking and communication skills in children.* New York: Wiley, 1968.

FREUD, S. *The interpretation of dreams.* In *The standard edition of the complete works of Sigmund Freud.* Vols. 4–5, 1953. London: Hogarth Press, 1953. (Originally published 1900)

FROSCH, J. The relation between acting out and disorders of impulse control. *Psychiatry*, 1977, *40*, 295–314.

GOVE, F., AND AREND, R. *Competence in preschool and kindergarten predicted from infancy.* Paper presented at the biennial meeting of the Society for Research in Child Development, San Francisco, March, 1979.

GREEN, B. F. In defense of measurement. *American Psychologist*, 1978, *33*, 664–670.

GUILFORD, J. P. Factors and factors of personality. *Psychological Bulletin*, 1975, *82*, 802–814.

HARRINGTON, D., BLOCK, J. H., AND BLOCK, J. Intolerance of ambiguity in preschool children: Psychometric considerations, behavioral manifestations, and parental correlates. *Developmental Psychology*, 1978, *14*, 242–256.

HARTMANN, H., KRIS, E., AND LOEWENSTEIN, R. M. Comments on the formation of psychic structure. *The Psychoanalytic Study of the Child*, 1946, *2*, 11–38.

HUMPHREYS, L. G. Notes on the multitrait-multimethod matrix. *Psychological Bulletin*, 1960, *57*, 86–88.

HUNT, J. MCV. *Intelligence and experience.* New York: Ronald Press, 1961.

JONES, E. E., KANOUSE, D. E., KELLEY, H. H., NISBETT, R. E., VALINS, S., AND WEINER, B. *Attribution: Perceiving the causes of behavior.* Morristown, N.J.: General Learning Press, 1972.

JUNG, C. G. *Psychological types.* New York: Pantheon, 1923.

KAFRY, D. Fire survival skills: Who plays with matches? Technical Report for Pacific Southwest Forest and Range Service, U.S. Department of Agriculture, 1978.

KAGAN, J. Body build and conceptual impulsivity in children. *Journal of Personality*, 1966, *34*, 118–128.

KAGAN, J. Biological aspects of inhibition systems. *American Journal of Disadvantaged Children*, 1967, *114*, 507–512.

KAGAN, J., AND KOGAN, N. Individual variation in cognitive processes. In P. Mussen (Ed.), *Carmichael's manual of child psychology* (3rd ed., Vol. 1). New York: Wiley, 1970.

KAGAN, J., AND MESSER, S. B. A reply to "Some misgivings about the Matching Familiar Figures Test as a measurement of reflection-impulsivity." *Developmental Psychology*, 1975, *11*, 244–248.

KAGAN, J., ROSMAN, B. L., DAY, D., ALBERT, J., AND PHILLIPS, W. Information processing in the child: Significance of analytic and reflective attitudes. *Psychological Monographs*, 1964, *78*, no. 1. (1, whole no. 578)

KELLER, A., FORD, L. H., AND MEACHAM, J. A. Dimensions of self-concept in preschool children. *Developmental Psychology*, 1978, *14*, 483–489.

KLEIN, G. S. Need and regulation. In *Nebraska Symposium on Motivation*, ed. M. R. Jones, vol. 2. Lincoln: University of Nebraska Press, 1954.

KREBS, D., AND STURRUP, B. *Altruism, egocentricity, and behavioral consistency in children.* Paper presented at the meeting of the American Psychological Association, New Orleans, September 1974.

KRIS, E. *Psychoanalytic explorations in art.* New York: International Universities Press, 1952.

LEWIN, K. *A dynamic theory of personality.* New York: McGraw-Hill, 1935.

LEWIN, K. *Principles of topological psychology.* New York: McGraw-Hill, 1936.

LEWIN, K. *The conceptual representation and the measurement of psychological forces.* Durham, N. C.: Duke University Press, 1938.

LEWIN, K. *Field theory in social science.* New York: Harper, 1951.

LOWENFELD, M. *The Lowenfeld Mosaic Test.* London: Newman Neame, 1954.

MACCOBY, E., AND JACKLIN, C. *The psychology of sex differences.* Stanford, Calif.: Stanford University Press, 1974.

MCREYNOLDS, P. The Rorschach concept evaluation technique. *Journal of Projective Techniques*, 1954, *18*, 60–74.

MURPHY, L. B. A longitudinal study of children's coping methods and styles. *Proceedings of the Fifteenth International Congress of Psychology*, Brussels, 1957, pp. 433–436.

MURPHY, L. B. *The widening world of childhood: Paths toward mastery.* New York: Basic Books, 1962.

PIAGET, J. *The construction of reality in the child.* New York: Basic Books, 1954.

PIAGET, J., AND INHELDER, B. *The child's conception of space.* London: Routledge and Kegan Paul, 1956.

REVELLE, W. Personal communication. December 16, 1976.

ROBINS, L. N. *Deviant children grown up.* Baltimore: Williams & Wilkins, 1966.

ROSENTHAL, D. *Genetic theory and abnormal behavior.* New York: McGraw-Hill, 1970.

ROTTER, J. B. Generalized expectancies for internal versus external control of reinforcement. *Psychological Monographs,* 1966, *80,* no. 1 (whole no. 609).

RUBIN, K. H., AND SCHNEIDER, F. W. The relationship between moral judgment, egocentrism, and altruistic behavior. *Child Development,* 1973, *44,* 661–665.

RUTHERFORD, E., AND MUSSEN, P. H. Generosity in nursery school boys. *Child Development,* 1968, *39,* 755–765.

SANDER, L., JULIA, H., STECHLER, G., AND BURNS, P. Continuous 24-hour interactional monitoring of infants reared in two caretaking environments. *Psychosomatic Medicine,* 1972, *34,* 270–282.

SANDER, L., STECHLER, G., JULIA, H., AND BURNS, P. Early mother-infant interaction and 24-hour patterns of activity and sleep. *Journal of American Academy of Child Psychiatry,* 1970, *9,* 103–123.

SCHILLER, J. *Child care arrangements and ego functioning: The effects of stability and entry age on young children.* Ph.D. dissertation, University of California, Berkeley, 1978.

SIEGELMAN, E., BLOCK, J., BLOCK, J. H., AND VON DER LIPPE, A. Antecedents of optimal psychological adjustment. *Journal of Consulting and Clinical Psychology,* 1970, *35,* 283–289.

SMITH, R. J. *The psychopath in society.* New York: Academic Press, 1978.

THOMAS, A., CHESS, S., AND BIRCH, N. G. *Temperament and behavior disorders in children.* New York: New York University Press, 1969.

TVERSKY, A., AND KAHNEMAN, D. Judgment under uncertainty: Heuristics and biases. *Science 185,* September 27, 1974.

WATERS, E., AND SROUFE, A. The stability of individual differences in attachment. In *The Organization of development and the problem of continuity in adaptation,* ed. A. Sroufe (Chair). Symposium presented at the meeting of The Society for Research in Child Development, New Orleans, 1977.

WHALEN, C. K., AND HENKER, B. Psychostimulants and children: A review and analysis. *Psychological Bulletin,* 1976, *83,* 1113–1130.

WHITE, R. W. Motivation reconsidered: The concept of competence. *Psychological Review,* 1959, *66,* 297–333.

WITKIN, H. A., AND GOODENOUGH, D. R. *Field dependence revisited* (ETS RB-76-39). Princeton, N.J.: Educational Testing Service, 1976.

WITKIN, H. A., AND GOODENOUGH, D. R. Field dependence and interpersonal behavior. *Psychological Bulletin,* 1977, *84,* 661–689.

ZIGLER, E., AND TRICKETT, P. K. IQ, social competence, and evaluation of early childhood intervention programs. *American Psychologist,* 1978, *33,* 789–798.

19

Developmental Analysis of the Role of Social Comparison in Self-Evaluation

Diane N. Ruble, Ann K. Boggiano, Nina S. Feldman, and Judith H. Loebl

Recent theoretical approaches to social development have emphasized a kind of self-socialization process (Maccoby and Jacklin 1974; Hartup, note 1) in which children are viewed as active processors of social information, seeking norms or guidelines to define appropriate behavior and to evaluate themselves. One particularly important source of information during this self-socialization process is the peer group—that is, how one's own behavior compares to relevant others. This social comparison process is thought to be central to self-evaluation in adults (Festinger 1954; Suls and Miller 1977), but there has been little attention directed to its role in the development of children's knowledge about themselves. Yet the impact of peers would seem to be of special interest in the study of early self-socialization. Not only do peers represent a major category of socializing agents (along with parents, teachers, and the media), but they also are likely to be an increasingly salient source of information with age, since the amount of time children spend with peers expands dramatically as children leave home and enter school.

The purpose of the present investigation was to examine age-related changes in the role of peers in children's self-evaluations in an achievement context. Since awareness of the importance of realistic self-evaluation may be viewed as a major and implicit goal of socialization, the point at which social comparison information begins to have an impact on children may be considered as a kind of milestone in the self-socialization process. In addition, age-related changes in the information used for achievement-related self-evaluation may be relevant to understanding such important developmental shifts as an increased correlation between test anxiety and test performance during the early years of school (Hill and Sarason 1966) and age-related decreases in positive evaluations of the self (e.g., Nicholls 1978; Ruble, Parsons, and Ross 1976). The few previous studies relevant to this issue suggest that children may not begin to use social comparison information until after about 8 years of age (Nicholls 1978, 1979; Ruble, Parsons, and Ross 1976; Veroff 1969). However, such studies have not been directly concerned with the role of peer comparison in self-evaluation, and the methods used may not have been adequate tests of these processes in young children.

In the present two studies, an attempt was made to maximize the availability of social comparison and to examine directly the changing role of this kind of information in children's self-evaluations. In contrast to the earlier research, in the present studies the information was presented concretely in terms of specific comparison to others (e.g., other children or performance representations were actually present) rather than abstractly in terms of general social norms (e.g., how most children of a given age perform), a distinction shown to have a major effect on adults' use of information (e.g., Borgida and Nisbett 1977). Also, multiple response measures were used to minimize the possibility of artifactual null effect findings for young children because of failures to understand a particular measure. Finally, extensive pilot testing and manipulation checks insured that the children at all ages understood and remembered the information provided.

In the first study, subjects performed a task in the presence of three peers. After they had finished, they were told how well they had done (outcome information), how well their peers had done (social comparison information), and were asked to make evaluative judgments about themselves and the task.

Method

Subjects.   The subjects were 52 first graders and 52 second graders from a racially mixed (10%–15% nonwhite)[1] public school serving a primarily middle-class area. The children were tested in the spring of the school year. Equal numbers of girls and boys in each grade participated in the study. First and second graders were chosen as subjects, since this is the time period during which a number of cognitive and social changes possibly related to social comparison are thought to occur (Veroff 1969).

Procedure.   The children were tested in groups of four (two boys and two girls of the same grade) by a white female experimenter during a 30-minute session. Children were randomly assigned to groups and to Outcome × Social Comparison conditions. The children were seated at separate desks some distance apart. Large pieces of cardboard served as screens, or partitions. The experimental task that the children were to perform was to arrange a series of five cartoon cards (similar to the cards used in the Wechsler Intelligence Scale) to form a story. Actual performance on the task was ambiguous enough for perceived outcome to be manipulated by the experimenter through verbal feedback.

Before the children did the story task, they were given instructions in the use of the rating scales. Special training and test booklets were constructed containing both a series of 5-point ratings scales (which were used to measure ability, effort, and task difficulty ratings) and a series of yes-no scales (which were used for memory check questions). Each scale was illustrated by a cartoon relevant to the judgment. For example, the scale used to rate effort was illustrated by a cartoon of a boy lifting weights. The measure of affect was a cardboard face with a movable mouth which could be easily bent by the children into smiles or frowns. This kind of rating scale has been used previously and has been matched with observer ratings of facial expressions (Ruble, Parsons, and Ross 1976). All children were able to respond appropriately to practice questions contained in the training booklet.

The children were then instructed about the task and were told to begin. When each child had arranged the cards to make a story, the experimenter looked at and collected the cards. Feedback was given to the children about their own outcome (whether they had successfully arranged the cards in the correct order) and about the performance of the other three children (all succeed/all fail/ no information). The experimenter spoke very quietly and music was played in the background, so the feedback given to each child was not overheard by the others. The order of presenting the outcome and social comparison was counterbalanced.

After the presentation of feedback, the children were instructed to use the face and the test booklet to answer questions about the task. All questions were read out loud and were similar to those used in previous studies (e.g., Ruble, Parsons, and Ross 1976). For example, to assess affect the experimenter asked, "How do you feel about how you did in the story-card game? Show me by moving the mouth on the face." The order of presentation of these questions was counterbalanced. The children then responded to the memory check questions concerning their own and the others' outcomes. A second task (hidden pictures) was given to all children at this time, using the same procedures, to assess the generality of effects. At the end of the session, children in failure conditions were given a hidden picture task for which they received success feedback; all children were warmly praised, thanked, given small prizes, and asked not to discuss the study with their friends.

Results

Preliminary analyses examining the consistency of the children's judgments across the two tasks showed that the correlations between the two ratings for affect, effort, and ability were all greater than .50 ($p < .001$) and were strong within each grade. Correlations between task difficulty ratings were somewhat lower, though significant (.30, $p < .01$). These results suggest that the dependent measures were fairly reliable and that the effects were generally due to the independent variables rather than to specific tasks. Thus, to avoid redundancy and because the data are similar for both tasks, only data for the first task (the story task) are discussed, though the means for Task 2 are available for inspection in Table 1.

The dependent measures were analyzed by means of a 2 × 2 × 3 multivariate analysis of variance, with grade, outcome, and social compari-

Table 1 Mean ratings as a function of grade level, outcome, and social comparison information—study 1

Type of rating and social comparison condition	Grade level and outcome condition							
	First				Second			
	Success		Failure		Success		Failure	
	M	SD	M	SD	M	SD	M	SD
Task 1								
Ability								
Others fail	4.1	1.5	3.6	1.6	4.1	1.1	3.2	1.0
Others succeed	5.0	.0	3.2	1.1	4.7	.5	2.0	1.0
No information	4.8	.7	2.8	1.2	4.3	1.0	3.4	1.7
Effort								
Others fail	4.6	1.3	3.9	1.8	4.0	1.7	5.0	.0
Others succeed	4.3	1.4	4.6	.9	4.0	1.3	4.2	1.4
No information	3.5	2.1	4.5	.9	4.4	.7	5.0	.0
Task difficulty								
Others fail	2.4	1.7	3.6	1.6	2.4	1.7	3.8	1.4
Others succeed	2.3	2.0	3.3	1.4	1.4	.7	2.4	1.3
No information	3.5	2.1	3.0	1.2	1.4	.7	3.3	1.2
Affect								
Others fail	2.6	2.6	1.3	2.6	3.3	.9	−.9	3.6
Others succeed	3.6	.5	.1	2.4	2.8	1.2	.9	2.9
No information	2.9	2.8	1.4	2.6	2.9	1.2	.1	3.6
Task 2								
Ability								
Others fail	5.0	.0	3.8	1.4	4.6	.9	3.8	.8
Others succeed	5.0	.0	3.0	1.0	5.0	.0	2.6	1.2
No information	4.5	1.4	3.4	1.3	4.0	.9	3.4	1.5
Effort								
Others fail	4.1	1.5	4.3	1.4	3.6	1.9	4.2	1.4
Others succeed	4.2	1.4	4.4	.9	4.2	1.0	4.3	1.4
No information	3.3	2.0	4.8	.7	4.1	1.0	5.0	.0
Task difficulty								
Others fail	2.9	1.6	3.6	1.3	1.6	.9	3.0	1.4
Others succeed	1.9	1.5	3.1	1.4	3.1	1.6	3.0	1.5
No information	2.4	1.9	3.3	1.3	2.4	1.7	3.8	1.5
Affect								
Others fail	3.6	.7	1.1	2.9	3.2	1.3	−1.0	3.0
Others succeed	3.4	.7	1.3	2.2	3.1	.9	.9	2.9
No information	1.3	3.4	2.6	1.4	3.0	1.3	.4	3.6

Note. The higher the number, the greater the judged ability, effort, task, difficulty, and positive affect. Ratings of affect range from −4 to +4. Ratings of the other measures range from 1 to 5. $n = 9$ for others fail and others succeed conditions; $n = 8$ for control groups.

son as the three between-subjects factors. (See Table 1 for cell means.) Not surprisingly, the analysis revealed that the children's judgments were strongly affected by their own success/failure outcome, $F(5,88) = 24.59$, $p < .001$. Univariate analyses revealed that the predicted effects were significant for all dependent variables except effort.

If the subjects' self-evaluations were also affected by the information regarding the other children's performance, then a main effect of social comparison would be expected. That is, the children should perceive their level of affect, ability, and effort and the difficulty of the task to be higher when others did poorly at the task than when others did well. In contrast to these predictions, neither a main effect of social comparison nor a Grade × Social Comparison interaction emerged as significant from the analysis. Instead, the Grade × Outcome × Social Comparison interaction reached significance, $F(10, 176) = 1.96$, $p < .05$. The only significant univariate interaction was Outcome × Social Comparison for ratings of ability, $F(2, 92) = 4.11$, $p < .05$. Post hoc tests of these means revealed the nonsignificant tendency ($p < .20$) for children in the failure condition to rate their ability as lower when told that others succeeded than when told that others failed, as expected, whereas counter to predictions, the children who succeeded tended ($p < .20$) to rate their ability higher when told that the other children also succeeded.

Within-grades analyses were also performed because of the three-way interaction with grade found in this study and because developmental differences were a central focus of the study. There were significant ($p < .01$) effects of success/failure outcome for both grades for ratings of affect, ability, and task difficulty. No other effects were significant for the first graders. The second graders made use of the social comparison information in the predicted direction for task difficulty ratings ($p < .05$), rating the task as more difficult when others failed. In addition, the Outcome × Social Comparison interaction for ability ratings was significant ($p < .01$). Children who failed rated their ability lower when others succeeded ($p < .025$), as predicted. Thus, consistent with previous research, only the second graders made any use at all of the social comparison information.[2]

Memory checks.   Correct recall of the information provided was high. Less than 15% of the children made any errors at all. A series of 2 × 2 chi-square comparisons revealed no significant differences on frequency of errors between grade levels, type of information, or order of information presentation. Thus, forgetting per se does not seem sufficient to explain the generally low use of the social comparison information. An additional analysis of variance using only subjects who recalled all the information correctly revealed no changes in the pattern of results.

Sex and order effects.   Analyses including sex and order of information presentation yielded no effects for sex of subject. Only one significant effect of order was found, the Order × Social Comparison interaction for ratings of affect, $F(2, 80) = 4.34$, $p < .05$. The use of the social comparison information tended to be in the predicted direction only when presented second or most recent, consistent with recency effects observed in moral judgment studies with young children (e.g., Feldman, Klosson, Parsons, Rholes, and Ruble 1976).

Discussion

The results of Study 1 are consistent with the hypothesis derivable from previous research that the self-evaluations of young children are essentially unaffected by social comparison. Relative to success/failure outcome information, the effect of the social comparison information was weak. In fact, this study showed almost no use of social comparison information by the first graders and unpredictable use of that information by the second graders.

Study 2

Although the results of Study 1 are consistent with previous studies, it may be premature to conclude that information about the performances and abilities of others is not at all important to children below the second-grade level. Previous work has indicated that the most important result of social comparison is not ability level per se, but rather maximizing future outcomes based on knowledge of ability relative to others (Festinger 1954; Jones and Regan 1974). Procedures used in previous studies have promoted evaluation simply for evaluation's sake, without making salient the future utility of accurate ability evaluation. Young children's use of social comparison information may be enhanced when accurate self-appraisal becomes a purposive tool for obtaining maximum outcomes. Because young children may prefer a more objective or autonomous basis for self-evaluation (Veroff 1969), it is not clear whether social comparison is irrelevant to the evaluative judgments of young children, or whether the information search process may simply have been truncated by the sufficiency of the more concrete or familiar objective (outcome) feedback provided in Study 1.

The purpose of Study 2 was to reexamine conclusions regarding age-related increases in use of social comparison for self-evaluation in a situation that provided a strong incentive to engage in the social comparison of abilities and in which objective information about a success/failure outcome was unavailable. Children at three age levels were required to make a competence-related decision affecting the number of prizes obtained ("Can I beat the other children?"). Maximum outcome depended on an accurate ability appraisal. In an attempt to decrease the impact of outcome information inferred from absolute level of performance, all subjects were given ambiguous performance feedback (50% correct), thereby increasing the potential impact of the comparative information. In addition to the behavioral prediction measure, ratings of affect and ability level comparable to Study 1 were included. Performance differences of self and others were concretely displayed and available throughout the experimental session to increase the salience of the comparative information and to ensure that any differences in use of the information did not result from differential retention abilities.

Method

Subjects.   The subjects were 90 kindergarten (K), second-, and fourth-grade children from a middle-class area recruited through their schools and through a local newspaper, who were tested during the spring of the school year. Subjects were randomly assigned to one of three social comparison conditions (relative success, relative failure, or no information control). There were an approximately equal number of males and females in each condition across various grade levels.

Procedure.   Children were escorted into the experimental room by a white female experimenter and were told that they would be playing a ball-throwing game. They were also told that a number of children their age from another school had played the game. The object of the game was to successfully throw four balls into an upright basketball hoop placed 1 foot (.3 m) from a corner of the wall in the experimental room. The hoop was purposefully concealed by a 3-foot (.9-m) curtain to manipulate performance, and the children had to throw the ball over the curtain to make a basket. The children were instructed to look carefully at the target hoop when the curtain opened and to remember its location, since they would not be able to see the hoop when the curtain was closed and the ball tossing began. They were told that the purpose of concealing the target hoop was to provide information to teachers and researchers about how well children *remember* the location of an object (the target hoop) after it is no longer visible. To make the task more enjoyable the children were told that they could win prizes if they played the game well.

After a brief practice session without performance feedback to acquaint the children with the general procedure, the game began. Each child was given four chances to throw the ball into the hoop concealed behind the curtain, and all children were told that they successfully made baskets after the second and fourth shots, with feedback given after each try.

To make children's scores salient, the experimenter pasted two paper balls signifying the two successful shots and two paper x's signifying unsuccessful shots on a piece of white cardboard and mounted each child's score under his or her name on an upright scoreboard. The scores of eight hypothetical other players were then shown to the subjects, according to condition, by placing the other children's cards indicating their scores on the same scoreboard. Subjects assigned to the relative failure condition were shown scores of others indicating that all of the other children had successfully scored more than the subjects—That is, seven children had scored four and one child had scored three out of the possible four hits. Children assigned to the relative success condition were shown scores indicating that only one of the eight children had managed to hit the target area once. Children assigned to the control conditions were not given information about the other players' scores. To ensure comprehension of the performance level of self and others, all subjects were asked how many successful shots they had made and, for those assigned to the experimental conditions, how many others had played and how many successful baskets each of the other children had made. All but one fourth-grade girl reported the scores of self and others (when appropriate) accurately. She was replaced by another fourth-grade girl.

To assess use of social comparison information in making ability-related decisions, the children were provided with the following instructions.

Tomorrow you will have the chance to play the ball-throwing game again, and two girls [boys] your age will be playing the game in this room with you. Now, I want you to think about how good you are at the ball-tossing game [as the experimenter pointed to the scoreboard], because I am going to ask you whether you think you could beat *both* of the other two children who will be here tomorrow to play the ball game, whether you think you could beat just *one* of the two children, or whether you don't think you could beat *either* of the two children when you play the game with them tomorrow. But before you tell me your decision, I want you to listen carefully to the rules of the game.

The "rules" were designed to provide the incentive to consider the comparative information when making the ability-related decision. The number of prizes that could be won for each subject, depending on condition, was made contingent on accurate self-appraisal by means of social comparison. Specifically, children were told that they would have to beat *exactly* how many other children they said they could beat on the second game to win *any* prizes at all. Thus, a penalty was imposed for underestimating or overestimating ability level relative to others. To illustrate, children were given the following instructions: "See the prize that is wrapped on the bottom shelf here? You can win that prize if you say you can't beat the other two children on the second game and really *don't* beat either of them tomorrow." The experimenter then pointed to a second shelf displaying one "extra" wrapped prize next to a cartoon drawing of one child and said, "See the extra prize on this shelf here? You can win the extra prize—two prizes in all—if you say you can beat and really do beat just one of the two children playing the game tomorrow." Finally, children were shown a third shelf holding two extra prizes adjacent to pictures of two other children and were told,

> And you can win these two extra prizes—three prizes in all—if you say you can beat both children and really do beat the two children tomorrow in the ball-tossing game. But think carefully about how good you are at the game, because if you don't beat *exactly* how many children you say you can beat on the second game, then you won't win any prizes at all.

After the rules had been thoroughly described and subjects indicated that they understood the costs of inaccurate predictions (both for underestimating or overestimating their own relative ability level), subjects' comprehension of the rules was tested by asking them to describe the three alternative choices presented by the experimenter and the number of prizes they would win if they did or did not accomplish each goal. All children demonstrated full comprehension of the rules.[3] Subjects' decisions regarding the number of children they thought they could beat were then recorded. Afterwards, subjects were asked to rate how sure they were that they could beat one or both of the other children on 4-point scales ranging from "not at all" to "very sure." The scale was made of rectangles of increasing colored areas, comparable to a bar graph, and the order of presenting the questions was counterbalanced.

After these measures were taken, the experimenter pointed to the scoreboard and asked subjects to rate on the same 4-point scale how good they thought they were at this task and how happy they felt about how they did on the first game. The order of presenting these two questions was also counterbalanced. Also, subjects were asked open-ended questions as to why they rated their affect and ability levels as they did.

The last major dependent variable concerned children's recognition of an element of strategy in social comparison—choice of comparison others. Subjects were asked whether they would prefer to play against two of the children whose scores they had seen on the board or against two children whose scores they had not seen. This measure was included to test the ability of children of different ages to make inferences regarding the probability of successfully beating children whose skills at the task relative to their own were known or unknown after being successful or unsuccessful relative to the known others.

Subjects in the experimental group were then asked, "Did you or the others make more baskets on the first game?" to see whether they could compare the performance of others to their own when called on to do so. All subjects correctly reported whether they or the others had demonstrated superior performance on the first game. Finally, subjects in the relative failure condition were given a puzzle task for which they received feedback indicating relative competence, and all subjects were warmly thanked and praised.

One week after the experimental session, the experimenter dispensed the prizes. The children were told that they would all be given the maximum number of prizes that could have been won on the second game, since scheduling the last few weeks of the school year made it impossible for each child to have the opportunity to play the additional game. They were then allowed to select three prizes and were praised for their cooperation.

Results

Prediction decisions. A Grade (K, 2, 4) × Social Comparison Condition (failure/control/success) analysis of variance was performed on children's decisions to try to beat zero, one, or two others in the subsequent game. The results revealed a main effect for condition, $F(2, 81) = 4.40, p < .05$, such that overall predictions of beating others was highest under success and least under failure, as expected. This use of the information should be interpreted in the context of a significant Grade × Condition interaction, $F(4, 81) = 2.90, p < .05$, demonstrating the predicted increased use of the information with grade level, as shown in Table 2. Within-grades analyses revealed that significant differences in predictions across conditions were evidenced only for the fourth graders, with significant differences between all pairs of cells at this age level.[4]

Certainty ratings. In accordance with predictions, a Grade × Condition × Certainty Level (with repeated measures on subjects' certainty in beating one or both others) analysis of variance demonstrated a main effect of condition, $F(2, 80) = 4.12, p < .05$, indicating that subjects were more certain of beating others under success, followed by control, and then failure. A main effect of confidence level also emerged, $F(2, 80) = 56.70, p < .001$, indicating, as expected, that subjects were more certain of beating one other than of beating two others.

The Grade × Condition × Certainty Level interaction also approached

Table 2 Mean ratings on the dependent variables as a function of grade level and social comparison condition—study 2

	Condition					
	Failure		Control		Success	
Grade and dependent variable	M	SD	M	SD	M	SD
Kindergarten						
Predictions	1.1	.74	1.1	.88	1.1	.88
Certainty	2.9	.91	2.8	1.1	3.0	.85
Ability	2.9	.88	2.7	.82	3.3	.48
Affect	3.2	.92	3.3	.95	3.0	.82
Preference for unknown others	.40	.52	—		.56	.53
Second						
Predictions	.5	.71	1.0	.67	.7	.82
Certainty	2.4	.63	2.3	.64	2.7	.50
Ability	2.5	.71	2.8	.42	2.8	.63
Affect	2.9	.32	3.0	.74	2.9	.74
Preference for unknown others	.89	.33	—		.20	.42
Fourth						
Predictions	.4	.52	1.1	.32	1.7	.48
Certainty	2.1	.55	2.4	.81	3.1	.37
Ability	2.2	.63	2.8	.42	2.7	.48
Affect	2.4	.70	2.7	.68	3.0	.67
Preference for unknown others	.90	.32	—		.57	.54

Note. The prediction measure ranges from 0 to 2, and the preference measure represents proportions of subjects who responded in the cell. All other measures range from 1 to 4. $n = 10$ per cell.

significance, $F(4, 80) = 2.44$, $p = .054$; and within-grades analyses were performed. These analyses revealed a main effect of certainty ($p < .05$) for each age group such that subjects felt more certain of beating one other than of beating two others. Although subjects at all grades thus appeared to be considering their general probability of success in beating one or two others in this response, only the fourth graders' predictions were significantly influenced by social comparison information, $F(2, 27) = 7.06$, $<.01$. (See Table 2.)

Ability and affect ratings. A Grade × Condition analysis of variance revealed a main effect for grade, $F(2, 81) = 3.14$, $p < .05$, indicating that kindergartners rated their ability level higher than second and fourth graders. The effect for condition was only marginally significant, $F(2, 81) = 3.06$, $p = .053$, though consistent with the direction of the other measures. Within-grades analyses, however, indicated that significant differences across conditions in rating ability level were evidenced only for fourth graders, $F(2, 27) = 3.82$, $p < .05$ (see Table 2), with success ratings higher than failure ratings. No significant effects were found for affect in either the overall analysis or the within-grades analyses. However, the means were in the predicted direction only for fourth graders, consistent with the earlier analyses.

Open-ended. Open-ended reasons as to why the children rated their ability and affect levels the way they did were coded as social-comparison relevant (e.g., "I must be pretty good because I beat all the others"), absolute (e.g., "2 out of 4 baskets is a good score"), or neither absolute nor comparative (e.g., "I did my best"; "I don't know"). The latter category of irrelevant answers were most frequently used by the children to explain both ability and affect ratings (57% and 71%, respectively). Answers related to absolute level of performance were used somewhat frequently (33% and 24%), whereas social-comparison relevant responses were used least often by the children (10% and 5%). However, consistent with fourth graders' use of the social comparison information in making ability evaluations, this age group demonstrated more frequent use of social-comparison relevant responses to explain ability evaluations (40%) than both kindergartners (5%) and second graders (0%; $p < .01$, using a Fisher exact test.)

Preference for known versus unknown comparison others. A Grade × Condition (failure/success) analysis of variance, using an arc sine transformation, was performed on the proportion of subjects who preferred to play against others whose ability levels were known or unknown. A main effect of condition emerged, $F(1, 49) = 5.63$, $p < .05$, indicating that the social comparison information had the predicted effect on preference behavior. A greater proportion of subjects who had experienced relative failure tended to choose unknown others more as future competitors than did subjects who succeeded. As expected, however, this strategical use of social comparison information was found to vary with grade level. (See Table 2.) A significant Grade × Condition interaction, $F(2, 49) = 4.08$, $p < .05$, revealed that in contrast to the direct self-evaluative measures, the second graders as well as the fourth graders were found to base strategy decisions on social comparison.

Additional analyses. Although several marginally significant interactions with sex of subject were found, no consistent pattern of these effects emerged. The only significant effect was a Sex × Condition × Level of Certainty interaction, $F(4, 136) = 3.55$, $p < .01$; in the control condition, males were more certain of beating two others than females, whereas the reverse occurred in the success condition.

General Discussion

Evaluation of one's achievements is theoretically influenced by social comparison processes (Festinger 1954; Suls and Miller 1977). Yet in spite of the importance of achievement evaluation once children enter a classroom environment, the present two studies found that the impact of social comparison information was weak and in fact did not consistently and systematically affect self-evaluations until surprisingly late (i.e., fourth grade).

Although these findings are consistent with previous studies relevant to developmental changes in the use of social comparison information for self-evaluation (e.g., Nicholls 1978; Ruble, Parsons, and Ross 1976), they seem to conflict with other types of studies. For example, Masters (1971) has reported that even nursery school children are influenced by social comparison, as measured by self-reinforcement after a child has been differentially reinforced relative to a peer. Similarly, children as young as 5–6 years of age show interest in comparing their performances with others (Dinner 1976; Ruble, Feldman, and Boggiano 1976) and make decisions about choice of comparison others in a manner predictable from Festinger's (1954) original formulations (Feldman, see note 2).

How may these apparent discrepancies across studies in the development of social comparison processes in young children be reconciled? We suggest viewing social comparison as a multifaceted process, similar to recent models of the development of perspective taking (Flavell 1977), such that several levels in the social comparison process develop at different times. Some of these steps include (a) motivation to seek information about others' performances, (b) strategies employed in the information seeking, (c) use of the information for tangible rewards, and (d) use of the information for abstract assessment and behaviors based on such assessment. For example, children's initial comparisons seem to be at an overt physical level, such as equalizing the number of rewards received (Masters 1971), and do not involve inferences that are removed from concrete differences, such as self-evaluation or behavior based on self-evaluations (Boggiano and Ruble 1979; Spear and Armstrong 1978). Thus, it is not that the present results are inconsistent with other studies of social comparison in young children, but rather that these studies are concerned with different steps in the process.

Why the use of social comparison may be a relatively late-developing phenomenon may be better explained by differences in the weighting of information for self-evaluation than by changes in children's capacities to evaluate themselves or to compare others' performances with their own. Young children's capacity to evaluate themselves has been documented in a number of studies, including for example, (a) the present finding of young children's differential response to success/failure outcome (Study 1) and certainty of beating competitors (Study 2), (b) children's differential self-reward on the basis of relative outcomes (Masters, 1971), and (c) kindergarten-aged children's ability to use social comparison in the evaluation of another child shown on videotape (Shultz and Butkowsky 1977; Feldman, Akst, Higgins, and Ruble, see note 3).

Differential weighting of the social comparison information may have occurred for several reasons. First, the children's focus of attention was most likely directed externally toward the specific features of the task that they (as actors) were engaged in. Thus, their assessment of performance based on direct experience with the task may have dominated evaluations, and such salience effects are likely to be especially pronounced in young children (Feldman et al. 1976; Pryor, Rholes, Kriss, and Ruble, see note 4). A second possible explanation concerns social-environmental changes with age in the emphasis placed on social comparison, such as teachers' criteria for grades or praise. Finally, young children's perceptions that their abilities are unstable or rapidly changing may make relative performance information essentially meaningless, in that their concern is more with how to improve their skills (e.g., to get more correct answers) than with evaluating their current level of competence (Feldman and Ruble 1977).

A word of caution is in order at this point. It is possible that children younger than 8 years of age do use social comparison information for self-evaluation in more familiar settings where comparative information is repeatedly available. Indeed, research is currently under way to examine these processes in more naturalistic settings. However, it may also be argued that social comparison information is more ambiguous and more obscured in natural settings and that the present experiments are a necessary initial test of children's inclinations to use such information when it is highly salient and relevant to the judgments at hand.

Although the specific reasons for a shift in the use of social comparison information cannot as yet be pinpointed, noting the existence of this shift is important for several reasons. For example, these findings suggest that the role of peers in the self-socialization process undergoes significant qualitative as well as quantitative changes. That is, children's initial comparisons are apparently not concerned with self-evaluation or self-definition, but rather with making sure that they are getting their fair share of rewards or with desiring to be similar to others. Thus, until children recognize that the outcomes of comparisons have deeper implications for the self, competition or comparative evaluation may have little long-lasting impact.

This research was supported in part by a Biomedical Science support grant and by Grant MH 27196-01, both from the National Institutes of Health. Some of the results were previously reported at the Society for Research in Child Development meetings at Denver, Colorado, April 1975. We thank D. Axsom for helpful comments on an earlier draft.

NOTES

1. Hartup, W. W. *Toward a social psychology of childhood.* Presidential Address to Division 7 at the annual meeting of the American Psychological Association, Washington, D.C., September 1976.
2. Feldman, N. S. *Developmental changes in social comparison interest.* Paper presented at the annual meeting of the American Psychological Association, San Francisco, August 1977.
3. Feldman, N. S., Akst, L., Higgins, E. T., and Ruble, D. N. *Young children's use of social comparison for self vs. other ability evaluations.* Unpublished manuscript, 1978. (Available from N. S. Feldman, Educational Testing Service, Princeton, N.J. 08541.)
4. Pryor, J. B., Rholes, W. S., Kriss, M., AND Ruble, D. N. *A developmental analysis of rational vs. nonrational forms of attribution.* Unpublished manuscript, 1978. (Available from J. B. Pryor, Department of Psychology, University of Notre Dame, Notre Dame, Ind. 46556.)

REFERENCES

BOGGIANO, A. K., AND RUBLE, D. N. Competence and the overjustification effect: A developmental study. *Journal of Personality and Social Psychology,* 1979, *37,* 1462–1468.
BORGIDA, E., AND NISBETT, R. E. The differential impact of abstract vs. concrete information on decisions. *Journal of Applied Social Psychology,* 1977, *7,* 258–271.
DINNER, S. H. Social comparison and self-evaluation in children (Doctoral dissertation, Princeton University, 1976). *Dissertation Abstracts International,* 1976, *37,* 1968B. (University Microfilms No. 76-22, 634)
FELDMAN, N. S., KLOSSON, E., PARSONS, J. E., RHOLES, W. S., AND RUBLE, D. N. Order of information presentation and children's moral judgments. *Child Development,* 1976, *47,* 556–559.
FELDMAN, N. S., AND RUBLE, D. N. Awareness of social comparison interest and motivations: A developmental study. *Journal of Educational Psychology,* 1977, *69,* 579–585.
FESTINGER, L. A theory of social comparison. *Human Relations,* 1954, *7,* 117–140.
FLAVELL, H. H. *Cognitive development.* Englewood Cliffs, N.J.: Prentice-Hall, 1977.
HILL, K. T., AND SARASON, S. B. The relation of test anxiety and defensiveness to test and school performance over the elementary school year: A further longitudinal study. *Monographs of the Society for Research in Child Development,* 1966, *31,* (2, Serial No. 104).
JONES, S. C., AND REGAN, D. T. Ability evaluation through social comparison. *Journal of Experimental Social Psychology,* 1974, *10,* 133–146.
MACCOBY, E. E., AND JACKLIN, C. N. *The psychology of sex differences.* Stanford, Calif.: Stanford University Press, 1974.

MASTERS, J. E. Social comparison by young children. *Young Children,* 1971, *27,* 37–60.

NICHOLLS, J. G. The development of the concepts of effort and ability, perception of academic attainment, and the understanding that difficult tasks require more ability. *Child Development,* 1978, *49,* 800–814.

NICHOLLS, J. G. The development of perception of own attainment and causal attribution for success and failure in reading. *Journal of Educational Psychology,* 1979, *71,* 94–99.

RUBLE, D. N., FELDMAN, N. S., AND BOGGIANO, A. G. Social comparison between young children in achievement situations. *Developmental Psychology,* 1976, *12,* 192–197.

RUBLE, D. N., PARSONS, J. E., AND ROSS, J. Self-evaluative responses of children in an achievement setting. *Child Development,* 1976, *47,* 990–997.

SHULTZ, T. R., AND BUTKOWSKY, I. Young children's use of the scheme for multiple sufficient causes in the attribution of real and hypothetical behavior. *Child Development,* 1977, *48,* 464–469.

SPEAR, P. S., AND ARMSTRONG, S. Effects of performance expectancies created by peer comparison as related to social reinforcement, task difficulty, and age of child. *Journal of Experimental Child Psychology,* 1978, *25,* 254–266.

SULS, J. M., AND MILLER, R. C. (Eds.). *Social comparison processes: Theoretical and empirical perspectives.* Washington, D.C.: Hemisphere, 1977.

VEROFF, J. Social comparison and the development of achievement motivation. In C. P. Smith (Ed.), *Achievement-related motives in children.* New York: Russell Sage Foundation, 1969.

20

The Emergence
of Gender Differences

Juanita H. Williams

It makes no difference whether pink is for girls and blue for boys, emotionality for girls and rationality for boys, or the other way round. What does make a difference is that a difference is made. . . . . It is the bifurcation by sex that is the fundamental fact.

—Jessie Bernard, *Women and the Public Interest,* 1971

· ·

At birth infants are identified by their biological sex as female or male. This is probably the most important category to which humans can be assigned, and it is the only one other than race which is invariant, except in rare instances. Why is this characteristic of the person so important? Perhaps nothing else so surely attests to the sexually dimorphic nature of human experience; sex is important because it is one of the major determinants of who and what the baby will be, and the kinds of life experiences it will have.

The question of whether males and females are different psychologically, and if so, what are the differences and their determinants, is presently eliciting much comment from both scientists and non-scientists. Widely held beliefs based both on myths and on research are being challenged. In this chapter we shall consider the nature, extent, and importance of observable sex differences in infancy and childhood, and some explanations for their development.

Reprinted from *Psychology of Women,* 2nd ed., by Juanita H. Williams, by permission of W. W. Norton & Company. Copyright 1983, 1977, 1974 by Juanita H. Williams.

Defining Gender Differences

In examining and evaluating the research on gender differences we want to keep in mind what we mean by "gender differences." When we speak of a gender difference we mean a difference in the *average* performance of females and males in a given area of behavior. For example, a difference in spelling ability means that the *average* performance of one sex is higher than the *average* performance of the other. The performance of individuals of each sex varies around the average for the sex so that some persons in the high group score lower than some persons in the low group. The two sexes overlap in this way on all human intellectual and behavior characteristics. Therefore, the important general rule is that a given psychological gender difference is never absolute, in the sense that one sex has the characteristic and the other does not. Rather, individuals regardless of sex vary greatly in the extent to which they manifest a particular characteristic, such as verbal ability or dependency behavior. This means that when we look at measures of such behavior we invariably find that differences within a sex category, for example, differences *among* women, are greater than differences *between* women and men.

In addition, there are certain limitations to the literature on gender differences that can make interpretation problematic (Hoffman 1972). First, judgments about the behavior of a particular individual or individuals may be relevant to a given group. For example, if some girls in a nursery school setting are rated high on "aggressiveness" it may mean that they are high compared to other girls in the group, or to the rater's conception of what constitutes aggressiveness among girls in general. Similar behaviors by boys in the group might be seen as average, since aggressive behavior, as we shall see later, is more normative for boys than for girls. Second, it is risky to generalize results obtained from one sample or population to another. Most generalizations are valid only within certain contexts and under certain conditions. It has been found, for instance, that under certain conditions white females are more easily influenced by others than are white males; yet the case is reversed for black females and males, such that white females and black males are more easily influenced by others than are their counterparts. This and other studies indicate that race, social class, family structure, and other variables can make generalizations from one group to another inappropriate and misleading.

A third problem in interpreting gender differences is the differential maturity rate of boys and girls. Girls are physically and developmentally more mature than boys are from birth through puberty, and this difference complicates comparisons between the sexes. Finally, there is the problem, common to many fields, of the definition of concepts. Studies of dependency behavior, for example, may use different definitions of dependency, so that they are actually looking at different phenomena, leading to inconsistencies in the interpretations of the results (Hoffman 1972). These problems and limitations will be pointed out in appropriate contexts as we go along.

Infancy

Few aspects of human development are so impressive as the growth and individuation of the infant during the first year of life. Observing the relatively helpless, supine, and asocial neonate[1] whose behavioral repertoire consists of a small collection of unlearned responses, one is awed by the transformation a few months later into a mobile, curious, imitative, and socially responsive young person who often wields a Promethean power to shape the behavior of others and to manipulate the environment. As a function of maturation and interaction with the contingencies of the environment, the infant's behavior becomes increasingly diversified, differentiated, and complex. Do certain aspects of this behavior become differentiated along sexually dimorphic lines in infancy? Do boys and girls differ behaviorally from birth? . . .

Social and Affective Behavior

The earliest manifestations of affect, or emotional response, in infants are crying, including fretfulness and irritability, and smiling to social stimulation. Studies based on naturalistic observation of infants in their homes tend to report that boys sleep less than girls and cry more during the first three months (Moss 1967). The difference in irritable crying diminishes, however, as a function of age, and later crying in older babies is more likely to be a reaction to fear, anxiety induced by separation, or some other exogenous event.

There is an interesting difference in maternal response to crying of boy and girl babies at three weeks and three months. Mothers were more likely to respond to irritability in girl babies at both ages, whereas at three weeks maternal contact did not vary with irritability of boy babies; in fact, by three months, mothers were less likely to contact the more irritable boys (Moss 1967). A learning-theory explanation for this seems plausible: mothers' contact response, contingent upon babies' response, is reinforced by girls more than by boys. That is, boys are less likely to quiet in response to handling. Of course, such a negative relationship may also reflect the mother's belief that boys should learn to endure discomfort, to rely less on comforting. Such a belief in the desirability of fostering toughness in boys could mediate maternal stoicism to their early wailing.

The so-called social smile appears in infants between two and eight weeks old. It is most often elicited by the human face and voice, and peaks in frequency around four months. There is no indication of a sex difference in readiness or frequency of smiling; rather, smiling seems to be a function of temperament interacting with experience. One study revealed a tendency for smiling to be related to slow tempo and chubby body build in girls, but not boys. Also, smiling behavior was more stable for girls across time. Those who smiled more at thirteen months did so also at twenty-seven months. This relationship did not occur for boys (Kagan 1971).

The data on susceptibility to fear arousal in male and female infants are interdeterminant. How does one infer fearfulness in a preverbal infant? Typically, the behaviors include crying, "freezing," clinging to mother, or trying to reach her if separated. Are these reactions to fear-eliciting stimuli more typical of female than male infants? A few studies bear on this, and show the ambiguity of the results of the research. For example, one study considered reaction to separation in 67 babies of each sex at age eight months. The child was placed on the floor with a toy. When the child was involved with it, the mother, on signal, rose and left the room, closing the door behind her. The child was observed for two minutes. During this period, 52 percent of the girls and 47 percent of the boys continued to play happily with the toy. Of the remainder, half fretted somewhat but did not cry intensely, while the other half cried very hard during the mother's absence. No significant difference was observed for these various reactions (Kagan 1971). While gender differences in irritability or fear did not occur within age groups, there were differences in the derivatives of these reactions when the infants were studied at twenty-seven months. Boys who had been most irritable at four months had lower vocabulary scores and less well-developed speech. Boys who were fearful at eight months were later more inhibited and apprehensive, staying closer to their mothers, than were the nonfearful controls. By contrast, girls who were irritable at four months became restless and active two-year-olds, and girls who were fearful at eight months were more verbal than the controls at twenty-seven months, and showed no need to stay close to their mothers. Thus irritability and distress seemed to have different meanings and different derivatives for the sexes. The crying, fearful boys became inhibited, shy two-year-olds; the same behaviors in four-month-girls were predictive of verbal, outgoing, precocious two-year-olds. Mothers are likely to react differently to fearful boys than to fearful girls, and this may account for the later observed differences.

Dependency is an extensively researched behavioral concept which has been widely held to characterize females more than males (Mischel 1970). To ask the question, Are infant girls more dependent than infant boys? points up a problem in evaluating the research on child development. Different observations may have quite different behaviors in mind when they are studying dependency in young children, so that the results may not be directly comparable to each other. For example, clinging, help-seeking, staying close to the mother, touching, wanting to be babied, crying in response to strangers, may all be part of a concept of dependency, but researchers may emphasize different aspects of it. Also, two hypothetical children might be equally dependent but one might manifest it by staying near the mother, the other by attention-getting behavior. In general, studies of dependency in young children have focused on proximity seeking, touching, and resistance to separation as indications of a child's need for reassurance in an anxiety-provoking situation.

When such studies use infants as subjects, they are usually conducted in a test situation in which the child's behavior and the mother-child interaction can be observed. Almost no studies include fathers. A recent review of studies of touching and proximity to parent and resistance to separation from parent included 22 studies of children aged three months to two years. Two-thirds of the measures showed no gender differences. Of the rest, girls had higher scores in the dependency direction on five measures, while boys had higher scores on six (Maccoby and Jacklin 1974). Clearly, for these kinds of infant dependence behaviors, boys and girls are more alike than they are different.

Some studies have sought the precursors of gender differences in later life in mothers' affective behavior toward boy and girl babies. Attachment behavior was studied between mothers and their infants at age twelve weeks, six months, and thirteen months. The researcher distinguished between two classes of attachment behavior: proximal and distal. Proximal behavior included physical contact, such as holding, kissing, touching, and caressing; distal behavior was contact other than physical, such as talking, smiling, and looking at each other. In these studies, mothers looked at and talked to their girl infants more from the earliest age. For the first six months they had more proximal contact with boy infants, perhaps because of their greater wakefulness. But after six months a reversal occurred, and girl babies had more of both proximal and distal contact with their mothers. By age thirteen months, the boys ventured farther from their mothers, stayed away longer, and returned to touch her less frequently. In the same situation, girls vocalized more, stayed closer, and touched their mothers more often (Lewis 1972). The results appeared to show a stronger tendency for mothers of sons to encourage separation, exploration, and autonomy, while maintaining a closer interpersonal bond with daughters.

On factors such as warmth, nurturance, and acceptance, however, mothers evidently treat boy and girl babies about the same. Studies of parental warmth toward children, including 12 studies in which the children ranged in age from newborn to two years have been reviewed. Some of the studies measured more than one kind of parental behavior, such as affectionate touching, smiling at infant, and expression of positive attitude. Of 18 measures of such behavior, no difference was observed for 12. Of the remaining 6, 3 were in favor of girls and 3 of boys (Maccoby and Jacklin 1974).

In infancy, then, the conclusion is that gender differences in social and affective behaviors, including irritability, smiling, fear and anxiety, and dependency, have not been demonstrated. In early infancy boys may be awake more and be more fretful, but this difference does not persist. The derivatives of early behavior may differ, however, for the two sexes; for example, fearful eight-month-old boys were fearful two-year-olds, but the same was not true for girls (Kagan 1971). Perhaps because of different developmental time-tables a given behavior may have a different meaning for boys and girls at the same age.

The Emergence of Gender Differences

We want to look now at that period in the life span which includes childhood and early adolescence. By this time the young person has formulated an identity, and is discernibly different in personality and behavior from all other persons. Contributions from the uniquely given biological features and the uniquely experienced environmental events are inextricably meshed by this time, and one can hope only to discern the relative importance of one or the other to the observed manifestations of behavior. . . .

Social and Affective Behavior

Stereotypes about the ways that males and females are or ought to be as they interact with others in the social world are even more numerous and persistent than are those held to describe their intellectual differences. In our society females are supposed to inhibit aggression and sexual urges, to be passive, nurturant, attractive, and to maintain a poised and friendly posture with others. Males should be sexually aggressive, independent, and suppressive of strong emotions, especially anxiety (Kagan 1964). This discussion will concentrate on a few areas which seem especially important for the psychology of women, areas which not only have attracted much research attention but also have served as focal areas for strongly held beliefs about the differences between males and females. These areas are fearfulness and anxiety, dependency, nurturance and maternal behavior, and aggression.

Fearfulness and anxiety.   Most of the research does not make a definitive distinction between fear and anxiety. At the physiological level, they are closely related to each other. Both describe an arousal state which includes body changes, such as increased heart and respiratory rates, trembling, muscle tension, and sweating. Studies of fearfulness in children usually refer to a specific object or situation, such as fear of strangers or fear of being left alone. Anxiety often means a more generalized state of arousal, sometimes with nonspecific causes. A highly unpleasant state, anxiety is sometimes described as a feeling of impending disaster or of threat to one's well-being or self-esteem. People differ in their readiness to experience anxiety. Some become anxious only rarely or in certain situations such as stage fright; others feel anxious most of the time. All persons at times experience both fear and anxiety. Those who have a generally fearful outlook on life, who are timid and hesitant in their approach to most situations, and who have frequent and intense anxiety are impaired in their psychological functioning. Research on gender difference in fearfulness and anxiety uses three basic methods: observation of subjects' behavior in certain situations, subjects' self-report of their feelings, and physiological measures.

Studies of children who have not learned to read and write have used reports of observations by parents and teacher rating scales. For example, one classic study had parents keep a diary for three weeks of all the occasions when their children showed fear. In another study two- to six-year-old children were asked to do "frightening" things: approach a large dog, walk on an elevated board, go into a dark place, or investigate a loud noise. In neither of these studies was there any difference in the frequency of fear responses of boys and girls. In the latter, however, the girls were seen as displaying a greater intensity of fear than the boys. In other words, those girls who were afraid were more afraid, according to the observers, than those boys who were afraid (Jersild and Holmes 1935). More recent observational studies have not found consistent differences in fear or timidity for boys and girls (Maccoby and Jacklin 1974).

With subjects who can read and write, the most frequently used method of assessing levels of fear and anxiety is some kind of self-report. Typically the subject is presented with a set of items which reflect fearful and anxious feelings and behavior, such as "I am nervous about being alone at night," or "I am afraid of dying." There are many such inventories to measure anxiety in both children and adults. Of 26 such studies on subjects aged six and over,

9 found no gender differences. Where differences were found, girls scored higher (Maccoby and Jacklin 1974).

There are several possible explanations for these results. The first is that females are more fearful and anxious than males. But there are at least two reasons why this conclusion may not be valid. The first is the possibility that girls are more willing to admit to such feelings than boys are (Hill and Sarason 1966). Related to this is also the possibility that some of the tests are weighted with items which are closer to the kinds of things that boys get anxious about, thus arousing their defenses more and eliciting negative answers. For example, an item such as "Are you afraid something might happen to your body?" might arouse castration fears in more boys than girls, but the boys' defensiveness about castration fears could cause them to respond in the negative. Another suggestion is that the tests might be weighted with items which are more likely to elicit anxiety responses from girls. Girls are constantly being warned about strange men, lonely places, and other possible risks of sexual molestation. Such warnings and the fear they generate could generalize to other men, such as the doctor, and to a variety of unusual settings. One 45-item test had 10 items which were believed to elicit such fears. Such a test would be biased in favor of higher scores for girls (Maccoby and Jacklin 1974).

Some attempts have been made to learn about gender differences in anxiety by measuring the physiological responses of the body to induced fear. Subjects in the laboratory may be told that they are going to receive an electric shock or that they must take an important intelligence test. The body changes associated with anxiety are then measured. While some differences in physiological arousal have been reported, their relationship to fear states is not known (Duffy 1962). Such measures are not strongly related to self-report measures; that is, subjects with the strongest body arousal do not necessarily make the highest scores on an anxiety inventory.

In conclusion, the research on fear and anxiety indicates that females report themselves as more anxious than males. While they may in fact be more susceptible to anxiety, it is also likely that greater willingness to admit feelings, and factors in the tests themselves, contribute to the feelings. Observational and physiological studies have not revealed differences in behavior or body changes.

Dependency.   Infant studies of dependency behaviors such as seeking proximity with the mother, touching, and clinging, did not reveal gender differences. Studies of dependency in older children have dealt with a greater variety of behaviors, such as frequency of contact with teachers, help seeking, proximity to age-mates, and social interactions with adults and peers. Such studies usually rely upon observation, teacher or parent ratings, and self-report questionnaires. For example, three- and four-year-old children were given a puzzle that was too difficult for them to solve to observe their coping behavior. Boys were more likely to become emotional and disorganized, and more of them sought help with the problem. Girls asked for information, continued attempts to solve the problem alone, and sought contact with the experimenter (Zunich 1964). It was interpreted that the girls were more dependent in this study. However, others pointed out that the girls' contact-seeking was a coping attempt rather than an escape from threat (Maccoby and Jacklin 1974). A review of eight observational studies of children's dependency behavior with adults other than family revealed that five of them found no differences, while the rest were inconsistent (Maccoby and Jacklin 1974).

Studies which use ratings as contrasted to direct observation of behavior more often find girls higher in dependency, leading these reviewers to caution against over-reliance on such measures. A culturally imposed bias to perceive girls as more dependent than boys could operate to influence ratings in that direction. For example, if a teacher is asked to rate each child in her class for dependency on a five-point scale, her cultural assumptions about dependency in girls and boys could bias her ratings so that the girls appeared more dependent than the boys. The fact that dependency is less pejorative as a descriptor of girls than of boys would tend to enhance this effect.

Studies of social interaction with peers and affiliative behavior have revealed some different trends for boys and girls. Boys have been found to have more extensive social interaction with age-mates, and to play in larger groups in middle childhood, while girls of similar age are more likely to have intense personal relationships with one or two close friends (Waldrop and Halverson 1973). Further evidence that girls' friendships involve greater intimacy was found in a study of self-disclosure or the willingness to be open with others in a self-revealing encounter (Rivenbark 1971). Both sexes were more self-disclosing to their best same-sex friends than to their best opposite-sex friends, but girls were more disclosing to both male and female friends than boys were. Also, girls disclosed more to their mothers than boys did to their fathers. In a related study, it was found that girls would permit more areas of their bodies to be touched by female and male friends, and by parents, than boys would (Jourard 1968).

These studies support a generalization that girls are more interested in the personal qualities of relationships and are more comfortable with intimacy than boys are. Other research found girls more oriented toward the gentler aspects of interpersonal relations and less toward the active aggressive possibilities. Also, they became interested in boys at an earlier age than boys became interested in them, and cared more about their personal appearance (Maccoby 1966).

Although varying in definitions of dependency, more studies find females to be higher on measures of dependency behavior (Mischel 1970). A longitudinal study of 44 males and 45 females over a twenty-five-year period found that dependency was a stable dimension for females but not for males (Kagan and Moss 1962). That is, girls who were considered to be dependent as children continued to be seen as dependent as they matured, while dependent boys did not necessarily grow up to be dependent men. It is reasonable to assume the cultural pressures operate differentially on the sexes with regard to dependency behavior. The experimental data suggest that one sex is not more emotionally dependent than the other during the first few years of life, but a continuation or persistence of dependent behavior is less likely to be tolerated in boys. If such behavior in girls is viewed more benignly by parents and reinforced later by males who are socialized to be helpful and to alleviate distress in females, then its continuity into maturity, such that those girls who were dependent grow into women who report themselves to be less self-sufficient and higher in need to be cared for, is not surprising.

While such findings propose different trends for the two sexes in various kinds of behavior commonly thought to reflect dependency, they cannot be interpreted as conclusive evidence for sex differences in dependency. The biggest problem in understanding the meaning of the research results was mentioned in the discussion of dependency in infants. Researchers in a general area of behavior, such as dependency, include different behaviors in their conceptualization, and use different methods for obtaining knowledge about the occurrence of such behaviors, with the result that inconsistencies and inconclusive results are common. Also, there is no consistent agreement on just what behaviors under what conditions constitute dependency. Whether a greater interest in intimacy in relationships is a sign of dependency is a matter of definition.

An example of terms being defined differently is the following: sometimes *attachment* is used to signify those behaviors that seek to maintain proximity and to resist separation, and *dependency* is reserved to mean physical dependency, as of the infant (Bowlby 1969). The term *dependency* has negative connotations, implying that it is culturally undesirable and should be eliminated from the child's repertoire. Attachment behavior, by contrast, is natural and functional for humans. Its continuation into adult life does not necessarily imply psychological pathology. Separating attachment behavior from the dependency concept would allow for more precise definition and would rid the research and its interpretation of the negative meaning which dependency gives it.

This approach is of special interest to studies of gender differences. If *dependency*, including all the behaviors subsumed under it, has pejorative connotations and if more studies find girls dependent, then it follows that the pejorative connotations become associated with girls and their behavior. The statement, "girls are more dependent than boys," has a certain stigma for girls, because in our society "dependent" qualities are less valued than "independent" qualities in behavior. The illogic of this is apparent when one looks at the behaviors that are considered to reflect "dependency" in the research. Some of them, such as interest in the interpersonal qualities of relationships and greater willingness to be open and self-disclosing, are positively valued even though the dependency rubric has meanings which are not. Future researchers in this area might do well to look more closely at the twin problems of definitions and values which characterize the literature on dependency.

Nurturance and maternal behavior. "*Nurturance*" means a readiness to give care and comfort to others, especially to those whose condition manifests such a need: the young, the weak, the sick. Much maternal behavior is nurturant involving taking care of and ministering to the needs of infants and children. Women throughout the world have always been far more likely than men to perform such a role and to be perceived as more nurturant by nature than men are. To the question, "Which sex is observably more nurturant?" on the basis of actual behavior, the answer is obvious. The question whether females have a greater readiness to be nurturant, perhaps on a biological basis, is more difficult to answer. Because of the current interest in women's roles and questioning of the traditional assignment to women of child care, the research in this area of gender differences may be the most socially relevant of all. Do males ever display "maternal" behavior, and if so, under what conditions? Is it feasible to consider a restructuring of society to include male involvement in the care of children, or is there a fateful bias which would run counter to such a shift?

Animal studies of maternal behavior are more plentiful than human studies. Because of the biological relationships between humans and other mammals, it is important to learn the extent to which maternal behavior in animals is sex linked; that is, the extent to which it is inevitably linked to the female condition, by hormones or other biological mechanisms.

The development of maternal behavior in rats is partially under hormonal control, but it is also affected by experience. It was shown that virgin females treated with blood plasma from females who had just given birth would develop such maternal behaviors as nest-building and licking and retrieving pups in about half the time it took untreated virgin females. This study also found that pregnant rats increased their maternal behavior toward other pups, but that the increase did not appear if the ovaries were removed. But experience with the young was also a factor. Both males and virgin females, deprived of gonads, developed maternal behaviors after a few days if presented with a fresh litter of pups each day. This finding suggests that there is a base level of readiness to respond to young that is independent of hormonal control and can be elicited by the stimulus of contact with the young (Rosenblatt 1969). Another study reported that the adult male's aggressiveness toward pups diminished after several fresh litters were supplied, and that nurturing behavior then appeared (Rosenberg et al. 1971).

The response of preadolescent rhesus monkeys to infants revealed that when young male-female pairs were presented with an infant, the females showed four times as much positive behavior toward it, including body contact, grooming and play, as the males did. The males, by contrast, showed ten times as much hostility to the infant (Chamov et al. 1967). In an earlier study if only a male was available, the infant persisted in its attempts to make body contact and eventually the male relented and held it for long periods (Harlow 1962).

Child-care participation by males varies much among subhuman primate species. For example, one study described a high level of involvement with juvenile care among young male hamadryas baboons. In that group, males display nurturant behavior toward the young before they themselves are adult (Kummer 1968). This child-care rehearsal seems to be preparatory for the male adult role, which includes a protective attitude toward his first consort, a juvenile female. His "maternal" behavior toward her seems to be a continuation of earlier practiced behaviors toward the very young of the group.

Such studies of other species indicate that maternal behavior is promoted to some degree by the sex hormones so that the females have a greater readiness to release such behavior when stimulated by the presence of young. Both sexes have the potential for appropriate child-care responses, however, and both virgin females and males can develop maternal behavior with continued exposure to infants, although in some species male aggres-siveness toward the young competes with the development of more positive behavior. When adult males participate in the care of children, as in the hamadryas, the juvenile males also show interest in them.

In humans very little is known about gender differences in nurturing potential. In most societies little girls receive early training for the mother role. In Indonesia they become surrogate mothers for their infant siblings when they are still children themselves. In our society they have dolls to play with to imitate the rituals of their mothers as they care for real babies. Given such initiations beginning early in life, it is difficult to learn what the con-tribution of nature is. Certainly among humans both sexes are able to behave in nurturing ways toward the young. Given that some base level of potential exists for both, it may be that the behaviors are simply elicited and reinforced earlier and more consistently for girls. Does male aggressiveness inhibit nurturing behavior in humans? The only hint of an answer to this question comes from observations of the androgenized girls reviewed in the last chapter (Money and Ehrhardt 1972). These girls were reported to be less interested in dolls than their nonandrogenized sisters were. Their interest in dolls was not measured systematically, however, but was based on their mothers' report. Since the mothers knew that the daughters had been influenced by male hormones, their observations were likely to be affected. Furthermore, girls differ greatly in their interest in dolls and doll play. The repertoire of nurturing behaviors which young girls have and boys do not, or which is larger and more predictable in girls, has not been demonstrated.

One study provides a sequel to the research on the nurturant behavior in childhood. Its findings challenge the often-repeated assertion that men are naturally uninterested and inept when exposed to newborn infants. Fathers and mothers of newborns were observed in the hospital. When the baby was brought in, the nurturant behavior, looking, holding, smiling, rocking, of each parent was observed. Except for smiling, fathers exhibited more such behavior than mothers did. When the parents were observed separately with the baby, fathers were at least as nurturant in their behavior as mothers were. The sample consisted of two groups of different backgrounds. The first group was well educated; and half the fathers had attended classes in childbirth and some had been present at their chil⅃'s delivery. The second group observed was in a working-class hospital; the group was racially mixed. None of the fathers in this group had been present at his child's birth. Yet all displayed interest in their infants, and a high level of nurturant behavior (Parke et al. 1972).

The question of the basis for and the relative strength of nurturing behavior in women compared to men continues to be the subject of vigorous debate. Since women are having fewer children, and some are choosing to have none at all, less of their lives is bound up in the nurturant role. Also, as mothers are increasingly occupied outside the home, their babies and chil-dren are being nurtured by mother surrogates, as they have traditionally been in some other parts of the world (Kitzinger 1978). Roles, too, are blurring, so that young fathers may be more involved in the care of their children than were their own fathers. For many, these changes may be superficial and may reflect necessity rather than desire, having nothing to do with natural proclivities, let alone parental instincts.

Some wonder if these egalitarian trends, accompanied by assertions that mothering is not for women alone and that fathers too can nurture their young, are not going against nature. Even feminists have been taking a second look at possible biological contributions to women's ubiquitous involvement in infant and child care (Lambert 1978; Rossi 1977; and in Goy and McEwen 1980). Feminist sociologist Alice Rossi, noting that 99 percent of human tenure on earth has been spent in hunter-gatherer bands, has asserted that the sexual division of labor, whereby lactating women carried and cared for babies and young children, was adaptive for group survival and therefore became genetically embedded in the species (Rossi 1977). Changes in social forms do not wipe out such predispositions. After examining the evidence for a biological potential for greater maternal investment in the child, exceeding any paternal investment, she concluded that an egalitarian ideology would run into profound difficulties when applied to child-rearing. Social and technological interventions that tend to minimize gender dimorphism in fundamental aspects of human life have the potential for interfering seriously in the process of mother-infant attachment—with critical implications for such human welfare issues as child abuse, delinquency, and other kinds of social and individual psychopathology. While not a call for a return to the asymmetries of traditional family roles, Rossi's proposal is for a better understanding of the possible biological substrates for the primary mother-child dyad.

A further example of the widely disparate positions taken by feminists on the nature-nurture spectrum is the recent work of psychoanalyst Nancy Chodorow (1978). She examined Rossi's (and others') "argument from nature" and the role-training argument (girls "learn" mothering by observation, imitation, and subtle ideological coercion) and found them either unsupported or too simplistic in their data and theoretical formulations. Instead, she has developed a psychoanalytic analysis to explain the pervasiveness of mothering by women:

> Women's capacities for mothering and abilities to get gratification from it are strongly internalized and psychologically enforced, and are built developmentally into the feminine psychic structure. Women are prepared psychologically for mothering throughout the developmental situation in which they grow up, and in which women have mothered them (p. 39).

She argues that development in the infantile period, particularly the resolution of the oedipus complex, entails different psychological patterns, which attenuate possibilities for parenting in boys, and enhance and extend them in girls. Because mothers have themselves been girls and have been mothered by women, they tend to sense a oneness and continuity with daughters, experiencing a daughter as an extension or double of the mother herself. Thus girls continue to remain part of the primary mother-child relationship longer, continuing the preoedipal attachment characterized by primary identification with the mother. Boys, by contrast, are experienced by their mothers as "male opposites," and are more likely to have been pushed out of the preoedipal relationship, having to curtail their empathic tie with their mother and to develop a more differentiated self.

Girls' identification processes are more continuously mediated by their ongoing relationship with their mother, whereas boys' are discontinuous owing to the necessity for them of earlier resolution of the oedipal conflict. Since girls do not need so strongly to deny preoedipal relational modes, continuation of or regression to these modes is not such a threat to their egos. They emerge, according to Chodorow's theory, with a basis for "empathy" built into their definition of self in a way that boys do not: "Because women are themselves mothered by women, they grow up with the relational capacities and needs, and psychological definition of self-in-relationship, which commits them to mothering. Men, because they are mothered by women, do not. Women mother daughters who, when they become women, mother" (p. 209).

Finally, in an early precursor to Chodorow's work, Margaret Mead, writing about the distinctions that societies make between boys and girls, suggested how boys raised by women must renounce their early experiences; and, poignantly, how girls raised with boys and men may hunger for theirs:

> Girls as well as boys may spend most of their time with men, busying themselves with masculine activities and pastimes. Or the children may spend most of their time with women. Then the boys also will learn to care for babies and cook, and they will go with their mothers and sisters to visit the newborn and mourn the dead. Later, all men will be left with a nostalgia for the childhood they shared with girls and women, but they will guard against it by renouncing all forms of tenderness, by speaking in loud, harsh voices, by making their stance aggressively masculine. . . . Or women may be left hungry for activity, . . . restless when they are confined to their homes, and chafing against their feminine tasks of tending the hearth and caring for the children. . . . (Mead and Heyman 1965, p. 100).

Aggression. The term *aggression* is used to apply loosely to a collection of behaviors whose general intent is to threaten or hurt another individual. In animal studies it usually covers acts of physical threat or attack, while in human studies it can mean these as well as negativistic, hostile acts, quarreling, and verbal abuse. The conditions under which aggressive behavior will occur and the sanctions for and against it vary widely across species, individuals, and cultures. A given individual often is inconsistent from time to time in his aggressive behavior even under similar conditions. Therefore an examination of the gender differences in aggressive behavior must begin with an understanding that such behavior, like other classes of behavior, has many sources of variation, of which sex is only one.

The evidence is very persuasive that males are more aggressive than females are. This generalization is supported by a large body of research including studies of a variety of human cultures and animal species. Reviews of more than a hundred studies of human sex differences in aggression revealed that males were more aggressive beginning around age two (Oetzel 1966; Maccoby and Jacklin 1974). In a cross-cultural analysis of differences in the behavior of children aged three to eleven, it was found that boys engaged in more rough-and-tumble play than girls, were more verbally aggressive, and were likely to react to an attack with counteraggression (Whiting and Pope 1973).

Evidence from primate studies echoes observations on humans. Male ground-dwelling Old World monkeys observed in their natural habitat engaged in much more rough-and-tumble play than females did (De Vore

1965). Such play in monkeys is a rehearsal for the adult role of dominance-seeking and defense of the group. Young male macaques (monkeys) reacted more aggressively to attack than young females did (Harlow 1962).

It has been suggested that differences in aggression are brought about by differential treatment of children (Feshbach 1970). This argument rests upon the idea that aggression is an acceptable component of the masculine model in our society but is not desirable or appropriate when incorporated by females. It is thought that because of this differential valuing, parents reinforce or at least permit the display of aggression in boys and punish or discourage it in girls. This explanation for the observed gender differences in aggression has been challenged. A review of studies on parental permissiveness for aggression (Maccoby and Jacklin 1974) revealed that there was no consistent evidence that parents were more tolerant of aggression in boys. There were some cross-sex effects, however. Fathers were especially severe in reprimanding sons for aggressive behavior, and were more permissive with daughters. Mothers, on the other hand, were more more lenient with sons' aggression or insolence than with daughters'. On the whole, the evidence does not support the hypothesis that differences in aggression are primarily the result of socialization practices. But if girls' universally observed lower level of verbal and physical aggressive behavior is not altogether or mostly the result of social inhibitions, then what is its origin? One alternative explanation is that these differences between the sexes, variable and modifiable as they are, come from a biological substratum. Though not as potent a determinant for human behavior as for animal behavior, this substratum accounts for the consistency of the gender differences in aggression across cultures and human groups.

The contention that the differences in aggression have a biological basis is centered on the following points: first of all, males are more aggressive than females in all societies for which evidence is available; second, the differences appear early in life, around age two to two and a half at a time when the available evidence indicates no differences in parental reward or punishment for aggressive behavior; third, similar differences are found in both human and subhuman species; and fourth, aggression is related to levels of sex hormones and can be changed by changing the levels of these hormones (Maccoby and Jacklin 1974). We have already considered material relating to the first three of these points. Evidence for the last point comes mostly from animal studies of the relationship between the sex hormones and behavior (Lunde 1973, and Money and Ehrhardt 1972). A few examples are presented here to suggest a possible parallel between animal and human behavior.

As we saw in the last chapter, when pregnant females are administered male sex hormones, their female offspring show masculine patterns of behavior. For example, masculinized female rhesus monkeys engaged in more rough-and-tumble play than is usual for the young female of the species (Young, Goy, and Phoenix 1965). Such play is functionally related to later aggressiveness in animals, although no such relationship has been established for humans. In the "tomboy" syndrome of girls androgenized *in utero,* an increased level of such play was observed (Money and Ehrhardt 1972). But the girls were not more aggressive in the sense of being antagonistic or hostile. The main component seemed to be an increased activity level

with liking for vigorous outdoor play. In these studies, prenatal androg-
enization did not result in a higher level of threatening or assaultive acts
toward others, the kind of aggression more frequently shown by boys.

The aggressive response of female monkeys treated with the male
hormone testosterone from age 6½ months has been recorded (Joslyn
1973). Three treated females and three untreated males were placed together and observed for thirty minutes a day during three time periods, at
ages 5–9½ months, 13½–16 months, and 25–27½ months. Before the testosterone treatment of the females, the males were dominant and more aggressive than the females. After the treatment began, the females became more
aggressive, and two of them attacked and subdued the two most dominant
males. These two females maintained their dominance until the end of the
study, long after the administration of testosterone was discontinued. Although the females became more aggressive vis-à-vis the males, their
rough-and-tumble play did not increase; rather, the male rough-and-tumble
play decreased from its earlier level. Thus the treatment of the female did
not change *her* rough-and-tumble play, but did change that of her male
playmate. A possible explanation for this is that the increase in aggression
and dominance by the females had the effect of subduing the normal
ebullience of the young males.

Some studies have shown correlations between levels of testosterone
and aggression in males; that is, higher levels of testosterone have been
found in more aggressive males, and vice versa. For example, one study
revealed that male prisoners with higher testosterone levels had committed
more violent crimes (Kreuz and Rose 1972). On the other hand, there is
some evidence that behavior affects testosterone level. When single male
monkeys were placed with all-female groups, they immediately assumed the
dominant role. Tested later, their testosterone level had risen to about four
times its pre-experimental level. When these same males were placed separately with mixed-sex groups where the dominance hierarchy was already
established and they had to assume a peripheral nondominant role, their
testosterone levels dropped sharply (Rose et al. 1972). Thus in males the
relationship between testosterone and aggression can work both ways. High
levels of aggression can be both an effect and a cause of elevated levels of
testosterone.

What do these data mean for explanations of gender differences in
aggression in humans? The differences are real, but they cannot be accounted for by placing the sole responsibility on differential socialization nor
by deducing a proposition that testosterone rules all. Aggression, like spatial
ability, is not something that males have and females do not have. There exist
aggressive and unaggressive persons, and in-between variations, in both
male and female populations. The suggestion from the data on gender
differences in aggression is that a biological substratum exists which predis-
poses males to be more aggressive in situations which elicit such behavior.
The threshold for aggressiveness in males seems to be lower so that under
certain stimulus conditions aggressive behavior is more likely to appear. The
empirically demonstrated link between male hormones and active aggression, and the physical superiority of males in build, strength, and muscle
mass provide a biological basis for a readiness to behave aggressively.

Yet in humans it is obvious that much behavior is acquired. Specific aggressive acts are learned, and the inhibition of such acts is also learned. Boys are probably more primed to learn them and in some environments are less likely to be taught to inhibit, while the reverse may be true for girls. Again, cross-cultural studies are helpful in gaining perspective on the issue. Although children regardless of sex are reported to show aggressive behavior in most societies, each society has its own way of dealing with it (Whiting and Child 1953). And children, again regardless of sex, reflect their culture's approach. As Margaret Mead showed, the Mundugumor reared aggressive, hostile children of both sexes. By contrast, today's Chinese children, reared in state-run nurseries, are taught cooperative behavior and are not punished physically (Sidel 1973). Observers marvel at the absence of hostile and aggressive behavior in their play groups.

Further evidence for the role of environmental influences in the acquisition of aggression as a personality trait in boys and girls appeared in a longitudinal study (Eron 1980). Begun in 1960, this study of 875 third graders and their parents living in a semirural county in New York State demonstrated that the aggressive behavior displayed by the children in school was related to the learning conditions for aggression that were present in the home. The less nurturant and accepting the parents were, the more aggressive the child was in school; the more a child was punished for aggression at home and the less he or she identified with either or both parents, the more aggressive the child was in school. A major contributing factor for aggression seemed to be a lack of favorable support from both parents.

Ten years later, the researchers were able to study again almost half their original sample, about equally divided among boys and girls, now about nineteen years old. One of the most striking findings was the persistence of aggressive behavior (or lack of it) over the years. Children who had been rated aggressive by their peers at age eight continued to be rated as more aggressive by their peers ten years later (see Figure 1). At this follow-up, although parental behaviors continued to be important, the single best predictor of aggressiveness for the nineteen-year-old young men was the rated violence of the television programs they had watched as eight-year-olds.

The differences between the boys and girls in this series of studies are especially interesting. Consistent with the other studies we have reviewed, the girls were much less aggressive at all times than the boys were. Also, the effect of early viewing of television violence and later aggressive behavior was either nonexistent for the girls, or went in the opposite direction; that is, girls who viewed more violence on television as children tended to be rated less aggressive as they matured. The authors thought that reasons for this gender difference include differential socialization whereby girls are less responsive to aggressive cues in the environment, and also the fact that in the 1960s there were hardly any female role models for aggression; rather, females in aggressive scenes were most likely to be victims. Related findings for girls, however, were that girls in the second wave of the study who expressed masculine interest patterns and who watched contact sports on television rated as more aggressive. In other words, when young females are aggressive, some of their interests and activities seem to deviate from those typical of their sex and to be more like those of males.

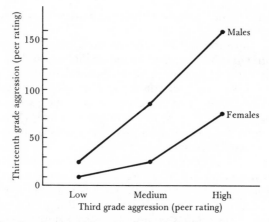

FIGURE 1   Consistency of aggression across time.

From Eron, L., "Prescription for Reduction of Aggression," *American Psychologist* 35 (1980):244–52. Copyright 1980 by the American Psychological Association. Reprinted by permission of the publisher and author.

Studies currently being conducted by Eron and his colleagues on first- and third-grade children show that those who score high on preference for masculine activities, regardless of sex, are likely to be more aggressive, and that the effect is cumulative across time. One intriguing finding was that the more aggressive boys tended to have aggressive fantasies, that is, fantasies in which they daydreamed about fighting or killing someone. The more aggressive girls, however, had few if any such fantasies; rather, they fantasized about action—heroes and heroines, winning games, and achievement.

The author concludes from these studies that if we want to reduce the level of aggression in society we should begin to reward boys for unaggressive behaviors; that we should, in fact, socialize boys more like girls, encouraging the development of socially positive qualities such as tenderness, sensitivity to feelings, nurturance, and cooperation (Eron 1980, p. 251).

What Do We Know about Gender Differences?

The foregoing discussion of psychological differences between the sexes has presented current knowledge in areas where differences have been shown to exist, and in a few others, where the findings are not conclusive and where misconceptions are common. Differences in other areas, such as achievement, will be discussed in other contexts later on. In general, then, we can conclude that:

1. Behavioral differences between boy and girl neonates have not been demonstrated.
2. Clearcut differences in cognitive ability and in social and affective behavior in the first two years have not been conclusively demonstrated. However, patterning of cognitive development is more consistent with age for girls, and is more strongly related to social class. Irritability and fearfulness are more consistent with age for boys.

Mothers are equally warm, nurturing, and accepting of boy and girl babies.

3. Gender differences in cognitive abilities emerge in middle to late childhood. Girls have higher verbal abilities, and boys have higher mathematical and spatial abilities. Several biological explanations have been advanced to account for these differences, especially in spatial ability. Biological components, however, would account for only a small part of differences between males and females in cognitive abilities, since these have also been shown to be affected by environmental and socialization factors.

4. The evidence for gender differences in fearfulness, dependency, and nurturance is inconclusive. Teacher ratings and self-reports tend to show girls more fearful, but it is not known to what extent cultural expectations and girls' greater willingness to admit feelings affect these results. Girls seem to be more oriented toward intimacy in interpersonal relations, but they do not exhibit more of the behaviors usually included in definitions of dependency in the research. While girls are more often in a nurturant role, as in doll play, it is not known to what extent nurturant behavior is innate in females. Both males and females can display nurturant behavior. There is some evidence that early exposure of males to infants and child care enhances their nurturant behavior as they mature.

5. From early childhood, boys have a higher level of aggressive behavior than girls. This difference has been observed in other cultures as well as in animal species. It is probable that a hormonally induced pattern of readiness to respond aggressively, as well as other physical characteristics, contribute initially to this difference. Human behavior, however, is highly malleable, and within-sex and cross-cultural differences are significant also.

NOTES

1. The *neonatal period* is usually defined as the first month of life and is part of *infancy*, the first year or two of life. These terms are loosely used to designate newborn infants and babies who have not acquired language.

REFERENCES

BOWLBY, J. 1969. *Attachment*. New York: Basic Books.

CHAMOV, A., HARLOW, H. F., AND MITCHELL, G. D. 1967. Sex differences in the infant-directed behavior of preadolescent rhesus monkeys. *Child Development* 38: 329–35.

CHODOROW, N. 1978. *The reproduction of mothering: psychoanalysis and the sociology of gender*. Berkeley: University of California Press.

DE VORE, I., ed., 1965. *Primate behavior: Field studies of monkeys and apes*. New York: Holt, Rinehart & Winston.

DUFFY, E. 1962. *Activation and behavior*. New York: Wiley.

ERON, L. D. 1980. Prescription for reduction of aggression. *American Psychologist* 35: 244–52.

FESHBACH, S. 1970. Aggression. In *Carmichael's manual of child psychology*. ed. P. F. Mussen. New York: Wiley.

GOY, R. W., AND MCEWEN, B. S. 1980. *Sexual differentiation of the brain*. Cambridge, Mass.: The MIT Press.

HARLOW, H. 1962. The heterosexual affectional system in monkeys. *American Psychologist* 17: 1–9.

HILL, K. T., AND SARASON, S. B. 1966. The relation of test anxiety and defensiveness to test and school performance over the elementary school years. *Monographs of the Society for Research in Child Development* 31, no. 104.

HOFFMAN, L. W. 1972. Early childhood experiences and women's achievement motives. *Journal of Social Issues* 28: 129–55.

JERSILD, A. T., AND HOLMES, F. B. 1935. Children's fears. *Child Development Monographs* 20.

JOSLYN, W. D. 1973. Androgen-induced social dominance in infant female rhesus monkeys. *Journal of Child Psychology and Psychiatry* 14: 137–45.

JOURARD, S. M. 1968. *Disclosing man to himself.* Princeton, N.J.: Van Nostrand.

KAGAN, J. 1964. Acquisition and significance of sex typing and sex role identity. In *Review of Child Development Research,* ed. M. Hoffman and L. Hoffman, vol. 1. New York: Russell Sage.

KAGAN, J. 1971. *Change and continuity in infancy.* New York: Wiley.

KAGAN, J., AND MOSS, H. A. 1962. *Birth to maturity: A study in psychological development.* New York: Wiley.

KITZINGER, S. 1978. *Women as mothers: how they see themselves in different cultures.* New York: Random House.

KREUZ, L. E., AND ROSE, R. M. 1972. Assessment of aggressive behavior and plasma testosterone in a young criminal population. *Psychosomatic Medicine* 34: 321–32.

KUMMER, H. 1958. Two variations in the social organizations of baboons. In *Primates—studies in adaptation and variability,* ed. P. C. Jay. New York: Holt, Rinehart & Winston.

LAMBERT, H. H. 1978. Biology and equality: a perspective on sex differences. *Signs: Journal of Women in Culture and Society* 4: 97–117.

LEWIS, M. 1972. Parents and children: Sex-role development. *School Review* 80: 229–40.

LUNDE, D. T. 1973. Sex hormones, mood, and behavior. Paper presented at the 6th Annual Symposium, Society of Medical Psychoanalysis, New York.

MACCOBY, E. E. 1966. Sex differences in intellectual functioning. In *The development of sex differences.* ed. E. E. Maccoby. Stanford, Calif.: Stanford University Press.

MACCOBY, E. E., AND JACKLIN, C. 1974. *The psychology of sex differences.* Stanford, Calif.: Stanford University Press.

MEAD, M., AND HEYMAN, K. 1965. *Family.* New York: Macmillan.

MISCHEL, W. 1970. Sex typing and socialization. In *Carmichael's manual of child psychology.* ed. P. H. Mussen. New York: Wiley.

MONEY, J., AND EHRHARDT, A. 1972. *Man and woman, boy and girl.* Baltimore: The Johns Hopkins University Press.

MOSS, H. A. 1967. Sex, age, and state of determinants of mother-infant interaction. *Merrill Palmer Quarterly* 13: 19–36.

OETZEL, R. M. 1966. Classified summary of research in sex differences. In *The development of sex differences.* ed. E. E. Maccoby. Stanford, Calif.: Stanford University Press.

PARKE, R., O'LEARY, S., AND WEST, S. 1972. Mother-father-newborn interaction: Effects of maternal medication, labor, and sex on infant. *Proceedings of the 80th Annual Convention of the American Psychological Association.*

RIVENBARK, W. H., III. 1971. Self disclosure among adolescents. *Psychological Reports* 28: 35–42.

ROSE, R. M., GORDON, T. P., AND BERNSTEIN, I. S. 1972. Plasma testosterone levels in the male rhesus: Influences of sexual and social stimuli. *Science* 178: 643–45.

ROSENBERG, K. M., DENENBERG, V. H., ZARROW, M. X., AND BONNIE, L. F. 1971. Effects of neonatal castration and testosterone on the rat's pup-killing behavior and activity. *Physiology and Behavior* 7: 363–68.

ROSENBLATT, J. S. 1969. The development of maternal responsiveness in the rat. *American Journal of Orthopsychiatry* 30: 36–56.

ROSSI, A. 1977. A biosocial perspective on parenting. *Daedalus* 106: 1–22.

SIDEL, R. 1973. *Women and child care in China.* Baltimore: Penguin.

WALDROP, M. F., AND HALVERSON, C. F., JR. 1973. Intensive and extensive peer behavior: Longitudinal and cross-sectional analyses. Unpublished manuscript, Child Research Branch, National Institute of Mental Health, Washington, D.C.

WHITING, A. W. M., AND CHILD, I. L. 1953. *Child training and personality.* New Haven, Conn.: Yale University Press.

WHITING, B. B., AND POPE, C. P. 1973. A cross-cultural analysis of sex differences in the behavior of children aged three through eleven. *Journal of Social Psychology* 91: 171–88.

YOUNG, W. C., GOY, R. W., AND PHOENIX, C. H. 1965. Hormones and sexual behavior. In *Sex research: New developments.* ed. J. Money. New York: Holt, Rinehart & Winston.

ZUNICH, M. 1964. Children's reactions to failure. *Journal of Genetic Psychology* 104: 19–24.

21

Differential Socialization of Girls and Boys in Light of Cross-Cultural Research

Carolyn Pope Edwards and Beatrice Blyth Whiting

Any review of current research on sex differences in children's behavior suggests that there are three major competing explanatory systems for the origins of sex differences in social behavior: the biological model, which points to constitutional (usually hormonal) factors as the major source of sex differences; the cognitive-developmental stage model, which considers that girls' and boys' cognitive discovery of their gender identity leads them to choose different patterns of behavior; and the socialization model, which looks to the direct and indirect actions of socializing agents as the primary cause of sex role differentiation. The third model, predominant for a long time in the social sciences, has recently lost ground, especially in developmental psychology. A recent review by Maccoby and Jacklin (1974), for instance, concludes that there is no strong evidence that parents consistently act differentially toward sons versus daughters. Although not all authorities agree with Maccoby and Jacklin (see, for example, Birns 1976; Block 1976; Brooks-Gunn and Matthews 1979), the socialization explanation has tended to lose force while the other two models have received much more attention than before.

We believe that the study of socialization has been faulty because of its

From C. P. Edwards and B. B. Whiting, "Differential Socialization of Girls and Boys in Light of Cross-Cultural Research." In *New Directions for Child Development: Anthropological Perspectives on Child Development*, no. 8, ed. Charles M. Super and Sara Harkness (San Francisco: Jossey-Bass, 1980). Reprinted by permission.

lack of an integrated cross-cultural perspective. This perspective is required first, to broaden the foundation of empirical information in a crucial way and second, to offer a more complete analysis of the environments in which children learn than can be gained from working within our home culture only. In this paper we shall discuss how these two gains of the cultural perspective can greatly strengthen our understanding of the differential socialization of girls and boys. As an example, we shall offer a few of the findings of an ongoing collaborative cross-cultural project under our direction and funded by the Ford Foundation (Whiting et al., forthcoming). While our data do not address the validity of the biological and cognitive stage models, they do illustrate the advantages of a cultural perspective when conducting research on sex role socialization.

The first gain of the cultural perspective, broadening the data base, has been addressed by many earlier authors, including ourselves (Whiting and Edwards 1973). Cross-cultural research provides a greater range of variation than does single-culture research and thus offers a way to gain leverage on antecedent variables. For example, cross-cultural research has suggested that children in U.S. households, relative to children in some other cultural settings, may show a reduced degree of sex difference in certain kinds of social behavior, notably aggression, nurturance, responsibility, and help and attention seeking. These findings were obtained in an analysis of the social behavior of 134 children aged three to eleven, who were interacting in natural settings in six communities—Taira (Okinawa), Juxtlahuaca (Oaxaca, Mexico), Tarong (Philippines), Qhalapur (Uttar Pradesh, India), Nyansongo (Kenya), and Orchard Town (in the New England area of the United States). (A detailed description of the methodology and results can be found in Whiting and Edwards 1973; see also Edwards and Whiting 1974; Whiting and Whiting 1975). In the Six Cultures study, social interaction scores of boys and girls were compared for fifteen behaviors of prosocial responsibility, dominance, dependency, compliance, nurturance, and aggression. In each cultural sample, t-tests were performed to compare the boys and girls at two age levels—three to six and seven to ten. The sample from the New England community (called Orchard Town) showed the fewest number of mean differences in the predicted direction (17/30 versus 21, 23, 23, 23, and 24 for the other samples) and was also one of the samples that showed the fewest number of statistically significant comparisons (1 versus 0, 1, 2, 4, and 5; setting significance level at $p < .05$, two-tailed). Generally, fewer sex differences were found for the three samples in which boys and girls were treated similarly in terms of being assigned care for their younger siblings and being asked to do household and economic work. Those three samples were from communities in New England, the Philippines, and Kenya. In contrast, greater numbers of statistically significant sex differences were found for the three samples in which girls and boys were treated dissimilarly: Girls, much more often than boys, were asked to do household tasks, to take care of infants, or to do work that kept them close to home and in the company of adult females. Those three samples were from communities in India, Mexico, and Okinawa. Because the general American pattern in urban and suburban areas is for neither girls nor boys to be assigned many childcare, household, or economic tasks, we can expect the extent of sex differences in social behavior of American children to be minimized relative to children in many other cultures. Thus, in the present example, comparative research offered a way to obtain samples in which the extent of sex differences was much greater than in typical American samples. The method of study provided leverage on the antecedent variable of task assignment.

The second gain of the cultural perspective, offering a more complete analysis of the learning environment of the child, concerns coming to understand better how cultural processes affect children's development. In discussions of social development, much lip service tends to be paid to the concept of culture, but usually only the vaguest understanding of how culture works lies behind commonly voiced opinions of the type, "Children are encouraged by American culture to be competitive and independent." How encouraged? Who or, more likely, what encourages them? Most psychologists have little working knowledge of the ways in which cultural processes set the stage for individual development. A more comprehensive analysis of these processes can come from a comparative cultural perspective, which enables one to specify the functional dimensions of the learning environment of the child. As J. Whiting and others (1966, p. 83) succinctly put it, "certain aspects of the childrearing process seem to have the effect of, if not creating, at least strengthening values far beyond the conscious intent of the agents of socialization." Without a concept of culture as a learning environment, it is difficult to conceptualize socialization pressures in more than a very partial and fragmented way.

Using a comparative cultural perspective to understand better the important dimensions of children's learning environments can be illustrated by the cross-cultural data from a recent collaborative project that we directed (Whiting et al., forthcoming). Let us first briefly explain the project and the kind of data that our group obtained (see also Whiting 1979). Then we will discuss one set of findings and explain their relevance to the question of the differential socialization of boys and girls.

The current project was based on recent observations of the social interaction and daily activities of children aged two to twelve years and, secondarily, on a reanalysis of the Six Cultures data. The more recent data on social interaction were collected by a number of different anthropologists and psychologists who worked in six communities in Kenya, one in India, and one in Liberia (see Table 1). In 1976, the Ford Foundation sponsored a project to analyze jointly the data on both social interaction and daily activities, and a group of twelve met in Cambridge to develop a plan of attack. Thus our collaborative project was born, to study sex differences in the social behavior of children and to examine the effects of modernization on mother-child interaction.

To assess sex differences in social interaction, the group agreed to examine twenty-one categories of social behavior, grouped into seven larger categories of *nurturance, dependence, prosocial dominance, egoistic dominance, aggression,* and *sociability.* The categories are based on the judged conscious intent of the actor toward the person with whom he or she is observed to be interacting and whose ongoing behavior the actor wishes to affect. According to our approach (Whiting 1979; Whiting and Whiting 1975), social interaction is conceived to involve the seeking or offering of goods and services to recipients who may accept or reject them. Different types of

Table 1 Characteristics of the samples

Location	Field Researcher	Year of Field Work	Sample	Linguistic Group
1. Kien-taa, Liberia	Gerald Erchak	1970–1971	15 households; 20 children aged 1–6 (360 minutes observation/child)	Kpelle
2. Ngecha, Kenya	Beatrice Whiting	1968–1970 1973	42 homesteads; 104 children aged 2–10 (at least 45 minutes observation/child)	Kikuyu
3. Oyugis, Kenya	Carol Ember	1968–1969	10 children aged 8–12 (135 minutes observation/child)	Luo
4. Kisa, and 5. Kariobangi, Kenya	Thomas Weisner	1970–1972	24 urban and rural families matched by age, education, and kinship ties; 68 children aged 2–8 (120 minutes observation/child)	Abaluya
6. Kokwet, and 7. Urot, Kenya	Sara Harkness and Charles Super	1972–1975	Kokwet: 64 children aged 3–10; Urot: 64 children aged 3–10 (120 minutes observation/child)	Kipsigis
8. Bubaneswar, India (State of Orissa)	Susan Seymour	1965–1967	36 households (24 upper class, 12 lower class); 103 children aged 0–10 (16 hours of observation/household)	Oriya

interaction involve benefit to the actor, the recipient, both of them, or some other person or persons. The goods and services exchanged in social interaction include such things as food and material goods as well as intangibles (information, instrumental help, comfort, attention, privilege, control, physical pain, psychological pain, friendship, social participation, and competition). For example, *prosocial dominance* involves the seeking of control through acts such as assigning chores or reprimanding whose apparent goal is to benefit the recipient and/or the social group. *Dependent* behaviors involve the seeking of services such as help, attention, and information to benefit the actor.

It was assumed that the intention of the actor could be judged in the majority of instances by observers who were native to the culture. The observations for all samples were done in naturally occurring situations, usually in the house or yard. Observers were trained to record, in running

English sentences, social interaction between the sample child and/or the sample mother and the other individuals in the environment identified by age, sex, and kinship relation. The length of observation periods varied from one sample to another (the longest period, one hour, was in Bubaneswar, India; the shortest in the Six Cultures samples, five minutes). There was also variation in the focus of observations (in most cases the sample child was the focus; in India the mother or mother surrogate was the focus; and in the Ngecha, Kenya sample, the focus was on children in most observations but on mothers in others). Finally, coding procedures varied in terms of who coded the running protocols into behavioral categories. In most cases, local observers performed this task; however, field researchers Harkness and Super, Erchak, and Seymour coded their own data, and in the Six Cultures study, the narrative records were forwarded from the field to the Laboratory of Human Development at Harvard for coding. Reliability of coding was monitored by all of the researchers. On the average reliability probably never fell below the 70 percent level (see Whiting and Edwards 1977). Table 1 displays the number and ages of children in each sample.

The set of findings concerning *nurturance* (defined as behavior in which a person offers a service or resource to meet the needs of another) can be used to demonstrate the way in which we conceptualize culture, as an independent variable, in terms of learning environments for children. The failure of American research to elucidate the learning of nurturant behavior can be traced to the fact that, as Maccoby and Jacklin (1974, p. 220) point out, "existing research has seldom focused on a child's offering of nurturance to an infant or younger child." Rather, naturalistic studies of nurturance and all other kinds of social behavior of children are based almost entirely on mother-child and same-aged peer observations. Little or no American material exists that is directly comparable to our project's data—that is, observations including children's interaction with infants and older and younger children as well as with their mothers. Certainly we are not the first in recent years to express the need for more study of children's cross-age interaction (see, for example, Edwards and Lewis 1979; Hartup 1976; Konner 1975), but here the point concerns the importance of cross-age peer studies for understanding the development of sex differences in social behavior.

Our findings indicate that sex differences in nurturant behaviors are more prominent in some kinds of dyadic interaction than in others. We made nurturance comparisons by the following procedure. We constituted a summary category offering of material goods, physical care, help, comfort, and attention. Within each cultural sample we then added together all of the nurturant versus non-nurturant social acts done by girls versus boys to specific target groups of people. For example in the Kien-taa, Liberia community sample, the girls, ($n = 8$) made a total of 7 nurturant versus 227 non-nurturant acts to mothers whereas the boys ($n = 7$) made 2 nurturant versus 179 non-nurturant acts (*phi* nonsignificant for boys versus girls). In that same sample girls made 44 nurturant acts versus 64 non-nurturant acts to infants (under 1.5 years of age), whereas boys made 22 nurturant versus 52 non-nurturant acts (*phi* = .10, nonsignificant). Thus in both comparisons girls scored proportionately higher than boys but nonsignificantly so. Tables 2, 3, 4, and 5 display the results of all of the comparisons, that is, they indicate which sex in each cultural sample displayed proportionately more nurturance to a specific target group, as well as whether the *phi* value of the comparison is statistically significant. Although our methodology has the weakness of having lumped together all the acts of girls (and boys) in a sample regardless of their ages, it has the strength of having separated out acts to various target groups—mothers, infants, children a defined number of years younger than the actor child, children a defined number of years older than the actor child, and children relatively close in age to the actor child.

The findings (Tables 2 to 5) suggest that, overall, girls behave more nurturantly than boys. There are twelve comparisons in the four tables in which girls score significantly higher than boys but only three of the reverse. What is further evident is that the sex difference in behavior favoring girls is most consistently found in the behavior of children to infant/toddlers (see Table 2). Table 4, presenting behavior to children older than the actor, has the fewest number of significant sex differences. To summarize, sex differences in nurturance are most consistent in behavior directed to very young children (infant/toddlers), least prevalent and consistent in behavior directed to mothers and older children, and intermediate in behavior directed to younger children or to children close in age to the actor. In no type of dyadic interaction are boys consistently more nurturant than girls; rather,

Table 2 Sex differences in nurturant[a] behavior I

| | Type of Social Interaction | |
Sample	*To Mothers*[b]	*To Infant/Toddlers*[c]
Kien-taa	B	G
Urot	G	—
Kokwet	G	G
Kisa	G	—
Kariobangi	B	G*
Ngecha	G	G
Oyugis	—	—
Bubaneswar–Lower Class	G = G	—
Bubaneswar–Upper Class	B	—
Nyansongo	B	B
Tarong	G	B
Juxtlahuaca	G	G***
Taira	—	G***
Khalapur	G	—
Orchard Town	B	—

Note: This table presents the sex of child showing the higher percentage of nurturance in behavior directed to mothers and behavior directed to infant/toddlers.

[a] Nurturance is the summed category including the offering of food, material goods, physical care, help, comfort, and attention.

[b] For each cultural sample, nurturant versus non-nurturant acts of all girls (G) to their mothers were summed; the same was done for boys (B). The resulting scores for girls versus boys were tested for significance using the phi coefficient. A dash (—) indicates that there were fewer than twenty social acts by girls to the target or less than twenty by boys to the target, for a particular sample. *$p<.05$, **$p<.01$, ***$p<.001$.

[c] Infant/toddlers were less than eighteen months old for the first set of samples and less than two years old for the Six Cultures samples. Sex differences were tested following the same procedure outlined in footnote b.

Table 3 Sex differences in nurturant behavior II

Sample[b]	Type of Social Interaction[a]	
	To Younger Child[c] of the Same Sex	To Younger Child[c] of the Opposite Sex
Kien-taa	B***	—
Urot	G***	—
Kokwet	G*	B
Kisa	G	—
Ngecha	B**	B = G
Acts by Children in Older Age Group to Children in Younger Age Group[d]		
	of Same Sex	of Opposite Sex
Nyansongo	G	G
Tarong	G*	G*
Juxtlahuaca	G	G
Taira	G**	B
Orchard Town	G	—

Note: This table presents the sex of child showing the higher percentage of nurturance in behavior directed to children younger than the actor child.

[a] Comparisons and significance tests done as in Table 2, using phi coefficients *$p<.05$, **$p<.01$, ***$p<.001$.
[b] Samples have been omitted where frequency of interaction for thse dyad types were too low for comparisons to be made. It is interesting to note in this and all following tables the greater prevalence of same-sex versus cross-sex interaction (column 1 versus 2).
[c] Here, data include all behavior directed by actor children to targets three or more years younger than they are (excluding infants).
[d] Here, data include all behavior directed by children classified in the older group (age 7–10) to children in the younger group (age 3–6). Thus the procedure varies from that for samples above, necessitated by the way in which the Six Cultures data were originally coded.

Table 4 Sex differences in nurturant behavior III

Sample[b]	Type of Social Interaction[a]	
	To Older Child[b] of the Same Sex	To Older Child[b] of the Opposite Sex
Kien-taa	G	—
Urot	G	—
Kokwet	G	G
Kisa	G	—
Ngecha	G = B	G**
Oyugis	—	—
Acts by Children in Younger Age Group to Children in Older Age Group[c]		
	of the Same Sex	of the Opposite Sex
Nyansongo	G	—
Tarong	B	G
Juxtlahuaca	B	B
Taira	G = B	—
Orchard Town	B	—

Note: This table presents the sex of child showing the higher percentage of nurturance in behavior directed to children older than the actor child.

[a] Comparisons and tests of significance follow procedures in Table 2, *$p<.05$, **$p<.01$, ***$p<.001$.
[b] Here data include all behavior directed by actor children to targets three or more years older than they were (but not older than age 12).
[c] Here data include all behavior directed by younger age group (3–6) to older age group (7–10). (See Table 3, footnote d.)

Table 5 Sex differences in nurturant behavior IV

| | Type of Social Interaction[a] | | | |
| | To Slightly Younger Child[b] | | To Slightly Older Child[b] | |
Sample	*Same Sex*	*Opposite Sex*	*Same Sex*	*Opposite Sex*
Kien-taa	—	—	G	—
Kokwet	B	G	B	G
Kisa	G	—	B	—
Kariobangi	G	—	—	—
Ngecha	G**	G	G	G
Oyugis	—	—	G	—
	Acts Between Children Both in Older Age Group[c]		Acts Between Children Both in Younger Age Group[c]	
	Same Sex	*Opposite Sex*	*Same Sex*	*Opposite Sex*
Nyansongo	G	G	B	B
Tarong	G*	G	B*	G
Juxtlahuaca	G**	—	G	G
Taira	B	B	G	G
Khalapur	B	—	—	G
Orchard Town	G	G	G	B

Note: This table presents the sex of child showing the higher percentage of nurturance in behavior directed to children close in age to the actor child.

[a] Comparisons and tests of significance follow procedures in Table 2, $*p<.05$, $**p<.01$, $***p<.001$.

[b] Here *slightly younger* and *slightly older* are defined as two years or less age difference.

[c] Older age group includes children aged 7–10, younger age group includes children aged 3–6. (See Table 3, footnote d.)

sex differences favoring girls on this dimension appear in all dyadic contexts but to a greater or lesser extent depending on the specific type of interaction.

What might be the cause of girls' greater display of nurturance? It does not appear to be the result of extensive differences in treatment by mothers of daughters versus sons. Like Maccoby and Jacklin (1974), we find few behaviors that mothers consistently direct more to one sex than to another (although *reprimanding* or *correcting* is one such behavior; see Whiting 1979). Nevertheless, while mothers may behave relatively similarly to boys and girls, it is clear that in many cultures girls spend much more time in the dyadic contexts that elicit nurturance—that is, in the company of infants and young children (Whiting and Whiting 1975). Our data do not suggest that this is necessarily due to mothers assigning more child care chores to girls but rather that, when mothers do request such tasks, girls are more likely to comply. Thus, we suggest the following two-part scenario for the socialization of sex differences in nurturance: (1) During the early years (perhaps ages three to six), girls are not more nurturant than boys but they are more willing to play with and take responsibility for younger children, especially infants, toddlers, and younger sisters. (A large number of studies conducted on U.S. samples have found females of various ages, including preschoolers, to display more interest than males in babies. See, for example, Berman, Monda, and Myerscough 1977; Berman et al. 1978; Edwards and Lewis 1979; Feldman, Nash, and Cutrona 1977; Frodi and Lamb 1978; Lamb 1978.) (2) By middle childhood (age seven to eight and above), sex differences in nurturance toward infants and younger sisters begin to appear as a result of girls having learned to be responsive to the needs of others in those dyadic contexts.

The relevance of this scenario for the comparative study of human development is that cultures differ greatly in the amount of time that children, especially girls, spend in the company of very young children. As targets of interaction, infants and toddlers are much more available to children of some cultures than to children of others. For example, in the Six Cultures communities of Nyansongo, Kenya, and Juxtlahuaca, Mexico, an average of 25 percent of all children's social acts were directed to infants, whereas in Orchard Town, that amount was only 3.5 percent (Whiting and Whiting 1975). Thus, different cultural groups can magnify, minimize, or perhaps even eliminate any sex differences in nurturance to the extent that they place girls and boys in the settings that promote the development of nurturant behavior.

To conclude, we believe that different kinds of social behavior are learned in interaction with different sex/age groups of people, and that cultures shape the behavior of their children by selecting the company they keep and the activities that engage their time. Parents do, of course, consciously attempt to transmit certain behaviors and values to their children; but without the support of that complex of dyadic contexts and activities that we call the cultural learning environment, those socialization pressures would probably have little force. This is true in the area of sex role socialization as much as in any other, and consequently, if we limit our study of children to only a few social contexts and activities (such as mother-child interaction and same-age peer interaction at school), we may miss much of the action where sex role learning occurs.

The study of the relative distribution of different social contexts and activities in the daily lives of children is a critical but largely ignored subject in most current socialization research. The recent shift in developmental psychology away from socialization explanations of sex differences may, therefore, reflect more the inadequacy of present research strategies than a basic weakness of the socialization model itself for predicting and explaining sex differences in children's social behavior.

A report of the collaborative research of Beatrice Whiting, Carolyn Edwards, Lawrence Baldwin, Charlene Bolton, Ralph Bolton, Carol Ember, Gerald Erchak, Sara Harkness, Amy Koel, Carol Michelson, Ruth Munroe, R. L. Monroe, Sara Nerlove, Barbara Rogoff, Susan Seymour, Charles Super, and Thomas Weisner.

REFERENCES

BERMAN, P. W., GOODMAN, V., SLOAN, V. L., AND FERNANDER, L. "Preference for Infants Among Black and White Children: Sex and Age Differences." *Child Development*, 1978, *49*, 917–919.

BERMAN, P. W., MONDA, L. C., AND MYERSCOUGH, R. P. "Sex Differences in Young Children's Responses to an Infant: An Observation Within a Daycare Setting." *Child Development*, 1977, *48*, 711–715.

BIRNS, B. "The Emergence and Socialization of Sex Differences in the Earliest Years." *Merrill-Palmer Quarterly*, 1976, *22*, 229–254.

BLOCK, J. H. "Issues, Problems, and Pitfalls in Assessing Sex Differences: A Critical Review of *The Psychology of Sex Differences*." *Merrill-Palmer Quarterly*, 1976, *22*, 383–308.

BROOKS-GUNN, J., AND MATTHEWS, W. S. *He and She: How Children Develop Their Sex-Role Identity.* Englewood Cliffs, N.J.: Prentice-Hall, 1979.

EDWARDS, C. P., AND LEWIS, M. "Young Children's Concepts of Social Relations: Social Functions and Social Objects." In M. Lewis and L. A. Rosenblum (Eds.), *The Child and Its Family.* Genesis of Behavior, vol. 2. New York: Plenum, 1979.

EDWARDS, C. P., AND WHITING, B. B. "Women and Dependency." *Politics and Society*, 1974, *4*, 343–355.

FELDMAN, S. S., NASH, S. C., AND CUTRONA, C. "The Influence of Age and Sex on Responsiveness of Infants." *Developmental Psychology*, 1977, *13*, 675–676.

FRODI, A. M., AND LAMB, M. E. "Sex Differences in Responsiveness to Infants: A Developmental Study of Psycholphysiological and Behavioral Responses." *Child Development*, 1978, *49*, 1182–1188.

HARTUP, W. W. "Cross-Age Versus Same-Age Peer Interaction: Ethological and Cross-Cultural Perspectives." In V. L. Allen (Ed.), *Children as Teachers.* New York: Academic Press, 1976.

KONNER, M. "Relations Among Infants and Juveniles in Comparative Perspective." In M. Lewis and L. A. Rosenblum (Eds.), *Friendship and Peer Relations.* Origins of Behavior, vol. 4. New York: Wiley, 1975.

LAMB, M. E. "The Development of Sibling Relationships in Infancy: A Short-Term Longitudinal Study." *Child Development*, 1978, *49*, 1189–1196.

MACCOBY, E. E., AND JACKLIN, C. N. *The Psychology of Sex Differences.* Stanford, Calif.: Stanford University Press, 1974.

WHITING, B. B. "Maternal Behavior in Cross-Cultural Perspective." Paper presented at Annual Meeting of the Society for Cross-Cultural Research, Charlottesville, Virginia, February 20, 1979.

WHITING, B. B., AND EDWARDS, C. P. "A Cross-Cultural Analysis of Sex Differences in the Behavior of Children Aged Three Through Eleven." *Journal of Social Psychology*, 1973, *91*, 171–188.

WHITING, B. B., AND EDWARDS, C. P. "The Effect of Age, Sex, and Modernization on the Behavior of Mothers and Children." Report to the Ford Foundation, January 1977.

WHITING, B. B., EDWARDS, C. P., EMBER, C. R., ERCHAK, G., HARKNESS, S., SEYMOUR, S., SUPER, C., AND WEISNER, T. *The Company They Keep.* Manuscript in progress, Harvard University.

WHITING, B. B., AND WHITING, J. W. M. *Children of Six Cultures: A Psycho-Cultural Analysis.* Cambridge, Mass.: Harvard University Press, 1975.

WHITING, J. W. M., CHASDI, E. H., ANTONOVSKY, H. F., AYRES, B. C. "The Learning of Values." In E. Z. Vogt and E. M. Albert (Eds.), *People of Rimrock.* Cambridge, Mass.: Harvard University Press, 1966.

Part VII

Adolescent Social and Moral Development

In adolescence, peer relations multiply and intensify, cognitive and moral beliefs are restructured, and the adolescent participates seriously, almost as an equal, in the basic institutions of society. Yet through all of this, family ties remain critically important for the teenager. The adolescent's often exhilarating sense of increasing social power and equality with peers and adults alike is still accompanied by the adolescent's need for parental guidance and support.

The readings in this section focus on the changing peer world of the adolescent and on the major reorganizations in moral judgment that occur throughout the teen years. There is no question that the two topics are related. The increasing intimacy of the peer relation fosters a closer awareness of interpersonally oriented values such as trust, honesty, responsibility, and care. Further, peer engagements offer the adolescent another forum to try out new ideas and question old ones. This reexamination of belief is a critical instigator of moral change. The adolescent years are marked by frequent assertions of one's values followed by ruthless self-critiques of these same values. Through this process of experimentation and critical examination, the adolescent finally constructs systems of moral beliefs with some coherence and stability.

Harry Stack Sullivan's classic treatment of preadolescent and adolescent youth emphasizes the psychological significance of the adolescent's changing peer relations. During the transition from childhood to adolescence, Sullivan writes, "full-blown" intimacy is first experienced in a friendship.

This is Sullivan's famous notion of a "chum"—one whose welfare becomes of "practically equal importance" to that of the self. In a chumship, one develops such sensitivity to the other's needs that, in effect, one asks not what one can do for oneself but rather what one can do for one's chum. This leads to genuine collaboration between chums. In Sullivan's words, this means "clearly formulated adjustments of one's behavior to the expressed needs of the other person in pursuit of increasingly identical—that is more and more nearly mutual—satisfactions, and in the maintenance of similar security operations." Among the many personal fruits of such collaboration is a "validation of self worth." In other words, through the processes of responding to another's needs, sharing one's innermost needs, and constructing mutual goals with another, one establishes a sense that one's own needs and goals are legitimate and worthy of respect. From his psychiatrist's viewpoint, Sullivan places great value in terms of mental health on this adolescent confirmation of self-worth.

Sullivan's account is reminiscent of the literature on friendship presented in the readings on childhood. Sullivan, however, characteristically digs deeper into the emotional and psychological consequences of peer relations. In his other writings, he describes some maladaptive patterns that pose psychotherapeutic problems for clinicians: these being what Sullivan calls "warps" in interpersonal behavior and personality development. In the present reading, Sullivan goes on to note some difficulties encountered by normal adolescents when sexuality becomes an inevitable part of their peer social world. At this point, the task of the adolescent is to integrate the intimacy discovered in earlier chumships with the expression of sexual desire. This is one of the most challenging and rewarding tasks of social development, and often is not satisfactorily resolved until years beyond adolescence.

In a sociological analysis, Dexter Dunphy traces many of the same changes that psychological accounts of adolescent friendships have documented. Dunphy, however, adds insights into how developing friendship patterns are manifested in the changing social structure of adolescent peer groups. Dunphy, like other sociologists before him, identifies two types of group structure commonly found in adolescent peer society: cliques and crowds, the former being more close-knit and intimate than the latter. In his observations of adolescents at home, in parties, on street corners, and in other places where teenagers congregate, Dunphy found five age-related stages of adolescent clique and crowd development. These stages go from the single-sex cliques, isolated within themselves, to more complex associations between cliques, to a loose crowd formation, to a final break-up of the crowd and the formation of heterosexual couples, the most intimate sort of "clique."

In Dunphy's account, therefore, we see adolescents moving from close single-sex friendships through a series of casual same-sex and heterosexual contacts, to a final phase of heterosexual intimacy. This progression may be viewed psychologically in terms of the adolescent's needs for secure exploration into the attractive but threatening possibilities of intimacy. The adolescent's initial forays into intimacy are on the safe ground of small, single-sex cliques. When cliques join together to become crowds, this offers opportunities for casual and safe encounters with the opposite sex. As these acquaintances become gradually more intimate, the crowd structure is reorganized and finally done away with in favor of the couple. The peer world's social organization has followed the adolescent's shifting psychological needs.

Although both friends and family are of primary importance to the adolescent's psychosocial development, in many ways the adolescent ventures beyond the confines of intimate peer and parental relations. As the adolescent anticipates a career and the full responsibilities of citizenship, a new awareness of societal institutions and a new interest in the workings of the system emerges. As a consequence, the adolescent realizes that one's social interactions may have legal, economic, or political significance beyond their interpersonal meanings. In short, the transition to adolescence requires a perspective on collective social concerns; the laws, norms, and procedures of the social system becomes a focus of attention. This new orientation influences adolescent values of every kind.

Lawrence Kohlberg describes how adolescent moral values are transformed in a series of developmental stages through the adolescent's emerging awareness of broad societal considerations. The critical transitions in the adolescent years are the shifts from Stage 2 to 3, 3 to 4, and 4 to 5. At Stage 3 begins a social-relational perspective that values the mutual expectations that derive from interpersonal relationships. One's reputation in society becomes a focal point for one's moral concerns. At Stage 4, one adopts a "member of society" perspective that engenders a respect for the law and the social order. At Stage 5, one still values the social system as a necessary institution, but believes that certain of its existing codes or laws may well be changed. In other words, one understands the necessity of entering into a "social contract" with others, but always strives to improve the workings of the existing social arrangements. Kohlberg has launched a twenty-five-year research program to demonstrate that these moral changes occur predictably and in sequence as the individual develops. Kohlberg also believes that the moral sequence he describes is universal, although there is much controversy about this point in the psychological and anthropological literature.

22

Preadolescence and Early Adolescence
Harry Stack Sullivan

Need for Interpersonal Intimacy

Just as the juvenile era was marked by a significant change—the development of the need for compeers, for playmates rather like oneself—the beginning of preadolescence is equally spectacularly marked, in my scheme of development, by the appearance of a new type of interest in another person. These changes are the result of maturation and development, or experience. This new interest in the preadolescent era is not as general as the use of language toward others was in childhood, or the need of similar people as playmates was in the juvenile era. Instead, it is a specific new type of interest in a *particular* member of the same sex who becomes a chum or a close friend. This change represents the beginning of something very like full-blown, psychiatrically defined *love*. In other words, the other fellow takes on a perfectly novel relationship with the person concerned: he becomes of practically equal importance in all fields of value. Nothing remotely like that has ever appeared before. All of you who have children are sure that your children love you; when you say that, you are expressing a pleasant illusion. But if you will look very closely at one of your children when he finally finds a chum—somewhere between eight-and-a-half and ten—you will discover something very different in the relationship—namely, that your child begins to develop a real sensitivity to what matters to another person. And this is not in the sense of "what should I do to get what I want," but instead "what should I do to contribute to the happiness or to support the prestige and feeling of worth-whileness of my chum." So far as I have ever been able to discover, nothing remotely like this appears before the age of, say, eight-and-a-half, and sometimes it appears decidedly later.

Thus the developmental epoch of preadolescence is marked by the coming of the integrating tendencies which, when they are completely developed, we call love, or, to say it another way, by the manifestation of the need for interpersonal intimacy. Now even at this late stage in my formulation of these ideas, I still find that some people imagine that intimacy is only a matter of approximating genitals one to another. And so I trust that you will finally and forever grasp that interpersonal intimacy can really consist of a great many things without genital contact; that intimacy in this sense means, just as it always has meant, closeness, without specifying that which is close other than the persons. Intimacy is that type of situation involving two people which permits validation of all components of personal worth. Validation of personal worth requires a type of relationship which I call collaboration, by which I mean clearly formulated adjustments of one's behavior to the expressed needs of the other person in the pursuit of increasingly identical—that is, more and more nearly mutual—satisfactions, and in the maintenance of increasingly similar security operations.[1] Now this preadolescent collaboration is distinctly different from the acquisition, in the juvenile era, of habits of competition, cooperation, and compromise. In preadolescence not only do people occupy themselves in moving toward a common, more-or-less impersonal objective, such as the success of "our team," or the discomfiture of "our teacher," as they might have done in the juvenile era, but they also, specifically and increasingly, move toward supplying each other with satisfactions and taking on each other's successes in the maintenance of prestige, status, and all the things which represent freedom from anxiety, or the diminution of anxiety. . . .[2]

Preadolescent Society

Except in certain rural communities, there occurs in preadolescence the development of at least an approach to what has long been called by sociologists "the gang." I am again speaking rather exclusively of male preadolescents, because by this time the deviations prescribed by the culture make it pretty hard to make a long series of statements which are equally obviously valid for the two sexes. The preadolescent impersonal relation is primarily, and vastly importantly, a two-group; but these two-groups tend to interlock. In other words, let us say that persons *A* and *B* are chums. Person *A* also finds much that is admirable about person *C*, and person *B* finds much that is admirable about person *D*. And persons *C* and *D* each has his chum, so that there is a certain linkage of interest among all of these two-groups. Quite often there will be one particular preadolescent who is, thanks to his having been fortunate in earlier phases, the sort of person that many of these preadolescent people find useful as a model; and he will be the third member, you might say, of many three-groups, composed of any one of a number of two-groups and himself. At the same time, he may have a particular chum just as everybody in this society may have. Thus these close two-groups, which are extremely useful in correcting earlier deviations, tend at the same time to interlock through one person or a few people who are, in a very significant sense, leaders. And incidentally, let me say that many of us are apt to think of leadership in political terms, in terms of "influence" and the "influential." We overlook the fact that influence is exerted by the influential in certain conspicuous areas other than that of getting people to do what the leader wants done. The fact is that a very important field of leadership phenomena—and one that begins to be outstandingly important in preadolescence—is opinion leadership; and understanding this and developing techniques for integrating it might be one of the few great hopes for the future.

Thus some few people tend to come out in leadership positions in preadolescent society. Some of them are the people who can get the others to collaborate, to work with understanding and appreciation of one another toward common objectives or aims, which sometimes may be crimes, or what not. And others are the leaders whose views gradually come to be the views of a large number in the group, which is opinion leadership. This kind of leadership has certain fairly measurable and perhaps some imponderable aspects. One of its reasonably measurable aspects is that people whose development, combined with their intellectual abilities, has given them the ability to separate facts and opinions, tend to be considered by the others as well informed, right in their thinking about things of interest at that particular stage, and thus tend to do the thinking for a good many of the others because of the latter's unfortunate personality warp. And the time when these leaders in opinion do the thinking almost exclusively is when there are serious problems confronting the members of the group. The level of general insecurity about the human future is high at this stage of development, and in any case probably increases when serious problems arise, whether they occur in the preadolescent gang or in society as a whole. It is at those times that perhaps far more than half of the statistical population—handicapped by lack of information, by lack of training, and by various difficulties in personal life which call out a good deal of anxiety, which in turn interferes with practically everything useful—has to look to opinion leadership for anything like reassuring views or capable foresight. Thus an important part of the preadolescent phase of personality development is the developing patterning of leadership-led relationships, which are so vital in any social organization and which are, theoretically at least, of very great importance in relatively democratic organizations of society.

I have suggested that an important aspect of the preadolescent phase is that, practically for the first time, there is consensual validation of personal worth. Now it is true that some children are fortunate, indeed; through the influences to which they have been subjected in the home and school, they are about as sure as they can be that they are worth while in certain respects. But very many people arrive in preadolescence in the sad state which an adult would describe as "getting away with murder." In other words, they have had to develop such remarkable capacities for deceiving and misleading others that they never had a chance to discover what they were really good for. But in this intimate interchange in preadolescence—some preadolescents even have mutual daydreams, spend hours and hours carrying on a sort of spontaneous mythology in which both participate—in this new necessity for thinking of the other fellow as right and for being thought of as right by the other fellow, much of this uncertainty as to the real worth of the personality, and many self-deceptive skills at deceiving others which exist in the juvenile era, may be rectified by the improving communication of the chums and, to a much lesser extent but nonetheless valuably, by confirmatory relations in the collaboration developed in the gang. . . .

[From "Early Adolescence"]

The earlier phase of adolescence as a period of personality development is defined as extending from the eruption of true genital interest, felt as lust, to the patterning of sexual behavior which is the beginning of the last phase of adolescence. There are very significant differences, in the physiological substrate connected with the beginning of adolescence, between men and women; but in either case there is a rather abrupt change, relatively unparalleled in development, by which a zone of interaction with the environment which had been concerned with excreting waste becomes newly and rapidly significant as a zone of interaction in physical interpersonal intimacy. In other words, what has been, from the somatic viewpoint, the more external tissues of the urinary-excretory zone now become the more external part of the genital zone as well. The change, from the psychological standpoint, pertains to new needs which have their culmination in the experience of sexual orgasm; the felt tensions associated with this need are traditionally and quite properly identified as *lust*. In other words, lust is the felt component of integrating tendencies pertaining to the genital zone of interaction, seeking the satisfaction of cumulatively augmented sentience culminating in orgasm.

There is, so far as I know, no necessarily close relationship between lust, as an integrating tendency, and the need for intimacy, which we have previously discussed, except that they both characterize people at a certain stage in development. The two are strikingly distinct. In fact, making very much sense of the complexities and difficulties which are experienced in adolescence and subsequent phases of life, depends, in considerable measure, on the clarity with which one distinguishes three needs, which are often very intricately combined and at the same time contradictory. These are the need for personal security—that is, for freedom from anxiety; the need for intimacy—that is, for collaboration with at least one other person; and the need for lustful satisfaction, which is connected with genital activity in pursuit of the orgasm.

The Shift in the Intimacy Need

As adolescence is ushered in, there is, in people who are not too much warped for such a development, a change in the so-called object of the need for intimacy. And the change is from what I shall presently be discussing as an isophilic choice to what may be called a heterophilic choice—that is, it is a change from the seeking of someone quite like oneself to the seeking of someone who is in a very significant sense very different from oneself. This change in choice is naturally influenced by the concomitant appearance of the genital drive. Thus, other things being equal and no very serious warp or privation intervening, the change from preadolescence to adolescence appears as a growing interest in the possibilities of achieving some measure of intimacy with a member of the other sex, rather after the pattern of the intimacy that one has in preadolescence enjoyed with a member of one's own sex.

The degree to which the need for intimacy is satisfied in this heterophilic sense in the present-day American scene leaves very much to be desired. The reason is not that the shift of interest toward the other sex in itself makes intimacy difficult, but that the cultural influences which are borne in upon each person include very little which prepares members of different sexes for a fully human, simple, personal relationship together. A great many of the barriers to heterophilic intimacy go back to the very beginnings of the Western world. Just to give a hint of what I am talking about, I might mention the so-called double standard of morality and the legal status which surrounds illegitimate birth. One can get an idea of the important influence of cultural organization and cultural institutions of the possibilities of relationships in adolescence which are easy and, in terms of personality development, successful, by studying a culture very significantly different from our own in this respect. For some years I have recommended in this connection Hortense Powdermaker's *Life in Lesu.*[3] There, the institutions bearing on the distinction between the sexes are very significantly different from ours, and the contrast between our institutions and theirs perhaps sheds some light in itself on unfortunate aspects of the Western world.

But to return to our culture: The change in the need for intimacy—the new awakening of curiosity in the boy as to how he could get to be on as friendly terms with a girl as he has been on with his chum—is usually ushered in by a change of covert process. Fantasy undergoes a rather striking modification—a modification almost as abrupt and striking as the sudden acceleration of somatic growth which begins with the puberty change and leads, for instance, to the awkwardness which I have mentioned. And there may also be a change of content in overt communicative processes, both in the two-group and in the gang. That is, if the preadolescents are successfully progressing toward maturation and uniformly free from personality warp, this interest in members of the other sex also spreads into the area of communication between the chums, even though the one chum may not be quite up to the other and may be somewhat opposed to this new preoccupation with girls. In the more fortunate circumstances, this is presently a gang-wise change, and those who are approximately ready for it profit considerably from this last great topic of preadolescent collaboration—the topic of who's who and what's what in the so-called heterosexual world. If the group includes some members whose development is delayed, the social pressure in the group, in the gang, is extremely hard on their self-esteem and may lead to very serious disturbances of personality indeed. As I have previously hinted, it is not uncommon for the preadolescent phase to fade imperceptibly into the early adolescent phase, and for gang-wise genital activity to become part of the pattern of the very last stage of preadolescence or the verge of adolescence. Thus one not uncommonly finds at this point that the lust dynamism is actually functioning and governing a good part of group activity, but this is very definitely oriented to that which is to follow with members of the other sex.

In this change from preadolescence to adolescence, there has to be a great deal of trial-and-error learning by human example. A considerable number of those at the very beginning of adolescence have some advantage in this learning by virtue of having already acquired data from their observation of and experience with a sibling of the other sex not very far removed from them in developmental age; these data which had been previously unimportant are now rapidly activated.

I believe that according to conventional, statistical experience, women undergo the puberty change somewhat in advance of men; in a great many instances, this leads to a peculiar sort of stutter in developmental progress between the boys and the girls in an age community so that by the time most of the boys have gotten really around to interest in girls, most of the girls are already fairly well wound up in their problems about boys. From the standpoint of personality development, it would be convenient if these things were timed slightly better; but I suppose that in the beginning when everything was arranged—I've never had any private information on the subject, by the way—procreation was fully as important as a feeling of self-esteem is now in a highly developed civilization. And so women get ready for procreation quite early; in fact one of the important problems of adolescence is how to avoid the accident of procreation. . . .

NOTES

1. [*Editor's note:* Sullivan's use of the terms "collaboration" and "cooperation" should be kept in mind throughout this section. By cooperation, he means the usual give-and-take of the juvenile era; by collaboration, he means the feeling of sensitivity to another person which appears in preadolescence. "Collaboration . . . is a great step forward from cooperation—*I* play according to the rules of the game, to preserve *my* prestige and feeling of superiority and merit. When we collaborate, it is a matter of *we*." (*Conception of Modern Psychiatry*, [W. W. Norton, 1953], p. 55.]

2. [*Editor's note:* Up to this point, this chapter is taken from 1944–45 lectures, rather than from the series on which this book is primarily based, since this portion is missing in the latter series because of failures of recording equipment. The material corresponds, however, to the outline in Sullivan's Notebook.]

3. [Hortense Powdermaker, *Life in Lesu: The Study of a Melanesian Society in New Ireland* (New York: W. W. Norton, 1933.)]

23

The Social Structure of Urban Adolescent Peer Groups

Dexter C. Dunphy

Most writers on adolescence emphasize the influence of peer groups on the course of adolescent social maturation. Indeed some regard the peer group as of comparable significance to the family and the school in the socialization of urban adolescents. Parsons, for example, states: "The family offers a wide enough range of role participations only for the young child. He must learn by actual participation, progressively more roles than his family of orientation can offer him. It is at this point that the peer group and school assume paramount importance."[1] Existing research has established that a major difference in sex composition exists between typical preadolescent and adolescent groups. Preadolescent groups are almost universally unisexual in composition with play centering around sex-categorized activities and role models.[2] The "gang age" thus appears to consolidate the oedipal crisis by reinforcing the child's learning of his basic sex role, such learning taking place mainly at this stage through identification with the parent of the child's own sex. Adolescence by contrast is marked by an increasing volume of heterosexual choices of preferred associates. During adolescence most persons achieve membership in a heterosexual group and acquire a heterosexual role.[3]

With some notable exceptions, field studies of adolescent peer groups have been few and inadequate and most studies of adolescent groups have

From Dexter C. Dunphy, "The Social Structure of Urban Adolescent Peer Groups," *Sociometry* 26 (1963):230–46. Reprinted by permission of The American Sociological Association.

aimed to assess the importance of isolated factors rather than to study groups as functioning entities. With the exception of studies of delinquent gangs, the literature is practically devoid of thorough analyses of particular groups and their dynamics. Consequently documented information on the forms and functions of adolescent peer groups is limited. Many writers distinguish two types of adolescent groups, usually referred to as "cliques" and "crowds." The most obvious difference between these two groups is their size. Hurlock, for instance, refers to the crowd as "the largest of the social units formed by adolescents."[4] The clique is usually regarded as smaller, more clearly defined and more cohesive than the crowd. Hollingshead states: "When there is a lack of homogeneity the peer group may be a clique, which is smaller and more purposefully organized than is the crowd. Exclusion of those who do not belong is the express purpose of the clique."[5] A wide survey of the use of these two terms in the literature on adolescence reveals no clear indication of the relative size limits of the two types of group nor agreement on what different functions, if any, these two groups perform for their members. While Hurlock suggests that cliques are the basic elements in a crowd,[6] Cole states that the clique "prevents many social contacts from taking place and reduces the effectiveness of those that do occur."[7] Similarly no clear picture exists of the internal structural properties of adolescent peer groups (e.g., leadership) nor of the dynamics by which groups function to induce the learning of a mature heterosexual role. The study reported here was therefore undertaken to provide some detailed information on the types, sizes, structure, and dynamics of adolescent peer groups in non-institutionalized urban setting.

The Research Design

This article summarizes some of the results of a field study undertaken in Sydney, Australia, between February, 1958, and December, 1960. Informal peer associations of adolescents were located in the community and studied in their natural settings. The research methods were developed in a pilot project with 60 adolescents. The subjects of the investigation itself were 303 adolescents amongst whom boys and girls were included in approximately equal numbers.[8] Ages ranged from 13 to 21 years. The groups were scattered throughout the Sydney Metropolitan area, were from differing socioeconomic backgrounds (although predominantly middle class) and were in most cases connected in some way with sponsored youth organizations. These clubs were used as points of departure for an exploration of the natural groups to which their members belonged, each group being studied for a period of from four to six months. Two natural associations of "unattached" youth were included to check a possible bias arising from the method of choosing subjects: no important differences were found between the structure and dynamics of these groups and the other groups in the study.[9]

The main problem in investigating the structural properties of adolescent groups is to find an appropriate method of research. Because of their informal nature, the most satisfactory method is participant observation. However, since these are adolescent peer groups, the adult observer is denied membership and full participation in them. A modified version of the participant-observer approach was developed in a pilot study. This consisted in making initial contacts with youth through institutional settings, establishing rapport and subsequently moving out into non-institutional settings. The author spent many hours on streetcorners, in milkbars and homes, at parties and on Sydney beaches with the groups being studied. All groups were informed of the nature of the study and agreed to cooperate. Other more formal methods were used in conjunction with informal observation and participation. Questionnaires were administered to all subjects, diaries were kept concurrently by the members of each group in which interaction with peers for a period of 1 week were recorded in detail; the majority of the subjects were interviewed at length, their answers to questions being recorded on tape. The result was a flexible method of observation designed to gather a large amount of detailed information with as little interference as possible to the normal functioning of the groups under study.

Results

Group Types.   An initial attempt to locate group boundaries through sociometric means proved confusing because of a considerable lack of correspondence between individual subjects' responses when asked to list those who belonged to their "crowd." However, observation of interaction, and interviewing, revealed a high level of consensus on the boundaries of membership groups. Groups were clearly recognized as definite entities, and high status members of these groups could give accurate (i.e., verifiable by observation of interaction) descriptions of group boundaries and could also list members in status terms. In fact, while many members could not accurately describe their own positions in the group structure, they could usually describe the positions of others with some precision.

Two kinds of groups were located by participant observation, by interview, and by analysis of the diaries. These correspond fairly close with those referred to as cliques and crowds in the literature, and this terminology will be applied to them here. Both types of groups are true peer groups since group members are of similar age and regard each other as acceptable associates.

The first and most obvious basis of differentiation between the group types was size, the clique being smaller than the crowd. Forty-four cliques were located varying in size from three to nine members and having an average membership of 6.2. Crowds were considerably larger. Twelve crowds were located have a range of membership from 15 to 30 and an average size of 20.2. On the average then, the clique is only about one-third the size of a crowd. No group was observed with a membership in the range ten to 14. Therefore, if these groups are typical, cliques and crowds are not two ends on a continuum of size but two distinct groups on a numerical basis alone. An examination of the two types of groups shows why this is so. *The crowd is essentially an association of cliques.* There was little variation in the number of cliques within the twelve crowds. No crowd had more than four or less than two component cliques. The average number of cliques forming a crowd was 3.1.

The distinct upper limit of nine members for the clique suggests the intimacy of the relationships between members. The limited membership makes possible the strong cohesion which is a marked characteristic of these groups. Their similarity in size to the family possibly facilitates the transference of the individual's allegiance to them and allows them to provide an alternative center of security. The larger number in the crowd obviously precludes such close relationships between members. Interviews showed that from the point of view of a member within one clique within a crowd, members of other cliques are acceptable associates but not "real buddies" like the members of his own clique.

While the cliques are the basic units in crowd structure, not all cliques were associated with crowds. This held for five of the 44 cliques in the study whose members either were not accorded or did not seek, status in a crowd. They were outside the crowd structure as some individuals (isolates) were outside the clique structure. Clique membership appears to be a prerequisite of crowd membership, since no case was found of an individual possessing crowd membership without at the same time being a member of a clique. On the other hand, one could be a clique member without being a crowd member. The members of cliques normally lived in close residential proximity and this appeared to be the main ascriptive requirement for clique membership. The cliques associated in a crowd were from adjacent residential localities and their members were of similar age and level of social development. Contrary to Cole's view, quoted above, cliques do not limit social contacts, but, on the contrary, the acquirement of clique membership is virtually the only way in which such contacts can be established and expanded.

Within localities, crowds were differentiated on an age basis, with two or three crowds associated in a status hierarchy. Five of these hierarchies, each in a different suburb, were objects of investigation in the study. Invariably, the mean age of members of a crowd higher in the hierarchy was higher than the mean age of members of a crowd lower in the hierarchy. All but one of the crowds in the study formed part of a hierarchy of two or three crowds, and in some hierarchies, upper status members of one crowd occupied low status positions in the crowd above. The difference between age means of crowds adjacent in such hierarchies varied from seven months to three years and seven months, but averaged about two years.

Since age was a major factor underlying crowd differentiation, it is not surprising that where two crowds were adjacent in a crowd hierarchy, the social distance between them (as measured by relative frequency of interaction) varied with the difference between the mean ages of their members. When there was a large gap between the mean ages of adjacent crowds, interaction between the members of the two crowds was extremely limited. Where the gap was small, interaction was far more frequent and the upper status members of the lower crowd tended to hold low status positions in the crowd above.

All crowds were heterosexual, and within crowds there was a consistent difference between the ages of boys and girls. In all crowds boys were older on the average than the girls with whom they associated. Differences between the mean ages of boys and girls in the same crowd ranged from three months to one year and ten months but averaged ten months. Many of the cliques of later adolescents were heterosexual and in all these the same age relationship between the sexes was apparent. The differentiation of the sexes along age lines parallels the typical age relationship between spouses in marriage.

Cliques and crowds perform different functions for their members. The clique centers mainly around talking. The members of one hierarchy, for example, recorded 69 clique settings and 25 crowd settings in their diaries. Of the 69 clique settings, the predominant activity in 56 of them was talking, while it was the main activity in only five of the 25 crowd settings. A similar trend was found in all groups. Analysis of the content of conversation in the clique shows that it performs an important instrumental function in that it is the center for the preparation of crowd activities, for dissemination of information about them, and for their evaluation after they are over. The crowd, on the other hand, is the center of larger and more organized social activities, such as parties and dances, which provide for interaction between the sexes. It acts as a reservoir of acceptable associates who can be drawn on to the extent required by any social activity. Thus cliques and crowds are not only different in size; they are also different in function.

There is a tendency for clique and crowd settings to be distributed differently throughout the week. In the hierarchy mentioned above, 16 of the 25 crowd settings took place at the weekend and only nine during the week. Of the clique settings, however, 47 occurred during the week and only 22 at the weekend. In all hierarchies the majority of crowd settings occurred at weekends, while the majority of clique settings occurred on weekdays.

Structural Change. In considering the hierarchical arrangement of crowds, certain general trends in the structural development of peer groups through the adolescent period become apparent. Some structural characteristics consistently appear before others in all hierarchies. An abstract ideal-typical outline of structural development is portrayed in Figure 1.

The initial stage of adolescent group development appears to be that of the isolated unisexual clique: i.e., isolated in terms of any relationship with corresponding groups of the opposite sex. This primary stage represents the persistence of the preadolescent "gang" into the adolescent period. Stage 2 introduces the first movement towards heterosexuality in group structure.[10] Unisexual cliques previously unrelated to cliques of the opposite sex now participate in heterosexual interaction. At this stage, however, interaction is considered daring and is only undertaken in the security of a group setting where the individual is supported by the presence of his own sex associates. Interaction at this stage is often superficially antagonistic. Stage 3 sees the formation of the heterosexual clique for the first time. Upper status members of unisexual cliques initiate individual-to-individual heterosexual interaction and the first dating occurs. Those adolescents who belong to these emergent heterosexual groups will maintain a membership role in their unisexual clique, so that they possess dual membership in two intersecting cliques. This initiates an extensive transformation of group structure by which there takes place a reorganization of unisexual cliques and the reformation of their membership into heterosexual cliques (stage 4). While the

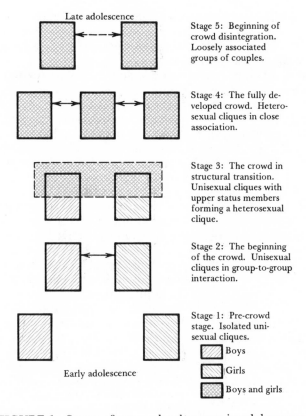

Late adolescence

Stage 5: Beginning of crowd disintegration. Loosely associated groups of couples.

Stage 4: The fully developed crowd. Heterosexual cliques in close association.

Stage 3: The crowd in structural transition. Unisexual cliques with upper status members forming a heterosexual clique.

Stage 2: The beginning of the crowd. Unisexual cliques in group-to-group interaction.

Stage 1: Pre-crowd stage. Isolated unisexual cliques.

Boys

Girls

Boys and girls

Early adolescence

FIGURE 1   Stages of group development in adolescence.

cliques persist as small intimate groups, their membership now comprises both sexes. Stage 5 sees the slow disintegration of the crowd and the formation of cliques consisting of couples who are going steady or engaged. Thus there is a progressive development of group structure from predominantly unisexual to heterosexual groups. In this transition, the crowd—an extended heterosexual peer group—occupies a strategic position. Membership in a crowd offers opportunities for establishing a heterosexual role. The crowd is therefore the most significant group for the individual, but crowd membership is dependent upon prior membership in a clique. In fact, the crowd is basically an interrelationship of cliques, and appears to consolidate the heterosexual learning appropriate to each stage of development. The majority of clique members, therefore, possess a determinate position in an extended hierarchical arrangement of cliques and crowds, in which high status is accorded to groups most developed in heterosexual structure. The course of the individual's social development appears to be strongly influenced by his position within this structure.

Internal Properties.   Boundaries of peer groups were clearly defined and boundary definition operated as a form of social control. Crowd boundaries were most rigidly defined. When peer group members were asked to choose associates to join them in a number of situations, only four to eight per cent of choices were directed outside the crowd. On the other hand 37 to

47 per cent of choices were directed outside the members' own cliques to members of cliques within the same crowd. The majority of choices were made within the respondent's own clique. Clique boundaries were less sharply defined than crowd boundaries since some individuals were willing to choose members of other cliques in the same crowd. Very few were prepared to choose outside their own crowd.

Boundary definition was a constant process which could be observed in recurring decisions such as who would be invited to parties or on swimming excursions. The meaning of boundary definition in practice can be illustrated by describing a party in which members of two crowds from the same hierarchy were involved. The hierarchy consisted of three crowds, the upper and middle crowds being fairly narrowly differentiated by age and therefore having two "marginal" members in common. At the instigation of the author, members of these two crowds were invited to a party held by one of the members of the upper crowd. Clique boundaries were most obvious at the beginning and the end of the evening. Members arrived and left in cliques. At the party itself, however, the cliques within each crowd showed a tendency to merge and members interacted across clique boundaries. The crowds were strongly differentiated. Although everyone was initially in the lounge room, the younger crowd gradually relegated itself to the kitchen, leaving the upper crowd in possession of the lounge room. This arrangement persisted throughout the rest of the evening. The two marginal members were clique leaders in the middle crowd, low status followers in the upper. Their behavior reflected their position in the hierarchy, for they oscillated from one room to the other throughout the evening. Two isolates, whom the author had arranged to be invited, showed contrasting ways of adjusting to the situation. The girl made no attempt to relate herself to either group, remained seated in one corner of the lounge room all evening, rarely spoke, and was left to make her own way home, unaccompanied. The boy attempted to relate himself to the upper crowd leader, was ignored, and remained on the fringe of those who gathered around this status figure. Thus both cliques and crowds are boundary maintaining systems in certain situations. When together, cliques in the same crowd tend to merge. However, only boundaries between cliques are relaxed. Those who did not possess membership in a component clique were not accepted into the crowd, whether or not they attempted to relate themselves to it.

In order to acquire a membership role, an individual has to pass from outside through the boundary into the group. This is definitely a matter of achievement. Members of groups reported that they had to "push themselves forward" to enter a group. A typical statement was: "Someone who gets in and pushes, gets into a group easiest. You just have to get in and push. People who stand back just don't make the grade." Acceptance into a group was not just a matter of achievement but also of conformity. It was reported by those who had achieved membership that a new member had to "fit in," "be the same to us." Or, as one boy put it: "All groups have a certain temperament of their own. Anyone new has to fit in; he must have similar aspects and outlooks and like similar things." By demanding initial conformity to peer group standards, members ensured that the crowd would be a cohesive entity capable of controlling the behavior of those in it in the interests of the dominant majority. The basic consensus of values which results is a major factor in the strong *esprit de corps* of most adolescent peer groups.

It is possible to lose a membership role and to pass through the group boundary out of the group. This was due to one of two causes, as was shown by an examination of a number of concrete cases. Firstly, ostracism was sometimes the result of a member's rejection of the authority of the group. A member who regarded himself as superior to others in the group, or his judgment as superior to the judgment of the group, was quickly cut down to size. Persistence in such an attitude involved exclusion from the group and the redefinition of the boundary to exclude the offender. Loss of a membership role could also occur where an individual failed to maintain achievement, especially heterosexual achievement, at the level of his peers. This involved at first a loss of status. Continued failure to achieve meant that the member was simply dropped from the group with a consequent readjustment of the group boundary.

Entrance to a peer group depends on conformity, and failure to continue to conform at any stage means exclusion from the group. Thus the definition of the group boundary is an important means of social control which ensures the maintenance of a high level of achievement in social development.

Role differentiation: Leader and Sociocenter.   Most adolescents claimed that their groups did not possess leaders. ("We don't like to think that there's a boss over us.") However, cliques were normally referred to by the name of one person in the group, e.g., "John Palmer's group." Other statements showed that while adolescents strongly denied that they had leaders, they did in fact implicitly recognize one person in the group as the incumbent of a leadership position. The following statement is typical of many made when adolescents discussed the groups they knew. "Rod has a group at Waverton, Joanne down there at North Sydney, and Julia up at Crows Nest. The groups revolve around them." In each peer group in the study there was one individual who occupied the major leadership position and who played an important and distinctive role in relating the group to its environment.

The structure of the external system of the cliques was basically composed of the relationship of the clique leaders' positions to each other, and these positions were integrated primarily through a common relationship with a crowd leader. In fact, the clique leaders assumed group representative roles in the external system of the clique. They were better known outside their group than any of their followers—a finding consistent with Whyte's account[11] of gang structures. Thus there were two types of leadership position differentiated, corresponding with the two main types of adolescent groups. There were both clique and crowd leaders. Clique leaders were more socially mobile than their followers and were in more frequent contact with others outside the clique. The communication structure of the crowd consisted in the interrelationship of the clique and crowd leadership positions. Consequently clique leaders were better informed than their followers about what was going on in the crowd, and played a decisive part in decision making. The high status accorded the crowd leader's position is reflected in verbal and written comments about those who occupied these positions. The crowd leader appeared to be a coordinating and integrating figure in the social structure of the crowd whose presence set the seal of success on a crowd event. The incumbent of this position was always a male, and usually the leader of the largest and most heterosexually advanced clique in the crowd. Thus he had already shown his organizational capacity in a clique setting. Each clique leader was also the focus of intra-clique interaction. He was thus not only the best informed person in his clique about events and people in the crowd but also the best informed person about what was going on in his own clique. As such, he occupied a strategic position between the external and the internal systems of his own group. His followers realized this and relied on the leader for information about others in the clique and in the crowd and about clique and crowd activities. While the clique leader's position is subordinate to that of the crowd leader, it is also invested with power and high status.

The clique leader's role in the coordination of his clique with others in the crowd exposes him to two sources of role expectations. In his position as leader of the clique he is expected by members of the clique to perform essential leadership functions. As a key figure in the crowd structure, he is subject to the expectations of the other clique leaders in the crowd. His subordinate position in relation to the crowd means that he is particularly susceptible to influence from that source. He is thus in a position where he relays the general wishes and attitudes of his followers to others in the crowd and the influence of others, particularly status superiors, to his followers. The leader role consists of organizational skills required for the coordination of clique activities with the activities of other cliques in the crowd. It also consists of personality traits allowing the leader to mix freely with others outside his clique and maintain friendly relations within the clique. *Most importantly he has to play an advanced heterosexual role since the crowd is essentially a heterosexual association.* Leaders dated more often, were more likely to be going steady, and had achieved this relationship earlier than other members of their cliques. Where a follower attained a superior level of heterosexual achievement than the leader, there was a change of leadership or a splitting of the group structure. The admired form of heterosexual role varies with the stage of structural development of the group. For instance, an aggressive role towards the opposite sex is admired at stage 2 (see Figure 1), but results in loss of a leadership position if maintained by the leader at stage 3.

Leaders were not only superior in heterosexual development but were responsible for maintaining the general of heterosexual development in their cliques. They acted as confidants and advisors in matters of heterosexual behavior and even organized "partners" for "slow learners." They thus brought about a progressive development in heterosexual relationships on the part of those in their groups. The clique leaders, one of whom is also the crowd leader, form an elite within the extended peer group or crowd. An elite is a small proportion of the population who together exercise a degree of control over persons and resources disproportionate to their number. The leaders are an elite in this sense in that, together, they strongly influence the behavior of those in thier cliques by consistently maintaining the pressure to achieve higher levels of social development. They do this through their centrality in the communication structure and their possession of the most valued "resources" of their groups: organizational skills, desired personality traits, and the ability to play an advanced sex role.

Within the crowd, role differentiation occurred also along the expressive dimension. Just as there was a central instrumental role in the crowd (the crowd leader), so there was a major expressive role referred to here as a "sociocenter." The sociocenter was a specialist in humor. While the status accorded this position varied from one crowd to another, the position was well established in all crowds. The incumbent was always popular, well-liked and the most extroverted member of the crowd. When the crowd gathered he usually dominated the center of the group's attention with a continual flow of witticisms and practical jokes. Because of the attention paid him in crowd settings, adults frequently regarded the sociocenter as the leader and inferred that the group was therefore essentially frivolous in character.

The degree to which the sociocenter role was differentiated varied considerably from one crowd to another, and the extent of the differentiation appeared to be influenced by the character of the crowd leader's role. In crowds where the crowd leader was seen by the members as playing an authoritarian, directive role, the sociocenter was highly differentiated. Where the crowd leader was seen as non-directive, as leading simply by virtue of superior social skills, the role was less differentiated. The more the crowd leader directly or indirectly forced the pace of social achievement in the crowd, the more highly differentiated the role of the sociocenter appeared.

This bears a similarity to R. F. Bales' finding[12] that differentiation in small problem-solving laboratory groups occurred along two axes, instrumental and expressive, and resulted in the emergence of a "task specialist" and a "best-liked man." These types appear to correspond to the "crowd leader" and the "sociocenter" reported above. Bales suggested that[13]

> a certain amount of ambivalence tends to center on the task specialist. He tends to be liked because he is satisfying needs in relation to the task area. But he also tends to arouse a certain amount of hostility because his prestige is rising relative to the other members, because he talks a large proportion of the time, and because his suggestions constitute proposed new elements to be added to the common culture, to which all members will be committed if they agree. Whatever readjustments the members have to make in order to feel themselves committed will tend to produce minor frustrations, anxieties and hostilities. These are centered to some degree on the object most active in provoking the disturbance—the task specialist.

In the adolescent peer group, the leader is the person who plays the most advanced heterosexual role. He moves the group to participate in heterosexual activities and encourages members to develop more natural heterosexual roles. While the members are generally motivated to achievement, this still implies new levels of conformity and commitment. The crowd leader's role is therefore particularly analogous to that of the task specialist who is similarly concerned with increased performance and similarly induces culture change. like the task specialist, also, the peer group leader is the center of the communication pattern and high in status relative to the other members. It seems likely that the sociocenter performs the system function of relieving the tension created in the group by the leader, tension which is at its highest in the heterosexual crowd situation. His specialization in humor, a form of tension release, supports this interpretation. The more the leader dominates, the more tension is created and the more differentiated the sociocenter role becomes. If this did not occur, the tension would tend to destroy the cohesion of the group and thus impede progress towards higher goals. Bales has noted the interdependence of these two roles in his groups and this was apparent in the peer groups. They are by nature high consensus groups since only members who conform to the culture of the group are admitted. The crowd leader and the sociocenter play mutually supportive roles in the crowd structure, the complementarity of the two roles preserving the equilibrium of the crowd.

Socialization Process in the Adolescent Peer Group.   The primary stage of socialization, which occurs in the family, is largely achieved through the identification of the child with his parents and his consequent incorporation of their norms. This stage has a strong effect on the acquisition of a basic sex role. The peer group at adolescence assumes many of the functions previously performed for the individual by the family and is thus of considerable significance in promoting his increasing independence from the family. If there is an internal consistency in the whole process of socialization through childhood and adolescence, we would expect socialization to take place through an identification with the peer group leaders similar to that with the parents. At the beginning of this article it was mentioned that discrepancies were observed when subjects were asked to name those in their crowd. The list given by an individual usually did not match very well the group others named as his associates and which could actually be observed in concrete situations. However, in the social structure of these membership groups as identified by participant observation, through interviews, and through analysis of diary records, these discrepancies showed up as a highly consistent and meaningful trend. When clique members were asked to name those in their crowd, they tended to name those in their own clique and the leadership elite in their crowd. The leadership elite was in fact highly "overchosen" in the sense that they received many more choices than they themselves made. There was a consistent discrepancy in the direction of high status between the groups in which the individuals actually participated and the groups to which they referred themselves.

By using a chi square technique, the probability of this trend occurring by chance could be tested. However, the test could be applied only to hierarchies where there were proportionately few intercrowd choices so that the crowds could be treated as if they were independent entities. Four of the five hierarchies met this criterion. Two hypotheses were tested. (a) Leaders, when choosing outside their own clique and within the same crowd, choose other clique leaders significantly more than they choose followers, when allowance is made for the relative proportion of leaders to followers. (b) Followers, when choosing outside their own clique and within the same crowd, choose clique leaders significantly more than they choose followers, when allowance is made for the relative proportion of leaders to followers. Hypothesis (a) was supported in three of the four hierarchies at the 0.1%, 1%, and 2% levels respectively, but the chi square was not significant in the fourth. Inspection of the fifth hierarchy shows that those choices made within the crowd boundaries show the same trend. Hypothesis (b) was supported in all four hierarchies at the .1%, .1%, .01%, and 5% levels respectively. Inspection of those choices made within crowd boundaries in the fifth hierarchy shows the same trend.

In some cases, choices were made of members of other crowds in the same hierarchy. These were usually choices between high status members of one crowd and low status members of another older crowd. Fifty-three choices of this kind were made in all the hierarchies. Forty-nine of these were directed upwards to members of crowds higher in status than the ones to which the choosers belong. The remaining four were directed downwards to members of crowds lower in status. Thus an examination of all extra-% choices reveals a strong and highly significant tendency to list clique leaders in the same crowd and members of a crowd higher in the status hierarchy when naming associates. In particular, those lower in status than the chooser tend to be omitted. Members of the leadership elite within crowds were particularly overchosen. These results can be interpreted as showing a general upward trend in status terms in the pattern of identification in these groups. In naming those who belong to their "crowd," therefore, these adolescents apparently listed their *reference* rather than their *membership* groups, suggesting that the social structure is stabilized by the ego-involvement of clique members with the clique and crowd leaders.

These data lend support to Freud's notion, advanced particularly in his *Group Psychology and the Analysis of the Ego*,[14] that a primary group is a number of individuals who have taken the same person, the leader, as their ego-ideal. "We already begin to divine that the mutual tie between members of a group is in the nature of an identification of this kind, based upon an important emotional common quality; and we suspect that this common quality lies in the nature of the tie with the leader."[15] Thus Freud's view emphasizes that the bond with the leader is of more importance to group stability than are the ties between the members and that, in fact, it is the former which confers significance on the latter. "A primary group of this kind is a number of individuals who have put one and the same object in the place of their ego ideal and have consequently identified themselves with each other in their ego."[16] Freud regarded the family as the prototype of every human group and the leader as a parent substitute. Certainly the position of the leader in the peer group is analogous in some ways with that of the parent and a similar identification appears to occur. However, the evidence above does suggest that there is identification not only with the leader of one's clique, but beyond that an identification with a number of status figures in the wider peer group—the crowd. The interviews suggested that there is a progressive differentiation of this object system. Generally speaking, the lower a member's status in the social structure, the less differentiated the mental picture he possessed of the positions of others and their relationships with each other. It seems reasonable to deduce from this that the first stage of socialization into a group of peers, the clique, is dependent on the differentiation by the initiate of the leader, and his identification with him. From this stage the pattern of identification suggests that there is a progressive differentiation of the whole object system and a single reference idol (the clique leader) is replaced by a system of social objects which consists basically in the pattern of crowd leadership positions and roles in their interrelationships.

Discussion

In the socialization of the individual his transition from the nuclear family to wider adult society can take place in many ways. In western urban society, the peer group is one important avenue through which this can occur. In Sydney, for instance, where this study was undertaken, it appears that about 70 per cent of boys and 80 per cent of girls at ages 14 and 15 belong to peer groups similar to those dealt with here.[17] If the groups reported are typical, socialization within the peer group system is an extension of socialization within the family system and shows important resemblances in pattern. There is, for instance, a similar differentiation of structure along instrumental and expressive lines with both high status instrumental and expressive roles functioning to preserve the equilibrium of the peer group system. As in the family, the individual proceeds through a series of successively more complex systems of relationships and in the process identifies with status figures, internalizing their roles. Thus his personality continues to expand through the progressive differentiation of his object system.

It appears of some significance that socialization within the adolescent peer group system begins as the stable state the individual enjoyed as latency child in the family is upset by new social expectations at puberty, leading him to establish an increased dependence on the peer group. Initially this group is the unisexual clique, which represents the continuation of the preadolescent "gang" and at this stage is a group comparable in size to the family. In order to achieve and maintain membership in this group, the individual must show his readiness to conform to the group's authority. This is made easier through his identification with the clique leader who embodies many of the social skills and personality traits admired in the group. The clique establishes and reinforces the individual's drive to achieve heterosexuality, since it is, or becomes, a subsystem of the crowd; the crowd in its turn is only a subsystem of a hierarchy of crowds. Thus through clique membership the individual is inducted into an external peer group system markedly different from the family in size. About middle adolescence there is a major transformation of the clique system which has persisted in a relatively stable form. A new clique system evolves from this structurally unstable stage. Groups become heterosexual, members having established a significant relationship with a member of the opposite sex. The crowd persists long enough to ensure that the basic role characteristics underlying this relationship are thoroughly acquired. It then breaks into cliques of loosely associated couples as members move towards marriage. The social structure of urban adolescent peer groups has the effect of maintaining a high level of achievement which ensures that most adolescents progressively acquire an increasingly mature heterosexual role.

NOTES

1. Talcott Parsons and Robert F. Bales, *Family, Socialization and Interaction Process* (London: Routledge & Kegan Paul, 1956), p. 38.
2. David P. Asubel, *Theory and Problems of Adolescent Development* (New York: Grune & Stratton, 1954); James H. Brossard, *The Sociology of Child Development* (New York: Rinehart, 1948); Paul H. Furfey, *The Gang Age: A Study of the Preadolescent Boy and His Recreational Needs* (New York: Macmillan, 1926); Jacob L. Moreno, *Who Shall Survive?* (Washington, D.C.: Nervous and Mental Disease Publishing Company, 1934); Frederic M. Thrasher, *The Gang* (Chicago: Chicago University Press, 1936); William F. Whyte, *Street Corner Society* (Chicago: Chicago University Press, 1943).

3. Luella Cole, *Psychiatry of Adolescence* (New York: Rinehart, 1948); William F. Connel, Elizabeth P. Francis, and Elizabeth E. Skilbeck, *Growing up in an Australian City* (Melbourne: Australian Council for Educational Research, 1957); Paul H. Furfey, "The Group Life of the Adolescent," *Journal of Educational Sociology* 14 (December 1940); 195–204; August B. Hollingshead, *Elmstown's Youth* (New York: McGraw-Hill, 1949); Elizabeth B. Hurlock, *Adolescent Development* (New York: McGraw-Hill, 1949); Moreno, *Who Shall Survive?*

4. Hurlock, *Adolescent Development,* p. 173.

5. Hollingshead, *Elmstown's Youth,* p. 448.

6. Hurlock, *Adolescent Development,* p. 173.

7. Cole, *Psychiatry of Adolescence,* p. 264.

8. In natural groups such as these, there are some membership changes over time. The numbers refer to the total membership of the groups at the time the sociometric questionnaire was administered.

9. However, the extent to which this sample of Sydney youth is "typical" is not known. Of the "natural associations," one is a hierarchy consisting of two crowds, the other a lower-class gang at Stage 1 (see Figure 1).

10. I have deliberately not specified modal ages for the onset of the stages outlined in Figure 1. The variation in the ages at which these phases of group development are encountered is so great that measures of central tendency, by themselves, would be misleading; and any useful estimate of standard deviations would require a much more comprehensive study than that described here. The average age of members in one isolated clique of girls (Stage 1), for example, was 16 years 0 months. On the other hand, Stage 3 had been reached by another clique of girls with an average age of only 13 years ten months, and the average age of the interacting clique of boys was 14 years six months. The figure suggests the order of structural changes in the adolescent peer group but the differing rates, and the conditions affecting these rates, need further, more extensive investigations.

11. Whyte, *Street Corner Society.*.

12. Parsons and Bales, *Family, Socialization and Interaction Process*.

13. Ibid., p. 297.

14. Sigmund Freud, *Group Psychology and the Analysis of the Ego* (New York: Liveright, 1922).

15. Ibid., p. 108.

16. Ibid., p. 120.

17. William F. Connel et al., *Growing up.*

24

The Development of Children's Orientations Toward a Moral Order: Sequence in the Development of Moral Thought

Lawrence Kohlberg

Since the concept of a moral attitude forms the basic building block of the social psychological theories of Freud (1922), Durkheim (1906), Parsons (1960) and others, there is reason to agree with McDougall (1908) that "the fundamental problem of social psychology is the moralization of the individual by the society."

Following the leads of Freud and Durkheim, most social scientists have viewed moralization as a process of *internalizing* culturally given external rules through rewards, punishments, or identification. Without questioning the view that the end point of the moralization process is one in which conduct is oriented to internal standards, one may well reject the assumption that such internal standards are formed simply through a process of "stamping in" the external prohibitions of the culture upon the child's mind. From the perspective of a developmental psychology such as that of Piaget (1932) or J. M. Baldwin (1906), internal moral standards are rather the outcome of a set of transformations of primitive attitudes and conceptions. These transformations accompany cognitive growth in the child's perceptions and orderings of a social world with which he is continuously interacting.

Directed by this developmental conception of the moralization process, our research has been oriented to the following tasks:

From L. Kohlberg, "The Development of Children's Orientations Toward a Moral Order: I. Sequence in the Development of Moral Thought," *Vita Humana* 6 (1963):11–33, by permission of S. Karger AG, Basel.

1. The empirical isolation of sequential stages in the development of moral thought.
2. The study of the relation of the development of moral thought to moral conduct and emotion.
3. The application of a stage analysis of moral judgment to subcultural differences as well as pathological deviance in moral orientations.
4. The isolation of the social forces and experiences required for the sequential development of moral orientations.

In the present paper, we shall summarize our findings as they relate to moralization as an age-developmental process, and we shall compare this characterization with that of Piaget.

The Isolation of Six Stages of Development in Moral Thought

Our developmental analysis of moral judgment is based upon data obtained from a core group of 72 boys living in Chicago suburban areas. The boys were of three age groups: 10, 13, and 16. Half of each group was upper-middle class; half, lower to lower-middle class. For reasons to be discussed in the sequel to this paper, half of each group consisted of popular boys (according to classroom sociometric tests), while half consisted of socially isolated boys. All the groups were comparable in I.Q.

We have also used our procedures with a group of 24 delinquents aged 16, a group of 24 six-year-olds, and a group of 50 boys and girls aged 13 residing outside of Boston.

The basic data were two-hour tape-recorded interviews focused upon hypothetical moral dilemmas. Both the content and method of the interviews were inspired by the work of Piaget (1932). The ten situations used were ones in which acts of obedience to legal-social rules or to the commands of authority conflicted with the human needs or welfare of other individuals. The child was asked to choose whether one should perform the obedience-serving act or the need-serving act and was then asked a series of questions probing the thinking underlying his choice.

Our analysis of results commenced with a consideration of the action alternatives selected by the children. These analyses turned out to shed little light on moral development. Age trends toward choice in favor of human needs, such as might be expected from Piaget's (1932) theory, did not appear. The child's reason for his choice and his way of defining the conflict situations did turn out to be developmentally meaningful, however.

As an example, one choice dilemma was the following:

Joe's father promised he could go to camp if he earned the $50 for it, and then changed his mind and asked Joe to give him the money he had earned. Joe lied and said he had only earned $10 and went to camp using the other $40 he had made. Before he went, he told his younger brother Alex about the money and about lying to their father. Should Alex tell their father?

Danny, a working class 10-year-old of I.Q. 98 replied: "In one way it would be right to tell on his brother or his father might get mad at him and spank him. In another way it would be right to keep quiet or his brother might beat him up."

Obviously whether Danny chooses to fulfill his "obligation" to adult authority or to peer loyalty will depend on which action he perceives as leading to the greater punishment. What interests us most, however, is the fact that Danny does not appear to have a conception of moral obligation. His judgments are predictions. From one to the next of the situations presented him, Danny was not consistently "authoritarian" or "humanistic" in his choices, but he was consistent in choosing in terms of the physical consequences involved.

A careful consideration of individual cases eventually led us to define six developmental types of value-orientation. A Weberian ideal-typological procedure was used to achieve a combination of empirical consistency and logical consistency in defining the types. The six developmental types were grouped into three moral levels and labeled as follows:

Level I. Pre-Moral Level

Type 1. Punishment and obedience orientation.
Type 2. Naive instrumental hedonism.

Level II. Morality of Conventional Role-Conformity

Type 3. Good-boy morality of maintaining good relations, approval of others.
Type 4. Authority maintaining morality.

Level III. Morality of Self-Accepted Moral Principles

Type 5. Morality of contract and of democratically accepted law.
Type 6. Morality of individual principles of conscience.

These types will be described in more detail in subsequent sections of this paper. The typology rests upon 30 different general aspects of morality which the children brought into their thinking. One such aspect was the child's use of concept of rights, another his orientation toward punitive justice, a third his consideration of intentions as opposed to consequences of action, etc. Each aspect was conceived as a dimension defined by a six-level scale, with each level of the scale corresponding to one of the six types of morality just listed.

A "motivational" aspect of morality was defined by the motive mentioned by the subject in justifying moral action. Six levels of motive were isolated, each congruent with one of the developmental types. They were as follows:

1. Punishment by another.
2. Manipulation of goods, rewards by another.
3. Disapproval by others.
4. Censure by legitimate authorities followed by guilt feelings.
5. Community respect and disrespect.
6. Self-condemnation.

These motives fall into three major levels. The first two represent on the verbal level what McDougall (1905) termed "the stage in which the operation of the instinctive impulses is modified by the influence of rewards and punishments." The second two correspond to McDougall's second stage "in which conduct is controlled in the main by anticipation of social praise and blame." The fifth, and especially the sixth, correspond to McDougall's third and "highest stage in which conduct is regulated by an ideal that enables a man to act in the way that seems to him right regardless of the praise or blame of his immediate social environment."

A more cognitive aspect of morality, conceptions of rights, was defined in terms of the following levels:

1. No real conception of a right. "Having a right" to do something equated with "being right," obeying authority.
2. Rights are factual ownership rights. Everyone has a right to do what they want with themselves and their possessions, even though this conflicts with rights of others.
3. Same as the second level concept but qualified by the belief that one has no right to do evil.
4. Recognition that a right is a claim, a legitimate exception, as to the actions of others. In general, it is an earned claim, e.g., for payment for work.
5. A conception of unearned, universal individual or human rights in addition to rights linked to a role or status.
6. In addition to level 5 conceptions, a notion of respecting the individual life and personality of the other.

Each of the 50 to 150 moral ideas or statements expressed by a child in the course of an interview could be assigned to one of 180 cells (30 dimensions × 6 levels per dimension) in the classification system. This classification yielded scores for each boy on each of the six types of thought based on the percentage of all his statements which were of the given type. Judges were able to assign responses to the moral levels with an adequate degree of agreement, expressed by product moment correlations between judges ranging from .68 to .84.

In spite of the variety of aspects of morality tapped by the 30 dimensions, there appeared to be considerable individual consistency in level of thought. Thus 15 boys in our original group of 72 were classified (in terms of their modal response) as falling in the first of our six types. On the average, 45% of the thinking of these 15 boys could be characterized as Type 1.

The differences between our age groups offer evidence concerning the developmental nature of the typology. The age trends for usage of the six types of thought are presented in Figure 1.

It is evident that our first two types of thought decrease with age, our next two types increase until age 13 and then stabilize, and our last two types increase until age 16. Analyses of variance of the percentage usage of each type of thought by the 10-, 13-, and 16-year-old groups were carried out.[1] The differences between the three age groups in usage of all types of thought but one (Type 3) were found to be significant beyond the .01 level.

If our stages of moral thinking are to be taken as supporting the developmental view of moralization, evidence not only of age trends, but of sequentiality is required. While the age trends indicate that some modes of

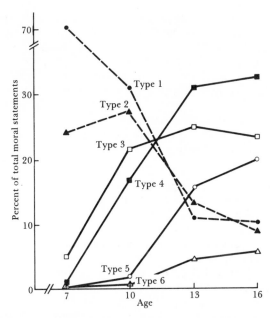

FIGURE 1   Use of six types of moral judgments at four ages.

thought are generally more difficult or advanced than other modes of thought, they do not demonstrate that attainment of each mode of thought is prerequisite to the attainment of the next higher in a hypothetical sequence.

Because the higher types of moral thought replace, rather than add to, the lower modes of thought, the Guttman (1950) scaling technique used by other investigators to establish certain cognitive developmental sequences (Schuessler and Strauss 1950; Wohlwill 1960) is not appropriate for our material. A more appropriate statistical model is derived from Guttman's (1954) quasi-simplex correlation matrix. The "simplex" pattern of intercorrelations derives from the expectation that the more two types of thought are separated from one another in a developmental sequence, the lower should be the correlations between them. This expectation can be compared with the actual intercorrelations obtained among the six types of thought.

Each child had a profile showing the percent of his responses that fell within each of the six types of thought. These profiles permitted us to correlate each of the six types of thought with each of the others across the sample of 72 boys, aged 10 to 16. The resulting product-moment correlation matrix is presented in Table 1. Each correlation reflects the extent to which the individuals who use the type of thought identified by the numbers at the left margin of the matrix also use a second type of thought identified by the numbers above the matrix.

The expectation applied to the matrix is that the correlations between two types of thought should decrease as these two types are increasingly separated in the developmental hierarchy. The matrix presented in Table 1 indicates general agreement with the expectation. The correlations diminish as we move away from the main diagonal entries, whether we go across the columns or down the rows. (The correlations are markedly negative, par-

Table 1 Matrix of intercorrelations between six types of moral judgment

Type	1	2	3	4	5	6
1	x					
2	55	x				
3	−41	−19	x			
4	−52	−41	18	x		
5	−52	−58	09	00	x	
6	−37	−43	−29	−07	23	x

tially because of the necessity for one percentage score to decrease as another increases.) Furthermore, correlations of types within the three main levels are higher than between levels, supporting our distinction of levels.[2]

The First Two Stages Compared with Piaget's Stages

Our proposed sequence of stages must have logical as well as empirical support. In characterizing our stages, we shall attempt a logical justification of their location in the hierarchy and at the same time, a comparison of our stages and concepts with Piaget's (1932) theory of developmental stages of moral judgment.[3]

Piaget (1932) starts from a conception of morality as respect for rules, a respect derived from personal respect for the authorities who promulgate and teach the rules. The young child's respect for authority and rules is originally unilateral and absolutistic, but in the 8- to 12-year-olds, this respect becomes mutual, reciprocal and relativistic. Unilateral respect for adults is said to inspire a *heteronomous* attitude toward adult rules as sacred and unchangeable. This attitude is believed to be supported by two cognitive defects in the young child's thought. One defect, egocentrism, the confusion of one's own perspective with that of others, leads to an inability to see moral value as relative to various persons or ends. The other defect, realism, the confusion of subjective phenomena with objective things, leads to a view of moral rules as fixed, eternal entities rather than as psychosocial expectations. The moral ideology resulting from the interaction of heteronomous respect and cognitive realism is described as "moral realism."

Piaget believes that the development of mutual respect toward other individuals in the 8- to 12-year-olds leads to an "autonomous" regard for the rules as products of group agreement and as instruments of cooperative purposes. "Mutual respect" is believed to be associated with the cognitive capacity to differentiate one's own value perspective from that of others (decline of egocentrism) and both of these trends are believed to arise largely through peer-group interaction.

Several of the thirty dimensions characterizing our six types are based on Piaget's conceptions. Our Moral Type 1 shares such characteristics of Piaget's heteronomous as concern for consequences rather than intentions, lack of awareness of relativity of value, definition of right as obedience to authority. These and othe Type 1 characteristics are illustrated by an excerpt from an interview with Tommy (age 10, working class, I.Q. 128). The excerpt also illustrates how the interview method traces back the child's immediate judgments to the unstated but basic assumptions or "principles" behind them.

This portion of the interview is in response to the third of the 10 moral dilemmas:

In Europe, a woman was near death from a special kind of cancer. There was one drug that the doctors thought might save her. It was a form of radium that a druggist in the same town had recently discovered. The drug was expensive to make, but the druggist was charging ten times what the drug cost him to make. He paid $200 for the radium and charged $2000 for a small dose of the drug. The sick woman's husband, Heinz, went to everyone he knew to borrow the money, but he could only get together about $1000 which is half of what it cost. He told the druggist that his wife was dying and asked him to sell it cheaper or let him pay later. But the druggist said: "No, I discovered the drug and I'm going to make money from it." So Heinz got desperate and broke into the man's store to steal the drug for his wife. Should the husband have done that?

The interview proceeded as follows:

"His wife was sick and if she didn't get the drug quickly, she might die. Maybe his wife is an important person and runs a store and the man buys stuff from her and can't get it any other place. The police would probably blame the owner that he didn't save the wife. That would be like killing with a gun or knife."

(Interviewer: Would it be all right to put the druggist in the electric chair for murder?)

"If she could be cured by the drug and they didn't give it to her, I think so, because she could be an important lady like Betsy Ross, she made the flag. And if it was President Eisenhower, he's important, and they'd probably put the man in the electric chair because that isn't fair."

(Should the punishment be more if she's an important person?)

"If someone important is in a plane and is allergic to heights and the stewardess won't give him medicine because she's only got enough for one and she's got a sick one, a friend, in back, they'd probably put the stewardess in a lady's jail because she didn't help the important one."

(Is it better to save the life of one important person or a lot of unimportant people?)

"All the people that aren't important because one man just has one house, maybe a lot of furniture, but a whole bunch of people have an awful lot of furniture and some of these poor people might have a lot of money and it doesn't look it."

On the one hand we notice Tommy's reasoning ability, his utilitarian calculation of the economics of the greater good. On the other hand we notice that the calculation of value is based on a "primitive" assumption as to the basis of moral values. A prosaic and commendable concern about the wife's life is eventually based on the notion that the value of a life is determined by its "importance" and that such importance is essentially a function of the amount of furniture owned.

Why are we justified in using the term "primitive" in describing the derivation of the value of life from the value of furniture? Awarding moral value to furniture involves a failure to differentiate the self's point of view from that of others, or to differentiate what the community holds as a shared or moral value (the value of life) and what the individual holds as a private value (the desire for furniture). Such a lack of sense of subjectivity of value is also suggested by Tommy's definition of culpability in terms of conse-quences rather than intentions (the wickedness of the druggist depends on his causing the loss of an important life).

It seems warranted then to view our Type 1 responses as reflecting cognitively primitive value assumptions.

Type 1 value assumptions, furthermore, are externalized from the motivational point of view, as indicated by definitions of right and wrong in terms of punishment and conformity to power-figures. As an example, Tommy defines the druggist's wrong in terms of a prediction with regard to punishment, and in terms of conformity to the wishes of important persons.

Such an interpretation of Tommy's responses as involving external motives is open to question, however. Piaget would see those responses as reflecting the young child's deep respect for authority and rules. Piaget sees the young child's morality as externally oriented only in a cognitive sense, not in a motivational sense. According to Piaget, the strong emotional respect the young child feels for authority and rules makes him feel unable to judge for himself, and forces him to rely on external adult sanctions and commands to define what is right and wrong. In the Piaget view, the child is oriented to punishment only because punishment is a cue to what is disap-proved by adults or by the "sacred World-Order."

In contrast to Piaget's interpretation, it has seemed to us simpler to start with the assumption that the Type 1 definition of wrong in terms of punish-ment reflects a realistic-hedonistic desire to avoid punishment, rather than a deep reverence for the adult "World-Order." The children of 10 and older who represent Type 1 morality did not in fact seem to show strong respect for adult authority. A case in point is Danny who, in a situation of conflict between brother and father, defined the right choice in terms of a prediction as to which one would retaliate more heavily. Danny went on to say:

"My brother would say, 'If you tell on me, I'll whip you with my belt real hard.' "

(What would you do then?)

"Well, if I was to tell my Dad if my brother Butchie was still hurting me, my brother Butchie would go find another house to live in."

Danny scores high on various attributes of Piaget's "moral realism," but it is hard to see Danny as expressing what Piaget terms "the sacredness of rules," "unilateral respect for adults," or a "belief in a World-Order."

We have concluded that it is possible to interpret all our observations with regard to "moral realism" without invoking Piaget's notion of the child's sense of sacredness of authority and rules. This conclusion is consistent with the findings of other studies of Piaget's moral judgment dimensions, as is documented elsewhere (Kohlberg 1963).

Regardless of the validity of Piaget's interpretation of "moral realism," Piaget's assumption that the young child feels a strong idealized moral respect for adult authority requires direct investigation. Piaget shares this assumption with psychoanalysts, and some form of the assumption seems critical for widely accepted notions as to the early childhood origins of adult neurotic guilt. In collaboration with B. Brener, we attempted a direct study of the validity of the Piaget assumption of "heteronomous respect" to explain the moral judgments of children aged four to eight. Earlier work with children of six and seven indicated that these children defined right and wrong mainly by reference to punishment when faced with simplified versions of our moral dilemmas. Did this indicate a basically "hedonistic" view of right or wrong or did it rather reflect a lack of cognitive resources for answering "why" questions in the context of a concern for conformity to sacred authority (Piaget's view)?

To investigate this issue, 96 children, aged 4, 5, and 7 were confronted with doll-enactments of stories in which disobedience to a rule (or adult) was followed by reward, and other stories in which obedience to a rule was followed by punishment. One such story was of a boy who was ordered to watch a baby on a couch while his mother left the house. The boy in the story proceeded to run out of the house and play outside. The S was asked to complete the story. The S was told that the mother returned and gave the disobedient boy some candy. S was then asked whether the child-doll had done good or bad, and a series of related questions.

In general, the 4-year-olds defined the story act as good or bad according to the reward or punishment rather than according to the rule or adult command. The older children showed considerable conflict, some of the 7-year-olds defining right and wrong in terms of the rule and showing concern about the "injustice" of punishing good and rewarding evil. These older children, however, still explained the rightness and wrongness of the act in relation to sanctions, but took a long-range or probabilistic view of this relation. Disobedience might have been rewarded in that situation, the children said, but in general it would still lead to punishment.

These results, while not consistent with Piaget's assumptions, should not be used to conclude that the moral decisions of 4–5-year-olds are based on crafty hedonism. Only as children reach a level of cognitive development at which the meaning of moral concepts can be differentiated from punishment can they attain either a definite hedonism or a degree of disinterested respect for authority.

The emergence of individualistic hedonism out of such growing cognitive differentiation is suggested by the responses which fall in our Type 2. Just as our first stage of morality coincides descriptively with Piaget's "heteronomous stage" but differs from it in interpretation, so our second stage coincides descriptively with Piaget's autonomous stage but differs from its interpretation. Like Piaget and others, we found an increase in the use of reciprocity (exchange and retaliation) as a basis for choice and judgment in the years six to ten, though not thereafter. We also found age increases in notions of relativism of value, and in egalitarian denial of the moral superiority of authorites.

These reactions were common enough and well enough associated in our 10-year-olds to help define our Type 2. The tendency to define value relative to private needs is reflected in the response of Jimmy (a 10-year-old working-class boy, I.Q. 105) to our test situation about mercy-killing. The story continues the plight of the wife dying of cancer as follows:

The doctor finally got some of the radium drug for Heinz's wife. But it didn't work, and there was no other treatment known to medicine which could save her. So the doctor knew that she had only about six months to live. She was in terrible pain, but she was so weak that a good dose of a pain-killer like ether or morphine would make her die sooner. She was delirious and almost crazy with pain, and in her calm periods, she would ask the doctor to give her enough to kill her. She said she couldn't stand the pain and she was going to die in a few months anyway.

Should the doctor do what she asks and make her die to put her out of her terrible pain?

Jimmy replied, "It's according to how you look at it. From the doctor's point of view, it could be a murder charge. From her point of view, it isn't paying her to live anymore if she's going to be in pain."

(How about if there were a law against it?)

"It should be up to her; it's her life. It's the person's life, not the law's life."

In this situation Jimmy defines right action instrumentally, as means to individual values; he defines it relativistically, in relation to the conflicting values of various individuals; and he defines it hedonistically, in terms of "paying" in pleasure and pain. The woman has ownership rights over herself, she is her own property. In more mature types of thought rights are defined relative to duties, the law is seen as defending and defining rights, and the law's respect for the woman's rights represents a respect for her personality and life.

Jimmy also relied heavily on reciprocity in defining role relations as indicated by such remarks as the following:

(Why should someone be a good son?)

"Be good to your father and he'll be good to you."

The advance in cognitive differentiation of this type of response over that of Type 1 seems evident. It seems clear that such definition of value in terms of ego-need and reciprocity of needs is in a sense internal; i.e., it is not simply a reflection of direct teaching by others. It reflects rather Type 2's increasing awareness of its own ego-interests and of the exchange of ego-interests underlying much of social organization.

It also seems evident, however, that the Type 2 modes of thought are far from constituting an adequate or mature basis for morality. We find in a number of our older delinquent boys that further intellectual development seems to carry this Type 2 morality to the cynicism which is its logical endpoint. For example, John, a bright 17-year-old working-class delinquent (I.Q. 131), said in response to the story about stealing a drug for one's wife:

"Should the husband steal the drug for his wife? I would eliminate that into whether he wanted to or not. If he wants to marry someone else, someone young and good-looking, he may not want to keep her alive."

John's hedonistic relativism was also associated with a view of rights and law which was the systematic endpoint of Jimmy's views:

(Should the law make a worse punishment for stealing $500 or for cheating that amount by making a personal loan with no intention to repay it?)

"I don't see that they have a right to decide anything. Who are they?

They didn't get robbed and they don't do the stealing. It's vanity, they like the feeling of saying what's right. Laws are made by cowards to protect themselves."

Insofar as John was willing to make judgments not based completely on hedonistic relativism, they involved some notion of equality or reciprocity, e.g.:

"If a buddy of mine loans me something I'd do anything for him. If he double-crosses me, I'll do anything against him."[4]

From a developmental view, then, the Type 2 morality of need and reciprocity reflects both cognitive advance and a firmer internal basis of judgments than does the Type 1 morality. It does not, however, give rise to any of the characteristics usually attributed to moral judgment, or to a sense of obligation. While possessing the basic attributes stressed by Piaget as characterizing the stage of moral autonomy, this type of thought is not based on mutual (or any other type) moral respect (as Piaget had hypothesized).

The Intermediate Stages of Moral Development

It is clear that Type 1 and Type 2 children do not express attitudes toward "the good" and "the right" like those we take for granted in adults and which we often regard as moral cliches or stereotypes. These stereotypes first appear in our Type 3 and Type 4 preadolescents, whose verbal judgments and decisions are defined in terms of a concept of a morally good person (the implication of labelling Type 3 as a "good boy" morality).

A fairly typical Type 3 "good boy" response to the story about stealing the drug is the following response by Don (age 13, I.Q. 109, lower-middle class):

"It was really the druggist's fault, he was unfair, trying to overcharge and letting someone die. Heinz loved his wife and wanted to save her. I think anyone would. I don't think they would put him in jail. The judge would look at all sides, and see that the druggist was charging too much."

Don's response defines the issues in terms of attitudes toward the kinds of people involved; "the loving husband," "the unfair druggist," "the understanding judge," "what anyone would do," etc. He assumes that the attitudes he expresses are shared or community attitudes.

Don carries his moral-stereotypical definition of the social world into material not explicitly moral, e.g. into a series of questions we asked concerning the status of various occupational roles. Don tells us:

"President Eisenhower has done a good job and worked so hard he got a heart attack and put himself in the grave, just about, to help the people."

Don sees expected role-performances as expressions of a virtuous self, and bases respect for authority on a belief in the good intentions and wisdom of the authority figure, rather than in his power. It is also clear that his definition of the good and right has moved from a simple classification of outward acts (Type 1) and their need-related consequences (Type 2) to a definition in terms of "intentions," of inner attitudes of liking and "helping other people" (Type 3), or attitudes of "showing your respect for authority" (Type 4). These concerns imply a definition of good and right which goes beyond mere obedience to rules and authority, and which involves an active concern for the social goals behind the rules.

In terms of motivation, this second level is one in which conduct is controlled in the main by anticipation of praise and blame. Praise and blame are, of course, effective reinforcers even in the child's earliest years. In these early years, however, disapproval is but one of the many unpleasant external consequences of action that are to be avoided. In contrast, our Type 3 and Type 4 pre-adolescents attempt to make decisions and define what is good for themselves by *anticipating* possible disapproval in thought and imagination and by holding up approval as a final internal goal. Furthermore, the pre-adolescent is bothered only by disapproval if the disapproval is expressed by legitimate authorities. This attitude is naively expressed by Andy (age 16, working class, I.Q. 102) in his reply to the second story about telling one's father about one's brother's lie:

"If my father finds out later, he won't trust me. My brother wouldn't either, but I wouldn't have *a conscience* that he (my brother) didn't."

Andy equates his "conscience" with avoidance of disapproval by authorities, but not by peers. The growth of self-guidance in terms of consciously anticipated moral praise or blame seems to be part of a larger process of development expressed in the active use of moral praise and blame toward others expressed at this stage. There is also a close relationship between approval-sensitivity and what is often termed "identification with authority." This is evident with regard to Andy who tells us:

"I try to do things for my parents, they've always done things for you. I try to do everything my mother says, I try to please her. Like she wants me to be a doctor and I want to, too, and she's helping me to get up there."

Unlike the statements of compliance to the wishes of superiors (as in Level I), Andy's statements imply an identification of his own goals with his parent's wishes and a desire to anticipate them, somewhat independent of sanctions.

To summarize, we have mentioned the following "cognitive" characteristics of moral definitions at our second level:

a) Moral stereotyping. Definition of the good in terms of kinds of persons and a definition of persons and roles in terms of moral virtues.

b) Intentionalism. Judgments of moral worth based on intentions.

c) Positive, active and empathic moral definition. Duty and moral goodness defined in terms going beyond mere obedience to an actual service to other persons or institutions, or to a concern about the feelings of others.

On the motivational side we have mentioned:

d) Sensitivity to and self-guidance by anticipated approval or disapproval.

e) Identification with authority and its goals.

All of these characteristics imply that moral judgments at this level are based on *role-taking*, on taking the perspective of the other person with legitimate *expectations* in the situation, as these expectations form part of a *moral order*.

For children dominantly Type 3, this order and its associated role-taking is mainly based on "natural" or familistic types of affection and sympathy, as our examples have suggested. For children of Type 4, the moral order is seen as a matter of rules; and role-taking is based on "justice," on regard for the rights and expectations of both rule-enforcers and other rule-obeyers. The distinction between Type 3 and Type 4 styles of role-taking in moral judgment may be illustrated by two explanations as to the wrong of stealing from a store. Carol (13, I.Q. 108, lower-middle class, Type 3) says:

"The person who owns that store would think you didn't come from a good family, people would think you came from a family that didn't care about what you did."

James (13, I.Q. 111, lower-middle class, Type 4) says:

"You'd be mad, too, if you worked for something and someone just came along and stole it."

Both Carol and James define the wrong of stealing by putting themselves in the role of the victim. James, however, expresses the "moral indignation" of the victim, his sense that the rights of a community member have been violated, rather than expressing merely the owner's disapproval of the thief as a bad and unloved person. In both, Type 3 and Type 4, regard for rules is based upon regard for an organized social order. For Type 3, this order is defined primarily by the relations of good or "natural" selves; for Type 4 it is rather defined by rights, assigned duties, and rules.

Moral Orientation at the Third Developmental Level

It is often assumed by psychologists that moral conflicts are conflicts between community standards and egoistic impules. If this were true, it seems likely that the Type 3 and 4 moral orientations would persist throughout life. The story situations we used, however, placed in conflict two standards or values simultaneously accepted by large portions of the community. Many of the children at stages 3 and 4 went to great lengths to redefine our situations in such a way as to deny the existence of such conflicts between accepted norms, no matter how glaringly this conflict was presented. Both types of children took the role of the authority figure in defining right and wrong, tending to insist that the authority figure would adjust the rule in the interests of the various individuals involved.

In contrast, children of Types 5 and 6 accept the possibility of conflict between norms. This is most clear in our Type 6 children who attempt to choose in terms of moral principles rather than moral rules. Conventional examples of moral principles are the Golden Rule, the utilitarian principle (the greatest good for the greatest number) and Kant's categorical imperative. A moral principle is an obligatory or ideal rule of choice between legitimate alternatives, rather than a concrete prescription of action (Dewey and Tufts 1936; Kohlberg 1958). Philosophically such principles are designed to abstract the basic element that exists in various concrete rules, and to form an axiomatic basis for justifying or formulating concrete rules.[5] Moral principles, of course, are not legally or socially prescribed or sanctioned, they are social ideals rather than social realities.

An example of the use of the utilitarian maxim as a moral principle is provided by Tony (age 16, I.Q. 115, upper-middle class). He is replying to a situation involving a choice of leaving or staying at a civilian air-defense post after a heavy bombing raid may have endangered one's family:

"If he leaves, he is putting the safety of the few over the safety of many. I don't think it matters that it's his loved ones, because people in the burning buildings are someone's loved ones too. Even though maybe he'd be miserable the rest of his life, he shouldn't put the few over the many."

Tony says that leaving the post is wrong, not because of the actual consequences, but because he evaluated the situation wrongly, and "put the few over the many." This is not merely a matter of utilitarian economies but of the requirement of justice that all lives be treated as of equal value.

Moral principles are principles of "conscience," and Type 6 children tend to define moral decisions in these terms. When Type 6 children are asked "What is conscience?," they tend to answer that conscience is a choosing and self-judging function, rather than a feeling of guilt or dread.

A more easily attained "rationality" in moral choice than that of Type 6 is embodied in the Type 5 orientation of social contract legalism. Type 5 defines right and wrong in terms of legal or institutional rules which are seen as having a rational basis, rather than as being morally sacred. Laws are seen as maximizing social utility or welfare, or as being necessary for institutional functioning. It is recognized that laws are in a sense arbitrary, that there are many possible laws and that the laws are sometimes unjust. Nevertheless, the law is in general the criterion of right because of the need for agreement.

While Type 5 relies heavily on the law for definitions of right and wrong, it recognizes the possibility of conflict between what is rationally "right" for the individual actor, and what is legally or rationally right for the society. George (16, upper-middle class, I.Q. 118) gives a fairly typical response to the questions as to whether the husband was wrong to steal the drug for his dying wife:

"I don't think so, since it says the druggist had a right to set the price since he discovered it. I can't say he'd actually be right; I suppose anyone would do it for his wife though. He'd prefer to go to jail than have his wife die. In my eyes he'd have just cause to do it, but in the law's eyes he'd be wrong. I can't say more than that as to whether it was right or not."

(Should the judge punish the husband if he stole the drug?)

"It's the judge's duty to the law to send him to jail, no matter what the circumstances. The laws are made by the people and the judge is elected on the basis that he's agreed to carry out the law."

George's belief is that the judge must punish even though the judge may not think the act is wrong. This is quite consistent with his belief that the act was individually "just," but legally wrong. It reflects a typical distinction made at this level between individual person and social role, a distinction which contrasts with the earlier fusion of person and role into moral stereotypes. The judge's role is seen as a defined position with a set of agreed-upon rules which the role-occupant contractually accepts on entering office. At the level of definition of role-obligation, then, contract replaces earlier notions of helping the role-partner, just as legality replaces respect for social authority in defining more general norms.

All these aspects of a Type 5 orientation seem to be, in part, reactions to a cognitive advance in social concepts to what Inhelder and Piaget (1958) describe as the level of formal operations. Such a cognitive advance permits a view of normative judgment as deriving from a formal system derived from a set of agreed-upon assumptions. Any given set of norms or roles is then seen as one of many possibilities, so that the major requirement of normative definition becomes that of clarity and consistency.

Implications of the Stages for Conceptions of the Moralization Process

We may now briefly consider some of the implications of our stages for conceptions of the process and direction of moral development. Our age trends indicate that large groups of moral concepts and ways of thought only attain meaning at successively advanced ages and require the extensive background of social experience and cognitive growth represented by the age factor. How is this finding to be interpreted?

From the internalization view of the moralization process, these age changes in modes of moral thought would be interpreted as successive acquisitions or internalizations of cultural moral concepts. Our six types of thought would represent six patterns of verbal morality in the adult culture which are successively absorbed as the child grows more verbally sophisticated.

In contrast, we have advocated the developmental interpretation that these types of thought represent structures emerging from the interaction of the child with his social environment, rather than directly reflecting external structures given by the child's culture. Awareness of the basic prohibitions and commands of the culture, as well as some behavioral "internalization" of them, exists from the first of our stages and does not define their succession. Movement from stage to stage represents rather the way in which these prohibitions, as well as much wider aspects of the social structure, are taken up into the child's organization of a moral order. This order may be based upon power and external compulsion (Type 1), upon a system of exchanges and need satisfactions (Type 2), upon the maintenance of legitimate expectations (Type 3 and 4), or upon ideals or general logical principles of social organization (Types 5 and 6). While these successive bases of a moral order do spring from the child's awareness of the external social world, they also represent active processes of organizing or ordering this world.

We have cited two major results from our quantitative analyses which support this developmental interpretation. The first result was the approximation of the matrix of type intercorrelations to a quasi-simplex form. This suggested that individual development through the types of moral thought proceeded stepwise through an invariant sequence. If our moral types form an invariant sequence, acquisition of a higher type is not likely to be a direct learning of content taught by cultural agents, but is rather a restructuring of preceding types of thought. This interpretation is strengthened by the trend toward negative correlations between the higher and lower types of thought. Such negative relations suggest that higher modes of thought replace or inhibit lower modes of thought rather than being added to them. This in turn suggests that higher types of thought are reorganizations of preceding types of thought.

More strongly than the quantitative data, we believe that the qualitative data and interpretations contained in our stage descriptions make the notion of developmental transformations in moral thought plausible and meaning- ful. We have described characteristics of the types which suggest that each type is qualitatively different than previous types. Such qualitative differ- ences would not be expected were development simply a reflection of greater knowledge of, and conformity to, the culture. We have also attemp- ted a logical analysis of the characteristics of the types which allows us to see each type as a conceptual bridge between earlier and later types.

The developmental conception of the moralization process suggested by our analysis of age changes has some definite further implications. Impli- cations as to relations of the development of moral thought to social envi- ronmental factors on the one hand, and to the development of moral conduct on the other, will be considered in the sequel to this paper.

Summary

The paper presents an overview of the author's findings with regard to a sequence of moral development. It is based on empirical data obtained mainly from boys aged 10, 13, and 16 in lengthy free interviews around hypothetical moral dilemmas. Ideal-typological procedures led to the con- struction of six types of moral thought, designed to form a developmental hierarchy. The first two types parallel Piaget's heteronomous and autonom- ous moral stages, but various findings fail to support Piaget's view that these stages are derived from heteronomous or mutual respect.

More mature models of thought (Types 4–6) increased from age 10 through 16, less mature modes (Types 1–2) descreased with age. Data were analyzed with regard to the question of sequence, e.g., to the hypothesis that attainment of each type of thought is the prerequisite to attainment of the next higher type. A quasi-simplex pattern of intercorrelations supported this hypothesis.

Such evidence of developmental sequence in moral attitudes and con- cepts is believed to be of great importance for conceptions of the process of moralization. It indicates the inadequacy of conceptions of moralization as a process of simple internalization of external cultural rules, through verbal teaching, punishment, or identification. In contrast, the evidence suggests the existence of a series of internally patterned or organized transformations of social concepts and attitudes, transformations which constitute a devel- opmental process.

NOTES

1. The means in figure 1 for age 7 are based on only 12 boys and a limited number of responses per child, compared to the older group.
2. These cross-sectional findings need to be supplemented by a longitudinal analysis if we are to accept the stages as a genuine developmental sequence. We are presently engaged in a semilongitudinal analysis, in which we have reinterviewed 54 of our original subjects after a three-year interval. The findings will be reported in a subsequent publication.
3. There are a number of other recent typologies of moral judgment relevant to our own, briefly discussed elsewhere (Kohlberg 1963).

4. Such use of reciprocity by delinquents should not be considered evidence of a genuine morality of peer loyalty or "mutual respect" however. John says elsewhere, "I'm a natural leader. I understand how kids are made and I just pull the right strings and make monkeys out of them."

5. It is historically true that all philosophic formulations of moral principles, such as those mentioned, are variations of a basic prescription to take the role of all others involved in the moral situations.

REFERENCES

BALDWIN, J. M. Social and ethical interpretations in mental development (Macmillan, New York 1906).

DEWEY, J. AND TUFTS, J. Ethics (Holt, New York 1932).

DURKHEIM, E. Sociology and philosophy (Free Press, Glencoe, Illinois 1953). Originally published 1906.

FREUD, S. Group psychology and the analysis of the ego (Liveright, New York 1949). Originally published 1922.

GUTTMAN, L. The basis for scalogram analysis; in Stoufer, S. A. et al., Measurement and prediction; pp. 60–90 (Princeton University Press, Princeton 1950).—In Lazarsfeld, P. (Ed.), Mathematical thinking in the social sciences (Free Press, Glencoe 1954).

INHELDER, B. AND PIAGET, J. The growth of logistical thinking (Basic Books, New York 1958).

KOHLBERG, L. The development of modes of moral thinking and choice in the years 10 to 16; unpublished doctoral dissertation, (Chicago (1958).—Moral development and identification; in Stevenson, H. (Ed.), Child psychology, 1963. Yearbook of Nat. Soc. for the Study of Education (University of Chicago Press, Chicago 1963).

MCDOUGALL, W. An introduction to social psychology (Methuen, London 1905).

PARSONS, T. The superego and the theory of social systems; in Bell, N. and Voegl, E. (Eds.), A modern introduction to the family (Free Press, Glencoe 1960).

PIAGET, J. The moral judgment of the child (Free Press, Glencoe 1948). Originally published 1932.

SCHUESSLER, K. AND STRAUSS, A. L. A study of concept learning by scale analysis. Amer. Soc. Rev. *15*, 752–762 (1950).

WOHLWILL, J. A study of the development of the number concept by scalogram analysis. J. Genet. Psychol. *97*, 345–377 (1960).

Part VIII

Adolescent Personality and Identity Formation

MANY psychologists define the adolescent period as the time for intensely examining and constructing one's personal identity. In this view, adolescence is not a set age-range but rather the period during which one consciously searches one's individual nature and eventually derives a consolidated self-identity. Although this typically occurs during the late teens and early twenties in our society, it may well last until middle age for some individuals. We might also expect wide cultural variation in the timing and nature of the identity search.

Erik Erikson writes of identity formation as a "psycho-social task," meaning that the process serves a dual function. On the one hand, it is a psychological endeavor, the goal of which is to understand one's experience of individuality. On the other hand, it is a social endeavor, responding to the demands of others to define oneself in terms of chosen familial, occupational, and societal roles. For internal reasons, the adolescent must establish an identity that is consistent, comprehensive, and systematic. For external reasons, one's chosen identity must unambiguously define productive roles in the various social networks to which one belongs. Identity formation, therefore, entails a combined process of self-examination, experimentation with selected roles, and critical reevaluation in light of social feedback.

During the identity formation process, adolescents construct a new totality out of their earlier childhood identifications and anticipations of future plans. Once constructed, a personal identity not only establishes one's social role but also guides one's future choices. An identity therefore is more than just a static label. It is a dynamic force in one's life, bearing implications for future directions in one's career, one's interpersonal relations, and one's participation as a citizen in society.

Erikson calls the identity search a "crisis," but in many ways his descriptions sound more like a prolonged trial, resolved in piecemeal fashion over years. The adolescent tries out new opinions and behaviors, always with an eye to their appropriateness for the adolescent's desired self-image. Many attitudes and behaviors are rejected along the way, until finally the adolescent can anticipate the appropriateness of particular decisions for the chosen self-image before the decisions are actually made and acted out. This is a sign of a consolidated identity. Other signs include a general acceptance of oneself, feelings of comfort in one's self-image, extensive self-knowledge, and what Erikson calls "a sense of psycho-social well-being." This Erikson defines as "a feeling of being at home in one's body, a sense of 'knowing where one is going,' and an inner assuredness of anticipated recognition from those who count." Erikson also writes eloquently about symptoms of identity confusion in adolescents who have not yet been able to achieve a consolidated identity. He does point out, however, that this is more of a developmental than a clinical problem, in that most adolescents over time spontaneously grow out of these problems and establish a consolidated identity without the need for special therapy.

Social interactions during all phases of life have consequences for personality and identity formation, but in adolescence there is a particularly marked tendency to use social interaction to project one's personality, thereby bolstering one's sense of self. The adolescent's social behavior often becomes self-conscious and guarded, imbued with strategy and caution. Words and acts are guided with a view towards their effects on others' view of the self. David Elkind uses the term "strategic interaction" to capture this quality in adolescent social behavior.

Elkind believes that, for the adolescent, the main goal of the strategic interaction during adolescence is enhancing one's self-esteem. At a time of crisis in one's identity search, and in between the emotional support system of one's current family and one's future career and adult family, the adolescent's sense of self is on shaky ground. Strategic interactions may temporarily bolster this sense of self by offering the adolescent an opportunity to assert the self in a positive way to a valued audience. Elkind's insightful analysis reveals how many mundane adolescent activities—telephoning, dating, "cutting" one's peers—serve the double function of the strategic interaction.

Strategic interactions of one sort or another continue throughout life. They are commonplace in business negotiations and other manipulative encounters. But, according to Elkind, the use of strategic interactions for the sake of enhancing one's self-esteem continues only for those whose "ego-gratification" needs remain at the adolescent level of maturity. For most, the normal process of identity consolidation resolves the need constantly to create social episodes whose main purpose is the dramatic enhancement of self.

Does a young woman's search for identity differ from that of a young man? Most research has found little difference in the pace or pattern of identity formation in women and men. On most psychological measures of identity formation, women and men appear more similar than different. Ruthellen Josselson's clinical study, however, leaves some open questions as to whether feminine identity may have some special features, at least among the cohort of women represented by Josselson's sample.

Josselson notes that the women that she interviewed often emphasized interpersonal concerns over achievement-oriented concerns. Nurturance was often a "shared ideal" for many of these women's sense of self. This, of course, conforms with the sex-related socialization patterns described by Edwards and Whiting in reference to childhood. Related to this, Josselson also points to the special quality of her women's identity commitments. These commitments were abstract and fundamental rather than narrowly linked to particular occupations or ideologies. The sense of direction in these women's lives were less sharply defined but more encompassing of basic life goals than those of young men. "Identity in women," writes Josselson, "centers far more on what kind of a person to be than on occupational or ideological choice." Of course we should keep in mind Edwards and Whiting's comments about the impact of culture on any sex differences in social and personality development. Social changes in times to come may well alter the unique quality that Josselson found in young women's identities. And the causal influence likely could work in an additional way: changes in feminine identity, already a fact of contemporary social life, well might force key social changes in our culture.

25

The Life Cycle
Epigenesis of Identity
/Identity Confusion
in Life History and
Case History
Erik H. Erikson

Among the indispensable co-ordinates of identity is that of the life cycle, for we assume that not until adolescence does the individual develop the prerequisites in physiological growth, mental maturation, and social responsibility to experience and pass through the crisis of identity. We may, in fact, speak of the identity crisis as the psychosocial aspect of adolescing. Nor could this stage be passed without identity having found a form which will decisively determine later life.

Let us, once more, start out from Freud's far-reaching discovery that neurotic conflict is not very different in content from the "normative" conflicts which every child must live through in his childhood, and the residues of which every adult carries with him in the recesses of his personality. For man, in order to remain psychologically alive, constantly re-resolves these conflicts just as his body unceasingly combats the encroachment of physical deterioration. However, since I cannot accept the conclusion that just to be alive, or not to be sick, means to be healthy, or, as I would prefer to say in matters of personality, *vital,* I must have recourse to a few concepts which are not part of the official terminology of my field.

I shall present human growth from the point of view of the conflicts,

From Erik H. Erikson, *Identity: Youth and Crisis,* by permission of W. W. Norton & Company. Copyright 1968 by W. W. Norton & Company. This material comes from two of the chapters in the book, "The Life Cycle: Epigenesis of Identity," which begins on this page, and "Identity Confusion in Life History and Case History," which begins on page 423.

inner and outer, which the vital personality weathers, re-emerging from each crisis with an increased sense of inner unity, with an increase of good judgment, and an increase in the capacity "to do well" according to his own standards and to the standards of those who are significant to him. The use of the words "to do well" of course points up the whole question of cultural relativity. Those who are significant to a man may think he is doing well when he "does some good" or when he "does well" in the sense of acquiring possessions; when he is doing well in the sense of learning new skills and new knowledge or when he is not much more than just getting along; when he learns to conform all around or to rebel significantly; when he is merely free from neurotic symptoms or manages to contain within his vitality all manner of profound conflict.

There are many formulations of what constitutes a "healthy" personality in an adult. But if we take up only one—in this case, Marie Jahoda's definition, according to which a healthy personality *actively masters* his environment, shows a certain *unity of personality,* and is able to *perceive* the world and himself *correctly*[1]—it is clear that all of these criteria are relative to the child's cognitive and social development. In fact, we may say that childhood is defined by their initial absence and by their gradual development in complex steps of increasing differentiation. How, then, does a vital personality grow or, as it were, accrue from the successive stages of the increasing capacity to adapt to life's necessities—with some vital enthusiasm to spare?

Whenever we try to understand growth, it is well to remember the *epigenetic principle* which is derived from the growth of organisms *in utero.* Somewhat generalized, this principle states that anything that grows has a ground plan, and that out of this ground plan the parts arise, each part having its time of special ascendancy, until all parts have arisen to form a functioning whole. This, obviously, is true for fetal development where each part of the organism has its critical time of ascendance or danger of defect. At birth the body leaves the chemical exchange of the womb for the social exchange system of his society, where his gradually increasing capacities meet the opportunities and limitations of his culture. How the maturing organism continues to unfold, not by developing new organs but by means of a prescribed sequence of locomotor, sensory, and social capacities, is described in the child-development literature. As pointed out, psychoanalysis has given us an understanding of the more idiosyncratic experiences, and especially the inner conflicts, which constitute the manner in which an individual becomes a distinct personality. But here, too, it is important to realize that in the sequence of his most personal experiences the healthy child, given a reasonable amount of proper guidance, can be trusted to obey inner laws of development, laws which create a succession of potentialities for significant interaction with those persons who tend and respond to him and those institutions which are ready for him. While such interaction varies from culture to culture, it must remain within "the proper rate and the proper sequence" which governs all epigenesis. Personality, therefore, can be said to develop according to steps predetermined in the human organism's readiness to be driven toward, to be aware of, and to interact with a widening radius of significant individuals and institutions.

It is for this reason that, in the presentation of stages in the development of the personality, we employ an epigenetic diagram analogous to the one employed in *Childhood and Society* for an analysis of Freud's psychosexual stages.[2] It is, in fact, an implicit purpose of this presentation to bridge the theory of infantile sexuality (without repeating it here in detail) and our knowledge of the child's physical and social growth.

The diagram is presented on [p. 411]. The double-lined squares signify both a sequence of stages and a gradual development of component parts; in other words, the diagram formalizes a progression through time of a differentiation of parts. This indicates (1) that each item of the vital personality to be discussed is systematically related to all others, and that they all depend on the proper development in the proper sequence of each item; and (2) that each item exists in some form before "its" decisive and critical time normally arrives.

If I say, for example, that a sense of basic trust is the first component of mental vitality to develop in life, a sense of autonomous will the second, and a sense of initiative the third, the diagram expresses a number of fundamental relations that exist among the three components, as well as a few fundamental facts for each.

Each comes to its ascendance, meets its crisis, and finds its lasting solution in ways to be described here, toward the end of the stages mentioned. All of them exist in the beginning in some form, although we do not make a point of this fact, and we shall not confuse things by calling these components different names at earlier or later stages. A baby may show something like "autonomy" from the beginning, for example, in the particular way in which he angrily tries to wriggle his hand free when tightly held. However, under normal conditions, it is not until the second year that he begins to experience the whole critical alternative between being an autonomous creature and being a dependent one, and it is not until then that he is ready for a specifically new encounter with his environment. The environment, in turn, now feels called upon to convey to him its particular ideas and concepts of autonomy in ways decisively contributing to his personal character, his relative efficiency, and the strength of his vitality.

It is this encounter, together with the resulting crisis, which is to be described for each stage. Each stage becomes a crisis because incipient growth and awareness in a new part function go together with a shift in instinctual energy and yet also cause a specific vulnerability in that part. One of the most difficult questions to decide, therefore, is whether or not a child at a given stage is weak or strong. Perhaps it would be best to say that he is always vulnerable in some respects and completely oblivious and insensitive in others, but that at the same time he is unbelievably persistent in the same respects in which he is vulnerable. It must be added that the baby's weakness gives him power; out of his very dependence and weakness he makes signs to which his environment, if it is guided well by a responsiveness combining "instinctive" and traditional patterns, is peculiarly sensitive. A baby's presence exerts a consistent and persistent domination over the outer and inner lives of every member of a household. Because these members must reorient themselves to accommodate his presence, they must also grow as individuals and as a group. It is as true to say that babies control and bring up their families as it is to say the converse. A family can bring up a baby only by being brought up by him. His growth consists of a series of challenges to them to serve his newly developing potentialities for social interaction.

	1	2	3	4	5	6	7	8
VIII								INTEGRITY vs. DESPAIR
VII							GENERATIVITY vs. STAGNATION	
VI						INTIMACY vs. ISOLATION		
V	Temporal Perspective vs. Time Confusion	Self-Certainty vs. Self-Consciousness	Role Experimentation vs. Role Fixation	Apprenticeship vs. Work Paralysis	IDENTITY vs. IDENTITY CONFUSION	Sexual Polarization vs. Bisexual Confusion	Leader- and Followership vs. Authority Confusion	Ideological Commitment vs. Confusion of Values
IV				INDUSTRY vs. INFERIORITY	Task Identification vs. Sense of Futility			
III			INITIATIVE vs. GUILT		Anticipation Of Roles vs. Role Inhibition			
II		AUTONOMY vs. SHAME, DOUBT			Will to Be Oneself vs. Self-Doubt			
I	TRUST vs. MISTRUST				Mutual Recognition vs. Autistic Isolation			

411

Each successive step, then, is a potential crisis because of a radical change in perspective. Crisis is used here in a developmental sense to connote not a threat of catastrophe, but a turning point, a crucial period of increased vulnerability and heightened potential, and therefore, the ontogenetic source of generational strength and maladjustment. The most radical change of all, from intrauterine to extrauterine life, comes at the very beginning of life. But in postnatal existence, too, such radical adjustments of perspective as lying relaxed, sitting firmly, and running fast must all be accomplished in their own good time. With them, the interpersonal perspective also changes rapidly and often radically, as is testified by the proximity in time of such opposites as "not letting mother out of sight" and "wanting to be independent." Thus, different capacities use different opportunities to become full-grown components of the ever-new configuration that is the growing personality.

Infancy and the Mutuality of Recognition

For the most fundamental prerequisite of mental vitality, I have already nominated a *sense of basic trust,* which is a pervasive attitude toward oneself and the world derived from the experiences of the first year of life. By "trust" I mean an essential trustfulness of others as well as a fundamental sense of one's own trustworthiness.

In describing a development of a series of alternative basic attitudes, including identity, we take recourse to the term "a sense of." It must be immediately obvious, however, that such "senses" as a sense of health or vitality, or a sense of the lack of either, pervades the surface and the depth, including what we experience as consciousness or what remains barely conscious or is altogether unconscious. As a conscious experience, trust is accessible to introspection. But it is also a way of behaving, observable by others; and it is, finally, an inner state verifiable only by testing and psychoanalytic interpretation. All three of these dimensions are to be inferred when we loosely speak of "a sense of."

As is usual in psychoanalysis, we learned first of the "basic" nature of trust from adult psychopathology. In adults a radical impairment of basic trust and a prevalence of *basic mistrust* is expressed in a particular form of severe estrangement which characterizes individuals who withdraw into themselves when at odds with themselves and with others. Such withdrawal is most strikingly displayed by individuals who regress into psychotic states in which they sometimes close up, refusing food and comfort and becoming oblivious to companionship. What is most radically missing in them can be seen from the fact that as we attempt to assist them with psychotherapy, we must try to "reach" them with the specific intent of convincing them that they can trust us to trust them and that they can trust themselves. . . .

Early Childhood and the Will to Be Oneself

. . . .
The over-all significance of this second stage of early childhood lies in the rapid gains in muscular maturation, in verbalization, and in discrimina-

tion and the consequent ability—and doubly felt inability—to co-ordinate a number of highly conflicting action patterns characterized by the tendencies of *"holding on"* and *"letting go."* In this and in many other ways, the still highly dependent child begins to experience his *autonomous will.* At this time sinister forces are leashed and unleashed, especially in the guerrilla warfare of unequal wills, for the child if often unequal to his own violent will and parent and child are often unequal to one another. . . .

This stage, therefore, becomes decisive for the ratio between loving good will and hateful self-insistence, between co-operation and willfulness, and between self-expression and compulsive self-restraint or meek compliance. A sense of self-control without loss of self-esteem is the ontogenetic source of a sense of *free will.* From an unavoidable sense of loss of self-control and of parental overcontrol comes a lasting propensity for *doubt* and *shame.*

For the growth of autonomy a firmly developed early trust is necessary. The infant must have come to be sure that his faith in himself and in the world will not be jeopardized by the violent wish to have his choice, to appropriate demandingly, and to eliminate stubbornly. Only parental firmness can protect him against the consequences of his as yet untrained discrimination and circumspection. But his environment must also back him up in his wish to "stand on his own feet," while also protecting him against the now newly emerging pair of estrangements, namely, that sense of having exposed himself prematurely and foolishly which we call shame or that secondary mistrust, that "double take," which we call doubt—doubt in himself and doubt in the firmness and perspicacity of his trainers. . . .

Childhood and the Anticipation of Roles

Being firmly convinced that he is a person on his own, the child must now find out what kind of a person he may become. He is, of course, deeply and exclusively "identified" with his parents, who most of the time appear to him to be powerful and beautiful, although often quite unreasonable, disagreeable, and even dangerous. Three developments support this stage, while also serving to bring about its crisis: (1) the child learns to move around more freely and more violently and therefore establishes a wider and, to him, unlimited radius of goals; (2) his sense of language becomes perfected to the point where he understands and can ask incessantly about innumerable things, often hearing just enough to misunderstand them thoroughly; and (3) both language and locomotion permit him to expand his imagination to so many roles that he cannot avoid frightening himself with what he himself has dreamed and thought up. Nevertheless, out of all this he must emerge with a *sense of initiative* as a basis for a realistic sense of ambition and purpose.

What, then, are the criteria for an unbroken sense of initiative? The criteria for the development of all the "senses" discussed here are the same: a crisis beset with some new estrangement is resolved in such a way that the child suddenly seems to be "more himself," more loving, more relaxed, and brighter in his judgment—in other words, vital in a new way. Most of all, he seems to be more activated and activating; he is in the free possession of a certain surplus of energy which permits him to forget many failures rather quickly and to approach new areas that seem desirable, even if they also seem dangerous, with undiminished zest and some increased sense of direction. . . .

School Age and Task Identification

Such is the wisdom of the ground plan that at no time is the child more ready to learn quickly and avidly, to become big in the sense of sharing obligation, discipline, and performance than at the end of the period of expansive imagination. He is also eager to make things together, to share in constructing and planning, instead of trying to coerce other children or provoke restriction. Children now also attach themselves to teachers and the parents of other children, and they want to watch and imitate people representing occupations which they can grasp—firemen and policemen, gardeners, plumbers, and garbage men. If they are lucky they live at least part of their lives near barnyards or on safe streets around busy people and around many other children of all ages so that they can observe and participate as their capacities and their initiative grow in tentative spurts. But when they reach school age, children in all cultures receive some systematic instruction, although it is by no means always in the kind of school which literate people must organize around teachers who have learned how to teach literacy. In preliterate people much is learned from adults who become teachers by acclamation rather than by appointment, and much is learned from older children, but the knowledge gained is related to the basic skills of simple technologies which can be understood the moment the child gets ready to handle the utensils, the tools, and the weapons (or facsimiles thereof) used by the big people. He enters the technology of his tribe very gradually but also very directly. More literate people, with more specialized careers, must prepare the child by teaching him things which first of all make him literate. He is then given the widest possible basic education for the greatest number of possible careers. The greater the specialization, the more indistinct the goal of initiative becomes, the more complicated the social reality, and the vaguer the father's and mother's role in it. Between childhood and adulthood, then, our children go to school, and school skills seems to many to be a world all by itself, with its own goals and limitations, its achievements and disappointments. . . .

While all children at times need to be left alone in solitary play or, later, in the company of books and radio, motion pictures and television, and while all children need their hours and days of make-believe in games, they all, sooner or later, become dissatisfied and disgruntled without a sense of being able to make things and make them well and even perfectly: it is this that I have called the *sense of industry*. Without this, even the best-entertained child soon acts exploited. It is as if he knows and his society knows that now that he is psychologically already a rudimentary parent, he must begin to be something of a worker and potential provider before becoming a biological parent. With the oncoming latency period, then, the advancing child forgets, or rather quietly "sublimates"—that is, applies to concrete pursuits and approved goals—the drives which have made him dream and play. He now learns to win recognition by producing things. He develops perseverance and adjusts himself to the inorganic laws of the tool world and can become an eager and absorbed unit of a productive situation.

The danger at this stage is the development of an estrangement from himself and from his tasks—the well-known *sense of inferiority*. This may be caused by an insufficient solution of the preceding conflict: the child may still want his mommy more than knowledge; he may still prefer to be the baby at home rather than the big child in school; he still compares himself with his father, and the comparison arouses a sense of guilt as well as a sense of inferiority. Family life may not have prepared him for school life, or school life may fail to sustain the promises of earlier stages in that nothing that he has learned to do well so far seems to count with his fellows or his teacher. And then again, he may be potentially able to excel in ways which are dormant and which, if not evoked now, may develop late or never.

It is at this point that wider society becomes significant to the child by admitting him to roles preparatory to the actuality of technology and economy. Where he finds out immediately, however, that the color of his skin or the background of his parents rather than his wish and will to learn are the factors that decide his worth as a pupil or apprentice, the human propensity for feeling unworthy may be fatefully aggravated as a determinant of character development.

Good teachers who feel trusted and respected by the community know how to alternate play and work, games and study. They know how to recognize special efforts, how to encourage special gifts. They also know how to give a child time and how to handle those children to whom school, for a while, is not important and is considered something to endure rather than enjoy, or even the child to whom, for a while, other children are much more important than the teacher. But good parents also feel a need to make their children trust their teachers, and therefore to have teachers who can be trusted. For nothing less is at stake than the development and maintenance in children of a positive identification with those who know things and know how to do things. Again and again in interviews with especially gifted and inspired people, one is told spontaneously and with a special glow that *one* teacher can be credited with having kindled the flame of hidden talent. Against this stands the overwhelming evidence of vast neglect.

The fact that the majority of teachers in our elementary schools are women must be considered here in passing, because it can lead to a conflict with the nonintellectual boy's masculine identification, as if knowledge were feminine, action masculine. Bernard Shaw's statement that those who can, do, while those who cannot, teach, still has frequent validity for both parents and children. The selection and training of teachers, then, is vital for the avoidance of the dangers which can befall the individual at this stage. The development of a sense of inferiority, the feeling that one will never be "any good," is a danger which can be minimized by a teacher who knows how to emphasize what a child *can* do and who recognizes a psychiatric problem when she sees one. Obviously, here lies the best opportunity for preventing the particular identity confusion which goes back to incapacity or a flagrant lack of opportunity to learn. On the other hand, the child's budding sense of identity can remain prematurely fixed on being nothing but a good little worker or a good little helper, which may by no means be all he might become. Finally, there is the danger, probably the most common one, that throughout the long years of going to school a child will never acquire the enjoyment of work and pride in doing at least one kind of thing really well.

Regarding the period of a developing sense of industry, I have referred to outer and inner hindrances in the use of new capacities but not to aggravations of new human drives, nor to submerged rages resulting from their frustration. This stage differs from the earlier ones in that it is not a swing from an inner upheaval to a new mastery. Freud calls it the latency stage because violent drives are normally dormant. But it is only a lull before the storm of puberty, when all the earlier drives re-emerge in new combinations.

On the other hand, this is socially a most decisive stage. Since industry involves doing things beside and with others, a first sense of division of labor and of differential opportunity—that is, a sense of the *technological ethos* of a culture—develops at this time. Therefore, the configurations of culture and the manipulations basic to the *prevailing technology* must reach meaningfully into school life, supporting in every child a feeling of competence—that is, the free exercise of dexterity and intelligence in the completion of serious tasks unimpaired by an infantile sense of inferiority. This is the lasting basis for co-operative participation in productive adult life.

Two poles in American grammar school education may serve to illustrate the contribution of the school age to the problem of identity. There is the traditional extreme of making early school life an extension of grim adulthood by emphasizing self-restraint and a strict sense of duty in doing what one is told to do, as opposed to the modern extreme of making it an extension of the natural tendency in childhood to find out by playing, to learn what one must do by doing what one likes to do. Both methods work for some children in some ways, but impose on others a special adjustment. The first trend, if carried to the extreme, exploits the tendency on the part of the preschool and grammar school child to become entirely dependent on prescribed duties. He thus may learn much that is absolutely necessary and he may develop an unshakable sense of duty. But he may never unlearn an unnecessary and costly self-restraint with which he may later make his own life and other people's lives miserable, and in fact spoil, in turn, his own children's natural desire to learn and to work. The second trend, when carried to an extreme, leads not only to the well-known popular objection that children do not learn anything any more but also to such feelings in children as those expressed in the by now famous question of a metropolitan child: "Teacher, *must* we do today what we *want* to do?" Nothing could better express the fact that children at this age do like to be mildly but firmly coerced into the adventure of finding out that one can learn to accomplish things which one would never have thought of by oneself, things which owe their attractiveness to the very fact that they are not the product of play and fantasy but the product of reality, practicality, and logic; things which thus provide a token sense of participation in the real world of adults. Between these extremes we have the many schools which have no styles at all except grim attendance to the fact that school must be. Social inequality and backwardness of method still create a hazardous gap between many children and the technology which needs them not only so that they may serve technological aims, but, more imperatively, so that technology may serve humanity.

But there is another danger to identity development. If the overly conforming child accepts work as the only criterion of worthwhileness, sacrificing imagination and playfulness too readily, he may become ready to submit to what Marx called "craft-idiocy," i.e., become a slave of his technology and of its dominant role typology. Here we are already in the midst of identity problems, for with the establishment of a firm initial relationship to the world of skills and tools and to those who teach and share them, and with the advent of puberty, childhood proper comes to an end. And since man is not only the learning but also the teaching and above all the working animal, the immediate contribution of the school age to a sense of identity can be expressed in the words "I am what I can learn to make work." It is immediately obvious that for the vast majority of men, in all times, this has been not only the beginning but also the limitation of their identity; or better: the majority of men have always consolidated their identity needs around their technical and occupational capacities, leaving it to special groups (special by birth, by choice or election, and by giftedness) to establish and preserve those "higher" institutions without which man's daily work has always seemed an inadequate self-expression, if not a mere grind or even a kind of curse. It may be for that very reason that the identity problem in our time becomes both psychiatrically and historically relevant. For as man can leave some of the grind and curse to machines, he can visualize a greater freedom of identity for a larger segment of mankind.

Adolescence

As technological advances put more and more time between early school life and the young person's final access to specialized work, the stage of adolescing becomes an even more marked and conscious period and, as it has always been in some cultures in some periods, almost a way of life between childhood and adulthood. Thus in the later school years young people, beset with the physiological revolution of their genital maturation and the uncertainty of the adult roles ahead, seem much concerned with faddish attempts at establishing an adolescent subculture with what looks like a final rather than a transitory or, in fact, initial identity formation. They are sometimes morbidly, often curiously, preoccupied with what they appear to be in the eyes of others as compared with what they feel they are, and with the question of how to connect the roles and skills cultivated earlier with the ideal prototypes of the day. In their search for a new sense of continuity and sameness, which must now include sexual maturity, some adolescents have to come to grips again with crises of earlier years before they can install lasting idols and ideals as guardians of a final identity. They need, above all, a moratorium for the integration of the identity elements ascribed in the foregoing to the childhood stages: only that now a larger unit, vague in its outline and yet immediate in its demands, replaces the childhood milieu— "society." A review of these elements is also a list of adolescent problems.

If the earliest stage bequeathed to the identity crisis an important need for trust in oneself and in others, then clearly the adolescent looks most fervently for men and ideas to have *faith* in, which also means men and ideas in whose service it would seem worth while to prove oneself trustworthy. (This will be discussed further in the chapter on fidelity.) At the same time, however, the adolescent fears a foolish, all too trusting commitment, and will, paradoxically, express his need for faith in loud an l cynical mistrust.

If the second stage established the necessity of beii g defined by what one can *will* freely, then the adolescent now looks foi an opportunity to decide with free assent on one of the available or unavoidable avenues of duty and service, and at the same time is mortally afraid of being forced into activities in which he would feel exposed to ridicule or self-doubt. This, too, can lead to a paradox, namely, that he would rather act shamelessly in the eyes of his elders, out of free choice, than be forced into activities which would be shameful in his own eyes or in those of his peers.

If an unlimited *imagination* as to what one *might* become is the heritage of the play age, then the adolescent's willingness to put his trust in those peers and leading, or misleading, elders who will give imaginative, if not illusory, scope to his aspirations is only too obvious. By the same token, he objects violently to all "pedantic" limitations on his self-images and will be ready to settle by loud accusation all his guidelines over the excessiveness of his ambition.

Finally, if the desire to make something work, and to make it work well, is the gain of the school age, then the choice of an occupation assumes a significance beyond the question of remuneration and status. It is for this reason that some adolescents prefer not to work at all for a while rather than be forced into an otherwise promising career which would offer success without the satisfaction of functioning with unique excellence.

In any given period in history, then, that part of youth will have the most affirmatively exciting time of it which finds itself in the wave of a technological, economic, or ideological trend seemingly promising all that youthful vitality could ask for.

Adolescence, therefore, is least "stormy" in that segment of youth which is gifted and well trained in the pursuit of expanding technological trends, and thus able to identify with new roles of competency and invention and to accept a more implicit ideological outlook. Where this is not given, the adolescent mind becomes a more explicitly ideological one, by which we mean one searching for some inspiring unification of tradition or anticipated techniques, ideas, and ideals. And, indeed, it is the ideological potential of a society which speaks most clearly to the adolescent who is so eager to be affirmed by peers, to be confirmed by teachers, and to be inspired by worth-while "ways of life." On the other hand, should a young person feel that the environment tries to deprive him too radically of all the forms of expression which permit him to develop and integrate the next step, he may resist with the wild strength encountered in animals who are suddenly forced to defend their lives. For, indeed, in the social jungle of human existence there is no feeling of being alive without a sense of identity.

Having come this far, I would like to give one example (and I consider it representative in structure) of the individual way in which a young person, given some leeway, may utilize a traditional way of life for dealing with a remnant of negative identity. I had known Jill before her puberty, when she was rather obese and showed many "oral" traits of voracity and dependency while she also was a tomboy and bitterly envious of her brothers and in rivalry with them. But she was intelligent and always had an air about her (as did her mother) which seemed to promise that things would turn out all right. And, indeed, she straightened out and up, became very attractive, an easy leader in any group, and, to many, a model of young girlhood. As a clinician, I watched and wondered what she would do with that voraciousness and with the rivalry which she had displayed earlier. Could it be that such things are simply absorbed in fortuitous growth?

Then one autumn in her late teens, Jill did not return to college from the ranch out West where she had spent the summer. She had asked her parents to let her stay. Simply out of liberality and confidence, they granted her this moratorium and returned East.

That winter Jill specialized in taking care of newborn colts, and would get up at any time during a winter night to bottle feed the most needy animals. Having apparently acquired a certain satisfaction within herself, as well as astonished recognition from the cowboys, she returned home and reassumed her place. I felt that she had found and hung on to an opportunity to do actively and for others what she had always yearned to have done for her, as she had once demonstrated by overeating: she had learned to feed needy young mouths. But she did so in a context which, in turning passive into active, also turned a former symptom into a social act.

One might say that she turned "maternal" but it was a maternalism such as cowboys must and do display; and, of course, she did it all in jeans. This brought recognition "from man to man" as well as from man to woman, and beyond that the confirmation of her optimism, that is, her feeling that something could be done that felt like her, was useful and worth while, and was in line with an ideological trend where it still made immediate practical sense.

Such self-chosen "therapies" depend, of course, on the leeway given in the right spirit at the right time, and this depends on a great variety of circumstances. I intend to publish similar fragments from the lives of children in greater detail at some future date; let this example stand for the countless observations in everyday life, where the resourcefulness of young people proves itself when the conditions are right.

The estrangement of this stage is *identity confusion,* which will be elaborated in clinical and biographic detail in the next chapter. For the moment, we will accept Biff's formulation in Arthur Miller's *Death of a Salesman:* "I just can't take hold, Mom, I can't take hold of some kind of a life." Where such a dilemma is based on a strong previous doubt of one's ethnic and sexual identity, or where role confusion joins a hopelessness of long standing, delinquent and "borderline" psychotic episodes are not uncommon. Youth after youth, bewildered by the incapacity to assume a role forced on him by the inexorable standardization of American adolescence, runs away in one form or another, dropping out of school, leaving jobs, staying out all night, or withdrawing into bizarre and inaccessible moods. Once "delinquent," his greatest need and often his only salvation is the refusal on the part of older friends, advisers, and judiciary personnel to type him further by pat diagnoses and social judgments which ignore the special dynamic conditions of adolescence. It is here, as we shall see in greater detail, that the concept of identity confusion is of practical clinical value, for if they are diagnosed and treated correctly, seemingly psychotic and criminal incidents do not have the same fatal significance which they may have at other ages.

In general it is the inability to settle on an occupational identity which most disturbs young people. To keep themselves together they temporarily overidentify with the heroes of cliques and crowds to the point of an apparently complete loss of individuality. Yet in this stage not even "falling in love" is entirely, or even primarily, a sexual matter. To a considerable extent adolescent love is an attempt to arrive at a definition of one's identity by projecting one's diffused self-image on another and by seeing it thus reflected and gradually clarified. This is why so much of young love is conversation. On the other hand, clarification can also be sought by destructive means. Young people can become remarkably clannish, intolerant, and cruel in their exclusion of others who are "different," in skin color or cultural background, in tastes and gifts, and often in entirely petty aspects of dress and gesture arbitrarily selected as the signs of an in-grouper or out-grouper. It is important to understand in principle (which does not mean to condone in all of its manifestations) that such intolerance may be, for a while, a necessary defense against a sense of identity loss. This is unavoidable at a time of life when the body changes its proportions radically, when genital puberty floods body and imagination with all manner of impulses, when intimacy with the other sex approaches and is, on occasion, forced on the young person, and when the immediate future confronts one with too many conflicting possibilities and choices. Adolescents not only help one another temporarily through such discomfort by forming cliques and stereotyping themselves, their ideals, and their enemies; they also insistently test each other's capacity for sustaining loyalties in the midst of inevitable conflicts of values.

The readiness for such testing helps to explain . . . the appeal of simple and cruel totalitarian doctrines among the youth of such countries and classes as have lost or are losing their group identities—feudal, agrarian, tribal, or national. The democracies are faced with the job of winning these grim youths by convincingly demonstrating to them—by living it—that a democratic identity can be strong and yet tolerant, judicious and still determined. But industrial democracy poses special problems in that it insists on self-made identities ready to grasp many chances and ready to adjust to the changing necessities of booms and busts, of peace and war, of migration and determined sedentary life. Democracy, therefore, must present its adolescents with ideals which can be shared by young people of many backgrounds, and which emphasize autonomy in the form of independence and initiative in the form of constructive work. These promises, however, are not easy to fulfill in increasingly complex and centralized systems of industrial, economic, and political organization, systems which increasingly neglect the "self-made" ideology still flaunted in oratory. This is hard on many young Americans because their whole upbringing has made the development of a self-reliant personality dependent on a certain degree of choice, a sustained hope for an individual chance, and firm commitment to the freedom of self-realization.

We are speaking here not merely of high privileges and lofty ideals but of psychological necessities. For the social institution which is the guardian of identity *is* what we have called *ideology*. One may see in ideology also the imagery of an aristocracy in its widest possible sense, which connotes that within a defined world image and a given course of history the best people will come to rule and rule will develop the best in people. In order not to become cynically or apathetically lost, young people must somehow be able to convince themselves that those who succeed in their anticipated adult world thereby shoulder the obligation of being best. For it is through their ideology that social systems enter into the fiber of the next generation and attempt to absorb into their lifeblood the rejuvenative power of youth. Adolescence is thus a vital regenerator in the process of social evolution, for youth can offer its loyalties and energies both to the conservation of that which continues to feel true and to the revolutionary correction of that which has lost its regenerative significance.

We can study the identity crisis also in the lives of creative individuals who could resolve it for themselves only by offering to their contemporaries a new model of resolution such as that expressed in the works of art or in original deeds, and who furthermore are eager to tell us all about it in diaries, letters, and self-representations. And even as the neuroses of a given period reflect the ever-present inner chaos of man's existence in a new way, the creative crises point to the period's unique solutions.

We will in the next chapter present in greater detail what we have learned of these specialized individual crises. But there is a third manifestation of the remnants of infantilism and adolescence in man: it is the pooling of the individual crises in transitory upheavals amounting to collective "hysterias." Where there are voluble leaders their creative crises and the latent crises of their followers can be at least studied with the help of our assumptions—and of their writings. More elusive are spontaneous group developments not attributable to a leader. And it will, at any rate, not be helpful to call mass irrationalities by clinical names. It would be impossible to diagnose clinically how much hysteria is present in a young nun participating in an epidemic of convulsive spells or how much perverse "sadism" in a young Nazi commanded to participate in massive parades or in mass killings. So we can point only most tentatively to certain similarities between individual crises and group behavior in order to indicate that in a given period of history they are in an obscure contact with each other.

But before we submerge ourselves in the clinical and biographic evidence for what we call identity confusion, we will take a look beyond the identity crisis. The words "beyond identity," of course, could be understood in two ways, both essential for the problem. They could mean that there is more to man's core than identity, that there is in fact in each individual an "I," an observing center of awareness and of volition, which can transcend and must survive the *psychosocial identity* which is our concern in this book. In some ways, as we will see, a sometimes precocious self-transcendence seems to be felt strongly in a transient manner in youth, as if a pure identity had to be kept free from psychosocial encroachment. And yet no man (except a man aflame and dying like Keats, who could speak of identity in words which secured him immediate fame) can transcend himself in youth. We will speak later of the transcendence of identity. In the following "beyond identity" means life after adolescence and the uses of identity and, indeed, the return of some forms of identity crisis in the later stages of the life cycle.

Beyond Identity

The first of these is the crisis of *intimacy*. It is only when identity formation is well on its way that true intimacy—which is really a counterpointing as well as a fusing of identities—is possible. Sexual intimacy is only part of what I have in mind, for it is obvious that sexual intimacies often precede the capacity to develop a true and mutual psychosocial intimacy with another person, be it in friendship, in erotic encounters, or in joint inspiration. The youth who is not sure of his identity shies away from interpersonal intimacy or throws himself into acts of intimacy which are "promiscuous" without true fusion or real self-abandon.

Where a youth does not accomplish such intimate relationships with others—and, I would add, with his own inner resources—in late adolescence or early adulthood, he may settle for highly stereotyped interpersonal relations and come to retain a deep *sense of isolation*. If the times favor an impersonal kind of interpersonal pattern, a man can go far, very far, in life and yet harbor a severe character problem doubly painful because he will never feel really himself, although everyone says he is "somebody."

The counterpart of intimacy is distantiation: the readiness to repudiate, isolate, and, if necessary, destroy those forces and people whose essence seems dangerous to one's own. Thus, the lasting consequence of the need for distantiation is the readiness to fortify one's territory of intimacy and solidarity and to view all outsiders with a fanatic "overvaluation of small differences" between the familiar and the foreign. Such prejudices can be utilized and exploited in politics and in war and secure the loyal self-sacrifice and the readiness to kill from the strongest and the best. A remnant of adolescent danger is to be found where intimate, competitive, and combative relations are experienced with and against the selfsame people. But as the areas of adult responsibility are gradually delineated, as the competitive encounter, the erotic bond, and merciless enmity are differentiated from each other, they eventually become subject to that *ethical sense* which is the mark of the adult and which takes over from the ideological conviction of adolescence and the moralism of childhood.

Freud was once asked what he thought a normal person should be able to do well. The questioner probably expected a complicated, "deep" answer. But Freud simply said, *"Lieben und arbeiten"* ("to love and to work"). It pays to ponder on this simple formula; it grows deeper as you think about it. For when Freud said "love," he meant the generosity of intimacy as well as genital love; when he said love and work, he meant a general word productiveness which would not preoccupy the individual to the extent that he might lose his right or capacity to be a sexual and a loving being.

Psychoanalysis has emphasized *genitality* as one of the developmental conditions for full maturity. Genetality consists in the capacity to develop orgastic potency which is more than the discharge of sex products in the sense of Kinsey's "outlets." It combines the ripening of intimate sexual mutuality with full genital sensitivity and with a capacity for discharge of tension from the whole body. This is a rather concrete way of saying something about a process which we really do not yet quite understand. But the experience of the climactic mutuality of orgasm clearly provides a supreme example of the mutual regulation of complicated patterns and in some way appeases the hostilities and the potential rages caused by the daily evidence of the oppositeness of male and female, of fact and fancy, of love and hate, of work and play. Such experience makes sexuality less obsessive and sadistic control of the partner superfluous.

Before such genital maturity is reached, much of sexual life is of the self-seeking, identity-hungry kind; each partner is really trying only to reach himself. Or it remains a kind of genital combat in which each tries to defeat the other. All this remains as part of adult sexuality, but it is gradually absorbed as the differences between the sexes become a full polarization within a joint life style. For the previously established vital strengths have helped to make the two sexes first become similar in consciousness, language, and ethics in order to then permit them to be maturely different.

Man, in addition to erotic attraction, has developed a selectivity of "love" which serves the need for a new and shared identity. If the estrangement typical for this stage is *isolation,* that is, the incapacity to take chances with one's identity by sharing true intimacy, such inhibition is often reinforced by a fear of the outcome of intimacy: offspring—and care. Love as mutual devotion, however, overcomes the antagonisms inherent in sexual and functional polarization, and is the vital strength of young adulthood. It is the guardian of that elusive and yet all-pervasive power of cultural and personal style which binds into a "way of life" the affiliations of competition and co-operation, production and procreation. . . .

[From "Identity Confusion in Life History and Case History"]

Diffusion of Time Perspective

In extreme instances of delayed and prolonged adolescence, an extreme form of a disturbance in the experience of time appears which, in its milder form, belongs to the psychopathology of everyday adolescence. It consists of a sense of great urgency and yet also of a loss of consideration for time as a dimension of living. The young person may feel simultaneously very young, and in fact babylike, and old beyond rejuvenation. Protests of missed greatness and of a premature and fatal loss of useful potentials are common among our patients, as they are among adolescents in cultures which consider such protestations romantic; the implied malignancy, however, consists of a decided disbelief in the possibility that time may bring change, and yet also of a violent fear that it might. This contradiction is often expressed in a general slowing up which makes the patient behave, within the routine of his activities and of his therapy, as if he were moving in molasses. It is hard for him to go to bed and face the transition into a state of sleep, and it is equally hard for him to get up and face the necessary restitution of wakefulness; it is hard to come to the therapeutic appointment, and hard to leave it. Such complaints as "I don't know," "I give up," and "I quit" are by no means mere habitual statements reflecting a mild depression; they are often expressions of the kind of despair discussed by Edward Bibring[3] as a wish on the part of the ego "to let itself die."

The assumption that life could actually be made to end with the end of adolescence or at tentatively planned later "dates of expiration" is by no means entirely unwelcome, and, in fact, can become the only condition on which a tentative new beginning can be based. Some of our patients even require the feeling that the therapist does not intend to commit them to a continuation of life if treatment should fail to prove it really worth while. Without such a conviction the moratorium would not be a real one. In the meantime, the "wish to die" is a really suicidal wish only in those rare cases where "to be a suicide" becomes an inescapable identity choice in itself. I am thinking here of a pretty young girl, the oldest of a number of daughters of a mill worker. Her mother had repeatedly expressed the thought that she would rather see her daughters dead than become prostitutes, and at the same time she suspected "prostitution" in the daughters' every move toward companionship with boys. The daughters were finally forced into a kind of conspiratorial sorority of their own, obviously designed to elude the mother, in order to experiment with ambiguous situations and yet probably also to give each other protection from men. They were finally caught in compromising circumstances. The authorities, too, took it for granted that they intended to prostitute themselves, and they were sent to a variety of institutions where they were forcefully impressed with the kind of "recognition" society had in store for them. No appeal was possible to a mother who, they felt, had left them no choice, and much of the good will and understanding of social workers was sabotaged by circumstances. At least for the oldest girl—for a number of reasons—no other future was possible except that of another chance in another world. She hanged herself after having dressed nicely and written a note which ended with the cryptic words "Why I achieve honor only to discard it . . ."

Diffusion of Industry

Severe identity confusion is regularly accompanied by an acute upset in the sense of workmanship, either in the form of an inability to concentrate on required or suggested tasks or in a self-destructive preoccupation with some one-sided activity, i.e., excessive reading. The way in which such patients sometimes, under treatment, find the one activity in which they can reemploy their once lost sense of workmanship is a chapter in itself. Here it is well to keep in mind the stage of development which precedes puberty and adolescence, namely, the elementary school age, when the child is taught the prerequisites for participation in the particular technology of his culture and is given the opportunity and the life task of developing a sense of workmanship and work participation. As we saw, the school age significantly follows the Oedipal stage: the accomplishment of real, not merely playful, steps toward a place in the economic structure of society permits the child to reidentify with parents as workers and tradition bearers rather than as sexual and familial beings, thus nurturing at least one concrete and more "neutral" possibility of becoming like them. The tangible goals of the elementary practice of skills are shared by and with age mates in places of instruction (sweathouse, prayer house, fishing hole, workshop, kitchen, schoolhouse) most of which, in turn, are geographically separated from the home, from the mother, and from infantile memories; here, however, there are wide differences in the treatment of the sexes. Work goals, then, by no means only support or exploit the suppression of infantile instinctual aims; they also enhance the functioning of the ego, in that they offer a constructive activity with actual tools and materials in a communal reality. The ego's tendency to turn passivity into activity thus acquires a new field of manifestation, in many ways superior to the mere turning of passive into active in infantile fantasy and play, for now the inner need for activity, practice, and work completion is ready to meet the corresponding demands and opportunities in social reality.

Because of the immediate Oedipal antecedents of the beginnings of a work identity, however, the attitude toward work in our young patients reverses gears toward Oedipal competitiveness and sibling rivalry. Thus identity confusion is accompanied not only by an inability to concentrate, but by an excessive awareness of as well as an abhorrence of competitiveness. Although the patients in question usually are intelligent and able and have often shown themselves successful in office work, scholastic studies, and sports, they now lose the capacity for work, exercise, and sociability and thus lose the most important vehicle of social play and the most significant refuge from formless fantasy and vague anxiety. Instead, infantile goals and fantasies are dangerously endowed with the energy emanating from matured sexual equipment and vicious aggressive power. One parent, again, becomes the goal; the other, again, the hindrance. Yet this revived Oedipal struggle is not and must not be interpreted as exclusively or even primarily a sexual one. It is a turn toward the earliest origins, an attempt to resolve a diffusion of early introjects and to rebuild shaky childhood identifications—in other words, a wish to be born again, to learn once more the very first steps toward reality and mutuality and to be given renewed permission to develop again the functions of contact, activity, and competition.

A young patient who had found himself blocked in college nearly read himself blind during the initial phase of his treatment, apparently in a destructive overidentification with father and therapist, both of whom were professors. Guided by a resourceful "painter in residence," he came upon the fact that he had an original talent to paint, an activity which was prevented only by his advancing treatment from becoming a self-destructive overactivity. As painting proved to be a valuable asset in the patient's gradual acquisition of a sense of identity of his own, one night he dreamed a different version of a dream which previously had always ended in frightened awakening. As always, he was fleeing from fire and persecution, but this time he fled into a stand of trees which he had sketched himself, and as he fled into it the charcoal drawing turned into a real forest with infinite perspectives.

The Choice of the Negative Identity

The loss of a sense of identity is often expressed in a scornful and snobbish hostility toward the roles offered as proper and desirable in one's family or immediate community. Any aspect of the required role, or all of it—be it masculinity or femininity, nationality or class membership—can become the main focus of the young person's acid disdain. Such excessive contempt for their backgrounds occurs among the oldest Anglo-Saxon and the newest Latin or Jewish families; it can become a general dislike for everything American and an irrational overestimation of everything foreign, or the reverse. Life and strength seem to exist only where one is not, while decay and danger threaten wherever one happens to be. This typical fragment from a case report illustrates the superego's triumph of depreciation over a young man's faltering identity: "A voice within him which was disparaging him began to increase at about this time. It went to the point of intruding into everything he did. He said, 'If I smoke a cigarette, if I tell a girl I like her, if I make a gesture, if I listen to music, if I try to read a book—this third voice is at me all the time—"You're doing this for effect; you're a phony." ' This disparaging voice became rather relentless. One day on the way home to college, his train crossed through the New Jersey swamplands and some poorer sections of cities, and he felt overwhelmingly that he was more congenial with people who lived there than he was with people on the campus or at home. Life seemed to exist only in those places, and the campus, in contrast, was a sheltered, effeminate place."

In this example, it is important to recognize not only an overweening superego, overclearly perceived as a deprecating inner voice (but not integrated enough to lead the young man into an alternative career), but also the acute identity confusion as projected on segments of society. An analogous case is that of a French-American girl from a rather prosperous mining town who felt panicky to the point of paralysis when alone with a boy. It appeared that numerous superego injunctions and identity conflicts had, as it were, short-circuited in the obsessive idea that every boy had a right to expect from her a yielding to sexual practices popularly designated as "French."

Such estrangement from national and ethnic origins rarely leads to a complete denial of *personal identity,* although the angry insistence on being called by a particular given name or nickname is not uncommon among young people who try to find refuge in a new label. Yet, confabulatory reconstructions of one's origin do occur. An especially inventive high school girl from Middle-European stock secretly sought the company of Scottish immigrants, carefully studying and easily assimilating their dialect and their social habits. With the help of history books and travel guides she reconstructed for herself a childhood in a given milieu in an actual township in Scotland, which was apparently quite convincing to some descendants of that country throughout long evening talks. She spoke of her American-born parents as "the people who brought me over here," and when sent to me introduced herself as "Lorna" and described her childhood "over there" in impressive detail. I went along with the story, saying that it had more inner truth than reality to it. And indeed the inner truth turned out to be a memory, namely, the girl's erstwhile attachment to a woman neighbor who had come from the British Isles and who had given her more of the kind of love she wanted than her parents did or could. The force behind the near-delusioned power of the invented "truth" was in turn a death wish against her parents, which is latent in all severe identity crises. The semideliberateness of the delusion came to the fore when I finally asked the girl how she had managed to marshall all the details of life in Scotland. "Bless you, sir," she said, in a pleading Scottish brogue, "I needed a past." Needless to say, with such gifts for language, histrionics, and personal warmth, a "delusion" is very different in nature and prognosis from a truly psychotic condition.

On the whole, however, our patients' conflicts find expression in a more subtle way than the abrogation of personal identity. They choose instead a *negative identity,* i.e., an identity perversely based on all those identifications and roles which, at critical stages of development, had been presented to them as most undesirable or dangerous and yet also as most real. For example, a mother whose first-born son died and who, because of complicated guilt feelings, had never been able to attach to her later surviving children the same amount of religious devotion that she bestowed on the memory of her dead child, aroused in one of her sons the fateful conviction that to be sick or dead was a better assurance of being "recognized" than to be healthy and about. A mother who was filled with unconscious ambivalence toward a brother who had disintegrated into alcoholism again and again responded selectively only to those traits in her son which seemed to point to a repetition of her brother's fate, with the result that this "negative" identity sometimes seemed to have more reality for the son than all his natural attempts at being good. He worked hard at becoming a drunkard, and, lacking the necessary ingredients, ended up in a state of stubborn paralysis of choice.

In other cases the negative identity is dictated by the necessity of finding and defending a niche of one's own against the excessive ideals either demanded by morbidly ambitious parents or indeed actualized by superior ones. In both cases the parents' weaknesses and unexpressed wishes are recognized by the child with catastrophic clarity. The daughter of a man of brilliant showmanship ran away from college and was arrested as a prostitute in the Negro quarter of a southern city, while the daughter of an influential southern Negro preacher was found among narcotic addicts in Chicago. In such cases it is of utmost importance to recognize the mockery and vindictive pretense in such role playing, for the white girl had not really prostituted herself, and the colored girl had not really become an addict—yet. Needless to say, however, each of them had put herself into a marginal social area, leaving it to law enforcement officers and psychiatric agencies to decide what stamp to put on such behavior. A corresponding case is that of a boy presented to a psychiatric clinic as "the village homosexual" of a small town. On investigation, it appeared that the boy had succeeded in assuming this fame without any actual acts of homosexuality except one, much earlier in his life, when he had been raped by some older boys.

Such vindictive choices of a negative identity represent, of course, a desperate attempt at regaining some mastery in a situation in which the available positive identity elements cancel each other out. The history of such a choice reveals a set of conditions in which it is easier for the patient to derive a sense of identity out of a total identification with that which he is least supposed to be than to struggle for a feeling of reality in acceptable roles which are unattainable with his inner means. The statement of a young man that "I would rather be quite insecure than a little secure" and of a young woman that "at least in the gutter I'm a genius," circumscribe the relief following the total choice of a negative identity. Such relief is, of course, often sought collectively in cliques and gangs of young homosexuals, addicts, and social cynics.

Some forms of upper-class snobbism must be included here because they permit some people to deny their identity confusion through recourse to something they did not earn themselves, such as their parents' wealth, background, or fame, or to some things they did not create, such as styles and art forms. But there is a "lower lower" snobbism too, which is based on the pride of having achieved a semblance of nothingness. At any rate, many a sick or desperate late adolescent, if faced with continuing conflict, would rather be nobody or somebody totally bad or, indeed, dead—and this by free choice—than be not-quite-somebody. The word "total" is not accidental in this connection . . . a human proclivity to a "totalistic" reorientation when, at critical stages of development, reintegration into a relative "wholeness" seems impossible. The totalistic solution of a psychotic break cannot be discussed here. . . .[4]

Having offered a picture of the whole condition of acute identity confusion, I would like to take up each of the part-symptoms described and relate it to two phenomena seemingly remote from one another: the individual's childhood and cultural history. Since we take it for granted that the conflicts we meet in our case histories in vastly aggravated form are, in principle, common to all individuals, so that the picture presented is only a distorted reflection of the normal adolescent state, we may now inquire, first, how this state can be shown to revive old childhood conflicts and, second, what are the various avenues which cultures offer to "normal" youths so that they may overcome the forces that pull them back into infantile regressions and find ways of mobilizing their inner strength for future-oriented pursuits.

First, then, the pull back into childhood, the regressive aspects of adolescent conflict. I hope I will not complicate this matter unbearably by reintroducing the chart in order to "locate" regressive trends in our scheme of psychosocial development. I know that some readers will have wondered what to do with the as yet unassigned parts of the chart. Others would probably prefer to read on and leave the diagram to those interested in such charting. I will, therefore, insert here a paragraph intended only for chart fanciers, explaining to them the way in which, throughout this section, the numbers after certain items refer to the chart. Other readers may ignore this next paragraph as well as all subsequent numbers in parentheses. To them, I hope, the text will speak for itself.

Only the *diagonal* of the epigenetic chart [p. 411] has been fully discussed. . . . It depicts, we said, the ontogenetic unfolding of the main components of psychosocial vitality (I.1–VIII.8). We have also filled in some aspects of the vertical leading from infancy to identity, from I.5 to V.5. These are the specific contributions which previous stages make directly to the development of identity, namely, the primitive *trust* in mutual recognition; the rudiments of a *will* to be oneself; the *anticipation* of what one might become; and the capacity to *learn* how to be, with skill, what one is in the process of becoming. But this also means that each of these stages contributes a particular estrangement to identity confusion: the earliest would come about with an "autistic" inability to establish mutuality. The most radical forms of identity confusion, we have just seen, can be traced back to such early disturbances. Here, a basic confusion of contradictory introjects undermines, as it were, all future identifications and thus also their integration in adolescence. Taking our cues, then, from the clinical picture just described, and experimenting with the chart, we will now distribute the various *part-symptoms* of confusion on horizontal V of the chart, and indicate how we would trace them downward along the "regressive" verticals 1, 2, 3, and 4 to their antecedents in childhood. The reader need only let his eye wander along these verticals to find the location of the numbers which appear after the major items.

Let us begin with the first item of pathology just described, the mistrust of time itself and the dominance of *time confusion* (V.1). A loss of the ego's function of maintaining perspective and expectancy is a clear regression to a time in early infancy when time did not exist. The experience of time arises only from the infant's adaptation to initial cycles of need tension, delay of satisfaction, and satiation. In the infant, as tension increases, future fulfillment is anticipated in a "hallucinatory" way; as fulfillment is delayed, moments of impotent rage occur in which trust seems obliterated; any signs of an approaching satisfaction gives time again a quality of intense hope, while further delay causes redoubled rage. Our patients, as we saw, do not trust time and are not convinced that sufficient satisfaction is sufficiently predictable to make wanting and "working" worth while.

Our most malignantly regressed young people are in fact clearly possessed by general attitudes which represent something of a mistrust of time as such: every delay appears to be a deceit, every wait an experience of impotence, every hope a danger, every plan a catastrophe, every possible provider a potential traitor. Therefore, time must be made to stand still, if necessary by the magic means of catatonic immobility. These are the extremes which are manifest in few but latent in many cases of identity confusion, and every adolescent, I would believe, knows at least fleeting moments of being thus at odds with time itself. In its normal and transitory form, this new kind of mistrust quickly or gradually yields to outlooks permitting and demanding an intense and even fanatic investment in a future, or a rapid succession in a number of possible futures. These, to the elders, often seem quite inconsistent with each other and at any rate quite "utopian," that is, based on expectations which would call for a change in the laws of historical change. But then, again, youth can attach itself to seemingly utopian world images which somehow prove to be realizable in part, given the right leader—and historical luck. Time confusion, then, is more or less typical for all adolescents at one stage or another, although it becomes pathologically marked only in some.

What does the social process do about this, from culture to culture, and from one era to another? I can only offer some suggestive examples. Thus, there was the romantic period, when youth (and artists and writers) were preoccupied with the ruins left by a dead past which seemed more "eternal" than the present. To be emphasized here, however, is not the mere turning to a distant past, but a concomitant change in the whole quality of temporal experience. This, under different cultural or historical conditions, can be acquired in settings as different (to choose from examples already mentioned in this book) as a vision-quest in the blinding prairie sun or dancing to drumbeat throughout the night; in utterly passive drug-induced floating in "absolute" time or in goose stepping to blaring trumpets in preparation for the Thousand Year Reich. There is, in fact, an indispensable temporal aspect of all ideology, including the ideological significance which the goals and values of different civilizations have for youth, be they bent on salvation or reform, adventure or conquest, reason or progress, in accordance with newly developing identity potentials. For among the essentials which they provide for youth is a sensually convincing *time perspective* compatible with a coherent world image. It makes supreme sense that today, when the standardization of anticipated futures is at its height, thousands of young people would choose to behave as if the moratorium were a way of life and a separate culture. As they choose to forget about their future, society forgets that theirs is only a modern—that is, more populous and more publicized—

form of an old phenomenon, as is clearly revealed by the quality of revival in some of our young people's display.

We also diagnosed *identity-consciousness* among the ingredients of identity confusion, and we meant by it a special form of painful self-consciousness which dwells on discrepancies between one's self-esteem, the aggrandized self-image as an autonomous person, and one's appearance in the eyes of others. In our patients an occasional total obliteration of self-esteem contrasts sharply with a narcissistic and snobbish disdain of the judgment of others. But again, we see corresponding, if less extreme, phenomena in that sensitivity of adolescents which alternates with defiant shamelessness in the face of criticism. Again, these are primitive defenses, upholding a shaky self-certainty against the sense of *doubt* and *shame* (II.2) which we discussed in the last chapter. While this is normally a transitory matter, it persists in some character formations and remains characteristic of many creative people who experience, according to their own testimony, repeated adolescences and with them the full cycle of sensitive withdrawal and forceful self-exhibition.

Self-consciousness (V.2) is a new edition of that original doubt which concerned the trustworthiness of the parents and of the child himself—only in adolescence, such self-conscious doubt concerns the reliability of the whole span of childhood which is now to be left behind and the trustworthiness of the whole social universe now envisaged. The obligation now to commit oneself with a sense of free will to one's autonomous identity can arouse a painful over-all ashamedness somehow comparable to the original shame and rage over being visible all around to all-knowing adults—only such shame now adheres to one's having a public personality exposed to age mates and to be judged by leaders. All of this, in the normal course of events, is outbalanced by that *self-certainty* (V.2) now characterized by a definite sense of independence from the family as the matrix of self-images, and a sureness of anticipation.

Among the societal phenomena corresponding to this second conflict there is a universal trend toward some form of uniformity either in special uniforms or in distinctive clothing through which incomplete self-certainty, for a time, can hide in a group certainty. Such certainty has always been provided by the age-old badges as well as the sacrifices of investitures, confirmations, and initiations, but it can also be temporarily and arbitrarily created by those who care to differ, radically, and yet must evolve a certain uniformity of differing (zoot-suiters, beatniks). These and less obvious uniformities are enforced by comprehensive shaming among peers, a judgmental give-and-take and a cruel banding together which leaves outsiders "holding the bag" in painful, if sometimes creative, isolation.

The display of a total commitment to a *role fixation* (V.3) as against a free *experimentation* with available roles has an obvious connection with earlier conflicts between free initiative Oedipal guilt in infantile reality, fantasy, and play. Where our patients regress below the Oedipal crisis to a total crisis of trust, the choice of a self-defeating role often remains the only acceptable form of initiative on the way back and up, and this in the form of a complete denial of ambition as the only possible way of totally avoiding guilt. The normal expression of relatively guilt-free and in fact more or less "delinquent" initiative in youth, however, is an experimentation with roles which follows the unwritten codes of adolescent subsocieties and thus is not lacking a discipline of its own.

Of the social institutions which undertake to channel as they encourage such initiative and to provide atonement as they appease guilt, we may point here, again, to initiations and confirmations: they strive within an atmosphere of mythical timelessness to combine some badge of sacrifice or submission with an energetic push toward sanctioned ways of action—a combination which, where it works, assures the development in the novice of an optimum of compliance with a maximum sense of free choice and solidarity. This special proclivity of youth—namely, the achievement of a sense of free choice as the very result of ritual regimentation—is, of course, universally utilized in army life.

Extreme *work paralysis* (V.4) is the logical sequence of a deep sense of the inadequacy of one's general equipment. Such a sense of inadequacy, of course, does not usually reflect a true lack of potential; it may, rather, convey the unrealistic demands made by an ego ideal willing to settle only for omnipotence or omniscience; it may express the fact that the immediate social environment does not have a niche for the individual's true gifts; or it may reflect the paradoxical fact that an individual in early school life was seduced into a specialized precocity which out-distanced his identity development. For all these reasons, then, the individual may be excluded from that experimental competition in play and work through which he learns to find and insist on his own kind of achievement and his work identity. This can become especially relevant in an early turn to delinquency—delinquents being, in many ways, the "positive" counterparts of our patients because at least they act out in company what the isolate suppresses. Some mockery of work and yet a competition with it is obvious in such delinquent phrases as "doing a job" (that is, a burglary) or "making a good job of it" in the sense of completing the destruction. From here it is only one step to another obvious consideration, namely, that young people must have learned to enjoy a sense of *apprenticeship* (IV.4) in order not to need the thrill of destruction. Schizoids and delinquents have in common a mistrust of themselves, a disbelief in the possibility that they could ever complete anything of value. This, of course, is especially marked in those who, for some reason or other, do not feel that they are partaking of the technological identity of their time. The reason may be that their own gifts have not found contact with the productive aims of the machine age or that they themselves belong to a social class (here "upper-upper" is remarkably equal to "lower-lower") that does not partake of the stream of progress.

Social institutions support the strength and distinctiveness of the budding work identity by offering those who are still learning and experimenting a certain status of *apprenticeship*, a moratorium characterized by defined duties and sanctioned competitions as well as by special license.

These, then, are the regressive trends in the identity crisis which are particularly clearly elaborated in the symptoms of identity confusion and some of the social processes which counteract them in daily life. But there are also aspects of identity formation which anticipate future development. The first of these is what we may call a *polarization of sexual differences* (V.6), i.e., the elaboration of a particular ratio of masculinity and femininity in line with identity development. Some of our patients suffer more lastingly and malignantly from a state not uncommon in a milder and transient form in all adolescence: the young person does not feel himself clearly to be a member of one sex or the other, which may make him the easy victim of the pressure emanating, for example, from homosexual cliques, for to some persons it is more bearable to be typed as something, anything, than to endure drawn-out bisexual confusion. Some, of course, decide on an ascetic turning away from sexuality which may result in dramatic breakthroughs of bewildering impulses. For *bisexual confusion* (V.6) in adolescence joins *identity-consciousness* in the establishment of an excessive preoccupation with the question of what kind of man or woman, or what kind of intermediate or deviate, one might become. In his totalistic frame of mind, an adolescent may feel that to be a little less of one sex means to be much more, if not all, of the other. If at such a time something happens that marks him socially as a deviant, he may develop a deep fixation, reinforced by the transvaluation of a negative identity, and true intimacy will then seem dangerous. Here the sexual mores of cultures and classes make for immense differences in the psychosocial differentiation of masculine and feminine and in the age, kind, and ubiquity of genital activity. These differences can obscure the common fact discussed above, namely, that the development of psychosocial intimacy is not possible without a firm sense of identity. Induced by special mores, young people in confusion may foreclose their identity development by concentrating on early genital activity without intimacy; or, on the contrary, they may concentrate on social, artistic, or intellectual aims which underplay the genital element to an extent that there is a permanent weakness of genital polarization with the other sex.

Social institutions here offer ideological rationales for widely different patterns of partial sexual moratoria such as complete sexual abstinence for a specified period, promiscuous genital activity without personal commitment, or sexual play without genital engagement. What a group's or an individual's "libido economy" will stand depends both on the kind of childhood left behind and on the identity gain which accrues from such preferred sexual behavior.

But youth also makes an important step toward parenthood and adult responsibility in learning to take *leadership* as well as to assume *followership* (V.7) among peers and to develop what often amounts to an astonishing foresight in the functions thus assumed. Such foresight can be, as it were, ahead of the individual's over-all maturity precisely because the prevailing ideology provides a framework for an orientation in leadership. By the same token, the common "cause" permits others to follow and to obey (and the leader himself to obey higher leaders) and thus to replace the parent images set up in the infantile superego with the hierarchy of leader-images inhabiting the available gallery of ideals—a process as typical for delinquent gangs as for any highly motivated group. Where a youth can neither obey nor give orders he must make do with an isolation which can lead to malignant withdrawal but which also, if he is lucky and gifted, will help him respond to guiding voices who speak to him (as if they knew him) over the centuries, through books, pictures, and music.

We now come to that system of ideals which societies present to the young in the explicit or implicit form of an ideology. From what has been said so far we can ascribe to ideology the function of offering youth (1) a simplified perspective of the future which encompasses all foreseeable time and thus counteracts individual "time confusion"; (2) some strongly felt correspondence between the inner world of ideals and evils and the social world with its goals and dangers; (3) an opportunity for exhibiting some uniformity of appearance and behavior counteracting individual identity-consciousness; (4) inducement to a collective experimentation with roles and techniques which help overcome a sense of inhibition and personal guilt; (5) introduction into the ethos of the prevailing technology and thus into sanctioned and regulated competition; (6) a geographic-historical world image as a framework for the young individual's budding identity; (7) a rationale for a sexual way of life compatible with a convincing system of principles; and (8) submission to leaders who as super-human figures or "big brothers" are above the ambivalence of the parent-child relation. Without some such *ideological commitment,* however implicit in a "way of life," youth suffers a *confusion of values* (V.8) which can be specifically dangerous to some but which on a large scale is surely dangerous to the fabric of society. . . .

NOTES

1. Marie Jahoda, "Toward A Social Psychology of Mental Health," *Symposium on the Healthy Personality, Supplement II: Problems of Infancy and Childhood,* Transactions of Fourth Conference, March 1950, ed. M. J. E. Benn (New York: Josiah Macy, Jr., Foundation, 1950).
2. See Erik H. Erikson, *Childhood and Society,* 2nd ed. (New York: W. W. Norton, 1963), Part I.
3. Edward Bibring, "The Mechanism of Depression" in *Affective Disorders,* ed. P. Greenacre (New York: International Universities Press, 1953), pp. 13–48.
4. I owe my orientation in this field to Robert Knight, "Management and Psychotherapy of the Borderline Schizophrenic Patient" in *Psychoanalytic Psychiatry and Psychology,* Austen Riggs Center, Vol. 1, ed. R. P. Knight and C. R. Friedman (New York: International Universities Press, 1954), pp. 110–22; and Margaret Brenman, "On Teasing and Being Teased: and the Problem of 'Moral Masochism' " also in *Psychoanalytic Psychiatry and Psychology,* pp. 29–51.

26

Strategic Interactions in Early Adolescence
David Elkind

Erving Goffman has described a variety of human interaction patterns in an impressionistic yet consensually valid way (Goffman 1969). One type is what he calls *strategic interactions,* interpersonal encounters that have as their aim the acquisition, concealment, or revelation of information through indirect means. In effect, strategic interactions involve calculation about the other person's thinking on the part of at least one of the people involved. Goffman quotes Chesterfield's advice to his son regarding diplomacy as an example of strategic thinking and performance:

> There are some additional qualifications necessary, in the practical part of the business, which may deserve some consideration in your leisure moments—such as, an absolute command of your temper, so as not to be provoked to passion upon any account; patience to hear frivolous, impertinent and unreasonable applications; with address enough to refuse, without offending; or by your manner of granting, to double the obligation; dexterity enough to conceal a truth, without telling a lie; sagacity enough to read other people's countenance; and serenity enough not to let them discover anything by yours—a seeming frankness with a real reserve. These are the rudiments of a politician; the world must be your grammar. [Chesterfield cited in Goffman 1969, p. 97]

Goffman's description of strategic interactions is essentially sociological and non-developmental. His description holds for adult members of the society. Looked at from the standpoint of cognitive development, however, true strategic interactions become possible only in early adolescence, thanks to the emergence of formal operations. Moreover, because the imaginary audience and the personal fable play so large a part in the young adolescent's behavior, strategic interactions have a personal egocentric quality that is lacking in Chesterfield's description. Put differently, from a developmental standpoint one might expect the quality of these interactions to change as the individual matures.

This developmental change in the nature of strategic interactions may be explained as follows. The adolescent, much more than the child or the adult, seeks to enhance, maintain, and defend self-esteem in relation to the audience. Because he or she is breaking away from the security of parental ties, that continuing source of acceptance and self-esteem is weakened. And because the young adolescent does not yet have an occupation or supportive friendships, the usual sources of adult self-esteem and support are absent. That is why the young adolescent is so concerned with audience reactions. It is, for a brief period in life, the primary source of self-esteem enhancement.

Accordingly, strategic interactions in early adolescence have a different purpose and quality than they do in later adolescence and adulthood. In adulthood, the period Goffman (1969) writes about, strategic interactions are for the purpose of acquiring, retaining, or revealing information for some strategic purpose, such as winning a game, besting a foe, or gaining a business advantage. Although self-esteem is involved in such interactions, it is secondary to the other aims. But, in early adolescence, the prime aim of strategic interactions is the enhancement, maintenance, or defense of self-esteem.

It needs to be said, however, that some forms of strategic interaction characteristic of early adolescence are carried over to late adolescence and adulthood. But, in such instances, the interactions are clearly recognizable for what they are, egocentric interactions in the service of the imaginary audience and the personal fable. Those who are the victims of such interactions will often speak of them as "childish" or as "immature."

Strategic Interactions in Early Adolescence

The development of strategic interactions from early adolescence to adulthood parallels other cognitive developments, that is to say, development is usually from a stage of undifferentiation and hierarchical organization (Werner 1948). Young children, for example, do not distinguish clearly between what is physical and what is psychic; they regard dreams as physical things at the same time as they endow physical things with life. By adolescence, physical and mental are clearly differentiated and ordered in relation to one another. In the same way, young adolescents' initial efforts at strategic interactions are marked by a failure to distinguish clearly between their thoughts and those of the person being interacted with. Strategic interactions become more differentiated and more subtle with increasing age. We can now look at some of these interactions.

Phoning and Being Phoned

Among children and adults, phoning is largely a communicative activity. One calls to get or to give information. But in adolescence phoning and being phoned become indices of popularity and hence are bound up with self-esteem. Many young adolescents, therefore, engage in certain strategic interactions in order to make certain that they will receive phone calls. For example, some young people insist, at school, that they have important secret information that they will impart to a friend if the friend will call that evening.

Phoning someone else has its own strategic patterns. In calling another young person, one wants to avoid the impression that the call is made out of loneliness and a desire for friendship and companionship. If the boy or girl being phoned is not free to engage in the proposed activity, it is again necessary to avoid any show or expression of disappointment. This is what in contemporary adolescent parlance is called "cool." It means that you give no indication as to your needs or emotions and that you take whatever happens with equanimity.

Once on the phone, other strategems come into play. One of these is to stay on the phone a long, long time. Parents often assume that these long-winded discussions are solely devoted to projects or gossip. But they also have another purpose, to give other potential callers the *busy signal.* A phone in use signifies a popular person and the busy signal is a sign of popularity. Sometimes, of course, the adolescent may cut a conversation short because he or she is "expecting some other calls," which gives the caller the message that he or she is nothing special and that others are waiting to call the popular person.

These are only a few of the strategic interactions that center around phoning and being phoned in early adolescence. It is important to emphasize that this type of strategic interaction does not really persist into adulthood. Adults, for example, do not try to prove popularity by the number of calls they get. Nor do they show no emotion when friends decline to come over or to go out with them. For adults the appropriate response here is one of regret. Anything else would simply be rude.

Friendships

In early adolescence, friendship patterns often take on a strategic coloration. An attractive girl may befriend a less attractive one, in part, at least, to enhance the impression of attractiveness to the imaginary audience. But the contrast also confirms her sense of being specially, uniquely attractive. Similar motives operate for the less attractive girl, who hopes to impress the audience by the very fact of being associated with the attractive girl. And the fact of being the attractive girl's friend confirms the less attractive girl in *her* sense of specialness.

It is not surprising, then, that early adolescent friendships tend to be rather cliquish. Belonging to a special clique is impressive to an audience who admires such things (and the adolescent believes that everyone does). Likewise, belonging to the special group confirms the young person in his specialness—one would not belong unless one were special. And the adolescent who is not accepted by the clique suffers for the same reason that clique members rejoice, the audience knows he or she does not belong and the sense of being special in a negative way, the outsider, is very strong and very painful.

The foregoing paragraphs have suggested just some of the ways in which friendships are used strategically at early adolescence. Other patterns can be briefly noted. Some adolescents befriend others, again probably in part only, because the friend's parents are wealthy, well known, or both. Sometimes outsiders befriend other outsiders to demonstrate to the audience that they do have friends and to confirm their sense of specialness, in that they are the only ones to see the special qualities of the other outsider they have befriended.

It should be said, too, that the dynamics of friendship patterns can be seen within as well as between groups. This often occurs when there are three boys or girls who are rather good friends. Sociologically three is a bad number and two of the friends usually band together to ostracize the third. Here again the rejecting couple impresses the audience and confirms the fable of being special; the adolescent on the outside suffers from the public ouster and the private humiliation. Interestingly, the couples in the threesome may change so that an outsider becomes an insider and vice versa.

On Cutting and Being Cut

Recognizing another person in a public place is an important social act to both parties. By giving or withholding recognition a person can enhance or diminish self-esteem in others. This is true because to be recognized in a public place is recognition in front of an audience and a boost to self-esteem. Failure to be recognized has, of course, the opposite effect. Hence the giver or withholder of recognition has a sort of power, the use of which enhances that person's sense of specialness. But the use of that power is also seen by an audience and hence serves to impress others as well.

Young adolescents, thanks to formal operations, come to appreciate the power of recognition in public places. Nothing is so devastating to a person as to go through all the motions of public recognition—movement toward the other person, smiling, eyes clearly focused on the other person—and to have these overtures ignored by the other. On campus one day, I saw a young woman walk toward a young man, smiling and in the process of saying, "Hi, how are you?" when he turned on his heel and walked away. She was crushed, seemed to shrink into herself, looked about to see how large the audience had been and slowly walked away in a different direction from the one she had been walking in.

The power of cutting and the humiliation of being cut are largely a function of the imaginary audience that is assumed to monitor the actions of both parties involved. To be sure, cutting occurs at all later developmental periods, but it is basically an adolescent phenomena. The adult who is greeted by someone he would not prefer to meet is usually cool but polite. It is only the adult who has not matured who continues to use cutting as a strategic interaction. For most adults, cutting is a rude and immature way of dealing with difficult social interactions.

Dating

Dating involves a series of complex behavior patterns from the initial request to the final parting.

For young adolescents, dating is fraught with strategic interactions. There is, first of all, the matter of asking for a date. The problem is how to ask so as to avoid rejection. One of the first strategies young people have to learn is to ask first whether the other person is doing anything on the afternoon or evening in question. If the person *is* busy, then one has really not asked the other person out and so has not been rejected. This strategy also permits the datee to decline in advance by saying that he or she has "other plans." This strategy permits the dater to ask for a date indirectly and for the datee to refuse, equally indirectly.

Of course, not all young people are proficient in these strategies. If a young man calls up and, without preliminaries, asks a young woman to go out with him one night and she says she has other plans, he does not know if this is the truth or whether it is an evasion. This communication can be made clearer if the girl says that she would like to and would he please call again. If she does not encourage him to call again, this communication is less clear but is decidedly in the direction of rejection. Accordingly, the strategy of first asking the to-be-invited person whether they are busy offers both parties more flexibility than a direct invitation. It is a strategic interaction.

Asking for a date is, however, but one in a series of strategic interactions that will occur if the engagement is accepted. It is not necessary to discuss all of those interactions, but two are of particular interest from the standpoint of acquiring, retaining, and revealing information. These are the "pass" and the "parting gesture." We need to look at these in a little more detail.

Among older adolescents and adults, the function of a date is to bring two people together for a period of time in pleasurable circumstances and for entertainment and enjoyment. In early adolescence, however, dating is as much for the imaginary audience as it is for the pleasure of the other person. Many teenagers of the opposite sex have very little to say to one another. The idea of having a date, and of other people knowing about the date, is often more exciting than the date itself.

For the boy and for the girl as well, much of the anxiety of the date centers around the physical interaction that it entails. The boy's strategy is to try and "get" as much as he can with the girl's permission, or at least without violent protest. A usual strategy for the boy is to test the limits nonverbally with the aid of slowly moving arms and crawling fingers. The girl communicates equally nonverbally by either moving toward or away from the boy and by accepting or pushing away the troublesome hands.

How different this is from older adolescents and adults who use a variety of subtle body cues to communicate sexual attraction and willingness to engage in sexual encounter. One is reminded here of the difference, described earlier, between preadolescents and adolescents trying to solve the combinatorial problem with four chips of different colors that are to be put together in different ways. The preadolescents have to manipulate the materials themselves in order to arrive at the correct combinations. But the adolescents can do the manipulations mentally. In the same way, the early physical groupings of the young adolescent are prelude to the more subtle and covert means of communicating attraction and willingness at later stages of development.

The parting is another facet of dating that requires strategic interactions. Initiating and terminating interpersonal encounters are often the most difficult part of those encounters, and successful terminations, like successful initiations, require effective strategies. The aim of an effective termination is to leave both parties feeling good about themselves and one another and desirous of another interchange, or at least not aversive to one.

The most effective strategy for termination is to prepare for it in advance. The girl may say, as they are driving home, "My parents usually wait up for me and don't like me to ask people in at this hour." Usually, both boy and girl prepare in advance by rehearsing a few set lines such as, "Thank you very much. I had a very nice time." If either one wants to leave the door open for future engagements, one will say, "Let's do it again sometime." Often, however, young adolescents muff their lines and partings are likely to end with the boy rushing off and tossing an abrupt "See ya." into the wind.

In young adolescents, perhaps the greatest anxiety is encountered in the matter of the good-night kiss. First there are all the rules, frequently broken, about not kissing on the first date. Then there is the problem of finding out, on the boy's side, whether or not it will be permitted. What the boy has to decide is whether to ask first or simply to try it. In some ways, the verbal request invites a verbal rejection even if the girl is willing, because she may not be willing to verbalize it. On the other hand, if the boy tries to kiss the girl without asking first and she rejects the kiss, he is put in the position of being sexually aggressive and a roughneck.

Consequently, young adolescents do not usually handle terminations very well. Here again, their concern for the audience ("Hey, look at him, he kissed her!" or "Hey, look at him, she didn't let him kiss her!"—in the case of the boy. And "Hey, look at her, he really kissed her!" or "Look at her, she wouldn't let him kiss her!") makes these interactions awkward in the extreme. Indeed, the young adolescent is often so concerned with the audience reaction that he or she ignores cues that would make this interaction more successful.

These are but a few of the interactions that emerge in the course of dating. I have hardly touched on the complex strategic interactions involved in petting and being petted, but here again each individual is trying to get information from the other in order to know how to proceed. Since both parties are inexperienced at this sort of communication, the interactions tend to be clumsy and unsatisfying. As young people gain in experience and practice, their strategic interactions around dating become more polished and proficient.

Forbidden Acts

Some of the most interesting and ingenious strategic interactions practiced by young adolescents have to do with the concealment or disguise of forbidden acts. Such acts include smoking, drinking, sexual intercourse, stealing from local stores, and skipping school. Because these acts are punishable to various degrees, adolescents go to great lengths to conceal or to disguise them. Many of these strategic interactions are based on the adolescent's assumptions about adult behavior patterns.

A strategic interaction engaged in by the author when he was a young teenager is illustrative of these strategems. I grew up in Detroit, where being able to drive a car was a sign of mature status. Beginners' licenses were then available at age 14. But before that, many of us at the age of 12 or 13 would "borrow" the family car to practice, driving it around the block. I usually tried to do this Sunday afternoons when my father was taking a nap and my mother was off visiting friends. Then I would take the keys off the dresser and a friend and I would be off for a few turns around the block.

Once, however, I failed to reckon on a party at a neighbor's house. When I returned to park the car in the spot where it had been parked before, I found the place taken! Panic quickly set in and my friend and I proceeded to push three cars back to make the correct spot open again. Tired but triumphant, I parked the car and started toward the house on my way to returning the keys to their position on the dresser. But there was my father standing on the porch! He had witnessed the whole procedure. I shall spare you the details of what followed, but I did not take the car without permission and without a permit again.

Smoking, whether it be tobacco or marijuana, is another act that young adolescents go to lengths to conceal. Finding a place to smoke that will be undiscovered presents a challenge in itself. Out of doors and in public places, of course, there is the danger of being seen and reported. Indoors there is the problem of odors, particularly if the parents do not smoke. Adolescents usually try to find a place that is not frequented by adults, such as a cellar or an attic as a place to smoke. At school, the bathroom is most often the place, but this is often policed by school officials. For young adolescents, finding a place to smoke that is free of detection is far from easy.

Concealing the fact that one has been smoking is not easy either. Breath mints are usually taken in large quantities, but they don't help the odor that attaches to clothes, hair, and skin. Some adolescents bathe and change clothes after smoking for just this reason. Obtaining new supplies is another problem that has been solved for the adolescent with the advent of cigarette machines. Store people are less cautious about selling minors cigarettes than they are about selling them beer and liquor.

Drinking presents some of the same strategic problems as smoking. It is necessary to find a place that will not be intruded on, it is necessary to get a supply of the beverage to be consumed, and it is necessary to hide or conceal the fact that any of this has taken place. The place is often someone's home that has been vacated for a known period of time. The beverage may be taken from parental reserves, but this means concealing the fact that some of those reserves are depleted. Here the adolescent's knowledge about parents comes in handy. If the parent is casual about how much beer, liquor, and wine he has on hand, it is easier for the adolescent to take some than if the parent keeps close tabs on his liquor cabinet.

A variety of strategies are employed to get supplies from stores. Fake ID cards are in great demand and some young people become quite adept at manipulating identity papers. Another strategy is to have someone who is older buy it for the younger participants. Other strategies are forging a note from parents to the effect that the vendor should sell the young person beer to take home to his parents. Still other young people dress and make themselves up to look older so that no questions will be asked.

Concealing the effects of drinking presents problems similar to those of smoking, except in the case when the young person is rather high. The strategy that is often decided on, but that often does not work, is avoidance. The young person tries to get to his or her room as quickly as possible and with as few interchanges as possible. A remark to the effect that he or she is not feeling well or has a headache, although tempting, has to be avoided because parents might become oversolicitous. A better strategy is to say that there is much homework to be done and that it has to be got at immediately.

It is interesting that in communities where alcohol is not permitted, adults have institutionalized some of the strategic interactions devised by adolescents. In Utah, for example, alcohol is sold only in state liquor stores and is not available in restaurants. But there are many private clubs where one can keep one's own liquor in a cabinet and have it served at the table. The private club is a strategy for having alcoholic beverages available in eating places when this is prohibited by law in public eating places.

One last example of strategic interactions around forbidden acts is that of skipping school. This involves a number of different strategies. One is to leave home in the morning giving no telltale signs in dress or demeanor that something is up. This is not as easy as it might appear. If the young person is too easy to awaken, dressed too quickly, and too compliant to parental requests, this could signal that something is not as it should be. Instead the adolescent has to make sure that he or she is as usual so that the parent will not suspect anything out of the ordinary. But playing one's usual self is not easy, and adolescents miscues can alert parents to the fact that something is afoot.

Finding a place to go is another problem. A movie is dark and offers concealment, but most movies do not open till mid-afternoon. In larger cities, the students can travel to another part of the city and find anonymity there. With the demise of downtown areas, many young people spend their unofficial leaves from school at shopping centers or malls. If the parents of one or another adolescent work, they can sometimes spend the day at home listening to records and watching television. It is necessary, however, to make sure that they leave no telltale signs of their full-day occupancy.

Perhaps the most difficult part of taking an unofficial day off from school comes in forging the note from parents. This is a delicate matter because the note must sound like a parent and not like a teenager. Also the notepaper must be the type that the parent would use. Trying to write neatly and to copy the style of the parental writing is still another challenge. Finally, handing the note in with the appropriate casual demeanor, when your heart is pounding against your ribs, is still another strategy that the adolescent who would engage in this type of forbidden action must master.

I hope that, in discussing the strategic interactions that surround forbidden acts, I have not given the impression of condoning these acts. I do not. For many different reasons, health, legal, and moral, I do not believe that young adolescents should smoke, or drink, or skip school. But, at the same time, I know that they do do these things and that in part, but only in part, it is because of the challenge of the strategic interactions they entail. Strategic interactions provide young people with challenge and excitement that are motivating in and of themselves, quite apart from the often dubious pleasure of the forbidden act.

That is to say, in engaging in forbidden acts and outwitting adults, adolescents are again performing for an audience. Their success impresses the audience and confirms the personal fable of uniqueness and specialness. In understanding the psychology of forbidden acts, therefore, we need to take account of the pleasure and rewards that come from successfully engaging in strategic interactions as well as the rewards associated with the forbidden acts themselves.

The Development of Strategic Interactions in Older Adolescents and Adults

In this chapter I have argued that strategic interactions have a developmental dimension and that some types of strategic interactions are particularly characteristic of the young adolescent. What happens to these types of interaction as young people grow older? In general, their development moves in one of several different directions: automatization, legalization, and transformation.

Automatization

Some of the interactions that young adolescents engage in with great conscious deliberation eventually become automatic. For example, as phoning and being phoned becomes a more common experience, patterns of verbal interaction over the phone become more or less automatic and do not need to be thought about. To be sure, some conscious aspects of phoning and being phoned still linger on. Being called is still an ego booster. But for the adult, such popularity usually means that he or she is successful in his or her career, not necessarily in interpersonal relations.

Dating skills also become more sophisticated and automatic with increasing age. This permits young people to be more natural with one another once the mechanics of dating becomes routine. Also, as teenagers become older they verbalize more about these interpersonal relationships and there is less need for nonverbal communication to ask and answer questions about physical interactions. And more generally, relationships in later adolescence become more comprehensive, more inclusive of the total persons involved and less focussed on the sensual alone.

The automatization of some strategic interactions does not mean that all such interactions are at an end. Far from it. Young adults need to learn how best to present themselves when applying for a job, when asking for a raise, and so on. As adults we have to engage in a whole new set of strategic interactions that revolve primarily around our work, our relationships with our friends and family. Like the automatization of other skills, the automatization of strategic interactions of adolescence frees and prepares us for more complex, higher order strategic interactions that must be engaged in later in life.

Legalization

Some forms of strategic interaction, particularly those associated with some forbidden acts, are rendered unnecessary by virtue of the fact that young people have reached the age of 18 or 21. At this age it is no longer necessary to use strategems to obtain cigarettes or liquor or to find a place where they can be used without detection and to disguise the fact that they have been used.

To be sure, adults find new forms of forbidden acts to take their place. Illegal gambling, dope trafficking, and prostitution are forbidden acts that adults engage in strategic interactions to conceal. Prostitution is somewhat unique in this regard because the prostitute must reveal what it is she is vending in order to make a sale. Strategies must then be devised to avoid being picked up by the police but to enhance being picked up by a "John." Accordingly, the coming-of-age that makes some forbidden acts legal does not eliminate the phenomenon of strategic interactions about forbidden acts. There are simply new kinds of acts that are forbidden among adults and new types of strategic interactions that are substituted for those employed in adolescence.

Transformation

Some types of strategic interaction are transformed into more elaborate procedures as young people grow older. Cutting and being cut is a case in point. Adults continue to engage in cutting in public places, but it has new meaning and different consequences. Among adults cutting and being cut is often related to social and professional status. That is to say, the cutting is done to what the person represents as much as the person himself or herself. In adolescence, cutting is always personal and lacks the social dimension.

As adults become more and more identified with occupational and social status roles, their self-esteem comes from these roles as much as it does from personal achievement. Cutting in public places for adults is often a matter of asserting one's occupational or professional role, rather than a personal slight. Administrators, for example, whether they be factory foremen or university deans, tend to be less than effusive in greeting their workers or faculty in public places. It is not that they wish to put down the particular individuals as much as it is that they wish to make clear the difference in their respective status.

Friendship patterns also undergo transformation as young people mature. Friendships tend to become less egocentric and more based on mutual interests and compatibility of temperament rather than for more exploitive purposes. Certainly, even adult friendships can have an exploitive dimension, but this is usually a secondary factor in the relationship. Strategic interactions in mature friendships often center about how best to provide support and encouragement when the friend is having a hard time and how best to rejoice in the friend's happiness and success. Mature friendships lack the egocentrism they had in early adolescence.

Summary and Conclusion

The aim of the present chapter was both methodological and substantive. With regard to methodology, I tried to demonstrate an alternative approach to current studies of social cognition. Rather than trying to *extend* concepts derived from developmental psychology of interpersonal phenomena, I tried to *analyze* a construct taken from sociology—namely Erving Goffman's concept of strategic interaction—from a developmental perspective. To this end, I reviewed the developmental changes coincident with formal operations to demonstrate that only when these operations are present can true strategic interactions take place.

With regard to substance, I described a number of interactions peculiar to early adolescence. These included phoning and being phoned, cutting and being cut, dating, and forbidden acts. In contrast to adults, adolescents engage in strategic interactions largely to maintain, defend, or enhance self-esteem. Many of the strategic interactions of early adolescence are modified with increasing age as a consequence of automatization, transformation, or legalization. In adulthood, new and different forms of strategic interaction come into prominence.

In his own work Piaget has always recognized the fruitfulness of borrowing from different disciplines to find problems for developmental psychology. This point has somehow been lost in contemporary studies of social cognition. I hope the present discussion has demonstrated the potential fruitfulness of starting a developmental analysis from properly sociological concepts.

REFERENCES

BALDWIN, J. M. *Thought and things or genetic logic* (2 vols.). New York: Macmillan, 1906–1908.

BOOLE, G. *The laws of thought.* New York: Dover, 1950. (Originally published, 1854.)

ELKIND, D., AND BOWEN, R. Imaginary audience behavior in children and adolescents. *Developmental Psychology,* 1979, *15,* 38–44.

ELKIND, D., BAROCAS, R., AND ROSENTHAL, H. Combinatorial thinking in adolescents from graded and ungraded classrooms. *Perceptual and Motor Skills,* 1968, *27,* 1015–1018.

FLAVELL, J. H. *The developmental psychology of Jean Piaget.* Princeton, N.J.: Princeton University Press, 1963.

FLAVELL, J. H. *The development of role-taking and communication skills in children.* New York: Wiley, 1968.

GINSBURG, H., AND OPPER, S. *Piaget's theory of intellectual development: An introduction.* Englewood Cliffs, N.J.: Prentice-Hall, 1969.

GOFFMAN, E. *Strategic interaction.* Philadelphia: University of Pennsylvania Press, 1969.

INHELDER, B., AND PIAGET, J. *The growth of logical thinking in children and adolescents.* New York: Basic Books, 1958.

PIAGET, J. *The moral judgment of the child.* New York: Free Press, 1948.

PIAGET, J. *The judgment of reasoning of the child.* London: Routledge & Kegan Paul, 1951.

PIAGET, J. *The language and thought of the child.* London: Routledge & Kegan Paul, 1952.

SELMAN, R. The relation of role-taking to the development of moral judgment in children. *Child Development,* 1971, *42,* 79–91.

WERNER, H. *Comparative psychology of mental development.* New York: Harper & Row, 1948.

27

Psychodynamic Aspects of Identity Formation in College Women

Ruthellen L. Josselson

Introduction

While subtle and complex clinical observation has bequeathed richness to the understanding of psychopathology, the phenomenon of normal development lies scattered among piecemeal and often unrelated variables, is shrouded behind obscure part-theories, or, at best, is designated as the obverse of pathology. This observational and theoretical lacuna seems to become most apparent whenever the larger culture struggles to comprehend and assimilate "problematic" societal subgroups. Then, stereotypes are pitted against projected images, ideals against modal realities, and the lack of carefully compiled data hinders informed judgment.

The late 1960s was the age of crisis among youth, a visible and mystifying occurrence which the mass media leaped to overformulate. In the absence of a reliable developmental theory of its own, psychological research obligingly adopted popular categorizations, and a spate of poorly conceptualized studies on "activists" and "the alienated" appeared. Not surprisingly, these studies found "significant" differences among the behaviorally defined groups, but these were differences which hung in isolation, unable to advance very far the construction of an heuristic theory which could

From Ruthellen L. Josselson, "Psychodynamic Aspects of Identity Formation in College Women," *Journal of Youth and Adolescence* 2, no. 1 (1973). Reprinted by permission of Plenum Publishing Corporation.

absorb and explain time-bound behavioral shifts in an essentially timeless process of ontogenesis.

Similarly, the "crisis" among women in the early 1970s has laid bare the fundamental weakness in our understanding of the development of a woman. And, again, once the communications network of the culture had provided labels, psychologists obediently began conceptualizing and researching the differences between "liberated" and "traditional" women. As with the problem of youth, questions of incidence, of phenomenology, of the relationship of superficial attitudes to deep psychological processes were largely ignored.

The one theory within psychology elaborate and powerful enough to generalize beyond its own particular brand of data is that of psychoanalytic thought. This framework, however, is tied to a reductionistic metapsychology and, in addition, is unable to account for the vagaries of social influence and change. Psychoanalytic formulations of such problems as restless youth and angry women seemed to necessitate the transformation of these groups into recognizable pathologies before analysis could be attempted. Responsive to these weaknesses, ego analytic and social analytic schools of thought were engaged in inventing inductive and holistic concepts which would extend and/or modify the parent theory in order to account for later stages of growth, to integrate social reality and internal dynamics, and to, more generally, provide a more viable model of nonpathological development.

Erikson's concept of identity, which evolved within this historical effort, was of particular interest to those interested in the phenomenon of normal adolescent growth. In delineating a developmental epoch with a phenomenology deducible from a larger developmental schema, Erikson provided a truly psychosocial construct which is sensitive to the vagaries of intraindividual conflicts and resolutions and also responsive to age-specific societal demands to which the individual must accommodate. Identity, then, seemed to provide a theoretically derived guidepost to orient research into late adolescent development.

Erikson (1956), however, couches the identity construct in connotative and suggestive items. He defines identity as the embodiment of (1) the conscious sense of individual identity, (2) the silent doings of ego synthesis, (3) the unconscious striving for continuity of personal character, and (4) the maintenance of inner solidarity with a group's ideals and identity. The *process* of identity formation embraces an evolving configuration "established by ego syntheses and resyntheses . . . integrating constitutional givens, idiosyncratic libidinal needs, favored capacities, significant identifications, effective defenses, successful sublimations and consistent roles" (Erikson 1968, p. 71). These, at least, are the stuff of which identity is made.

In his expositions, Erikson grapples with the problem of identity from three directions. His biographical analyses, which have defined his preferred mode of dealing with the topic, articulate the organizing function of identity within the lives of historical giants. These men, Shaw, William James, Luther, Gandhi, were exemplary in the originality of the identities they forged, identities which were to have profound effects on their societies and, therefore, identities which were clearly visible. Erikson's pathographic discussions explore the ramifications of identity diffusion, the vulnerability to regression, and the availability to negative identities which mark those who are overwhelmed by the identity task. Finally, his genetic approach to identity formation focuses on the sociotheoretical necessity for the concept. Given the limited usefulness of the mechanism of identification, the crystallization of identity is necessary for the individual to identify himself, at the end of adolescence, within a community. Thus Erikson presents us with case studies at the extremes and a metapsychology. He remarks, however, that his approach is incomplete and that "in order to describe the universal genetics of identity, one would wish to be able to trace its development through the life histories of 'ordinary' individuals" (1968, p. 155).

Operationalizing the Concept of Identity

In order to determine the usefulness of Erikson's formulation of identity as a means of diffracting the late adolescent experience, it was first necessary to operationalize the concept. Several researchers (Block 1961; Bronson 1959; Gruen 1960) relied on primarily intrapsychic criteria to anchor the construct, but Marcia (1964, 1966) devised a structured interview format which preserved the inherently psychosocial nature of identity formation. His paradigm evolved from Erikson's view that identity is essentially a kind of contract that the individual makes with society, commitments to be and to do in certain ways and not in others, commitments which are made following a psychosocial moratorium, or crisis period.

Utilizing the criteria of crisis and commitment in regard to occupational and ideological choices, Marcia isolated four identity statuses:

Achievements—those who have seriously considered occupational and ideological alternatives and made a decision on their own terms.

Foreclosures—those who have made commitments in the absence of crisis, largely holding to childhood or parentally derived choices.

Moratoriums—those in an active crisis period, struggling to make commitments.

Diffusions—those who lack commitments and appear unconcerned about it.

In addition to the face validity of this categorization, Marcia and his associates provided for construct validity in demonstrating that those persons within each of these identity statuses would behave consistently and differentially on independent measures such as anxiety, authoritarianism, and cooperation in a prisoner's dilemma game (see Table 1, part A).

All of this work in its validational stages was performed with male subjects. The attempt to transpose it to female subjects led to difficulties, a rather frequent occurrence in psychological research. Given the existing theoretical and empirical writings on female development which stress the preeminence of the interpersonal sphere for women (Douvan and Adelson 1966; Coleman 1961; Sanford 1956; Deutsch 1944), it seemed clear, as the work on the identity statuses progressed, that the identity status interview must reflect interpersonal identity to accurately assess the identity "status" of a woman. With the addition of a set of questions regarding decisions about premarital sexual behavior, the identity status distribution among women

Table 1 Summary of empirical results regarding identity statuses

A. Males		
Achievements:	Highest performance on concept attainment task under stress[a]	⎰ Least vulnerable to self-esteem manipulation,[b] reflective cognitive style[d]
Moratoriums:	Most anxious,[b] least cooperation with high-authority opponent in prisoner's dilemma[c]	
Foreclosures:	Most authoritarian,[a] unrealistically high goals[a]	⎰ Impulsive cognitive style[d]
Diffusions:	Most vulnerable to self-esteem manipulation[a]	
B. Females		
Achievements:	Most difficult college majors[e]	⎰ Low in self-cognition,[g] field independent,[h] more resistant to conformity
Foreclosures:	Highest self-esteem,[e] most authoritarian,[e] lowest anxiety[e]	
Moratoriums:	Least authoritarian,[e] most cognitively complex,[g] highest anxiety[h]	⎰ High in self-cognition,[g] field dependent[h]
Diffusions:	Highest anxiety[e]	

[a] Marcia (1966).
[b] Marcia (1967).
[c] Podd *et al.* (1970).
[d] Waterman (1972).
[e] Marcia and Friedman (1970).
[f] Toder and Marcia (1971).
[g] Josselson (1972).
[h] Schenkel (1973).

produced discrete and consistent groups similar to those for men (Schenkel 1972). (The major difference, however, was that, as research evidence accumulated, it became clear that where male Foreclosures behaved much like male Diffusions and male Moratoriums much like Achievements, female Foreclosures behaved much like female Achievements and female Moratoriums were more similar to Diffusions (see Table 1, part B.)

The identity status mode of investigation thus proved to be a reliable means of differentiating diverging paths through the late adolescent period of growth. The work to date, however, in its focus on attitudinal and behavioral measures, has produced what is becoming a rather uninterpretable mass of findings. The thrust of this previous investigative effort was one of defining the concomitants of identity positions, and often strayed from theoretical underpinnings which might guide interpretations of results. In short, research to date on these identity statuses has asked the useful question "Given that we know an individual's identity status, what else does that tell us about him/her?"

The Present Research

The present study is oriented to the question "What developmental and psychodynamic factors determine which path the individual will take through the identity stage?" The approach employs clinical interviewing and analysis in order to develop psychodynamic portraits of each of the statuses and, in a broader sense, to follow Erikson's instruction to study identity development among ordinary individuals.

Women were chosen to be the subjects of this research partly in response to the general dearth of data on women and partly in hopes that this study would also contribute to the understanding of the nature of female identity.

Sample

Subjects were 48 college senior women, all in their early 20s, drawn at random from three universities in Boston. More detailed information on the sample follows in the "Overview" section.

Procedure

Each subject was given the identity status interview, modified for women (see Marcia 1964; Schenkel 1972). Briefly, this interview was oriented to assess the presence or absence of crisis and commitment in regard to occupational, religious, political, and sexual standards choices. Using a two-raters-out-of-three criterion of rater agreement, reliability of *overall* identity status (a weighted combination of ratings in each of the four categories) was 100%. Interviewing continued until there were 12 women in each of the four identity statuses.

Each subject was then interviewed by a clinical psychologist for approximately 1–1½ hr. This interview followed a semistructured format, focusing on biographical information, salient developmental influences, prominent areas of conflict and their management, history of significant object relationships, descriptions of and attitudes toward family members, early memories, dreams, and recurrent fantasies.

These tape-recorded interviews were transcribed and qualitatively rated by two clinical psychologists. Because identity is a unique juxtaposition of elements for each individual, the analysis of these data was *first* intraindividual; i.e., "What are the unique and dominant forces and concerns for this woman?" Once these individual profiles were compiled, generalizations were made in an hypothesis-generating manner, focusing on the question "What common developmental forces and concerns are characteristic of the women in this group and different from those of women in other statuses?"

The Sample as a Whole—An Overview

While the women in this study are extraordinarily diverse, it will facilitate the understanding of the identity status groups to describe the most general psychosocial aspects of their lives. They are all about to graduate from college; most are looking for jobs. They have high hopes, are idealistic in their goals, yet are fearful of not being able to accomplish enough. Occupationally, they have chosen rather low-aspiration careers, with few of them planning to go to graduate school. Often there is a tentativeness about their commitments in regard to the question of job or more schooling. Many plan to work for a while, with the recognition that graduate school is always possible if they are dissatisfied with their jobs. For some, graduation means the first step toward financial autonomy. After years of working part-time and scrimping to get through school, a first full-time job means their own apartment, or a car, or clothes, or travel.

The distribution of the sample with regard to college attendance of parents and occupational status of mothers is presented in Table 2. Because there were no significant differences between the statuses on these variables, data are given for the sample as a whole. The majority of the women in the sample are the first generation of women in their families to attend college. For most, this is a source of pride to them and to their families, representing the attainment of parents' hopes for them and the possibilities of upward social mobility.

Table 2 Educational and occupational background of parents

	Fathers (%)	Mothers (%)
A. Educational background of parents		
College	52	17
Noncollege	48	83
B. Occupational status of mothers		
Recent return to work		25
Long-term part-time work		28
Career involvement		6
Never worked		41

While parents often pressured their daughters toward college, they seldom steered them in a particular occupational direction. Most of the women report that their parents are happy with their occupational plans but are, at this point, more interested in having them marry than succeed professionally. Their parents seem to have viewed their daughters' college education as a means of self-improvement or husband-catching and seem somewhat unnerved when their daughters, as a result of their education, begin to take occupational commitments seriously.

Many of the women are involved in long-standing relationships with men, and several are engaged. Surprisingly, the majority of the sample feel no press to get married, a startling change in social mores from just a few years ago (see Bardwick 1971, p. 153), when women felt it to be a kind of duty to marry after college graduation. None of these women seems to consider it a failure not to have immediate marriage prospects. Most wish to be on their own for a while, and some plan to live with their boyfriends; few seem to feel that marriage promises them additional benefits at this point in their lives. Often their reluctance to marry immediately upon graduation is a source of friction with their parents. With the exception of two women, all wish to marry "eventually." They explain that their main reason for wishing to marry is related to their needs for long-term companionship; they seem to have few romantic ideas in regard to marriage.

When asked about their plans for having children, the almost unanimous response is "That's so far off." All but three wish to have children "eventually," and two of the excepted three are ambivalent. The majority of these women see their life plans as a sequence of a few years of nonmarriage and career involvement, several years of childless marriage in which both partners work, several years of child-rearing, followed by a return to some sort of involvement in a career, a part-time job, or volunteer efforts. There is no woman on the sample who plans a full-time career of homemaking and mothering. Only three of the 48 women are connected to organized Women's Liberation groups. Yet the question of motherhood *vs.* career seems, for the majority of them, to have been stably resolved in the direction of combining them. Whatever and however attitudes toward sexual roles transmit themselves through the culture, these women, diverse as they and their backgrounds are, seem to have made a unanimous and unconflicted choice to experience occupational achievement, homemaking, and motherhood—eventually.

The content of religious concerns varies within religions, for those women who have experienced religious conflict. Catholics are engaged with questions of the authority of the Church and the meaning of their parochial schooling. The Jews in the sample were, for the most part, raised in the tradition of "cultural Judaism," and for them religion is confounded with issues of family closeness. Protestants are the most heterogeneous, sometimes resembling the Catholics, other times more akin to the Jews in their religious concerns. The most profound question across religious affiliation is that of the existence of God. While the interviewers did not ask about this directly, almost all of the women brought it up, and it seems that once this issue is settled, the remainder of religious decisions fall into place.

For almost 80% of the sample, politics is simply an irrelevant area. Interestingly enough, many were guilty to admit that they just do not have time or cannot be bothered. It was as if they felt that the interviewer expected them to have strong political convictions and, given their membership in a much-publicized generation, that they *should* have them. But, for the most part, neither they nor their parents had strong party loyalties or strong beliefs in regard to issues. To our amazement, several women had trouble thinking of any contemporary political question on which they had any views at all.

Boston did not have a highly politicized student population except during the Cambodian crisis in the spring of 1970. If these women mentioned any political activism at all, they related their experiences during the city-wide student antiwar strike which occurred in 1970. Their involvement with this, however, was often part of the tidal wave that swept through their universities ("It was the thing to do") rather than a part of deeply felt conviction. Not to mention the fact that the success of the student strike made it impossible to give finals that term. Those who had been significantly involved with political activism often expressed despair over its ineffectiveness. Feeling that politics held little promise of influence on their lives or the lives of others, most of these more idealistic women have turned to their occupational goals to implement their ideas of social change.

In terms of sexual standards, there is again a majority view among very diverse women. For most, sex is a natural concomitant of love, to be enjoyed as an expression of deep feeling. Sex is to be treated with respect and engaged in with careful discrimination and proven emotions in regard to partners. (At least, this is the view they believe in theoretically.) Almost one-quarter of the sample were virgins; less than one-eighth had experimented with or were involved in free, nondiscriminating sexuality. Perhaps the most interesting generalization to be made here regards these women's views of how their parents would react to knowledge of their sexual behavior. Descriptions of this imaginary disclosure range from the fantasy of parents, particularly mothers, having a heart attack on the spot, to parents, particularly fathers, committing hara-kiri. In this day of the overreported sexual revolution, it seems slightly unrealistic to expect one's parents to cling quite so tightly to Victorian standards. Yet this seems to serve an important maturational function for these women, an element which will be discussed later.

By and large, the investments of these women focused on what was most immediate in their lives—papers, exams, boyfriends, girlfriends, money. Their identities, if one may think of a composite identity, are unimaginative and conventional. The plethora of choice that seems to surround them is really not so multifaceted—instead, it is a series of variations on a theme. Few of them are deeply committed to ideology or political values, the center of Erikson's concept of identity. The ideologies they do have are primarily interpersonal; the system of ideas by which they organize their lives emphasizes being a good person—values of honesty, openness, caring for others. They are loath to presume to see their lives as part of history, feeling in general that they as individuals are too insignificant to affect the lives of any but a few chosen others. They also appear more willing to choose among extant social alternatives than to create new ones, even where they feel dissatisfied with what exists. There is also a kind of flexibility in their sense of themselves and their futures. Identity for them seems to be a preparedness for the vagaries of social circumstance and a readiness to deal with whatever might come. Most cannot imagine their future in 5 years, even with respect to a geographical locale; asked about the future in 10 years, most mention that they expect to have one or two children, but the rest is cloudy.

These were women who were delightful to interview. Most of them came to the testing session with a mixture of apprehension and curiosity, but they relaxed and warmed up quickly when they realized that all was just what they had been told it would be. They talked openly about their thoughts and feelings, and several commented perceptively on the particularly intense kind of discussion that is sometimes possible only with an interested and uncritical stranger. The "research relationship" (Offer 1969) thus established seemed to succeed in providing an atmosphere for revealing and discovering. Those few women who remained highly controlled and bent on presenting themselves as other than they were seemed to be acting out of characterological needs rather than responding to the artificiality of the situation. This technique of data collection, then, seems to be a viable, though cumbersome, means of understanding psychological development among those who do not become subjects by virtue of being patients.

The Foreclosures

"I am loved and cared for; therefore, I am."

Case Material

FERN

Fern is a senior at a large private university, majoring in nursing. She has never doubted any of her strong religious beliefs and feels that premarital intercourse is wrong, but that if she ever felt it necessary to sleep with someone before marriage, she would ask her mother to get her birth control pills.

From her earliest years, she has felt great sympathy toward those less fortunate than herself, and she would repeatedly resolve to do everything she could to help them. One of her earliest memories concerns a crippled child who lived next door who had no playmates in the neighborhood. Fern preferred to spend her time with this child rather than join in the games of the other children. While her parents never encouraged her in any one particular occupational direction, the helping pattern was firmly entrenched in her family.

Born and still living in an Irish Catholic section of Boston, Fern continually emphasized the closeness of her family. Throughout her childhood, her father was plagued by an untreatable illness, and he finally died when she was 11 years old. Much of the family closeness centered around him and caring for him. Her mother was the dominant member of the family—she was Catholic and raised her two children in this religion, enlisting their support in her efforts to influence her husband to accept Catholicism. Nightly, mother and daughters would pray for the conversion of Fern's father and for his recovery from his illness. For Fern, these two things were clearly confused.

Fern described her father as friendly and outgoing, as the one to take problems to. Her mother was more introverted and had no friends outside the family, but she was practical and loving and saw that the family remained close even after the death of Fern's father. Fern saw her parents and their relationship in an idealized way. She spoke of how they never fought once, how they were always fair and just with their children, convening family councils to settle problems of chores and money. Of them, she said, "I don't think I could pick parents who have given more to their children than my parents gave to me." Of herself, Fern gave the impression of having been a model child, eager to please her parents and convinced of their ultimate wisdom. At times she felt that her sister was allowed to balk at chores without adequate punishment and, unlike herself, did not have to work so hard for everything she got.

To almost all questions, Fern responded with reference to her family.

Her life outside her family was fraught with difficulty. In her first friendship with a neighborhood playmate, she encountered rejection because of religious difference. She remembers returning home to her mother crying and of "becoming aware of what kinds of things exist." Her mother was very protective of her and "never pushed me to cope with the neighborhood." As a result, Fern retreated to the safety and security of the warm, close-knit family. Through high school she had few friends, and of her experiences in college she says, "I have lots of acquaintances but few friends." Her strict moral code makes it difficult for her to join in pleasurable activities with others. She cannot understand why, for example, her acquaintances drink or smoke pot; she "can get high on life." Similarly, she was very angry when a friend of hers cut classes, because she felt that this was unfair when she was working so hard.

A predominant theme throughout the interview is her need for an idealized male figure. In high school, the most important person to her was a drama teacher who rescued her from her isolation and got her involved in producing plays. "If it weren't for him, I'd probably be a very dull person," she says, and goes on to describe him in a highly romanticized way. The substitution of this man for her father is fairly conscious in that she plans to ask him to give her away when she marries. Her relationships with men of her own age are more conflicted. She has dated little, and the one serious relationship she had ended when the man was unable to tolerate her moral perfectionism. She does, however, retain an intense fantasy involvement with a patron saint, again an easily distinguishable displaced father. She worries about spinsterhood, sometimes seriously reconsidering her childhood wish to become a nun. She feels that she could not compromise on her standards for a man and could not love a man who did not respect her scruples.

The central dynamic pattern of Fern's life seems to have been her idealization of her fallen-saint father, a person of whom she strove to be worthy. Her continued and unquestioning investment in the religion of her childhood cements her closeness to him. But she lost him before she could ever win him or, through maturation, give him up. One of her dreams evinces this unconscious theme:

> I dreamt I met B [the boyfriend] again and I was very cool to him. I told him I was going to walk and he came along. We walked to the beach and we began to talk about what had happened and he was just about to tell me what he felt and then I woke up. So I'll never know what he would have said.

At the same time, the moral rectitude that was the strength of her family preserves the source of childhood narcissistic gratification, the approval of her parents.

Fern's romanticism of the past allows her no room to express any anger or resentment against her parents. They are security and protection; the outside world means danger and threat and cannot be trusted. This projected fear is evident in her early memories:

> The first day of school—kindergarten—a girl going down the slide and her leg got caught on a piece of metal.

> The first day of school—a rainy day—my neighbor was standing at the bus stop.

I was running down the street for the bus and he wouldn't tell the bus driver to stop and it drove away.

On listening to Fern, one has the strong suspicion that her father's illness represented some early trauma for her. While her voice is confident and her manner relaxed, though eager to convince the interviewer of her goodness, the unconscious threads belie a massive fear of helplessness and intense needs for defense against it. A recurrent dream:

People are running back and forth in chaos, yelling and screaming. I am standing in the middle and I don't know what's going on. I'm watching all these people running around and I don't know why I'm standing there instead of running with everyone else. And I don't know where anyone's going or why they're so frightened. And I want to get out.

And another:

They were putting up a telephone pole and I was standing there and I don't know why and a telephone pole hit me on the head. . . . They took me to the hospital and I was dead. . . .

In Fern's unconscious fantasies, events happen, threatening her, totally outside of her control. Her favored means of dealing with this is to retreat to what, in her earliest development, provided security. For her, the regression and rethinking necessary for progressive identity formation would present the dangers inherent in renouncing the safety of her parents, now firmly implanted symbolically in her own superego.

Discussion

This case illustrates several themes which characterize development among the Foreclosures. Without exception, Foreclosure women emphasize the closeness of their families and their need for the security they had in them. Examination of the meaning of this security for these women suggests a need to rekindle an early union where primary narcissism prevailed. This thread is most apparent in their concern with omnipotence or, at least, with allying themselves with an object who can do everything and protect them from anything. The early lives of these women are marked by a relationship, usually with the father, in which all is given to them in magical ways through the power of this person. Their task, then, is only to continue to please the objects in order to maintain supplies.

Individuation is scarcely suggested by these data, and these subjects often have difficulty even conceptualizing their parents as distinct from themselves. There is almost no distance between their idealization of one or both parents and their own ego ideal. From the earliest time, being a very good girl for very good parents has been a source of self-esteem; at the close of the oedipal period, this ideal itself seems to have become sexualized such that living up to an ideal of goodness is symbolic of attaining the desired object. At the same time, achievement of such goodness allows participation in the fantasies omnipotence of the internalized object.

There is, of course, nothing unusual about this developmental pattern; all children preserve omnipotence through the internalization of the omnipotent parents. Yet, at adolescence, this ego ideal is generally severely shaken by the realization that parents are, after all, fallible. The crucial question, then, is why this adolescent process seems not to occur among these women.

One important aspect of adolescent development stressed by all writers irrespective of school of thought is that of peer support. The need for ego support from peers derives from the loosening of ego ties to the parents of childhood. Peer support provides the bulwark from which to rework the superego and ego ideal, to form new identifications, and to shake loose from dependency on the parents. Among the Foreclosures, attempts at meaningful relationships with peers continually fail. In general, the Foreclosures seem to be unable to establish enough trust outside the family for friendships to form.

The dynamics of trust are not well understood. Erikson sees trust as ensuing from the mutuality of the earliest mother-child bond and considers it to be necessary for the foundation of any other relationship. In Freudian terms, disturbances of this early oral stage engender the most profound malfunction in later life. There is nothing to suggest that these women are psychotic or that they lack basic trust; to the contrary, their memories tend to romanticize the early mutual, all-giving, all-having state. Yet they continually show marked fears of the nonfamilial world. The trust they established in early relationships does not generalize; rather, it becomes split such that the family is all good and the nonfamily is dangerous.

One reason for this is the inability of Foreclosure women to tolerate ambivalence. For them, things tend to be all good or all bad. They cannot, for the most part, experience anger, disappointment, envy, or even mild criticalness toward their parents, probably because to do so would be to devalue the major source of narcissistic supplies. As a result, negative affect toward primary objects is repressed and projected outward; their families love them while the rest of the world represents all that is rejecting and disapproving.

The theme of betrayal runs through the early memories of the Foreclosures, and while it usually occurs at the hands of the parents, it is not specifically attributed to them. For example, one woman remembers moving to a new house without having been told it was going to happen, then quickly says she did not really miss the old one. Another remembers a favorite puppy she had at the age of 3 and "the night they took it away from me." The passivity and helplessness inherent in these early memories seem to have been defended against by massive identifications with the powerful forces and the anger repressed and externalized.

Foreclosure women also seem to have had particularly possessive mothers. This is apparent in the case of Fern, whose mother allowed her to retreat after her first encounter with the hostility in the world. Another Foreclosure woman describes how her mother always warned her not to trust girls, and she was therefore prepared when the girls at school made her the object of scorn and gossip. The mother of yet another similarly feared that schoolmates would corrupt her daughter, and she therefore provided her daughter with the support to resist doing whatever the high school crowd did. These women, therefore, seem to have had mothers who demanded an exclusivity in their intimacy, mothers who themselves were isolated and fearful and passed on to their daughters their own fears of rejection. The ensuing pact, I love you and you love me and the rest of the world be damned, provides a highly gratifying source of narcissistic supplies for the developing girl and obviates the need to develop other relationships.

Fathers of these women seem to have struck a similar bargain, although this had its most profound effect on their daughters' superego. With only one exception, each of these women had an intensely affectionate relationship with her father, whom she both identified with and tried to please. If there was frustration in the father-daughter romance, it is securely repressed. Rather, these women have the sense of having been loved by the perfect man whom they would rather die for than displease. Again the narcissistic gratification makes it unnecessary to search beyond the family for satisfaction of needs.

It is also characteristic, as is suggested in the case of Fern, for Foreclosure women to have been the good child in a family with an identifiable bad child. Examples:

1. Felicia had a sister who, early in her life, became psychotic but could not be institutionalized. Although this sibling terrorized her, it drove her closer to her mother in their mutual effort to control her sister. Felicia grew up quite fearful of becoming like her sister and had a profound sense of her responsibility to be good to compensate her mother for having such a bad child.
2. Frances' sister became pregnant when Frances was 15, and this was the source of family humiliation and an ugly public law suit. At the time, Frances had been tentatively exploring her own developing sexual interests and independence, but guiltily returned to comfort and soothe her parents, vowing that she, at least, would never hurt them.

Thus whatever cements the bond between daughter and parent, be it love, guilt, or fear, tends to mediate against the loosenings of childhood psychic organization necessary for the identity process to unfold.

There is, in addition, a self-seeking, hungry attitude in these women. In content, their concerns focus on what they have or are seeking to be given. Where they are involved in beginning to care for others, their givingness has a hollow ring or, as in the case of Fern, a highly defensive quality. They are clearly central in their own universe, collecting supplies and jealous of them, eager to gain more. Some appear to have been overgratified as children, whose early years were so satisfying that life becomes a quest for what is lost; others are striving to create a fantasied fulfilled state, to replace what was not rather than give up the dream. In either case, this seems to account for their self-assured, goal-oriented qualities—they know what they want.

The inability to experience ambivalence, the absence of internal conflict, and the relative lack of individuation from their parents are all factors in their general uninsightful approach to themselves. They take themselves for granted; they are what they are because that is the way it is, and they have little capacity to reflect on it very much. There is something of an emptiness to their conscious mental life. This in part stems from the absence of conscious conflict, such that everything is described in apple-pie terms. If you ask a Foreclosure woman whether she experiences conflict over this or that issue, she will most likely tell you about the last person who tried to make her change her ways. Life, then, is a struggle between the self and the world; the parts of the self are always kept in harmony.

On an unconscious level, however, things are not so rosy and placid. Five of the Foreclosure women report recent rape or near-rape experiences, only one of which sounds completely real and not laden with elements of fantasy. Another two have dreams in which they are being attacked by men. One woman, after detailing a rather serene and nontraumatic life history, reported the following dream:

> I dreamt I was at the office. There was a cigar store Indian who suddenly grabbed an axe and began hacking up this woman. I stood there fascinated by the whole thing.

This dream, although a bit more primitive than the others, typifies the unconscious preoccupation with aggression characteristic of the Foreclosures. This aggression is usually at the hands of men. The theme of punishment recurs among their fantasies and dreams, and appears generally in the context of a triangular relationship:

> A bear was chasing me and I screamed for my mother [recurrent dream].

> I used to be afraid of my father's cousin. Whenever he'd come, I'd hide, but he'd find me and I would scream for my mother [early memory].

> I dreamt a friend snuck out with someone besides her fiancé. The dream punished her [recent dream].

The aggression in these dreams seems to derive chiefly from a highly primitive superego and is consistent with the general retributive nature of archaic guilt among these women. They dare not transgress or question, not only because of the loss of narcissistic supplies, but also because of the potency of force with which their superego promises to retaliate. With such a double-edged sword to fight against and with the lack of supportive relationships, these women at adolescence stand powerless and can only surrender to the overwhelming superego. It is also no wonder that they so intensely feel the need for security and protection.

It must be emphasized, however, that these women do not experience themselves as dependent. The unconscious identification with parental superegos is so deep and so massive that ego boundaries between themselves and their parents are fused. The object of dependency is thereby internalized, leading to a sense of independence, and, with so much internal support (which still must be maintained by external support from the parents), Foreclosure women have great strength to resist group pressure and can forge their own paths as long as they are in harmony with superego strictures.

Another major thrust for growth at adolescence is the libidinal upsurge which demands a restructuring of the superego. Given the psychodynamic organization of these women, this does not occur. For them, the superego itself is eroticized: pleasure consists of being good, and they are, as a group, uninterested in sexuality except as a means of recreating a secure, protected, and loved state. Through early identifications with their mothers, they have all made the commitment to become wives and mothers. This does not seem to have involved much psychic rearrangement. Their choice of heterosexual partner is most commonly a simple substitution for one or the other parent, and their investment in their boyfriends is, most often, for protection and security. As one woman described her boyfriend of 3 years, "He's just something to cling to." Their boyfriends are parental substitutes and poor ones at that. Sexuality is tolerated and primarily ungratifying. The case of Joyce Kingsley, reported by Robert White (1966), is yet another example of the Foreclosure pattern of relationships.

Psychologically, then, these women remain children. While they appear to be confident and self-assured, they derive their self-esteem from the same source as does a latency-age child, from the uncompromising adherence to a parentally derived superego which they please symbolically as they once pleased the parents. They have settled for parental modes of thought and behavior partly because they were unable to form relationships outside the home deep enough for identifications to form.

Most of the theoretical writing on adolescence cautions against the precocious crystallization of identity, suggesting that identities formed without a period of loosening and conflict are brittle, fragile, and less able to withstand the jockeyings of life (Freud 1958; Beres 1961; Blos 1962; Grinker 1962; Spiegel 1961). It is, therefore, surprising that Foreclosure women resemble Achievement women on cognitive and behavioral measures and that they demonstrate the same independence of judgment, resistance to conformity pressure, and high self-esteem. Marcia and Friedman (1970) theorize that the moratorium period is more fraught with difficulty for women in that they are given less social support for testing new modes of being and that perhaps they are actually rewarded for remaining Foreclosures.

The relative scarcity of Foreclosures in this particular sample would not support the view that foreclosed positions are differentially rewarded by the larger society, although it is conceivable that in less urban and cosmopolitan settings this could be true. Society has always provided a certain amount of social support for women to remain childlike and dependent, which would at least allow the Foreclosures to live without feeling that they are at odds with social expectations of them (as a male Foreclosure might feel). As to the adaptiveness of this form of identity resolution, these data suggest that these women are paying a fairly high price for their stability in terms of ego constriction and somewhat limited interpersonal relationships. But, as Erikson repeatedly asserts, success of an identity depends on the ability of the individual to make the society adapt to him as well as to adapt himself to society. The purposefulness, intelligence, and general stubborn perseverance of the Foreclosures seem to give them even odds at success in arranging a comfortable niche for themselves.

The Achievements

"I have an effect on the world and on others; therefore, I am."

Case Material

ALICE

Alice is a slim, attractive woman from a small town in Massachusetts. She plans to go into social work and chose a large private university on that basis. Her parents never had plans for her, but she had given a great deal of thought to the question of what to be since the time she was a child. Religiously, her primary struggle was with her belief in God, and, despite her feeling that it was nice to "have someone to go to for help," she now considers herself an agnostic and continues to study many religions in order to "see if I can put together things I can accept." While she has strong political opinions, schoolwork has kept her too busy to be able to participate in political action.

In regard to sex, Alice went through several distinct phases of change. At the end of high school, she had a very strict set of standards in regard to virginity which, during the following summer, she totally abandoned. For a time she indulged in indiscriminate sexuality, which she later found to be incompatible with her standards for self-respect. This led to her present belief that, for her, sex is only permissible in the context of a loving relationship.

Alice describes herself as always having been more of a leader than a follower. She always had high standards for herself, and, as a child, she thought it particularly important to get high grades, to be in plays, and to play baseball well. Her sole sibling, an older brother, was himself very successful, and Alice always felt it crucial to do at least as well as he. The satisfaction she got from her achievements seemed, in this retrospection, to have been paramount in her life from the time she started school.

In the town where she grew up, few girls went to college. Like many of her classmates, she was engaged during her senior year of high school. However, the importance of academic achievement in her life caused her to have some serious misgivings about immediate marriage, and she decided to postpone it and apply to college. Her fiancé remained in the town and took a job. Within a year, Alice felt that she had changed so much that they had little basis for continuing their relationship. It was the trauma caused by giving up a person that had been important to her for so long that led Alice to "go wild" and throw off, experimentally, all the vestiges of the person she had been. This led her into drugs as well as promiscuity until she discovered the core of those things which really mattered to her.

Alice described her parents as having been loving but distant; they seem to have been rather American Gothic in flavor—hard-working people who were proud of her accomplishments but never got overinvolved or interfered with her life. Her mother she saw as passive and withdrawn, and Alice always wished for greater closeness to her. It was her father who was the disciplinarian in the family, and Alice feels that he was always reasonable but set definite limits. Although she never felt particularly close to him either, she did feel that it was from him that she had to win her independence. This battle was fought over the issue of her going to Europe for a summer, and she went despite his wishes. She feels that neither of her parents ever did anything outstanding, and while she yearns to be closer to them, she fears that she has grown too far away.

Because Alice's parents seemed to have expected her to be independent from a relatively early age, Alice seems always to have hungered for greater nurturance. Her intense needs "to be perfect" and to be accomplished were partly in the service of her attempt to win greater interest and love from them. Failing to do this, her successes were transformed into a gratification in their own right. Alice was able to defend against her dependent longings by becoming a leader and being a success. She was also able to salve the feelings of deprivation by making friends. With little activity at home, Alice turned to her peers for closeness and interest. The one dream she reports echoes the theme that people can make up for disappointments:

It was my girlfriend's birthday party and somehow her cake got smashed. Then her boyfriend came and she was happy again.

At the age of 12 she began the relationship with the boy to whom she was later engaged. He promised to fulfill her needs for parenting in that he "made a groove for me to fit into" and was very demanding. While she had other friends during this period, her boyfriend was primary in her life, and he set for her definite standards against which she could continually test herself. This relationship continued through her high school years. Her breaking away from him after her first year of college was at the same time a break with the symbolic tie to her parents, an abandonment of the need for the neat, ordered, and intense parental expectations and authority.

At the end of this period of her life, Alice again turned to her own abilities and to other friends for self-esteem. This time, however, she was more realistic in both areas. In terms of her work, she was able to temper her ideal of being perfect and "to help everyone for free" and to admit to herself that there were times when she was acting out of "just plain selfishness." She also became less idealistic in regard to relationships and no longer demanded that one person be everything to her. She has several close friends and has had a variety of boyfriends whom she feels she can turn to for support.

Her goals now are "to be on my own for awhile, to do things and see things before I settle down." Her work remains important to her. While she has become more realistic in regard to her parents, she still experiences the old wishes for closeness, this time in the form of hoping to take good care of them in their old age. In many ways, she appears to be attempting to mourn the ultimate loss of what she never had, and the resultant depression is not far below the surface. She feels keenly aware of the fact that her parents' image of her does not match what she is, and while she longs to tell them about some of her less conventional experiences, she feels that they could not understand. While she says that they never had definite expectations for her, she seems to have identified with them just enough so that being so different from them is, at least unconsciously, a betrayal of them. She saw her parents as quiet people who, while not outstanding, at least did no wrong, and it was a joy of her childhood to feel their pride in her. Her maturation has resided in compromising with this old internalized superego and the old identifications which were bound to what there was of her parents' love.

What is more striking about Alice is the effectiveness of her defenses. At times she appeared quite anxious and rather depressed, but she seems to have been able to utilize her capabilities and her relationships in the service of guarding against these negative feelings. She also feels a great deal of control over her own life and responsibility for the decisions she makes. This seems to have developed early. Her earliest memory:

When I was 3, my nose was split open. My brother was swinging a stick and he told me to get out of the way and I said no. And it hit me and I had to have stitches. I remember running in the house and being scared to death.

While this memory contains a portent of her later conflicts over independence, its most interesting aspect is the recall of her own part in getting hit by the stick. This is the active, striving, managing side of Alice, a quality which she has been able to utilize when conflict or circumstance has been ready to overwhelm her. Despite her insightfulness and sensitivity, Alice does not keep a tight lid on her feelings and, in a most characteristic way, gets "angry and acts, to avoid crying."

ANDREA

Andrea plans to go to medical school. Her father had encouraged her interest in science, a field she particularly enjoyed because it was "hard and a challenge." She maintains some contact with the Protestantism she was raised with but is allied with a newer, less conventional practice of it. Politically, she has been involved in some local campaigns, has strong political opinions. She feels that sex is permissible in the context of a strong commitment to a person, and while she knows her parents would vociferously disagree, she feels that "that's the way they are and I'm different."

A goal-oriented woman, Andrea decided on her course in life through a fairly gradual process of consolidating independence. She portrayed her family as having been very close and overprotective, but very important to her in terms of the many experiences they shared together. Her father was the source of her intellectual interests, and she fondly remembered the hours they would spend discussing what she was learning in school. She struggled more with her mother, primarily over hours and friends and other issues of freedom.

Until she went to college, Andrea felt she was a lot like her parents—she had their morality and their religion and their values of hard work and success. She had few friends during her school years, since her peers considered her to be "the studious one." She grew up without serious challenge to her parents' values or standards for her. It was a surprise for her when, in college, she met many people with different views and eventually came to realize that hers was "not necessarily the only right way to be."

An extremely intelligent woman, Andrea was interested in the varieties of her new friends' experiences, who, she found, were not rejecting of her because of her eagerness for knowledge. At this point, she seemed almost to be searching for a vehicle by which to achieve greater independence from her parents. It came in the form of a man with whom she developed her second serious relationship. "He made me more sure of myself, more self-confident and willing to try new things. It was important just having someone there who thought a lot of me. He helped me to grow up." Her relationship with him made it possible for her to define herself as different from her parents; the potential loss of their love was replaced by his.

Throughout her life, especially the most recent years, Andrea showed a pattern of complex and varied identifications with many people. Teachers, in particular, were very influential, as well as several close friends. She has always emulated strong, decisive people. While she once viewed her father as strong and active, she came to feel he was rather under her mother's control, and she feels that an important part of her commitment to her fiancé is that he is different from her father in this respect. Andrea showed a range of human beings. All this lays a groundwork of basic ego strength which, at the appropriate time and under the right set of circumstances, allows her to renounce earlier forms of narcissistic gratification and to struggle for maturity. This happens, for Andrea and for the other Achievements like her, with gradualness rather than identifiable and intense crisis. The testing of identity possibilities is largely silent and internal; how much internal conflict is experienced during this process we cannot judge on the basis of these data. Andrea's developmental pattern at the identity stage most closely approximates the norm for growth at late adolescence discussed in the psychoanalytic literature (e.g., Blos 1962).

Alice exemplifies the other primary road to identity achievement, the one closer to that outlined by Erikson, who stresses the experience of the moratorium phase. Unlike Andrea, Alice presents a clearly conflicted and visible period of uncertainty, a time of testing and trial followed by a period of decision. Women such as Alice tend to have a history of a sense of deprivation, of parents who basically loved them but whom, try as they would, they could never please enough. They sometimes experienced extreme anxiety or psychosomatic symptoms during their middle adolescence or experimented with extreme actions that they knew their parents would vigorously oppose. Yet they also seemed to have consolidated enough ego strength to be able to turn to their own abilities and to be able to begin the process of mourning for what they felt they missed. This is clear in the case of Alice. Lacking the sense of real closeness to her parents, she, fairly early in her development, attempted to substitute another person for all those experiences she wished for. But her own self-esteem drawn from her own abilities finally made that solution untenable, and she was able to give up a relatively secure and comfortable relationship and cope with the ensuing depression. Another woman with a somewhat similar history was able to recognize, with the aid of psychotherapy, that her need to be perfect was making her life impossible and was able to give up what was, early in her development, her means to finally winning her parents' total love.

Despite the variance among the Achievements, the predominant theme in each interview is the struggle for independence. Achievements, more often than any other group, are apt to speak of experiences in which they discovered that they could be on their own and survive. Or they describe times when they made decisions contrary to their parents' will and found that, although they felt guilty, they were also solidly committed to "having my own life." A striking feature of these women is their extraordinary skill in manipulating the environment to support their nascent independence. Teachers, trips to Europe, and roommates are all employed in the service of providing new modes of being and legitimizing the attempt to "do my own thing." Their lives are devoted to seeking identity-confirming experiences. Coehlo et al. (1963) point to the use of the interpersonal environment to broaden the basis of self-esteem as a hallmark trait of freshman college students making a successful adjustment. The particular way in which Achievements make use of the support of their peers confirms the importance of this mechanism in the process of identity formation.

Most of all, Achievements form relationships with men who will help them become less dependent on their parents. Unlike the Foreclosures, who feeling in regard to each of her parents, admiring some of their characteristics, resenting others. At the same time that she feels love for them, she gets angry at them for overprotecting her. Her parents, then, were not wholly gratifying—at least by the time she reached adolescence. Then, her mother seemed restrictive and her father too passive to intervene. Through her relationship with her fiancé, she was able to give up her dependency on her parents without simply substituting him for them and without having to untie completely her emotional bonds to them. With his support, she could move forward. This is the theme of a recurrent childhood daydream she reports:

> I used to daydream about a castle out in the woods with dungeons; it was spooky, but exciting, with things there trying to attack me. But I was looking for the treasure. I was with a friend, and as long *as someone is with me I don't get scared.*

Discussion

These two cases illustrate the variation to be found among the Achievements. Unlike the Foreclosures, who are characterized by their failure to confront a developmental struggle, the Achievements are, by definition, people who have experienced both crisis and commitment. It is not surprising, then, that the Achievements are more heterogeneous than the Foreclosures; they take varied routes to psychosocial crisis and negotiate diverse obstacles on the way to commitment.

Although the distinction is somewhat arbitrary, one might conclude on the basis of these clinical data that there are two major "paths" to identity achievement and that these are distinguishable by the relative intensity of the crisis and the relative precrisis investment in primary objects.

Andrea is typical of one of these paths. Her middle adolescent development followed in a somewhat characteristic Foreclosure pattern, and although her postcrisis identity is formulated on her own terms, it is less distant from her parents' identities than, for example, is Alice's. Andrea has integrated her basic trust in and love for her parents with her own needs for self-differentiation and novel experiences, and her psychological development shows clear differences from the Foreclosures'. For one thing, she demonstrates an ability to turn to her own intellectual capacities and talents for self-esteem rather than relying exclusively on love and approval from her parents. While these resources were partly inherent and partly developed originally to gain parental esteem, they became at some point relatively autonomous, and later became central to her sense of purpose and identity. When she met with frustration at the hands of her classmates, she did not retreat. Instead, she was able to wait it out, confident of at least some of her own worth, without experiencing the entire external world as hostile.

A second major difference from the Foreclosures that Andrea demonstrates is her realistic appraisal of her parents and her ability to experience ambivalence toward them. This seems to produce a concomitant ability to form what Erikson calls "part identification" such that she wishes to be like each parent in some ways, wishes to be not like them in others. She can also express anger toward them and, unlike the Foreclosures, has no need to find some extrafamilial agent to project it onto. Similarly, she is clearly individuated from them and can experience her parents as distinct and separate choose men as substitute objects of dependency, people who will "care for" them as their parents did, Achievements choose men who will "care about" them and replace some of the self-esteem that will inevitably be lost as distance from their parents increases.

Guilt over the separation from their parents is evident in the Achievements. But it is partly counterbalanced by their sense that what they are moving toward is right and meaningful. As one woman put it, "My whole outlook on life has changed. I've learned that other people can be important—that there's more to life than just my family. There's work and school and Bob and living for myself. As much as I love my family and like to be with them, I've also got my own life. And they won't be around forever and I have to learn to take care of myself."

Achievements, though no more intelligent than the other groups, did learn through their experiences to gain self-esteem through their own efforts. Thus their work and their relationships tend to be the bootstraps by which they disengage from old object ties or from old wishes which were not fulfilled.

In the resultant identity, one finds both defensive and autonomous elements. Decisions, especially in regard to issues of religion and sex, tend to combine resolutions of old psychosexual conflict as well as to integrate self-representations and provide a plan for the future. While the advent of autonomy from the parents allows for new possibilities of being or, more precisely, becoming, these possibilities have somewhat distinct limits. Alice, for example, found her brief sexual rebellion too guilt-producing and moved back to more moderate standards. Another woman in the group demonstrates this even more clearly. Prepared to break away from her mother's control, she found herself fascinated by her wild and uninhibited roommate. She spent several months agonizing over her enchantment with this girl, who was the polar opposite of her mother. But she finally found a less drastic means of asserting her individuality by getting involved with a nouveau campus religious sect. Like Alice (and others), she could not override her superego but was able to strike a compromise with it. Identity, then, is crystallized within the bounds of what is most fundamental to the people they were in the past.

A recurrent pattern among the Achievements is a relatively unconflicted relationship to one parent (usually, but not always, the father) and a relatively charged and ambivalent relationship to the other. It is usually the latter parent who was the primary source of superego strictures, while the 'good parent' had more influence on the ego ideal. The superego parent is the one from whom separation is more difficult. This appears most clearly in the case of Andrea. While she retained many of the ideals she gained from her father, her struggle for autonomy caused her to abandon her mother's religion and sexual standards. It is toward her mother, also, that Andrea feels the most guilt.

Sibling rivalries figure prominently in the families of Achievements, and these are most often rivalries with brothers. There are several other Achievement women who, like Alice, spent much of their early lives trying to beat out their brothers' accomplishments. This seems to coincide with the feistiness in these women, their ability to bounce back from frustrations and keep trying. For most of them, maturity has meant giving up the hope of being as good as brother (at his own game, anyway), but the struggle to do so seems to have been yet another bootstrap for them and another source of internal energy.

Achievements do not show great availability of affect or insight; they tend to prefer reality considerations to introspection. Those Achievements who have struggled through clearly defined moratorium periods retain their awareness of feelings and are exceptionally insightful. Those, like Andrea, whose development was more gradual and silent tend to be less expressive emotionally and to resemble the Foreclosures in their propensity to repress, isolate, and intellectualize.

Achievements' dreams do not show the drive-laden quality of the Foreclosures' dreams. In general, they are more reflective of current issues and have less suggestion of early concerns. One dream epitomizes the developmental crisis:

> I dreamt I was driving down a hill with my father. Then I stopped the car and let him out and kept driving down the hill. Sometimes I would think I would just drive around the block and pick him up again, but I didn't.

In their daydreams, Achievements repeatedly report fantasies of great success, imagining themselves as great composers or revered scientists. Then they often go on to speak of the fact that they have drastically scaled down their aspirations and laugh at their own abandoned ideals. Again this reflects the Achievements' tendency to lean on their own capacities and to look for satisfaction and self-esteem in doing. Their ego ideal, now modified, seems to have focused on what they might be rather than whom they might be loved by.

Among their early memories is a common theme of individual action and control:

> I'd lean out my window at night after my parents thought I'd gone to sleep. I was jealous that everyone else was up and I used to look out and see what was going on out in the garden.

> My older brother and I slept in the same room and we'd have a good time and my mother would come in and tell us to shut up but we'd start jumping between the beds.

> Taking walks with my brother early in the morning—we used to go out before my mother and father got up.

> I was less than 2. My sister and I were playing with a red rubber ball in the kitchen and my mother was cooking dinner. The ball rolled under the stove and we were trying to get it. She got very upset because we were going to get burned.

This portrait perhaps suggests more commonality among the Achievements than is in fact the case. Their backgrounds and life circumstances vary. Some show characteristics of the Foreclosures; others at times speak in ways more reminiscent of the Moratoriums. Yet the basic self-reliance and capacity to form progressive relationships, winding as they will through the twists of experience, emerge as the ego capacities which are fundamental to late adolescent autonomy and the integration of identity.

The Moratoriums

"I am Right; therefore, I am."

Case Material

MILLIE

Millie was raised in Philadelphia, came to college at a small private school, and has switched her major four times. She had originally planned to be a nurse like her mother, then found that she did not like it. She switched to physical therapy but found she became overinvolved with "how badly everyone was treated." Next she tried psychology, but this field "got me very into myself," and she became afraid it would "screw me up," so she switched one more time, this time to sociology.

She also has a great many religious conflicts. Raised in the strictest Catholic tradition, she now feels very aware of its "hypocrisy." When she noticed that many people were going to church only to see what other people were wearing, she stopped going to church. "I know my parents would like me to go to church and I'd like to do it for them, but I couldn't because I'd be a hypocrite and I'd be deceiving them into thinking I'm a good Catholic girl again when I'm not." Nevertheless, she feels that "things are ingrained in me and that makes me not sure what I believe. I want to believe in God, although I'm not sure I do. Because just to believe in reality is not so nice because there are a lot of things about reality that are not so nice."

Millie had intense political struggles last year during the student strike, with which she became involved after witnessing a policeman beat up some students. "I was believing what people were saying—that you can give up your grades for people who are over in Viet Nam dying. You can make a sacrifice for them and I felt, 'Yeah, that's what I'm going to do.' But there's no correlation between me not going to class and them dying over there. It's not doing them any good. And I really got screwed. And nothing came of it. The summer came and everyone went home and that was it. And I had three incompletes. I'm apathetic now. I really did get involved and all I could see was I was getting screwed and nothing was coming of it. I don't know what I'd do now. Things aren't the way I'd like them to be in my ideal society."

The question of marriage is also conflicted for her. "I don't like to think of myself as 40 and unmarried. But right now I can't imagine it. I can imagine loving someone or living with someone but as soon as I know there's a legal bond—that this is the way it's going to be, I get scared." In regard to sexual standards, however, she has quite definite feelings—she feels that "anyone who is 21 and a virgin is perverted." At the same time, she is afraid that "there are a lot of guys who can't handle a sexual relationship and will just think that the girl's a slut." She is also not completely sure she has gotten over the idea "that if you have sex before you're married, you'll go straight to hell."

Asked to describe herself, Millie began right off talking about her persistent conflict over being a child or an adult. "I don't think I act my age. I think I act like a kid. Maybe it's that I don't act the way I thought I would act at this age. I used to think that when I was 20—I don't know—that I'd walk around discussing Plato or something." This feeling that things in the present—especially the way she is—are not what she had hoped for or expected is a continual theme throughout her interview. One of her early memories reflects the same feeling of wishing for and fearing the privileges of the next stage:

> The day before I went to kindergarten, which I was really looking forward to—very apprehensive but very excited about being a "big girl." And my mother said I had to get up at 7 a.m. and I began to think twice about it.

Part of this conflict stems from Millie's quest to be right about things. She has little to say about her childhood except that she was always a very good girl. She remembers her early life as a harmonious, secure environment where she was just like her parents, who were like everyone else's parents, and all the other kids were just like her. Success was easy. Her movement into the more complex world of Boston and of college startled her because there was no longer the ready, ubiquitous social agreement that she was always right. In her words, "It starts when you're little. You think your parents are gods. Then you find out they're only human, but you still believe what they say because they're your parents. . . . The more I learn, the more middle of the road I become, and it's hard that way because I like to have the answers. But it seems like that's the way it's going—that you just can't say that this is right and this is wrong."

Millie describes her parents as having been affectionate and generous. She felt that her mother often gave her more than she deserved and feels very guilty about this. Her father, whom she saw as strong and stable, was the authority in the home, and she remembers being frightened of him. He set definite limits for her, and she never felt able to disobey him. Although she did not give extensive material in regard to her early life, the atmosphere seems to have been one of living up to fairly stringent internal and external demands. "I always want to run away, but I never do. My mother once told me that if you shirk responsibility once, you'll just do it all the time, so I never do." She remembers a time when she cheated on a test and later felt very relieved when it did not help her do better.

As a result of these internal and external pressures, Millie seems always to have felt a great need for structure, for something she could bounce against to test if she were right or wrong. In high school, she would become very dependent on the boys she dated, trying to live up to what they wanted her to be. Then she would get very depressed when they would break up with her.

When she first entered college, she felt rather adrift at the loss of structure and got involved with a boy who was to be the focus of her life for the next 3 years. He was, like her father, a strong authoritarian figure who set out to mold her and teach her. However, he was also somewhat sadistic, and, because of many of his attitudes and habits, her parents particularly despised him. Millie, therefore, became caught in a complex struggle between her parents and her boyfriend, unable to give up her dependency on either of them. While she feels that her boyfriend was most helpful in terms of making her less dependent on her parents, she simply shifted her conflicted dependency needs onto him. She idealized him as she had once idealized her parents and tried in every way to be like him. Now that he has left her once again, she wishes only "to be completely in love with someone." Again she yearns for someone who will take the choices away from her and provide the Answers. And again she feels a sense of failure because she was never able to fulfill her boyfriend's expectations of her.

Millie's struggle for individuation thus seems to have failed. Instead of being able to dispense with authority and make decisions, she is caught up with a search for authorities to comply with or rebel against. While she managed to disengage from some of the content of the internalized demands, the tone of her superego remains the same. In trying to grow away from her parents, she unconsciously chose someone who would impose opposite demands with equivalent force to those which her father once used to have her obey. (This is also evident in her totalistic statement regarding sexual morality.) She also feels that she cannot live up to her own expectations—she can never be "as big" a girl as she had hoped. It is, therefore, anxiety reducing to be able to live up to the expectation of others. This might be a successful solution to the identity problem were it not for the intensity of her ambivalence, especially toward men, which does not allow her to maintain a dependent relationship for long.

Having chronically low self-esteem, Millie seems unable to conceive of herself as existing as an individual. Her entire life is centered on how people are reacting to her, whether she is pleasing them or shocking them (which she also enjoys). She appears to need others not so much in the service of security (as the Foreclosures do) but in order to feel in control. Her fantasies are impulse laden, and she seems to fear that, given too much choice, she could not contain herself: she might become a sexual glutton, terribly aggressive, or just irresponsible. She needs relationships, then, to check her, to keep her on leash, and to serve the function her father once did. It seems, then, that Millie's is a problem of a harsh but vulnerable superego, which her ego cannot master in search of an external voice. Were she able to find such a spokesman in a benign person, she might be able to resolve the conflict and achieve an independent identity. Without such an object, she is left to the plethora of choice which surrounds her, where no choice bears the stamp of Right.

Discussion

Of the four groups, Moratoriums show the greatest psychodynamic homogeneity. Most outstandingly, they share an omnipresent sense of guilt. The actual content of the guilt varies but most often centers on their feeling of disappointing their parents, or on the potential for doing so. Almost to a one, they describe their parents, particularly their mothers, as overprotective and go on to recount episodes of extreme guilt induction at their hands. These tales sometimes border on a caricature, marked by a persistent plaint on the mothers' part of "How could you do this to me?" Many of these women speak of the early indulgence they received from their mothers, but they are sensitive to the price their mothers paid for the close mother-daughter bond: "I'm all she has and now she has nothing left." And, unspoken, "It's my fault and I feel I have to make it up to her." They are also sensitive to the price they themselves are paying for having taken so much from their mothers, feeling at times that they did not deserve to have so much, at other times that, having taken, they do not have the right not to repay their mother by doing as she wishes. As one woman expressed it, "When they give me something, I really appreciate it and try to deserve it. I feel I have to be the good girl they wanted me to be." They seem to feel like infidels who have betrayed their mothers' love. A number of these women also had mothers whom they never wanted (consciously) to be like. Where they felt, for example, that their mothers had unpleasant lives, the struggle to disavow their dependency on their mothers is intensified by their feeling that compliance with their mothers might cause them, against their will, to become like them.

If they reject their identifications with their mothers, the Moratoriums cling to their identifications with their fathers, betraying their mothers a second time. Seen as strong and authoritarian though warm and loving, their fathers represent a romanticized ideal of strength and success. Where the mother seems to have been internalized as the prohibiting, retaliating part of the superego, the father forms the core of the ego ideal.

It cannot be determined on the basis of these data whether in fact this group had particularly guilt-inducing parents or whether, because of the developmental crisis, they perceive them that way. Some of their descriptions of their mothers' prohibitions, particularly in regard to sex, raise the question of whether they might be projecting the introjected superego back onto the primary objects in order to be better able to fight it. This process seems to allow some to reduce their anxiety (e.g., "It's not that I wish to remain a little girl, it's that she's trying to make me") while they build independence in less conflicted areas. For example, one woman who had always had high expectations of herself says, "My father still expects me to be a doctor. I know my capabilities and they're not medical school. *He just won't admit I have limitations.*" This is a woman who is making some strides in establishing meaningful, satisfying relationships with men, which she is better able to do when the conflict over achievement is externalized. Others similarly complain that their parents have an "ideal vision" of them and that this (somehow) prevents them from being what they really are.

The wish to regain an early form of omnipotence is also reflected in their choice of new identifications. Unlike the other groups, Moratorium women idealize one or more of their peers. They wish to be like "my roommate who has no problems," or "my friend who does everything right." Millie's relationship with her boyfriend was also partly based on a projection of perfection and her attempt to incorporate it through identification.

More often than any of the other groups, the Moratoriums report daydreams, often continuing from childhood, of wondrous success. To be an opera star, the first female Supreme Court justice, ambassador to Russia, to discover a cure for cancer—these are the fantasies that filled the heads of the little girls they once were, and they remain reluctant to give them up even yet. (These fantasies have much more specificity and uniqueness than those of the Achievements.) These visions of glory seem to have originated from the father, from being perfect to win him or incorporate him. Such perfection, however, is impossible for them to attain. Yet they cling to their ideal, feeling that if they can reach it they will somehow be absolved from failing the mother. As a result, these women are under attack from both sides; they have failed both internalized parents, for different reasons, and they suffer an increasing loss of self-esteem. They suffer guilt through violation of the prohibitions of their mothers and guilt from not attaining the ideals of their fathers, and they can find no neutral stronghold to rest on. Their moratorium phase is an attempt to compromise with these forces.

Another important aspect of the intense guilt is to be found in the structure of the ego ideal itself. For these women, goals tend to be formulated in an imperious, totalistic tone. They seek "The Answers." From childhood, they derived satisfaction and self-esteem from being Right, and through adolescence they have remained convinced of the essential Rightness of themselves, their families, and their beliefs. What seems to induce the moratorium state is the shock at finding other modes of Rightness which cannot, of course, all be The Right. As in the case of Millie, this experience tarnishes the old ego ideal and prompts or promotes the autonomy struggle from the parents. Instead of liberalizing the demanding superego, however, the Moratorium woman embarks on a kind of crusade, determined to discover what is Really Right, and until she either finds something which she can embrace or gives up the quest, she can make no choices around which to construct an identity. Erikson discusses this process in terms of adolescent vulnerability to false gods and heroes. There is always an omnipresent They or It which was to have promised all—but usually fails. If and when they do find another mode of life or belief or values that seem Right, they set up the choice in an all-or-none fashion. Compromise, at least in the thick of the woods of this stage, does not appear possible: "I'm in the middle of two societies, a liberal one and a very, very strict one. I don't think I can decide ever."

Another striking commonality among the Moratoriums is their single-minded focus on and need for relationships. Unlike the Achievements, who look both to their own capacities and to significant relationships to bolster self-definition, the Moratoriums show little purposeful investment in personal achievement. (If I can't be an opera star, why be anything?) They experience themselves primarily in relation to other people—gaining approval, respect, love, being used, being left, being taught, etc.—and almost never speak of themselves as knowing themselves through what they do.

Asked to describe themselves in a hypothetical situation, the Moratoriums often replied that it would depend on who they were speaking to. It was as if they experience such marked fluctuations in their self-images that their sense of self is contingent on the qualities of the other person. At the same time, this response indicates that what the Moratoriums would tell someone about themselves would depend on what was most likely to win the approval of this other person, whether that person's approval was worth having or not.

There is often a desperate quality to the Moratoriums' search for object relationships, as though in attempting to renounce their childhood ties to their parents, there appears an enormous void to be filled. Unlike the Foreclosures, who are seeking to replace parental security, the Moratoriums seem primarily to hunger for new identifications. Each relationship provides a potential mirror, a way of saying to themselves, "This is what I would be if that is what I choose to become." Each relationship also provides raw material for the endless introspection that marks the Moratoriums, and they tend to ruminate a great deal over how they "really" felt or how they are the same or as different from those they know. All this is in the service of defining themselves. The Moratoriums were unique among the groups in asking the interviewers for personal feedback at the end of the study, and they were especially curious to know "what other people said." Erikson comments on this obliquely in the following passages:

> The search for a new and yet reliable identity can perhaps best be seen in the persistent adolescent endeavor to define, overdefine, and redefine themselves and each other in often ruthless comparisons, while a search for reliable alignments can be recognized in the restless testing of the newest of possibilities and the oldest of values. (1968, p. 87)

The relationships are also necessary to provide solace from the internal war. Unable to approve of themselves, the Moratoriums look to others to reassure them of their worth, to tell them that they are right and good. However, relationships tend to be transient, because the other person generally gets swallowed up in the developmental conflict, aligned with one side or the other, or, having served as a brief buoy to the ego, outlives his usefulness as the Moratorium moves on to other aspects of the conflict.

Part of the definition of the Moratorium group included that they be conflicted in regard to sexual standards. While this issue is not always consciously central to their identity struggles, it does serve as an unconscious keystone. For the Moratoriums, commitment to adult sexuality would involve burning the last bridge which links them to childhood. It is as though commitment to adult sexuality means admitting forever that childhood is a land of no return. This seems to be why it is so necessary for the Moratoriums to make sure that their parents maintain "their ideal vision of me" (as pure and innocent); telling their parents, and "meaning it," that they are adults means their parents may no longer be willing to accept them back as a child. If the rest of their lives is devoted to covertly telling their parents (or their internalized parents) to go away, their conflicts over sexual standards add, "but not too far."

Sexual taboos are also the cornerstones of the primitive superego, and, because the Moratoriums are not yet ready to disengage from it, the obligation falls on their parents to keep it alive and visible enough to be fought. One woman gives a clear statement of this process:

> I told my mother that if I had strong feelings for some one, I would sleep with them. And she said, OK, she agreed with me. *But I didn't believe her,* because they have an ideal vision of their daughter and they'll never see the bad (!) parts anyway. [Italics mine.]

If their parents attempt to help them learn to fly, the Moratoriums become frightened that they are being banned from the nest.

The Moratoriums, then, are straddling two major and distinct sets of ego organization, unable to opt for one side or another and managing with an enormous expenditure of energy to keep all possibilities open.

Impulses are relatively conscious in these women, and as they fight their old superego they begin to feel extremely vulnerable to inappropriate impulse expression. The loosening of old defenses also awakens earlier psychosexual conflicts, which appear primarily in recurring oedipal themes in their dreams.

At times the Moratoriums appear to have very weak ego boundaries.

They have difficulty maintaining relationships partly because their loss of distance from the other person becomes frightening. There is also a remarkable fluidity between what is internal and what is external, such that they are often uncertain whether the feelings toward themselves that they seem to perceive in others are coming from the other person or from themselves. Given, however, that this is a recent development, the permeability of the ego boundaries seems to result from the cataclysm that shook the previous personality structure and to act in the service of increasing self-differentiation.

The Moratoriums are without question the most sensitive and insightful of the groups, and, in some ways, the most likable. Some experience torrents of feeling so intensely that it is often painful to listen to the tapes. At the same time, they do capture in reality the clinician's perceptions of what adolescence should be all about; they have the acuity of vision, the responsiveness to social problems, and the psychological closeness to the great philosophical issues of life that have so often been sentimentalized by observers of youth. The healthier ones often have developed an acute sense of humor which allows them some distance from their conflicts and which they seem to use in the service of delay—to allow them to carry on with life without having to erect permanent and constricting defenses.

Clinically, the Moratoriums resemble the Diffusions more than the Achievements in their anxiety, their intensity of affect, and their low level of self-esteem. Yet they show more energy and less depression than the Diffusions. Where both groups do contain troubled, conflicted women, the Moratoriums are fighting to stay above water. The Diffusions are barely floating and allowing themselves to be pulled by the currents.

The Diffusions

"I feel; therefore, I am."

The Diffusions, in previous studies as well as in this one, are continually the most mixed group and the hardest to understand as a group. This is explicable partly on the basis of the fact that the Diffusions are defined as a group by the *absence* of crisis and the *absence* of commitment. Logically, one would expect to find more homogeneity where the criterion is the presence of something rather than the absence of it.

From the 12 women in this category, there emerge four subgroupings which may represent different stages or types of identity diffusion. There probably are, in the population, many more types. Each of these subgroups will be briefly described, and an attempt will be made to formulate some general underlying characteristics.

Type I. Severe Psychopathology

There are two women who are diagnosably borderline psychotics. Their psychosexual and psychosocial dynamics are those traditionally seen clinically, and these have been amply described in the literature. Erikson has already described the phenomenon of identity diffusion among hospitalized patients, and much of his analysis would be applicable here. In many ways, however, these two women seem more disturbed and less involved with clear-cut identity struggles than those described by Erikson. They are more concerned with whether to be or not to be rather than with what or how to be. If this is indeed a true crisis of identity, it is at least radically different in quality and structure from the developmental task facing the other women under discussion. In these two women, what identity issues do exist are obscured by long-standing attempts to cope with massive ego failures.

Type II. Previous Developmental Deficits

There are three women, who form the subgroup of those with previous developmental deficits, whose lives show the scars of early severe psychological trauma. The loss of a favored parent or early emotional neglect due to family disorganization has resulted in a general sense of futility and instability. These women have parents with whom they were unable to form any lasting positive identifications, the absence of identity crisis in this group seems to be partly attributable to their lack of any solid, workable psychic structure to reorganize. Instead, their entire lives have been characterized by a search for some remedy to the ego deficits; they have tried one thing after another, and nothing seems to work very well for them. Impulsive, avoiding guilt at all costs, they are preoccupied with unrepressed early struggles. Their inability to make identity commitments results from the inability of the ego to integrate the aspects of the self which are highly charged and poorly defended. Rather than try to make something of themselves, these women, when they think of the future at all, wish to make something *else* of themselves. As one woman, in a moment of hope put it, "It isn't necessary to build on the past. You can go outside the past and make a new past." They experience their lives as a succession of events, unrelated to each other, feeling that they are one person today, another person 2 weeks from now. To this extent, they attempt to live outside of their own histories, disavowing a past that they cannot come to terms with, and this means disavowing parts of themselves. This splitting which occurs both within the self at present and between the selves at different time periods renders integration impossible. [For case material regarding this subgroup, see Josselson (1972).]

Type III. Moratorium Diffusions

THE CASE OF DEBBIE

Debbie was the most articulate woman in the entire sample, and it would be an injustice to paraphrase her.

On occupation:

> I don't know what I want to do—join the circus, a gypsy camp, I don't know. Yesterday I was thinking of starting a day care center in Vermont. I guess I'm about 50% serious about it. I'm terrible at planning. I can't do long-range things very well. When the time comes, I'll do something.

On religion:

> I've always believed in God, but God has changed.

On politics:

I got involved like everyone else in petitions and marches, then I thought it was all absurd and I don't bother with it anymore.

On sexual standards:

I don't know. The first time I see a person, if I want to sleep with them, something clicks—the vibrations he gives off. If he doesn't mention it and I would like to go to bed with him, I just ask him. I just trust my instincts.

I always think it would be so easy if I were an artist. Then I could say, "I'm an artist and I'm driven to create this art." But I'm not. I'm just an average sort of person and—I don't know. I used to think I was mystically endowed and had cosmic consciousness. I felt that everyone could see, but I could *really* see. Everyone knew things, but I *really* knew things. Almost as if I had seen the light, and of course, it couldn't be explained, it could just be felt.

Up to a certain age, I believed everything my parents said. Then, in college, I saw all these new ideas and I said, "Okay, I'm not going to believe all that stuff you told me," and I rejected everything and said to myself, "Okay, now I'm going to make a new Debbie which has nothing to do with my mother and father. I'm going to start with a clean slate," and what I started to put on it were all new ideas and these ideas were opposite to what my parents believed. But slowly, what's happening is that I'm feeling incomplete and I realize that what's happening is that I'm adding on a lot of the things which they've told me and I'm taking them as my own and I'm coming more together with them.

When I went to live in England, I met this woman who was very mystical. She was my mentor. I look at people a lot like that—like they're going to teach me something. And she took it for granted that I was equal to her, so this image I had of her—wonderful, gifted, mystical person—and she treated me as an equal and I began to feel that I must be like her. And we were both into Eastern religion and everything is all one—it's a wonderful unified cosmos and we're all part of it and all there is is to love each other and I was really feeling it. I was feeling at one with trees. I kept changing my name. I could be anything I wanted. It was all one.

Then I came back to America. It's like you can't afford to have stars in your eyes in America or any of that mystical stuff. In India, people go up to the mountains and for years they try to reach these heightened states of consciousness. And in Cambridge, for the mere price of $149.95 you can go home and practice biofeedback—your alpha level will go right up to your potential. You just go to the seminar every Saturday and pay your money and *you* are going to reach nirvana. It made me feel foolish to have believed what I did. I just became cynical.

You have to make up your mind. If you want to be in the clouds you can't be half-assed about it and keep one foot on the ground just in case those are only just clouds.

For a while I just believed what I wanted to believe and I had my own reality. Then I came back to my house and it was, "Debbie, will you help me dust?" "Sure." And that was reality and I couldn't sit there having vibrations. I've become cynical.

The summer before I came to college, I hung around this corner all summer. This was life to me. What did I know? Then I came to college and there were all these people who came from all different places and there were really rich people and smart people and freaky people and people who didn't believe in God and there were so many things, drugs, sex, hippies. It was all very confusing.

Debbie described her parents as having been opposite in character. Her mother was warm, soft, and quiet, while her father was loud, aggressive, and demanding. She feels she has elements of both in her nature. Although she describes her family as having been close, she seems to have little emotional investment in them, as though they never had much importance in her life. She recalls, at age 13, telling her parents that she did not need parents anymore except for food and shelter. Debbie had always been very involved in peer culture, and when her parents tried to impose restrictions as to hours or friends, she fought them until they relented.

From an early time, Debbie had the sense of being very special. She and her sisters were the smartest pupils in their school, and her father had great pride in and expectations of his daughters. While Debbie always admired her mother, she always felt different from her. Where she saw her mother was gentle, sure of herself, peaceful, and calm, Debbie felt in herself an aggressiveness and adventurousness that never left her satisfied with herself, her friends, or her world.

DISCUSSION

For Debbie, as for the other two women in this subgroup, struggle with important questions is central to her life. Although conflict does not focus specifically on psychosocial identity issues—at least, not the ones used to define the statuses they are not passively resigning themselves to amorphousness. Their lives tend to be marked by movement between moratorium and diffusion states as they try new modes of being, search for answers, quest for meaning, then give up for a while only to begin again.

There are, however, some important differences between these three women and the Moratoriums. For one thing, they are not involved in the separation-autonomy struggle central to the other group. They have, to the contrary, rejected their parents and their lifestyles and are conscious of no conflict about this. They have disowned their pasts and have decided what they are not going to be. In this respect, they are more like the type II Diffusions. But they are healthier and less overwhelmed by the pressures of earlier periods and the ties of primary object relationships. Unlike the Achievements, who have worked these problems through, these Diffusions repress and deny them, which gives them an appearance of freedom. This is clearest in regard to the structural relationship between the ego and superego. The Diffusions behave as though the superego, internalized long ago, could simply be turned off. Their impulsivity is in the service of keeping the superego out of service, and it is no wonder that none of the avenues they choose feels right to them. Choices tend to be the choices of parts of themselves, while the remaining parts are left to object. In this vein, Debbie speaks of feeling "incomplete." What they have of their ego ideal is its tone, to be something very special, but the goals they aspire to are unrealistic and do not take account of the people they have already been.

The parents of these women all seem to have had high expectations of their daughters (particularly the fathers). Yet these expectations of greatness and specialness tended to have an amorphous tone, such that these women seem never to have had a concrete sense of what they were supposed to have been. This ego ideal, given its vagueness, also appears to have been immune to the experiences in reality which tend to force revisions. As Debbie expressed it, they can have their own reality—at least, for a time. These women—all three of them—have lived a kind of double life, existing and coping in reality while maintaining a strong investment in a private world. Like Debbie, they tend to search for totalistic experiences where they can exist at a pinnacle of feeling (unlike the Moratoriums, who want to be Right), at one with the romanticized ego ideal. These experiences tend to take them outside the social mainstream, which requires too much compromise and delivers too little emotional pitch.

If they are "alienated," it is because reality, not society, does not promise to fulfill the exciting dreams of childhood. In this respect, they are reminiscent of Keniston's (1960) Inburn. But these particular women have internalized just enough of the more defined expectations of their families to be unable to fully commit themselves to wholly unconventional lifestyles. Debbie, for example, found that her mystical reality was a fulfilling interlude which she could not maintain back on her home turf.

There is a striking developmental theme among these women in regard to their mothers. Whereas the type II Diffusions could not form positive identification with their mothers, these women show a different pattern. They have idealized their mothers, discovering in latency that they are completely unlike them. They speak of having always wished to be like their mothers, who were warm, loving, giving, and extremely talented domestically or artistically. And they feel great disappointment when they find that they do not have her gifts. Again reality does not provide what has been wished for.

Toward their fathers, these women feel intense ambivalence, and some of their acting out is traceable to conflicts in this relationship. More important, perhaps, is that the father is the chief object of identification, and these identifications are themselves ambivalent ones. Unable to be like their mothers and wishing to be less like their fathers, these women seem to have no other recourse besides casting around among the multitude of possibilities in the larger society for a totally new mode of being. Lacking solid and trusted introjects against which to test "what they really are," their quest is a difficult one.

Type IV. Foreclosed Diffusions

Foreclosed Diffusions are women who are uncommitted and drifting with their noncommitment, but women whose parents seem to have equally diffuse identity resolutions.

The four women in this group all seem to experience themselves as a leaf blown by the wind. Acting for the moment, unable to define a consistent direction, they seem to suffer from atrophy of the will.

These are women whose parents always left decisions up to them, never pushed them into or out of anything. Yet these daughters seem to have sensed that their parents, rather than encouraging them to be independent, were merely expressing their own lack of convictions and inability to make decisions. Such vacillation seems to have induced their daughters to cling even tighter to them for some small measure of security. These women share a kind of fatalistic passivity, feeling that they have so little control over their own lives that there is no point in trying to plan.

Like the Foreclosures, these Diffusions describe their families as having been close, and they remain emotionally involved with them. However, their bond with their families has less intensity than that of the Foreclosures and is not tied to fulfilling familial expectations. They also differ from the Fore-closures in that they have a plethora of friends and activities and seem to gravitate toward whatever will define their lives and tell them what to do. But after a short period of time, they begin to feel trapped by this structure and move on to a new friend or a new involvement.

The difficulty these women experience in describing their past lives is that they feel that the past was much like the present—a succession of diverse people and events that did not add up. They were, in general, very close to their mothers and had highly romantic and sexualized relationships with their fathers. Even in the family romance, they seem to have felt no controls applied to them.

These women have been denied the opportunity to accept or rebel. Whatever they wanted or did was fine, and their parents provided no taboos or beliefs around which they could build a sense of exclusivity at the center of their sense of self. Their identity diffusion, then, results from a dearth of internalized cornerstones on which to hang identity elements. The tone of the identity they do have mirrors their parents' inconsistency and opportunism.

The absence of guilt is remarkable among this group. Affect is primarily isolated, intellectualizations are prominent, and internal conflict does not appear either in their histories or in the more projective material. There is, however, a strong suggestion of underlying depression which is defended against by activity.

Discussion

There are, then, many paths to identity diffusion. Anything that seri-ously interferes with development also tends to mediate against identity formation. It is possible, however, to abstract a few more specific threads from these diverse groups in order to characterize the Diffusions.

What seems to be most salient is the failure of internalization of objects. In each of these subgroups, for one reason or other, the individuals have been unable to form viable positive identifications with either parent. In their preidentity stages, they had little goal for "what to be when they grew up"—only a commitment to what not to be or a wish to be what they could not be. They had parents who set no realistic expectations, so they could never win self-esteem through pleasing them. Since their parents either did not set or did not enforce reasonable limits, they were also forced into indepen-dence when they needed structure. In a sense, they are daughters of parents who continually told them, overtly or covertly, not to be like them, but to be very special.

The Diffusions, then, must come to terms with their developmental dilemma by a variety of splitting maneuvers—splitting an unrealistic superego from the ego, splitting poorly controlled impulses from the ego, and splitting the ego itself. Guilt intensifies impulsivity, which further intensifies guilt, and this they cannot allow themselves to experience. Unable to give up their attempt to placate the romanticized ego ideal, they seek fulfillment in whatever salvation happens to appear; when this fails, they simply find something else. Early developmental struggles which are only poorly resolved keep them acting in their attempt to avoid anxiety and regression. Given these burdens, their weakened egos manage to juggle these elements but cannot begin to integrate them. Commitment itself appears frightening as though standing still for a moment might mean being overwhelmed.

Possibilities, diverse and confusing as they are, are cherished by the Diffusions. Their long-standing involvement in fantasy serves to produce a succession of images of themselves being any one of a profession of things. Commitment to something would involve giving up some of these possibilities, and that would endanger the Diffusions' self-esteem, which is largely built on fantasy. Unique to the Diffusions is the concern with all the things that one could become, and they speak of all the possibilities they could choose from as though potential itself provided a kind of omnipotence.

The Diffusions are very much aware of their feelings and somewhat preoccupied with them. As one woman put it, "Feeling something is better than feeling nothing." Feelings do seem to form the rudimentary core of the Diffusions' identity.

The ego of the Diffusions, then, is incapable, at least at this point in time, of the integration necessary for identity formation. Because of their need to obliterate the past (or, in the case of the Foreclosed Diffusions, where the past is vacuous), the Diffusions exist only within the present. Their failure of time integration is clearly visible in these interviews in that most feel alienated from their futures as well as their pasts. Erikson suggests that the identity diffuse individual seeks to counterpoint rather than synthesize his sexual, ethnic, occupational, and typological alternatives, and this is evident in the Diffusions' denial that they are indeed inexorably bound to an irrevocable history. Guttman (1970), in discussing alienation, similarly suggests that the hippies' essential argument is with a fate that has assigned them the limitations of a single sex, a single body, and a single set of parents. These existential limitations are experienced as unacceptable boundaries which curtail future choice. Debbie describes just such a feeling in her attempts to abolish her history as well as the separateness which intrudes between her ego and others. In feeling at one with trees, time and existence itself are conquered.

Theoretical Implications

The Psychodynamic Basis of Ego Identity Development

Before summarizing and exploring these themes, it must be reiterated that there are exceptions in each group. Ultimately, identity formation must be understood as a process unique to the individual. Identity is, in a sense, a solution to a jigsaw puzzle where each person has different pieces to fit together. Nevertheless, there is enough similarity within each group to warrant an attempt at generalization.

A second caution to theory resides in the fact that the identity status groups are by definition relatively unstable states. They are positions at a point in time, and there is every reason to suppose that in a year's time these positions might change. Of course, this holds more true for some groups than others. Achievements might go through another moratorium state or, if their lives treat them roughly enough, could become Diffusions. Foreclosures could evolve into any of the other three statuses. As for the Moratoriums and Diffusions, they might trade places or become Achievements; it is also conceivable that some of the Moratoriums might become overwhelmed by conflict, seal it over, and return to foreclosed positions. Yet again the consistency which does appear among the groups suggests that these are not random distributions at a point in time. They are, instead, distributions at an important point in time where social forces are exacting certain choices and commitments. How these women choose to cope with that particular set of social circumstances may, in fact, be reflective of more stable and permanent characteristics than the theory of transitional stages might predict.

It is conceivable that these identity status groups contain stable character types rather than developmental positions. What few longitudinal data are available on these identity statuses would support the view that, over time, there is movement toward higher levels of identity resolution (Waterman et al. in press).

The assumption inherent in this paper is that personality configurations predispose the individual to certain styles of approaching and resolving the identity task. At the same time, identity formation is seen as a process where movement toward and away from commitment is to be expected.

The developmental enigma which confronts these women in the identity stage seems to be the realization that the id-ego-superego organization consolidated through middle adolescence cannot serve into adulthood. What one was supposed to be is no longer valid. Archaic superego prohibitions compromise the development of new ego skills; childhood ego ideals are threatened with nonfulfillment. The ego's task, then, is to modify, mollify, and integrate these other structures. Where once the ego had to enlist the superego's support to redirect the organism from "What I want to do" toward "What I should do," now it must disengage from the superego such that the ego alone can move the organism based on "What it is reasonable for me to do." From the data presented here, it seems that the ego's means of wresting control from the superego is the central dynamic determinant of the process which identity formation will take.

In the Foreclosures, the superego is the incorporation of the loving but strict parents. It is a structure associated with self-esteem and narcissistic supplies. The Foreclosure ego seems to have had little need or experience of developing skills that were not in the service of pleasing the superego. Therefore, they are not particularly competent interpersonally with peers but do well at satisfying teachers and other authorities. They have pursued few innate talents but succeed at doing whatever task is required of them. For them, the choice presented by this developmental stage jeopardizes a too-harmonious intrapsychic balance and the ego works to avoid the stage altogether, seeking instead to recreate an environment where the old balance will be effective. The ego, then, chooses to remain subordinate to the superego. It is as though the ego feels that it could never bring as much gratification again, so why disrupt a good thing. As a result, crisis does not occur, and the ego attempts to preserve an external climate favorable to the internal balance rather than reshuffling internal structures.

The Achievements start with a similar ego-superego configuration, but the superego never has as much of a monopoly of narcissistic supplies. These are women who enjoy competence for its own sake and make use of talents and friends in the service of self-esteem. Their ego has the armaments to challenge the superego in the interests of modifying rather than destroying it. While they must tolerate a certain amount of anxiety and guilt, they have the ego reserves to be able to renounce certain kinds of older self-esteem incomes and, through intricate and complex negotiations, can effect a workable compromise with the internalized expectations from childhood. This gives them a range of freedom within which to work to construct a new identity.

The Moratoriums, with a less diplomatic ego, attempt to battle their superego head on, to set up all-or-nothing choices for themselves or to replace the superego's content without modifying its power. They have less ego strength than the Achievements, and what they seem to be trying to do is to hold on to the loving functions of the superego with one hand and abolish it with the other. Feeling that they cannot afford to give up the experience of "being good," they are nevertheless too driven toward growth to give in entirely to the superego's demands. As a result, they swing back and forth or try to construct a new superego. Meanwhile, the ego goes in search of more arms for the struggle. When and if their ego develops enough of its own skills to be able to bargain effectively with the inner voice, they are headed toward identity achievement.

In this last statement seems to lie the crux of the matter. Whatever resolves this "crisis," which is a crisis between the ego and the superego, will become a cornerstone of identity. Be it person, place, or thing, that which the ego can enlist in its struggle against superego domination is experienced as self-enhancing, i.e., "This is right for me" or "This is what I stand for." This, I believe, is the mechanism by which identity joins the society and the individual. Where once the superego was internalized as a representation of society's demands, identity at this stage represents all those activities and relationships which can be effectively utilized in this second major internal struggle. Similarly, those ego elements which are most successful in disengaging the ego from the superego are highlighted and accentuated and given a more prominent role in the resultant identity. To carry the military analogy to its limit, those soldiers that fight the best are promoted.

The Diffusions, by contrast, do not experience this choice or struggle. Their primitive, repressed superego historically held only retributive power and was never fully integrated with the ego in its struggle against the id. The ego organization never really had a satisfactory balance to disrupt, and the behavior of the Diffusions during this developmental stage reflects the same pattern of depression, action, then punishment which they have experienced for most of their lives. Since their ego was never very adept at internal integration, the external social pressures of this stage tend only to make matters worse.

The superego's importance has been largely minimized in writings on adolescence, or attention has been given it only in terms of its relationship to impulse expression. The psychoanalytic focus on the attainment of genital primacy has crowded out consideration of the many other aspects of human individuation (Lichtenstein 1970). While the prohibition of instinctual expression at the hands of the superego is a central issue in middle adolescence, there seems to be a broader, less instinctually focused aspect of the superego which must be modified in late adolescence.

To some degree, the original internalization of the superego in women is less specific in regard to content than in regard to tone. Pederson (1961) suggests that the tone of the superego and the ego ideals is far more critical developmentally than their content. The Moratoriums in their effort to construct an equal but opposite superego provide an example of this. Being good, however that is defined in the family, is what is important in the early development of women. Pleasing the parents is always the basis of being good, and the studies on adolescence have documented the predilection of girls to continue to look to their parents for guidance even through adolescence (Douvan and Adelson 1966). The problem of late adolescence, the establishment of an independent, autonomous identity, requires an effort to give up this source of self-love.

It is not surprising, in view of this, that the Foreclosures show the least depression of any of the groups. Having decided against risking the old balance, their self-esteem derives from childhood sources. The others, however, must mourn the loss of a stable, loving solacing introject and are also more vulnerable to experiences of failure.

The process of this struggle is also influenced by the history of identification, since identification affects the superego as well as the ego. Again, there are distinct patterns among the identity status groups. The Foreclosures are unique in forming positive, unambivalent identifications with their mothers. They want to be, not so much what their mothers are, but what their mothers wanted to be; they can feel loved only in the context of a loving relationship with their (internalized) approving mothers. The Achievements, by contrast, have both positive and negative identifications with both parents, a situation which increases the number of introjects and the complexity of the ego-superego structure. They have had a choice from early times of pleasing either mother or father, and their superego tends to be a composite of aspects of both parents. This allows for more structural flexibility and gives the ego more room to negotiate.

Both the Achievements and the Moratoriums (groups which have formulated or are trying to formulate the autonomous identity), in contrast to the Foreclosures, have ambivalent identifications and a history of conflict with their mothers. Middle adolescent conflict with the mother, then, seems to be a preparation for the internal struggle which accompanies identity growth. Haan et al. (1968) also found that increasing development of morality among women was related to conflict with mothers.

It is important, however, for these women not to go too far in such conflict. The Achievements seem to have discovered in the course of their struggle that introjects are not infinitely flexible. They take certain aspects of their past identifications as boundaries of the possibilities, using them as anchor points to disengage themselves from the less appropriate or less satisfying identifications. This stands in contrast to the Moratoriums, who are trying to overthrow the old structure completely, to disavow any identification with the mother, and to find some way of living up to the idealized father.

The failure of identifications in the Diffusions is conjoint with the failure of superego integration. Never having had a parent they felt it worthwhile to please, the Diffusions are plagued by punitive introjects which they can neither emulate nor escape from.

Freedom from superego restrictions seems to be a prerequisite for forming new, meaningful identifications. These new identifications tend to be diffused among a very large group of peers and significant others. While the Moratoriums often try to find (or have found) one person whom they are consciously striving to be like (a totalistic identification), the Achievements can seldom pinpoint particular people whom they wanted to be like or else they name a great many people who had attributes they emulated. The ego, free of superego domination, is then highly selective and finely tempered in its new identifications. It seems to bend what it sees outside itself to fit what already is. The Moratorium and Diffusion ego, however, in its struggle with the superego, seems more consciously to try to bend the self to be like what it admires.

Erikson was sensitive to the role of the superego in identity formation and saw its influence in the ideology aspect of identity. Underlying his concept of totalism is the image of an infantile superego winning back its prominent role in identity. The Moratoriums' attraction to totalistic commitments, even though they have not yet made them, would be consistent with Erikson's view of the superego's role in identity. Elsewhere, he speaks of the "complete denial of ambition as the only possible way of totally avoiding guilt" (1968, p. 184), which, if modulated a bit, is a fair description of the ego-superego structure to be found among the Diffusions. The inability to work, he continues, may reflect the unrealistic demands of an ego ideal unwilling to settle for anything less than omnipotence or omniscience. Traces of such a process may be found among both Moratoriums and Diffusions. In addition, Erikson notes that "a positive sense of identity permits the individual to forego irrational self-repudiation" (p. 89). This statement is in many ways the inverse of the process I described earlier whereby those identity elements which serve to support the ego against the irrational superego become central to identity.

Where we had expected to find the greatest problem of integration to lie in the choice among so many potential identities, we find instead a more clear-cut choice between the pulls of the past and relatively conventional choices for the future. Erikson discusses the polarity of identity diffusion at this stage, and this danger awaits the individual in the moratorium stage who goes too far in dissociating the superego. The other pitfall is regression, for the person who becomes too overwhelmed by conflict to continue to grow.

This, hopefully, sheds some light on the dynamics of identity crisis. But what of commitment? The thesis of this paper has been that whatever serves to adaptively resolve a crisis will invoke a simultaneous commitment. Yet there is another aspect to this which has not been discussed: the fear of commitment itself. Those women who most keenly appreciate the variety of choice at their disposal and are overwhelmed by it (a rarity in the sample) are generally bent on avoiding choice altogether. Appearing most commonly among the Moratoriums and Diffusions, this fear is expressed as the fear of the permanence of adulthood, the sense that choice is irrevocable, the terror of being "trapped" or "caught in a rut." Growth itself is experienced as evil, and what looms as most ominous is a state where there is an absence of choice. The magical belief in growing up as a never-never-land where all wants are fulfilled is a casualty of the late adolescent period (Galdston, undated). Dreams do not "come true," and the late adolescent often feels cheated out of what she had felt was promised her. Millie offers a fine illustration of a disappointed faith in growing up. Diffusions, who have perhaps suffered more childhood frustration than the others, seem to regard their own growth as a waiting for the story to have a happy ending. Commitment through their own actions might prevent the magic; if they are in a mundane rut, no fairy godmother will ever appear.

On Feminine Identity

Given the current cultural chaos in regard to the acceptable modes of being a woman, it is reasonable to search these data for some clues as to what is fundamental to these women's sense of their feminine identity. Much has been written on the importance of the inner space, on the greater emphasis on interpersonal attributes over achievement in women. To some extent, these observations are supported by the women in this sample.

Identity in women centers far more on what kind of a person to be than on occupational or ideological choice. Where identity in men is confirmed or denied by objective yardsticks such as degrees received or financial success, identity substantiation in women is dependent on the responses of important others. In order to feel giving, the woman must find someone willing to receive; to feel lovable, she must have someone to love her. The work of this period for women is to sort out those ego states and ego ideals that can be validated in experience from those that cannot. Thus the woman who had always been shy and wished to be gregarious must accept that her attempts to be outgoing have continually failed and that she is, after all, a shy person.

It has been widely assumed that this emphasis on the interpersonal context is in the service of developing the skills needed to become a wife and mother. This teleological reasoning seems unwarranted. These women seem to value interpersonal competence for its own sake, and getting along well with different kinds of people brings an autonomous sense of satisfaction. Curious about other people, these women enjoy closeness *qua* closeness and form relationships for the sake of the relationship rather than as preparation for anything else.

Nurturance is the shared ideal for these women. It comprises the core of both affiliative and achievement needs. When they speak of what is important to them in their lives and careers, whatever they mention revolves around a means "of helping others, of working with others." Even a goal as abstract as biochemical research is conceived in terms of the cancer patients such research might contribute toward curing. Erikson's (1968) concept of inner space has to some extent been misunderstood. He, too, recognizes the active component of nurturance, seeing it as a means of productivity as well as receptivity.

Earlier research on the achievement drive in woman focused on masculine achievement-competition and aggressiveness (Horner 1970). Such traits are antinurturant and women do tend to avoid them, but this does not negate their desire to achieve in the sense of being productive and making a positive contribution to society through personal achievements. Women are less likely to think of their work in terms of getting ahead or being the best for the sake of competition. Rather, they emphasize the more private satisfactions of service for its own sake and doing well to maximize their potential for positively affecting the lives of others.

Of the 48 women in the present sample, not one ever mentioned conflict between achievement aspirations and relationships with men. True, some of them did lose some popularity during high school for their academic commitments, but these women do not seem to carry deep scars from the experience. Those who have high achievement aspirations have found men who support their ambitions, and competition does not seem to be a problem. If, indeed, women seek to suppress their achievement needs in order not to scare away eligible husbands, one would expect such a theme to appear at least once in 48 clinical interviews. It does not.

Some writers have placed much stress on the differential importance of *which* parent the woman is primarily identified with, attempting to tease out differences between father-identified and mother-identified women. The data presented here suggest that all of these women have significant identifications with both parents and that it makes little sense to speak of which parent the subject identified with *more*. Obviously, the qualities and intensities of these identifications are significant within the psychodynamic scheme, but it seems to make little difference for identity formation whether adaptive traits are derived from the mother or the father.

Others have suggested that because of the fact that much of a woman's life depends on whom she marries, intimacy may precede identity in women. This view assumes a great amount of passivity on the part of women in the ultimate choice of marriage partner. Erikson comments that much of a woman's identity resides in the kind of man she wishes to be sought by, suggesting that it is the identity choice which precedes intimacy. In today's culture, women are even less passive than that, often doing the seeking themselves. The data in this study would suggest a third view, namely, that the identity and intimacy stages are merged in women. As was discussed previously, women who have achieved identities have often accomplished this via a relationship which supported their independence from their parents, opened new possibilities for identifications, or helped them consolidate previous ego ideals. To the extent the relationship boosted her sense of identity, the woman was more likely to feel greater commitment to it. Only in a few cases among the Achievements did it appear that the woman was resolving the crisis by borrowing identity from the person she was intimate with. The more common pattern was one of using the relationship to sharpen and strengthen identity, then using the increased sense of identity to deepen the relationship. Because interpersonal competence is so central to female identity formation, it seems necessary to have an intimate relationship where possibility for self-confirmation is maximized. At the same time, others of these women demonstrate that there are avenues for intimacy outside of a simple heterosexual relationship which serve equally well for identity-enhancing experiences. The Achievements also exemplify the importance of the industry stage in identity formation. Their accomplishments, talents, and skills are often equally as significant as their relationships in heightening self-differentiation and self-esteem. Erikson (1959) suggests that the industry, identity, and intimacy stages are highly interrelated, and the Achievements would bear this out. The question of which comes first becomes rhetorical. The important distinction remains, however, that identity in women is far more punctuated by intimacy considerations than in men.

These data also suggest that female identity is different in quality from male identity. Where identity in men is metaphorically a straight line that may twist and turn but moves ever forward, identity in women is a series of concentric circles. Life, for these women, feels cyclical. They see their future as a succession of stages, in which each stage will have a slightly different focus, but all will be integrated into a whole that makes sense. Their experience of who they are and where they are going is multifaceted; they are and will be many things, but not all at the same time. Their commitments are abstract rather than narrow, and they have a flexibility in their expectations. They say, for example, "I would like to use the law to help people," rather than "I would like to be a lawyer in a big New York corporation law firm." Or they say, "At some point in my career I will take time off to have children. How and for how long I will do this depends on where we are living and what kind of child care is available." While some writers have viewed this as vagueness of identity commitment, it seems rather to be a commitment to fundamentals, with the details to be worked out later. In order to do and be many things in the course of a lifetime, these women recognize that they must leave some integration to the arrival of circumstances and that they must exercise control where they can but also be able to wait.

Erikson has stated that the history of a culture can be told in the history of the identity crisis. These women are clearly operating in the context of the cultural present, choosing options from those available. As this context changes, so may change the very nature and process of female identity.

Concluding Remarks

The search for the dynamics of identity formation has led us to the dynamics of the autonomy-individuation process, of the ego-superego struggle, and of character synthesis. Starting with Erikson's psychosocial concept of identity, we have found relevant many of the elements of late adolescent character formation discussed by Blos and other psychoanalytic writers. We have, in a sense, found the mutuality of these streams of development.

The method employed in this clinical survey allowed for the discovery of important dynamics. But the task remains to test these findings systematically and to develop less cumbersome research tools that can be sensitive to the enormous complexity of a concept such as identity.

The author wishes to thank her thesis chairman, Dr. Joseph B. Adelson, for his inspiration and guidance. Special thanks are also due to the members of the thesis committee: Dr. Fredrick Wyatt, Mrs. Selma H. Fraiberg, Dr. Sheila G. Baler, and Dr. Marvin Felheim. Dr. Susi Schenkel and Mrs. Susan Novick were invaluable for their thoughtful and careful assistance in the analysis of the clinical tapes.

REFERENCES

BARDWICK, J. (1971). *Psychology of Women,* Harper and Row, New York.

BERES, D. (1961). Character Formation. In Lorand, S., and Schneer, H. I. (eds.), *Adolescents: Psychoanalytic Approach to Problems and Therapy,* Hoeber, New York.

BLOCK, J. (1961). Ego identity, role variability and adjustment. *J. Consult. Psychol, 25:* 392–397.

BLOS, P. (1946). Psychological counseling of college students. *Am. J. Orthopsychiat. 16:* 571–581.

BLOS, P. (1954). Prolonged adolescence. *Am. J. Orthopsychiat. 24:* 733–742.

BLOS, P. (1962). *On Adolescence: A Psychoanalytic Interpretation,* Free Press of Glencoe, New York.

BLOS, P. (1967). The second individuation process of adolescence. In *Psychoanalytic Study of the Child,* vol. XV, International Universities Press, New York.

BLOS, P. (1968). Character formation in adolescence. In *Psychoanalytic Study of the Child,* Vol. XXIII, International Universities Press, New York.

BRONSON, G. W. (1959). Identity diffusion in late adolescents. *J. Abnorm. Soc. Psychol. 59:* 414–417.

COCHLO, G. V., HAMBURG, D. A., AND MURPHY, E. G. (1963). Coping strategies in a new learning environment. *Arch. Gen. Psychiat. 9:* 433–443.

COLEMAN, J. S. (1961). *The Adolescent Society,* Free Press of Glencoe, New York.

DEUTSCH, H. (1944). *Psychology of Women,* Vol. 1. Grune and Stratton, New York.

DOUVAN, E., AND ADELSON, J. (1966). *The Adolescent Experience,* Wiley, New York.

ERIKSON, E. (1956). The problem of ego identity. *J. Am. Psychoanal. Ass. 4:* 56–121.

ERIKSON, E. (1958). *Young Man Luther,* W. W. Norton, New York.

ERIKSON, E. (1959). Late adolescence. In Funkenstein, D. H. (ed.)., *The Student and Mental Health,* World Federation for Mental Health, Cambridge, Mass.

ERIKSON, E. (1968). *Identity, Youth and Crisis,* W. W. Norton, New York.

ERIKSON, E. (1969). *Gandhi's Truth,* W. W. Norton, New York.

FENICHEL, O. (1945). *The Psychoanalytic Theory of Neurosis,* W. W. Norton, New York.

FREUD, A. (1958). Adolescence. In *Psychoanalytic Study of the Child,* Vol. XIII, International Universities Press, New York.

GALDSTON, R. Idealism in adolescence. Unpublished paper provided by the author.

GRINKER, R. R. (1962). "Mentally healthy" young males. *Arch. Gen. Psychiat. 6:* 405–453.

GRUEN, W. (1960). Rejection of false information about oneself as an indication of ego identity. *J. Consult. Psychol. 24:* 231–238.

GUTTMAN, D. (1970). Female ego styles and generational conflict. In *Feminine Personality and Conflict,* Wadsworth, Belmont, Calif.

HAAN, N., SMITH, N. B., AND BLOCK, J. (1968). Moral reasoning of young adults. *J. Personal. Soc. Psychol. 10:* 183–201.

HORNER, M. (1970). Femininity and successful achievement: A basic inconsistency. In *Feminine Personality and Conflict,* Wadsworth, Belmont, Calif.

JOSSELSON, R. (1972). Identity formation in college women. Unpublished doctoral dissertation, University of Michigan.

KENISTON, K. (1960). *The Uncommitted: Alienated Youth in American Society,* Harcourt, Brace and World, New York.

LAMPL-DE-GROOT, J. (1960). On adolescence. In *Psychoanalytic Study of the Child,* Vol. XV, International Universities Press, New York.

LAUFER, M. (1964). Ego ideal and pseudo-ego-ideal in adolescence. In *Psychoanalytic Study of the Child,* Vol. XIX, International Universities Press, New York.

LICHTENSTEIN, H. (1970). Changing implication of the concept of psychosexual development: An inquiry. *J. Am. Psychoanal. Ass. 18:* 300–318.

MARCIA, J. (1964). Determination and validation of ego-identity status. Unpublished doctoral dissertation, Ohio State University.

MARCIA, J. (1966). Development and validation of ego-identity status. *J. Personal. Soc. Psychol. 34:* 551–558.

MARCIA, J. (1967). Ego identity status: Relationship to change in self-esteem, "general maladjustment," and authoritarianism. *J. Personal. Soc. Psychol. 35:* 118–133.

MARCIA, J. AND FRIEDMAN, M. (1970). Ego identity status in college women. *J. Personal. Soc. Psychol. 38:* 249–263.

OFFER, D. (1969). *The Psychological World of the Teenager.* Basic Books, New York.

PEDERSON, I. (1961). Personality formation in adolescence and its impact upon the psychoanalytical treatment of adults. *Internat. J. Psychoanal. 42:* 381–388.

PODD, M., MARCIA, J., AND RUBIN, B. (1970). The effects of ego identity status and partner perception on a prisoner's dilemma game. *J. Soc. Psychol. 82:* 281–287.

SANFORD, N. (1956). Personality development during the college years. *J. Soc. Issues 12:* 117–126.

SCHENKEL, S. (1972). Attitudes toward premarital intercourse in determining identity status in college women. *J. Personal. 40:* 472–482.

SCHENKEL, S. (1973). The relationship between ego identity status, field independence and conventional femininity in college women. Unpublished doctoral dissertation, State University of New York at Buffalo.

SHAPIRO, R. L. (1963). Adolescence and the psychology of the ego. *Psychiatry 26:* 77–87.

SPIEGEL, L. A. (1958). Comments on the psychoanalytic psychology of adolescence. In *Psychoanalytic Study of the Child,* Vol. XIII, International Universities Press, New York.

SPIEGEL, L. A. (1961). Disorder and consolidation. *J. Am. Psychoanal. Ass. 2:* 78–92.

TODER, R., AND MARCIA, J. (1971). Ego identity status and response to conformity pressure in college women (in press).

WATERMAN, A. S., GEARY, P., AND WATERMAN, C. A longitudinal study of changes in ego identity status from the freshman to the senior year at college (in press).

WATERMAN, C. (1972). The relationship between ego identity status and the cognitive style dimension of reflection-impulsivity. Paper presented at the Eastern Psychological Association meeting.

WHITE, R. W. (1966). *Lives in Progress,* Holt, New York.